Information Technology and Law Series

Volume 38

The *Information Technology & Law Series* was an initiative of IT *e* R, the national programme for information Technology and Law, which was a research programme set up by the Dutch government and The Netherlands Organisation for Scientific Research (NWO) in The Hague. Since 1995 IT *e* R has published all of its research results in its own book series. In 2002 IT *e* R launched the present internationally orientated and English language *Information Technology & Law Series*. This well-established series deals with the implications of information technology for legal systems and institutions. Manuscripts and related correspondence can be sent to the Series' Editorial Office, which will also gladly provide more information concerning editorial standards and procedures.

Ot van Daalen

From Encryption to Quantum Computing

The Governance of Information Security and Human Rights

ASSER PRESS

Springer

Ot van Daalen
Institute for Information Law (IViR)
University of Amsterdam
Amsterdam, The Netherlands

ISSN 1570-2782 ISSN 2215-1966 (electronic)
Information Technology and Law Series
ISBN 978-94-6265-637-6 ISBN 978-94-6265-635-2 (eBook)
https://doi.org/10.1007/978-94-6265-635-2

Published by T.M.C. ASSER PRESS, The Hague, The Netherlands www.asserpress.nl
Produced and distributed for T.M.C. ASSER PRESS by Springer-Verlag Berlin Heidelberg

This T.M.C. ASSER PRESS imprint is published by the registered company Springer-Verlag GmbH, DE, part of Springer Nature.
The registered company address is: Heidelberger Platz 3, 14197 Berlin, Germany

Acknowledgements

One added benefit of writing a book is getting a chance to acknowledge the family, colleagues and friends who make such an undertaking possible. I am deeply thankful to my parents—Rineke for reviewing the book in its various iterations and for nurturing my curiosity when I was young, and Bas, for his unfailing appreciation of my work, which made writing an extra pleasant task.

I am also deeply grateful to my supervisors, Joris, Mireille and—in the first half of this trajectory—Nico van Eijk. Joris, thank you for guiding me through this endeavor with gentle and clear guidance. Your input was invaluable, and I cherish our friendship. Mireille, your years-long experience and broad knowledge of the legal field has elevated this book to a level I couldn't have achieved without you. Nico, thank you for giving me the chance to do this project in the first place and for your supervision during the first half. And lastly, Harry Buhrman, thank you for entrusting this project with me—it has been a true privilege to work on this for the past years.

I am also very grateful to the people who shared their expertise with me. Jeroen van Beek, our regular cups of coffee were an important source of inspiration, and your detailed feedback on the security-related aspects of the book made it much better. Similarly, I am very grateful to Matthijs Koot and Jaap-Henk Hoepman for reviewing parts of my book. My gratitude also goes out to Brendan Newitt, for giving feedback the section on criminal law, and to Joran van Apeldoorn, for providing input on some of the quantum-related parts. Yvonne Donders, thank you for reviewing an early draft of the part of this book on encryption as part of the Ph.D. process. I am also indebted to the people who in interviews brought me up to speed on the topics discussed in this book: fukami, Rickey Gevers, Jeroen van der Ham, Christian van 't Hof, Bart Jacobs, Karst Koymans, Cees de Laat, Christian Schaffner and Aristoteles Tzafalias. As you will see, many of the points raised during those interviews are reflected in the book. My thanks also go out to the participants of the '19 workshop in Berkeley for providing feedback on an early draft of the encryption analysis, and to the participants of the '19 PLSC workshop on encryption policy and quantum technologies for providing inspiration on the issues developed in this book. This also goes for my quantum reading group—Geoff, Joran and Joris—for the discussions on all things quantum. And thanks to Erica Moore for editing part of my book and to

Melinda Rucz for helping with the research—you saved me a ton of work. Of course, all errors and omissions remain mine alone.

Let me also thank the wonderful colleagues and students at the IViR. I am truly privileged to work among such an excellent group of curious and kind people. In particular, thank you to those who stood in for me when I was finishing the book, and thank you to Margriet Pauws-Huisink and Anja Dobbelsteen for their help in the background.

This is also the place for a shout out to the b03k3nc7ub, Alexander, Maurits, Axel, Jeroen and Hans—I thoroughly enjoy our meetings and look forward to having many more of them. Hans, thank you for the feedback on my book and for helping me getting my technical infrastructure in order, and for the numerous times I typed in as I was writing this. Sjoera, thanks for kickstarting my career in digital rights, which ultimately led me to this book. Martijn, our working together in an early part of my career made a long-lasting impression and shaped my idea of excellence in work and life in general. My thanks also go out to my anonymous font-dealer, for providing feedback on the design and generally being there to help in various ways. And the same goes for my parents-in-law, Cees and Gisela de Groot, for their support. Thank you also to Michel for our monthly meetings, which I enjoy very much and helped me stay on track. And thank you to my sister Noor, for always being there for me.

Finally, I want to thank my wife Anne—for encouraging me in my decision to write this book, for enabling me to write it and for always supporting what I was doing. And thank you for your love, strength, integrity and kindness.

This book is based on my Ph.D., which is called "Making and Breaking with Science and Conscience: The human rights-compatibility of information security governance in the context of quantum computing and encryption". I defended the Ph.D. in October 2022 at the University of Amsterdam. I also published parts of the Ph.D. (and thus this book) in separate papers.[1] The Ph.D. was supported by the Dutch Research Council (NWO) through the Gravitation-grant Quantum Software Consortium (no. 024.003.037).

January 2024 Amsterdam, The Netherlands

[1] Van Daalen O (2022) In Defense of Offense: Information Security Research under the Right to Science, Computer Law & Security Review 46: 105706; Van Daalen O (2023) The Right to Encryption: Privacy as Preventing Unlawful Access, Computer Law & Security Review 49:105804; Van Daalen O (2023) The Right to Root: Constructing a Claim to Control Devices from the Right to Privacy, JIPITEC, vol. 14, iss. 2023: 4, pp: 580-593; and Van Daalen O (2024) Developing a human-rights compatible governance framework for quantum computing, Research Directions: Quantum Technologies, vol. 2, 2024.

Contents

Chapter 1
Introduction

Contents

Abstract This chapter explains the scope, relevance and structure of the research presented in this book. The scope of the research is on the application of the human rights to privacy (and data protection), to freedom of expression and to science, to the domains of information security, encryption and quantum computing. The analytical framework for this exercise understands information security as a continuous cycle of making and breaking, and the relationship between encryption and quantum computing as an example of this.

Keywords Privacy · Freedom of expression · Right to science · Information security · Quantum computing · Encryption

1.1 Introduction

If you squint, *everything* is information—and the rest are computers in disguise. Genes, guns, vaccines, viruses—all digitised, available at the click of a button. And what about cars, skyscrapers, fridges, bikes? They are basically elaborate structures built around silicon chips. One of the important questions of the twenty-first century then is: who gets to access and control these information and systems?

First, laws have an important role to play here. If you want to know what data your phone collects, you can invoke data protection rules. If someone steals your phone, you can go to the police to hopefully get it back. And if the police then wants to listen in on a suspect's conversation, the telecommunications company has to let them do so.

O. van Daalen, *From Encryption to Quantum Computing*, Information Technology and Law Series 38, https://doi.org/10.1007/978-94-6265-635-2_1

But organisational rules are also important. The telecommunications company requires its employees to keep information confidential. The police are likely to prohibit employees from sticking passwords to their screen. And the phone manufacturer might have policies in place to prevent intelligence agencies from introducing a backdoor in their software.

And finally, technology is important. The software on your phone limits what you can do with it. You can change the settings on your phone to prevent a thief from viewing you pictures. And although telecommunication companies may have to grant access to the police, they also take technical measures to protect their network from attacks by others.

Determining who can gain access and control is an important part, perhaps even the main function, of the field of information security. This is done by *taking* measures. An organisation can, for example, install a firewall to determine which information may enter, and which may leave the network. Or it can implement access management measures to control who gets to use a system. But these measures are also constantly under attack. From criminals to corporations, from governments to academics, it looks like everyone is trying to *break* all the things, all the time. This, too, is part of the field of information security.

In fact, an accurate description of information security would have to involve this continuous cycle of making and breaking. Decades ago, when computers were the size of rooms and their global number could be counted on two hands, users were already battling with administrators over who was allowed to gain access. As these machines have shrunk, multiplied and gained in importance, these battles remain, and their impact has greatly increased.

In response, states have in the past decades adopted rules on information security. Some require organisations to take information security measures. Some rules prohibit attackers from breaking these measures. And some rules are aimed at mitigation, for example obliging organisations to notify authorities of data breaches.

However well-intentioned most of these policies might be, when you look at them as a whole, they tend to focus on the *making* side of things, often at the neglect of the *breaking* side. This approach is incomplete. Software and hardware will continue to contain weaknesses, and people will continue to find and exploit them. This dynamic of making and breaking is inherent to information security and cannot be rooted out. In this book, building on best practices in information security, I call this process of making and breaking the *information security cycle*.[1] And I argue that, in order for policies in this domain to be compatible with human rights, those policies must be developed around this continual cycle of discovery and mitigation.

Now, this dynamic of making and breaking plays out in various fields of information security, but one domain in particular attracts the attention of governments: encryption technologies. This technology is a fundamental building block of many

[1] See for instance, Article 32(1)(d), which refers to a process of regularly evaluating and if necessary, updating security measures; the ISO/IEC 27001:2013 standard on information security management systems, in which a similar approach can be found, ISO, ISO/IEC 29147:2014—Information technology—Security techniques—Vulnerability disclosure, 15 February 2014; and the now-deprecated Guidelines on securing personal data of the Dutch Data Protection Authority, CBP 2013.

information security measures, because it allows users to restrict access to information and information systems. But this power to keep information confidential also poses an obstacle for governments, who have traditionally been able to gain access to the information they require in the course of investigations. In response, governments have over the past decades fought back to ensure they retain access, by subverting and regulating these technologies. Because encryption is such a foundational information security technology, the stakes in this technological-regulatory battle are high.

Another technological development, however, promises to raise the stakes in this particular cycle of making and breaking significantly: the development of quantum computers. These new kinds of computers, built with fundamentally different technologies from today's computers, may in the next decades provide enormous computing power to their users. And one of the potential applications of this power is to break a widely used form of encryption, public key encryption, something I'll explain further in this book.

These developments are not only highly relevant for policy—they also have an important human rights angle. First, this information security cycle of making and breaking is *itself* strongly related to human rights, leading to significant questions. For instance: to what extent is the work by information security researchers protected by the right to science and the right to communications freedom (a concept I explain further below)? And can you limit the development of quantum computers as such, to protect private communications?

But the issue of who gets access to information, and who gets to control information systems—in other words: the *application* of information security measures—is obviously also important to the enjoyment of human rights. Policies in this domain have a bearing in particular to the human rights to privacy, data protection and communications freedom. This perspective also leads to important questions. To what extent do governments have an obligation to limit unauthorised access to your private data? Or are they actually allowed to limit information security measures, in order to maintain access to your data when necessary? And what do human rights say about who gets to control your phone—to what extent can companies restrict the functionality of devices?

The relationship between information security and human rights has not been developed in depth in the literature yet, and especially not while viewing information security as this cycle of making and breaking (I discuss the most important books and articles below). In this book, I explore the relationship between human rights and this cycle of making and breaking, using the arms race between encryption technologies and quantum computing as an important case study. There is one aspect of this relationship that I am particularly interested in, namely the obligations of states under human rights instruments. This book thus centers around the following question: what constitutes human rights-compatible governance of the information security cycle, encryption technologies and quantum computing?

1.2 Scope, Terminology and Limitations

In answering this question, a number of restrictions apply. One important restriction lies in the way I look at the *function* of information security (and encryption and quantum computing), as well as *research* into these domains. I take what you could call an "information based" perspective: I am primarily interested in how governmental measures and technologies enable and restrict the flow of information, and—related to this—how these measures restrict the use of information systems. This is why I emphasise how information security measures impose conditions on the creation, distribution and use of information and discuss how the information security cycle is dependent on the possibility of researching and sharing information. This perspective was chosen because it fits well with the primary function of information security technologies, which is to channel information flows and restrict the use of systems (I will get to the concept of information security in Chap. 2, but this description suffices for now). It also fits well with the dominant function of science, which is to develop and share knowledge, which is a particular form of information.

Because of this "information based" perspective, this book is also restricted to three human rights: the rights to privacy (and data protection), to communications freedom and to science. These rights are for a large part about the extent to which governments may, or must restrict information flows. Other human rights are, of course, also relevant for determining what governments may and must do in these domains. These include the classical rights, such as the right to human dignity, to physical and mental integrity, to freedom of thought and to assembly. These also include economic and social rights, such as the right to just conditions of work (where information security measures may enforce unjust conditions) and the right to strike (which might be made more difficult by information security measures). In some contexts, these specific rights may be even more directly applicable than the rights to privacy, communications freedom and science. Where a state is, for instance, jamming encrypted communications of protesters, this would probably be evaluated primarily under the right to assembly, not the right to communications freedom. But the reasoning with regard to these human rights will roughly mirror the three human rights discussed in this book, in particular when it comes to the more classical human rights.

Territorially, governmental measures at the European Union (EU) level are the main focus of this book. Most of the issues surrounding information security are global in nature, and thus require at least a regional response. I further argue that the EU bloc can play an important role as a pioneer, setting a global standard for human rights-compatible governance in the domain of information security, similar to what it did with regard to data protection. In fact, as we will see, the EU is also already quite active in this domain. I occasionally discuss policies and practices in specific member states, to the extent that these are relevant for determining the scope of EU policy, for example because member states implemented the rules originating from the EU, because a national constitutional court issued a judgment which is relevant at an EU level or because enforcement often takes place at the national level. There is of course an issue of competence here: many of these rules also affect national security, and national security falls within the remit of each member state. Moreover, to the extent that I conclude that states have a positive obligation to intervene, it is questionable whether this conclusion can be based on the Charter. I devote attention to these issues in Chap. 8.

This focus on the EU also means that I focus on the human rights instruments which are particularly relevant to EU and its member states, namely the European Convention of Human Rights (the Convention), the European Charter of Fundamental Rights of the European Union (the Charter) and the International Covenant on Social, Economic and Cultural Rights (the Covenant).[2] The Convention and the Charter play an important role for courts across Europe when assessing the compatibility of state measures. The Covenant, relevant for the right to science, is almost never applied in court, but it is generally considered to be an important source in policymaking, also in the EU.

From a substantive perspective, I discuss only a limited part of the broader field of information security: I focus on how information security technologies *restrict access* to information and *restrict control* of systems. But, as explained in Chap. 2, information security is about much more. For example, information security is also about the availability of information—whether a website is up or down—and about the authenticity of information—whether it has not been tampered with. However, assessing the connection between human rights and these other functions of information security would require a significantly different analysis, and is best suited for a different book.

In addition, information security is not only about technological measures in a narrow sense it is also about measures which are more organisational in nature, such as confidentiality obligations in contracts with employees, and organisational policies relating to access of systems. My analysis revolves around those aspects of information security which have a more technological character, such as encryption algorithms and changes to user software, because the policy debate is focused on these aspects. I will, however, occasionally also discuss the organisational framework in which these measures are embedded.

Part of this book is about developing a framework for substantive policy in the domain of information security. Throughout the book, I group governmental policies and practices under the header of *governance*, a term many will associate with a broader meaning, encompassing public and private institutions as much as rules.[3] I thus discuss only a part of what falls under the broader header of *governance—substantive governance*, if you will. This means I also leave a lot of things out

[2] Council of Europe (1950) European Convention on Human Rights (as amended by Protocols Nos. 11 and 14 and supplemented by Protocols Nos. 1, 4, 6, 7, 12, 13 and 16); European Union (2009) Charter of Fundamental Rights of the European Union; United Nations (1976) International Covenant on Economic, Social and Cultural Rights.

[3] See for example Möllers 2006. Under one oft-cited definition, this is the manner in which power is exercised in the management of a country's economic and social resources for development; The World Bank 1994, p. vii. This includes topics such as transparency surrounding policymaking, accountability of executive power, and the strength of civil society.

which are especially relevant in the context of information security. In particular, I barely touch on the administrative aspects of institutions which are tasked with safeguarding information security. For instance, I do not discuss the powers which are accorded to national cybersecurity centers and intelligence agencies, the role of public-private initiatives and how tasks are divided between these bodies. I also do not discuss in depth the role of the private sector in information security, for example through standardisation and market power. I acknowledge that these play a significant role in shaping the information security landscape, also historically. The reason for restricting my research this way has to do with space and clarity: the book already touches on a broad ranges of topics and including these aspects would not be helpful for the analysis. Connecting these aspects to human rights is, however, a valuable topic for further research.

Following up on this theme: in writing about substantive policy, I often refer to the *government* or *state* as if it were a monolithical unit. I acknowledge that things are usually not that simple. There are various institutions within a government, with often conflicting interests, and there sometimes are also competing teams within one institution. For example, intelligence agencies have already for a long time had the conflicting tasks of securing communication of some, while intercepting communication of others. This also explains why governance sometimes is inconsistent or illogical. Still, human rights law is not really concerned with the explanations as to *why* governance is the way it is—courts when applying human rights instruments view the state as the main unit of policy making, and I will do the same.

1.3 Structure and Approach

In answering what constitutes human rights-compatible governance of the information security cycle, encryption technologies and quantum computing, I employ a simple structure, distinguishing between the facts, the rules and the application of those rules. This book thus consists of three main parts. In Part I, I answer the question how governments are, and could be shaping the domains of information security, encryption and quantum computing. Because I review the human rights-compatibility of governance measures, the "facts" in this case not only consist of the technological landscape, but also the legal framework shaping this technological landscape. In Part II, I then discuss the rules by which these governance measures need to be assessed: this is the human rights framework which imposes limits on what governments *may* do and provides obligations on what governments *should* do. And then in Part III, I apply this human rights framework to each of the domains of information security, encryption technologies and quantum computing.

Zooming in on each of the chapters, the structure is as follows. In, on the technological landscape, I first describe the continuous cycle of making and breaking ingrained in information security—the information security cycle. I also discuss how encryption technologies are an important information security measure and explore how broad adoption of these technologies potentially impedes access to information by governments. I then discuss how quantum computing works, how this technology can break encryption and how these technologies can be expected to develop in the future.

In Chap. 3, on the legal landscape, I then provide an overview of current and potential governance measures in these domains. Here, I investigate how governmental policies and practices impact the information security cycle, again also focusing on encryption and quantum computing. I do this by discussing what the rules are, whether these rules are enforced, and whether uncertainty on the rules and their enforcement may make people more fearful to do things which would actually be legal or not enforced. I also explore how governments may steer future development through a broad range of potential interventions, for example by giving grants, investing in education and providing information on security threats. The goal is not to be complete—rather it is to provide an analysis of the most important governance approaches in these domains and illustrate the interests at play.

This chapter is partly a mere description of the rules. It is, however, also an analysis of *gaps* in regulation, particularly when it comes to information security. I conclude in the synthesis that states have an obligation under the human rights to privacy and communications freedom to close gaps in the information security cycle, so it is important to understand what these gaps are. For this gap analysis, I take as a starting point that many of the regulations discussed in this chapter are aimed at strengthening information security measures. And where these rules fail to do so in practice, I consider this a gap. My analysis is further based on the assumption that a smooth-functioning feedback loop in finding and fixing vulnerabilities is important for strengthening information security measures. Where this feedback loop is not functioning well, I also consider this a gap. To be clear: whether a gap needs fixing in view of human rights requirements is not part of this chapter—those questions will be discussed in the third part of this book.

After having described the landscape in Part I, I then develop the normative framework in Chaps. 4, 5, 6 and 7. As noted above, the yardstick by which I measure governmental policies and practices is human rights law, in particular the right to privacy (and data protection), the right to communications freedom (a term I explain further in Chap. 6), and the right to science. For the rights to privacy, data protection and communications freedom, I apply the Convention and the Charter. I only discuss national law when it is relevant for furthering the understanding of similar concepts as laid down in these European instruments. For the right to science, the Covenant and the Charter are relevant. In Chap. 5, I then discuss the rights to privacy and data protection under the Convention and the Charter. In Chap. 6, I review the right to communications freedom under these instruments. And in Chap. 7, I explore the right to science under the Covenant.

Finally, in Chaps. 8–11, I apply the human rights framework to the landscape described in Part II. For each chapter, I mirror the structure employed throughout this book—first laying out the factual and legal considerations for a specific domain, then summarising the conclusions with regard to human rights in this domain, and then developing policy recommendations. These chapters build on what has already been said in the earlier parts of the book—the sources are thus limited, while some of the earlier conclusions are reiterated. But the emphasis lies on the conceptual insights: what do the particular human rights imply for human rights-compatible governance in each domain. For each chapter, I also mention topics for further research. The book will end with the conclusion in Chap. 11, summarising my main findings.

I have frozen the description of the technological landscape, governance developments and analysis of case law around the beginning of 2023, and have incorporated only major developments in these fields afterwards.

This book is based on my Ph.D., which is called "Making and Breaking with Science and Conscience: The human rights-compatibility of information security governance in the context of quantum computing and encryption". I defended the Ph.D. in October 2022 at the University of Amsterdam. Parts of the Ph.D. (and thus this book) were published in separate papers.[4]

1.4 Relevance of This Book

The most important contribution of this book lies in the in-depth analysis of information security from the perspective of human rights. Academics have paid little attention to human rights in the context of information security, let alone understanding it as a dynamic process. Burkart and McCourt performed a somewhat similar analysis in *Why hackers win: power and disruption in the network society*, but this is focused more on the US, with less attention devoted to legal aspects.[5] Dizon, in his book called *Breaking and Remaking Law & Technology*, describes information security governance but does not pay as much attention to human rights as well.[6] Porcedda's book on the relation between "cybersecurity" and the right to privacy and data protection also deserves to be mentioned, but it has a narrower focus and a different goal, namely resolving the apparent tension between privacy and cybersecurity.[7] Arnbak in his 2015 book also touches on information security and human rights, but focuses more on an analysis of the development of different policy instruments in this field.[8] This focus on human rights also sets my book apart from currently dominant approaches to research in the field of information security, which are mostly about the economics, psychology and technology of information security.[9] For completeness, there have been some articles on the concept of *human security*, opposing it with *cybersecurity*,

[4] Van Daalen 2022, 2023 and two forthcoming papers, one on digital autonomy and the right to privacy, and one on quantum computing policy.

[5] Burkart and McCourt 2019.

[6] Dizon 2016.

[7] Porcedda 2017.

[8] Arnbak 2016.

[9] See Anderson 2020, Chap. 3 (psychology), Chap. 8 (economics) and referenced literature; see for an analysis of vulnerability disclosure policy from an economics perspective ENISA.

but this concept could be more grounded in human rights law.[10] And while human rights do play an important role in the context of encryption technologies, there is no recent literature analysing how encryption regulations should be assessed under European human rights law: the last in depth analysis, by Schulz and Van Hoboken, stems from 2016.[11] Finally, there is very little analysis of the legal implications of quantum computing, let alone of the human rights aspects of quantum computing. The major work in this field is *Law and Policy for the Quantum Age* of Hoofnagle and Garfinkel, but it has a decidedly US slant and touches on human rights issues only tangentially.[12]

In this book, I take the cycle of making and breaking as a central point in my analysis. While information security experts indeed view their work as part of this cycle, this generally is not how governance in the field of information security is devise. Dizon, mentioned above, also explores how the law affects the work of security experts, but does not emphasise the cyclical nature of information security itself. I believe that focusing on the offensive and defensive side of information security equally provides new insights as to how policy in the domain of information security—as well as in the domains of encryption and quantum computing—should be devised. It means, for example, that you need to actively provide room in governance for doing research on how to break things. This approach also emphasises the risk mitigation aspects that are involved when exercising human rights: if you know that vulnerabilities will continue to be found, it makes more sense to focus on mitigating the risks when they are found, then on finding them in the first place.

Another contribution of this book, is that I provide an up-to-date overview of EU governance measures in the domains of information security, encryption and quantum computing, taking the cyclical nature of information security as a starting point. Parts of these measures have already been mapped separately. See in particular, Arnbak's analysis of information security policy in the context of data protection, telecommunications, digital signatures and certificates, cybercrime and critical infrastructure, and Hofman's analysis of security measures in the context of data protection (see further the sources in Chap. 3).[13] There are furthermore many overviews of encryption governance, but this study provides a relevant contribution by discussing some of the more recent proposals from a human rights perspective and further developing the positive obligations of states in this regard. And when it comes to quantum computers, this is the first book which provides an overview on the limited governance measures in this domain in the EU (Hoofnagle and Garfinkel in their book mentioned above only touch on this in passing).[14]

---

[10] See for example Cavelty 2014; see also Salminen and Hossain 2018.

[11] Schulz and van Hoboken 2016.

[12] Hoofnagle and Garfinkel 2021.

[13] Arnbak 2016; Hofman 2022.

[14] Hoofnagle and Garfinkel 2021. Some papers have been written outlining a broad vision on governance of quantum computing, but there is no comprehensive attempt yet to map this governance space; see Perrier 2021; Johnson 2019; de Wolf R (2012) What Quantum Computing Can Do for You. Inaugural lecture; de Wolf 2017.

This broad mapping of governance measures also allows for a comprehensive gap analysis, resulting in a number of important insights. First, an insight from this analysis is that information security governance measures should be applied across all systems which are vulnerable to attacks—something which is not currently the case. This has already been suggested by BEUC in 2019, but without a legal analysis.[15] Also, the introduction of the *attack surface* as an atomic unit for policymaking is new: from an information security perspective, this is where the action takes place, so this is where governance measures should be directed. This has not been proposed previously. Lastly, my suggestion to introduce an exception for information security research has been proposed in other places before, but in this book I also provide the legal backing for this, basing it on the right to science and the right to communications freedom.[16]

On the human rights side, an important analytical tool developed in this book is the focus on the risk of *unlawful access*. Human rights courts have in the past emphasised the safeguards for *lawful access* to interests protected by privacy and communications freedom, mostly disregarding states' obligations when it comes the other type of access, *unlawful access*. But in fact, information security measures are mostly about preventing unlawful access. My conclusion is that measures which significantly increase the risk of unlawful access to information or systems, or unlawful control of information and systems, should be considered an interference. Furthermore, the conclusion that in many cases this interference is disproportionate, given the current state of information security, is important in future analyses of states' obligations in this domain.

With this book, I also draw attention to the double-edged nature of information security measures for human rights. Information security measures may in certain instances protect human rights, when the *human in question* is in control of the application of the measures, or when they benefit from this application. You might be able to determine yourself when you want to apply strong encryption, or strong encryption is built in the device you're using by default: in both cases you benefit from the privacy-protecting properties of encryption. But these measures may also negatively impact human rights, by restricting the freedom of people to access information and use systems. This perspective is already important for the analysis of the relationship between information security and human rights.

My analysis of the right to science also provides useful insights. The most relevant conclusion is that the duty of care that comes with the right to science has a role to play in steering policy debates. This duty of care under the right to science implies that policymakers and researchers have an obligation to mitigate the risks of potentially dangerous technologies. For information security, this means that the right to science also imposes on researchers a duty to disclose their findings. This is completely new and has not been proposed in literature before (it also leads to a number of practical questions on the boundaries of this duty). For quantum computing, the implication

[15] Oliveira da Silva 2019.

[16] See for example Schaake et al. 2018; ENISA (2015), para 6.3; and ENISA (2013), p. 10.

that governments must on the basis of human rights obligations invest in alternative, quantum resistant technologies, is also an important insight.

Now, although I limit myself mostly to information security in this book, the conclusions on states' obligations with regard to the right to science do not remain limited to information security only. These can also be translated to other fields where research can have positive or negative impacts.[17] For example, advances in artificial intelligence technologies can be used to impersonate people, but also to detect fake news. Virology research can be used to make viruses more deadly, but also to make vaccines. Understanding these technologies as part of a cycle makes it possible to develop governance steering their development and use in the public interest. In particular, the emphasis in information security on risk mitigation can also be useful for other fields—it could imply that experimenting with viruses can only be allowed if vaccines are developed simultaneously. I touch on this question in the conclusion.

References

Articles, Books and Other Documents

Anderson R (2020) Security Engineering: A Guide to Building Dependable Distributed Systems, 3rd edn. John Wiley and Sons, Indianapolis.

Arnbak AM (2016) Securing Private Communications: Protecting Private Communications Security in EU Law: Fundamental Rights, Functional Value Chains, and Market Incentives. Kluwer Law International, Alphen aan den Rijn, The Netherlands.

Burkart PC, McCourt TM (2019) Why Hackers Win: Power and Disruption in the Network Society. University of California Press, Oakland.

Cavelty MD (2014) Breaking the Cyber-Security Dilemma: Aligning Security Needs and Removing Vulnerabilities. Science and Engineering Ethics 20:701–715. https://doi.org/10.1007/s11948-014-9551-y

CBP (2013) Richtsnoeren: Beveiliging van persoonsgegevens. https://www.autoriteitpersoonsgegevens.nl/uploads/imported/beleidsregels_beveiliging_van_persoonsgegevens.pdf. Accessed 14 December 2023.

de Wolf R (2017) The Potential Impact of Quantum Computers on Society. arXiv:171205380 [quant-ph].

Dizon MAC (2016) Breaking & Remaking Law and Technology: A Socio-Techno-Legal Study of Hacking. Tilburg University, Tilburg.

ENISA (2013) The Directive on Attacks against Information Systems: A Good Practice Collection for CERTs on the Directive on Attacks against Information Systems. https://www.enisa.europa.eu/publications/the-directive-on-attacks-against-information-systems. Accessed 14 December 2023.

ENISA (2015) Good Practice Guide on Vulnerability Disclosure: From Challenges to Recommendations. https://www.enisa.europa.eu/publications/vulnerability-disclosure/at_download/fullReport. Accessed 14 December 2023.

ENISA (2018) Economics of Vulnerability Disclosure. https://www.enisa.europa.eu/publications/economics-of-vulnerability-disclosure. Accessed 14 December 2023.

[17] See on the governance of other types of dual-use technologies Harris 2016, comparing nuclear and biological technologies with the governance of vulnerabilities in cyberweapons.

Harris ED (ed) (2016) Governance of Dual-Use Technologies: Theory and Practice. American Academy of Arts & Sciences. https://www.amacad.org/publication/governance-dual-use-technologies-theory-and-practice/section/7. Accessed 14 December 2023.

Hofman JA (2022) De beveiliging van persoonsgegevens: Over de juridische invulling van art. 5 lid 1 onder f en 32 AVG. Kluwer Juridische Uitgevers, Deventer.

Hoofnagle CJ, Garfinkel S (2021) Law and Policy for the Quantum Age, 1st edn. Cambridge University Press, New York.

ISO, *ISO/IEC 29147:2014 - Information technology - Security techniques - Vulnerability disclosure*, February 15, 2014.

Johnson WG (2019) Governance Tools for the Second Quantum Revolution. Jurimetrics 59:4.

Möllers C (2006) European Governance: Meaning and Value of a Concept. Common Market Law Review 43: 313–336.

Oliveira da Silva F (2019) Keeping Consumers Secure. How to Tackle Cybersecurity Threats through EU Law, BEUC-X-2019-066. https://www.beuc.eu/sites/default/files/publications/beuc-x-2019-066_keeping_consumers_secure_-_how_to_tackle_cybersecurity_threats_through_eu_law.pdf. Accessed 14 December 2023.

Perrier E (2021) Ethical Quantum Computing: A Roadmap. arXiv:210200759 [quant-ph].

Porcedda MG (2017) Cybersecurity and Privacy Rights in EU Law: Moving beyond the Trade-off Model to Appraise the Role of Technology. European University Institute.

Salminen M, Hossain K (2018) Digitalisation and Human Security Dimensions in Cybersecurity: An Appraisal for the European High North. Polar Record 54:108–118. https://doi.org/10.1017/S0032247418000268

Schaake M, Pupillo L, Ferreira A, Varisco G (2018) Software Vulnerability Disclosure in Europe: Technology, Policies and Legal Challenges. https://www.ceps.eu/ceps-publications/software-vulnerability-disclosure-europe-technology-policies-and-legal-challenges/. Accessed 14 December 2023

Schulz W, van Hoboken J (2016) Human Rights and Encryption. UNESCO.

van Daalen O (2022), In Defense of Offense: Information Security Research under the Right to Science, Computer Law & Security Review 46: 105706.

van Daalen O (2023) The Right to Encryption: Privacy as Preventing Unlawful Access, Computer Law & Security Review 49:105804.

The World Bank (1994) Governance: The World Bank's Experience. The International Bank for Reconstruction and Development/World Bank, Washington, DC. https://elibrary.worldbank.org/doi/abs/10.1596/0-8213-2804-2, Accessed 3 January 2024.

Regulation (EU) 2016/679 of the European Parliament and of the Council of 27 April 2016 on the protection of natural persons with regard to the processing of personal data and on the free movement of such data, and repealing Directive 95/46/EC (General Data Protection Regulation).

Part I
The Landscape

Chapter 2
The Technological and Societal Landscape

Contents

Abstract This chapter explores the technological landscape, focusing on three topics: information security, encryption and quantum computing. With regard to information security, it highlights the ongoing struggle between creating secure systems and finding their weaknesses. It further underlines that the current state of information security is notably poor, with the complexity of IT systems providing ample opportunities for attackers. The chapter also touches on the dilemma faced by researchers who discover vulnerabilities on how to responsible disclose their findings. It finally examines the relationship between encryption technologies and quantum computing, suggesting that the development of quantum-resistant technologies is

O. van Daalen, *From Encryption to Quantum Computing*, Information Technology and Law Series 38, https://doi.org/10.1007/978-94-6265-635-2_2

crucial. The discussion intertwines technology and human rights, seeking a balance between government access to encrypted information and protecting individual rights.

Keywords Information security · Encryption · Quantum computing · Vulnerabilities · Coordinated vulnerability disclosure

2.1 Introduction

To most legislators, information security is something you *have*, not something you *do*. Your computer is either secure, or it is not, and when it is not—well, that's a problem. Politicians and victims often respond by assigning blame—the hacker who entered the system did so unlawfully, or the company left a gaping hole in its server because it did not patch it in time. But if we take a step back, it is clear that this unpatched server was not the first in the history of computing—millions have come before it, and millions will follow. What we see instead is a recurring process of finding weaknesses and fixing them, only for the next weakness to be discovered and fixed, and so on. That cat-and-mouse game between offence and defence? *That is* information security.

In this chapter, I take look at this continuous process, which I call the information security cycle.[1] In the first section, I describe the cycle itself. Then I describe an important measure which many organisations use to protect themselves: encryption technologies. In the final section, I review a technology which is expected to undermine many of these encryption technologies: quantum computing.

2.2 The Information Security Cycle

A central point of this book is that for policymaking, information security should be considered to be a continuous process. In this section, we look at this feedback loop from various vantage points. We first take the perspective of an organisation that wants to defend itself through its information security policy. Then we zoom out and take the perspective of a historian, showing how the cycle of making and breaking is ingrained in the user culture associated with different generations of computers, from mainframes in the seventies to current cloud services. Next, we take a deep dive into the life of a vulnerability, from initial discovery to final fix. And we acquaint ourselves with the work of those on the bug-hunting trail, from intelligence services to criminals, from companies to academic researchers. Lastly, we look through the eyes of the user and consider the devastating effects that the exploitation of a vulnerability

[1] Parts of this chapter have already been published in Van Daalen 2022, 2023a, 2023b, 2024.

can have on people's lives, and on IT infrastructure, but we also touch on some of the positive aspects of weaknesses in information security systems.

2.2.1 What Is Information Security?

This book is about information security—but what *is* information security exactly? In the literature, information security is often framed in terms of desirable *security properties* (also called *security objectives*). Three properties are commonly seen as fundamental building blocks: *confidentiality* (preventing unauthorised access to information), *integrity* (preventing unauthorised alteration of information) and *availability* (ensuring that information remains accessible to authorised users), often abbreviated as the CIA-triad.[2] There is an ongoing debate about whether other security properties should also be regarded as fundamental, or whether they are merely a combination of lower-level functions. For example, some authors include *authentication* (identifying an originating entity or the origin of data) and *non repudiation* (preventing the denial of previous commitments or actions) under this header as well.[3]

It is not necessary to resolve this debate here—all these security properties are just building blocks. For this book, a more interesting question is: what do you *use* those properties for? In this book, I am focusing on a particular function of information security—the function of (i) *access* and (ii) *control*, to and of, (iii) *information* and (iv) *systems*. Let me explain these four aspects. First, when I say information security is about restricting *access* to information, I am primarily talking about the building block of *confidentiality* described above. And then secondly, I'm broadening this notion of access to also include access to *systems*—to your phone, your computer, to your account, etc. Third, when I say *control* of information, I am talking about ways in which the use or distribution of this information can be restricted—this, for instance, is what digital rights management measures are aimed at. Obviously, information security plays an important role in those settings as well. And finally, when I talk about control of *systems*, I mean how information security measures can be aimed at restricting their functionality—think of an e-bike with a digitally imposed maximum speed.

To be clear: information security is about more than this. For example, I'm not touching on the function of information security for ensuring trust. But for this book, this limited notion of information security as access and control, to and of, information and systems, plays an important role in my analysis in subsequent chapters.

There is also another aspect to the notion of information security which is worth discussing upfront—*whose* information security are we talking about? When Apple takes information security measures to restrict users from installing apps outside of

---

[2] See Arnbak 2016, Chap. 5 for an in depth discussion of these concepts; and Menezes et al. 1997, p. 4 for the definition of the first two.

[3] Menezes et al. 1997, p. 4; see also Arnbak 2016, Chap. 5.

the app store, you could argue that this is done to keep the user secure: this way you can prevent malicious apps from being installed on the phone. But it also limits the user in what it can do with the phone. In fact, perhaps this measure benefits Apple even more than it benefits the user—Apple can ensure that it takes a cut of the income from all apps which are installed on this phone and exclude apps which compete with its own apps. We often see that the organisations which take information security measures consider the user to be an adversary—and this has implications for human rights as well.

This notion of who is the beneficiary of an information security measure is also relevant for a final distinction I want to discuss at the outset: the difference between information security and cybersecurity. Unfortunately, there is no clear line between the two. For one, cybersecurity is a buzzword, sometimes used to attract the readers' attention or to frame an old topic in a new way. It's also a vague term. As a result, you will sometimes see the term *cybersecurity* used in a way which is similar to my description of *information security* above. More often, though, the term *cybersecurity* is used to refer to a particular application of information security, namely to further specific, mostly state-related interests.[4] In those cases, it's about protecting critical infrastructure, about protecting against online terrorism, about online attacks by nation states, etc. And it can also be used in a context where it is more focused on preventing crime, gaining access to encrypted data in an investigation, even about preventing the stealing of intellectual property. For this book, however, it is not so important to delineate the two exactly, because I will avoid the term altogether, precisely because it has no clear meaning.

2.2.2 *Taking Information Security Measures*

Now, many organisations will, at some point in their development, take information security measures to defend against attacks. But it can be difficult to determine which measures make the most sense. Over the past decades, standard practices have emerged to help organisations make the best choices, even in the face of changing circumstances. These are generally subsumed under the *plan-do-check-act* cycle, originally developed for quality assurance in manufacturing, but applied in other contexts since, including in information security.[5]

In the first phase of the cycle, the *plan*-phase, an organisation will decide which measures are necessary in view of the risks. These decisions are usually laid out in an information security policy. In this policy, the *security requirements* (e.g. that certain information must remain confidential) are described in view of the *risks* to certain

[4] See Nissenbaum 2005.

[5] In the GDPR, controllers and processors are required to implement "a process for regularly testing, assessing and evaluating the effectiveness of technical and organisational measures for ensuring the security of the processing", Article 32(1)(d); in the ISO/IEC 27001:2013 standard on information security management systems, a similar approach can be found; see also the now-deprecated Guidelines on securing personal data of the Dutch Data Protection Authority; CBP 2013.

files (e.g. that intelligence agencies might hack the servers). The security *measures* (e.g. encryption) then follow logically from that scenario. In the second phase, the *do*-phase, the organisation then implements these measures.

Security policies are generally couched in terms of required security properties. For example: if you want to ensure the continuous availability of a website (a *requirement*) which might be attacked by people attempting to bring the website down (a *risk*), you might buy services to add bandwidth and capacity to your servers to mitigate this risk (a *measure*). That does not mean, of course, that these measures are always sufficient: perhaps the attack is bigger than expected and *still* brings your website down. These breaches, if detected, usually call for a response to address the newly exposed risks.

That is why information security policies need to be tested and reviewed periodically—the *check* and *act* phases of the cycle. You periodically check whether the measures are commensurate with the risks, then adjust as needed. This approach reflects the reality of the continuous cycle of making and breaking, which was already present in the early computing days, and is still with us, as we will see in the very short history of computing and hacking which follows.

2.2.3 Three Generations of Hackers; from Mainframes, to PCs, to the Internet

First a word of caution. This history is by no means complete. It merely serves to underline the argument that making and breaking security measures is as old as computing. It focuses mostly on the United States, partly because many accounts of hacking history, including Levy's *Hackers*, are situated in the United States, but also because the United States had, and still has, a significant influence on computing and the internet.[6]

The first generation of computer users—and the first to call themselves *hackers*, an honorific signifying a high degree of creativity and virtuosity with technology—came of age in the seventies, among giant computers in well-funded research institutions, one of the most prominent being MIT. Left to their own devices, these hackers developed one of the first ethical frameworks for computers—later summarised as the Hacker Ethic, which prescribed that: access to computers should be unlimited and total, all information should be free, mistrust authority, and promote decentralisation.[7] The best way to promote the latter, was "to have an open system, something that presents no boundaries between a hacker and a piece of information or an item

[6] Levy 2010; see for a European history of hacking Alberts and Oldenziel 2014; see for a recent analysis of the hacking landscape Burkart and McCourt 2019; see for a study focusing on hackers and free software Coleman 2013.

[7] Levy 2010, pp. 28–29.

of equipment".[8] You can see that the concept of information security was not really part of this mindset.

Yet these academic institutions were funded by the military; a culture which espoused compartmentalisation, hierarchy and authority.[9] While hackers in the very early days had been able to insulate themselves from this uneasy truth, it was only a matter of time before the military mindset presented itself in the form of mainframe systems with *access control*: two multi-user access systems were installed at MIT—CTSS and Multics—both containing password protection.[10] MIT hackers quickly found a way around it, and also developed an alternative operating system called the Incompatible Time-Sharing System, which did not have passwords and was designed to allow maximum access to any users' file.[11] A similar system at Stanford did not require passwords either, but did give users the option to keep files private. The hackers at Stanford took a particular interest in those privacy-conscious users. "Anybody that's asking for privacy must be doing something interesting", one hacker noted.[12]

Then, in the early eighties, computers became *personal* computers.[13] A second generation of hackers was born. Commerce imposed itself on the Hacker Ethic; hippies turned entrepreneurs, and started companies such as Apple.[14] The focus of hacking shifted, from accessing multi-user systems, to copying software on tapes and floppy disks, in some instances improving it to circumvent rules in games for example.[15] Bill Gates' famous Open Letter to Hobbyists on the unauthorised copying of his version of BASIC, back when Microsoft was still just two people, drives the point home: "most of you steal your software. [...] Who cares if the people who worked on it get paid?"[16] This did not stop hackers from bypassing copy-protection, though, if only to be able to understand the code and improve it.[17] In fact, Levy reports that most copy-protection experts who worked for companies, simultaneously moonlighted at home, figuring out ways to circumvent the protection measures of

---

[8] Ibid., p. 29.

[9] Thomas 2002, pp. 14–15.

[10] See Levy 2010, Chap. 6.

[11] Ibid., pp. 113–114, 118.

[12] Ibid., p. 137. One of the more principled hackers at the MIT Lab was Richard Stallman, the founder of the Free Software Foundation and the inventor of the GNU Public License, who generally objected to the use of passwords on the systems. He broke into one such system, decrypted the passwords of all users, and sent messages to them, suggesting that they switch to "carriage return" as their password; ibid., p. 439. Stallman changed the next iteration of the program to show the password on a display whenever you logged in, exposing it to bystanders.

[13] See Thomas 2002, p. 15.

[14] Ibid., pp. 30–34.

[15] See for example Alberts and Oldenziel 2014, para 2.4 (the Netherlands), Chap. 4 (Greece), paras 6.3 and 6.10 (Poland).

[16] Levy 2010, p. 233.

[17] Ibid., p. 391.

other organisations.[18] There is evidence that companies were hacking the copy-protection schemes of competitors, publishing the results online to advance their own interests.[19]

From the eighties onwards, personal computers were also increasingly outfitted with network technologies. First, people used them to connect to privately run servers, mostly bulletin board systems (BBS). But in the early nineties, internet access providers also started to offer the public at large a way to connect to the internet. People soon started hooking up their personal computers to these new networks, but quickly found out that increased connectivity was a double-edged sword. The internet is a gigantic copying machine—files can be duplicated without much effort across various systems. But the internet is also an excellent infrastructure for remote system intrusion: it provided outsiders a way into all kinds of computers connected online. The cat-and-mouse game thus expanded to accessing systems remotely.[20] And just as hackers had been hired to develop copy protection systems, the question for companies now arose whether hackers could be hired as security consultants to protect against *remote intrusion*.[21] Many hackers probably did both.

This arms race has not abated since. On the contrary, more parties are now involved and the stakes are higher than ever. Billions of devices have come online, and all kinds of people and organisations are interested in breaking information security for any number of reasons. Stories about governments hacking the IT systems of other states make headlines just about every week, from Iranian uranium enrichment facilities to the 2018 Winter Olympics in South Korea.[22] Data breaches are a daily occurrence. Weak spots in software and hardware, or *vulnerabilities*, are so common, and they are so often exploited, that it is possible to describe the standard lifecycle of a vulnerability. This will be done below, giving an overview of the actors and interests involved—through the story of the *Life and Death of a Zero Day*.

---

[18] Ibid., p. 392.

[19] See the account of a NewsCorp subsidiary hacking the TV smartcards of competitors; Burkart and McCourt 2019, p. 19.

[20] See a quote from Dutch hacker Rop Gonggrijp: "Computer security is like a chess-game, and all these people that say breaking into my computer systems is like breaking into my house: bull-shit, because securing your house is a very simple thing, you just put locks on the doors and bars on the windows and then only brute force can get into your house, like smashing a window. But a computer has a hundred thousand intricate ways to get in, and it's a chess game with the people that secure a computer"; Jordan and Taylor 1998, p. 774. See also for an account of Wau Holland and Steffen Wernéry's hack of Germany's *Bildschirmtext* in 1984, transferring DM 135,000 from the *Hamburger Sparkasse* to their own account; Alberts and Oldenziel 2014, Chap. 8; and for an account of the early days of the internet in the Netherlands, ibid., Chap. 9.

[21] Jordan and Taylor 1998, pp. 770–771.

[22] Zetter 2014; Greenberg 2019a.

2.2.4 The Life and Death of a Zero Day

Much of the information security discourse centres around the "vulnerability" or weakness, in software or hardware. An attacker can exploit a vulnerability to make a system act in a way which it is not supposed to do, or to be more precise: to violate a *security policy* discussed above.[23]

While you might in theory be able to make software and hardware without vulnerabilities, in practice it is virtually impossible. Making a product involves hundreds, if not thousands of suppliers, and suppliers of those suppliers.[24] Chips are built by one manufacturer, components and libraries built by others, with often some open source code thrown in as well. It is not doable to independently verify all of these components, and there are techniques for hiding backdoors in chips which are next to impossible to detect.[25] But more fundamentally, even such verification only provides limited assurance that a component can actually be trusted.[26]

As a result, many vulnerabilities are found in most widely used products after they are shipped, and even if they are shipped without vulnerabilities, the deployment by users might create new weaknesses. One particular attack underlines the complexity of the current IT ecosystem: supply chain attacks. These attacks target a supplier of components used by downstream customers. These attacks allow for gaining access at scale. For example, if you take over the software which is used to administer the networks of thousands of organisations, this is the equivalent of taking over the networks of these organisations themselves, but for a fraction of the effort. Some recent high-profile attacks have been carried out this way.[27]

---

[23] A vulnerability is defined as "a set of conditions or behaviors that allows the violation of an explicit or implicit security policy"; Householder et al. 2017, p. 2. The 2014 ISO/IEC standard on vulnerability disclosure defines a vulnerability as a "weakness of software, hardware, or online service that can be exploited"; ISO 2014 (since replaced), p. 2; see also Grance et al. 2002, pp. D–3: "A flaw or weakness in system security procedures, design, implementation, or internal controls that could be exercised (accidentally triggered or intentionally exploited) and result in a security breach or a violation of the system's security policy." See also the definition of Anderson: "A vulnerability is a property of a system or its environment which, in conjunction with an internal or external threat, can lead to a security failure, which is a breach of the system's security policy. By security policy I will mean a succinct statement of a system's protection strategy (for example, 'in each transaction, sums of credits and debits are equal, and all transactions over $1,000,000 must be authorized by two managers')"; Anderson 2020, Sect. 1.7.

[24] See for instance ENISA 2017.

[25] Levine 2020; Becker et al. 2014.

[26] See Thompson 1984 for a principled argument.

[27] Possibly Russian and Chinese attackers gained entry to thousands of high profile governmental organisations and companies through supply chain attacks, including network management tools; Sanger et al. 2021; Perlroth et al. 2021; Sanger and Perlroth 2020; Schneier 2021a, 2021b; Attackers were able to take control of Asus' servers and started pushing malicious software through its update mechanism, infecting hundreds of thousands of computers; Zetter 2019a; Kaspersky 2019; A year earlier, anti-virus software CCleaner was backdoored Steckler and Vlcek 2017; see also Greenberg 2019b.

One particular type of vulnerability is called the "zero day vulnerability", or simply the "zero day". It is a weak spot for which no fix has been created yet, usually because the vendor doesn't know of its existence. Of all vulnerabilities, zero days are the most coveted by attackers, because by definition there is not yet a direct defence for them, and that is why zero days can wreak the most havoc. Let's follow a zero day from inception to extinction.[28]

2.2.4.1 The Birth of a Zero Day

Our story begins with the *creation* of a vulnerability. A coder introduces a security bug in the system: perhaps a random number generator is not creating truly random numbers, or an online form does not have measures which prevent the unauthorised execution of submitted code. Of course, most of these bugs will be introduced accidentally. However, there are examples of vulnerabilities that appear to have been introduced intentionally.[29] Computer code often contains bugs, and the larger the program, the more bugs it probably contains.

Regardless of intent, another important distinction which we will draw upon further in this book, is the difference between *shipped* vulnerabilities, and *deployment* vulnerabilities. A package of software for a web server might be vulnerable—that is a shipped vulnerability. Or the way that server has been installed or configured on a particular computer leaves open a way to get in—that is a vulnerability in the deployment. The distinction is relevant, because shipped vulnerabilities generally have the potential to affect many more users than deployment vulnerabilities—the latter only affect the *instances* of products with an incorrect deployment. Shipped vulnerabilities on the other hand are a form of *class breaks*: vulnerabilities which affect all instances of a product.[30]

If you want to get a sense of your security exposure, it is usually not enough to look at vulnerabilities in isolation. IT systems are comprised of various components. For an attacker trying to enter a system, it can often be enough to find only one weak spot, in one of those components: the security of the system is as weak as the weakest link.[31] But the weakest link in what, exactly? This is where another

---

[28] See for a schematic overview Householder et al. 2017; Frei et al. 2010; and for earlier literature McHugh et al. 2000; and Schneier 2000. Not all of the phases described below neatly follow each other, and some are iterative; see Householder et al. 2017, p. xi.

[29] There is convincing evidence that the NSA introduced a backdoor in a random number generator used for encryption and it is possible that the NSA also introduced a backdoor in Juniper routers. There is the suggestion that someone covertly tried to install a backdoor in GNU/Linux around 2003; Corbet 2003. And the father of Linus Torvalds (one of the lead developers of GNU/Linux), who is a Finnish MEP, has even claimed in a European Parliament hearing that his son has been asked by the NSA to introduce backdoors in the source code; Falkvinge 2013. See furthermore an analysis of open source software supply chain attacks, which demonstrates that attackers have been able to insert malicious code in software repositories, for example by becoming a maintainer; Ohm et al. 2020, or through package squatting; Birsan 2021.

[30] See Schneier 2016, 2018, Chap. 1.

[31] See Schneier 2003, Chap. 8.

concept is useful, that of the *attack surface*. This concept also plays a role in later chapters, so it is useful to explain it further. The term was introduced in 2003 by a Microsoft developer, Michael Howard, who wanted to calculate the "attackability" of a product, or "its exposure to attack".[32] Howard applied the idea to products which could be somewhat clearly circumscribed, such as a certain version of Microsoft Windows. Since then, however, it has been used in the context of more than just a particular set of code. Theisen et al. reviewed hundreds of papers in which the term was used, and distinguish six themes. These range from a "programming-centric" definition—focusing on particular implementation methods in code—to a "user-centric" approach—focusing on data flow and control flow.[33]

However, the one which best captures the concept for purposes of this book, is what the authors call the "features" theme: the attack surface is an "enumeration of all available attack avenues to a target system". This definition emphasises the *problem* (exposure to attack), not the *cause*. Under this definition, the "surface" is not a technical boundary between the inside and outside world (as this distinction between inside and outside is hard to make in a highly connected world). It is a functional surface, a metaphorical surface, a mere collection of all the ways in which systems can get attacked.

This broad definition is useful for our purposes, because systems are increasingly built in a modular fashion, with different components provided by different organisations. This means that a growing part of this attack surface is not under the direct control of the organisation which offers the system. And from the perspective of the user or organisation which is exposed, it does not really matter whether an attack was performed through hardware, software, through external libraries or through code developed by the direct supplier. What matters is that their system was attacked. Yet, regulations are not built around this idea of the attack surface. In Chap. 8, I then propose a solution, where I will also discuss questions on the boundaries of this definition, in particular on what constitutes a *system* and what constitutes an *attack*.

2.2.4.2 The Unearthing of a Zero Day

After inception, many vulnerabilities will lie dormant, undiscovered for months if not years. But researchers are continuously on the lookout for bugs. Some work for the vendor: a researcher might work for Microsoft, looking to find holes in Windows. More often, however, vulnerabilities will be discovered by an outsider: as we will see, thousands of outside researchers around the world are constantly on the prowl, hunting for bugs, for a wide range of reasons and with a diverse range of backgrounds.

In more professional settings, researchers will, in some cases, determine the boundaries and conditions for an investigation into potential vulnerabilities beforehand, to ensure that the research complies with legal and ethical requirements. This at least is the case in certain universities, where security researchers are required to

[32] Howard 2003.

[33] Theisen et al. 2018, p. 99.

consult an ethical committee beforehand, usually requiring an analysis of the legality and proportionality of the research.[34] But in other settings, for example in the case of independent researchers, such formalities will sometimes be skipped.

Researchers hunt by disassembling hardware, trawling through lines of code and remotely testing online services. This used to be done manually, and still often is. However, many tools and services have come available which enable automatic testing. These range from tools cracking passwords to online services indexing potentially vulnerable connected devices; from tools mapping devices on large networks to sophisticated software analysing code with the help of artificial intelligence.[35] Some of these tools are developed and maintained within academia; some are developed by commercial companies, and some by individuals as a side project. Some are available for free, and some for a commercial fee.

Many of these tools have a *dual use*: they can be used by organisations defending their systems in order to check for vulnerabilities, *and* they can be used by malicious attackers to find and then exploit vulnerabilities.[36] This is unavoidable: you cannot draw a clear line between tools which are intended to search for a vulnerability with the goal of *exploiting* it, and tools which are intended to *fix* it. That's also the case for tools which execute an exploit: the best way to test whether something is vulnerable, even for defensive purposes, is to actually exploit it.

This is an important point throughout the book, so let me rephrase it: if there is an offensive purpose for a tool, there's also a defensive purpose. For example: a software tool which allows for the cracking of passwords can at first sight be used only offensively, by criminal organisations to gain unauthorised access to online services. However, it is also useful for a system administrator to know whether the password of one of its users can be easily cracked or, has been cracked, and then prohibit the user from using that password. The law is struggling with this dual nature of tools and vulnerabilities, as we will see in Chap. 3.

Since the information security of a system is as strong as its weakest link, researchers who are looking for vulnerabilities generally have the upper hand. The attacker only needs one vulnerability in the attack surface to gain access, whereas the defender needs to close every potential gap. This is called the *Defender's Dilemma*.[37]

---

[34] See for an early discussion on the topic Buchanan et al. 2011; Aycock et al. 2012.

[35] See for password cracking for example; for a connected device search engine Shodan Team. The Shodan.io website. https://www.shodan.io/. Accessed 15 January 2020; for mapping tools ZMap Team The ZMap Project. https://zmap.io/. Accessed 15 January 2020.

ZMap Team; Herpig 2019; Buchanan et al. 2020; and Schneier 2021b for a discussion of artificial intelligence in information security.

[36] See Bratus et al. 2014, p. 10: underlining the importance of offensive research for information security: "Without a concerted effort to claim its place, offensive computing will end up being further marginalized, nearly impossible to practice outside of costly legal protection, and completely impossible to practice as a citizens' science"; and see Geer 2014: "Part of my feeling stems from a long-held and well-substantiated belief that all cyber security technology is dual use. Perhaps dual use is a truism for any and all tools from the scalpel to the hammer to the gas can—they can be used for good or ill—but I know that dual use is inherent in cyber security tools."

[37] There is also the Attacker's Dilemma—defenders have the upper hand when it comes to *detection*, because they can set surveillance measures within their network in advance, and tripping over only

As discussed in the introduction, this dilemma was always there. But because there now are many people with various interests in attacking widely used software and hardware, armed with tools that automatically scan for vulnerabilities, the balance has tilted even more towards offence, increasing the chances of a vulnerability being found. This has profound implications for the information security cycle, which will be further discussed in Chap. 3.

2.2.4.3 The Discovery and Disclosure of a Zero Day

After the research has started, there comes the moment of discovery, and—in most cases—subsequent disclosure. This is an important moment in the life of a zero day, because how the zero day will be disclosed depends on who has found it. When the vendor itself discovers a weakness in its own product, it might fix it before others become aware of it. But most vulnerabilities are in fact discovered by *others* than the vendor. In that case, several scenarios are possible. It occurs quite frequently that an outside researcher might come across a vulnerability, but will not do anything with it—for example because it was found while breaking the law, and reporting the vulnerability might lead to liability. But it can also happen that a researcher will choose to use it to attack—in this case you can head directly to Sect. 2.2.4.4 on the weaponisation of a zero day. Or the researcher will disclose it in one way or another. To *whom* the disclosure is done makes a lot of difference, as we will see.

Some researchers aim for public disclosure, usually after giving the vendor time to fix the problem. Highly specialised research groups at universities spend years looking for bugs in widely used systems.[38] These university researchers will generally want to disclose their research in academic papers, to be published at conferences. But there are also groups of experts working within private companies who share their work widely: Project Zero, for example, is a team of expert security researchers at Google who focus on finding zero days in their own products and the products of others, publicly disclosing the found weaknesses on their blog.[39] Lastly, there are independent researchers who share their findings with the public.[40]

Some researchers will, on the other hand, not disclose the vulnerability to the outside world, but only disclose it to the vendor. There are, for example, many companies and researchers which offer security assessments as a consulting service. These researchers often also do research on their own initiative, not on the basis

---

one wire is already sufficient for them to get noticed. Still, sometimes even when you are noticed, you still have the possibility to do damage.

[38] In the Netherlands, for example, Radboud University has found weaknesses in NXP's Mifare-chip used globally for authentication in locks and public transport systems, and in SSD hardware encryption (see Chap. 3).

[39] Evans 2014; Stone 2019.

[40] See for example the work of the Dutch Institute for Vulnerability Disclosure, https://www.divd.nl/.

of an engagement.[41] Some researchers top up their income or even provide in their livelihood with rewards from bug hunting through *bug bounty* programs, through which companies can offer a reward to anyone who tips them off to a vulnerability.[42] Sometimes, the reporter is allowed to also publish her findings after publication, but that will depend on the vendor's policy. Companies also offer intermediary services, publishing bug bounty programs for its partners, and handling bug notifications and payouts—prominent examples of this are HackerOne and Bugcrowd.[43] This is a significant market: HackerOne in 2020 reported paying out USD 100 million since its inception.[44]

Some researchers only focus on the in-house development of zero days *without* disclosure to the vendor and the public, instead opting to sell what they've found to interested parties.[45] There is a motley crew of government institutions, researchers, companies, and criminals, as well as companies selling vulnerabilities to those parties. The business is controversial and is sometimes compared to the arms trade.[46] It is also a world about which we know very little. What we *do* know, is that this market is driven by some serious money. We can get a glimpse into the value of zero days through the companies that buy these unfixed vulnerabilities. Zerodium, formerly called Vupen, is such a company. It touts itself the world's leading zero-day acquisition platform, and offers to pay up to USD 2.5 million for weaknesses in systems.[47] Some of the other high-profile outfits are Dubai-based Crowdfense (offering bounties in the millions to supply "institutional Customers with a steady stream of actionable Cyber Capabilities"), Australia-based Azimuth Security (reported to provide in-house developed exploits to countries such as the US, UK and Australia) and Exodus Intelligence (buying and providing vulnerabilities as well as exploits to its customers).[48] The price of bug bounty programs has come to mirror—to a certain

---

[41] For example, Security Research Lab, which has done extensive work on the security of mobile phone communications, calls itself "a hacking research collective and think tank working on consultancy and in-house projects as well as tools at the cutting edge of security research"; Security Research Labs Security Research Labs. Corporate Website. https://srlabs.de/. Accessed 3 December 2019.

[42] See for an early empirical study Finifter et al. 2013.

[43] Hackerone Bug Bounty—Hacker Powered Security Testing. https://www.hackerone.com/index.php/. Accessed 26 November 2019.

Bugcrowd About. https://www.bugcrowd.com/about/. Accessed 4 December 2019.

[44] Mickos 2020.

[45] See Ablon and Bogart 2017; and for earlier reports Fidler 2015; Greenberg 2014, 2012a, 2012b; Ablon et al. 2014; Zoller 2011; Radianti et al. 2009; Miller 2007. Other firms mentioned in these reports are Netragard, Arc4dia, ExploitHub, Errata Security, iDefense, Revuln and Endgame, but it is uncertain whether they are still active in the zero-day market.

[46] Fidler 2015; The Economist Staff 2013.

[47] Zerodium 2019a, 2019b, 2019c; Although it expected prices to drop mid-2020 because of surplus in iOS-exploits; Zerodium 2020.

[48] Crowdfense Bug Bounty program. https://www.crowdfense.com/bug-bounty-program.html. Accessed 26 November 2019. Crowdfense Customers. https://www.crowdfense.com/customers.html. Accessed 26 November 2019; Franceschi-Bicchierai 2018a, 2018b; Exodus Intelligence Research Sponsorship Program. https://rsp.exodusintel.com/#about. Accessed 26 November 2019;

extent at least—the rates offered by these zero day-firms: Apple offers up to USD 2 million for some vulnerabilities.[49]

Not all of the researchers are in it for the money, of course. Academics are probably after academic acclaim. Companies might want to improve security, improve their reputation and perhaps even hurt competitors. Some, mostly consulting outfits, are after publicity: a good hack can generate precious attention. Individuals might be motivated by an addiction to computers, curiosity, thrill-seeking, the desire for power, the 'lulz' or as a political act.[50] Others might wish to improve security for the general public.[51]

2.2.4.4 The Weaponisation of a Zero Day

We have seen that, after discovery, the lives of zero days diverge sharply, depending on who found them. When an intelligence agency finds a zero day, it might keep it to itself. When it is found by one of the commercial outfits specialising in the sale of zero days, it might end up in a vulnerability feed, through which customers, usually governments and companies, are informed that there is a weakness in a system. Some of these zero day-platforms pay lip service to the idea that the information they are peddling is used by customers to shore up their defenses.

This is unlikely, however, where the zero days are related to software and hardware which is not developed or maintained by the recipient of this information. This because customers of these vulnerability feeds will have only a limited array of responses available: they can either stop using the affected product or create a workaround. When the vulnerability is in software which is available in source code, a customer would in theory be able to develop a patch to fix the code itself—but in most other cases they are not, or they have to build a complicated fix. It is therefore quite likely that customers will instead use the zero day to attack. Likewise, if an intelligence agency found the zero day, it may not disclose it to others but instead keep the vulnerability to itself to attack—as we will see in Chap. 3, there is a heated debate on whether this is desirable. And where an organisation decides to attack, we move on to the next phase of a zero day: the weaponisation.

This is done by converting the vulnerability into a working 'exploit': executable code which allows for the circumvention of a security policy. Some intelligence services and criminals will develop these exploits themselves to break into systems. If we zoom in on those exploits which are turned into weapons, you will notice that these also contain a propagation method (e.g. an attachment in a mail or an infected

---

Exodus Intelligence About us. https://www.exodusintel.com/about.html. Accessed 26 November 2019.

[49] Apple Security Research (2023) Bug bounty categories. https://security.apple.com/bounty/categories/. Accessed 14 June 2023.

[50] Jordan and Taylor 1998, p. 768; Coleman 2014, pp. 31, 263.

[51] See Thomas 2002, p. 44; van't Hof and Messers 2016.

advertisement) and a payload.[52] An exploit is intended to gain access in the broader sense—a preliminary action—whereas a payload is intended to do something *after* having gained access (exfiltrating or deleting data).

Many organisations operate weaponised exploits. The NSA is known to stockpile vulnerabilities and has created an automated system for infecting targets, but other intelligence services likely do the same.[53] Not only governments and criminals do this, though: there are also companies which make money by weaponising vulnerabilities, and then selling them. The Israel-based NSO group offers a mobile spyware suite called Pegasus, which allows for the remote surveillance of mobile phones with zero days, used by governments and others around the world, some to deadly effect, as we will see.[54] In 2018, another spyware suite called FinFisher, developed by now-bankrupt Pegasus competitor Gamma International, operated command-and-control servers in 25 countries, ranging from Australia to Indonesia, with, in some cases, strong indications of politically-motivated targeting.[55] Gamma Group advertised "access to a large library of 0-day and 1-Day Exploits for popular software like Microsoft Office, Internet Explorer, Adobe Acrobat Reader and many more", to use with its surveillance technologies, even *guaranteeing* four viable exploits.[56] Lastly, Citizen Lab in 2014 identified 21 suspected government users of another spyware suite offered by Italy-based Hacking Team (since called Memento Labs).[57] I discuss some of the effects of this exploitation in the section that follows.

It is not always necessary for an organisation to go to great lengths to develop an exploit: you can sometimes just steal the exploits from others. For instance, it is suspected that Chinese intelligence agencies discovered an attack by the NSA on its own systems. They then not only stopped the attack, but are suspected of repurposing those tools for their own offensive purposes, attacking EU and Asian targets in 2016.[58] Some of these exploits later turned up on the internet as well through a leak by a group calling itself the Shadow Brokers (see below). And this also works the other way: Huawei has been suspected of backdooring routers it has sold to mobile networks globally, which would enable China to listen in on, or disrupt

---

[52] Herr and Rosenzweig 2014, p. 304.

[53] See the description of the FOXACID system; Schneier 2013a, 2013b. In 2017, WikiLeaks released a trove of documents, allegedly from the CIA, which also contained exploits, including one zero day for Cisco routers, which Cisco investigated and then patched; Cisco 2017; Cisco IOS and IOS XE Software Cluster Management Protocol Remote Code Execution Vulnerability. https://tools.cisco.com/security/center/content/CiscoSecurityAdvisory/cisco-sa-20170317-cmp. Accessed 18 September 2019.

[54] Citizen Lab reported in 2018 that operators in 45 countries were using Pegasus, and at least 10 of these appeared to be actively engaged in cross-border surveillance; Marczak et al. 2018a, 2018b. Of these, six operators were linked to countries with a dubious human rights record. It has even impersonated a security page of Facebook to infect victims; Cox 2020.

[55] Marquis-Boiré et al. 2013; see Chaos Computer Club 2022.

[56] Privacy International 2018.

[57] Marczak et al. 2014; Franceschi-Bicchierai 2019. This group also appears to sell and use zero day exploits; Privacy International 2018.

[58] Perlroth et al. 2019b.

mobile communications.[59] This has been the topic of much controversy, as Huawei is a major provider of equipment for 5G networks currently being rolled out. But at the same time, the NSA is reported to have hacked Huawei's servers because, according to the NSA, they want to make sure that they know how to exploit these products, to "gain access to networks of interest" as well.[60]

2.2.4.5 The Gradual Disclosure of a Zero Day

Fortunately, not all zero days end up in a weaponised exploit—some are discovered by public-minded researchers who want to fix the hole and will disclose the vulnerability. But these security researchers have to perform a tricky balancing act. Security researchers want to push knowledge of the vulnerability out in the open quickly—perhaps partly for fame or academic acclaim, but primarily because they want to make users aware of the existence of the vulnerability. While they are waiting for a patch, users can then decide to either not use the service or tool, or develop a patch themselves. The need for a speedy release becomes more pressing as knowledge of the vulnerability spreads, because the risk of exploitation by others then also increases.[61] If a vulnerability is being exploited in the wild, immediate release might even be called for.[62] And in some high-stakes cases, the longer security researchers have to sit on a vulnerability, the greater the risk that they might themselves become a target.[63] On the other hand, disclosing a vulnerability which is not fully fixed exposes users to serious security risks. Sometimes, the political implications of security research, such as that Russia was involved in taking down the power grid in Ukraine, can also be a reason for not exposing it.[64]

This is why *coordinated vulnerability disclosure* (CVD) procedures have been developed.[65] CVD processes are the outcome of a fierce debate over the past decades on the best approach to disclosure. Some in this debate feared that waiting for

---

[59] Reichert 2020.

[60] Sanger and Perlroth 2014.

[61] For example, researchers at the Vrije Universiteit reported that after not publishing their findings on CPU-weaknesses, they were getting reports that information on the vulnerabilities was being shared; Zetter 2019b.

[62] For example, Google Project Zero employed a seven day-deadline for disclosure of vulnerabilities which were being exploited in the wild; Stone 2019.

[63] There is one reported incident of a Belgian cryptography professor, Jean-Jacques Quisquater, being hacked, but is uncertain who was behind the hack; Constantin 2014; Eeckhout and Vanhecke 2014; see more recently for a campaign targeting security researchers; Weidemann 2021.

[64] See for example private researchers coming to an agreement with the US government to not publish their findings with regard to the Ukraine; Greenberg 2019c, pp. 60–61.

[65] Forms of limited disclosure were initially called "responsible disclosure", but because the term "responsible" meant different things to different people, the term "coordinated vulnerability disclosure" was embraced; see MSRC 2010; see for an older legal analysis of when disclosure helps security Swire 2004.

the vendor to develop remediating measures before publicly disclosing a vulnerability would stall the process. They argued for full disclosure. Full disclosure means publishing all information on a vulnerability to everyone at the same time, usually before the vulnerability is fixed.[66] Others were highly critical of full disclosure, arguing that it creates "information anarchy" and only helps the attackers.[67]

Disclosing vulnerabilities does indeed increase the frequency of attacks.[68] But on the other hand, it also incentivises vendors to release patches.[69] CVD is a middle-ground solution that gave vendors time to come up with a fix, after which the vulnerability would be disclosed.[70] The process is not entirely uncontroversial, with reputable security experts undecided on how CVD procedures should be shaped, as we will also see below.

As a consequence, not all disclosure will proceed without a hitch. Sometimes, researchers are obstructed by court cases. There are several examples of security researchers being sued for exposing vulnerabilities in their research. In 2008, chip-maker NXP sued Radboud Universiteit and its researcher, who were intending to publish an article describing how they cracked the security of the widely used Mifare-chip (the court denied the request to prohibit publication).[71] In another high-profile case, Volkswagen was granted an injunction in a UK high court relating to the publication of research into keyless theft.[72] After two years of negotiation, Volkswagen eventually agreed the paper could be published, albeit with one sentence struck out.[73] Apart from these high-profile cases, there are also examples of people being sued for publishing information security research (or intending to do so).[74] There is also an example of a security researcher proactively suing before publication.[75] Not only are researchers impeded by court cases—sometimes, they are also denied the opportunity to present their work with other experts. There are instances of researchers being

---

[66] See Schneier 2007, at least as a fallback option to incentivise vendors to embrace other kinds of disclosure policies. It should be noted that in addition to the audience to which you're disclosing, there is also a debate on the information you're disclosing. Full-disclosure in this context would mean that not only information on a vulnerability, but also particular exploits would be published, which would allow others to actually use the information to breach a system very easily.

[67] See for example Culp 2001.

[68] Arora et al. 2007.

[69] Nizovtsev and Thursby 2007; Arora et al. 2008, 2010. It might even spur further research into the security of a product; Jo 2019. See also Swire 2004, for an early, less economics based model for when disclosure helps security. See for other analyses; Choi et al. 2010; Ransbotham and Mitra 2013.

[70] See for example ISO 2013; ENISA 2015; and NCSC 2018.

[71] District Court of Arnhem, ECLI:NL:RBARN:2008:BD7578, NXP/RUN (Mifare-chip), Judgment of 18 July 2008; see also Garcia and Jacobs 2016. A vivid description of the events leading up to the court case regarding Mifare can be read in Van't Hof's account; van't Hof and Messers 2016, Chaps. 3 and 4.

[72] EWHC 1832 (Ch), HC13C02168, Volkswagen Aktiengesellschaft v Garcia & Ors, Judgment of 25 June 2013; O'Carroll 2013; Verdult et al. 2013.

[73] Grierson 2015.

[74] See for example Whittaker 2017a; Zetter 2015; Rey 2015; FireEye 2015.

[75] See Electronic Frontier Foundation 2016.

denied visas to speak at conferences.[76] There is also one known instance where the programme committee of a government-sponsored conference interfered with the content of talks.[77] And there are examples of employers prohibiting their employees from presenting their findings at security conferences.[78]

2.2.4.6 The Fixing of a Zero Day

But even when there is no court case, no conference blocking publication and no employer taking measures, the application of CVD procedures is not always straightforward. The increasing interdependence of all parties in the supply chain makes it difficult to coordinate disclosure processes, let alone assign responsibility for making a patch available. When researchers at Radboud University found a vulnerability in the hardware encryption of Samsung, Crucial and Sandisk SSDs, it wasn't the hard drive vendors who made a patch. It was Microsoft. That is because Microsoft had been turning off software-based encryption automatically if it determined that an SSD already offered hardware-based encryption. So *Microsoft* could most easily provide a patch for what was essentially a hardware problem. And ultimately, they did.[79]

But some vulnerabilities cannot be fixed, and others are very hard to fix, or can be fixed only with a significant performance hit. This is particularly the case with hardware based-vulnerabilities, because it is more difficult to replace chips than programs. In one example, researchers found a flaw in a key security component, a TPM module, which could only be addressed by changing the chip, which is next to impossible for hardware which is already built.[80] We have seen multiple attacks on Intel and AMD CPUs, allowing for unauthorised reading of memory, which could only be remedied (partly) by software which slowed the processor down significantly, which then also were circumvented, and required additional mitigations.[81] Another example is software which allowed users to gain full access to their phone (called jailbreaking) with the telling title *checkm8*, affecting a wide range of iPhone and iPad models.[82] Because the attack involved a hardware component of the phones, it was simply unpatchable.

Meanwhile, many cheap embedded devices have only limited support from their vendor: a Chinese producer of connected children's toys will not always bother with pushing updated firmware to its devices if a bug is found.[83] As a result, hacked

[76] See for example Whittaker 2017b; Spring 2019; Thomson 2019; Aftergood 2013.
[77] See Schneier 2019; Taylor 2019.
[78] See Zetter 2005, 2010; Schwarz 2012.
[79] Meijer and van Gastel 2019.
[80] Moghimi et al. 2019.
[81] Kocher et al. 2019; Lipp et al. 2020; Larabel 2021; Ren et al. 2021; University of Virginia School of Engineering and Applied Science 2021.
[82] Potuck 2019; Lee 2019.
[83] See for an analysis of manufacturers' firmware update provision; Rodríguez et al. 2021.

fridges have been observed sending spam, and security cameras have been recruited in DDoS-attacks.[84]

Because it is sometimes difficult to develop a patch, and because some companies go into damage control mode when confronted with a vulnerability, the period that security researchers grant to vendors for fixing a vulnerability is still heavily contested. The desired policy is rather delicate, because in the phases between the discovery of a vulnerability and the deployment of remediation measures, the vulnerability remains exposed. The window of exposure opens when a vulnerability is discovered and grows as knowledge of the vulnerability spreads. Only when remediation measures are developed and applied, does the window start closing again.[85]

From a security perspective, the idea is to keep the window of exposure as short as possible—by delaying disclosure while patching swiftly. This is evidenced by the debate around vulnerabilities in Intel CPUs, where the researchers held off on publicly disclosing the vulnerabilities for months in order to give Intel the time to develop patches, but when the patches didn't address the root cause of the vulnerabilities—a faulty hardware design of their chips—Intel asked them to postpone publication for some additional months.[86] Ultimately, the team of researchers decided to publish their findings regardless of whether Intel brought out a patch, also because the vulnerabilities were starting to become known among the wider community of researchers: "*Anybody can weaponize this. And it's worse if you don't actually go public, because there will be people who can use this against users who are not actually protected*", one of the researchers said.[87]

The period granted for fixing a vulnerability depends in part on how likely it is that a vulnerability will be discovered independently. This is the "collision rate"—the likelihood of two people finding the same vulnerability. Ablon and Bogart find that exploits and their underlying vulnerabilities have an average "life expectancy" of 6.9 years (the time between first discovery and public disclosure), and that for a given stockpile of zero-day vulnerabilities, after a year, approximately 5.7% have been independently discovered.[88] Herr, Schneier and Morris report for their dataset, in the period between 2009 and 2016, a rediscovery rate of 12.7%, where "for Android and Chrome, more than 60% of all rediscovery takes place in the first month after the original vulnerability's disclosure".[89] Where there is already evidence that a vulnerability is actively being exploited, this would of course favour speedy disclosure.[90] But even when a company is confronted with attacks using its vulnerability in the wild, it may still hold off with bringing out a patch: Microsoft waited two years

---

[84] Corera 2014; Graff 2017.

[85] Schneier 2000.

[86] Zetter 2019b.

[87] Ibid.

[88] Ablon and Bogart 2017.

[89] Herr et al. 2017, p. 22. See further earlier research; Ozment 2005 which concludes that "vulnerability rediscovery occurs 'in the wild' and that it is not particularly uncommon".

[90] See on the prevalence of zero-day attacks before disclosure Bilge and Dumitraş 2012.

before patching a serious vulnerability in the program signature validation code of Windows.[91]

Even when a patch has been developed, users still have to apply the patch, something they often fail to do in time, or fail to do at all. And while most operating systems have automated systems for installing security updates, they too require an action on the part of the user. Many people do not install security updates as a result.[92] Large organisations will generally only install updates in regular update cycles, in order to first test the effects of an update and only then roll it out across the system. These cycles may take months, and the internal processes are not always in place to identify high priority security updates which require quicker fixes.[93] Smaller organisations may not have an update policy in place, and some organisations will avoid updating their systems because they fear it might break something. Furthermore, many embedded devices are coming online which are more difficult to patch. It is harder to update your smart lamp, than it is to update your laptop, if only because most lamps and other consumer products tend to have a poor user-interface. This all means that while the risk that a zero day poses might be mitigated in theory when a vendor offers a patch, the vulnerability can still live on in systems that fail to apply the patch. This is sometimes called a N-day. And while zero day vulnerabilities might often be more newsworthy because of their novelty, these will eventually become N-days, and many of the breaches we read about can be attributed to these N-days.

2.2.5 *The Devastating Effects of Exploits and Other Breaches*

Now, all these breaches may seem harmless—clever digital tricks affecting an abstract, mathematical world. But that does not do justice to the severity of their consequences, as these attacks affect people and organisations in real ways. Some of these will be discussed. To be fair, not all of these examples of attacks make use of exploits, but some of them do and the point remains valid, regardless of whether the attack involved an exploit or not. Take data breaches, for instance.[94] Some breaches, such as the Yahoo-breach of 2013, involve data on *billions* of users, and many affect *millions*.[95] Meanwhile, for each record obtained, there is potential for misuse. This

[91] Krebs 2020.

[92] See for example Koot 2020, which describes the situation where a security-critical patch was not installed by large organisations, even months after a patch was made public.

[93] For example, a high-risk vulnerability in VPN software was already discovered and fixed in April 2019 by the vendor, but turned out to be exploited in August 2019, with hundreds of large organisations not having installed the patch; Koot 2019; Modderkolk 2019.

[94] Many data breaches have occurred because the information systems were badly secured and a good number became accessible through the use of exploits: of the top ten data breaches between 2005 and 2018 in terms of quantity of leaked data, seven are a result of hacking; Hammouchi et al. 2019, p. 1006.

[95] See Perlroth 2017; Hammouchi et al. 2019, p. 1006. Data breaches are a recurring theme in the Internet Organised Crime Threat Assessment of Europol; see Europol 2019 and earlier years.

data can be used by criminals to steal an identity, open accounts or make fraudulent purchases.[96] This can lead to financial loss, emotional distress and lost time (to deal with the incident).[97] And if spies are behind a breach, the data could be used to blackmail diplomats and recruit new informants. A 2018 data breach of the Marriott-hotel chain, which exposed the data of roughly 500 million guests, is suspected for instance of being a Chinese intelligence-gathering effort.[98]

And intelligence services also use exploits to collect data in other ways. Exploits are used by intelligence services to intercept communications and do other kinds of spying. The NSA uses these technologies to inject exploits into rerouted communications, enabling them to take over the computer of a target.[99] But there are also reports of the CIA and MI5 being able to secretly spy on people through their Samsung smart TVs.[100]

Some exploits are not used to gather data, but to gain control over a system. These can be industrial targets, such as critical infrastructure. The 2015 attack on the Ukrainian power grid is an example.[101] On 23 December of that year, in the middle of winter, power stations across Ukraine were shut off remotely, cutting off the lights and heat of almost a quarter of a million people for up to six hours. A year later, the power grid was attacked again.[102] In places with harsh winters, cutting of the heat for an extended period can prove life-threatening. Russia is suspected of being behind the attacks, flexing its muscles in a smaller country as a deterrent measure: an "expensive light flicking" operation to signal to the West that it has real cyberweapons.[103] The US has also accused Russia of being behind attacks disrupting the broadcasts of two television channels (and two thousand websites) in the country of Georgia.[104] But to be clear, not only Russia has the ability to execute these kinds of attacks. The US has leaked that it has code within the Russian electricity infrastructure which it can use to shut down the grid.[105] And many systems are in fact vulnerable: a study found that almost one thousand industrial control systems in the Netherlands have multiple, highly severe vulnerabilities, which could be fixed by taking measures

96 ENISA 2010.

97 See for example Li et al. 2019.

98 Sanger et al. 2018.

99 Schneier 2013c.

100 Franceschi-Bicchierai 2017.

101 See Zetter 2016a; see also Greenberg 2019c. Another high-profile example is Stuxnet, the malware used to disrupt uranium enrichment facilities in Natanz, Iran, which exploited four zero-day vulnerabilities in Microsoft Windows; Naraine 2010; Zetter 2014. It is suspected that Iran and the United States were involved in developing the malware. There are also reports of attacks on US utilities; Raggi and Schwarz 2019. The US further claims that Russia-backed hackers have attempted to attack US nuclear facilities and the electricity grid; Perlroth 2020.

102 Greenberg 2016; Zetter 2016b.

103 Greenberg 2019c, p. 133.

104 Greenberg 2020a.

105 Sanger and Perlroth 2019.

which are relatively easy to deploy.[106] Not only industrial control systems can be at risk. Attackers have been able to (remotely) take over a car while it was being driven, steering the wheel, braking and shutting off the transmission.[107] And attackers have been able to clone digital keys of widely used car models, including those of Toyota, Hyundai and Kia.[108]

Sometimes, exploits end up being used for multiple purposes over time, as is demonstrated by the story of EternalBlue. In August 2017, a group called The Shadow Brokers published Unix- and Windows-exploits, allegedly stolen from the NSA, who likely had stockpiled them for use in their operations.[109] Part of the dump was an exploit dubbed EternalBlue, which targeted certain versions of Windows. Even though Microsoft made a patch available within a day of learning about it, the exploit has continued to wreak havoc on the internet for years.[110] In particular, a virulent strain of ransomware called WannaCry, which was based on EternalBlue, infected up to 300,000 computers in over 150 countries.[111] The Trump administration later announced that North Korea was behind the attacks.[112] This attack was rapidly followed by the Petya/NotPetya attack, which used some of the same exploits as WannaCry and infected machines in more than 60 countries (with over 70% of the infections in Ukraine).[113] These attacks had far-reaching economic impact: the Petya/NotPetya-attack destroyed the fleet management system used by Mærsk shipping. This left nearly 800 vessels dead in the water (representing one fifth of the world's shipping capacity), with total damage for Mærsk alone amounting to USD 250–USD 300 million.[114] While these two strands of malware are thought to have been developed by groups connected to the government, later iterations which incorporated the EternalBlue exploit, such as cryptomining malware WannaMine and malware setting up malicious proxy networks, were likely developed by non-state actors.[115] Years later, in 2019, these exploits were still damaging the IT systems of organisations in cities across the US.[116] And this was no isolated incident: as crime moves increasingly online, criminals will use vulnerabilities more often to take over computers, for example to hold data ransom.[117]

---

[106] Ceron et al. 2019; see for an example of an Indian nuclear plant infected by malware; Gallagher 2019; see for hack of a Florida water plant Mathews 2021.

[107] Golson 2016; Greenberg 2015.

[108] Greenberg 2020b.

[109] Cox 2017. It was later confirmed on the basis of documents leaked by Snowden, that some of the exploits were indeed "cyberweapons" used by the NSA, as a unique ID mentioned in internal NSA-documents was found in an exploit published by The Shadow Brokers; Biddle 2016.

[110] MSRC 2017.

[111] Europol 2017, p. 19.

[112] Bossert 2017.

[113] Europol 2017, p. 20.

[114] Greenberg 2018.

[115] Serper (undated); Whittaker 2018.

[116] Perlroth and Shane 2019.

[117] See for an overview of developments in online crime from 2019 Anderson et al. 2019.

Finally, exploits can be used for targeted abuse and murder, often of political dissidents.[118] In 2019, multiple zero-days were found on a website targeting the Uyghur community, just as stories on Uyghur Muslim concentration camps run by the Chinese government were coming out.[119] A phone could become infected simply by visiting the website, and then the attackers—likely to be the Chinese government—would gain full access to all data on the phone, including messages, pictures and locations. Whether this exploit was used to round up dissidents is not known. Then there's the story of Citizen Lab, who investigated the use of NSO Group spyware in Mexico against citizens who were politically active, either speaking out in favour of a tax on soft drinks, or against corruption or the drug trade.[120] In all those instances, the target was sent messages with a link which, when clicked on, installed spyware on their phone. But it is the tale of Saudi-Arabian dissident and writer Jamal Khashoggi that is perhaps the best documented. In 2018, Khashoggi was lured into the Saudi consulate in Istanbul, never to re-emerge. It was later discovered that he had been killed inside and dismembered with a bone saw. When Citizen Lab investigated the phone of Khashoggi's friend Omar Abdulaziz, a Saudi dissident living in Canada, they found it infected with NSO's Pegasus spyware.[121] The researchers believe that the Pegasus operator is linked to the Saudi government. The United Nations special rapporteur investigating the murder of Khashoggi subsequently linked the infection of this phone to the interception of chat messages between Abdulaziz and Khashoggi, and it is believed that the interception played a role in his murder.[122] The UN rapporteur in the context of this investigation also concluded that the phone of Amazon's owner Jeff Bezos was likely to have been hacked via a WhatsApp account used by Saudi Crown Prince Mohammed bin Salman. As a result, the special rapporteur called for "a moratorium on the global sale and transfer of private surveillance technology".[123]

It should be said, meanwhile, that although there are strong suspicions as to who is behind an attack, it is notoriously difficult to attribute attacks to organisations. Attackers can easily hide their tracks or suggest that attacks originate from a different country. The CIA even allegedly maintains a library with malware and other attack technology stolen from adversaries' intelligence services for such false flag

---

[118] See for a theoretical attack on insulin pumps which could be used to kill people as well Newman 2019.

[119] Whittaker 2019; Perlroth et al. 2019a; Ramzy and Buckley 2019; see later Franceschi-Bicchierai 2020 for similar zero-days. See for how malware has been used to spy on politicians; Kirchgaessner 2020a, 2020b.

[120] See the series on the abuse of NSO Group's spyware in Mexico, Scott-Railton et al.; Kaye 2019, para 9; and Schilis-Gallego and Lakhani 2020; a large scale hack-for-hire scheme was later uncovered by CitizenLab; Scott-Railton et al. 2020.

[121] Marczak et al. 2018a, 2018b.

[122] Special Rapporteur on extrajudicial, summary or arbitrary executions, Chap. I.I; Kirkpatrick 2018; and dos Santos and Kaplan 2018.

[123] Special Rapporteur on extrajudicial, summary or arbitrary executions and Special Rapporteur on the promotion and protection of the right to freedom of opinion and expression; OHCHR 2020.

operations, using it to suggest, for example, that an attack comes from the Russian Federation, not the US.[124]

It can be expected that the impact of zero days will grow in the coming years. The software ecosystem is becoming less diverse: most consumer devices run Windows, Apple or Android, and most embedded devices run Linux-based operating systems. Furthermore, because of network effects, some apps have a very large user base. Meanwhile, the number of devices is still increasing: there are more mobile devices on this planet than there are people, and the growth of connected everyday objects (the "Internet of Things") is in its early days. Lastly, many of these devices are connected to the internet continuously. As a result, one zero day can impact billions of people, thus making it also more attractive to find them.

2.2.6 The Advantages of Exploits

It would be a mistake, though, to conclude that exploits are always bad. Vulnerabilities are an unavoidable part of information security, and information security benefits from the discovery and patching of vulnerabilities in the long run, as we have seen above. What's more, information security technologies enable control, for example over devices and information, and in some cases, it may be in the public interest to circumvent this control.

For example, the circumvention of information security measures can benefit whistleblowers. If the NSA had taken far-reaching security measures to ensure near-total control over its internal files, then Snowden would have never been able to exfiltrate the vast amounts of documents he did.[125] By contrast, whistleblower Reality Winner who shared documents on Russian hacking of US voting software was unmasked in part due to the use of invisible ink dots printed on the leaked documents, which identified the printer used to print them and included a timestamp.[126]

And there is also a host of other reasons why circumvention of security measures may be desirable. One example comes from certain rules prohibiting the circumvention of certain copy-protection measures for copyrighted works, or DRM. I discuss this prohibition further in Chap. 3, but for now I'm interested in the *exceptions* to this prohibition, particularly in the US. There, the Copyright Office decides each three years which activities are exempt from this circumvention prohibition for reasons of public interest. These exceptions range from jailbreaking iPads and Alexa home devices, allowing the user to install apps of their choice, to software that reads text aloud for the blind, from the ability to modify and repair cars to using third party feedstock for 3D printers.

[124] Wikileaks 2017.

[125] See Snowden 2019, in particular Chap. 20 on Heartbeat.

[126] Graham 2017; here, there is also a cycle of making and breaking between those who want identifying dots to be printed and those who want to remove them; see Anzuoni 2020.

All these activities are in the public interest. Jailbreaking can benefit innovation: Apple has taken a functionality first developed by the jailbreak community and copied it into its own operating system.[127] Modifying cars can make them go faster or run more efficiently. Third party feedstock can be cheaper and better. But all of this can be blocked by technological information security measures imposed by the manufacturer or the service provider.

Information security designers will generally not take into account these interests. For them, information security is about preventing attackers from using a system in contravention of the security policy. But what does it take to be considered an attacker? This is, essentially, everyone who might use the system in a way which is contrary to the security policy. This means that the user will often be considered an adversary as well.

This is an important point—some of the systems which we discuss in this book, such as DRM systems—are built around the assumption that its users—for example the people listening to music and movies—are its adversaries. And in the words of Doctorow: "If your world is made of computers, then designing computers to override their owners' decisions has significant human rights implications."[128] One such system taken in isolation can already be problematic; it becomes especially so if a system where the user is *not* considered the adversary (a desktop computer), collides with one where the user *is* considered a potential attacker (a piece of software enforcing DRM). One of the goals of this book is to explore how this fact, that users operate in information security environments where they are considered the adversary, should be understood from a human rights perspective.

2.3 The Encryption Landscape

But first, let us take a look at a particularly poignant example of the making and breaking cycle: the breaking of encryption technologies by quantum computers. Encryption technologies are widely used, but, as we will learn in the next subsection, many of these technologies will probably be broken in the coming decades by quantum computers. This wide adoption raises the stakes enormously, allowing us to better identify which parameters can be tweaked to optimise the information security cycle, so that it works *for*, not *against* humans. I will in this section first discuss the *making* part: encryption technologies, and then in the next section discuss the *breaking*, with quantum computers. I will discuss encryption technologies from two perspectives: those who use encryption as a security measure, and those who have an interest in breaking it. But first: what do I mean when talking about *encryption technologies*?

---

[127] Kazmucha 2010, 2011.

[128] Doctorow 2012; see also Doctorow 2020.

2.3.1 *Encryption Technologies as a Measure Against Unauthorised Access*

In the first section of this chapter, I discussed the role that desired *security properties* play in devising an information security policy. Confidentiality and integrity are two commonly required information security properties. For example: you might want to prevent people from accessing information without authorisation (a form of confidentiality), or you want to ensure that information is not changed when you send it over the internet (a form of integrity). But how do you ensure confidentiality and integrity?

This is where *cryptographic technologies* come in. These play an important role in safeguarding both confidentiality and integrity.[129] Cryptographic technologies are firstly involved in shielding off information from unauthorised users, thus safeguarding *confidentiality*, by enciphering information in such a way that only authorised users—users with the key—are able to access the decrypted data. And cryptographic technologies are applied to safeguard the *integrity* of information, enabling people to check whether a file has been tampered with.[130] Cryptographic technologies are also applied in *authentication systems*, by providing secure ways to identify users.[131] And cryptographic technologies can be used for *non repudiation* purposes. If one can with certainty prove the origin of information, this automatically makes it impossible for the sender to repudiate that.[132]

Of all these applications, it is safeguarding *confidentiality* that attracts the most attention of governments. That's because confidentiality measures can prevent governmental institutions, in particular law enforcement and intelligence agencies, from accessing information, including communications between people. In this book, cryptographical technologies for safeguarding *confidentiality* are generally called "encryption technologies".

From the perspective of the government, not all of these encryption technologies are the same. First, the degree of confidentiality afforded by them differs. Some

---

[129] Menezes et al. 1997 define *cryptography* as the "study of mathematical techniques related to aspects of information security such as confidentiality, data integrity, entity authentication, and data origin authentication"; Menezes et al. 1997, p. 4; see also Anderson 2020, Chap. 5.

[130] This is mostly done with one-way functions (hashing functions) which reduce large sets of information to almost unique fingerprints (hashes), which can be used to independently verify whether certain information has changed. For example, in order to certify that a certain file has not been tampered with in transit, one can compare the hash from a file as computed by the sender with the hash as computed by the recipient. Hashing functions are also used to create a time stamp, to prove that information was created before a certain moment.

[131] Digital signature schemes are an example of this: through the use of encryption and hashing functions, one can certify the origin of information. Cryptocurrencies use this function, because it has to be ascertained that only the owner of a digital currency may make a transaction with this currency.

[132] For example, if a cryptocurrency transaction is digitally signed with a certain key which only the sender has, all other parties should in most circumstances be able to trust that the sender made the transaction.

encryption technologies work with keys that are stored with the service provider, such as a telecommunications company. Other technologies allow issuing new keys to new users when necessary (polymorphic encryption).[133] If a government wants to access information encrypted with those technologies, it can ask a third party to hand over the key. Second, encryption might keep some information confidential, but still allow for a certain kind of *legibility* and subsequent *sorting*.[134] This is particularly the case for encryption technologies which allow for calculations on encrypted data without disclosing the data itself (homomorphic encryption). Say, for instance, that you store the salaries of all your employees with a cloud provider using homomorphic encryption. The cloud provider then might not be able to find out the exact salary of each employee in the dataset, yet it can still determine what the average or highest salary is. In other words, even those encryption technologies which provide *confidentiality* may in certain cases not protect against revealing information or then having others act on this information.

By contrast, technologies which give the *user* sole control over the data present a far more difficult challenge to governments.[135] The reason, of course, is this: if only users, not others, control when information may be decrypted, governments have no way to gain access to this information. For that, they would need help from the user, or they would need to compromise the user's system. In this book, these technologies are called "user-controlled encryption technologies".[136] As we will see, these are not only the most problematic for governments, they are also the most useful for individuals.

2.3.2 *The Difference Between Symmetric and Asymmetric Cryptography*

In the next section of this chapter, the effects of quantum computing on encryption technologies will be discussed. Before I do that, though, it is useful to make one further distinction within this broader set of *encryption technologies*. There are two fundamentally different kinds of cryptographical systems. They differ in how keys are handled, and in how easily they can be broken by quantum technologies. One

[133] Hoepman 2021, para 3.4.2.

[134] See Veale 2019.

[135] This description draws on the definition in Encryption Working Group, p. 3; see also Baker and Landau 2019. This could be called a subset of Privacy Enhancing Technologies as defined by Diaz et al., which are technologies specifically aimed at "enabling individuals to engage in online activities free from surveillance and interference"; Diaz et al., p. 924.

[136] This term was first coined by Encryption Working Group 2019, p. 3. It should be noted that the term "control" does not refer to "control" of the algorithms and software used—these might well be developed by the service provider, for example. The "control"-element refers to the keys with which the information can be decrypted: these keys are in control of the user. This definition thus does not include systems where the service provider has access to the keys: for those situations, it is usually possible in theory to access the keys through a service provider.

is *symmetric key* encryption (also called *shared key*, or *secret key* encryption).[137] In this type of encryption, the key is used to encrypt and to decrypt data is the *same*. For example: the hotline between Moscow and Washington during the Cold War was outfitted with copies of the same keys on each end.[138] This scheme has an important drawback. It requires the exchange of the keys beforehand, which means it is necessary to establish a secure communication channel in advance (e.g. you have to send a key book between communication partners by courier while ensuring that the courier does not make a copy of the book).

When the first contours of the information society were forming in the 1970s, several people realised that the ability to send messages to others in confidence was important for the development of telecommunications and computing.[139] Diffie and Hellman devised a novel system called "public key cryptography", or *asymmetric encryption*, which through the innovative use of mathematics made it possible to *decrypt* information with a key which was different from the one with which it was initially *encrypted*.[140] With public key cryptography, the sender *encrypts* a message with a key which the recipient has published or shared beforehand. This key is the public part of a *keypair*, and is generally called the *public key*. The recipient then *decrypts* the information with the *private* part of this keypair—called the *private key*.

These *public* key cryptography systems use *one-way functions*: functions which are very easy to perform one way, but very hard to reverse. These are based on specific mathematical problems in the field of number theory, such as the problem of factorisation of integers and the discrete logarithm problem.[141] The presumed security of these systems relies on the assumption that these mathematical problems have no efficient solution, that they cannot be "cracked". It is true that it is indeed difficult to solve these with classical computers and the current state of math which is publicly known (*outside* the intelligence agencies). But it's widely expected that with sufficiently advanced quantum computers, it will become possible to reverse these one-way functions. That will undercut the security of most systems based on public key cryptography, something I discuss further in the next section. Before I do that, though, I will discuss the adoption of encryption technologies and how this poses challenges to governments.

---

[137] Anderson 2020, p. 146.

[138] Kahn 1996, Chap. 19.

[139] In the words of Diffie and Hellman: "A private conversation between two people with no prior acquaintance is a common occurrence in business [...] and it is unrealistic to expect initial business contacts to be postponed long enough for keys to be transmitted by some physical means"; Diffie and Hellman 1976, p. 1976; see for a history of cryptography within DuPont and Fidler 2016.

[140] See Diffie and Hellman 1976; Anderson 2020, Chap. 5. It later was revealed that James Ellis and Clifford Cocks at GCHQ had made the same invention several years earlier; Levy 1999.

[141] See Chen et al. 2016, p. 2; ETSI 2015, p. 8 and further; Mavroeidis et al. 2018; Bernstein and Lange 2017. The algorithms most commonly used in public key cryptography are based on RSA, elliptic curve or finite field cryptography. As an example, the factorisation problem, implemented by the RSA-algorithm, is based on the mathematical reality that it is easy to multiply two given large primes, but if you are presented with a number which is the product of two large primes, then it is very difficult to calculate what the constituent primes are (*factorisation*).

2.3.3 The Adoption of Encryption Technologies

If we want to get a sense of the adoption of encryption technologies, it is useful to make one last distinction between types of encryption technologies: namely between *device encryption* and *end-to-end encryption.* Device encryption is intended to encrypt all or part of the information on a device, where the key is only available to the user of the system. For the purposes of this book, end-to-end encryption is defined as encryption of communication between two parties where *only the parties themselves* have the key to decrypt the data. End-to-end encryption generally employs a combination of symmetric and asymmetric encryption, whereas device encryption is generally only based on symmetric encryption.[142]

Most common operating systems provide device encryption, increasingly as the default. For *mobile phones*, the two major mobile operating systems currently have device encryption turned on by default. Apple by default in current versions of its iOS mobile operating system encrypts data on the device, and parts of key system apps are encrypted on a per-file basis using a key hierarchy.[143] Android turned on device encryption by default in Android 7.0 (Nougat), released at the end of 2016.[144] In 2017, Google reported that over 75% of its devices running Android 7.0 are fully encrypted, and this figure must have increased significantly since.[145] An industry-funded study from 2017 estimates that 21% of all mobile devices have full disk encryption, but this was before full disk encryption became the default option for iOS and Android, so this figure is likely to be significantly higher at the time of writing this book.[146] For *desktops and laptops*, the picture is mixed. Microsoft already by default turns on its device encryption software BitLocker for most computers using Windows 8.1 or newer, and it expects Bitlocker to be pervasive across modern Windows devices in the future.[147] Apple's device encryption for macOS, FileVault, is not enabled by default.[148] The same goes for Linux: most popular distributions offer device encryption, but not by default.[149]

End-to-end encryption is also becoming increasingly common, in particular in chat software. The more popular apps are WhatsApp, one of Facebook's messaging apps, and iMessage, Apple's app. WhatsApp's encryption is based on Signal's

142 Hoepman 2021, para 3.3.4. Where cryptographical technologies are used to sign information, this will be done by asymmetric encryption; ibid., para 5.1.

143 See Apple 2021.

144 Google 2016.

145 Martonik 2017.

146 Lewis et al. 2017, p. 9.

147 See Microsoft 2017.

148 Apple 2018.

149 See for instance Ubuntu, on which many popular distributions are based. Ubuntu Full Disk Encryption Howto. https://help.ubuntu.com/community/Full_Disk_Encryption_Howto_2019. Accessed 2 November 2021.

encryption library developed by Open Whisper Systems.[150] End-to-end encryption in WhatsApp has been introduced by default in all versions of WhatsApp after 31 March 2016.[151] At that time, WhatsApp was reported to have 1 billion users.[152] This figure has grown since then to 2 billion in 2020.[153] iMessage also applies end-to-end encryption.[154] As of June 2021, more than 90% of all of Apple's mobile devices run iOS 13 or 14, which include iMessage, and Apple recorded over 1.5 billion active iOS devices in 2020.[155]

These numbers do not, however, provide the full picture. These technologies are also applied in a wide range of contexts: from business to government, from lawyers to activists, from medical professionals to journalists, from families to lovers.[156] In a survey of 2016, the researchers identified more than 800 hardware or software products incorporating encryption technologies from over fifty different countries.[157] Sometimes they are adopted as a result of a deliberate choice, for example when journalists want to protect their sources. Sometimes they are applied in order to comply with organisational policies, such as when a bank requires data on USB flash drives to be encrypted. And sometimes they are applied as a result of regulations, such as when doctors are required by privacy rules to encrypt their data. I discuss these regulations further in Chap. 3.

2.3.4 The Challenges for Governments to Access Encrypted Data

As noted above, because encryption technologies can shield information from the government, ever since these technologies started spreading, governments have claimed that these technologies hamper their investigations, both in the context of intelligence gathering and of law enforcement.[158] European agencies indicate that they increasingly encounter encryption and consider it a challenge, because it affects their ability to perform their investigations. But—and this is important for the human rights analysis we will get to later—empirical data is limited and it is unclear to what

[150] See for Whatsapp WhatsApp (2020a); and WhatsApp (undated) WhatsApp FAQ—End-to-end encryption. https://faq.whatsapp.com/en/android/28030015/. Accessed 9 November 2018.

[151] WhatsApp (2020a), p. 3.

[152] Metz 2016.

[153] WhatsApp 2020a, 2020b.

[154] See Apple 2018, pp. 60–61.

[155] Apple (2021) Apple Developer Support. Apple App Store. https://developer.apple.com/support/app-store/. Accessed 2 November 2021. Apple 2020, 2021.

[156] See for instance Ra'ad Al Hussein 2016; Elsayed-Ali 2016; Kaye 2015.

[157] Schneier et al. 2016.

[158] See Koomen 2019 for an overview in the EU; see for the US Manhattan District Attorney's Office 2019; for an industry-funded study from 2017, see Lewis et al. 2017; see lastly the analysis in Gill and Parsons 2018.

extent there are investigations which couldn't be *solved*.[159] In fact, one report suggests that law enforcement agencies in the US can access device data more often than not, and that the situations where encryption blocks access are an exception to the rule.[160]

This is because encryption technologies never function in isolation. They are always part of a broader system, which means that many parts of the system can be attacked. In the words of Edward Snowden: "Encryption works. Properly implemented strong crypto systems are one of the few things that you can rely on. Unfortunately, endpoint security is so terrifically weak that NSA can frequently find ways around it."[161] So what is this *endpoint security* exactly?

Cryptographic building blocks already contain many potential targets. These include the *cryptographic cipher*, *key management*, *access policy*, *communication protocol*, *implementation*, the *host system* and the *usage* of the technologies. One method for evaluating the security of a system is through an 'attack tree', which is an overview of all the links which are relevant for attacking the system.[162] Let's walk through some of them:

- An important element is the *cryptographic cipher*. Here, the question is whether the cipher can be 'broken'—that is, can an attacker derive the input of the cipher from the output of the cipher? To date, most cryptographic ciphers are not so much mathematically proven to be secure, but have merely been tested—and found to be very difficult or impossible to break by reputable cryptographers, but even "with many seasoned eyes looking at the system, security deficiencies may not be uncovered for years."[163]

  Another part of such systems, related to the cipher, is the *key management*: the way keys are stored and distributed. If, for example, keys are not generated on the device, but instead are distributed by a central point, this opens up the possibility for using the keys without authorisation. And if keys are indeed stored on the device itself, measures should be taken to ensure that an attacker gaining access to the *device* does not gain access to the *keys* (for example by encrypting the key with a different key which is only available to authorised users).

  Furthermore, the *ways in which access can be gained* to the keys are highly relevant. In particular, if the system enforces a maximum number of login attempts, introduces delays between access attempts, or erases the encrypted data after a number of failed attempts, this will prevent brute-force attacks. For communication applications, the *communication protocol* is also an important element. Changing the communications protocol can weaken the security of a communication. For example, some communication protocols offer encryption ciphers with

---

[159] See for example Presidency of the Council of Ministers 2016, p. 3; European Commission 2017, p. 8; Europol and EC3 2019, p. 31; Europol et al. 2019, p. 23.

[160] Koepke et al. 2020; Landau 2020.

[161] Snowden 2013.

[162] Kohno et al. 2010, pp. 5 and 6. See Schneier's attack tree against PGP, which is more detailed; Schneier 1999; see also Kerr and Schneier 2018, in particular p. 1005 and further.

[163] Kohno et al. 2010, p. 13.

differing strengths. In *downgrade attacks*, the communication protocol is forced to use a weak encryption cipher.[164]

- The *implementation* of the cryptographic scheme can further defeat the theoretical protection afforded. If, for example, keys are stored in the device memory but the memory is not properly wiped or it is accessible by an attacker, the keys can be compromised.[165]
- The system in which the implementation is *embedded* also provides various attack avenues. For example, if an attacker can gain access to the input device of a system, it can record and later replay the user keys used for decryption. Or if an attacker gains access to the windowing system, it can manipulate the user interface to covertly harvest keys or view decrypted information. For example, browsers show a lock next to the URL when an HTTPS-connection is in place. Where the interface does not present an accurate picture of the internal security state of the system, this also affects the efficacy of the security technologies.
- Lastly, many things can go wrong in *using* the system. It might be that the organisational policies for gaining access to the system are not well-designed, increasing the risks of insider threats. Or the system is so difficult to use, that users write their passwords on post-its next to a computer. Or one can gain access through social engineering, for instance impersonating the support desk.

Since a system is only as secure as it weakest link, the effectiveness of real-life applications of cryptography depends on the strength of all these elements of the system.[166] And while it is already notoriously hard to devise secure cryptographical ciphers and implement them in code that is itself sufficiently secure, it is as least as hard to implement the other parts of the system securely. As a result, there are very few instances in which the cryptographical elements of a system are the weakest link. In other words: cryptography forms only a small part of the attack surface of a system. This affords governments with many avenues for gaining access to encrypted data, both through policies and practices. I discuss these further in Chap. 3. Even in those cases where encryption *is* the weakest link, governments may in the future have a way to gain access: with the use of sufficiently advanced quantum computers. That is the topic of the next section.

---

164 The FREAK, LOGJAM, DROWN and POODLE attack are examples of this, where browsers can be forced to downgrade to export-grade encryption ciphers (e.g. ciphers which the NSA deemed safe for export during the nineties, which can be easily broken); Heninger and Halderman 2016; Möller et al. 2014.

165 As an example of this, security researchers disclosed a flaw in software commonly being used to encrypt email (PGP/GPG), allowing an attacker to decrypt and exfiltrate messages without the victim being aware; Poddebniak et al. 2018. This attack did not exploit a vulnerability in the algorithms used, but in the software implementing the algorithm.

166 Kohno et al. 2010, pp. 4–5.

2.4 Quantum Computing: Crypto-killer App or Vapourware?

The origins of modern computing can be traced back to the efforts by Turing and his colleagues at Bletchley Park to crack the German Enigma-cipher.[167] And Claude Shannon, before writing "A Mathematical Theory of *Communication*" in 1948, one of the foundational theories on networked communications, first wrote a classified primer on "A Mathematical Theory of *Cryptography*" in 1946.[168] It is hardly a coincidence that the history of modern computing and communication begins with a race to crack an information security measure. From the Second World War onwards, "two of the primary functions of the computer would be code-making and code-breaking", as one author notes.[169] Now, history repeats itself, as one of the main drivers behind the development of quantum computing is the potential to break a large part of encryption currently used, which would shake the foundations of information security *and* disrupt the computing landscape. I explore this further below.

2.4.1 Quantum Mechanics

Classical physics describes the behaviour of objects *above* atomic scale: what happens when you drop two differently-sized lead balls from the tower of the Nieuwe Kerk in Delft? *Quantum* physics, or quantum mechanics, deals with the behaviour of nature on an *atomic and sub-atomic* scale: how do things such as electrons and photons behave when you bombard them with lasers? While classical mechanics have been studied for centuries, it was only in the beginning of the past century that researchers trained their focus on quantum mechanics. And what they discovered was startling: objects on a quantum level work differently than we would expect. They depart from our daily experience in three ways.[170]

First, particles are related to each other at a distance, a phenomenon called *entanglement*. For example: the measuring of the "spin" of a particle—the direction in which it turns—can influence the spin of another "entangled" particle, even when these particles are at a great distance from each other. This is what Einstein famously called "*spukhafte Fernwirkung*", or "spooky action at a distance".[171] Recent breakthroughs have allowed particles to be entangled over hundreds of kilometres, which enables secure exchange of cryptographic keys (further discussed below).

Moreover, they can exist in probabilities of two states at once (*superposition*). For particles in superposition, this means that you can only say that there is, for example,

[167] Thomas 2002, p. 13; see Marsh 2019 for the role of women in breaking German ciphers.

[168] Shannon 1948, 1949.

[169] Thomas 2002, p. 13.

[170] See Becker 2018 for a history.

[171] Born and Einstein 1971, p. 158; Buhrman et al. 2001.

a 40% chance that the spin of a certain particle is upwards, and a 60% chance that the spin is downwards, while multiple readings of identical particles would yield different results. In fact, without measurement, the particle spins neither 100% in one direction nor the other. Only after measurement does the particle spin 100% one way or the other—the act of measurement causes the probabilities to "collapse" towards one direction. The counterintuitive consequences of this were illustrated by Schrödinger with the now-famous thought experiment of a cat in a box whose fate depends on an atom in superposition. If quantum effects could be directly translated to events on supra-atomic scale, this would mean that the cat is alive *and* dead at the same time, because the atom would be spinning up *and* down at the same time. So simply observing the state of the atom, forcing it to "click" into an up- or downwards spin, could kill the cat.[172]

Lastly, these probabilities in superposition of the same quantum object can interact with each other. This is a phenomenon called *interference*. For example: a probability of 60% of a certain polarisation can interfere with a probability of 40% of an opposite polarisation, with their amplitudes cancelling each other out, just like waves in a pond.

2.4.2 The Application of Quantum Mechanics to Perform Calculations

Scientists aim to harness these peculiar characteristics of quantum mechanics for the development of new technologies, called quantum technologies.[173] One such technology is called *quantum communication*, which concerns the exchange of information over long distances via quantum properties. This is sometimes marketed as the *quantum internet*, which suggests that quantum technology could be used to send all kinds of information over the internet. In practice, however, quantum communication is a way to securely exchange random keys to encrypt communication, and is called quantum key distribution, or QKD. Another technology is *quantum sensing*, which allows for the measurement of physical phenomena, such as gravity, time, rotation and magnetic fields, on the basis of quantum effects. This is useful for improving things such as radar, location detection, optical measurement and building precise clocks.[174]

In this book, I focus on another quantum technology, namely quantum *computing*—performing calculations using the phenomena of entanglement, superposition and interference. Classical computers perform calculations through the transformation of "classical" bits, which can have a discrete value of either 1 *or* 0, on or off. Quantum computers transform quantum bits, or qubits, which as a result

[172] Schrödinger 1935, p. 812.

[173] See for a classification Acín et al. 2018; European Commission 2016.

[174] Acín et al. 2018, Sect. 5; German Federal Ministry of Education and Research 2019.

of superposition have a *simultaneous* value of 0 and 1, with different probabilities of coming out as one or the other at the moment of measurement.[175]

Just as classical computer gates are used to transform classical bits, transformations with qubits are performed with quantum gates.[176] But whereas classical computers can only be in one state at a time, quantum computers can as a result of superposition be in multiple states at the same time.[177] This adds up quickly: a computer with 1000 qubits can *simultaneously* represent more states than there are atoms in the universe.[178] Moreover, if qubits are entangled, which is not always the case, this ensures that an operation on one qubit also has an effect on the other qubits.[179]

Quantum computers could in theory be used like classical computers: to transform discrete qubits as if they were classical bits. But that would be a waste. They wouldn't be faster than normal computers, and they would be far more expensive, if only because it is so difficult to measure the outcome of calculations. No, the potential power of quantum computers lies in other applications, applications for which classical computers are not well suited.[180] Perhaps the best way to think about quantum computers, is that they are "supercomputers", computers with an extreme processing capacity, but that these supercomputers have limited functionality. So: special-purpose supercomputers.

One such special purpose is to *simulate* other quantum systems, for example in the realm of molecular chemistry. This is very difficult to do with classical computers: because quantum systems have to be described in terms of probabilities, the number of required calculations increases exponentially. But sufficiently advanced quantum computers would for example allow us to model the behaviour of molecules, which could lead to the development of new medicines and materials. Another application is in the field of *optimization and search*, such as searching rapidly within large sets, or finding the shortest route or solving some systems of linear equations.[181] But of all these applications, it is the deciphering of encryption that is spurring at least a significant part of the development of quantum computing, especially by

---

[175] See Chap. 1 of Nielsen and Chuang 2010; and Chap. 1 of Williams 2011 for an introduction.

[176] For completeness: some success factoring large numbers has also been reported using quantum annealing machines, such as the one developed by D-Wave; Peng et al. 2019. These work on the basis of a fundamentally different technology from gate-based quantum computing and it is contested whether they can achieve quantum speedup, at least with the current state of technology; German Federal Office for Information Security 2020, p. 24; see also National Academies of Sciences 2018, Sect. 2.4 for a discussion. For this reason, they will not be discussed further here.

[177] Quantum computations are also *reversible*, which has benefits for certain applications; see Möller and Vuik 2017, p. 260.

[178] De Wolf 2012, p. 12.

[179] Grover explains this well; see Grover 1999.

[180] See for an early analysis Preskill 1998. It is also likely that potential applications we are now considering for quantum computers will eventually be surplaced by applications which we haven't yet imagined, similar to the evolution of classical computers; Maslov et al. 2019.

[181] See Montanaro 2016; and de Wolf 2017.

governments. Code breaking is one of quantum computing's "killer apps", as we will see.

2.4.3 The Development of Quantum Computers

The idea to build computers based on quantum mechanics was suggested as early as the 1980s, but real-life quantum computers remained vapourware—long promised but never delivered—for much of the two decades that followed.[182] Then three discoveries by computer scientists kicked off scientific interest in quantum computing. Shor in 1994 developed the first quantum algorithm with practical application, namely the fast factorisation of large numbers (that is, finding the primes from which a number is composed), and the finding of discrete logarithms.[183] As discussed above, most current *asymmetric* cryptographic systems are built on the assumption that it is nearly impossible to factor large numbers and find discrete logarithms, so these are highly interesting applications, in particular for intelligence agencies (something I'll go into further in Chap. 3). Shor noted that "[i]f the only uses of quantum computation remain discrete logarithms and factoring, it will likely become a special-purpose technique whose only raison d'être is to thwart public key cryptosystems".[184] Two years later, Grover developed a general search algorithm for quantum computers, which increases in particular the speed of brute-force attacks on *symmetrical* key algorithms.[185] And in the same year, 1996, Lloyd proved that a quantum computer can be programmed to simulate any quantum-mechanical system.[186] This is useful, because, as noted above, modelling the behaviour of particles on an atomic and sub-atomic scale, for example the interaction between atoms, quickly becomes very complex with classical computers, whereas a smaller quantum computer could already suffice to perform such calculations.

Since then, not only has the number of yearly papers on quantum computing and the number of quantum algorithms grown significantly, but this has also resulted in the development of "working" quantum computers.[187] The power of these computers is still very limited, as we will see below, but they are used to gain experience in operating these computers. Noteworthy milestones are when scientists IBM built a

---

[182] Feynman 1982, 1986; Benioff 1980, 1982a, 1982b; see also Deutsch and Penrose 1985. Similar ideas were developed in Russia by Yuri Manin and others as well; see Hoofnagle and Garfinkel 2021, para 4.7.

[183] See Shor 1997.

[184] Ibid.

[185] Grover 1996.

[186] Lloyd 1996.

[187] The yearly number of academic papers with "quantum computing" in the name on the Dimensions dataset grew from less than hundred in the mid-nineties to more than 2000 in 2019, with especially significant growth since 2017 (1241 papers) and 2018 (1626 papers); Dimensions 2020. The number of algorithms which can in theory be used with a quantum computing has also grown significantly; Jordan 2019; see also Montanaro 2016.

7 bit quantum computer in 2001 and used Shor's algorithm to factor the number 15 (3×5), and others repeating the same feat in 2012 factoring the number 21 (3×7).[188] Since then, many organisations—from large companies such as Microsoft, Alibaba, Google and IBM, to lesser known ones such as Rigetti Computing and IonQ—have built these experimental quantum computers.[189] Many also offer access to their quantum computers via the cloud, some completely through their own hardware and development frameworks (e.g. IBM, Google, and Microsoft) and some in collaboration with others (e.g. Rigetti, in a hybrid cloud of Amazon).[190] Besides these commercial organisations, universities are also active in this space. QuTech, for instance, a collaboration between the Dutch University of Technology (TU Delft) and the Netherlands Organisation for Applied Scientific Research (TNO), has developed quantum computing and offers access through its cloud platform, as does the University of Bristol.[191]

Some of these *organisations* are in a race to achieve "quantum supremacy"—by developing a quantum computer that can do things no classical computer can.[192] But it is not only organisations that are vying for "supremacy"—significant developments are driven by *countries* competing for technological breakthroughs, hoping to achieve a tipping point where their military power allows them to dominate their counterparts. One reporter breathlessly described this as "the most important tech contest since the space race".[193] It was revealed in the Snowden leaks in 2014 that the NSA is developing a quantum computer with a budget of USD 80 million.[194] Later, the NSA's director Paul Nakasone in August 2018 said that the NSA "will make advances in encryption and in quantum computing to secure what we choose, and to unlock

---

[188] See Vandersypen et al. 2001; Martín-López et al. 2012.

[189] See Möller and Vuik 2017; Resch and Karpuzcu 2019; Gyongyosi and Imre 2019 for relatively recent overviews.

[190] See IBM Research Editorial Staff 2018 where IBM reports that over 3 million remote executions were performed by over 80,000 users between 2016 and 2018; Castellanos 2020a; see also LaRose 2019.

[191] QuTech About Quantum Inspire. In: Quantum Inspire. https://www.quantum-inspire.com/about-qi. Accessed 19 August 2020.

Bristol U of Quantum Computer. http://www.bristol.ac.uk/physics/research/quantum/engagement/qcloud/computer/. Accessed 19 August 2020.

[192] Preskill 2012. Google has claimed to have achieved *quantum supremacy* in 2019. However, the calculation did not result in something useful—it was merely the calculation of a semi-random number for which a quantum computing was faster than a classical computer. Moreover, IBM has disputed that Google has achieved it, and the original author of the term has not come to a definitive conclusion either; Arute et al. 2019; Pednault et al. 2019; Preskill 2019. Chinese scientists later claimed that their research on photon-based quantum computers led to quantum supremacy, albeit with a non-programmable quantum computer; Ball 2020; Aaronson 2020.

[193] Kania and Costello 2018, p. 1; See for a critical discussion Lindsay 2020b; they call the ability to break RSA a "formidable offensive advantage" (p. 55) but at the same time cautions that defensive technologies such as PQC and QKD are already being developed (see below); Nikias 2018.

[194] Rich and Gellman 2014.

what we need, and to maintain an operational advantage".[195] An official from GCHQ noted that same year: "If a state has invested a huge amount in a quantum computer, the logical thing is to attack cryptosystems".[196]

The potential power of quantum computers explains the significant government investments, mostly by the EU (and its member states), the US and China.[197] In 2018, the European Union pledged EUR 1 billion over a period of 10 years for the development of quantum technology, including quantum computing, under the Quantum Flagship program.[198] In 2020 the EU proposed to allocate EUR 8 billion until 2033 for the development of supercomputers, including quantum computers.[199] Germany in June 2020 invested EUR 2 billion for the funding of quantum technologies, "immediately" commissioning the building of two quantum computers.[200] The UK invested GBP 1 billion in quantum technologies between 2014 and 2019.[201] The Dutch National Growth Fund granted a sum of EUR 615 million to the Dutch Quantum Delta programme over a period of six years (until 2027), of which almost EUR 100 million is dedicated to quantum computing.[202] The US at the end of 2018 adopted the National Quantum Initiative Act which allocates USD 1.2 billion over a period of five years accelerating R&D at the federal level, and has since called to up the spending on quantum technologies to over USD 500 million per year.[203] While these are sizable investments, they are dwarfed by the spending of the Chinese government in co-operation with the commercial sector. Although it is difficult to estimate total investments in China, they likely amount to tens of billions of Euros, with the ongoing construction of the largest quantum technology lab in China already reportedly costing over EUR 9 billion.[204] And even these amounts are relatively small, in comparison to prior "moonshot"-projects: the Apollo space program is estimated to have cost USD 190 billion, the Manhattan project USD 28 billion and the development of the GPS location system USD 14 billion (adjusted for inflation).[205]

---

[195] Nakasone 2018. In the 2013 Congressional Budget Justification, James Clapper already wrote: "We are tackling hard problems in quantum computing"; Poulsen 2013.

[196] Johnson 2018.

[197] See for an outdated overview of investments also National Academies of Sciences 2018, Table 7.2; see also the discussion in Hoofnagle and Garfinkel 2021, Chap. 9.2.

[198] See European Commission undated; and Acín et al. 2018.

[199] Council Regulation (EU) 2021/1173 of 13 July 2021 on establishing the European High Performance Computing Joint Undertaking and repealing Regulation (EU) 2018/1488 2021 (OJ L) 256.

[200] German Government 2020, para 44.

[201] UK Government 2019.

[202] Quantum Delta Nederland 2021, Chap. 4.

[203] Subcommittee on Quantum Information Science of the National Science & Technology Council 2018; Loten 2020; Castellanos 2020b. It in 2019 also announced a co-operation with Japan; see Japan and United States 2019.

[204] Kania and Costello 2018, p. 6 and further; Chen 2017; See Zhang et al. 2019 for an overview of the state of scientific research on quantum technologies.

[205] See Hoofnagle and Garfinkel 2021, Fig. 9.1.

2.4.4 The Timeline for Developing a Quantum Computer that Can Break Encryption

Such high investments are needed because there are still many obstacles in the way of building a usable quantum computer, and overcoming these obstacles is expensive.[206] Quantum information can be encoded in various ways, for example using superconducting circuits or trapped ions.[207] Each architecture poses its own engineering challenges, but one of the main obstacles in all approaches is susceptibility to outside "noise" and something called *decoherence*. This means that a qubit tends to shift from a state of superposition into a classical state again, which would obviate the quantum effects.[208] To allow for more complex calculations, users need longer coherence times—how long a quantum state persists—and less susceptibility to outside noise. To achieve this, quantum computers currently must be cooled to temperatures just above absolute zero (0.1 K, – 273.15 °C).[209] As a result, today's quantum computers are fantastic gold, copper and steel contraptions straight out of a William Gibson novel, about the size of a small room.[210]

Even at these low temperatures, though, decoherence and noise are still a problem. Quantum computers currently remain coherent for only a very short period of time. The application of error correction algorithms should address this. These algorithms work by combining several *physical* qubits into one *logical* qubit: currently, it is estimated that for every logical qubit, depending on the error-correction scheme applied, you would need over a thousand physical qubits.[211] Unfortunately, engineers have not succeeded in using error correction at scale in quantum computing yet, which I explain further below.

Thus, quantum computers are now in what has been called the "Noisy Intermediate-Scale Quantum" (NISQ) era.[212] "Noisy", in the sense that these computers are still prone to errors. "Intermediate-scale" in the sense that the largest computers as of this writing have over a couple of hundred qubits.[213] And although these quantum computers do "work" in the narrow sense, they are not yet very useful.

---

[206] See National Academies of Sciences 2018, in particular the summary for an overview.

[207] See the overview Resch and Karpuzcu 2019, p. 12.

[208] See Acín et al. 2018, Sect. 3; see also Resch and Karpuzcu 2019, Chap. 3.2.

[209] See Lichfield 2020.

[210] See the picture in Metz 2019. The costs of building something which can remain this cold are very high and one of the fields of research is to build devices which operate at a higher temperature (around 1.5 K, – 271.65 °C), which would significantly decrease the costs, from millions of dollars versus thousands of dollars; Yang et al. 2020; Lindsay 2020a.

[211] Resch and Karpuzcu 2019, p. 11; see also National Academies of Sciences 2018, where approximately 3000 logical qubits are estimated to require over 4.5 million physical qubits; and Sevilla and Riedel 2020, Fig. 1 for a schematic overview.

[212] Preskill 2018.

[213] IBM claims to have developed a 433-qubit computer: IBM 2022; and another startup claims to have developed a computer with 256 qubits: Gent 2021; Roberts 2021.

The development of a quantum computer which can factor RSA encryption with a keysize of 2048 bits (RSA-2048) is generally considered to be the tipping point for the breaking of encryption. This is because of the widespread use of RSA-2048 and because it implies that other types of encryption can also be broken. It is estimated that in order to break RSA-2048, you would need a quantum computer with approximately 4098 *logical* qubits.[214] With current error rates and error-correction mechanisms, a quantum computer with over 4000 logical qubits would require millions of physical qubits. The largest computers at the time of writing have a couple of hundred of *physical* qubits.

Even if engineers succeed in applying error-correction, it would still be very challenging to take the technologies currently used to sustain *tens* of physical qubits and scale them up to *millions* of physical qubits.[215] A quantum computer of that scale using current technologies would be the size of a soccer field and require approximately all worldwide Helium 3 used industrially in a year to cool the machines.[216] That is not to say that development at this scale is impossible: the NSA has developed a data centre in Utah encompassing more than *ten* soccer fields, at a cost of some USD 2 billion, drawing 65 MW of electricity and 1.7 million gallons of water per day.[217] In other words, if the stakes are high enough, size and money are not the main issue. Currently, the main hurdles are technical in nature; we simply cannot get a computer this size to work.

Still, these challenges are being worked at. Google in 2023 reported for example a way to scale qubits while maintaining error correction capabilities.[218] So, assuming that the technical hurdles to build a quantum computer with thousands of *logical* qubits will be overcome, the next question is: *when?* Turns out that's difficult to pinpoint. Intel co-founder Gordon Moore famously predicted that the processing capacity of classical computer chips would double roughly every two years.[219] There is no corollary to Moore's law for quantum computing. In part because, much like the early days of classical computing, there are various competing hardware platforms, each with their own technological trajectory.[220] It also has to do with the limited number of quantum computers currently built and as a result, the limited

214 National Academies of Sciences 2018, Table 4.1.

215 Ibid., pp. 126–127.

216 Frank et al. 2019, Sect. 2.7.

217 Bamford 2012. And in 2017, New York University leaked documents on a large supercomputer called WindsorGreen built by NYU and IBM for the NSA, probably intended to crack password protected data or faking software signatures, running custom-developed chips called ASICS; Biddle 2017. This supercomputer according to one expert "pretty much wipes the floor" with publicly disclosed supercomputers at the time, and in all likelihood is also the size of a soccer field.

218 Acharya et al. 2023.

219 Moore 1965.

220 See German Federal Office for Information Security 2020, Chap. 2.2.1 for an overview. Whereas classical bits are only encoded through the voltage levels in silicon chips being either low or high, qubits are encoded in sub-atomic media, which differ wildly, ranging from the polarisation states of a photon to the spin directions of an electron. The way these qubits are encoded has significant implications for the technology being used, and hence the computer architecture.

number of datapoints on which predictions can be based. Most current estimates of the development timeline of quantum computers are based on surveys with experts.

In general, these experts do not underestimate the engineering challenges but many are confident that a quantum computer of that size will be ultimately built in the coming decades.[221] The US National Academies of Sciences in its 2018 report on quantum computers did not describe a timeline, merely concluding that a "scalable, fully error-corrected machine [...] capable of a larger number of operations appears to be far off".[222] Mosca in 2018 gave a more precise estimate, calculating a 1 in 7 chance of breaking RSA-2048 by 2026, increasing to 1 in 2 by 2031 (more on this below).[223] One group of experts estimated the approximate probability of the development of a computer which can break RSA-2048 in 24 h. While less than one third estimated that the chance that this would happen within 10 years is 50% or more, more than the majority of the experts consider this about 50% likely or more within 20 years (in a pessimistic interpretation of the responses).[224] RAND summarises a group of experts who on average estimate the oddly specific year "2033" to be the most likely for a "cryptographically relevant" quantum computer to be developed.[225] And the authors of one study estimate on the basis of technological advances so far that attacks on RSA-2048 "will become feasible between mid 2039 and mid 2058 with 90% confidence with the median in early 2050".[226]

How should we deal with this uncertainty? In a thorough study by the German Office for Information Security, the authors did not provide a development timeline, but instead give their advice on the basis of the assumption that such a computer will *eventually* be built.[227] In this book, I do the same: at some point in the coming decades, a quantum computer capable of factoring large numbers will be developed. This might seem far off, but as we will see it is important to start preparing for these developments now.

2.4.5 The Impact of Quantum Computing on Encryption

There are three applications of encryption where such a quantum computer possibly has an impact. The most serious risk is in the field of *asymmetric encryption*. This includes the widely used RSA and Diffie-Hellman protocols, which can be considered "broken" when sufficiently advanced quantum computers are developed. Currently, asymmetric encryption works, because with classical computers it is next

---

[221] See Clarke 2019 for an optimistic view.

[222] National Academies of Sciences 2018, p. 157.

[223] Mosca 2018, p. 2.

[224] Mosca and Piani 2019, p. 26, 2020.

[225] Vermeer and Peet 2020, p. 22.

[226] Sevilla and Riedel 2020, p. 30.

[227] Frank et al. 2019; German Federal Office for Information Security 2020.

to impossible to calculate the private key if you know the public key. Even if classical computers were to become much faster, defending against these attacks is a matter of lengthening the key size. Not so when quantum computers are developed—then doubling the key size does not really help you. The second application where quantum computing poses a risk, is *symmetric* encryption. This risk is much lower than for asymmetric encryption—generally the key size can be doubled to resist quantum attacks. The same goes for the third application, *hashing*, used for example to securely authenticate users. Here again, in order to defend yourself you need to lengthen the hash.[228]

As discussed, asymmetric encryption technologies are firstly used to *secure communications*, for example between individuals (e.g. you and your friend using WhatsApp), between a computer and a website (e.g. you visiting a banking site), between organisations (e.g. banks exchanging transactions) and within organisations (e.g. Google transferring data between its data centres).[229] Secondly, they are used for *signing*, ensuring that software and other kinds of data has not been tampered with. For instance, Windows uses signatures to automatically check if an update comes from Microsoft and has not been changed while it was being sent over the internet. So it is safe to say asymmetric encryption plays an important role in our information infrastructure.

It is thus tempting to think that undermining asymmetric encryption would also undermine that infrastructure. One expert warned that if the security of communications breaks down, "our way of life breaks down", another even calling it a "Cryptocalypse".[230] But are these concerns justified?[231]

Yes. That's partly because of the very *real* threat that *actual attacks* with quantum computers pose to the confidentiality and integrity of information. And it's in part because of the breakdown in *trust* stemming from the *potential* threat. Before I get to how this works, let me first define this discussion in an important way. In this book, I focus on the *confidentiality* that encryption technologies offer, not on the integrity, because that's what governments are primarily concerned about. And quantum computing may affect the confidentiality of information, as we will see. I do acknowledge, however, that integrity and signature forging is a topic to be explored further in other research.

As to the threat of *actual* attacks: I explore different scenarios below, but for all scenarios except for *quantum winter* (where quantum computers fail to develop further), attacks with quantum computers will initially probably be targeted.[232] Perhaps only intelligence agencies will use these computers at first—possibly even enlisting the computers built by private organisations. But as these computers become more widely available, you cannot rule out that a well-funded criminal organisation would also obtain access for that purpose. Eventually, it is to be expected that powerful

228 See National Academies of Sciences 2018, Chap. 4 for a discussion.

229 See Hoepman 2021, para 3.2.2.

230 Ornes 2017; Aan de Brugh 2016.

231 See for a similar critical analysis Lindsay 2020b; see also Lindsay 2020c.

232 See for a similar analysis Mulholland et al. 2017, p. 18.

quantum computers will be offered in the cloud, to be used by anyone, posing the risk that everyone could decrypt information (see Chap. 10 for policy recommendations in this regard).

But having access to a quantum computer which you can use for decryption is in itself not enough. You also need to have access to the data you want to decrypt. As explained in the previous section, devices are encrypted with symmetric encryption, whereas quantum computers break asymmetric encryption, used for communications. Thus, attacks by quantum computers will be focused on encrypted communications. And this means you will need access to communications channels and associated servers. The intercepting of internet communications in bulk is likely only within the purview of state actors. It is difficult to intercept fiberglass undersea cables covertly, and as far as we know only governments, such as the United States and the United Kingdom are doing so.[233] These surveillance programmes often combine the interception with the storing of data.[234] Others, such as criminal organisations, are less likely to pull this off. Perhaps they could hack telecommunication providers and intercept certain specific communications, but this would probably be detected quickly. Or they could intercept communications over the air, but they would probably not be able to do this in bulk—only within certain regions where they have antennas listening in on traffic. Thus, not all communications data is available for decryption.

But even if an organisation had a quantum computer *and* access to communication, it would still not be able to decrypt *all* communications. This is because each key requires separate decryption, and this takes time, at least at first. For example, decrypting an RSA-2048 key on a 4098 logical qubit quantum computer is expected to take more than 28 h (see Table 2.1). As quantum computers increase in size, the time to break a key will decrease. Still, as long as it is not in the order of seconds, it will probably be impossible to break keys in bulk. This means that an organisation, at least initially, will not decrypt all keys: it will focus on those keys which encrypt particularly valuable information or give access to particularly valuable systems. This also depends on whether the keypair changes over time. For example, if a string of communications is encrypted with the same keypair—this is the case for the encryption used traditionally for email, PGP/GPG—you only need to break one pair to decrypt the entire string. If each message is encrypted with a different key, one attack yields less decrypted information. And if organisations were to succeed in breaking keypairs in bulk—something which would become a possibility if quantum computers become big enough—vast swaths of data would become available as a result, and it's uncertain whether sufficient intelligence analysts would be able to handle all the information that would become available.[235] In sum: there is a risk

---

[233] See Khazan 2013 for a description of how this works; see MacAskill et al. 2013 on the British interception programme TEMPORA; and Angwin and Larson 2015; Angwin et al. 2015; NSA 2017 on the US interception programmes (usually called the "Upstream"-programmes).

[234] GCHQ (2014); MacAskill et al. 2013.

[235] Lindsay 2020b, p. 344.

Table 2.1 Literature-reported estimates of quantum resilience for current cryptosystems

System	Category	Key size	Algorithm	Logical qubits	Physical qubits	Time to break	Mitigation
AES-GCM	Symmetric encryption	128	Grover's	2,953	4.61×10^6	2.61×10^{12} years	Double keysize
		192		4,449	1.68×10^7	1.9×10^{22} years	
		256		6,861	3.36×10^7	2.29×10^{32} years	
RSA	Asymmetric encryption	1,024	Shor's	2,050	8.05×10^6	3.58 hours	Move to PQC
		2,048		4,098	8.56×10^6	28.63 hours	
		4,096		8,194	1.12×10^6	229 hours	
ECC	Asymmetric encryption	256	Shor's	2,330	8.56×10^6	10.5 hours	Move to PQC
		384		3,484	9.05×10^6	37.67 hours	
		521		4,719	1.13×10^6	55 hours	
SHA 256	Bitcoin mining	n/a	Grover's	2,403	2.23×10^6	1.8×10^4 years	
PBKDF2	Password hashing	n/a	Grover's	2,403	2.23×10^6	2.3×10^7 years	Move from passwords

Source Table adapted from Table 4.1 of National Academies of Sciences 2018; see also Chen et al. 2016, p. 2; and Bernstein and Lange 2017, Table 1 for other overviews

of attacks against encrypted communication once sufficiently powerful quantum computers become available, but these attacks will initially be *targeted*.

However, in addition to the risk of *actual* decryption, the *threat* of such targeted attacks is at least as worrisome. This threat is like a cloud hanging over the efficacy of these technologies, undermining public trust in encryption, affecting sectors from banking to health, from machine-to-machine communications to politics.[236] Encryption is seen by many as the last line of defence, the only thing that really works when it comes to ensuring that people cannot access information (see Chap. 3). If trust in that last line breaks down, this could further undermine the trust in information security in general. The effects of this are difficult to assess. In a sense, as discussed, information security is already "broken"—a determined attacker with sufficient resources can already gain access to most data without authorisation, and this hasn't resulted in the breakdown of our information society (yet). And as noted, encryption is rarely the weakest link in the attack surface of a system. But given the potential repercussions

[236] See for a similar argument de Wolf 2017, p. 3; and Mulholland et al. 2017, p. 19.

if our information security were to become more brittle, it is at least good policy to decrease this risk now.

This is why several government institutions already identified the threat quantum computing poses to public key cryptography years ago.[237] Some have even started giving advice on switching to "post-quantum cryptography", or PQC, and are preparing to use it themselves.[238] I discuss both in the following sections.

2.4.6 Post-quantum Cryptography as a Mitigation Measure

As the impending breaking of current asymmetric encryption looms, the race for new *quantum resistant* algorithms is on. Because asymmetric encryption is mostly used in communication between different parties, this means it is important to establish worldwide standards. The efforts to develop these standards are spearheaded by the US-based National Institute of Standards and Technology (NIST). In late 2016, NIST started a Post-Quantum Cryptography Standardization track to "specify one or more additional unclassified, publicly disclosed digital signature, public-key encryption, and key-establishment algorithms that are capable of protecting sensitive government information well into the foreseeable future, including after the advent of quantum computers".[239] Since then, the proposals have gone through a number of rounds of triage by internal reviews and public feedback, and in 2022 one public key and three digital signature solutions were selected.[240]

Since quantum computers that can break encryption are at least one to two decades away, you might ask why new algorithms are already being built. This is for two reasons. First, it takes time to replace the encryption protocols in a public key infrastructure—it took twenty years, for instance, to fully roll out the *first* generation of public key infrastructure, and other transitions were of a similar duration.[241] The other

---

[237] Chen et al. 2016, p. 2; ETSI 2015; The US Director of National Intelligence in 2019 concluded that "Foreign deployment of a large-scale quantum computer, even 10 or more years in the future, would put sensitive information encrypted with today's most widely used algorithms at greatly increased risk of decryption"; Coats 2019.

[238] See for example TNO et al. 2023; US legislation which manages migration to PQC for federal agencies: Khanna 2022; German Federal Office for Information Security 2020; AIVD 2022; Schneier 2015. The NSA in 2015 suggested that "For those partners and vendors that have not yet made the transition to Suite B algorithms, we recommend not making a significant expenditure to do so at this point but instead to prepare for the upcoming quantum resistant algorithm transition"; NSA 2015.

[239] Computer Security Division 2016.

[240] See NIST 2023.

[241] Computer Security Division 2017; the widespread adoption of ECC in public key cryptography also took more than two decades; see Koblitz et al. 2011; SHA-2 was standardised by NIST in 2002 and by 2016, 35% of all websites were still using an older standard, and AES was adopted as a standard in 2001 whereas the average adoption year for surveyed organisations was 2014; Vermeer and Peet 2020, p. 14.

reason is that organisations and individuals in many cases want to keep information secret for a considerable amount of time into the future.[242] Say that the Dutch government wants to maintain its diplomatic communications confidential for a period of thirty years. The encryption which Dutch embassies currently use is not necessarily quantum resistant (it might be, we do not know, but let's assume it is not).[243] We should also assume that this traffic is intercepted and stored by other governments. If a quantum computer is built within twenty years, it means the secrets of the Dutch government might be spilled before the end of this confidentiality period of thirty years. Put more generally, if (i) the time it takes to deploy quantum resistant algorithms and (ii) the confidentiality period required together are lower than (iii) the time it takes to make a quantum computer, there is a period where the confidentiality of information cannot be guaranteed.

There are multiple reasons why it takes so long to develop quantum resistant algorithms. The most fundamental reason is that the trust we have in currently used algorithms comes from the fact that they have not been broken over the past decades. The same trust in newly developed algorithms also simply requires time and a lot of attempts at breaking them. Moreover, they not only have to be secure, but also usable.[244] Most importantly, the computational costs of running the algorithm have to be acceptable: even if the costs of encrypting and decrypting information were to be small in absolute terms, if they for example doubled the load on CPUs compared to current algorithms, this could already pose significant problems. Where applications are based on CPUs with little processing power (e.g. smartcards, "Internet of Things"-appliances), this might exceed their available computing power. But the same applies to large computers, to the extent that they are processing high volumes (e.g. a webserver processing a large amount of client data simultaneously).[245] In addition, the implementation characteristics of any PQC algorithms are a key factor in choosing an algorithm: can it easily be implemented in a variety of existing platforms, protocols and applications? One last aspect which is non-technical, but important nonetheless, is whether the post quantum algorithms are subject to any patents and, if so, under what conditions they are licensed. This language is not entirely comforting, as it clearly allows the licensing of algorithms for a fee. In Chap. 9, I discuss policy recommendations in this regard.

The implementation of PQC algorithms is a formidable obstacle. Making the switch has been compared to "changing tires on a moving car", which is probably an understatement, since the Saudi have made a national sport out of doing exactly

[242] See Mosca 2018.

[243] The head of the Dutch department of the intelligence service for secure communications, Bas Dunnebier, in an interview suggests that the Dutch government already uses quantum-resistant algorithms; Dunnebier 2021.

[244] See National Institute of Standards and Technology (NIST) 2016, Sect. 4 for the evaluation criteria.

[245] See for example the discussion of the use of PQ-algorithms in TLS 1.3; Sikeridis et al. 2020; and for experiments in implementing NIST candidates in JavaScript Yuan et al. 2018.

that.[246] First, organisations need to have an overview of the systems where they are currently using vulnerable algorithms. That's challenging due to the widespread adoption of public key-technologies. Next, how those vulnerable algorithms are implemented can further complicate the replacement: Are communication partners also switching to the new algorithms? Is the encryption taking place in hardware or software? Can the algorithm be easily replaced? What are the terms imposed by the supplier and do new licenses need to be concluded? As for algorithms used in consumer devices—routers, thermostats, cars—some will require the owner to update the device manually (which many will not do) and some devices will not support updates at all. And what about updating the update mechanism itself? Furthermore, a switch to PQC can have an impact on how existing protocols function. They may require larger packet sizes, or result in a change in latency for instance. Also, software implementations may work on the assumption that keys have certain maximum size for security, whereas new PQC keys are potentially factors bigger, breaking the whole system.[247]

Not only is the *implementation* challenging from an organisational perspective: the switch to post quantum algorithms could also introduce *new* security vulnerabilities.[248] Even if an algorithm is believed to be secure, implementing it in a new library without vulnerabilities is hard; ensuring that the interaction of such a library with its environment does not introduce additional vulnerabilities is even harder. For example, the use of new PQC in hardware will open up possibilities for new side channel attacks, harvesting information from things such as power consumption, electromagnetic radiation and execution time.[249] Further, since not all devices will switch seamlessly to new PQC protocols, support for outdated protocols will have to be built in for some time, opening up the possibility of downgrading attacks, where you force the other party to use an outdated and less secure protocol. Moreover, something resonating through all these considerations is the ideal of *cryptography agility*—taking this opportunity to upgrade cryptographic infrastructure so that you are able to quickly replace algorithms as needed in the future.[250] If a cryptographic migration is to be automated—and this is unavoidable given the sheer scale of the use of cryptography in IT systems—this opens up the possibility of automated attacks against the updating systems as well. Lastly, as discussed, the security of some encryption standards adopted by NIST in the past has been cast into doubt as a result of potential (covert) influence by the NSA. The current open selection process prevents that to a certain extent, but still there will be fears that the protocols will contain an intentional weakness for intelligence agencies to exploit, a *backdoor*.

---

[246] See Misoczki 2018; Barker et al. 2020; Computing Community Consortium 2019; see World Village Cooking 2014. Some organisations, such as Amazon and IBM, are already implementing post-quantum algorithms for their services; Hopkins 2019; and IBM 2019.

[247] Vermeer and Peet 2020, p. 24.

[248] See Computing Community Consortium 2019, p. 7 and further for an overview.

[249] Taha and Eisenbarth 2015.

[250] Cyber Resilience Workshop Series Committee et al. 2017; Computing Community Consortium 2019.

2.4.7 *The Development of Quantum Key Distribution as a Mitigation Measure*

All in all, switching to PQC poses a formidable challenge. There's also an entirely different encryption technology which can resist attacks by quantum computers: quantum key distribution, or QKD, sometimes called "quantum cryptography".[251] (This is different from *post*-quantum cryptography discussed above.) The question is to what extent this technology provides a viable alternative to current public key cryptography.

QKD is not built around the assumption that some mathematical problems are very hard to break (e.g. factoring), but instead on the physical properties of shared quantum bits. In 1984, Bennett and Brassard developed a key distribution scheme which would allow for the exchange of a shared secret key via quantum properties, to be used for secure communications afterwards.[252] Since then, the "unconditional" security of this approach—that is the security regardless of the particular resources of the attacker—has been demonstrated in several papers.[253]

QKD works by sending a stream of random qubits encoded in photons over an optical link, such as fiberglass cable or through the air, and then relaying approximately half of the bits back to the sender via a classical channel to check whether the initial stream of qubits was intercepted.[254] Because this stream of qubits is exchanged using quantum properties, such a scheme makes it impossible to eavesdrop without detection: if an attacker observes the photons being exchanged, it will disturb the communication between the sender and the recipient, thereby noticeably increasing the error rate of the communications. If no eavesdropping is detected, then the rest of the exchanged key can be safely used for encryption using *symmetric* algorithms, which depending on the length of the key and the algorithm used is impossible to break, also with quantum computers (see above). Thus, QKD has only one application: to facilitate the secure exchanging of keys, an important current function of public key algorithms. It cannot, however, replace all functionalities of public key algorithms. In particular, it cannot be used for authentication or creating signatures: it is merely a way to exchange information while keeping it confidential.

But even for key exchange protocols, the range of applications of QKD is restricted and their security in real life cannot be fully guaranteed. Firstly, the distance over which QKD can currently be applied is limited: some 100 km over fiberglass cable, and over 1000 km through the air.[255] Moreover, the technology currently fits in a

---

[251] See Lo et al. 2014.

[252] Bennett and Brassard 1984; see also Wiesner 1983; and Ekert 1991. Since then, other QKD protocols have also been developed, see for an overview Al-Ghamdi et al. 2020.

[253] Shor and Preskill 2000; Mayers 2004; Lo and Chau 1999; Biham et al. 1999.

[254] Mink et al. 2009, p. 102.

[255] Yoshino et al. 2013; Ursin et al. 2007. Chinese researchers have even succeeded in exchanging pictures of Schrödinger and the Chinese philosopher Micius via QKD using a satellite between Vienna and Bejing in 2017; Liao et al. 2017; Yin et al. 2017, 2020; Giles 2018; University of Science and Technology of China 2018. The QKD products which can currently be bought, for

server rack the size of a coffee table, which means it will only be used by very specific customers who operate their own communications infrastructure, such as governments and financial institutions. Unless the technology can be shrunk to chip-size, it won't be used by consumers, for example to secure communications between phones, IoT devices or other small devices. Lastly, while in theory QKD cannot be attacked, real life QKD remains susceptible to attacks for three reasons. First, since high error rates are a sign that the QKD communications channel is compromised, this opens up the possibility for an attacker to actively insert errors in the communication, thereby blocking the secure exchange of keys altogether—a denial of service attack. Second: the sender and recipient need to authenticate each other beforehand: this cannot be done with QKD. This opens up other avenues of attack. And third: the implementation of QKD in hardware and software allows for various additional attack vectors, although it should be noted that ETSI in a study concluded that all implementation attacks can be mitigated.[256] In short: QKD might be a potential alternative for current asymmetric encryption, but only in limited cases: PQC will have to bear the brunt of resistance against quantum attacks.

2.4.8 *The Spin-Offs of the Quantum Race*

Now, the story that quantum computing will break encryption resonates well in the news—and it is the reason for this book. But it is not the only story you can tell about these new machines. Quantum computers are expected to have other uses besides breaking encryption. In fact, another reason why so many countries and governments are investing large sums in quantum computing, may well be because it carries a lot of promise in other fields.[257] As already alluded to above, quantum computers are expected to do two things well: simulating quantum mechanical systems, as well as solving search and optimisation problems. Quantum simulation may lead to breakthroughs in a wide range of fields related to chemistry, from health (developing better drugs), to agriculture (developing cheaper ways to create fertiliser) and materials (cheaper solar panels). And while search and optimisation solutions can be used to break encryption, these routines play an important role in other fields as well, for example in logistics (distribution and traffic planning) and finance (valuing derivatives). The most important take-away is: we simply do not know the potential applications of quantum computing precisely, but there is a chance that this technology will be seriously disruptive.

---

example produced by Toshiba (Japan) and IDQuantique (Switzerland) have a maximum distance of around 100 km.

Toshiba (2020) Quantum Key Distribution. https://www.toshiba.co.jp/qkd/en/products.htm. Accessed 15 September 2020 Toshiba 2020; ID Quantique 2020.

[256] ETSI 2018.

[257] Hoofnagle and Garfinkel 2021; Preskill 2018, para 6.9; de Wolf 2012, 2017; German Federal Ministry of Education and Research 2019; Quantum Delta Nederland 2019; Gerbert and Ruess 2018.

Another thing to keep in mind, is that research on quantum computing can also lead to breakthroughs in *other* disciplines. It is happened before with other "moonshot"-projects. The Manhattan Project resulted in advances in nuclear power and in applications for radioisotopes, including cancer treatment, genetics research and biochemistry.[258] NASA publishes a website and magazine called Spinoffs dedicated exclusively to technological innovations developed for space, but used on Earth, ranging from infrared thermometers to scratch-free lenses.[259] And the internet, used by people all over the world, is a byproduct of the development of a military communication system for the US Department of Defense.[260]

Quantum technologies arguably bear some resemblance to these other foundational technologies. The development of quantum technologies is expected to have direct results, e.g. in sensing and metrology. But they can also be expected to have indirect results, for example in manufacturing, in refrigeration, isolation, and lasers.[261] Given the enormous amounts of money currently being funnelled into quantum computing, and the fundamental science required to get this to work, this will probably lead to generally applicable scientific insights, not only in the narrow field of quantum computing per se, but also in other domains. This is relevant for the assessment under the human right to science in Chap. 7.

2.4.9 Different Scenarios for Quantum Computing

So, *if* scientists succeed in building large-scale quantum computers, these are still a long way off. In the meanwhile, there are a number of potential scenarios which may unfold. Of course, peering into the future is fraught with difficulty and not something I am necessarily qualified to do. Still, it is useful to get a better sense of the different options, and to also provide more depth to the analysis of quantum computing governance in Chap. 10. Building on the work of Hoofnagle and Garfinkel, I distinguish four different trajectories.[262]

In the first, let us call it *state takes all*, a large state such as China or the US is the first to build a useful quantum computer. This quantum computer could then be applied to further develop quantum computers, increasing the advantage of the initial development. In this scenario, the state not only developed the computer, but is also driving its use. And it will use it to consolidate its technological and geopolitical power. One of the obvious applications in this scenario will be breaking the encrypted communication of other states. But it could also be used to develop new nuclear, chemical and biological weapons, strengthening its military might.

[258] Atomic Heritage Foundation 2014; Meyers 2020.
[259] NASA (2020) Spinoff. https://spinoff.nasa.gov/. Accessed 17 September 2020 NASA 2020.
[260] Abbate 1999, in particular Chap. 1.
[261] See for example German Federal Ministry of Education and Research 2019.
[262] Hoofnagle and Garfinkel 2021, Sect. 8.2.

There is also a variation to this scenario, where instead the large investments of a *private* company pay off—let's call this *corporation takes all*. Here, the winner will use it to consolidate its commercial power, outcompeting other companies, also possibly entering new markets. For example, if Google were to develop a useful quantum computer, it could use it to strengthen not only its search technology, but also to develop new medicines.

Then there are scenarios where this cycle of improvement is not so strong that one winner takes all—instead multiple states and corporations develop these computers simultaneously, possibly in partnership. Let's call this *public-private development*. On one end of the spectrum, the state enlists a privately developed computer for its exclusive use, possibly even nationalising the technology. Here, military applications will then be the dominant theme. On the other end, the state develops the technology and makes it available for commercial purposes. Here, there will be a mixture of state-related and commercial uses for these computers. Possibly, companies would make this power available through cloud services, just as Google, IBM and Microsoft are already making it possible to experiment online with small-scale quantum computers offered as a cloud service.

And lastly, a possible scenario is *quantum winter*—a scenario where reality just cannot keep up with the hype, where quantum computers fail to materialise. The large sources of funding which are currently flowing to this field will dry out, and hosts of scientists specialised in parts of quantum computing will move on to other fields. This has happened before: the development of artificial intelligence went through similar phases.

It's impossible to tell which variation of these scenarios will play out. But the governance implications for these scenarios are different. I explore this further in Chap. 10.

2.5 Summing Up

At the heart of modern information security lies a paradox; a tension between making and breaking, between control and intrusion. Securing things and finding vulnerabilities are two sides of the same coin, and one is necessary for the other. The state of information security requires a continuous feedback loop in order to improve. But information security measures may also restrict human rights. One way to ensure that these measures respect human rights, is by tweaking this feedback loop. How to tweak this feedback loop is the main topic of this book.

An important starting point for tweaking this cycle is that the current state of information security is abysmal. As IT systems become more complex, the attack surface of these systems grows. Meanwhile, it is much easier to play offence than defence: defenders have to secure all potential avenues for unauthorised access, while attackers only need one weak spot to break in. As a result, the research into zero days has taken flight: governmental institutions, corporations and criminals have all become active in this crowded domain. One set of researchers find zero days to improve security. Another set of researchers looks for zero days to ultimately exploit these; the consequences of this are sometimes disastrous.

Tweaking the information security cycle towards certain forms of coordinated vulnerability disclosure can accelerate the fixing of vulnerabilities. This comes with a couple of practical obstacles, though. Experts do still not agree about the best practices for disclosure, especially since the information and technologies used to shore up defences are generally the same as those used to attack. Moreover, because vendors often are dependent on a complex network of suppliers, the coordination of mitigating measures is increasingly challenging. I discuss policy options for coordinated vulnerability disclosure from the perspective of human rights in Chap. 8.

All these questions are illustrated with the interplay between encryption technologies and quantum computing. Asymmetric encryption technologies are an important building block of information security because they are difficult to break with current computers. These technologies are used widely, in computers and phones and internet communications, by privacy activists and large corporations, by criminals and intelligence agencies. But governments also claim that the widespread use of encryption technologies hinders law enforcement departments and intelligence agencies in accessing information in the course of investigations.

Quantum computers may change this: these computers may break public key encryption technologies in the future. Since the development of such a computer will enable targeted attacks against encrypted communication and potentially further undermine trust in information security, some governments are already advising to switch to technologies which can resist quantum attacks. These quantum resistant technologies are now being developed.

And so, the cycle of making and breaking has been set into motion again. This time we might be able to steer its direction, though, taking into account the risks and benefits of the development of quantum computing from a human rights perspective. Yes, breaking encryption technologies would pose a serious problem for information security—and information security is used to protect several human rights, such as the right to privacy. Then again, governments have good reasons to want to access encrypted information in some cases. And furthermore, scientific research and development is also protected by human rights, such as the right to communications freedom and the right to science. These tensions are further explored in the rest of this book.

But in order to know where we should tweak the information cycle to protect human rights, we first need to understand the current governance of the information security cycle. This is the topic of the Chap. 3.

References

Articles, Books and Other Documents

Aan de Brugh M (2016) "De cryptocalypse komt eraan". NRC Handelsblad 4 September 2016. https://www.nrc.nl/nieuws/2016/09/04/de-cryptocalypse-komt-eraan-4086146-a1519706. Accessed 3 January 2024.

Aaronson S (2020) Quantum Supremacy, Now with BosonSampling. Shtetl-Optimized. https://www.scottaaronson.com/blog/?p=5122. Accessed 8 January 2021.

Abbate J (1999) Inventing the Internet. MIT Press, Cambridge, Mass.

Ablon L, Bogart A (2017) Zero Days, Thousands of Nights: The Life and Times of Zero-Day Vulnerabilities and Their Exploits. RAND Corporation.

Ablon L, Libicki MC, Golay AA (2014) Zero-Day Vulnerabilities in the Black and Gray Markets. In: Markets for Cybercrime Tools and Stolen Data. RAND Corporation, pp 25–28.

Acharya R, Aleiner I, Allen R et al. (2023) Suppressing Quantum Errors by Scaling a Surface Code Logical Qubit. Nature 614:676–681. https://doi.org/10.1038/s41586-022-05434-1

Acín A, Bloch I, Buhrman H et al. (2018) The Quantum Technologies Roadmap: A European Community View. New Journal of Physics 20:080201. https://doi.org/10.1088/1367-2630/aad1ea

Aftergood S (2013) Cryptographer Adi Shamir Prevented from Attending NSA History Conference. Federation Of American Scientists. https://fas.org/blogs/secrecy/2013/10/shamir/. Accessed 11 October 2019.

AIVD (2022) Prepare for the Threat of Quantum Computers, January 18, 2022. https://english.aivd.nl/binaries/aivd-en/documenten/publications/2022/01/18/prepare-for-the-threat-of-quantumcomputers/Prepare+for+the+threat+of+quantumcomputers.pdf. Accessed 3 January 2024.

Alberts G, Oldenziel R (2014) Hacking Europe: From Computer Cultures to Demoscenes. Springer, London.

Al-Ghamdi A-B, Al-Sulami A, Aljahdali AO (2020) On the Security and Confidentiality of Quantum Key Distribution. Security and Privacy 3:111. https://doi.org/10.1002/spy2.111

Anderson R (2020) Security Engineering: A Guide to Building Dependable Distributed Systems, 3rd edn. John Wiley and Sons, Indianapolis.

Anderson R, Barton C, Boehme R et al. (2019) Measuring the Changing Cost of Cybercrime. 2019 Workshop on the Economics of Information Security (WEIS 2019). https://doi.org/10.17863/CAM.41598

Angwin J, Larson J (2015) NSA Spying Relies on AT&T's "Extreme Willingness to Help". ProPublica. https://www.propublica.org/article/nsa-spying-relies-on-atts-extreme-willingness-to-help. Accessed 16 September 2020.

Angwin J, Savage C, Larson J et al. (2015) AT&T Helped U.S. Spy on Internet on a Vast Scale. The New York Times 5 August 2015.

Anzuoni M (2020) Tracing Paper. Logic Magazine. https://logicmag.io/security/tracing-paper/. Accessed 2 July 2021.

Apple, Apple Platform Security, May 2022. https://support.apple.com/guide/security/welcome/web. Accessed 3 January 2024.

Apple (2018) About Encrypted Storage on Your New Mac.Apple Support. https://support.apple.com/en-us/HT208344. Accessed 5 February 2019.

Apple, iOS Security: iOS 12. https://www.apple.com/business/site/docs/iOS_Security_Guide.pdf. Accessed 10 October 2018.

Apple (2021) Apple Developer Support.Apple App Store. https://developer.apple.com/support/app-store/. Accessed 2 November 2021.

Apple (2020) Apple Reports Record First Quarter Results. In: Apple Newsroom. https://www.apple.com/newsroom/2020/01/apple-reports-record-first-quarter-results/. Accessed 2 November 2021.

Arnbak AM (2016) Securing Private Communications: Protecting Private Communications Security in EU Law: Fundamental Rights, Functional Value Chains, and Market Incentives. Kluwer Law International, Alphen aan den Rijn, The Netherlands.

Arora A, Nandkumar A, Telang R (2007) Does Information Security Attack Frequency Increase with Vulnerability Disclosure? An Empirical Analysis. Information Systems Frontiers 8:350–362. https://doi.org/10.1007/s10796-006-9012-5

Arora A, Telang R, Xu H (2008) Optimal Policy for Software Vulnerability Disclosure. Management Science 54:642–656. https://doi.org/10.1287/mnsc.1070.0771

Arora A, Krishnan R, Telang R, Yang Y (2010) An Empirical Analysis of Software Vendors' Patch Release Behavior: Impact of Vulnerability Disclosure. Information Systems Research 21:115–132. https://doi.org/10.1287/isre.1080.0226

Arute F, Arya K, Babbush R et al. (2019) Quantum Supremacy Using a Programmable Superconducting Processor. Nature 574:505–510. https://doi.org/10.1038/s41586-019-1666-5

Atomic Heritage Foundation (2014) Peaceful Nuclear Innovations. https://www.atomicheritage.org/history/peaceful-nuclear-innovations. Accessed 17 September 2020.

Aycock J, Buchanan E, Dexter S, Dittrich D (2012) Human Subjects, Agents, or Bots: Current Issues in Ethics and Computer Security Research. In: Danezis G, Dietrich S, Sako K (eds) Financial Cryptography and Data Security. Springer Berlin Heidelberg, Berlin, Heidelberg, pp 138–145.

Baker J, Landau S (2019) New Perspectives on the Future of Encryption. In: Lawfare. https://www.lawfareblog.com/new-perspectives-future-encryption. Accessed 12 July 2019.

Ball P (2020) Physicists in China Challenge Google's "Quantum Advantage". Nature 588:380–380. https://doi.org/10.1038/d41586-020-03434-7

Bamford J (2012) The NSA Is Building the Country's Biggest Spy Center (Watch What You Say). Wired, 15 March 2012.

Barker W, Polk W, Souppaya M (2020) Getting Ready for Post-Quantum Cryptography: Explore Challenges Associated with Adoption and Use of Post-Quantum Cryptographic Algorithms, 26 May2020.

Becker A (2018) What Is Real?: The Unfinished Quest for the Meaning of Quantum Physics, 1st edn. Basic Books, New York.

Becker GT, Regazzoni F, Paar C, Burleson WP (2014) Stealthy Dopant-Level Hardware Trojans: Extended Version. The Journal of Cryptographic Engineering 4:19–31. https://doi.org/10.1007/s13389-013-0068-0

Benioff P (1980) The Computer as a Physical System: A Microscopic Quantum Mechanical Hamiltonian Model of Computers as Represented by Turing Machines. Journal of Statistical Physics 22:563–591. https://doi.org/10.1007/BF01011339

Benioff P (1982a) Quantum Mechanical Models of Turing Machines That Dissipate No Energy. Physical Review Letters 48:1581–1585. https://doi.org/10.1103/PhysRevLett.48.1581

Benioff P (1982b) Quantum Mechanical Hamiltonian Models of Turing Machines. Journal of Statistical Physics 29:515–546. https://doi.org/10.1007/BF01342185

Bennett CH, Brassard G (1984) Quantum Cryptography: Public Key Distribution and Coin Tossing. Proceedings of the IEEE International Conference on Computers, Systems and Signal Processing 560:175–179. https://doi.org/10.1016/j.tcs.2014.05.025

Bernstein DJ, Lange T (2017) Post-Quantum Cryptography. Nature 549:188.

Biddle S (2016) The NSA Leak Is Real, Snowden Documents Confirm. The Intercept. https://theintercept.com/2016/08/19/the-nsa-was-hacked-snowden-documents-confirm/. Accessed 18 September 2019.

Biddle S (2017) NYU Accidentally Exposed Military Code-Breaking Computer Project to Entire Internet.The Intercept. https://theintercept.com/2017/05/11/nyu-accidentally-exposed-military-code-breaking-computer-project-to-entire-internet/. Accessed 15 September 2020.

Biham E, Boyer M, Boykin PO et al. (1999) A Proof of the Security of Quantum Key Distribution. arXiv:quant-ph/9912053

Bilge L, Dumitraş T (2012) Before We Knew It: An Empirical Study of Zero-Day Attacks in the Real World. In: Proceedings of the 2012 ACM Conference on Computer and Communications Security. Association for Computing Machinery, New York, NY, USA, pp 833–844.

Birsan A (2021) Dependency Confusion: How I Hacked Into Apple, Microsoft and Dozens of Other Companies.Medium. https://medium.com/@alex.birsan/dependency-confusion-4a5d60fec610. Accessed 12 February 2021.

Born M, Einstein A (1971) The Born-Einstein Letters. The MacMillan Press, London and Basingstoke.

Bossert TP (2017) It's Official: North Korea Is Behind WannaCry. Wall Street Journal 19 December 2017.

Bratus S, Arce I, Locasto ME, Zanero S (2014) Why Offensive Security Needs Engineering Textbooks. Or, How to Avoid a Replay of "Crypto Wars" in Security Research.;login: 39:6–11.

Buchanan B, Bansemer J, Dakota C et al. (2020) Automating Cyber Attacks, CSET, November 2020.

Buchanan E, Aycock J, Dexter S et al. (2011) Computer Science Security Research and Human Subjects: Emerging Considerations for Research Ethics Boards. Journal of Empirical Research on Human Research Ethics 6:71–83. https://doi.org/10.1525/jer.2011.6.2.71

Buhrman H, Cleve R, van Dam W (2001) Quantum Entanglement and Communication Complexity. SIAM Journal on Computing 30:1829–1841.

Burkart PC, McCourt TM (2019) Why Hackers Win: Power and Disruption in the Network Society. University of California Press, Oakland.

Castellanos S (2020a) Amazon's Cloud Unit to Offer Quantum Computing from 3 Tech Companies. Wall Street Journal, 13 August 2020.

Castellanos S (2020b) White House Plans to Boost AI, Quantum Funding by 30%. Wall Street Journal, 14 August 2020.

CBP (2013) Richtsnoeren: Beveiliging van persoonsgegevens. https://www.autoriteitpersoonsgegevens.nl/uploads/imported/beleidsregels_beveiliging_van_persoonsgegevens.pdf. Accessed 14 December 2023.

Ceron JM, Chromik JJ, Santanna JJC, Pras A (2019) Online Discoverability and Vulnerabilities of ICS/SCADADevices in the Netherlands, WODC June 21, 2019.

Chaos Computer Club (2022) Stage Win: FinFisher Is Bankrupt.CCC.de. https://www.ccc.de/en/updates/2022/etappensieg-finfisher-ist-pleite. Accessed 31 March 2022.

Chen L, Jordan S, Liu Y-K et al. (2016) Report on Post-Quantum Cryptography, NIST IR 8105. NIST April 2016.

Chen S (2017) China Building World's Biggest Quantum Research Facility.South China Morning Post. https://www.scmp.com/news/china/society/article/2110563/china-building-worlds-biggest-quantum-research-facility. Accessed 25 August 2020.

Choi JP, Fershtman C, Gandal N (2010) Network Security: Vulnerabilities and Disclosure Policy. The Journal of Industrial Economics 58:868–894. https://doi.org/10.1111/j.1467-6451.2010.00435.x

Cisco (2017) The Wikileaks Vault 7 Leak—What We Know So Far. blogs@Cisco - Cisco Blogs. https://blogs.cisco.com/security/the-wikileaks-vault-7-leak-what-we-know-so-far. Accessed 18 September 2019.

Clarke J (2019) An Optimist's View of the 4 Challenges to Quantum Computing.IEEE Spectrum: Technology, Engineering, and Science News. https://spectrum.ieee.org/tech-talk/computing/hardware/an-optimists-view-of-the-4-challenges-to-quantum-computing. Accessed 28 May 2020.

Coats DR (2019) Worldwide Threat Assessment of the US Intelligence Community, 29 January ODNI, 29 January 2019.

Coleman EG (2013) Coding Freedom: The Ethics and Aesthetics of Hacking. Princeton University Press, Princeton.

Coleman EG (2014) Hacker, Hoaxer, Whistleblower, Spy: The Many Faces of Anonymous. Verso, London ; New York.

Computer Security Division ITL (2016) Public-Key Post-Quantum Cryptographic Algorithms: Nominations.CSRC | NIST. https://content.csrc.e1c.nist.gov/news/2016/public-key-post-quantum-cryptographic-algorithms. Accessed 4 September 2020.

Computer Security Division ITL (2017) Post-Quantum Cryptography. NIST. https://content.csrc.e1c.nist.gov/Projects/Post-Quantum-Cryptography. Accessed 4 September 2020.

Computing Community Consortium (2019) Identifying Research Challenges in Post Quantum Cryptography Migration and Cryptographic Agility, CCC Workshop. January 31, 2019.

Constantin L (2014) Prominent Cryptographers Targeted by Malware Attacks.PCWorld. https://www.pcworld.com/article/2093700/prominent-cryptographer-victim-of-malware-attack-related-to-belgacom-breach.html. Accessed 16 January 2020.

Corbet (2003) An Attempt to Backdoor the Kernel.LWN.net. https://lwn.net/Articles/57135/. Accessed 3 December 2019.

Corera G (2014) Fridge Sends Spam Emails. BBC News, 17 January 2014.

Cox J (2017) Shadow Brokers Dump Alleged Windows Exploits and NSA Presentations on Targeting Banks.Vice. https://www.vice.com/en_us/article/bmezja/shadow-brokers-dump-alleged-windows-exploits-and-nsa-presentations-on-targeting-banks. Accessed 13 September 2019.

Cox J (2020) NSO Group Impersonated Facebook to Help Clients Hack Targets.Vice. https://www.vice.com/en_us/article/qj4p3w/nso-group-hack-fake-facebook-domain. Accessed 17 September 2020.

Culp S (2001) It's Time to End Information Anarchy. Microsoft Security Response Center. https://web.archive.org/web/20011109045330if_/; http://www.microsoft.com:80/technet/treeview/default.asp?url=/technet/columns/security/noarch.asp. Accessed 19 September 2019.

Cyber Resilience Workshop Series Committee, Forum on Cyber Resilience, Computer Science and Telecommunications Board et al. (2017) Cryptographic Agility and Interoperability: Proceedings of a Workshop. National Academies Press, Washington, DC.

Deutsch D, Penrose R (1985) Quantum Theory, the Church–Turing Principle and the Universal Quantum Computer. Proceedings of the Royal Society of London A Mathematical and Physical Sciences 400:97–117. https://doi.org/10.1098/rspa.1985.0070

de Wolf R (2012) What Quantum Computing Can Do for You. Inaugural lecture. https://homepages.cwi.nl/~rdewolf/oratie-final.pdf. Accessed 3 January 2024.

de Wolf R (2017) The Potential Impact of Quantum Computers on Society. arXiv:171205380 [quant-ph].

Diaz C, Tene O, Gürses S (XXXX2013) Hero or Villain: The Data Controller in Privacy Law and Technologies. Ohio State Law Journal 74:42.

Diffie W, Hellman M (1976) New Directions in Cryptography. IEEE Transactions on Information Theory 22:644–654. https://doi.org/10.1109/TIT.1976.1055638

Dimensions (2020) Overview of quantum computing in title of academic publications.Dimensions. https://app.dimensions.ai/analytics/publication/for/aggregated?search_mode=content&search_text=quantumcomputing&search_type=kws&search_field=text_search. Accessed 18 August 2020.

Doctorow C (2012) The Coming Civil War over General Purpose Computing.Memex. https://memex.craphound.com/2012/08/23/the-coming-civil-war-over-general-purpose-computing/. Accessed 28 May 2021.

Doctorow C (2020) Descartes' God Has Failed and Thompson's Satan Rules Our Computers. Pluralistic. https://pluralistic.net/2020/12/05/trusting-trust/. Accessed 28 May 2021.

dos Santos N, Kaplan M (2018) Jamal Khashoggi's Private WhatsApp Messages May Offer New Clues to Killing.CNN. https://www.cnn.com/2018/12/02/middleeast/jamal-khashoggi-whatsapp-messages-intl/index.html. Accessed 15 January 2020.

Dunnebier B (2021), Interview for Cyberhelden Podcast, https://www.cyberhelden.nl/. Accessed 3 January 2024.

DuPont Q, Fidler B (2016) Edge Cryptography and the Codevelopment of Computer Networks and Cybersecurity. IEEE Annals of the History of Computing 38:55–73. https://doi.org/10.1109/MAHC.2016.49

Eeckhout M, Vanhecke N (2014) Belgian Professor in Cryptography Hacked (English Summary). De Standaard, 1 February 2014.

Ekert AK (1991) Quantum Cryptography Based on Bell's Theorem. Physical Review Letters 67:661–663. https://doi.org/10.1103/PhysRevLett.67.661

Electronic Frontier Foundation (2016) EFF Asks Court to Block U.S. From Prosecuting Security Researcher For Detecting and Publishing Computer Vulnerabilities.Electronic Frontier Foundation. https://www.eff.org/nl/press/releases/eff-asks-court-block-us-prosecuting-security-researcher-detecting-and-publishing. Accessed 15 October 2019.

Elsayed-Ali S (2016) Encryption: A Matter of Human Rights Amnesty International 2016.

Encryption Working Group (2019) Likely Future Adoption of User-Controlled Encryption, Carnegie Endowment for International Peace, April 2019.

ENISA (2017) Hardware Threat Landscape and Good Practice Guide ENISA January 2017.

ENISA (2015) Good Practice Guide on Vulnerability Disclosure: From Challenges to Recommendations, ENISA 2015.

ENISA (2010) Preventing Identity Theft, Presentation 3 April 2010, https://www.enisa.europa.eu/publications/archive/preventing-identity-theft_training-material. Accessed 3 January 2024.

ETSI (2015) Quantum Safe Cryptography and Security - An Introduction, Benefits, Enablers and Challenges ETSI White Paper, June 2015.

ETSI (2018) Implementation Security of Quantum Cryptography - Introduction, Challenges, Solutions, ETSI White Paper, July 2018.

European Commission (2016) Quantum Technologies Roadmap. https://qt.eu//app/uploads/2018/04/QT-Roadmap-2016.pdf. Accessed 21 August 2020.

European Commission (2017) Eleventh Progress Report Towards an Effective and Genuine Security Union, COM(2017)608 final, 18 October 2017.

European Commission (2020) About the Quantum Flagship.Quantum Technology. https://qt.eu/about/. Accessed 21 August 2020.

Europol, Internet Organised Crime Threat Assessment (IOCTA) 2019, 2019.

Europol, Internet Organised Crime Threat Assessment (IOCTA) 2017, 2017.

Europol, EC3, Internet Organised Crime Threat Assessment (IOCTA) 2018, 2018.

Europol, EC3, Eurojust, First report of the observatory function on encryption, 11 January 2019.

Europol, EC3, Eurojust, Second report of the observatory function on encryption, 18 February 2020.

Evans C (2014) Announcing Project Zero.Google Online Security Blog. https://security.googleblog.com/2014/07/announcing-project-zero.html. Accessed 26 November 2019.

Falkvinge R (2013) NSA Asked Linus Torvalds to Install Backdoors into GNU/Linux.Falkvinge on Liberty. //falkvinge.net/2013/11/17/nsa-asked-linus-torvalds-to-install-backdoors-into-gnulinux/. Accessed 3 December 2019.

Feynman RP (1982) Simulating Physics with Computers. International Journal of Theoretical *Physics* 21:467–488. https://doi.org/10.1007/BF02650179

Feynman RP (1986) Quantum Mechanical Computers. Foundations of Physics 16:507–531. https://doi.org/10.1007/BF01886518

Fidler M (2015) Regulating the Zero-Day Vulnerability Trade: A Preliminary Analysis. ISJLP 11:405–484.

Finifter M, Akhawe D, Wagner D (2013) An Empirical Study of Vulnerability Rewards Programs. Proceedings of the 22nd USENIX Security Symposium 2013.

FireEye (2015) Bug Bounties, (Non) Lawsuits and Working with the Research Community.FireEye. https://www.fireeye.com/blog/executive-perspective/2015/09/bug_bounties_non.html. Accessed 15 October 2019.

Flexera About Secunia Research. https://www.flexera.com/products/operations/software-vulnerability-research/secunia-research.html. Accessed 28 November 2019.

Franceschi-Bicchierai L (2017) VICE - The CIA Spied on People Through Their Smart TVs, Leaked Documents Reveal. https://www.vice.com/en_us/article/8qbq5x/the-cia-spied-on-people-through-their-smart-tvs-leaked-documents-reveal. Accessed 3 July 2020.
Franceschi-Bicchierai L (2018a) How a Tiny Startup Became the Most Important Hacking Shop You've Never Heard of.Vice. https://www.vice.com/en_us/article/8xdayg/iphone-zero-days-inside-azimuth-security. Accessed 26 November 2019.
Franceschi-Bicchierai L (2018b) Startup Offers $3 Million to Anyone Who Can Hack the iPhone.Vice. https://www.vice.com/en/article/pax987/crowdfense-offers-3-million-for-iphone-android-hacks. Accessed 18 October 2020.
Franceschi-Bicchierai L (2019) Hacking Team's New Owner: "We're Starting From Scratch".Vice. https://www.vice.com/en_us/article/neavnm/hacking-team-new-owner-starting-from-scratch. Accessed 13 September 2019.
Franceschi-Bicchierai L (2020) Mysterious Bugs Were Used to Hack iPhones and Android Phones and No One Will Talk About It.Vice. https://www.vice.com/en/article/xgzxmk/google-project-zero-bugs-used-to-hack-iphones-and-android-phones. Accessed 27 May 2021.
Frank KW, Rainer S, Brandon L et al. (2019) Entwicklungsstand Quantencomputer. German Federal Office for Information Security, July 2019.
Frei S and others (2010) 'Modeling the Security Ecosystem - The Dynamics of (In)Security' in Tyler Moore, David Pym and Christos Ioannidis (eds), Economics of Information Security and Privacy. Springer US, pp. 79–106.
Gallagher S (2019) Indian Nuclear Power Plant's Network Was Hacked, Officials Confirm.Ars Technica. https://arstechnica.com/information-technology/2019/10/indian-nuclear-power-company-confirms-north-korean-malware-attack/. Accessed 30 May 2021.
Garcia FD, Jacobs B (2016) The Fall of a Tiny Star. In: Ryan PYA, Naccache D, Quisquater J-J (eds) The New Codebreakers: Essays Dedicated to David Kahn on the Occasion of His 85th Birthday. Springer Berlin Heidelberg, Berlin, Heidelberg, pp 69–87.
GCHQ (2014) Leaked GCHQ Report on the Technical Abilities of Tempora. https://www.eff.org/nl/document/20140618-der-spiegel-gchq-report-technical-abilities-tempora. Accessed 4 January 2024.
Geer D (2014) Cybersecurity as Realpolitik, Blackhat, 6 August 2014.
Gent E (2021) IBM's 127-Qubit Eagle Is the Biggest Quantum Computer Yet.Singularity Hub. https://singularityhub.com/2021/11/22/ibms-127-qubit-eagle-is-the-biggest-quantum-computer-yet/. Accessed 14 January 2022.
Gerbert P, Ruess F (2018) The Next Decade in Quantum Computing - and How to Play, BCG, November 2018.
German Federal Ministry of Education and Research (2019) Quantum Technologies—from Basic Research to Market, December 3, 2019. https://www.quantentechnologien.de/fileadmin/public/Redaktion/Dokumente/PDF/Publikationen/Federal-Government-Framework-Programme-Quantum-technologies-2018-bf-C1.pdf. Accessed 4 January 2024.
German Federal Office for Information Security (2020) Migration zu Post-Quanten-Kryptografie - Handlungsempfehlungen des BSI, August 2020. https://www.bsi.bund.de/SharedDocs/Downloads/DE/BSI/Krypto/Post-Quanten-Kryptografie.pdf?__blob=publicationFile&v=1. Accessed 4 January 2024.
German Government (2020) Eckpunkte des Konjunkturpakets, June 3, 2020.
Giles M (2018) The Man Turning China into a Quantum Superpower.MIT Technology Review. https://www.technologyreview.com/2018/12/19/1571/the-man-turning-china-into-a-quantum-superpower/. Accessed 15 September 2020.
Gill L, Parsons C (2018) Shining a Light on the Encryption Debate: A Canadian Field Guide, Citizen Lab and the Canadian Internet Policy & Public Interest Clinic, May 2018.
Golson J (2016) Jeep Hackers at It Again, This Time Taking Control of Steering and Braking Systems.The Verge. https://www.theverge.com/2016/8/2/12353186/car-hack-jeep-cherokee-vulnerability-miller-valasek. Accessed 3 July 2020.

Google (2016) Android 7.0 Nougat: a more powerful OS, made for you. https://www.blog.google/products/android/android-70-nougat-more-powerful-os-made/. Accessed 11 October 2018.

Google Google Quantum Computing Service (2021). https://quantumai.google/cirq/google/concepts. Accessed 12 November 2021.

Graff G (2017) The Mirai Botnet Was Part of a College Student Minecraft Scheme. Wired, 13 December 2017.

Graham R (2017) How The Intercept Outed Reality Winner. https://blog.erratasec.com/2017/06/how-intercept-outed-reality-winner.html. Accessed 21 November 2020.

Grance T, Hash J, Peck S et al. (2002) Security Guide for Interconnecting Information Technology Systems, NIST SP 800-47.

Greenberg A (2012a) Meet The Hackers Who Sell Spies The Tools To Crack Your PC (And Get Paid Six-Figure Fees). Forbes, 21 March 2012.

Greenberg A (2012b) Shopping For Zero-Days: A Price List For Hackers' Secret Software Exploits. Forbes, 23 March 2012.

Greenberg A (2014) Inside Endgame: A Second Act For The Blackwater Of Hacking. In: Forbes. https://www.forbes.com/sites/andygreenberg/2014/02/12/inside-endgame-a-new-direction-for-the-blackwater-of-hacking/. Accessed 4 December 2019.

Greenberg A (2015) Hackers Remotely Kill a Jeep on the Highway—With Me in It. Wired, 21 July 2015.

Greenberg A (2016) How an Entire Nation Became Russia's Test Lab for Cyberwar. Wired, 20 June 2017.

Greenberg A (2018) The Untold Story of NotPetya, the Most Devastating Cyberattack in History. Wired, 22 August 2018.

Greenberg A (2019a) Inside Olympic Destroyer, the Most Deceptive Hack in History. Wired, 17 October 2019.

Greenberg A (2019b) A Mysterious Hacker Group Is On a Supply Chain Hijacking Spree. Wired, 3 May 2019.

Greenberg A (2019c) Sandworm. A New Era of Cyberwar and the Hunt for the Kremlin's Most Dangerous Hackers, 1st edn. Doubleday, New York.

Greenberg A (2020a) The US Blames Russia's GRU for Sweeping Cyberattacks in Georgia. Wired, 20 February 2020.

Greenberg A (2020b) Hackers Can Clone Millions of Toyota, Hyundai, and Kia Keys. Wired, 5 March 2020.

Grierson J (2015) Security Flaw Affecting More Than 100 Car Models Exposed by Scientists. The Guardian, 18 August 2015.

Grover LK (1999) Quantum Computing. The Sciences 1999:24–30.

Grover LK (1996) A fast Quantum Mechanical Algorithm for Database Search. arXiv:quant-ph/9605043

Gyongyosi L, Imre S (2019) A Survey on Quantum Computing Technology. Computer Science Review 31:51–71. https://doi.org/10.1016/j.cosrev.2018.11.002

Hammouchi H, Cherqi O, Mezzour G et al. (2019) Digging Deeper into Data Breaches: An Exploratory Data Analysis of Hacking Breaches Over Time. Procedia Computer Science 151:1004–1009. https://doi.org/10.1016/j.procs.2019.04.141

Heninger N, Halderman JA (2016) The Legacy of Export-Grade Cryptography in the 21st Century. https://summerschool-croatia.cs.ru.nl/2016/slides/NadiaHeninger.pdf. Accessed 4 January 2024.

Herpig DS (2019) Securing Artificial Intelligence: Part 1: The Attack Surface of Machine Learning and Its Implications Stiftung Neue Verantwortung, October 2019.

Herr T, Rosenzweig P (2014) Cyber Weapons and Export Control: Incorporating Dual Use with the PrEP Model. SSRN Journal 8:301. https://doi.org/10.2139/ssrn.2501789

Herr T, Schneier B, Morris C (2017) Taking Stock: Estimating Vulnerability Rediscovery, Belfer Center for Science and International Affairs, July 2017.

Hoepman J-H (2021) Privacy Is Hard and Seven Other Myths: Achieving Privacy through Careful Design. MIT Press, Cambridge, Massachusetts.
Hoofnagle CJ, Garfinkel S (2021) Law and Policy for the Quantum Age, 1st edn. Cambridge University Press, New York.
Hopkins A (2019) Post-Quantum TLS Now Supported in AWS KMS. Amazon Web Services. https://aws.amazon.com/blogs/security/post-quantum-tls-now-supported-in-aws-kms/. Accessed 24 September 2020.
Householder AD, Wassermann G, Manion A, King C (2017) The CERT Guide to Coordinated Vulnerability Disclosure, CMU/SEI-2017-SR-022.
Howard M (2003) Fending off Future Attacks by Reducing Attack Surface. MSDN Library. https://docs.microsoft.com/en-us/previous-versions/ms972812(v=msdn.10). Accessed 26 November 2021.
IBM (2020) Quantum Experience Documentation and Resources. https://quantum-computing.ibm.com/docs/. Accessed 19 August 2020.
IBM (2019) IBM Developing New Cloud Services and Technology to Help Keep Data Secured from Future Fault-Tolerant Quantum Computers.IBM News Room. https://newsroom.ibm.com/2019-08-23-IBM-Developing-New-Cloud-Services-and-Technology-to-Help-Keep-Data-Secured-from-Future-Fault-Tolerant-Quantum-Computers. Accessed 24 September 2020.
IBM (2022) IBM Unveils 400 Qubit-Plus Quantum Processor and Next-Generation IBM Quantum System Two. https://newsroom.ibm.com/2022-11-09-IBM-Unveils-400-Qubit-Plus-Quantum-Processor-and-Next-Generation-IBM-Quantum-System-Two. Accessed 14 June 2023.
IBM Research Editorial Staff (2018) IBM Collaborating with Top Startups to Accelerate Quantum Computing. IBM Research Blog. https://www.ibm.com/blogs/research/2018/04/ibm-startups-accelerate-quantum/. Accessed 19 August 2020.
ID Quantique (2020) Cerberis 3 QKD System. Quantum Key Distribution for enterprise, government and telco production environments. https://iopscience.iop.org/article/10.1088/1367-2630/16/1/013047. Accessed 15 September 2020.
ISO (2014) ISO/IEC 29147:2014 - Information technology - Security techniques - Vulnerability disclosure. https://www.iso.org/standard/45170.html. Accessed 4 January 2024.
ISO (2013) – https://www.iso.org/standard/27001. Accessed 4 January 2024.
Japan, United States (2019) Tokyo Statement on Quantum Cooperation. In: United States Department of State. https://www.state.gov/tokyo-statement-on-quantum-cooperation/. Accessed 23 November 2020.
Jo A-M (2019) Software Vulnerability Disclosure and Security Investment (Preliminary Draft Presented at WEIS 2019). https://weis2019.econinfosec.org/wp-content/uploads/sites/6/2019/05/WEIS_2019_paper_18.pdf. Accessed 4 January 2024.
Johnson L (2018) Computer Will Find EVERYTHING You've EVER Done Online & There's ZERO You Can Do to Stop It. Express.co.uk. https://www.express.co.uk/news/science/913998/quantum-computers-encryption-data-nsa-gchq-microsoft. Accessed 6 December 2018.
Jordan S (2019) Overview of Quantum Algorithms.Quantum Algorithm Zoo. https://quantumalgorithmzoo.org/. Accessed 19 August 2020.
Jordan T, Taylor P (1998) A Sociology of Hackers. The Sociological Review 46:757–780. https://doi.org/10.1111/1467-954X.00139
Kahn D (1996) The Codebreakers: The Story of secret Writing. rev. edn. Scribner, New York.
Kania EB, Costello JK (2018) Quantum Hegemony: China's Ambitions and the Challenge to U.S. Innovation Leadership Center for a New American Security 12 September 2018.
Kaspersky (2019) Operation ShadowHammer: A High Profile Supply Chain Attack. https://securelist.com/operation-shadowhammer-a-high-profile-supply-chain-attack/90380/. Accessed 28 May 2021.
Kaye D (2019) Surveillance and Human Rights. Report of the Special Rapporteur on the Promotion and Protection of the Right to Freedom of Opinion and Expression, United Nations, A/HRC/41/35, 28 May 2019.

Kaye D (2015) Report on Encryption, Anonymity, and the Human Rights Framework, United Nations, A/HRC/29/32, 22 May 2015.

Kazmucha A (2010) Top 8 Jailbreak Concepts Apple Should Implement in iOS 5.iMore. https://www.imore.com/innovative-jailbreak-concepts-apple-implement-ios-5. Accessed 21 November 2020.

Kazmucha A (2011) Jailbreak Innovation: Still the Future of iOS. iMore. https://www.imore.com/team-pure-jailbreak-benefits. Accessed 21 November 2020.

Kerr OS, Schneier B (2018) Encryption Workarounds. The Georgetown Law Journal 106:989.

Khazan O (2013) The Creepy, Long-Standing Practice of Undersea Cable Tapping.The Atlantic. https://www.theatlantic.com/international/archive/2013/07/the-creepy-long-standing-practice-of-undersea-cable-tapping/277855/. Accessed 16 September 2020.

Kirchgaessner S (2020a) WhatsApp Confirms Catalan Politician's Phone Was Target of 2019 Attack.The Guardian. http://www.theguardian.com/technology/2020/jul/28/whatsapp-confirms-catalan-politicians-phone-was-target-of-2019-attack. Accessed 30 May 2021.

Kirchgaessner S (2020b) Israeli Spyware Used to Target Moroccan Journalist, Amnesty Claims.The Guardian. http://www.theguardian.com/technology/2020/jun/21/journalist-says-he-was-targeted-by-spyware-from-firm-despite-its-human-rights-policy. Accessed 30 May 2021.

Kirkpatrick DD (2018) Israeli Software Helped Saudis Spy on Khashoggi, Lawsuit Says. New York Times, 2 December 2018.

Koblitz AH, Koblitz N, Menezes A (2011) Elliptic Curve Cryptography: The Serpentine Course of a Paradigm Shift. Journal of Number Theory 131:781–814. https://doi.org/10.1016/j.jnt.2009.01.006

Kocher P, Horn J, Fogh A et al. (2019) Spectre Attacks: Exploiting Speculative Execution. In: 2019 IEEE Symposium on Security and Privacy (SP). IEEE, San Francisco, CA, USA, pp 1–19.

Koepke L, Weil E, Janardan U et al. (2020) Mass Extraction: The Widespread Power of U.S. Law Enforcement to Search Mobile PhonesUpturn, 20 October 2020. https://www.upturn.org/work/mass-extraction/. Accessed 4 January 2024.

Kohno T, Ferguson N, Schneier B (2010) Cryptography Engineering: Design Principles and Practical Applications. Wiley Pub., Indianapolis, IN.

Koomen M (2019) The Encryption Debate in the European Union, Carnegie Endowment for International Peace, 30 May 2019.

Koot M (2019) Kwetsbare Pulse Connect Secure SSL-VPNs in Nederlandse IP-adresruimte: bevindingen en gedachten. In: Matthijs R. Koot's notebook. https://blog.cyberwar.nl/2019/09/dutch-kwetsbare-pulse-connect-secure-ssl-vpn-in-nederlandse-ip-adresruimte-bevindingen-en-gedachten/. Accessed 4 December 2019.

Koot M (2020) Field Note on CVE-2019-11510: Pulse Connect Secure SSL-VPN in the Netherlands. Digital Threats: Research and Practice 1:13:1–13:7. https://doi.org/10.1145/3382765

Krebs M (2020) Microsoft Put Off Fixing Zero Day for 2 Years — Krebs on Security.Krebs on Security. https://krebsonsecurity.com/2020/08/microsoft-put-off-fixing-zero-day-for-2-years/. Accessed 23 October 2020.

Landau S (2020) Law Enforcement Is Accessing Locked Devices Quite Well, Thank You.Lawfare. https://www.lawfareblog.com/law-enforcement-accessing-locked-devices-quite-well-thank-you. Accessed 8 January 2021.

Larabel M (2021) A Look At The CPU Security Mitigation Costs Three Years After Spectre/Meltdown.Phoronix website. https://www.phoronix.com/scan.php?page=article&item=3-years-specmelt&num=9. Accessed 8 January 2021.

LaRose R (2019) Overview and Comparison of Gate Level Quantum Software Platforms. Quantum 3:130. https://doi.org/10.22331/q-2019-03-25-130

Lee A (2019) The iOS Checkm8 jailbreak is hugely significant, but not for you. Wired UK, 1 October 2019.

Levine EV (2020) The Die Is Cast: Hardware Security Is Not Assured. ACMqueue 18:4.

Levy S (1999) The Open Secret. Wired, 1 April 1999.

Levy S (2010) Hackers. 1st ed. O'Reilly Media, Sebastopol, CA.
Lewis JA, Zheng DE, Carter WA et al. (2017) The Effect of Encryption on Lawful Access to Communications and Data. Rowman & Littlefield, Lanham.
Li Y, Yazdanmehr A, Wang J, Rao HR (2019) Responding to Identity Theft: A Victimization Perspective. Decision Support Systems 121:13–24. https://doi.org/10.1016/j.dss.2019.04.002
Liao S-K, Cai W-Q, Liu W-Y et al. (2017) Satellite-to-Ground Quantum Key Distribution. Nature 549:43–47. https://doi.org/10.1038/nature23655
Lichfield G (2020) Inside the Race to Build the Best Quantum Computer on Earth.MIT Technology Review. https://www.technologyreview.com/2020/02/26/916744/quantum-computer-race-ibm-google/. Accessed 18 August 2020.
Lindsay C (2020a) Quantum Computing Heats up Down Under as Researchers Reckon They Know How to Cut Costs and Improve Stability.The Register. https://www.theregister.com/2020/04/16/quantum_computing_cost_stability_paper/. Accessed 20 August 2020.
Lindsay JR (2020b) Demystifying the Quantum Threat: Infrastructure, Institutions, and Intelligence Advantage. Security Studies 29:335–361. https://doi.org/10.1080/09636412.2020.1722853
Lindsay JR (2020c) Surviving the Quantum Cryptocalypse. Strategic Studies Quarterly 2020:49–73.
Lipp M, Schwarz M, Gruss D et al. (2020) Meltdown: Reading Kernel Memory from User Space, Communications of the ACM 63:46–56. https://doi.org/10.1145/3357033
Lloyd S (1996) Universal Quantum Simulators. Science 273:1073–1078. https://doi.org/10.1126/science.273.5278.1073
Lo H-K, Chau HF (1999) Unconditional Security Of Quantum Key Distribution over Arbitrarily Long Distances. Science 283:2050–2056. https://doi.org/10.1126/science.283.5410.2050
Lo H-K, Curty M, Tamaki K (2014) Secure Quantum Key Distribution. Nature Photonics 8:595–604. https://doi.org/10.1038/nphoton.2014.149
Loten A (2020) Trump Wants to Double Spending on AI, Quantum Computing. Wall Street Journal, 10 February 2020.
MacAskill E, Borger J, Hopkins N et al. (2013) GCHQ Taps Fibre-Optic Cables for Secret Access to World's Communications.The Guardian. http://www.theguardian.com/uk/2013/jun/21/gchq-cables-secret-world-communications-nsa. Accessed 16 September 2020.
Manhattan District Attorney's Office (2019) Fifth Report on Smartphone Encryption and Public Safety. https://www.manhattanda.org/wp-content/uploads/2019/10/2019-Report-on-Smartphone-Encryption-and-Public-Safety.pdf. Accessed 4 January 2024.
Marczak B, Guarnieri C, Marquis-Boiré M, Scott-Railton J (2014) Mapping Hacking Team's "Untraceable" Spyware, Citizen Lab, 17 February 2014.
Marczak B, Scott-Railton J, McKune S et al. (2018a) HIDE AND SEEK: Tracking NSO Group's Pegasus Spyware to Operations in 45 Countries, Citizen Lab, 18 September 2018.
Marczak B, Scott-Railton J, Senft A et al. (2018b) The Kingdom Came to Canada: How Saudi-Linked Digital Espionage Reached Canadian Soil, Citizen Lab, 1 October 2018.
Marquis-Boiré M, Marczak B, Guarnieri C, Scott-Railton J (2013) You Only Click Twice: FinFisher's Global Proliferation, Citizen Lab, 13 March 2013.
Marsh A (2019) The Hidden Figures Behind Bletchley Park's Code-Breaking Colossus - IEEE Spectrum. Technology, Engineering, and Science News. https://spectrum.ieee.org/tech-history/dawn-of-electronics/the-hidden-figures-behind-bletchley-parks-codebreaking-colossus. Accessed 23 January 2020.
Martín-López E, Laing A, Lawson T et al. (2012) Experimental Realization of Shor's Quantum Factoring Algorithm Using Qubit Recycling. Nature Photonics 6:773–776. https://doi.org/10.1038/nphoton.2012.259
Martonik A (2017) More Android Phones Are Using Encryption And Lock Screen Security Than Ever Before. Android Central. https://www.androidcentral.com/more-android-phones-are-using-encryption-and-lock-screen-security-ever. Accessed 11 October 2018.
Maslov D, Nam Y, Kim J (2019) An Outlook for Quantum Computing [Point of View]. Proceedings of the IEEE 107:5–10. https://doi.org/10.1109/JPROC.2018.2884353

Mathews L (2021) Florida Water Plant Hackers Exploited Old Software and Poor Password Habits.Forbes. https://www.forbes.com/sites/leemathews/2021/02/15/florida-water-plant-hackers-exploited-old-software-and-poor-password-habits/. Accessed 30 May 2021.

Mavroeidis V, Vishi K, Zych MD, Jøsang A (2018) The Impact of Quantum Computing on Present Cryptography. ijacsa 9: https://doi.org/10.14569/IJACSA.2018.090354

Mayers D (2004) Unconditional Security in Quantum Cryptography. arXiv:quant-ph/9802025

McHugh J, Fithen WL, Arbaugh WA (2000) Windows of Vulnerability: A Case Study Analysis. Computer 33:52–59. https://doi.org/10.1109/2.889093

Meijer C, van Gastel B (2019) Self-Encrypting Deception: Weaknesses in the Encryption of Solid State Drives. In: 2019 IEEE Symposium on Security and Privacy (SP). IEEE, San Francisco, CA, USA, pp 72–87.

Menezes AJ, Van Oorschot PC, Vanstone SA (1997) Handbook of Applied Cryptography. CRC Press, Boca Raton.

Metz C (2016) Forget Apple vs. the FBI: WhatsApp Just Switched on Encryption for a Billion People. Wired, 5 April 2016.

Metz C (2019) Google Claims a Quantum Breakthrough That Could Change Computing. The New York Times, 23 October 2019.

Meyers C (2020) A Forgotten Legacy: How Nuclear Reactors Built for War Transformed Peacetime Science.Discover magazine. https://www.discovermagazine.com/the-sciences/a-forgotten-legacy-how-nuclear-reactors-built-for-war-transformed-peacetime. Accessed 17 September 2020.

Mickos M (2020) $100 Million Paid - One Billion in Sight for Hackers.HackerOne. /blog/100-million-paid-one-billion-sight-hackers. Accessed 28 May 2020.

Microsoft (2017) Overview of BitLocker Device Encryption in Windows 10. https://docs.microsoft.com/en-us/windows/security/information-protection/bitlocker/bitlocker-device-encryption-overview-windows-10. Accessed 10 October 2018.

Microsoft Azure Quantum.Microsoft Azure website. https://azure.microsoft.com/en-us/services/quantum/. Accessed 19 August 2020.

Miller C (2007) The Legitimate Vulnerability Market. 10. https://securitylab.disi.unitn.it/lib/exe/fetch.php?media=teaching:netsec:2016:miller-legitimate_vulnerability_market.pdf. Accessed 4 January 2014.

Mink A, Frankel S, Perlner R (2009) Quantum Key Distribution (QKD) and Commodity Security Protocols: Introduction and Integration. https://arxiv.org/abs/1004.0605. Accessed 4 January 2024.

Misoczki R (2018) Post-Quantum Cryptography—Challenges and Opportunities. https://crypto.iacr.org/2018/affevents/qsci/medias/Rafael_Misoczki.pdf. Accessed 4 January 2024.

Modderkolk H (2019) Intern netwerk honderden bedrijven en ministerie lag maandenlang wagenwijd open. De Volkskrant, 28 September 2018.

Moghimi D, Sunar B, Eisenbarth T, Heninger N (2019) TPM-FAIL: TPM meets Timing and Lattice Attacks. https://arxiv.org/abs/1911.05673. Accessed 4 January 2024.

Möller B, Duong T, Kotowicz K (2014) This POODLE Bites: Exploiting The SSL 3.0 Fallback. https://www.openssl.org/~bodo/ssl-poodle.pdf. Accessed 4 January 2024.

Möller M, Vuik C (2017) On the Impact of Quantum Computing Technology on Future Developments in High-Performance Scientific Computing. Ethics and Information Technology 19:253–269. https://doi.org/10.1007/s10676-017-9438-0

Montanaro A (2016) Quantum Algorithms: An Overview. npj Quantum Information 2:15023. https://doi.org/10.1038/npjqi.2015.23

Moore GE (1965) Cramming More Components Onto Integrated Circuits. Proceedings IEEE 86:1. https://doi.org/10.1109/JPROC.1998.658762

Mosca M (2018) Cybersecurity in an Era with Quantum Computers: Will We Be Ready? IEEE Security & Privacy 16:38–41. https://doi.org/10.1109/MSP.2018.3761723

Mosca M, Piani M (2020), Quantum Threat Timeline Report 2020. https://globalriskinstitute.org/publication/quantum-threat-timeline-report-2020/. Accessed 4 January 2024.

Mosca M, Piani M (2019), Quantum Threat Timeline Report 2019. https://globalriskinstitute.org/publication/quantum-threat-timeline/. Accessed 4 January 2024.
MSRC (2010) Coordinated Vulnerability Disclosure: Bringing Balance to the Force. Microsoft Technet. https://blogs.technet.microsoft.com/ecostrat/2010/07/22/coordinated-vulnerability-disclosure-bringing-balance-to-the-force/. Accessed 19 September 2019.
MSRC (2017) Protecting Customers and Evaluating Risk.Microsoft Security Response Center. https://msrc-blog.microsoft.com/2017/04/14/protecting-customers-and-evaluating-risk/. Accessed 13 September 2019.
Mulholland J, Mosca M, Braun J (2017) The Day the Cryptography Dies. IEEE Security & Privacy 15:14–21. https://doi.org/10.1109/MSP.2017.3151325
Nakasone P (2018) Insa Leadership Dinner with General Paul Nakasone. https://www.youtube.com/watch?v=6S6DA8L19qQ. Accessed 4 January 2024.
Naraine R (2010) Stuxnet Attackers Used 4 Windows Zero-Day Exploits.ZDNet. https://www.zdnet.com/article/stuxnet-attackers-used-4-windows-zero-day-exploits/. Accessed 18 September 2019.
National Academies of Sciences Engineering, and Medicine. (2018) Quantum Computing: Progress and Prospects. Washington, DC: The National Academies Press. https://doi.org/10.17226/25196
National Institute of Standards and Technology (NIST) (2016) Submission Requirements and Evaluation Criteria for the Post-Quantum Cryptography Standardization Process. https://csrc.nist.gov/csrc/media/projects/post-quantum-cryptography/documents/call-for-proposals-final-dec-2016.pdf. Accessed 4 January 2024.
National Security Agency | Central Security Service (NSA) (2015) NSA Suite B Cryptography. https://web.archive.org/web/20150815072948/; https://www.nsa.gov/ia/programs/suiteb_cryptography/index.shtml. Accessed 15 September 2020.
National Security Agency | Central Security Service (NSA) (2017) NSA Stops Certain Section 702 "Upstream" Activities. https://www.nsa.gov/news-features/press-room/Article/1618699/nsa-stops-certain-section-702-upstream-activities/. Accessed 16 September 2020.
NCSC (2018) Coordinated Vulnerability Disclosure: The Guideline. https://english.ncsc.nl/publications/publications/2019/juni/01/coordinated-vulnerability-disclosure-the-guideline. Accessed 4 January 2024.
Newman LH (2019) These Hackers Made an App That Kills to Prove a Point. Wired, 6 July 2019.
Nielsen MA, Chuang IL (2010) Quantum Computation and Quantum Information, 10th anniversary edn. Cambridge University Press, Cambridge; New York.
Nikias CLM (2018) This Is the Most Important Tech Contest Since the Space Race, and America Is Losing. Washington Post, 11 May 2018.
Nissenbaum H (2005) Where Computer Security Meets National Security. Ethics and Information Technology 7:61–73. https://doi.org/10.1007/s10676-005-4582-3
NIST (2023), 'Selected Algorithms 2022 - Post-Quantum Cryptography | CSRC | CSRC'. https://csrc.nist.gov/Projects/post-quantum-cryptography/selected-algorithms-2022. Accessed 14 June 2023.
Nizovtsev D, Thursby M (2007) To Disclose or Not? An Analysis of Software User Behavior. Information Economics and Policy 19:43–64. https://doi.org/10.1016/j.infoecopol.2006.10.001
O'Carroll L (2013) Scientist Banned from Revealing Codes Used to Start Luxury Cars. The Guardian, 26 July 2013.
OHCHR (2020) UN Experts Call for Investigation into Allegations That Saudi Crown Prince Involved in Hacking of Jeff Bezos' Phone. https://www.ohchr.org/EN/NewsEvents/Pages/DisplayNews.aspx?NewsID=25488. Accessed 24 January 2020.
Ohm M, Plate H, Sykosch A, Meier M (2020) Backstabber's Knife Collection: A Review of Open Source Software Supply Chain Attacks. arXiv:200509535 [cs].
Ornes S (2017) News Feature: Code Wars. PNAS 114:2784–2787. https://doi.org/10.1073/pnas.1702236114

Ozment A (2005) The Likelihood of Vulnerability Rediscovery and the Social Utility of Vulnerability Hunting. Fourth Workshop on the Economics of Information Security (WEIS) 2–3 June 2005.

Pednault E, Gunnels J, Maslov D, Gambetta J (2019) On "Quantum Supremacy".IBM Research Blog. https://www.ibm.com/blogs/research/2019/10/on-quantum-supremacy/. Accessed 28 May 2020.

Peng W, Wang B, Hu F et al. (2019) Factoring Larger Integers with Fewer Qubits via Quantum Annealing with Optimized Parameters. Science China Physics, Mechanics & Astronomy 62:060311. https://doi.org/10.1007/s11433-018-9307-1

Perlroth N (2017) All 3 Billion Yahoo Accounts Were Affected by 2013 Attack. The New York Times, 3 October 2017.

Perlroth N (2020) Russians Who Pose Election Threat Have Hacked Nuclear Plants and Power Grid. The New York Times, 24 October 2020.

Perlroth N, Shane S (2019) In Baltimore and Beyond, a Stolen N.S.A. Tool Wreaks Havoc. The New York Times, 25 May 2019.

Perlroth N, Conger K, Mozur P (2019a) China Sharpens Hacking to Hound Its Minorities, Far and Wide. The New York Times, 9 December 2020.

Perlroth N, Sanger DE, Shane S (2019b) How Chinese Spies Got the N.S.A.'s Hacking Tools, and Used Them for Attacks. The New York Times, 6 May 2019.

Perlroth N, Sanger DE, Barnes JE (2021) Widely Used Software Company May Be Entry Point for Huge U.S. Hacking. The New York Times, 11 January 2021.

Poddebniak D, Dresen C, Muller J et al. (2018) Efail: Breaking S/MIME and OpenPGP Email Encryption Using Exfiltration Channels. In: Proceedings of the 27th USENIX Security Symposium. USENIX, Baltimore, MD, p 19.

Potuck M (2019) "Unpatchable" iOS Exploit May Bring Permanent iPhone Jailbreak.9to5Mac. https://9to5mac.com/2019/09/27/ios-unpatchable-ios-exploit-jailbreak-iphone-x/. Accessed 27 November 2019.

Poulsen K (2013) New Snowden Leak Reports "Groundbreaking" NSA Crypto-Cracking. Wired, 29 August 2013.

Presidency of the Council of Ministers (2016) Encryption of Data: Mapping of the Problem - Orientation Debate. https://www.eerstekamer.nl/overig/20161122/encryption_of_data_mapping_of_the/meta. Accessed 4 January 2024.

Preskill J (1998) Quantum Computing: Pro and Con. Proceedings of the Royal Society of London 454:469–486. https://doi.org/10.1098/rspa.1998.0171

Preskill J (2012) Quantum Computing and the Entanglement Frontier. arXiv:12035813 [cond-mat, physics:quant-ph].

Preskill J (2018) Quantum Computing in the NISQ Era and beyond. Quantum 2:79. https://doi.org/10.22331/q-2018-08-06-79

Preskill J (2019) Why I Called It "Quantum Supremacy".Quanta Magazine. https://www.quantamagazine.org/john-preskill-explains-quantum-supremacy-20191002/. Accessed 28 May 2020.

Privacy International (2018) Exploiting Privacy: Surveillance Companies Pushing Zero-Day Exploits. http://privacyinternational.org/blog/1245/exploiting-privacy-surveillance-companies-pushing-zero-day-exploits. Accessed 13 September 2019.

Quantum Delta Nederland (2021) Projectvoorstel Nationaal Groeifonds. https://assets.quantum-delta.prod.verveagency.com/assets/proposal-that-was-submitted-to-the-national-growth-fund.pdf. Accessed 4 July 2024.

Quantum Delta Nederland (2019) Nationale Agenda Quantumtechnologie. https://www.rijksoverheid.nl/documenten/brochures/2020/02/17/nationale-agenda-quantumtechnologie. Accessed 4 January 2024.

Ra'ad Al Hussein Z (2016) Apple-FBI Case Could Have Serious Global Ramifications for Human Rights. https://www.ohchr.org/EN/NewsEvents/Pages/DisplayNews.aspx?NewsID=17138#sthash.o25R7Bqg.dpuf. Accessed 15 August 2019.

Radianti J, Rich E, Gonzalez JJ (2009) Vulnerability Black Markets: Empirical Evidence and Scenario Simulation.2009 42nd Hawaii International Conference on System Sciences, pp 1–10.

Raggi M, Schwarz D (2019) LookBack Malware Targets the United States Utilities Sector with Phishing Attacks Impersonating Engineering Licensing Boards. Proofpoint. https://www.proofpoint.com/us/threat-insight/post/lookback-malware-targets-united-states-utilities-sector-phishing-attacks. Accessed 3 July 2020.

Ramzy A, Buckley C (2019) "Absolutely No Mercy": Leaked Files Expose How China Organized Mass Detentions of Muslims. The New York Times, 16 November 2019.

Ransbotham S, Mitra S (2013) The Impact of Immediate Disclosure on Attack Diffusion and Volume. In: Economics of Information Security and Privacy III. Springer, New York, NY, pp 1–12.

Reichert C (2020) US Finds Huawei Has Backdoor Access to Mobile Networks Globally, Report Says. CNET. https://www.cnet.com/news/us-finds-huawei-has-backdoor-access-to-mobile-networks-globally-report-says/. Accessed 3 July 2020.

Ren X, Moody L, Taram M et al. (2021) I See Dead µops: Leaking Secrets via Intel/AMD Micro-Op Caches. https://www.cs.virginia.edu/venkat/papers/isca2021a.pdf. Accessed 4 January 2024.

Khanna R (2022) Quantum Computing Cybersecurity Preparedness Act. https://www.congress.gov/bill/117th-congress/house-bill/7535. Accessed 4 January 2024.

Resch S, Karpuzcu UR (2019) Quantum Computing: An Overview Across the System Stack. arXiv:190507240 [quant-ph].

Rey E (2015) Sending Mixed Signals—What Can Happen in the Course of Vulnerability Disclosure. https://insinuator.net/2015/09/sending-mixed-signals-what-can-happen-in-the-course-of-vulnerability-disclosure/. Accessed 15 October 2019.

Rich S, Gellman B (2014) NSA Seeks to Build Quantum Computer That Could Crack Most Types of Encryption. Washington Post, 2 January 2014.

Roberts S (2021) This New Startup Has Built a Record-Breaking 256-Qubit Quantum Computer. MIT Technology Review. https://www.technologyreview.com/2021/11/17/1040243/quantum-computer-256-bit-startup/. Accessed 14 January 2022.

Rodríguez E, Noroozian A, van Eeten M, Gañán C (2021) Superspreaders: Quantifying the Role of IoT Manufacturers in Device Infections. https://weis2021.econinfosec.org/wp-content/uploads/sites/9/2021/06/weis21-rodriguez.pdf. Accessed 4 January 2024.

Sanger DE, Perlroth N (2014) N.S.A. Breached Chinese Servers Seen as Security Threat (Published 2014). The New York Times, 22 March 2014.

Sanger DE, Perlroth N (2019) U.S. Escalates Online Attacks on Russia's Power Grid. The New York Times, 15 June 2019.

Sanger DE, Perlroth N (2020) FireEye, a Top Cybersecurity Firm, Says It Was Hacked by a Nation-State. The New York Times, 6 February 2021.

Sanger DE, Perlroth N, Thrush G, Rappeport A (2018) Marriott Data Breach Is Traced to Chinese Hackers as U.S. Readies Crackdown on Beijing. The New York Times, 11 December 2018.

Sanger DE, Perlroth N, Barnes JE (2021) As Understanding of Russian Hacking Grows, So Does Alarm. The New York Times, 28 May 2021.

Schilis-Gallego C, Lakhani N (2020) "It's a Free-for-All": How Hi-Tech Spyware Ends up in the Hands of Mexico's Cartels. The Guardian, 7 December 2020 http://www.theguardian.com/world/2020/dec/07/mexico-cartels-drugs-spying-corruption. Accessed 8 January 2021.

Schneier B (1999) Attack Trees: Modeling Security Threats. Dr Dobbs Journal, December 1999.

Schneier B (2000) Managed Security Monitoring: Closing the Window of Exposure. http://www.keystoneisit.com/window.pdf. Accessed 4 January 2024.

Schneier B (2003) Beyond Fear: Thinking Sensibly about Security in an Uncertain World. Copernicus Books, New York.

Schneier B (2007) Full Disclosure of Security Vulnerabilities a "Damned Good Idea".Schneier on Security. https://www.schneier.com/essays/archives/2007/01/schneier_full_disclo.html. Accessed 19 September 2019.

Schneier B (2013a) Attacking Tor: How the NSA Targets Users' Online Anonymity. The Guardian, 4 October 2013.

Schneier B (2013b) How the NSA Thinks About Secrecy and Risk. The Atlantic, 4 October 2013.

Schneier B (2013c) How the NSA Attacks Tor/Firefox Users with QUANTUM and FOXACID.Schneier on Security. https://www.schneier.com/blog/archives/2013/10/how_the_nsa_att.html. Accessed 22 June 2021.

Schneier B (2015) NSA Plans for a Post-Quantum World.Schneier on Security. https://www.schneier.com/blog/archives/2015/08/nsa_plans_for_a.html. Accessed 3 September 2020.

Schneier B (2016) Class Breaks. Edge. https://www.edge.org/annual-question/2017/response/27229. Accessed 8 January 2021.

Schneier B (2018) Click Here to Kill Everybody: Security and Survival in a Hyper-Connected World. W. W. Norton & Company.

Schneier B (2019) Speakers Censored at AISA Conference in Melbourne.Schneier on Security. https://www.schneier.com/blog/archives/2019/10/speakers_censor.html. Accessed 11 October 2019.

Schneier B (2021a) Why Was SolarWinds So Vulnerable to a Hack? The New York Times, 23 February 2021.

Schneier B (2021b) The Coming AI Hackers, https://www.belfercenter.org/publication/coming-ai-hackers. Accessed 4 January 2024.

Schneier B, Seidel K, Vijayakumar S (2016) A Worldwide Survey of Encryption Products. SSRN Journal. https://doi.org/10.2139/ssrn.2731160

Schrödinger E (1935) Die gegenwärtige Situation in der Quantenmechanik. Naturwissenschaften 23:807–812. https://doi.org/10.1007/BF01491891

Schwarz H (2012) Black Hatted. Henry Schwarz's ATM & EFT-POS Security Blog. https://henryschwarz.blogspot.com/2012/06/black-hatted.html. Accessed 18 October 2019.

Scott-Railton J, Hulcoop A, Abdul Razzak B et al. (2020) Dark Basin: Uncovering a Massive Hack-For-Hire Operation, Citizen Lab, 9 June 2020.

Serper A (undated) Wannamine Cryptominer That Uses EternalBlue Still Active.Nocturnus Cybereason. https://www.cybereason.com/blog/wannamine-cryptominer-eternalblue-wannacry. Accessed 13 September 2019.

Sevilla J, Riedel CJ (2020) Forecasting Timelines of Quantum Computing. arXiv:200905045 [quant-ph].

Shannon CE (1948) A Mathematical Theory of Communication. Bell Systems Technical Journal 379 and further.

Shannon CE (1949) Communication Theory of Secrecy Systems. Bell System Technical Journal 28:656–715. https://doi.org/10.1002/j.1538-7305.1949.tb00928.x

Shor PW (1997) Polynomial-Time Algorithms for Prime Factorization and Discrete Logarithms on a Quantum Computer. SIAM Journal on Computing 26:1484–1509. https://doi.org/10.1137/S0097539795293172

Shor PW, Preskill J (2000) Simple Proof of Security of the BB84 Quantum Key Distribution Protocol. Physical Review Letters 85:441–444. https://doi.org/10.1103/PhysRevLett.85.441

Sikeridis D, Kampanakis P, Devetsikiotis M (2020) Post-Quantum Authentication in TLS 1.3: A Performance Study. In: Proceedings 2020 Network and Distributed System Security Symposium. Internet Society, San Diego, CA.

Snowden E (2013) Edward Snowden: NSA Whistleblower Answers Reader Questions. The Guardian, 17 June 2013.

Snowden E (2019) Permanent Record. Henry Holt and Company.

Spring T (2019) RSA Conference Cryptographers' Panel Discus Latest Frontlines in Crypto Wars.Threatpost. https://threatpost.com/rsa-conference-2019-cryptographers-panel-decries-adi-shamirs-visa-issues/142533/. Accessed 11 October 2019.

Steckler V, Vlcek O (2017) Update to the CCleaner 5.33.6162 Security Incident.Avast. https://blog.avast.com/update-to-the-ccleaner-5.33.6162-security-incident. Accessed 28 May 2021.

Stone M (2019) Bad Binder: Android In-The-Wild Exploit.Project Zero. https://googleprojectzero.blogspot.com/. Accessed 26 November 2019.
Subcommittee on Quantum Information Science of the National Science & Technology Council (2018) National Strategic Overview for Quantum Information Science. https://www.quantum.gov/wp-content/uploads/2020/10/2018_NSTC_National_Strategic_Overview_QIS.pdf. Accessed 4 January 2024.
Swire P (2004) A Model for When Disclosure Helps Security: What Is Different About Computer and Network Security? https://papers.ssrn.com/sol3/papers.cfm?abstract_id=531782. Accessed 4 January 2024.
Taha M, Eisenbarth T (2015) Implementation Attacks on Post-Quantum Cryptographic Schemes. Cryptology ePrint Archive 14.
Taylor J (2019) Melbourne Cyber Conference Organisers Pressured Speaker to Edit "Biased" Talk. The Guardian 9 October 2019.
The Economist Staff (2013) The Digital Arms Trade. The Economist 30 March 2013.
Theisen C, Munaiah N, Al-Zyoud M et al. (2018) Attack Surface Definitions: A Systematic Literature Review. Information and Software Technology 104:94–103. https://doi.org/10.1016/j.infsof.2018.07.008
Thomas D (2002h) Hacker Culture. University of Minnesota Press, Minneapolis.
Thompson K (1984) Reflections on Trusting Trust. Communications of the ACM 1984 (August 1984):761–763.
Thomson I (2019) Adi Shamir Visa Snub: US Govt Slammed after the S in RSA Blocked from His Own RSA Conf. https://www.theregister.co.uk/2019/03/05/rsa_cofounder_us_visa_row/. Accessed 11 October 2019.
TNO, CWI, AIVD (2023) Het PQC-migratie handboek/. https://www.tno.nl/nl/newsroom/2023/04/pqc-migratie-handboek/. Accessed 4 January 2024.
UK Government (2019) £1 Billion Investment Makes UK a Frontrunner in Quantum Technologies. https://www.gov.uk/government/news/1-billion-investment-makes-uk-a-frontrunner-in-quantum-technologies. Accessed 25 August 2020.
University of Science and Technology of China (2018) Real-World Intercontinental Quantum Communications Enabled by the Micius Satellite. https://phys.org/news/2018-01-real-world-intercontinental-quantum-enabled-micius.html. Accessed 15 September 2020.
University of Virginia School of Engineering and Applied Science (2021) Computer Scientists Discover New Vulnerability Affecting Computers Globally.ScienceDaily. https://www.sciencedaily.com/releases/2021/04/210430165903.htm. Accessed 2 July 2021.
Ursin R, Tiefenbacher F, Schmitt-Manderbach T et al. (2007) Entanglement-Based Quantum Communication over 144 km. Nature Physics 3:481–486. https://doi.org/10.1038/nphys629
Vandersypen LMK, Steffen M, Breyta G et al. (2001) Experimental Realization of Shor's Quantum Factoring Algorithm Using Nuclear Magnetic Resonance. Nature 414:883–887. https://doi.org/10.1038/414883a
van Daalen O (2022), In Defense of Offense: Information Security Research under the Right to Science, Computer Law & Security Review 46: 105706.
van Daalen O (2023a) The Right to Encryption: Privacy as Preventing Unlawful Access, Computer Law & Security Review 49:105804.
van Daalen O (2023b) The Right to Root: Constructing a Claim to Control Devices from the Right to Privacy, JIPITEC 14(2023:4): 580–593.
van Daalen O (2024) Developing a human-rights compatible governance framework for quantum computing, Research Directions: Quantum Technologies 2: 2024.
van't Hof C, Messers P (2016) Helpende hackers: verantwoorde onthullingen in het digitale polderlandschap, Tek Tok 2015.
Veale M (2019) Privacy Preserving Power: Regulating Encrypted Data Analysis, Google PAIR Symposium, 14 September 2019. Google PAIR Symposium. Accessed 4 January 2024.

Verdult R, Garcia FD, Ege B (XXXX2013) Dismantling Megamos Crypto: Wirelessly Lock-picking a Vehicle Immobilizer. Supplement to the Proceedings of the 22nd USENIX Security Symposium 1.

Vermeer M, Peet E (2020) Securing Communications in the Quantum Computing Age: Managing the Risks to Encryption. https://www.rand.org/pubs/research_reports/RR3102.html. Accessed 4 January 2024.

Weidemann A (2021) New Campaign Targeting Security Researchers. https://blog.google/threat-analysis-group/new-campaign-targeting-security-researchers/. Accessed 27 January 2021.

WhatsApp (2020a) WhatsApp Encryption Overview: Technical White Paper. https://scontent-ams2-1.xx.fbcdn.net/v/t39.8562-6/384251896_820338303082371_851478598231004604 7_n.pdf?_nc_cat=100&ccb=1-7&_nc_sid=e280be&_nc_ohc=NJFOrMYERbIAX8eBkAV&_nc_oc=AQnp1IDjPdm_X8RjSbmzjSf4xqNMjZrQVMAvND7zE8Zi2ZmQsFkHIlk1bhQg3ntyvGI&_nc_ht=scontent-ams2-1.xx&oh=00_AfDzwbzvCCi28FUdX-yajkj02TLv_aEVZBCnCNTCudA3HA&oe=659AC511. Accessed 4 January 2024.

WhatsApp (2020b) Two Billion Users—Connecting the World Privately. WhatsApp.com. https://blog.whatsapp.com/two-billion-users-connecting-the-world-privately/?lang=en. Accessed 2 November 2021.

Whittaker Z (2017a) Security Firm Keeper Sues News Reporter over Vulnerability Story.ZDNet. https://www.zdnet.com/article/security-firm-keeper-sues-news-reporter-over-vulnerability-story/. Accessed 15 October 2019.

Whittaker Z (2017b) Black Hat Speaker Denied Entry to US in Another Needless Hit to Security Research.ZDNet. https://www.zdnet.com/article/denied-entry-united-states-black-hat-blow-to-security-research/. Accessed 11 October 2019.

Whittaker Z (2018) Hackers Are Using Leaked NSA Hacking Tools to Covertly Hijack Thousands of Computers.TechCrunch. http://social.techcrunch.com/2018/11/28/hackers-nsa-eternalblue-exploit-hijack-computers/. Accessed 13 September 2019.

Whittaker Z (2019) Sources Say China Used iPhone Hacks to Target Uyghur Muslims. TechCrunch. http://social.techcrunch.com/2019/08/31/china-google-iphone-uyghur/. Accessed 26 November 2019.

Wiesner S (1983) Conjugate Coding. SIGACT News 15:78–88. https://doi.org/10.1145/1008908.1008920

Wikileaks (2017) Press Release on Vault 7.Wikileaks. https://wikileaks.org/ciav7p1/index.html. Accessed 27 May 2021.

Williams CP (2011) Explorations in Quantum Computing. Springer London, London.

World Village Cooking (2014) Saudis Changing Tyres While Driving. https://www.youtube.com/watch?v=cIpBpGQ0XTI. Accessed 3 January 2024.

Yang CH, Leon RCC, Hwang JCC et al. (2020) Operation of a Silicon Quantum Processor Unit Cell above One Kelvin. Nature 580:350–354. https://doi.org/10.1038/s41586-020-2171-6

Yin J, Cao Y, Li Y-H et al. (2017) Satellite-Based Entanglement Distribution over 1200 Kilometers. Science 356:1140–1144. https://doi.org/10.1126/science.aan3211

Yin J, Li Y-H, Liao S-K et al. (2020) Entanglement-Based Secure Quantum Cryptography over 1,120 Kilometres. Nature 582:501–505. https://doi.org/10.1038/s41586-020-2401-y

Yoshino K-i, Ochi T, Fujiwara M et al. (2013) Maintenance-Free Operation of WDM Quantum Key Distribution System through a Field Fiber over 30 Days. Optics Express 21:31395–31401. https://doi.org/10.1364/OE.21.031395

Yuan Y, Xiao J, Fukushima K et al. (2018) Portable Implementation of Postquantum Encryption Schemes and Key Exchange Protocols on JavaScript-Enabled Platforms. Security and Communication Networks. https://www.hindawi.com/journals/scn/2018/9846168/. Accessed 4 September 2020.

Zerodium (2019a) Zerodium - About Us and Our Bug Bounties. https://zerodium.com/about.html. Accessed 26 November 2019.

Zerodium (2019b) FAQ About How to Sell Zero-Day (0day) Research and Exploits. In: Zerodium. https://zerodium.com/faq.html. Accessed 26 November 2019.

Zerodium (2019c) How to Sell Your 0day Exploit to ZERODIUM.Zerodium. https://zerodium.com/program.html#changelog. Accessed 26 November 2019.
Zerodium (2020) Tweet of 13 May 2020 on 2:05PM.Twitter. https://twitter.com/zerodium/status/1260541578747064326. Accessed 28 May 2020.
Zetter K (2005) Whistle-Blower Faces FBI Probe. Wired, 29 July 2005.
Zetter K (2010) Researcher Demonstrates ATM "Jackpotting" at Black Hat Conference. Wired, 28 July 2010.
Zetter K (2014) Countdown to Zero Day: Stuxnet and the Launch of the World's First Digital Weapon, 1st edn. Crown Publishers, New York.
Zetter K (2015) A Bizarre Twist in the Debate Over Vulnerability Disclosures. Wired, 11 September 2015.
Zetter K (2016a) Inside the Cunning, Unprecedented Hack of Ukraine's Power Grid. Wired, 3 March 2016.
Zetter K (2016b) Everything We Know About Ukraine's Power Plant Hack. Wired, 20 January 2016.
Zetter K (2019a) Hackers Hijacked ASUS Software Updates to Install Backdoors on Thousands of Computers.Vice. https://www.vice.com/en/article/pan9wn/hackers-hijacked-asus-software-updates-to-install-backdoors-on-thousands-of-computers. Accessed 28 May 2021.
Zetter K (2019b) Intel Fixes a Security Flaw It Said Was Repaired 6 Months Ago. The New York Times, 13 November 2019.
Zhang Q, Xu F, Li L et al. (2019) Quantum Information Research in China. Quantum Science and Technology 4:040503. https://doi.org/10.1088/2058-9565/ab4bea
Zoller T (2011) The Rise of Vulnerability Markets - History, Impacts, Mitigations, https://www.owasp.org/images/b/b7/OWASP_BeNeLux_Day_2011_-_T._Zoller_-_Rise_of_the_Vulnerability_Market.pdf. Accessed 4 January 2024.

Other Documents

Special Rapporteur on Extrajudicial, Summary or Arbitrary Executions, Annex to the Report of the Special Rapporteur on Extrajudicial, Summary or Arbitrary Executions: Investigation into the Unlawful Death of Mr. Jamal Khashoggi, A/HRC/41/CRP.1, 19 June 2019.
Special Rapporteur on Extrajudicial, Summary or Arbitrary Executions, Special Rapporteur on the Promotion and Protection of the Right to Freedom of Opinion and Expression, Analysis of the Evidence of Surveillance of Mr. Bezos' Personal Phone, 22 January 2020.

Table of Cases: National

District Court of Arnhem, ECLI:NL:RBARN:2008:BD7578, NXP/RUN (Mifare-chip), Judgment of 18 July 2008.

Chapter 3
The Governance Landscape

Contents

Abstract This chapter is about the governance relating to the information security cycle, encryption and quantum computing. It starts out with providing an overview of the rules relating to the taking of measures in the information security cycle, and the continues with a discussion of the breaking of those measures. It then focuses on the different governance approaches with regard to encryption. It ends with the limited governance relating to quantum computing. This exercise is all intended to create an inventory of the gaps in governance relating to these three domains, which can then be used for further assessment under the relevant human rights frameworks.

Keywords Information security measures · Encryption · Quantum computing · Governance · Hacking

O. van Daalen, *From Encryption to Quantum Computing*, Information Technology and Law Series 38, https://doi.org/10.1007/978-94-6265-635-2_3

3.1 Introduction

In Chap. 2, I discussed the information security cycle from various perspectives, focusing on two technologies in particular: encryption and quantum computing. This book is about how that cycle can be tweaked through governance in order to protect human rights. But doing so requires an understanding of the current situation: how are governments dealing with these domains *today*? That is the topic of this chapter.

In answering this question, I discuss both the applicable laws, such as rules prohibiting the export of encryption technologies, and governmental practices, such as the inserting of vulnerabilities into communications standards. The reason why I'm also interested in what governments *do*, not only what they *prescribe*, is that their non-legislative actions also have an impact on the enjoyment of human rights, as we will see. As discussed in the introductory chapter, I group these rules and practices together under the header of *governance*, although the term is often used to signify more than the rules and practices of governments. One of the governance elements not discussed in this book, is enforcement and the rules relating to competent authorities (for example on co-ordination and information sharing), because that would broaden the scope of the book too much.[1]

The goal of this chapter is to provide an overview of governance measures which I can then in the subsequent chapters assess for their human rights-compatibility.[2] This *tour d'horizon* will thus touch on a variety of governance measures, from criminal law to copyright law, from standardisation to export regulations. There is a risk of getting lost. The main question for each measure is, however, whether it is compatible with the human rights discussed in the subsequent chapters. Following the structure of the preceding chapter, I provide an analysis of the governance of the information security cycle, then an analysis of the governance of encryption and lastly an analysis of the governance of quantum computing.

3.2 Governance of the Information Security Cycle

Broadly speaking, the information security cycle consists of two phases: a *defensive side*, involving the taking of protective measures, and an *offensive* side, involving research into the vulnerabilities of those measures. The governance of the first stage of the cycle, the defensive stage, is about what organisations are required do to *secure* their systems.[3] The second stage of the cycle is about finding out whether things are *not* secure. I discuss both phases in turn.

---

[1] See for a discussion of this topic in the Netherlands Silfversten et al. 2020; and Cyber Security Raad 2021.

[2] Parts of this chapter have already been published in Van Daalen 2022 and 2023a, b and c and 2024.

[3] See for a similar mapping exercise Fuster and Jasmontaite 2020.

3.2.1 Regulation of the Measure-Taking Phase

Two questions can be discerned when it comes to the first phase, taking measures. First: which measures are organisations required to take *initially*? And second: how do organisations have to deal with subsequent knowledge of vulnerabilities *after* they have taken those initial measures? I discuss these questions in three different regulatory contexts: the processing of personal data, the protection of critical infrastructure and the offering of consumer services and devices.

The choice for discussing the processing of personal data and the offering of consumer services and devices needs little justification: these contexts have a strong relationship to the fundamental rights to privacy and data protection (as we will further see in Chap. 5). The protection of critical infrastructure has perhaps a less obvious connection to the fundamental rights discussed in this book.

There are two reasons why it is nevertheless useful to touch on this topic. First, the right to communications freedom as discussed in Chap. 6 is relevant to the extent that information security rules concern the protection of communications networks, and communications networks are a prime example of critical infrastructure. Second, from the perspective of information security, it is difficult to draw a clear line between domains like personal data protection and critical infrastructure. This is because of the growing insight that the impact of vulnerabilities does not remain confined to one domain. For example, vulnerabilities in online cameras for consumers may have an impact on critical infrastructure, and vice versa. So rules for one domain also have an impact on the other. But first, the processing of personal data.

3.2.1.1 Rules on Processing Personal Data

Before the second world war, computers wore skirts.[4] "Computers" were people, many of them women, all doing mechanically assisted manual calculations in the mathematical departments of large organisations.[5] Only in the decades that followed did the term "computer" come to signify machines.[6] And not only does the term "computer" have analogue roots—the term "data processing" also goes back to the days of punch cards: IBM salesmen in the mid-1950s started calling their punched card-gear "data processing systems", and their computers "*electronic* data processing systems".[7] At first these electronic data processing systems were still touted as "the highest form of mechanisation". It was only in the mid-1970s that the concept of "automated data processing" came to be primarily linked with *electronic* computers for the enterprise.[8] This is relevant, because the concepts used to regulate this domain

---

[4] Loff 2016.

[5] See Shetterly 2016.

[6] See Kennedy Jr. 1946, where the promises of a new "Electronic Computer" were already touted.

[7] Haigh 2001, p. 93.

[8] Theis 1954; Advisory Committee on Automated Personal Data Systems 1973.

still harken back to its analogue days, whereas the IT landscape has become infinitely more complex, as we will see.

The first generation of these new machines were so expensive that only universities, the military and a few large organisations could afford them—by the end of the 1950s only a few thousands had been installed globally.[9] But as technologies shrank and became more affordable, computers spread to other organisations that wanted to automate administrative tasks such as payroll, statistics and inventory. And these organisations were increasingly applying the power of computation not only to their *corporate* data, but also to repositories of *personal* data. It was this shift from manual to automated processing of personal data which led to growing concerns among legislators, eventually culminating in the mid-1970s in a host of policy instruments aimed at data protection.[10]

In those instruments of the late 1970s and 1980s, the *security* of processing of personal data was already deemed sufficiently important to be a distinct principle. An influential US-government report of 1973 setting out "Fair Information Principles" prescribed that record-keepers take "reasonable precautions to protect data in the system from any anticipated threats or hazards to the security of the system" and impose security requirements when transferring the data.[11] In the OECD Guidelines of 1980, the first time privacy principles were agreed upon at the international level, it was prescribed that personal data should be protected by "reasonable security safeguards against such risks as loss or unauthorised access, destruction, use, modification or disclosure of data".[12] A year later, in Convention 108, which focused on the EU and is regarded as the predecessor of contemporary data protection instruments such as the General Data Protection Regulation (GDPR), similar wording was employed: "appropriate" security measures should be taken to protect against "accidental or unauthorised destruction or accidental loss as well as against unauthorised access, alteration or dissemination".[13] In the decades since, this wording has barely changed.

The fact that security occupied such a prominent place in policy as early as the 1970s is perhaps surprising. Of course, the US military was already concerned about "penetrations" by the mid-1960s, but in the corporate world, threats were still quite manageable, especially by today's standards.[14] The *personal* computer was only slowly gaining momentum, local area networking was quite exotic and wide adoption of the public internet was still two decades away. Computers were available to only a small group of experts, so the threat of employees nosing through personal files

[9] Haigh 2001, p. 79.

[10] See for an example of these concerns Advisory Committee on Automated Personal Data Systems 1973; see for a historic account Gellman 2019; and van Alsenoy 2016, pt. III.

[11] Advisory Committee on Automated Personal Data Systems 1973, recommendation 1(b)(4) and (5).

[12] OECD 1980, para 11.

[13] (1981) Convention for the Protection of Individuals with regard to Automatic Processing of Personal Data (Convention 108), Article 7.

[14] See Warner 2015.

was limited. The greatest risks perhaps came from people crashing a timesharing mainframe and from careless employees leaving magnetic tapes out with the trash.[15]

One thing which certainly wasn't on the minds of legislators back then, was how computing infrastructure was set to become infinitely more complex in the future—with various suppliers offering products and services to be integrated and running on top of each other. But the outlines were already taking shape. The IBM S/360 mainframe, popular between the mid-1960s and the late 1970s, was not only compatible with IBM printers, IBM disk drives, IBM tape drives and IBM card readers—but also with the peripheral devices developed by *other* companies (called "plug-compatible manufacturers").[16] And while IBM in a 1968-memo still took the position that "hardware and software including programs are an indivisible product", it started unbundling its software that same year, selling it separately from its hardware, feeling the pressure of an antitrust investigation by the US government.[17] In the decades that followed, the computer industry has of course rapidly unbundled, and most computers now consist of hardware and software from thousands of providers.

This increased complexity in supply networks is, however, not reflected in data processing regulation. Forty years later, we still carry the consequences of that singular focus on large machines, located in separate rooms in office buildings, all manufactured by one organisation.[18] We still determine the application of data protection rules, laid down in the EU in the GDPR, on the basis of this punch-card concept of the "processing of personal data", even though the devices which do the processing are something completely different from these lab-sized calculators. And more importantly, the atomic unit of regulation in the GDPR, the *controller* or *processor*, can be traced back to the large organisations *running* these data processing machines.

These regulatory roots of the GDPR also explain an important gap in information security governance in the context of data protection. Under the GDPR, the "controller" and "processor" are required to take security measures.[19] The Court of Justice has given an extensive interpretation of this concept of a controller to ensure "the effective and complete protection" of data subjects.[20] And many organisations which cannot be considered a controller, but are processing personal data may be considered a "processor" under the GDPR. Thus, the obligation to secure your system applies

[15] See Yost 2015 on how the prospect of students crashing an IBM System 360 OS/MVT propelled an IBM user group to work on access control for IBM mainframes.

[16] Ceruzzi 2003, p. 164.

[17] Neubert, 2015, p. 27.

[18] Mayer-Schönberger 1997, p. 223.

[19] See (2016) Regulation 2016/679 of the European Parliament and of the Council of 27 April 2016 on the protection of natural persons with regard to the processing of personal data and on the free movement of such data, and repealing Directive 95/46/EC (General Data Protection Regulation), Article 32.

[20] CJEU, Case C-131/12, Google Spain, Judgment of 13 May 2014, para 34; CJEU, Case C-210/16, Wirtschaftsakademie, Judgment of 5 June 2018, para 28; CJEU, Case C-40/17, Fashion-ID, Judgment of 29 July 2019, para 66; CJEU, Case C-25/17, Jehova's witnesses, Judgment of 10 July 2018, para 73.

to most organisations which still are in one way or another administering systems processing personal data, either for themselves or for others.

But there is a limit as to how far this obligation extends, and that is particularly problematic when it comes to the security of personal data. As noted before, many organisations merely contribute hardware or software to a system processing personal data, such as CPUs, motherboards, memory chips, operating systems or applications—this was already so in the 1970s and is even more so now. When this contribution of an organisation has a certain proximity to the processing, such as an operating system, it can perhaps be argued that the supplier of that system is a controller, but this is far from clear. If, however, a flaw is found in components which are relatively distant from the actual processing, such as the encryption of SSDs, it is unlikely that the manufacturer of these SSDs would be required under the GDPR to provide a fix, because it cannot be considered the controller or processor of personal data. The only organisations who would, arguably, have an obligation to act on this vulnerability are organisations owning particular laptops with this particular vulnerability, but they are ill-equipped to do anything about it. And for those cases where the laptops are owned by persons, not organisations, this obligation to do anything about it is even less clear. In other words, the security rules under the GDPR do not directly cover the entire attack surface of a system—for many of those components, the security depends on the particular contractual arrangements concluded within the supply chain. But the security of such a system is only as strong as its weakest link. So, when Dutch consumer rights organisation *Consumentenbond* argued in one court case that Samsung had to properly secure its phones because of the GDPR, they had a point in principle, but no point in court: Samsung was not processing any personal data, merely assembling software and hardware of others and making it available it to its users.[21] As a result, users were paying the price of this legal lacuna, because their devices remained poorly secured. Fortunately, there are new regulatory initiatives which would close this gap, which are also discussed in this chapter.

3.2.1.2 Critical Infrastructure

The focus point of the governance measures described above centres around *the processing of personal data*. But as the digital revolution gained momentum, computers were also increasingly applied to control other processes, such as manufacturing and distribution—processes which do not necessarily involve the manipulation of personal data. This control was done partly with the help of so-called "industrial control systems" (ICSs). These systems used to be analogue, but became digital from the 1950s onwards.[22] Many of these systems have high *safety* requirements, so that people won't get hurt. But most of them were never designed with *security* in mind.

---

[21] District Court The Hague, ECLI:NL:RBDHA:2018:6310, Consumentenbond/Samsung, Judgment of 30 May 2018.

[22] See for a discussion in the context of electricity Cohn 2015; see further Stouffer et al. 2015, pp. 2–1b.

This perhaps has to do with the fact that the digital components for ICSs are often special purpose-devices: what works for an oil refinery, does not work for a sewage treatment plant, so breaches remain limited to only a limited number of devices, which supposedly make them less attractive to attack. Moreover, many organisations were slow to connect these facilities to the internet, which perhaps also made owners think the risk of attack was lower.

In hindsight, they were wrong.[23] The computers collecting and controlling industrial facilities in particular, called SCADA systems, are increasingly running on regular operating systems, and many have since been connected to the internet as well.[24] There is even a search engine dedicated to finding connected ICSs that are poorly secured.[25] Meanwhile, the lifecycle of these devices is measured in decades, not years, which means that devices still in use today are "secured" as if the internet did not exist. As a result, there have been numerous attacks on ICSs, leading to raw sewage spills into rivers, oil pipeline explosions, the destruction of nuclear enrichment facilities and the manipulation of power grids.[26]

Because these ICSs do not process personal data, the security requirements under the GDPR and similar instruments do not apply. So what rules are there to protect the power grid from failing and floodgates from opening?

The regulatory framework for ICSs revolves around systems for "critical infrastructure"—systems which have serious societal impact if they fail, such as electricity providers and telecommunications companies. The European Commission in 2004 kickstarted an overarching regulatory process for the protection of critical infrastructure, aptly called the European Programme for Critical Infrastructure Protection.[27] This resulted in a 2008 directive intended to map European critical infrastructure and assess its security.[28] The initiative was limited to the energy and transport sectors. The next year, the European Commission created a complementary programme for "Critical *Information* Infrastructure Protection", which eventually resulted in the Network and Information Security (NIS) directive.[29] In 2020, the European Commission then

[23] Byres et al. 2004.

[24] ENISA 2011, p. 5.

[25] Shodan Team. shodan.io. https://www.shodan.io/. Accessed 15 January 2020.

[26] See for example the timeline on p. 2 of McLaughlin et al. 2016; and Fauri et al. 2017, p. 5 and Section TODO.

[27] European Commission 2004, 2006, 2011.

[28] This was followed up by ENISA in 2011 with ENISA; see further European Commission 2019 for an evaluation. Member states have also adopted national legislation on ICS, see for an overview; ENISA 2015.

[29] European Commission 2009, 2011, (2016a) Directive (EU) 2016/1148 of the European Parliament and of the Council of 6 July 2016 Concerning Measures for a High Common Level of Security of Network and Information Systems Across the Union; with prior to this European Commission 2001; and 2006a, b; see for earlier policy documents focusing on CIIP; G8 Justice and Interior Ministers, G8 Principles for Protecting Critical Information Infrastructures, May 2003; OECD 2008; General Assembly United Nations, Resolution adopted by the General Assembly on the Creation of a Global Culture of Cybersecurity and the Protection of Critical Information Infrastructures, A/RES/58/199, January 30, 2004.

proposed a new cybersecurity strategy.[30] In 2022, the NIS Directive has been replaced by an updated version, commonly called the NIS2 Directive.[31]

The NIS 2 Directive obliges member states to ensure that certain providers of "essential" and "important services" take risk-based security measures and measures to mitigate incidents and ensure their continuity.[32] The directive extends not only to listed categories of entities providing essential or important services, but in some case also include non-listed organisations, for example extending it to services where a potential disruption of the service could have an impact on public safety, security or health or systemic risks.[33] Similar to the rules on the processing of personal data, the directive does not focus on the suppliers of components which make up a modern IT-infrastructure, only the providers *using* those components—thus leaving out a significant chunk of the attack surface.

3.2.1.3 Consumer Products and Services

The above category of rules relates to critical infrastructure. By contrast, a third category of regulations focuses on products and services which are offered to *consumers*. This is becoming more important, as computers are increasingly being integrated in products sold to individual people—from bicycles to sex toys, from talking dolls to webcams. I focus this analysis on specific duties of care in the consumer context, not general duties of care, for instance under tort law. This is firstly because of the legal principle that a *lex specialis*, a rule tailored to a specific situation, trumps a more general rule. Moreover, most of the obstacles present in the application of the specific laws discussed below, are also present in general tort law.[34]

Historically, the European Union only concerned itself with the "safety" of those products. The idea is that all products should meet with a certain baseline level of safety, to protect the consumer from physical harm. So, under the General Product Safety directive of 2001, only "safe products" may be put on the market.[35] And products are considered safe when they present "only the minimum risks compatible with the product's use, considered to be acceptable and consistent with a high level of protection for the safety and health of persons".[36] This regulation is then complemented by the general EU product liability framework, which describes who

---

[30] See High Representative of the Union for Foreign Affairs and Security Policy 2020.

[31] (2022a) Directive (EU) 2022/2555 of the European Parliament and of the Council of 14 December 2022 on Measures for a High Common Level of Cybersecurity Across the Union, Amending Regulation (EU) No 910/2014 and Directive (EU) 2018/1972, and Repealing Directive (EU) 2016/1148 (NIS 2 Directive).

[32] Ibid., Article 22.

[33] Ibid., Article 2(2).

[34] See also Verbruggen et al. 2016 which does not discuss general tort law in the context of cybersecurity of consumer devices.

[35] European Parliament and the Council (2001) Directive 2001/95/EC of the European Parliament and of the Council of 3 December 2001 on General Product Safety, Article 3(1).

[36] Ibid., Article 2(b).

can be held liable when a product is *not* safe.[37] Product liability furthermore extends to upstream suppliers and the importer.[38]

The central question is whether *information security* risks also fall under this header of product "safety". The European Commission in a 2020-report notes that the "concept of product safety encompasses protection against all kinds of risks arising from the product, including not only mechanical, chemical, electrical risks but also cyber risks and risks related to the loss of connectivity of devices".[39] But you could argue that a security vulnerability in a smart watch for children, which allows a kidnapper to locate a child, affects the child's *safety*.[40] In order to address this, the European Commission is at the time of writing in the process of updating the Product Liability Directive. Its proposal would clarify that product safety requirements include "safety-relevant cybersecurity requirements", and operators can be held liable for "lack of software updates or upgrades necessary to address cybersecurity vulnerabilities and maintain the product's safety".[41]

In addition, there are *some* consumer-oriented regulations for specific devices which also focus on security. One regulation applies to radio equipment.[42] This regulation affects all products wirelessly connected to the internet, including mobile phones, but also smart toys, home assistants, etc.[43] Under these rules, radio equipment is required to incorporate "safeguards to ensure that the personal data and privacy of the user and of the subscriber are protected".[44] This requirement is vague, does not extend to non-personal yet confidential information, and does not explain how to take into account the different phases of the information security cycle (e.g. discovery and mitigation).

Another set of regulations are embedded in the Directive on digital content and digital services, and the Directive on the sale of goods, under which certain content, services and goods incorporating those content and services must possess the security which the consumer "may reasonably expect" (and security updates must be applied to keep it that way).[45] These rules apply to all kinds of software (including

[37] (1985) Council Directive 85/374/EEC of 25 July 1985 on the approximation of the laws, regulations and administrative provisions of the Member States concerning liability for defective products, Articles 1 and 6.

[38] A "producer" is defined as "the manufacturer of a finished product, the producer of any raw material or the manufacturer of a component part and any person who, by putting his name, trade mark or other distinguishing feature on the product presents himself as its producer"; ibid., Article 3.

[39] European Commission 2020, p. 6.

[40] See ibid., p. 5.

[41] 2022b, Article 7(1)(f) and recitals 23 and 38.

[42] Similar legislation can be found with regard to medical devices and cars; European Commission, p. 6; a specific directive on the regulation of toys does not address security at all; (2009a) Directive 2009/48/EC of the European Parliament and of the Council of 18 June 2009 on the Safety of Toys; see further Whittle et al., which comes to conclusions somewhat similar as those in this paragraph.

[43] See for a similar analysis Hessel and Rebmann 2020.

[44] 2014, Article 3(3)(e).

[45] (2019a) Directive (EU) 2019/770 of the European Parliament and of the Council of 20 May 2019 on certain aspects concerning contracts for the supply of digital content and digital services, Articles

apps), services (such as hosting services) and connected products (like smart fridges). While it is laudable that the obligation to provide updates is made explicit, the security standard under this framework (the reasonable expectations of a consumer) is particularly unclear. This will arguably also depend on the extent to which the consumer has been warned that the product is not secure, for example.[46] More fundamentally, it is questionable whether the perspective of the expectations of the consumer is the best framework for determining security measures, as there is a risk that the broader societal interest in good security is not taken into account: what may be good enough for a consumer in terms of security, may not be good enough for society. *I* may find it acceptable to buy a cheap online camera which can be hacked, but *others* will have to deal with the consequences if my camera is involved in a botnet. And lastly, again this consumer-oriented approach does not cover the *incorporation* of products by businesses in end-user products (e.g. the incorporation of SSDs from another manufacturer in a laptop which is then sold to a consumer). As a result, these regulations do not address the allocation of responsibility between the different parties that contribute elements to the attack surface of a single product or service.

Another regulatory initiative from the European Commission, the Cybersecurity Act, is also worth mentioning.[47] Under this Regulation, the European Union Agency for Cybersecurity (ENISA) may adopt European cybersecurity certification schemes for products, services and processes. The idea behind this approach is that consumers will make their choices based on whether something is "certified".[48] This consumer-oriented approach will again not address the security issues outlined above. Most importantly, the certification scheme under the Cybersecurity Act is *voluntary*: companies are free to subject their products or services to an assessment for certification. While some certifications may become obligatory in certain settings, for example in public procurement or under the NIS 2 Directive, the paradigm is market-based: helping end users to make "informed choices".[49]

Finally, the most interesting regulatory initiative coming from the European Commission in recent years is the proposal for the Cyber Resilience Act (CRA).[50] The CRA would impose requirements on products with digital elements which are put on the market. Products with digital elements are defined as "any software or hardware product and its remote data processing solutions, including software or hardware

8(1)(b) and 8(2); (2019b) Directive (EU) 2019/771 on certain aspects concerning contracts for the sale of goods, amending Regulation (EU) 2017/2394 and Directive 2009/22/EC, and repealing Directive 1999/44/EC, Article 7(1)(d) and 7(3).

[46] See for an analysis van den Heuvel 2018, Section 6.2.1.

[47] (2019) Regulation (EU) 2019/881 of the European Parliament and of the Council of 17 April 2019 on ENISA (the European Union Agency for Cybersecurity) and on Information and Communications Technology Cybersecurity Certification and Repealing Regulation (EU) No 526/2013 (Cybersecurity Act).

[48] Ibid., Article 52.

[49] See ibid., recitals 91 and 92.

[50] European Commission (2022) Proposal for a Regulation on cybersecurity requirements for products with digital elements (Cyber Resilience Act). At the time of writing, this proposal is currently being negotiated.

components to be placed on the market separately".[51] These must be designed, developed and produced in such a way that they ensure an appropriate level of cybersecurity based on the risks, and delivered without any known exploitable vulnerabilities.[52] A more stringent regime applies to "critical products with digital elements", which would include things like password managers and network management systems.[53] Finally, market surveillance authorities of each member state may in certain situations where such a product presents a "significant cybersecurity risk" require the relevant operator to take measures to remove the risk.[54]

3.2.1.4 Dealing with Knowledge of Vulnerabilities

As we saw in the lifecycle of a zero day, for most vulnerabilities there comes a moment when they will be found. The rules relating to *finding* this vulnerability—the research stage—will be discussed later. But first, I want to discuss how organisations are required respond when they become aware of a vulnerability. Broadly speaking, one can distinguish between two kinds of required responses: fixing the security issue and notifying stakeholders.

The predominant response that may be required is patching the vulnerability. Under some of the more recent regulatory instruments discussed above, it is clear that the requirement to take measures to ensure security also implies an obligation to take mitigating measures when an organisation becomes aware of a potential risk. For the GDPR, this follows from the requirements to "ensure" the "ongoing" security, and to implement a procedure for testing, evaluating and assessing the security of systems.[55] This is even more pronounced in the NIS 2 Directive, where there is an explicit requirement to take measures in the domain of security in network and information systems acquisition, development and maintenance, including vulnerability handling and disclosure.[56] As noted above, in the Directive on digital content and digital services and the Directive on the sale of goods, the trader or seller is required to also provide security updates to ensure that the level of security which the consumer may reasonably expect is maintained. This obligation to take security measures, logically must include the obligation to apply updates when a vulnerability is found.

For the current product liability regime, it is less clear whether product liability for vulnerabilities found later in a product can be avoided because the defect was not

---

[51] Ibid., Article 3(1).

[52] Ibid., Annex 1 Section 1.

[53] Ibid., Annex III; see further Article 6(4) jo. Article 24(2) and (3).

[54] Ibid., Chap. V.

[55] (2016) Regulation 2016/679 of the European Parliament and of the Council of 27 April 2016 on the protection of natural persons with regard to the processing of personal data and on the free movement of such data, and repealing Directive 95/46/EC (General Data Protection Regulation), Article 32(1)(b) and (d).

[56] (2016a) Directive (EU) 2016/1148 of the European Parliament and of the Council of 6 July 2016 Concerning Measures for a High Common Level of Security of Network and Information Systems Across the Union, Artt. 21(2)(e).

there when the product was put into circulation, or because the defect was not foreseeable.[57] This would change under the new proposal for product liability, though, as the proposed directive provides that manufacturers can be held liable "for damage caused by their failure to supply software security updates or upgrades that are necessary to address the product's vulnerabilities in response to evolving cybersecurity risk".[58]

Finally, under the proposed Cyber Resilience Act, manufacturers of these products would have to comply with detailed process on discovering and handling vulnerabilities, including by having to maintain a list of the software dependencies of a product, by providing security updates without delay and informing users, having a policy on coordinated vulnerability disclosure and providing a contact address for reporting vulnerabilities.[59]

The second response is notification. Under the GDPR, controllers are obliged to document all data breaches (as defined in the GDPR), report most data breaches to the applicable data protection authorities and inform data subjects in the case of high-risk data breaches.[60] Under the NIS 2 Directive, regulated entities will without undue delay notify the competent authority of any incident that has a significant impact on the provision of their services and may under certain circumstances also have to inform the users of their services.[61] The NIS 2 Directive further cements this part of the information security cycle, as it obliges member states to adopt a policy to promote and facilitate coordinated vulnerability disclosure (CVD).[62] This CVD process should be supported by an organisation designated to coordinate the disclosure process in each member state, and should also provide for co-operation between each national organisation.[63] Furthermore, ENISA shall develop and maintain a vulnerability registry.

In the Cybersecurity Act, ENISA is accorded the task of strengthening capacity building in coordinated vulnerability disclosure, or CVD, but this is voluntary.[64]

---

[57] European Commission 2020, p. 15.

[58] (2022) Proposal for a Directive of the European Parliament and of the Council on Liability for Defective Products, recital 38; see also Article 10(2)(b) and (c).

[59] European Commission (2022) Proposal for a Regulation on cybersecurity requirements for products with digital elements (Cyber Resilience Act), Annex 1 Section 2.

[60] (2016) Regulation 2016/679 of the European Parliament and of the Council of 27 April 2016 on the protection of natural persons with regard to the processing of personal data and on the free movement of such data, and repealing Directive 95/46/EC (General Data Protection Regulation), Articles 32 and 33.

[61] (2022a) Directive (EU) 2022/2555 of the European Parliament and of the Council of 14 December 2022 on Measures for a High Common Level of Cybersecurity Across the Union, Amending Regulation (EU) No 910/2014 and Directive (EU) 2018/1972, and Repealing Directive (EU) 2016/1148 (NIS 2 Directive), Article 23.

[62] Ibid., Article 7(2)(c).

[63] Ibid., Article 12.

[64] (2019) Regulation (EU) 2019/881 of the European Parliament and of the Council of 17 April 2019 on ENISA (the European Union Agency for Cybersecurity) and on Information and Communications Technology Cybersecurity Certification and Repealing Regulation (EU) No 526/2013 (Cybersecurity Act), Article 6(1)(b).

There is no obligation to notify when you have *found* a vulnerability. Under the proposed Cyber Resilience Act, manufacturers of products with digital elements would have to report any actively exploited vulnerability as well as any incident having impact on the security of the product to ENISA.[65] Importers and distributors would also have certain reporting requirements in this regard.[66]

3.2.1.5 Subconclusion

Summing up, several issues can be identified in the current approaches to regulating the defensive stage of the information security cycle. Firstly, there are different rules for different contexts. The processing of personal data, the control of industrial systems and the consumer context all have their own rules when it comes to security. This makes it difficult to navigate the legal rules in this domain. Of course, if there are good reasons for distinguishing between the different contexts, that would be understandable. But the line between them is unclear, at best—"consumer devices are critical infrastructure", as Bruce Schneier writes.[67] Vulnerabilities do not remain confined in one domain: a vulnerability may at the same time be found in a software component that's used for personal data processing, critical infrastructure *and* consumer devices. Vulnerabilities in one domain may also affect other domains.

Second, in many of these regulations, the obligations to take security measures only extend to a limited group of organisations—leaving out the suppliers of components. This is problematic, because vulnerabilities in one component can affect the security of the entire attack surface, and vulnerabilities in one component can sometimes be fixed through a different component (a vulnerability in SSDs can be fixed through the operating system). The proposed Cyber Resilience Act would address both issues to a certain degree, as it covers all products with digital elements, and is not limited to certain sectors.

The third issue is that even where security requirements *do* apply, their content can be improved.[68] The risk-based security approach—the obligation to take measures "appropriate" to the risk—has now been adopted throughout many of the European regulations, in particular the GDPR and the NIS 2 Directive. The advantage of this standard is that it allows for some flexibility, leaving it up to organisations to determine which measures are suitable for their particular situation. But a narrow reading of the obligation would result in organisations only weighing the risk to the organisation itself, and not assessing the broader *societal* risks. For example, Marriott Hotels might take measures to address the risk that details on its guests could become available to hackers, but it will probably not consider the risk that intelligence agencies could use this data as leverage over a politician staying at the hotel with her lover.

---

65 European Commission (2022) Proposal for a Regulation on cybersecurity requirements for products with digital elements (Cyber Resilience Act), Article 11.

66 Ibid., p. Articles 13 and 14.

67 Schneier 2019a.

68 See also Arnbak et al. 2014, p. 79 and further.

Yet, there is a clear public interest in ensuring this risk is weighed as well. Taking large societal risks in account is also important when updating safety-oriented regulations to incorporate information security, because these regulations historically are focused on the risk to the *individual user or consumer*, not the society at large. When a hacked webcam is involved in a DDoS attack, this does not necessarily pose a risk to the user's security, but it does create problems for the victim of the attack. If these wider consequences are not addressed, we are offloading the effects of poor information security to the public at large.

More fundamentally, because information security policies are increasingly expected to balance conflicting interests, it is important to provide guidance on taking risk-based measures which are in conflict with each other. For example, the concept of resilience, which under the GDPR is considered an aspect of security, requires systems to continue working *after* an attack, whereas most of the other required measures are being taken to *prevent* an attack. An organisation thus will have to allocate its security budget between measures aimed at deterrence, and those aimed at mitigation. It is currently unclear how an organisation should balance these two interests.

The final issue is that current legislation at the time of writing places little emphasis on the cyclical nature of information security. Even when there are rules in place on information security, in many cases these are not clear on how to deal with knowledge of a vulnerability. As a result, organisations which play an important role in the attack surface are not subject to an obligation to fix vulnerabilities or to notify others when they become aware of one. And even where they are subject to such a requirement, the obligation to notify is limited. Under the GDPR and the NIS 2 Directive, organisations are not explicitly obliged to inform suppliers who play a role in the attack surface and might be able to fix the vulnerability. In particular, independent researchers who discover a vulnerability are not subject to a notification requirement. This aspect of the information security cycle, the research part, is discussed further in the next section.

3.2.2 Regulation of Security Research

In the section above, I discussed the regulatory instruments applicable to taking measures: which measures do organisations have to take to ensure "security"? In the following section, we shift to the other part of the cycle: what about activities that involve attacking security measures? How is this information security research regulated? Three specific sets of laws are relevant for information security research:

intellectual property rules, cybercrime laws and export regulations.[69] I discuss them in that order.

3.2.2.1 Intellectual Property Protection Rules

In the eighties, movies, music and software were shared over the "sneakernet"—friends passing copies of tapes or floppy disks to each other by hand. Copyright owners did employ copy protection measures, but most were easily defeated, and defeating them was only illegal in certain cases.[70] This changed in the mid-nineties, as the "Information Superhighway" evolved into the mainstream internet. This new world presented both a threat to existing distribution models, and new territory to be explored.[71] To exploit these uncharted grounds, entertainment companies contended, three things had to be done. First, the cables needed to be upgraded so more information could flow through them. And then, these series of empty tubes needed to be filled with "content"—music, movies, software and books. But this could only happen if the tubes didn't leak: the material should not be copied or accessed illegally during the voyage from server to eyeball.

This last aim turned out to be important for information security regulation.[72] Ensuring that content does not leak is a challenge, because digital technologies provide many opportunities to miscreants and tinkerers, especially from the moment when material enters someone's home. Without technical copy protection measures, a person could simply purchase a song, then copy it on their own device, and then republish the song for free. To plug these potential leaks, publishers envisaged gaining full control over the online distribution and use of digital information.

If you take this vision to its logical conclusion, however, this means extending publishers' reach into the living room of every internet user. It would require enlisting all computers, televisions and other communication devices, in order to impose restrictions on what users *could* do, while reporting back on what they *were doing*. A movie should be streamed securely to a browser on a device, but then the device should also prevent other software from copying the information as it flowed through memory, CPU and ultimately to the screen. Certainly, entertainment companies accepted *some* leakage—people could always find a way around copy protection—but the idea was to "keep honest users honest".[73]

Part of this vision required the development of security measures and standards to protect information from being copied and accessed illegally. But publishers also

---

[69] See for a discussion of US laws affecting security research Park and Albert; see for a similar mapping exercise of 2018 Schaake et al.; and for a more recent discussion OECD 2021, para 3.3. I will not focus on more generally applicable rules, such as tort law, because these more specific rules are more tailored to security research.

[70] See Brown 2006, p. 2; Koelman 2003, Chap. 3.

[71] See Litman 2006, Chap. 6; Koelman 2003, Chap. 3.

[72] See for a somewhat similar analysis Gillespie 2007.

[73] Hearing on Piracy Prevention and the Broadcast Flag 2003, p. 56.

pushed for a second line of defence: *legal* protection of *copy* protection. They wanted to make it illegal to defeat these technical measures aimed at unauthorised copying and access. At first glance, this perhaps seems logical: entertainment companies were merely protecting what was rightfully theirs. But that was only part of the story.

The other part of the story had to do with the growing awareness around that time that *code is law*: that our lives are increasingly shaped by the possibilities and constraints afforded by software and hardware.[74] In this case, the new *code*—the envisaged copy protection—would go much further than the old *law*. If fully enforced, this technological infrastructure would block ordinary citizens from sharing art and knowledge with friends and family, and prevent the re-use of information in new contexts, things which are considered perfectly legal. It would also requiring wrestling control from people over their own devices and require invasive tracking. And important for this book: it would make it difficult to research weaknesses in information security measures embedded in copy protection schemes.

The prospect that this highly problematic technological vision was to be fortified with the power of the legal apparatus was met with serious criticism. Opponents argued that in such a regime, media consumers users should at least have the option to *fight back*—to circumvent technological limitations which restricted their legitimate interests. A more fundamental argument, already present at that time, was that such a proposal is at odds with the cyclical nature of information security. Rules restricting the research and breaking of information security measures used for *commercial purposes*, also potentially prevent the improvement of information security measures *in the public interest*. Weaknesses in information security technologies used in critical infrastructure could in theory be prevented from being fixed due to regulation protecting these technologies in consumer devices.

Despite those controversies, these proposals gained political traction and were ultimately adopted. The entertainment lobby first attempted to push the rules in US Congress, but, facing pushback at that level, quickly shifted its efforts to the international stage, at the World Intellectual Property Organisation (WIPO), where work on an international copyright treaty fit for the digital age was underway.[75] There they succeeded in 1996, when for the first time legal protection to copy protection was granted.[76] These rules were then transposed, in Europe in the 2001 European

[74] See Lessig 2006; see for an earlier analysis of the anti-circumvention provisions of the DMCA Samuelson 1999; Samuelson 2003; see for the origins of this idea Reidenberg 1997; see for a recent and thorough analysis Diver 2021.

[75] Litman 2006, Chaps. 8 and 9.

[76] Article 11 of the WIPO Copyright Treaty obliges Contracting Parties to "provide adequate legal protection and effective legal remedies against the circumvention of effective technological measures that are used by authors in connection with the exercise of their rights under this Treaty or the Berne Convention and that restrict acts, in respect of their works, which are not authorized by the authors concerned or permitted by law"; (1996a) WIPO Copyright Treaty. Article 18 of the WIPO Performances and Phonograms Treaty contains a similar obligation; (1996b) WIPO Performances and Phonograms Treaty.

Copyright Directive and implementing legislation, and in the United States in the Digital Millennium Copyright Act (DMCA).[77]

The European rules effectuated this legal protection of copy protection in two ways, by prohibiting the actual *circumvention* of "effective technological measures" (which I discuss here) and by restricting the offering of circumvention *tools* (which I discuss below). Information security measures—the topic of this book—are almost always such "effective technological measures", because they restrict access to information or restrict the copying of information without authorisation.[78] Furthermore, while these rules may have been driven primarily by the desire to protect entertainment material, the scope of these rules extended to fields far beyond movies and songs, such as the verification of printer cartridges and keycard systems for locks.[79] That is because it has been argued that such systems restrict access to software, and software is protected by copyright as well.

Not only do the rules apply to virtually every kind of information with some security measure around it. The rules also apply to all circumvention, regardless of why you're doing it. Whether you are breaking encryption to start your illicit filesharing empire, or doing it to share an out-of-copy version of a Shakespeare sonnet with your English teacher, rules prohibiting circumventions and the tools for circumvention have difficulty taking this into account. This firstly affects the possibility of users to enjoy the rights granted to them via intellectual property right exceptions, such as the right to make a copy for private use, or to share information with family members, and because circumvention is necessary for testing security measures, these provisions also affect information security research.

This is why some room for exceptions has been built into these laws. In the US, explicit exceptions to the circumvention prohibition have been adopted for certain uses in the public interest, such as *jailbreaking*—taking over your own device to

---

[77] (2001) Directive 2001/29/EC of the European Parliament and of the Council of 22 May 2001 on the harmonisation of certain aspects of copyright and related rights in the information society, Article 6(1). The new Copyright in the Digital Single Market Directive has retained this provision; (2019d) Directive (EU) 2019/790 on copyright and related rights in the Digital Single Market and amending Directives 96/9/EC and 2001/29/EC, recital 7; (1998) Digital Millennium Copyright Act.

[78] Technological measures are considered "effective" where "the use of a protected work or other subject-matter is controlled by the rightholders through application of an access control or protection process, such as encryption, scrambling or other transformation of the work or other subject-matter or a copy control mechanism, which achieves the protection objective"; (2001) Directive 2001/29/EC of the European Parliament and of the Council of 22 May 2001 on the harmonisation of certain aspects of copyright and related rights in the information society, Article 6(3). The Court of Justice in *Nintendo* (2014) has ruled that "the concept of 'effective technological measures' is defined broadly", which also complies with the principal objective of the directive, which is to establish a high level of protection in favour authors; CJEU, Case C-355/12, Nintendo/PC Box, Judgment of 23 January 2014, para 27. The EFF has provided an overview of all the ways in which Section 1201 of the DMCA has stifled security research until 2014; Electronic Frontier Foundation 2014.

[79] NXP in its litigation against the disclosure of vulnerabilities regarding the Mifare-chip in the Netherlands also relied on this provision, but the district court did not consider it proven that the algorithm in question was protected by copyright; District Court of Arnhem, ECLI:NL:RBARN:2008:BD7578, NXP/RUN (Mifare-chip), Judgment of 18 July 2008.

be able to install all apps you want—and information security.[80] The EU prohibits all circumvention, but at the same time obliges member states to take measures to ensure that right holders under certain circumstances make available to users the means of benefiting from copyright exceptions.[81] It is furthermore clarified in recitals that these provisions "should respect proportionality and should not prohibit those devices or activities which have a commercially significant purpose or use other than to circumvent the technical protection", and in particular, "should not hinder research into cryptography".[82]

These measures, however, do not adequately address the problem that circumvention in the public interest is prohibited in the EU. A recital does not have the same binding force as actual provisions. More importantly, the carve-out is limited to devices or activities with another "commercially significant purpose or use" and "research into cryptography".[83] Information security research is not necessarily commercial in nature. Moreover, protected technological measures are not always cryptographic, and information security research into these other measures will not be affected by the specific carve-out for cryptography research.

Lastly, there are two other sets of intellectual property rules which deserve to be mentioned because they could in theory affect information security research. These relate to software "reverse engineering": taking a product and investigating how it works internally. In short, the Software Directive entitles the rightful user of a computer program to research how it works.[84] Contractual provisions contrary to these exceptions are considered null and void.[85] The rightful user may also reproduce and translate (e.g. decompile) parts of the code to the extent that this is "indispensable to obtain the information necessary to achieve the interoperability of an

[80] See U.S. Copyright Office 2000; Liu 2003. The US Library of Congress in 2015, 2018 and 2021 provided for an exemption on the circumvention prohibition for "good-faith security research"; Copyright Office of the Library of Congress 2021, p. 201.40.

[81] (2001) Directive 2001/29/EC of the European Parliament and of the Council of 22 May 2001 on the harmonisation of certain aspects of copyright and related rights in the information society, Article 6(4).

[82] See recital 48 of the ibid. This was introduced in the amended proposal of the European Commission 1999, recital 30; see for an analysis of the legislative history van Daalen 2003, Chap. 3.2.

[83] It is unlikely that "commercially significant" only relates to "purpose" and not to "use", because this would mean that "devices or activities which have a use other than to circumvent the technical protection", would not be prohibited. This would broaden the exception to all kinds of uses, even uses which are not considered legitimate.

[84] To be precise, it entitles the rightful owner to "observe, study or test the functioning of the program in order to determine the ideas and principles which underlie any element of the program" while doing "any of the acts of loading, displaying, running, transmitting or storing the program which he is entitled to do"; (2009b) Directive 2009/24/EC of the European Parliament and of the Council of 23 April 2009 on the Legal Protection of Computer Programs, Article 5(3).

[85] Ibid., Article 8 and recital 16; see also CJEU, Case C-406/10, SAS/World Programming, Judgment of 2 May 2012.

independently created computer program with other programs".[86] This exception may affect security research, because such research is not necessarily carried out to achieve interoperability, but in most cases to test the security measures of a system. Second, under the Trade Secrets Directive, it is allowed to acquire a trade secret when it is obtained by "observation, study, disassembly or testing of a product or object that has been made available to the public or that is lawfully in the possession of the acquirer of the information who is free from any legally valid duty to limit the acquisition of the trade secret".[87] This means, however, that it is possible to contractually limit the possibility of reverse engineering trade secrets.[88] This obviously can also affect security research, where the researcher obtains its research object directly from the manufacturer or distributor.

These rules have been in effect for around two decades now. During that period, ecosystems for movies, music and books have flourished, while the entertainment industry failed disastrously at plugging content leaks.[89] Unfortunately, the potentially negative effects of these rules on digital infrastructure and information security research are still felt. This raises the question whether the current rules should remain in place. I discuss this further in Chap. 8.

3.2.2.2 Cybercrime Rules

Copyright rules are enforced primarily through civil law—Nintendo took action against people who sold tools to copy their cartridges, and NXP took action against information security researchers. But when a researcher does not own the system or have permission to study it, they may also face criminal liability. This is discussed in the next section, focusing on two activities: gaining access and intercepting information.[90] These rules are a double-edged sword: on the one hand, their aim is to increase information security, by criminalising the circumvention of security measures. On the other hand, the circumvention of these measures can also be done in the public interest, in particular for information security research. This presents policymakers with a conundrum at the heart of the information security cycle: how do you deter undesired circumvention, while ensuring that information security measures can be improved? As we will see, the existing solutions are insufficient. I discuss policy options in Chap. 8.

[86] (2009) Directive 2009/24/EC of the European Parliament and of the Council of 23 April 2009 on the Legal Protection of Computer Programs, Article 6.

[87] (2016) Directive (EU) 2016/943 of the European Parliament and of the Council of 8 June 2016 on the Protection of Undisclosed Know-How and Business Information (Trade Secrets) against their Unlawful Acquisition, Use and Disclosure, Article 3(1)(b).

[88] See also recital 16 of ibid.

[89] Barnes 2019; Masnick and Beadon 2019; Waldfogel 2017.

[90] We will not discuss unauthorised system interference, or "computer sabotage"; see Council of Europe 2001, para 65.

3.2.3 Regulation of Unauthorised Access

Under the Cybercrime Directive, member states are obliged to criminalise the intentional access, to an information system, by infringing a security measure without the right to do so.[91] An "information system" is basically everything with a CPU, regardless of whether the system is offline or online—from servers to laptops, from smart thermostats to connected cars.[92] The question is thus what the terms "access", "without right" and "security measure" mean.

As to the term "access": *mere access* falls within the scope of this provision. It doesn't matter what will be done after having gained access, despite the fact that the drafters of the Cybercrime Convention were aware that access could be harmless or even beneficial, leading to "the detection of loopholes and weaknesses of the security of systems".[93] As a result, the scope of this provision is broad, potentially including many activities carried out in the public interest, including information security research.[94]

The term "without right" is defined as conduct "which is not authorised by the owner or by another right holder of the system or of part of it, or not permitted under national law".[95] Thus, "authorisation" is at the core of the definition.[96] Authorisation can be granted through a security policy or through contractual measures. Authorisation can arguably also be granted through CVD policies and bug bounty

---

[91] European Parliament (2013) Directive 2013/40/EU of the European Parliament and of the Council of 12 August 2013 on attacks against information systems and replacing Council Framework Decision 2005/222/JHA, Article 3. "Access" is "the entering of the whole or any part of a computer system (hardware, components, stored data of the system installed, directories, traffic and content-related data)"; Council of Europe 2001, para 46, on which the Cybercrime Directive is based.

[92] An "information system" is defined as "a device or group of interconnected or related devices, one or more of which, pursuant to a programme, automatically processes computer data, as well as computer data stored, processed, retrieved or transmitted by that device or group of devices for the purposes of its or their operation, use, protection and maintenance"; European Parliament (2013) Directive 2013/40/EU of the European Parliament and of the Council of 12 August 2013 on attacks against information systems and replacing Council Framework Decision 2005/222/JHA, Article 2(a).

[93] See Council of Europe 2001, para 44: "The mere unauthorised intrusion, i.e. 'hacking', 'cracking' or 'computer trespass' should in principle be illegal in itself" and para 49; see also Dizon 2016, pp. 211–212.

[94] See for a discussion Freitas and Gonçalves 2015. This is because information security measures for a significant part consist of measures *restricting* access, exactly the kinds of measures the Cybercrime Directive tries to protect. Researching the effectiveness—e.g. finding flaws in such measures—necessarily involves testing these access measures. If, in the course of testing a measure, a vulnerability is found, this in most cases means access is gained and the security measure is infringed.

[95] European Parliament (2013) Directive 2013/40/EU of the European Parliament and of the Council of 12 August 2013 on attacks against information systems and replacing Council Framework Decision 2005/222/JHA, Article 2(d).

[96] See for a discussion of the centrality of "authorisation" in the CIA-triad, Arnbak et al. 2014, para 5.2.

programs, but this does not appear to be common practice.[97] As a result, most of the information security research performed at the initiative of a third party will be done without authorisation. There is, however, another basis for such a right: if it is "permitted under national law". This again does not really address the interests of information security researchers, or others who want to circumvent security measures in the public interest. This firstly depends on the willingness of signatories to include an exception for information security research, and more importantly, there are no such exceptions in the legislation of EU member states, as far as I am aware (I touch on the way a public prosecutor can handle this prohibition in the section below).

The third condition is that a "security measure" must be circumvented. The question is how effective such a measure must be.[98] This issue has not been discussed in the legislative history of the directive. It is likely, that the bar for effectiveness is low, because if the security measures were really effective, then it would not be necessary to prohibit their circumvention (because they could not be circumvented).[99] For the purposes of this book, that is sufficient, because if one is to understand criminalised access as somewhat effective code-based restrictions, it is apparent that many types of security research fall within the scope of this provision.[100]

Meanwhile, there is no clear carve-out for the public interest, let alone for security researchers. The recitals mysteriously consider that the directive is "without prejudice to the right of access to information as laid down in national and EU law, while at the same time it may not serve as a justification for unlawful or arbitrary access to information"—a hollow phrase, as it does not clarify how to strike the balance between the two.[101] It is further clarified in the recitals that there is no criminal intent, and thus no criminal liability, "in the case of mandated testing or protection of information systems, such as where a person is assigned by a company or vendor to test the strength of its security system", the operative word being "mandated" (e.g. consultancy security research).[102] This leaves out information security research

[97] In one responsible disclosure policy sometimes used as a template in the Netherlands, authorisation is not granted, but it is merely promised that if certain conditions are complied with, the organisation will not take any legal steps against a reporter; Terra 2019.

[98] The European Parliament added this condition in first reading. The Cybercrime Convention leaves room to implementing states for adding this criterion; Hohlmeier (rapporteur) 2013; Council of Europe (2001) Convention on Cybercrime, Article 2. The Cybercrime Directive nor the legislative history sheds light on its meaning; see also Freitas and Gonçalves 2015, p. 59.

[99] In the Explanatory Report to the Convention, it is noted that "The most effective means of preventing unauthorised access is, of course, the introduction and development of effective security measures. However, a comprehensive response has to include also the threat and use of criminal law measures. A criminal prohibition of unauthorised access is able to give additional protection to the system and the data as such and at an early stage against the dangers described above"; Council of Europe 2001, para 45. See for the Netherlands District Court of The Hague, ECLI:NL:RBDHA:2018:10451, Vriendendatabase, Judgment of 30 August 2018.

[100] See Dizon 2016, pp. 209–210 for the same argument in the context of "hacking".

[101] European Parliament (2013) Directive 2013/40/EU of the European Parliament and of the Council of 12 August 2013 on attacks against information systems and replacing Council Framework Decision 2005/222/JHA, recital 17.

[102] Ibid., recital 17.

performed by outsiders—and much relevant research is in fact done by outsiders, as we saw. It is furthermore observed that the "identification and reporting of threats and risks posed by cyber attacks and the related vulnerability of information systems is a pertinent element of effective prevention of, and response to, cyber attacks and to improving the security of information systems", suggesting that "Member States should endeavour to provide possibilities for the legal detection and reporting of security gaps".[103] These suggestions are not further operationalised in the directive. We will discuss circumvention in the public interest and the need for a clear information security research exception in Chap. 8.

3.2.4 Regulation of Unauthorised Interception

Not only does the Cybercrime Directive regulate access, it also criminalises the intentional and unauthorised interception of "non-public transmissions of computer data to, from or within an information system, including electromagnetic emissions from an information system carrying such computer data".[104] This primarily encompasses all information flowing through and between computers.[105]

Three types of information security research are implicated in this provision. Firstly, the testing of communication protocols could run afoul of these laws: if one is to test the security of mobile communications, this will necessarily involve the interception (and perhaps even a *man-in-the-middle attack*) of communications traffic between a cell phone and a cell tower. Even if the researcher has gained authorisation from the owner of the cell phone, this does not necessarily imply that it also has gained authorisation from the telecommunications company operating the tower. Secondly, a more common example concerns the interception of traffic between a client and a server in order to better understand the traffic itself, not the protocol. This applies where a researcher wants to, for example, understand telemetry data sent by an operating system, which is transmitted encrypted to a server. In order to understand the data, one will have to intercept (and decrypt) the stream going to the server. A third kind of research involves examining offline systems, for example to extract keys from security components. This is sometimes done by intercepting the communications with other parts of a computer, for example through what are called *side-channel attacks*. In side-channel attacks, a researcher attempts to gain

---

[103] Ibid., recital 12.

[104] Ibid., Article 6.

[105] "Computer data" is defined as "a representation of facts, information or concepts in a form suitable for processing in an information system, including a programme suitable for causing an information system to perform a function"; ibid., Article 2(b). According to the Explanatory Report, the term "non-public" does not exclude communications via public networks; Council of Europe 2001, para 54. Further, the communication "can take place inside a single computer system (flowing from CPU to screen or printer, for example), between two computer systems belonging to the same person, two computers communicating with one another, or a computer and a person (e.g. through the keyboard)"; ibid., para 55.

information on the working of one channel through a related channel, such as power consumption. Since the directive also specifies the interception of "electromagnetic emissions", side-channel attacks will in some cases also fall within the scope of this provision.

Again, in order for the interception to fall within the scope of this provision, it must be done "without right", e.g. without consent from the owner or rights holder of the system. As we have seen above, this qualification still leaves room for snaring computer security research in its ambit.[106]

3.2.5 An Information Security Research Exception for Criminal Liability in Practice

The rules appear to be quite strict, leaving very little room for information security researchers accessing systems to access systems. However, a certain wiggle room arguably can be created through limits in *enforcing* these rules. For example, the Dutch public prosecutor has indicated that they will not start "in principle" a criminal investigation if the person reporting a vulnerability complies with the policy published on the website of the organisation they have investigated—a *coordinated vulnerability disclosure policy* or a *responsible disclosure policy*.[107] In determining whether to start proceedings, the public prosecutor will apply a human rights-related framework, which will be discussed further in this book. First, they will consider whether the actions were "necessary in a democratic society", proportionate to the goal of doing information security research, whether there were no less impactful alternatives to reaching the same goal, and whether the hack was reported immediately. Courts in the Netherlands have on multiple occasions in criminal cases left open the possibility that unauthorised access for information security research purposes could be legal, but that this requires disclosure to the vendor and that the actions *after* access are proportionate (e.g. not downloading entire databases).[108] Yet, the public prosecutor will only apply these exceptions "in principle", and researchers will take this possibility of prosecution in consideration when doing research, potentially limiting the scope of their work. As an example, ENISA in its report reviewing the directive notes that, when asked whether the rules were "sufficiently clear to ensure that CERTs, academic researchers, security professionals etc. could operate lawfully", law enforcement and policy makers considered the debate

[106] The Explanatory Report in the context of interception provides for the same understanding of this concept, Council of Europe 2001, para 58.

[107] Openbaar Ministerie 2020a; Openbaar Ministerie 2018; Openbaar Ministerie 2013; see for a discussion Harms 2017.

[108] See District Court The Hague, ECLI:NL:RBDHA:2018:10451, Centraal Bureau voor Genealogie, Judgment of 30 August 2018; District Court the Hague, ECLI:NL:RBDHA:2014:15611, Groene Hart Ziekenhuis, Judgment of 17 December 2014; District Court Oost-Brabant, ECLI:NL:RBOBR:2013:BZ1157, Henk Krol, Judgment of 15 February 2013.

largely academic.[109] Some CERTs, however, were less certain that they would not be held liable under these provisions.

3.2.6 Regulation of Disclosure, Exploits and Tools

Above, I discussed one element of the *offensive* part of the information security cycle: the research into information security measures. But many researchers will at some point disclose information on a vulnerability they have found, sometimes to a paying customer, sometimes to the public. Knowledge of vulnerabilities can not only be used to strengthen security measures, it can also be used to exploit them. The same goes for the tools used to do this research: the best way to find out whether a vulnerability exists, is by actually testing whether it can be exploited. Because of the potential for misuse, the disclosure of vulnerabilities, exploits and tools is also regulated. Three regimes—export regulations, copyright laws and cybercrime rules—potentially *restrict* the disclosure of vulnerabilities and the offering and use exploits and tools. By contrast, a fourth regime—the vulnerabilities equities process—*obliges* the disclosure of vulnerabilities under certain circumstances. These four legal frameworks will be discussed below.

3.2.6.1 Export Regulations

Export regulations are intended to control the export of conventional weapons and items which can be used for civilian and military purposes—also-called *dual-use technologies*. During the Cold War, this was done through the Coordinating Committee for Multilateral Export Controls (COCOM), intended to curtail exports from the West to the Soviet Union.[110] In 1996, COCOM was replaced by the Wassenaar Arrangement, a global non-proliferation regime for conventional weapons and dual-use technologies which currently has over 40 member countries around the world.

The Wassenaar Arrangement has to be implemented in local legislation. In Europe, the Wassenaar Arrangement is implemented in what is called the Dual-use Regulation.[111] For the export of most items covered under the Wassenaar Arrangement, it is necessary to obtain permission in advance from the relevant governmental agency (in the Netherlands, for example, this the Ministry of Foreign Affairs). The list of so-called "controlled items" under the Wassenaar Arrangement consists of physical objects, such as certain explosives, but also digital objects, such as software.

---

[109] ENISA 2013a, b, pp. 12–13.

[110] WA Secretariat 2020.

[111] (2021) Regulation of the European Parliament and of the Council Setting up a Union Regime for the Control of Exports, Brokering, Technical Assistance, Transit and Transfer of Dual-Use Items (Recast).

One type of software which was the object of much controversy in the nineties is encryption technology, discussed below. A more recent addition also has the potential to affect human rights more generally and information security research in particular—*intrusion software*.

The momentum for restricting international trade in surveillance and intrusion software increased when, after the fall of Gadhafi's regime in 2011, it was discovered that French, Chinese, South-African and American companies had supplied technologies to the Libyan government to surveil its population.[112] Simultaneously, research by Citizen Lab and others unearthed the use of zero days by governments to hack political adversaries. In response, policymakers pushed to curb the proliferation of surveillance tools to regimes with a history of human rights violations.[113] An initial attempt was made at the end of 2013: certain surveillance technologies were added to the list of controlled items, but "intrusion software" was also added to the list.[114] These rules allow for controlling the export of hacking software which weaponises malware. For example, in 2020, as a result of these rules, the German police raided the offices of Finfisher (one of the vendors of hacking software discussed in this chapter), in the course of an investigation into the export of surveillance software to countries such as Turkey.[115]

Although people in the information security research community appreciated the general thrust behind these regulations, they were also concerned because "intrusion" is what they do for a living.[116] While the list contained general exceptions for information and software "in the public domain", "basic scientific research" and software which is "generally available to the public", there were still fears that not all desirable vulnerability research could be done under this header, that the international exchange of knowledge on vulnerabilities would be curtailed and that the distribution of research tools could be affected.[117] This resulted in an update to the Wassenaar Arrangement in 2017, which clarified that the export restrictions do not apply to "vulnerability disclosure" or "cyber incident response".[118] Some argue, however, that it is still uncertain whether this covers all activities performed in information security

---

[112] Aikins 2012.

[113] See for example Marzouki 2012.

[114] See Schaake 2013; see further figure 3 of Ruohonen and Kimppa 2019 where an attempt is made to understand how the rule applies; see also Fidler 2019, p. 463 and further for an analysis.

[115] Meister 2020. A similar case brought by Amnesty in Israel against NSO group was dismissed; Holmes 2020.

[116] Saitta 2014; Bratus et al. 2014b; Zanero undated.

[117] WA Secretariat 2018, General Technology Note and General Software Note.

[118] WA Secretariat 2018, 4.E.1 and definitions; (2021a) Regulation of the European Parliament and of the Council Setting up a Union Regime for the Control of Exports, Brokering, Technical Assistance, Transit and Transfer of Dual-Use Items (Recast), 4E001 and definitions; vulnerability disclosure is defined as: "the process of identifying, reporting, or communicating a vulnerability to, or analysing a vulnerability with, individuals or organizations responsible for conducting or coordinating remediation for the purpose of resolving the vulnerability", and Cyber incident response is defined as "the process of exchanging necessary information on a cyber security incident with individuals or organizations responsible for conducting or coordinating remediation to address the cyber security incident".

research. In particular, the sharing of knowledge on vulnerabilities for trainings and classes, as well as information security research which is not intended to be used for vulnerability disclosure might be ensnared by this regulation.[119] The most important takeaway, though, is that even in relatively recent regulatory discussions on information security, policymakers have not sufficiently involved the research community itself. This will be discussed together with the policy recommendations.

3.2.6.2 Cybercrime Rules

Secondly, the Cybercrime Directive requires states to criminalise the intentionally making available of a computer password, access code, or similar data which enables access, with the intent to commit IT crimes.[120] Moreover, member states are obliged to criminalise the intentionally making available of "a computer programme, designed or adapted primarily for the purpose of" committing, in short, IT-related crime, and with the intention that the computer programme be used to commit IT-crimes.

In theory, information on vulnerabilities, exploits and tools containing exploits could fall within these provisions: it could be considered *data which enables access*, or *a programme designed to gain unauthorised access*. But this double "intent"-requirement should be interpreted narrowly in the context of tools.[121] The existence of intent is firstly derived from the purpose for which a certain tool is developed: if developed "for legitimate purposes", even if it is particularly suitable for criminal purposes, it shouldn't fall within this provision. It is also derived from the purpose for which it is made available—if it is not made available for criminal purposes, the intent requirement is also not satisfied. The German Supreme Court ruled in 2009 in constitutional complaints against the provision implementing this part of the Cybercrime Convention that its scope is limited to software whose purposes is committing a computer crime, and it does not concern security research tools—or dual-use tools more generally.[122] The court considered that software tools cannot be used for testing the security of systems without also allowing the possibility of being used for illegitimate purposes (referring to network testing tool *nmap* as an example).[123] This reasoning likely also applies to sharing vulnerabilities or exploits.

This means that disclosing vulnerabilities, exploits and tools containing exploits as part of purely scientific information security research will be legal. But where an organisation sells exploits as part of a criminal enterprise, for example to create a

[119] See Zanero undated, slide 23.

[120] See for a discussion of the regulation of tools under cybercrime laws also Iglezakis 2016, para 3.01[A].

[121] See recital 16 of the Cybercrime Directive and Explanatory Report to the Convention on Cybercrime, para 73.

[122] Bundesverfassungsgericht (BVerfG), 2 BVR 2233/07, 2 BVR 1151/08 and 2 BVR 1524/08, F.W. and K. gegen §202c Abs. 1 Nr. 2 StGB, Judgment of 19 June 2009a, para 31.

[123] Ibid., para 41; but see Hassemer 2010 for a critical reflection.

botnet, these prohibitions indeed apply. And the firms discussed which sell vulnerabilities and exploits to governments and other companies, operate in the grey area in between, because it is uncertain whether their customers will stay within the law.[124]

3.2.6.3 Copyright Rules

Thirdly, under the Copyright Directive, member states must provide legal protection against the production, distribution or possession for commercial purposes of certain circumvention "devices, products or components".[125] Whether these tools are prohibited depends on whether they are *promoted* as circumvention tools, have only a limited commercially significant *purpose* other than circumvention or are primarily *designed* to circumvent. A similar, but somewhat narrower provision can be found in the Software Directive, where member states are obliged to provide for appropriate remedies against a person committing "any act of putting into circulation, or the possession for commercial purposes of, any means the sole intended purpose of which is to facilitate the unauthorised removal or circumvention of any technical device which may have been applied to protect a computer program".[126]

Vulnerabilities, exploits and tools could in theory fall within the scope of this provision, because they allow for the circumvention of security measures. The first important condition is whether the disclosure is done for "commercial purposes". Some vulnerability research will be done for commercial gain, for example in order to attract attention with their research. Where vulnerabilities and exploits are offered for money, the commercial purpose is clear. Furthermore, many security research tools and exploits will be designed to circumvent; that is their main function. The fact that this circumvention also takes place for legitimate purposes, such as interoperability, legitimate copyright use, and installing other apps, does not matter. There have been numerous cases where this provision has been used to restrict the sale of devices which remove copy protection measures.[127] Given how broadly these provisions have been interpreted in the past, this could mean that for example an exploit which allows for the jailbreaking of a phone is considered a product or service intended to circumvent an "effective technological measure".

[124] See also Bratus et al. 2014a.

[125] (2001) Directive 2001/29/EC of the European Parliament and of the Council of 22 May 2001 on the harmonisation of certain aspects of copyright and related rights in the information society, Article 6.

[126] (2009) Directive 2009/24/EC of the European Parliament and of the Council of 23 April 2009 on the Legal Protection of Computer Programs.

[127] See for example CJEU, Case C-355/12, Nintendo/PC Box, Judgment of 23 January 2014; District Court of The Hague, ECLI:NL:RBSGR:2010:BN1963, Nintendo modchips, Judgment of 21 July 2010; Kabushiki Kaisha Sony Computer Entertainment Inc v Ball (Application for Summary Judgment), Judgment of 19 July 2004, [2004] EWHC 1738 (Ch); High Court of Justice, HC09C00988, Nintendo Co Ltd v Playables Ltd, Judgment of 28 July 2010, [2010] EWHC 1932; Landgericht München, 7 O 10502/12, TubeBox, Judgment of 26 July 2012.

3.2.6.4 Obligatory Disclosure under Vulnerabilities Equities Processes

Three of the the governance frameworks discussed above, potentially restrict disclosure of vulnerabilities. But there is one framework under which it is obligatory to *share* vulnerabilities: *vulnerabilities equities processes*, or VEPs.[128] These rules are intended to determine under what circumstances governments must use knowledge of weaknesses in the IT-infrastructure to strengthen it, instead of exploiting it. The momentum for these kinds of requirements grew when the public became more aware that not only criminals, but also governments themselves were hacking computers.[129] For example, the German government had already used software to enter suspects' computers via the internet in around 2010—software which could, as it turned out, also be taken over by criminals.[130] Around the same time, the Dutch police was also in the news with several investigations where it entered computers remotely.[131] Not only did this spur legislation to create a legal competence for hacking by governments, an example of which is discussed in Chap. 5, but it also put a spotlight on the fact that governments had an interest in keeping vulnerabilities secret. Now, as we have seen, it is unwise to assume that a vulnerability remains secret for long. Others may independently discover the same vulnerability, or the vulnerability may leak into the public domain. So the question is, how should governments weigh these competing interest? How do we balance the interests of being able to gain access to targeted devices in investigations, against the interest of ensuring that the devices of others—who are not a target—remain secure?

At first, this discussion was only a sideshow to the discussion on government hacking. But as a result of the Snowden revelations, the sheer scale of the vulnerabilities that governments had amassed soon became clear. The NSA could only perform many of its surveillance practices because it exploited information security holes.[132] In response to public concern, the Obama administration tasked a group of experts to review the NSA's practices. In its report, the experts also concluded that the government should only under limited circumstances keep knowledge of a vulnerability under wraps, which kickstarted the formation of an interagency process for dealing with vulnerabilities.[133] Then in 2014, a dangerous weakness was discovered in OpenSSL, a key internet communication security protocol.[134] When rumours started to spread that the vulnerability, called Heartbleed, had been known to the NSA for years, the White House felt compelled to respond. They published a blogpost, quite informal for such a hefty topic, in which they described the current status of

---

[128] See for a short overview of the history of VEPs Herpig and Schwartz 2019.

[129] See for an overview Li et al. 2018; and Gutheil et al. 2017.

[130] Chaos Computer Club 2011.

[131] In one case, it entered servers on the Tor-network containing images of sexual child abuse and made the pictures unavailable; Opstelten 2012; in another it entered the servers of a botnet and used the botnet to send a warning message to victims of malware; see Koning 2011, Chap. 1.

[132] See for example Gellman and Nakashima 2013.

[133] Clarke et al. 2013, recital 30.

[134] Durumeric et al. 2014.

the vulnerabilities equities process, noting that this is "a deliberate process that is biased toward responsibly disclosing the vulnerability".[135]

Yet two years later, a stockpile of NSA zero days fell into the hands of a hacker group called ShadowBrokers. This led to the development of malware that severely impacted organisations across the world, and people started to question how this bias towards disclosure actually had been applied in practice. "The National Security Agency is lying to us", wrote influential security expert Bruce Schneier.[136] Ultimately in 2017, the US government published a more formal memo describing its VEP, the VEP Charter, which was not laid down in a law.[137] It describes an interagency "Equities Review Board" which determines to what extent vulnerabilities should be disclosed, based on a list of considerations, such as the impact of a vulnerability, the possibilities for mitigation and its operational value. Under the VEP Charter, the secretariat must also produce an annual report (none have been published yet, four years later).[138]

In the EU, discussions on these VEPs are also gaining steam. A 2018-report recommended that all member states implement policies and practices on how to deal with knowledge of vulnerabilities, to be codified in law, with a default policy to disclose.[139] In another report, a detailed set of best practices for VEPs was described.[140] In the same year, GCHQ published a blog on its VEP, noting that the "default position is to disclose the problem and there has to be a very good reason not to—either an overriding intelligence case or the fact that disclosing could reduce the security of people who use the product".[141] In the Netherlands legislation for a VEP was proposed which would contain a "bias towards disclosure", but which allows for temporary secrecy under certain circumstances, but it never was put to a vote because of a lack of support.[142] Similarly, while it has been reported that Germany is also working on a formal policy, it appears to not have adopted one yet.[143]

Given the significant impact that withholding vulnerabilities may have on human rights, this leads to a number of observations. Firstly, the question is whether non-disclosure needs to have a legislative basis in view of human rights requirements. Then there is the question of under what circumstances the government may keep

---

[135] Daniel 2014; Riley 2014; see for an analysis and recommendations Schwartz and Knake 2016; and Healy 2016.

[136] Schneier 2016; others also directly connnected failures in the disclosure process with the impact of the hack; Greenberg 2016.

[137] US Government 2017.

[138] Wilson Thompson 2021.

[139] Schaake et al. 2018, p. 74.

[140] Herpig 2018.

[141] Levy 2018a.

[142] K. Verhoeven, Voorstel van wet van het lid Verhoeven houdende een regeling voor een afwegingsproces voor het gebruik van kwetsbaarheden in geautomatiseerde werken door de overheid (Wet Zerodays Afwegingsproces), 2018.

[143] Herpig and Schwartz 2019; see Bundesverfassungsgericht (BVerfG), IT-Sicherheitslücken, Judgment of 8 June 2021, 1 BvR 2771/18 for a German constitutional case on a VEP of the *Land* Baden-Württemberg, discussed in Section TODO.

vulnerabilities secret. On a positive note, the assumption underlying VEPs that information security is a process, and that it requires a periodic assessment of the decision to keep vulnerabilities secret, aligns closely with how information security works in practice. Lastly, it is notable that disclosure obligations are entirely absent in other domains—for example with regard to the surveillance software vendors discussed above. The human rights requirements regarding disclosure obligations, will be discussed further in Chap. 8.

3.2.7 Subconclusion

As we have now covered the complete information security cycle from taking measures to finding, disclosing and fixing vulnerabilities. A wide range of rules apply to this process, from copyright rules to export rules, from data protection to critical infrastructure protection.

In the first phase of the cycle, the governance frameworks relating to taking measures, fixing vulnerabilities and notifying stakeholders, have multiple gaps. Firstly, these obligations vary significantly, and for no good reason. They also do not apply to all organisations that play a role in the attack surface. This can be considered problematic because security is only as strong as its weakest link. Moreover, security standards do not explicitly take into account the impact that bad security can have on larger society, and there is no guidance on how to deal with conflicting obligations under these standards. Furthermore, the cyclical nature of information security receives only limited attention in this framework.

As for the second phase of the cycle, the research and disclosure part, security researchers will in many cases operate within a grey area of the law, sometimes even risking criminal liability. In particular, there is no clear, broadly applicable exception in the law for doing security research, which means that this risk mostly depends on assurances of the public prosecutor that it is not prosecuting those cases. A relevant question is whether offensive security research should have equal import and equal standing under the law.[144]

Furthermore, policymakers appear to be struggling with the dual-use nature of knowledge of vulnerabilities and tools used for information security research. Initial fears that export regulation and criminal provisions might stifle vulnerability disclosure and tools appear to be addressed—but only because of pushback from the research community. Policymakers appear to work from the assumption that publishing and circumventing weaknesses is the problem which needs to be addressed, whereas I argue that this is an intrinsic element of the information security cycle, which within boundaries needs to be embraced. I discuss in Chap. 8 how policymakers can devise policies which do justice to this dynamic from a human rights perspective. However, the governance of an important measure in the defensive stage of the information cycle, encryption technologies, will be discussed firstly.

---

[144] See also Bratus et al. 2014a.

The historical roots of this governance roots will be analyzed throughly because the core arguments have not changed over the past decades and thus also play a role in the analysis of human rights-compatible governance of encryption technologies in Chap. 9.

3.3 Governance of the Encryption Landscape

Nowadays, two interests drive restrictions of encryption, law enforcement agencies want access to communications for criminal investigations, and intelligence agencies want access for national security purposes. Law enforcement has not always been this concerned about encryption. The police targets criminals after all, and before the advent of the internet, criminals did not encrypt their communications. On the other hand, statesmen, spies and soldiers have been encrypting their communications for millennia. Encryption policy until the 1980s thus was predominantly a military affair, the domain of nations vying for power, and in this arena the US and UK reigned supreme.

This alliance between the US and the UK has its roots in the Second World War, when these countries successfully collaborated in joint signal intelligence, breaking Japanese and German ciphers.[145] This led the two countries to organise formally when the war ended, concluding a secret co-operation agreement in March 1946 (the UKUSA agreement).[146] In the decades that followed, this collaboration expanded to include other countries. The tightest collaboration is called the Five Eyes, and consists of the US and the UK, and the Commonwealth countries Canada, New Zealand and Australia.[147]

At the beginning of the Cold War, the Five Eyes and their allies directed their spying apparatus to the Communist bloc (e.g. the Soviet Union, China).[148] But as the political landscape became more complex, the collaboration also became more ambitious: in the seventies they set up a global secret spying network called Echelon, first intercepting satellite communications, later reportedly expanding to all kinds of communications over the air.[149]

In order to listen in on the communications of their adversaries, the Five Eyes had to do two things: collect communications and ensure that the encryption applied to these communications was vulnerable, preferably to them exclusively. To collect it, they scattered dozens of gigantic listening stations across earth and launched clusters

---

[145] Diffie and Landau 2007, p. 61.

[146] Norton-Taylor 2010.

[147] Other countries since then have also collaborated with the Five Eyes in various constellations, including the "Nine Eyes" (which includes the Netherlands, Denmark, Norway and France) and the "Fourteen Eyes" (which includes Germany, Sweden, Spain, Belgium and Italy); MacAskill and Ball 2013.

[148] See for a history which focuses on the spying towards the Global South Dover and Aldrich 2020.

[149] Campbell 2015; Campbell 1998; Schmid 2001.

of spying satellites into space. In order to exploit it they subverted the encryption available, and restricted what was exported, in particular to the Eastern bloc. These three governance measures—intercepting, subverting and restricting export—are still dominant in the encryption landscape, as we will see.

The lengths through which these agencies were willing to go defies the imagination. For instance, the CIA in the 1950s together with the West-German intelligence service, the *Bundesnachrichtendienst*, secretly acquired an entire company, Swiss cryptography provider Crypto AG, to rig encryption devices before selling them to friends and foes.[150] Eventually, they could listen in on the communications of more than 120 countries.[151] They also shared information on the backdoored algorithms with other allies, such as Denmark, Sweden, the Netherlands and France. This also happened closer to home as the Dutch intelligence agency at the end of the 1970s together with Dutch electronics firm Philips developed a microchip to decrypt the ciphers used in a machine actually sold by Philips (and Siemens).[152] Now, the Netherlands both profited from this arrangement and fell for it. Turns out that the encrypted phones it bought for special police units contained the backdoored Crypto AG chips as well.[153] Meanwhile, to further ascertain that adversaries would only use weak encryption, the West simultaneously restricted the export of encryption technologies to the Eastern bloc via COCOM. This was not really a matter of public debate at that time: the spying was all done in secret, and since encryption was used mostly for military purposes, regulating the export of encryption was hardly controversial.

This changed in the 1970s, as two developments started to pose an existential threat to the global signal intelligence hegemony of the Five Eyes and its allies.[154] First, communications were increasingly transmitted in digital form, and digital information can be more easily encrypted. For instance, the Amsterdam-based company TextLite launched a consumer device for sending small texts with a strong encryption algorithm (DES) in 1980. The NSA responded by purchasing the entire stock of devices directly from TextLite, in effect taking it off the market, while at the same time persuading the company to weaken its encryption for future devices.[155] Second, important scientific breakthroughs in cryptography were increasingly made by researchers *outside* the NSA, and not all of them were willing to abide by the NSA's demands. For example, when scientists at IBM discovered a technique in the seventies to defend against differential cryptanalysis, a method the NSA likely was already using to decrypt messages, the NSA could still just have the documents removed from the public domain. "We […] locked them up in safes, because they

---

[150] Miller 2020; another Swiss cryptography firm, Omnisec, is also alleged to have backdoored its technology at the request of the US; Editor 2021, Entry on Omnisec. Crypto Museum. https://www.cryptomuseum.com/manuf/omnisec/index.htm. Accessed 8 January 2021; SRF/jdp 2020.

[151] Jacobs 2020.

[152] Modderkolk 2020a.

[153] Jaspers et al. 2020.

[154] See on this Levy 2002.

[155] Metze 2014; Jaspers and Metze 2019.

were considered U.S. government classified. [The NSA] said do it. So I did it", one of the researchers said.[156] When Diffie and Hellmann published their groundbreaking discovery of public key encryption in 1976, things were different. The NSA's demand to their funder, the National Science Foundation, that future grants for encryption research needed prior approval fell on deaf ears.[157] What really shook the NSA to the core, though, was the advent of personal computing, combined with the internet, and with it the promise to put this power of unbreakable encryption in the hands of the masses.

3.3.1 The First Crypto Wars

The prospect of encryption becoming widely used ignited the first "Crypto Wars"—a publicly fought battle raging from the 1990s until the end of the millennium. On the surface, this was about the ability of ordinary citizens to have access to strong encryption, just as the Western military had had for decades. For some, it was also about the role of government in the nascent information society. On one side stood law enforcement and intelligence agencies, fearing that a vital tool in their toolbox was about to disappear. These agencies came from a world of virtually unfettered access where intercepting communications was a matter of tapping into real wires. They wanted to maintain this status quo: encryption was fine, as long as it could be broken when necessary. Part of this plan involved outlawing strong crypto, replacing it with deliberately weakened crypto, just as they had done in the past. But since strong encryption could now also be applied by domestic criminals, this required restricting not only its *export* but also its domestic *use*.

On the other side stood an eclectic collection of opponents. These ranged from self-styled "cypherpunks", libertarians who believed that encryption would finally herald an age of independence from government, to privacy activists, who feared that without encryption it would be impossible to keep things private online; from academics, who feared their information security research would be affected, to financial corporations, who needed confidentiality and integrity to support the burgeoning world of online transactions and e-commerce. What bound these groups together, was the conviction that weak encryption perhaps had sufficed in an analogue world but was not going to work in a world where everything was digitised and sent through networks around the globe.

Confronted with the prospect that domestic communications could become impenetrable, Joe Biden, then a US senator, introduced a bill in 1991 which required communication and equipment providers to ensure that government can always access the "plaintext contents of voice, data, and other communications"—a proto-backdoor.[158] Phil Zimmermann, a software developer involved in anti-nuclear

---

[156] Levy 2002, Chap. 4.

[157] Ibid., Chap. 6; Diffie and Landau 2007, pp. 71–72.

[158] Levy 2002, p. 236.

activism, was at that time working on a personal project called Pretty Good Privacy (PGP). He wanted to develop strong encryption software for use by the general public. Biden's proposal spurred Zimmermann to finish his project before the bill could be adopted. With the help of others, Zimmermann distributed the software for free via an online forum of peace activists, on the first weekend of June 1991.[159] In explaining why he developed PGP, Zimmermann writes how the information revolution leads to "a disturbing erosion of privacy", concluding that the "only way to hold the line on privacy in the information age is strong cryptography".[160] Biden's bill never became law, but Zimmermann did become the suspect in a criminal investigation for illegally exporting strong cryptography.[161]

The release of PGP was a strong symbol, but its reach was initially limited to tech-savvy activists. However, companies with a larger user base were also joining the movement. The inventors of the first practical implementation of public-key encryption, Rivest, Shamir and Adleman, had founded a company called RSA offering encryption modules for incorporation in other software. Netscape, the dominant browser at that time, started shipping public key encryption in the mid-nineties to support e-commerce transactions, and IBM started offering strong encryption in its popular office suite Lotus Notes.

These developments set off a string of protracted policy battles, in courts and parliaments throughout the world. In the US, the Clinton administration imposed a maximum on the key length—and thus the strength—of encryption technologies for export and proposed a backdoored standard for domestic phone calls. Cryptographers, engineers and academics quickly challenged the existing export regulations, and started lobbying against the backdoor proposal.[162] Other countries witnessed similar scenes. In France, for instance, legislation was adopted in the mid-nineties which only allowed the use of encryption technologies where the encryption keys are submitted to a third party, and which the government could then request when necessary.[163] Other countries, such as the UK, Germany and the Netherlands considered

[159] Singh, 2000, p. 609; Zimmermann 1996.

[160] Zimmermann 1991, 1996.

[161] The offending passage was removed in August 1991 after opposition from the Electronic Frontier Foundation, together with the Computer Professionals for Social Responsibility and other industry groups; Barlow 1992; Levy 2002, p. 356; Markoff 1996. The case was eventually dropped, presumably because MIT Press at the same time started globally distributing a 600-page book containing the source code of PGP, and the Department of Justice did not dare going after MIT, and didn't want to be seen as inconsistent; Diffie and Landau 2007, p. 230.

[162] Cryptographer Daniel Bernstein in 1992 started a court case because he wanted to share his cryptographic algorithms with academics outside of the US; engineer Philip Karn started a court case because he couldn't export Bruce Schneier's *Applied Cryptography* on disk; and university professor Junger wanted to publish information about encryption software on his website; 9th Cir., Bernstein v U.S. Dept. of Justice, Judgment of 6 May 1999, 176 F.3d 1132; D.D.C., Karn v U.S. Dept. of State, Judgment of 22 March 1996, 925 F.Supp. 1; 6th Cir., Junger v. Daley, Judgment of 4 April 2000, 209 F.3d 481. See for the failed initiative from the United States to push for an encrypted phone communications standard called the Clipper Chip; Levy 1994; Froomkin 1996; Blaze 2011.

[163] See Koops 1999, Chap. 5.3.3; and Koops 2013 on France.

doing the same, sparking a serious outcry from banks and NGOs.[164] The European Commission proposed introducing regulation on encryption in 1997, following up on policy guidelines from the OECD, which also emphasised the negative impact on global trade and economic development which encryption regulations may have.[165]

3.3.2 The Risks of Lawful and Unlawful Access

Crypto-proponents had two main objections against restrictions of encryption technologies. The first argument was fundamental. It had to do with *lawful access*: if a government can gain access to encrypted information, this undermines the promise of strong encryption to put access control in the hands of the user. For those with a libertarian streak, the possibility that a government could access encrypted data was already a showstopper: "*You can have my encryption algorithm [...] when you pry my cold dead fingers from its private key*".[166] However, the policy debate centred largely around the risk of *unlawful access*.

If you impose maximum key lengths or mandate weak algorithms, you make the encryption easier to break for law enforcement and intelligence agencies. But not only the governments imposing these regulations have advanced code-breaking capabilities. In order to break these ciphers, you just need to throw enough computing power at them or, in the case of a backdoor, have enough smart people study the algorithm long enough. Various intelligence agencies around the globe have those resources in full supply. So you should assume that other countries will also try to break the ciphers, stealing business secrets, listening on exiled dissidents and blackmailing politicians. What is more: even organised crime might muster the resources to decrypt messages, for instance to divert financial transactions to their own bank accounts. And even if a weakened cipher cannot be broken now, Moore's law suggests that it will be broken in the future, as the computational costs of brute-force attacks drop—which will make the communications more vulnerable in the future.[167]

These risks of unlawful access are also present for the alternative approach proposed at that time: submitting keys or parts of the key with a third party, or *key escrow*.[168] Crypto-proponents warned that such a central key repository would become a highly attractive target for attackers, with both trusted insiders abusing their position and outsiders breaking in. Moreover, incorporating this requirement in encryption systems would make them significantly more complex, increasing the costs and more importantly, potentially introducing additional vulnerabilities. Case in

164 See Koops 2013 on the United Kingdom, Germany and the Netherlands.

165 European Commission 1997; OECD 1997.

166 Barlow 1992.

167 For example, ciphers which the NSA deemed safe for export during the nineties can now be easily broken, yet browsers can still be forced to use these ciphers; Peterson 2015; Heninger and Halderman 2016; Möller et al. 2014.

168 Abelson et al. 1997.

point: some of the more advanced messaging algorithms employ *forward secrecy*—encrypting each message with a different key. This added layer of security ensures that even if an attacker breaks one message, the entire set of messages will not be cracked. It is generally impossible to retain this functionality while also ensuring that a government can access a master key—unless you covertly add the government as a participant to the conversation, something which GCHQ has proposed and which will be discussed further below.

A final argument which was raised, is that even if you restrict the spread of encryption, those who want to use it will get their hands on it anyway, especially in the age of the internet. Law-abiding citizens would then be forced to use weak versions of encryption technologies, whereas terrorists and criminals would use the strong version, regardless of the law—"if you outlaw encryption, only outlaws will have encryption".

These battles continued throughout the nineties and have been described elsewhere in gripping detail.[169] It is difficult to say which arguments carried the day, but at the end of the millennium, after years of Crypto Wars, proponents of strong encryption claimed victory.[170] The White House announced a relaxation of crypto export regulations in 1999, and it had already dropped its proposal for a domestic backdoored communications standard.[171] The 9 Circuit Court of Appeals handed down an important ruling that same year on a First Amendment challenge to these regulations.[172] Across the Atlantic, the UK shelved plans for a key escrow-requirement in 1999.[173] That same year, Germany announced that it would support the use of encryption and would not limit its availability.[174] And the French prime minister also around that time that the country would liberalise encryption policies.[175] "*It was official*", Levy summarised the prevailing sentiment at the time, "*public crypto was our friend*".[176] FIPR, a UK-digital rights group, was more cautious, but six years later, in 2005, they also claimed victory: "*The 'crypto wars' are finally over—and we've won!*"[177] But was this enthousiasm warranted? To some extent: yes, as we will see.

---

[169] See Levy 2002; Diffie and Landau 2007. See for a description of the European situation also Koops and Kosta 2018.

[170] See Diffie and Landau 2007, p. 257.

[171] White House 1999; Levy 1994; Froomkin 1996; Blaze 2011.

[172] Bernstein v. U.S. Dept. of Justice, 176 F.3d 1132 (9th Cir.1999). The case was later reheard *en banc*; see also McClure 1999.

[173] BBC News 1999.

[174] See German Government 1999; discussed in Acharya et al. 2017.

[175] Koops 2013; and Latrive 1999.

[176] Levy 2002.

[177] FIPR 2005.

3.3.3 *Regulatory Approaches in* Support *of Encryption*

European policymakers have embraced encryption as an important technology to safeguard information security since the start of the new millennium.[178] The encryption of personal data is explicitly listed as a required security measure under the GDPR.[179] Furthermore, under the ePrivacy rules, communication providers are required to inform users how they can protect the security of their communications, mentioning encryption technologies specifically.[180] Under the European Electronic Communications Code (EECC) communication providers must apply encryption where appropriate and promote encryption to its users.[181] The NIS 2 Directive also mentions encryption explicitly as one of the security measures which need to be taken.[182]

Encryption technologies furthermore have a prominent place in information security standards, which could partly be considered an implementation of these rules. For example, the international standard for securing creditcard information, PCI DSS, prescribes encryption as a way to prevent unauthorised access to information.[183] And the widely applied information security standard ISO 27001 also addresses the use of cryptography to protect confidentiality, authenticity and integrity of information.[184]

---

[178] Important to note, is that all these regulations do not provide guidance on the particular *kind* of encryption which should be applied, and the assessment *whether* encryption should be applied is a risk-based analysis. This is why I consider these regulations to *support*, not restrict encryption. Other regulations described below also prescribe the use of encryption, but mandate specific encryption technologies. This carries the risk of introducing mandatory backdoors, as a result *restricting* encryption.

[179] (2016) Regulation 2016/679 of the European Parliament and of the Council of 27 April 2016 on the protection of natural persons with regard to the processing of personal data and on the free movement of such data, and repealing Directive 95/46/EC (General Data Protection Regulation), Article 32(1)(a); see also recital 83; In assessing the compatibility of further processing, encryption is explicitly mentioned as one of the safeguards; ibid., Article 6(4)(e); And the application of encryption can also lead to the conclusion that an individual does not have to be notified of a data breach; ibid., Article 34(3)(a); see further the recommendations by ENISA in 2013 on cryptographic measures; ENISA 2013a, b; lastly, see EDPB 2020a, b.

[180] (2002) Directive 2002/58/EC of the European Parliament and of the Council of 12 July 2002 concerning the processing of personal data and the protection of privacy in the electronic communications sector as Amended by Directive 2006/24/EC and Directive 2009/136/EC, recital 20.

[181] (2018) Directive 2018/1972 of the European Parliament and of the Council of 11 December 2018 establishing the European Electronic Communications Code (Recast), Article 40(1), recitals 96 and 97.

[182] (2022a) Directive (EU) 2022/2555 of the European Parliament and of the Council of 14 December 2022 on Measures for a High Common Level of Cybersecurity Across the Union, Amending Regulation (EU) No 910/2014 and Directive (EU) 2018/1972, and Repealing Directive (EU) 2016/1148 (NIS 2 Directive), Article 21(2)(h).

[183] See PCI Security Standards Council, Payment Card Industry Data Security Standard 4.0, March 2022.

[184] See ISO, "ISO/IEC 27001:2013: Information Technology—Security Techniques—Information Security Management Systems—Requirements", ISO/IEC 2013.

EU policymakers have in the past also taken a public stance in favour of encryption. Germany (since 1999) and the Netherlands (since 2016) have moved to a principled position, promising that there will be no ban or limitation on encryption products.[185] Similarly, the European Commission, European Parliament, Council and other administrative bodies have in non-legislative documents taken a pro-encryption stance.[186] Some EU governments have even invested in the development of encryption technologies. The Dutch government has in the past donated EUR 1 million for the further development of open source encryption projects, such as OpenSSL—a symbolic amount, but still quite a powerful symbol.[187] And the European Commission and member states are investing in a host of encryption-related projects, including projects focused on developing post-quantum cryptographic techniques, quantum key distribution and homomorphic encryption.[188]

3.3.4 Regulatory Approaches **Restricting** *Encryption*

So, it was justified to a claim at least partial victory in the Crypto Wars, but it was too early to declare *total* victory. In particular, US and UK efforts to undermine encryption did not end with the Crypto Wars. On the contrary, American and British agencies doubled down. While they publicly feigned defeat, the NSA (under the Bullrun project) and GCHQ (under the Edgehill project) had been secretly weakening the effectiveness of widely used encryption technologies all along, running projects involving tens of thousands of people, with annual budgets exceeding a quarter of a billion dollars.[189] According to GCHQ in a leaked 2010 memo, the NSA

[185] Herpig and Heumann 2019, p. 1; Dutch government 2016, Kabinetsstandpunt Encryptie, p. 2; see for an analysis of the Dutch position Veen and Boeke 2020.

[186] See for the European Commission; European Commission and High Representative of the Union for Foreign Affairs and Security Policy 2017; European Commission 2017, p. 9; Hill 2017; for the European Parliament (2017) Resolution of 14 March 2017 on fundamental rights implications of big data: privacy, data protection, non-discrimination, security and law-enforcement, recital 16; and European Parliament (2017) Resolution of 3 October 2017 on the fight against cybercrime, recitals 30, 51; see for the Council Council of Ministers 2017.

[187] K. Verhoeven, Gewijzigd amendement van het lid Verhoeven ter vervanging van dat gedrukt onder nr. 14, 2015; K. Verhoeven en A. Kuiken, Gewijzigd amendement van de leden Verhoeven en Kuiken ter vervanging van dat gedrukt onder nr. 31, 2017.

[188] See for an overview of past and currently running projects the CORDIS website of the European Commission.

[189] See Perlroth et al. 2013; Ball et al. 2013; Larson 2013; see Kuner 2014 for a later assessment; see Bamford 2012 for an early scoop; see further Perlroth 2013a; Gellman and Miller 2013; Poulsen 2013. While this section discusses the NSA' and GCHQ's attempts to weaken encryption technologies, this does not imply that the NSA and GCHQ are the *only* countries doing so. It is quite likely that other countries running significant offensive cybersecurity operations, such as China, Russia and Israel, do the same. For example, a proposal for a Russian encryption standard is also suspected to be intentionally flawed; Cox 2019; moreover, there are also examples of the NSA sharing a vulnerability with vendors to fix it instead of using it for offensive purposes, such as with a major flaw in the Windows operating system in 2020; see Nakashima 2020.

in the past decades "has lead [sic] an aggressive, multi-pronged effort to break widely used Internet encryption technologies", and as a result, "[v]ast amounts of encrypted Internet data which have up till now been discarded are now exploitable".[190] For example, the NSA has been able to exploit key encryption technologies, such as SSL/TLS, SSH, IPSEC, PPTP, VPNs and VoIP. It also expected to shape "the world-wide commercial cryptography marketplace to make it more tractable to advanced cryptanalytic capabilities being developed by NSA/CSS". The GCHQ analysts who were present at the NSA presentation were "gobsmacked!"[191]

The NSA achieved part of these "breakthroughs" through hacking, tampering with hardware in transit to a customer, industry relationships, collaboration with other intelligence agencies and "advanced mathematical techniques".[192] One manufacturer, when asked to do so by the NSA, inserted a backdoor into new computer hardware for a foreign intelligence target before it was shipped.[193] Some companies have also been asked to hand the US government the encryption keys to all customer communications. The NSA even maintains an internal database of encryption keys for specific commercial products, which can automatically decode messages—and if a key is not available, a request goes to the "Key Provisioning Service", which tries to obtain it.[194]

The NSA also achieved these feats by undermining encryption standards, and in one case the agency's efforts are well-documented: those which were directed at the Dual Elliptic Curve Deterministic Random Bit Generator (Dual EC DRBG).[195] This standard was suspected as early as 2006 to contain a backdoor.[196] This standard plays an important role in certain encryption algorithms, and was drafted under the auspices of the US standardisation institute, NIST. In response to allegations of NSA meddling, NIST stated that it would "not deliberately weaken a cryptographic standard", but it simultaneously recommended people to not use the standard due to security concerns.[197] By then, however, the damage had already been done, and after this disclosure, further evidence came to the surface that this standard was compromised. In particular, security company RSA had, in 2004, already received USD 10 million from the NSA to set Dual EC DRBG as the default method for generating random numbers in its widely-used BSAFE crypto library (according to

[190] GCHQ, Presentation on Bullrun 2010; see further Poulsen 2013.

[191] Larson 2013.

[192] NSA 2010a, b.

[193] Perlroth et al. 2013; Greenwald 2014; NSA 2010a, b.

[194] See Perlroth 2013a; Perlroth et al. 2013.

[195] See for an excellent overview Bernstein et al. 2016. The Guardian and the Times in 2013 reported that the NSA "worked covertly to get its own version of a draft security standard issued by the US National Institute of Standards and Technology approved for worldwide use in 2006" and that the NSA's document stated: "Eventually, NSA became the sole editor"; Ball et al. 2013. The Times quotes from a memo of the NSA saying that developing the standard "was a challenge in finesse"; Perlroth 2013b; see for the standard NIST 2006.

[196] Schoenmakers and Sidorenko 2006; Brown and Gjøsteen 2007; Shumow and Ferguson 2007; Schneier 2007.

[197] NIST 2013a, b.

Reuters). Researchers then quickly confirmed that *dragnet* and *targeted* surveillance of traffic encrypted with the BSAFE TLS implementation of Dual EC DRBG was possible.[198] Router manufacturer Juniper, who was also using the flawed random number generator, had, after the discovery, tried to defang its vulnerability by setting the parameters to acceptable values. However, they later found out (in 2015) that they were inadvertently shipping code where the parameters were again reverted by an unknown party—possibly the NSA—to again enable the decryption of VPN-traffic.[199]

Parallel to these attempts to attack encryption through interference with standard setting, goverments also decrypt information through *brute-force attacks*, with extensive amounts of computing power. In 2020, EuroPol and the European Commission launched together a new decryption platform, as a result of an investment from the European Commission in decryption capabilities.[200] Little is known about the effectiveness of the platform—but it is reported that it is already being used by EU law enforcement authorities for device decryption, not communications decryption.[201] We know the US is also running large decryption operations. Of course, one of the drivers behind the development of quantum computers is to actually break encryption.

Lastly, governments have attacked parts of the system in which encryption technologies are embedded. Dutch law enforcement revealed in 2020 that it was able to intercept over 20 million encrypted chat messages, between suspects, sometimes in real time, because it had been able to infiltrate an encrypted chat service provider that was popular with criminals, EncroChat.[202] Criminals then switched to encrypted communications service Sky ECC, and judicial authorities in Belgium, France and the Netherlands started monitoring that service.[203] After that service was shut down, the FBI, DEA, Dutch police and the Swedish police together with 16 other countries developed and covertly operated their own encrypted communications company, to ensure that criminals would switch to a service they could monitor.[204] The authorities listened in on 12,000 encrypted devices used by over 300 criminal groups. The Dutch head of criminal investigations told the press that other communication means will also be disrupted, "like chess, you have to think several moves ahead to win", he boasted.[205]

---

198 Menn 2013; Checkoway et al. 2014. Shortly after the reports about the Dual EC DRBG containing a backdoor, RSA recommended customers to stop using it as a random number generator; Goodin 2013.

199 Checkoway et al. 2018; Green 2015; Weinmann 2015; later the NSA declined to confirm that it was involved; Menn 2020.

200 European Commission 2017, p. 9.

201 Stolton 2021.

202 Openbaar Ministerie 2020b; Modderkolk 2020b. Before, it had already infiltrated encrypted messaging services Ennetcom and Ironchat; van den Heuvel and van Wely 2019; NOS 2019.

203 Eurojust 2021.

204 Europol 2021; Graaf 2021.

205 Graaf 2021.

These activities obviously have a relation to human rights, something which we will explore in the chapters to come. One question is whether authorities are acting within their competence when doing these things. A more interesting question for our purposes, however, is whether these measures can under certain circumstances be considered proportionate. I explore this further in Chaps. 9 and 10.

3.3.5 The Second Crypto Wars

Perhaps, the Crypto Wars weren't won after all—governments had simply moved to fight on a different front while nobody was looking. Only after the revelations of Snowden did we learn to a certain extent what was happening at that other battlefield. And partly in response to the Snowden revelations, encryption is now applied increasingly *by default*. Apple, Google and Microsoft have begun to apply strong encryption in their operating systems for laptops and smartphones, and the most popular messaging services are applying end-to-end encryption to communications as well.[206]

This shift to encryption *by default* has changed the encryption landscape massively. Before only expert users actively turned on the encryption in their device, which meant that for most devices, information remained accessible by intelligence agencies and law enforcement, as well as determined criminal organisations. Granted, users had been able to encrypt their mail since the development of PGP, if they wanted to, but this required a deliberate choice and serious technical chops from both the sender and the recipient, so few people actually did it. Meanwhile, the most popular alternative communication channels were insecure by default: SMS-messages are plaintext, older mobile phone encryption is so weak it can be broken by the NSA (and possibly deliberately so), and TLS/SSL-certificates can be easily forged if you control a trusted certificate authority.[207] Now, as more users are communicating via these new messaging services, such as WhatsApp and Signal, law enforcement and intelligence agencies are signaling that this particular information source is drying up.

In response to this shift, the regulatory tides in the US and the EU are turning as well. Some even claim that we are in the midst of the Second Crypto Wars.[208] Institutions on both sides of the Atlantic are again pushing for new restrictions on encryption.

This change can be seen at the EU level, where several institutions are now moving in this direction. Most notably, the German Council Presidency in its 2020-memo on encryption sums up their position nicely: "security through encryption and security despite encryption".[209] The Council then in 2021 called on member states to "support

[206] See on Signal Veen and Boeke 2020.

[207] Reaves et al. 2018; Green 2013; Timberg and Soltani 2013; Pannu et al. 2015; Huang et al. 2014.

[208] See Koops and Kosta 2018; and Landau 2017 for a similar history.

[209] Presidency of the Council of Ministers 2020.

and contribute to the Commission's efforts in the process of identifying options for the way forward on encryption", and invited the Commission to "regularly inform delegations about possible next steps on encryption".[210] At a meeting at Europol in 2022, it was suggested that encryption could be circumvented through the "temporary retention of [software or hardware] vulnerabilities and their exploitation by the relevant authorities".[211]

This change can also be seen at the national level. France and Germany in 2017 in a joint letter to the European Commission called for new powers to deal with encrypted communications.[212] It was also announced in the media in May 2019 that the German Ministry of Interior Affairs was contemplating legislation which would oblige messenger services such as WhatsApp to provide plaintext communications on the basis of a court order, departing from its earlier hands-off approach with regard to encryption.[213] Simultaneously, there have been Dutch plans to limit encryption, although they do not appear to gain sufficient political traction.[214] And the UK has been publicly pushing for regulating encryption for some time already. The UK's former prime minister May over the course of 2017 and 2018 repeatedly stressed the importance of lawful access to encrypted content.[215] Meanwhile, across the Atlantic, the US Department of Justice has also pushed for limits on encryption in recent years. In particular, the department under Trump had asked Facebook to not roll out encryption, told Apple that it should create possibilities for law enforcement to gain access to its phones and tablets and proposed to create liability for providers who do not filter images of child sexual abuse—which would in effect prevent the application of encryption.[216]

Lawmakers this time around still want to gain access to encrypted information when necessary, but, in order to avoid the pitfalls of the first Crypto Wars, these measures may not weaken security of the encryption, for example through backdoors. Policymakers have suggested three approaches which ostensibly tackle the dilemma of gaining access while not affecting encryption. Two are directed at encrypted *communications*. The third approach is proposed to tackle device encryption.

---

[210] Presidency of the Council of the European Union 2021.

[211] Statewatch 3 October 2022, EU: Discussion on encryption ponders "retention of vulnerabilities and exploitation by the authorities". See also Monroy 2022.

[212] French Government and German Government 2017.

[213] Diehl et al. 2019; see for the background on the encryption debate in Germany Herpig and Heumann. A spokesman for the Ministry after heavy outcry suggested that this is merely under consideration, stressing that providers need to be able to determine how they encrypt communications as a rule, and that governmental access should be considered the exception; Holland 2019.

[214] Modderkolk 2020c.

[215] See for an overview of the UK's calls Hern 2018. This is relevant, because it one year before already adopted far-reaching legislation obliging communication providers to assist in granting access to encrypted information.

[216] Rosenstein 2017; FBI 2018, Going Dark. https://www.fbi.gov/services/operational-technology/going-dark. Accessed 30 November 2018; Savage 2018a; Geller 2019; Barr 2019; McCabe et al. 2019; BBC News 2020; Green 2020; Pfefferkorn 2020.

GCHQ has proposed changing the software of messaging applications in order to allow government actors to be covertly added to a chat.[217] Covertly adding a party to a conversation requires the co-operation of the service provider in two ways. First, the service provider would have to *add* a participant to the conversation. Second, the proposal would require providers to change their software, so that other users will not know when this participant joins the chat. By doing this, they argue, you do not have to weaken the encryption algorithm or store keys with a third party.

A second approach, which has been suggested in the fight against images of child sexual abuse, is to monitor communications on the device, e.g. *before the data is encrypted and transmitted to the other device*, in order to detect, block and possibly report illegal material (this is called *client-side scanning*, CSS).[218] This would also require the co-operation of the service provider, which would have to upload new functionality in software to do the monitoring, and more importantly, have to send regular updates of monitoring lists.

The third approach, focusing on device encryption, is to have organisations such as Apple and Microsoft store decryption keys with which the information can be decrypted when necessary.[219] This decryption key could for example be stored with the service provider, only to be provided when law enforcement can prove that it has the device in its possession.

The question is whether these new solutions are compatible with human rights. I discuss this further in Chap. 9. However, here I will discuss the relevant arguments in a way that can be weighed in the human rights assessment which follows. One central aspect of a human rights analysis of these proposals revolves around the risk of unlawful access and lawful access.[220] If you compare these proposals to the earlier ones which focused on the effectiveness of encryption *technologies*, these fare better when it comes to preventing unlawful access by organised crime. This is because the encryption *algorithm* is not undermined: if organised crime organisations intercept encrypted communications or obtain an encrypted device, they cannot decrypt it, at least not without co-operation of the service provider or device manufacturer.

What all these solutions have in common, however, is that they still introduce a certain risk of unlawful access. These solutions all create a new angle of attack—namely the channels intended for providing lawful access. There is a risk that these will be exploited by adversaries, particularly by intelligence agencies. If you create the possibility of silently adding people to a conversation, there is a chance that attackers will also add their participants to a conversation. If you develop the option

---

[217] Levy 2018b.

[218] See (2022c) Proposal for a Regulation of the European Parliament and of the Council laying down rules to prevent and combat child sexual abuse; and the analysis in van Daalen 2023a, b.

[219] See for example the CLEAR proposal of Ray Ozzie; Ozzie 2017; Levy 2018c; and Steven Savage's proposal; Savage 2018b.

[220] See for a discussion of the GCHQ proposal; Open Technology Institute 2019; see also Schneier 2019b; Landau 2018a; Green 2018a; Hoepman 2019; and Cardozo and Schoen 2019 for a critical discussion; see for a discussion of CSS Abelson et al. 2021; Rosenzweig 2020; Portnoy 2019. See for a discussion of the CLEAR proposal; Bellovin et al. 2018; Green 2018b; Landau 2018b; Tromer 2018.

to monitor conversations before encryption, there is a chance that attackers will also monitor these conversation. If you store device encryption keys with one provider, attackers might attack this storage. Of course, governments could take measures to minimise this risk by distributing the way in which these powers can be effectuated. For example, in those cases where using these powers depends on particular keys, these keys could be distributed across different repositories, making it more difficult to hack all of them (this is called *secret sharing*).

Still, it is uncertain whether these measures would be sufficient, as some fears from the first Crypto Wars have been borne out. Altering software to allow governments around the world to decrypt information is highly complex, and unavoidably introduces new vulnerabilities. While this concern was mostly theoretical during the first Crypto Wars, a vibrant market for weaknesses has now grown. And, just as it was argued that a central key repository is highly attractive to hackers, so too is a centralised way to gain access through other means an enticing attack avenue. We have meanwhile seen that the objections to central storage points were not purely theoretical: for instance, French SIM card provider Gemalto was hacked by the NSA and GCHQ between 2010 and 2011 to obtain millions of secret GSM keys, Dutch certificate provider Diginotar was hacked in 2012 by an intelligence agency to forge SSL certificates and RSA was hacked by Chinese spies who obtained millions of seeds used to create authentication tokens.[221] Silently pushing new software updates—required for the GCHQ proposal—adds to this risk. And if an intelligence agency from a political opponent has secretly hacked an updating system, you can rest assured they will also use this option to gain access to their victim's devices.

If governments resort to scanning messages *before* encryption instead of subverting to encryption algorithms, this would significantly expand the potential for unlawful access. If you can scan a device, instead of mere communications, you have access to much more data.[222] It also much easier to build in access for persons other than law enforcement and intelligence agencies: Apple in its client-side scanner also provides the option for parents to be informed when their child is sending pictures of nudes.[223]

The proposals aimed at changing the software on the device not only have a direct effect on the confidentiality of information encrypted by users—they also have an effect on the trust in the digital infrastructure in general, as well as in the trust in updating procedures.[224] When users cannot trust systems to effectively protect their information against unlawful access, this could have a chilling effect on the use of those systems.[225]

---

[221] Scahill and Begley 2015; Fox-IT; Greenberg 2021.

[222] See for a thorough evaluation Abelson et al. 2021; see for an earlier analysis Rosenzweig 2020.

[223] Apple 2021.

[224] See Encryption Working Group, branch 4 to that effect.

[225] Susan Landau points to a case study where erroneous reporting on potential flaws in the WhatsApp authentication system by The Guardian affected trust in the service—prompting users to consider less-secure alternatives; see Landau 2018a; Chadwick 2017. The signatories to the letter on GCHQ's ghosting proposal further point to a study from the encryption working group of the

Meanwhile the issues relating to *lawful access* have become more complex, because encryption technologies are incorporated in communication services and operating systems which are available globally. If you give governments access to encrypted information, the question is: which governments? Only the US and the EU? That would ensure an encryption standard is dead on arrival. So also China and Saudi-Arabia? That could lead to Uyghur or Saudi dissidents being dead on arrival at their local consulate. Both the Chinese and Saudi regimes already hack the devices of their targets, so it's a fair question to ask. This analysis not only applies to encrypted communications or devices; it also applies to client-side scanning, which works with lists of prohibited material—who is going to determine what is considered prohibited, who is going to keep the list updated, and which governments are informed when this material is found on a device? Moreover, it is trivially easy to expand the list—first child sexual abuse material, then terrorist content, but what then?[226] I explore the human rights implications of the difficulty in arranging a globally applicable lawful access framework in Chap. 9.

In addition, the *need* to regulate encryption technologies is unclear at best. As mentioned above, the police has over the past few years covertly entered multiple encrypted communications providers who had criminals as their customers.[227] This allowed the police to intercept valuable evidence in a number of cases. As long as criminals continue using these vulnerable services, the police will have access to more evidence, not less, due to misplaced trust in weak encryption. Moreover, the police has a host of other powerful tools at their disposal. These include remotely accessing servers, which they used to access information in several high-profile cases, as well as the authority to order the disclosure of decryption keys under certain circumstances.[228] These powers also include the possibility of accessing non-encrypted data—a resource which is growing by the day.

Lastly, the argument that *only outlaws will have strong crypto* still rings true, although it has shifted shape. Everyone—law-abiding citizen and criminal alike—has become reliant on a small group of hardware, software and service providers for many encryption technologies. Microsoft, Apple and Google apply device encryption. WhatsApp, Signal and Apple apply end-to-end encryption. Due to this centralised application of encryption, it will now be easier to covertly undermine these technologies at scale. At the same time, the increased globalisation of messaging services means there is a plethora of different encryption services around the world, all competing for customers, and presumably not all subject to the same encryption rules. So if criminals do not trust a service, there are plenty of alternatives. Meanwhile,

---

Obama administration, which noted that—in the context of operating systems—gaining remote access to devices through software updates "could call into question the trustworthiness of established software update channels", and could lead users, "concerned about remote access to their device", to "choose to turn off software updates, rendering their devices significantly less secure as time passed"; see the draft report referred to in Peterson and Nakashima 2015.

[226] Abelson et al. 2021, p. 21.

[227] See for example Andringa 2020; van den Heuvel and van Wely 2019.

[228] Sullivan and Satter 2019; AFP 2019; Redactie 2011; see on decryption orders Koops 2012.

the importance of encryption for ordinary citizens, governments and commerce has only grown, as we've discussed.

What this means for the human rights-compatibility of these new proposals will be discussed in Chap. 9.

3.3.6 Subconclusion

The story of encryption is the story of a military technology which from the 1980s onwards spread to the public at large and with it came the promise of a shift in power—the power to prevent access to information. For crypto proponents, this power was deemed a necessity in a developed world. But for agencies, this power also prevented access to their targets. In response, governments around the world between 1990 and 2000 frantically tried to stem the spread of strong encryption, even as the technology was being tightly integrated into our digital lives.

While the technology diffused into the civilian domain, the government response still bore the marks of its military roots: governments picked the most familiar tool in their toolbox, export restrictions, and complemented it with restrictions on domestic use. But this approach did not fit well with the new world, where the most important research and development is performed by maverick cryptographers outside of intelligence agencies, with no allegiance to governments, where encryption technologies could be easily shared on the internet, and where the economic need for strong encryption was now undeniable. Around 2000, the EU and US eventually backed off, abolishing restrictions on strong encryption for civilian use.

Or so it seemed. We have since learned that the US and UK had simply shifted their efforts to subverting important encryption technologies, something they had already been doing for decades. The only difference is that during the Cold War, encryption affected solely the military domain, whereas nowadays, it impacts the phones, laptops, and internet of everyone, while the importance of strong information security has only grown. Here again, the military mindset is on full display: secret, brazen operations with apparently very little concern for their wider impact.

Now, the dispersion of encryption has again entered a new phase. Governments are no longer concerned about encryption technologies making the jump from the military to the civilian domain—that ship has long sailed. They *are* concerned, however, about the application of strong encryption *by default* in consumer products and services. The makers of such devices and services—Apple, Google, Microsoft and Facebook—are today the focus of regulatory attention.

This new regulatory attention, however, is much like the old regulatory attention: governments may not want to weaken encryption or introduce a backdoor, but the new proposals carry similar risks. The introduction of a possibility to gain lawful access can be hacked, the added complexity may introduce new vulnerabilities, and the trust in updating mechanisms will be undermined. The need for such measures is unclear at best, and the effectiveness is disputed. Meanwhile, it is difficult to create a globally applicable lawful access framework. I discuss in Chap. 9 what this means for encryption governance.

There are also developments in the other direction as strong information security becomes more important, there are signs that governments are pushing for stronger encryption. EU rules promote the application of strong encryption in certain cases, and some countries are investing in the development of strong encryption. How this relates to human rights obligations will be further discussed in Chap. 9.

Now, as I've explained in the previous chapter, the effectiveness of encryption technologies depends partly on the future development of quantum computers. The question thus is, what the governance for this domain looks like. That is the topic of the next section.

3.4 Governance of Quantum Computing

From a regulatory perspective, quantum computers are at least two things: they are *powerful*, and they can be used for general as well as *military purposes* (which include surveillance by intelligence agencies). But they are also young. One measure used to determine the maturity of a technology is the *technological readiness level*, a standard originally developed for space technologies, but since embraced for all kinds of domains.[229] As discussed, useful quantum computers are still decades away. As an example, one source estimates quantum computing technologies to be somewhere between TRL 1 and 5, on a scale of 1–10.[230] As a result there are few policies and practices focused on quantum computing.[231] But the governance approaches that do exist, deal with these two aspects: supporting the development of the power of quantum computing, while restricting the export and use of this power for military uses.

The development of powerful computers. As discussed there are many governmental funding initiatives for the development of quantum computing. At the European level, one project in particular is worth mentioning. The European Union adopted a Regulation establishing an institutional structure for the support, through funding and co-ordination, of high-performance computing (the EuroHPC Joint Undertaking), which puts a lot of emphasis on quantum computing.[232] And in February 2022, the European Commission launched an iniative to develop European development and production capability for chips. One of the objectives for the proposed *Chips Act* is to build advanced technology and engineering capacities

[229] Olechowski et al. 2015.

[230] Gerbert and Ruess, (2018), p. 15.

[231] See also Johnson 2019 which does not discuss any rules, even though this topic is the subject of the article; and Perrier 2021, which is light on actual rules.

[232] Council Regulation (EU) 2021/1173 of 13 July 2021 on establishing the European High Performance Computing Joint Undertaking and repealing Regulation (EU) 2018/1488 2021 (OJ L).

for accelerating the innovative development of quantum chips, mainly by removing administrative obstacles.[233] The European Commission has also proposed to reallocate additional funding to this initiative, part of which will presumably be spent on quantum computing-related investments. Of course, governance through funding can have profound effects for the development trajectory of a technology. We discuss potential funding avenues in Chap. 10.

Regulating export. Second, there are rules restricting the export of some of the building blocks of quantum computers for military use. The European regulation implementing the Wassenaar Arrangement for instance regulates the export of superconducting digital circuits and Helium 3, both of which are necessary for quantum computers.[234] And while these regulations also restrict the export of certain powerful "digital computers", quantum computers do not fall within this definition. Furthermore, the export regulations have an impact on the scientific development of quantum computers. It is to be expected that more export regulation in view of national security risks will be adopted in the coming years, focusing on "chokepoint"-technologies without which a quantum computer cannot work, such as cryogenic refrigerators and quantum chips. The implications for policy of this are discussed in Chap. 10.

Conditions on use. Lastly, it is interesting to note that the European Union uses its funding to impose conditions on the use of these computers. In the EuroHPC Regulation, the use of these computers shall be open to users from the public and private sectors and shall focus on civilian applications, but direct access may be granted for other purposes in cases of "health- or climate-related or other crucial emergency support services for the public good, to emergency and crisis management situations or to cases that the Union considers essential for its security and defence".[235] This is relevant, because as we have seen in, quantum computers can be used to break public key encryption, which obviously also has a military application, for example to break the confidential communications of non-EU governments. With this proposal, the European Commission explicitly opens the door to funding computers that can be used for such purposes. Given the human rights implications of such use, it might be necessary to impose further restrictions.

---

233 Proposal for a Regulation of the European Parliament and of the Council establishing a framework of measures for strengthening Europe's semiconductor ecosystem (Chips Act) 2022, Article 4(2)(c).

234 (2021) Regulation of the European Parliament and of the Council Setting up a Union Regime for the Control of Exports, Brokering, Technical Assistance, Transit and Transfer of Dual-Use Items (Recast), Annex 1, 1C232, 3A001.d and 3E003.

235 (2021b) Council Regulation (EU) 2021/1173 of 13 July 2021 on establishing the European High Performance Computing Joint Undertaking and repealing Regulation (EU) 2018/1488, Articles 16(1) and 17(9).

3.5 Summing Up

In the preceding chapter, I discussed the *technological landscape*: what happens in the field of information security, and what role do encryption technologies and quantum computing play? In this chapter, I discussed the *governance landscape*: how do governments approach these topics? A couple of things stand out.

Governance of the information security cycle is a result of a mix of different, often conflicting interests. In the measure taking-phase, the interests of data protection, consumer protection and infrastructure protection play important roles. In the research stage, the interests of intellectual property protection and crime prevention drive policy. Yet, the conflicting interests of information security research are not well reflected in governance of the information security cycle. Similarly, encryption technologies are caught between the competing interest of, on the one hand, national security and crime prevention (pushing for increased access), and, on the other hand, the interests of everyone else (pushing for increased protection). Meanwhile, the governance of quantum computing is primarily driven by national security interests (ensuring access by breaking encryption) and industrial policy considerations (spurring innovation).

These different interests lead to a patchwork of different and sometimes conflicting obligations in the governance of the information security cycle. A key insight is that information security cuts across a wide range of sectors, yet legislators historically approached it piecemeal, although this may be changing. Where there *is* sectoral information security regulation, this often reflects historical roots. In data protection regulation, there are still traces of the enterprise roots of mainframes processing personal data. Likewise, the ruthless undermining of encryption by intelligence agencies undoubtedly comes from its military roots, even though these encryption technologies are now squarely in the civilian domain.

Another insight is that the cyclical nature of information security is not ingrained in regulatory governance. Doing research and disclosing vulnerabilities is still fraught with legal uncertainty. Only recently are policymakers focusing overarching processes for ensuring that knowledge on vulnerabilities is fed back into the cycle, but there is no obligation by researchers to disclose vulnerabilities. And policymakers have difficulty dealing with the dual use-nature of information security tools. The question is to what extent human rights require that the offensive part of the information security cycle is placed on equal footing with the defensive part of the cycle. In the coming chapters, I will connect these considerations to the human rights to privacy, communications freedom and science.

A further observation has to do with the role of the *public interest* in information security. Information security governance does not always reflect public interest considerations. Protecting private consumer devices also benefits the security of critical infrastructure. Encryption governance is intended to retain access for governmental institutions to information in a digitised world, but the public interest in preventing unauthorised access should also be taken into account when devising policy. Technical protection measures are intended to assert full control over content in the face of networked copying machines, but the public interest in enjoying copyright exceptions should also be considered. In the coming chapters, I explore the extent to which the rights to privacy and communications freedom play a role in safeguarding the public interest in these governance measures.

The last insight concerns the *process* by which governance affecting information security is created. There are but few instances where information security experts have been involved in the information security lawmaking process from the outset. Most often the experts are outsiders, who are confronted with a new policy in the final stages of the legislative process. They then have to go to great lengths to ensure that this policy reflects the public interest in doing information security research. Involving information security experts early in the policy making process is therefore important. Fortunately, the development of governance with regard to quantum computing is in its early stages, so there is still ample room for incorporating insights. These are discussed in Chap. 10.

But before we get to these considerations, however, I develop the standard by evaluating the required governance response. This will be done in Chaps. 8–11. Firstly, the general human rights framework will be discussed and applied in Chap. 4.

References

Articles, Books and Other Documents

Abelson H, Anderson R, Bellovin SM et al. (2021) Bugs in our Pockets: The Risks of Client-Side Scanning. arXiv:211007450 [cs] 2021.

Abelson H, Anderson R, Bellovin SM et al. (1997) The Risks of Key Recovery, Key Escrow, and Trusted Third-Party Encryption, 27 May1997. https://doi.org/10.7916/D8GM8F2W

Acharya B, Bankston K, Schulman R, Wilson A (2017) Deciphering the European Encryption Debate: Germany. https://www.newamerica.org/oti/policy-papers/deciphering-european-encryption-debate-germany/. Accessed 4 January 2024.

Advisory Committee on Automated Personal Data Systems (1973) Records, Computers and the Rights of Citizens, 1 July 1973. https://www.justice.gov/opcl/docs/rec-com-rights.pdf. Accessed 4 January 2024.

AFP (2019) German Police Smash Child Porn Ring on Darknet.Deutsche Welle. https://www.dw.com/en/german-police-smash-child-porn-ring-on-darknet/a-50043833. Accessed 18 December 2019.

Aikins M (2012) Jamming Tripoli: Inside Moammar Gadhafi's Secret Surveillance Network. Wired, 18 May 2012.

Andringa R (2020) Al tientallen strafzaken na EncroChat-hack en het einde is nog niet in zicht. https://nos.nl/l/2361112. Accessed 8 January 2021.

Apple (2021) Expanded Protections for Children. Frequently Asked Questions. v1.1. https://www.apple.com/child-safety/pdf/Expanded_Protections_for_Children_Frequently_Asked_Questions.pdf. Accessed 15 October 2021.

Arnbak AM, Asghari H, Van Eeten M, Van Eijk N (2014) Security Collapse in the HTTPS Market. Communications of the ACM 57:47–55. https://doi.org/10.1145/2660574

Ball J, Borger J, Greenwald G (2013) Revealed: How US and UK Spy Agencies Defeat Internet Privacy and Security. The Guardian, 6 September 2013.

Bamford J (2012) The NSA Is Building the Country's Biggest Spy Center (Watch What You Say). Wired, 15 March 2012.

Barlow JP (1992) Decrypting the Puzzle Palace. https://www.eff.org/nl/pages/decrypting-puzzle-palace. Accessed 4 January 2024.

Barnes B (2019) The Streaming Era Has Finally Arrived. Everything Is About to Change. The New York Times, 19 November 2019.

Barr W (2019) Transcript of Speech on Encryption and Cybersecurity. Barr W (2019) Transcript of Speech on Encryption and Cybersecurity. Accessed 4 January 2024.

BBC News (1999) E-Commerce "Key" Plan Shelved. http://news.bbc.co.uk/2/hi/business/290902.stm. Accessed 30 November 2018.

BBC News (2020) Trump Launches Fresh Attack on Apple Over Privacy. BBC News, 14 January 2020.

Bellovin SM, Blaze M, Boneh D et al. (2018) Analysis of the CLEAR Protocol per the National Academies' Framework, CUCS-003-18, 10 May 2018.

Bernstein DJ, Lange T, Niederhagen R (2016) Dual EC: A Standardized Back Door. In: Ryan PYA, Naccache D, Quisquater J-J (eds) The New Codebreakers. Springer, Berlin, Heidelberg, pp 256–281.

Blaze M (2011) Key Escrow from a Safe Distance: Looking Back at the Clipper Chip. In: Proceedings of the 27th Annual Computer Security Applications Conference on - ACSAC '11. ACM Press, Orlando, Florida, p 317.

Bratus S, Arce I, Locasto ME, Zanero S (2014a) Why Offensive Security Needs Engineering Textbooks. Or, How to Avoid a Replay of "Crypto Wars" in Security Research.;login: 39:6–11.

Bratus S, Capelis DJ, Locasto M, Shubina A (2014b) Why Wassenaar Arrangement's Definitions of Intrusion Software and Controlled Items Put Security Research and Defense At Risk—And How To Fix It. https://www.cs.dartmouth.edu/~sergey/drafts/wassenaar-public-comment.pdf. Accessed 4 January 2024.

Brown DRL, Gjøsteen K (2007) A Security Analysis of the NIST SP 800-90 Elliptic Curve Random Number Generator. In: Menezes A (ed) Advances in Cryptology - CRYPTO 2007. Springer, Berlin, Heidelberg, pp 466–481.

Brown I (2006) The Evolution of Anti-Circumvention Law. International Review of Law Computers & Technology. https://doi.org/10.1080/13600860600852119

Byres E, Eng P, Lowe J (2004) The Myths and Facts behind Cyber Security Risks for Industrial Control Systems. https://www.tofinosecurity.com/professional/myths-and-facts-behind-cyber-security-risks-industrial-control-systems. Accessed 4 January 2024.

Campbell D (2015) My Life Unmasking British Eavesdroppers.The Intercept. https://theintercept.com/2015/08/03/life-unmasking-british-eavesdroppers/. Accessed 6 October 2020.

Campbell D (1998) Somebody's Listening…and They Don't Give a Damn about Personal Privacy or Commercial Confidence. New Statesman 10–12.

Cardozo N, Schoen S (2019) Detecting Ghosts By Reverse Engineering: Who Ya Gonna Call?Lawfare. https://www.lawfareblog.com/detecting-ghosts-reverse-engineering-who-ya-gonna-call. Accessed 12 July 2019.

Ceruzzi PE (2003) A History of Modern Computing, 2nd edn. MIT Press, London, Eng.; Cambridge, Mass.

Chadwick P (2017) Flawed Reporting about WhatsApp. The Guardian, 28 June 2017.

Chaos Computer Club (2011) Chaos Computer Club Analyzes New German Government Spyware. https://www.ccc.de/en/updates/2011/analysiert-aktueller-staatstrojaner. Accessed 11 June 2021.

Checkoway S, Fredrikson M, Niederhagen R et al. (2014) On the Practical Exploitability of Dual EC in TLS Implementations. https://www.usenix.org/system/files/conference/usenixsecurity14/sec14-paper-checkoway.pdf. Accessed 4 January 2024.

Checkoway S, Shacham H, Maskiewicz J et al. (2018) Where Did I Leave My Keys?: Lessons from the Juniper Dual EC incident. Commun ACM 61:148–155. https://doi.org/10.1145/3266291
Clarke RA, Morell MJ, Stone GR et al. (2013) Liberty and Security in a Changing World, 12 December2013. https://obamawhitehouse.archives.gov/sites/default/files/docs/2013-12-12_rg_final_report.pdf. 4 January 2024.
Cohn J (2015) Transitions from Analog to Digital Computing in Electric Power Systems. IEEE Annals of the History of Computing 37:32–43. https://doi.org/10.1109/MAHC.2015.37
Copyright Office of the Library of Congress (2021) Exemption to Prohibition on Circumvention of Copyright Protection Systems for Access Control Technologies. https://www.federalregister.gov/documents/2021/10/28/2021-23311/exemption-to-prohibition-on-circumvention-of-copyright-protection-systems-for-access-control. Accessed 4 January 2024.
Council of Europe (2001) Explanatory Report to the Convention on Cybercrime, 23 November 23.
Council of Ministers (2017) Council Conclusions on the Joint Communication to the European Parliament and the Council: Resilience, Deterrence and Defence: Building Strong Cybersecurity for the EU.
Cox J (2019) Experts Doubt Russian Claims That Cryptographic Flaw Was a Coincidence.Vice. https://www.vice.com/en_us/article/43j3wm/experts-doubt-russian-encryption-standard-cryptography-backdoor-streebog-kuznyechik. Accessed 22 November 2019.
Cyber Security Raad (2021) Adviesrapport Integrale Aanpak Cyberweerbaarheid. https://www.rijksoverheid.nl/documenten/rapporten/2021/04/06/tk-bijlage-csr-adviesrapport-integrale-aanpak-cyberweerbaarheid. 4 January 2024.
Daniel M (2014) Heartbleed: Understanding When We Disclose Cyber Vulnerabilities.whitehouse.gov. https://obamawhitehouse.archives.gov/blog/2014/04/28/heartbleed-understanding-when-we-disclose-cyber-vulnerabilities. Accessed 19 September 2018.
Diehl J, Knobbe M, Rosenbach M, Wiedmann-Schmidt W (2019) Horst Seehofer greift WhatsApp an. Der Spiegel, 24 May 2019.
Diffie W, Landau SE (2007) Privacy on the Line: The Politics of Wiretapping and Encryption. Updated and expanded edn. MIT Press, Cambridge, Mass.
Diver LE (2021) Digisprudence: Code as Law Rebooted. Edinburgh University Press, Great Britain.
Dizon MAC (2016) Breaking & Remaking Law and Technology: A Socio-Techno-Legal Study of Hacking. Tilburg University, Tilburg.
Dover R, Aldrich RJ (2020) Cryptography and the Global South: Secrecy, Signals and Information Imperialism. Third World Quarterly 41:1900–1917. https://doi.org/10.1080/01436597.2020.1793665
Durumeric Z, Payer M, Paxson V et al. (2014) The Matter of Heartbleed. In: Proceedings of the 2014 Conference on Internet Measurement Conference - IMC '14. ACM Press, Vancouver, BC, Canada, pp 475–488.
EDPB (2020a) Letter on the relevance of encryption bans in third countries for assessing the level of protection in accordance with the GDPR when personal data are transferred to countries where these bans exist. https://edpb.europa.eu/sites/default/files/files/file1/edpb_letter_out2020-0061_mep_koernerencryption.pdf. Accessed 4 January 2024.
EDPB (2020b) Recommendations 01/2020 on measures that supplement transfer tools to ensure compliance with the EU level of protection of personal data.
Electronic Frontier Foundation (2014) Unintended Consequences: Sixteen Years under the DMCA. https://www.eff.org/wp/unintended-consequences-16-years-under-dmca. Accessed 4 January 2024.
Encryption Working Group (2019) Moving the Encryption Policy Conversation Forward. https://carnegieendowment.org/2019/09/10/moving-encryption-policy-conversation-forward-pub-79573. Accessed 4 January 2024.
ENISA (2011), Protecting Industrial Control Systems, 14 December 2011. https://www.enisa.europa.eu/publications/protecting-industrial-control-systems.-recommendations-for-europe-and-member-states. Accessed 4 January 2024.

ENISA (2013a), The Directive on attacks against information systems: a good practice collection for CERTs on the Directive on attacks against information systems. https://www.enisa.europa.eu/publications/the-directive-on-attacks-against-information-systems. Accessed 4 January 2024.
ENISA (2013b) Recommended cryptographic measures. Securing personal data., 10 September 2013. https://www.enisa.europa.eu/publications/recommended-cryptographic-measures-securing-personal-data. Accessed 4 January 2024.
ENISA (2015) Analysis of ICS-SCADA cyber security maturity levels in critical sectors. https://www.enisa.europa.eu/publications/maturity-levels. Accessed 4 January 2024.
ENISA (2020) Security Supervision under the EECC. https://www.enisa.europa.eu/publications/supporting-the-implementation-of-the-european-electronic-commmunications-code-eecc. Accessed 4 January 2024.
ENISA, Europol (2016) On lawful criminal investigation that respects 21st Century data protection - Europol and ENISA Joint Statement, 20 May 2016.
Eurojust (2021) New Major Interventions to Block Encrypted Communications of Criminal Networks. https://www.eurojust.europa.eu/new-major-interventions-block-encrypted-communications-criminal-networks. Accessed 9 June 2021.
European Commission (1997) Ensuring Security and Trust in Electronic Communication. Towards a European Framework for Digital Signatures and Encryption.
European Commission (2001) Network and Information Security: Proposal for A European Policy Approach, COM(2001)298 final, 6 June 6, 2001.
European Commission (2004) Critical Infrastructure Protection in the fight against terrorism., COM(2004) 702 final, 20 October 20, 2004.
European Commission (2006a) A European Programme for Critical Infrastructure Protection, COM(2006) 786 final, 12 December 12, 2006.
European Commission (2006b) A strategy for a Secure Information Society – —"Dialogue, partnership and empowerment", COM(2006) 251 final, 31 May 31, 2006.
European Commission (2009) Critical Information Infrastructure Protection. "Protecting Europe from large scale cyber-attacks and disruptions: enhancing preparedness, security and resilience", COM(2009) final, 30 March 30, 2009.
European Commission (2011) Critical Information Infrastructure Protection. "Achievements and next steps: towards global cyber-security", COM(2011) 163 final, 31 March 31, 2011.
European Commission (2017) Eleventh progress report towards an effective and genuine Security Union, COM(2017) 608 final, 18 October 18, 2017.
European Commission (2019) Evaluation of Council Directive 2008/114 on the Identification and Designation of European Critical Infrastructures and the Assessment of the Need to Improve Their Protection, SWD(2019) 308 final, 23 July 23, 2019.
European Commission (2020) Report on the safety and liability implications of Artificial Intelligence, the Internet of Things and robotics, COM(2020) 64 final, 19 February 19, 2020h.
European Commission (2022) Proposal for a Regulation on cybersecurity requirements for products with digital elements (Cyber Resilience Act).
European Commission, High Representative of the Union for Foreign Affairs and Security Policy (2017) Joint communication to the European Parliament and the Council: Resilience, deterrence and defence: building strong cybersecurity for the EU, JOIN/2017/0450 final.
Europol (2020) Europol and the European Commission inaugurate new decryption platform to tackle the challenge of encrypted material for law enforcement investigations. In: Europol. https://www.europol.europa.eu/newsroom/news/europol-and-european-commission-inaugurate-new-decryption-platform-to-tackle-challenge-of-encrypted-material-for-law-enforcement. Accessed 11 January 2021.
Europol (2021) 800 Criminals Arrested in Biggest Ever Law Enforcement Operation against Encrypted Communication. https://www.europol.europa.eu/newsroom/news/800-criminals-arrested-in-biggest-ever-law-enforcement-operation-against-encrypted-communication. Accessed 9 June 2021.

Fauri D, de Wijs B, den Hartog J et al. (2017) Encryption in ICS Networks: A Blessing or a Curse? In: 2017 IEEE International Conference on Smart Grid Communications (SmartGridComm). IEEE, Dresden, pp 289–294.
Fidler M (2015) Regulating the Zero-Day Vulnerability Trade: A Preliminary Analysis', 11 I/S: A Journal of Law and Policy for the Information Society 405.
FIPR (2005) The Crypto Wars Are Over! https://www.fipr.org/press/050525crypto.html. Accessed 30 November 2018.
Fox-IT (2012) Black Tulip. Report of the investigation into theDigiNotar Certificate Authority breach, 13 August 2012. https://respubca.home.xs4all.nl/pdf/besluit-wob-verzoek-totstandkoming-onderzoeksrapport-2011-fox-it-naar-diginotar.pdf. Accessed 4 January 2024.
Freitas PMF, Gonçalves N (2015) Illegal Access to Information Systems and the Directive 2013/40/EU. International Review of Law, Computers & Technology 29:50–62. https://doi.org/10.1080/13600869.2015.1016278
French Government, German Government (2017) Joint Letter of France and Germany to the European Commission, discussing inter alia encryption policy. https://regmedia.co.uk/2017/02/28/french_german_eu_letter.pdf. Accessed 12 June 2018.
Froomkin AM (1996) It Came from Planet Clipper: The Battle Over Cryptographic Key "Escrow". https://papers.ssrn.com/sol3/papers.cfm?abstract_id=2718996. Accessed 4 January 2024.
Fuster GG, Jasmontaite L (2020) Cybersecurity Regulation in the European Union: The Digital, the Critical and Fundamental Rights. In: Christen M, Gordijn B, Loi M (eds) The Ethics of Cybersecurity. Springer International Publishing, Cham, pp 97–115.
Geller E (2019) Trump Officials Weigh Encryption Crackdown.POLITICO. https://politi.co/2NkpsSO. Accessed 5 July 2019.
Gellman B, Miller G (2013) "Black Budget" Summary Details U.S. Spy Network's Successes, Failures and Objectives. Washington Post, 29 August 2013.
Gellman B, Nakashima E (2013) U.S. Spy Agencies Mounted 231 Offensive Cyber-Operations in 2011, Documents Show. Washington Post, 30 August 2013.
Gellman R (2019) Fair Information Practices: A Basic History. SSRN Journal. https://doi.org/10.2139/ssrn.2415020
Gerbert P, Ruess F (2018) The Next Decade in Quantum Computing - and How to Play, BCG 2018.
German Government (1999) Pressemitteilung des Bundesministerium des Innern und Bundesministerium für Wirtschaft und Technologie: Eckpunkte der deutschen Kryptopolitik. https://hp.kairaven.de/law/eckwertkrypto.html. Accessed 30 November 2018.
Gillespie T (2007) Wired Shut: Copyright and the Shape of Digital Culture. MIT Press, Cambridge, Mass.
Goodin D (2013) Stop Using NSA-Influenced Code in Our Products, RSA Tells Customers. Ars Technica. https://arstechnica.com/information-technology/2013/09/stop-using-nsa-influence-code-in-our-product-rsa-tells-customers/. Accessed 12 June 2019.
Graaf P de (2021) De politie runde anderhalf jaar lang een chat-app voor criminelen. Hoe trapten ze in de val? de Volkskrant. https://www.volkskrant.nl/gs-ba7acbe2. Accessed 9 June 2021.
Green M (2013) On Cellular Encryption. A Few Thoughts on Cryptographic Engineering. https://blog.cryptographyengineering.com/2013/05/14/a-few-thoughts-on-cellular-encryption/. Accessed 5 January 2021.
Green M (2015) On the Juniper Backdoor. A Few Thoughts on Cryptographic Engineering. https://blog.cryptographyengineering.com/2015/12/22/on-juniper-backdoor/. Accessed 12 July 2019.
Green M (2018a) On Ghost Users and Messaging Backdoors.A Few Thoughts on Cryptographic Engineering. https://blog.cryptographyengineering.com/2018/12/17/on-ghost-users-and-messaging-backdoors/. Accessed 3 July 2019.
Green M (2018b) A few thoughts on Ray Ozzie's "Clear" Proposal.A Few Thoughts on Cryptographic Engineering. https://blog.cryptographyengineering.com/2018/04/26/a-few-thoughts-on-ray-ozzies-clear-proposal/. Accessed 30 January 2020.

Green M (2020) EARN IT Is a Direct Attack on End-to-End Encryption. A Few Thoughts on Cryptographic Engineering. https://blog.cryptographyengineering.com/2020/03/06/earn-it-is-an-attack-on-encryption/. Accessed 25 September 2020.
Greenberg A (2016) The Shadow Brokers Mess Is What Happens When the NSA Hoards Zero-Days. Wired, 17 August 2016.
Greenberg A (2021) The Full Story of the Stunning RSA Hack Can Finally Be Told. Wired, 20 May 2021.
Greenwald G (2014) How the NSA Tampers with US-Made Internet Routers.The Guardian. http://www.theguardian.com/books/2014/may/12/glenn-greenwald-nsa-tampers-us-internet-routers-snowden. Accessed 5 January 2021.
Gutheil M, Liger Q, Heetman A et al. (2017) Legal Frameworks for Hacking by Law Enforcement: Identification, Evaluation and Comparison of Practices. https://www.europarl.europa.eu/RegData/etudes/STUD/2017/583137/IPOL_STU(2017)583137_EN.pdf. Accessed 4 January 2024.
Haigh T (2001) The Chromium-Plated Tabulator: Institutionalizing an Electronic Revolution, 1954-1958. IEEE Annals of the History of Computing 23:75–104. https://doi.org/10.1109/85.969965
Harms K (2017) Positieve uitlokking van ethisch hacken: Een onderzoek naar responsible-disclosurebeleid. Netherlands Journal of Legal Philosophy 46:196–207. https://doi.org/10.5553/NJLP/221307132017046002006
Hassemer IM (2010) Der so genannte Hackerparagraph § 202 c StGB - Strafrechtliche IT-Risiken in Unternehmen. WebDok 51/2010: https://doi.org/10.7328/jurpcb/201025351
Healy J (2016) The U.S. Government and Zero-Day Vulnerabilities: From pre-Heartbleed to Shadow Brokers. https://www.oodaloop.com/wp-content/uploads/2016/11/Healey-VEP.pdf Accessed 4 January 2024.
Heninger N, Halderman JA (2016) The Legacy of Export-Grade Cryptography in the 21st Century. https://summerschool-croatia.cs.ru.nl/2016/slides/NadiaHeninger.pdf. Accessed 4 January 2024.
Hern A (2018) May Calls again for Tech Firms to Act on Encrypted Messaging. The Guardian, 25 January 2018.
Herpig S (2018) Governmental Vulnerability Assessment and Management, Stiftung Neue Verantwortung 2018.
Herpig S, Heumann S (2019) The Encryption Debate in Germany, Stiftung Neue Verantwortung 2019.
Herpig S, Schwartz A (2019) The Future of Vulnerabilities Equities Processes around the World. Lawfare. https://www.lawfareblog.com/future-vulnerabilities-equities-processes-around-world. Accessed 11 June 2021.
Hessel S, Rebmann A (2020) Regulation of Internet-of-Things cybersecurity in Europe and Germany as exemplified by devices for children. International Cybersecurity Law Review 1:27–37. https://doi.org/10.1365/s43439-020-00006-3
Hill R (2017) EU: No Encryption Backdoors But, eh, Let's Help Each Other Crack That Crypto, Oui? Ja? The Register, 19 October 2017.
Hoepman J-H (2019) De Geest van Grapperhaus? On Privacy, Security & …. https://blog.xot.nl/2019/11/05/de-geest-van-grapperhaus/index.html. Accessed 23 November 2021.
Hohlmeier M (rapporteur) (2013) Report on the proposal for a directive of the European Parliament and of the Council on attacks against information systems and repealing Council Framework Decision 2005/222/JHA (COM(2010)0517—C7-0293/2010—2010/0273(COD)).
Holland M (2019) Angriff auf WhatsApp & Co.: Seehofer will Messenger zur Entschlüsselung zwingen. Heise, 14 May 2019.
Holmes O (2020) Israeli Court Dismisses Amnesty Bid to Block Spyware Firm NSO. The Guardian. http://www.theguardian.com/world/2020/jul/13/israeli-court-dismisses-amnesty-bid-to-block-spyware-firm-nso. Accessed 10 June 2021.
Huang LS, Rice A, Ellingsen E, Jackson C (2014) Analyzing Forged SSL Certificates in the Wild. In: 2014 IEEE Symposium on Security and Privacy, pp 83–97.
Iglezakis I (2016) The Legal Regulation of Cyber Attacks. Kluwer Law International.

Jacobs B (2020) Maximator: European Signals Intelligence Cooperation, from a Dutch Perspective. Intelligence and National Security. https://doi.org/10.1080/02684527.2020.1743538
Jaspers H, Metze M (2019) Hoe Philips een Nederlandse zaktelex "afluisterbaar" maakte voor de NSA.De Groene Amsterdammer. https://www.groene.nl/artikel/versleuteld-maar-niet-voor-amerika. Accessed 11 October 2020.
Jaspers H, Van Rosmalen L, Borm B (2020) "Eten en gegeten worden" in het spiegelpaleis van de geheime diensten.VPRO - Argos. https://www.vpro.nl/argos/lees/onderwerpen/cryptoleaks/2020/het-spiegelpaleis-van-geheime-diensten.html. Accessed 8 January 2021.
Johnson WG (2019) Governance Tools for the Second Quantum Revolution. Jurimetrics 59.
Kennedy Jr. TR (1946) Electronic Computer Flashes Answers, May Speed Engineering. New York Times, 15 February 1946.
Koelman KJ (2003) Auteursrecht en technische voorzieningen: juridische en rechtseconomische aspecten van de bescherming van technische voorzieningen. University of Amsterdam, Amsterdam.
Koning ME (2011) Terug-hacken als opsporingsmethode. https://merelkoning.nl/wp-content/uploads/2012/06/Terughacken-als-opsporingsmethode-scriptie-Merel-Koning-september-2011-nn.pdf. Accessed 4 January 2024.
Koops B-J (1999) The Crypto Controversy: A Key Conflict in the Information Society. Kluwer Law International.
Koops B-J (2012) Het decryptiebevel en het nemo-teneturbeginsel. Nopen ontwikkelingen sinds 2000 tot invoering van een ontsleutelingsplicht voor verdachten?, WODC 2012.
Koops B-J (2013) Crypto Law Survey - Country Overview. http://cryptolaw.org/cls2.htm#fr. Accessed 6 December 2018.
Koops B-J, Kosta E (2018) Looking for Some Light through the Lens of "Cryptowar" History: Policy Options for Law Enforcement Authorities against "Going Dark". Computer Law & Security Review 34:890–900. https://doi.org/10.1016/j.clsr.2018.06.003
Kuner C (2014) We Actually Lost the Crypto Wars.Media Policy Project. http://blogs.lse.ac.uk/mediapolicyproject/2014/11/12/we-actually-lost-the-crypto-wars/. Accessed 6 December 2018.
Landau S (2017) Listening in: Cybersecurity in an Insecure Age. Yale University Press, New Haven.
Landau S (2018a) Exceptional Access: The Devil Is in the Details. Lawfare. https://www.lawfareblog.com/exceptional-access-devil-details-0. Accessed 3 July 2019.
Landau S (2018b) What's Involved in Vetting a Security Protocol: Why Ray Ozzie's Proposal for Exceptional Access Does Not Pass Muster. Lawfare. https://www.lawfareblog.com/whats-involved-vetting-security-protocol-why-ray-ozzies-proposal-exceptional-access-does-not-pass. Accessed 30 January 2020.
Larson J (2013) Revealed: The NSA's Secret Campaign to Crack, Undermine Internet Security.ProPublica. https://www.propublica.org/article/the-nsas-secret-campaign-to-crack-undermine-internet-encryption. Accessed 24 May 2019.
Latrive F (1999) Le 19 janvier, Lionel Jospin a amorcé un revirement complet de la politique française en matière de cryptologie. Réactions. Les clés du secret. Libération.fr. https://www.liberation.fr/ecrans/1999/01/29/forum-le-19-janvier-lionel-jospin-a-amorce-un-revirement-complet-de-la-politique-francaise-en-matier_262430. Accessed 6 December 2018.
Lessig L (2006) Code, 2nd edn. Basic Books, New York.
Levy S (1994) Battle of the Clipper Chip. The New York Times, 12 June 1994.
Levy S (2002) Crypto: How the Code Rebels Beat the Government Saving Privacy in the Digital Age, 2nd edn. Penguin Books, New York.
Levy I (2018a) Equities Process. GCHQ. https://www.ncsc.gov.uk/blog-post/equities-process. Accessed 11 June 2021.
Levy I (2018b) Principles for a More Informed Exceptional Access Debate. Lawfare. https://www.lawfareblog.com/principles-more-informed-exceptional-access-debate. Accessed 6 December 2018.
Levy S (2018c) Cracking the Crypto War. Wired, 25 April 2018.

Li C, Huang C, Lai F et al. (2018) A Comprehensive Overview of Government Hacking Worldwide. IEEE Access 1–1. https://doi.org/10.1109/ACCESS.2018.2871762
Litman J (2006) Digital Copyright. Prometheus Books, Amherst, N.Y.
Liu JP (2003) The DMCA and the Regulation of Scientific Research. Berkeley Technology Law Journal 18:501.
Loff S (2016) When the Computer Wore a Skirt: Langley's Computers, 1935–1970.NASA. http://www.nasa.gov/feature/when-the-computer-wore-a-skirt-langley-s-computers-1935-1970. Accessed 15 October 2020.
MacAskill E, Ball J (2013) Portrait of the NSA: No Detail Too Small in Quest for Total Surveillance. The Guardian. http://www.theguardian.com/world/2013/nov/02/nsa-portrait-total-surveillance. Accessed 6 October 2020.
Markoff J (1996) Data-Secrecy Export Case Dropped by U.S. The New York Times, 12 January 1996.
Marzouki M (2012) Amesys - Complicity in Torture: Surveillance Tech Export Control Needed. European Digital Rights (EDRi). https://edri.org/our-work/edrigramnumber10-10amesys-complicity-in-torture/. Accessed 23 September 2020.
Masnick M, Beadon L (2019) The Sky is Rising. A Detailed Look at the State of the Entertainment Industry. https://skyisrising.com/. Accessed 4 January 2024.
Mayer-Schönberger V (1997) Generational Development of Data Protection in Europe. In: Agre P, Rotenberg M (eds) Technology and Privacy: The New Landscape. MIT Press, Cambridge, Mass.
McCabe D, Isaac M, Benner K (2019) Facebook and Barr Escalate Standoff over Encrypted Messages. The New York Times, 10 December 2019.
McClure D (1999) First Amendment Freedoms and the Encryption Export Battle: Deciphering the Importance of Bernstein v. United States Department of Justice, 176 F.3d 1132 (9th Cir. 1999). Nebraska Law Review 79:21.
McLaughlin S, Konstantinou C, Wang X et al. (2016) The Cybersecurity Landscape in Industrial Control Systems. Proceedings of the IEEE 104(5):1-19, https://doi.org/10.1109/JPROC.2015.2512235
Meister A (2020) Our Criminal Complaint: German Made State Malware Company FinFisher Raided. https://netzpolitik.org/2020/our-criminal-complaint-german-state-malware-company-finfisher-raided/. Accessed 10 June 2021.
Menn J (2013) Exclusive: Secret contract tied NSA and Security Industry Pioneer. Reuters, 20 December 2013.
Menn J (2020) Spy Agency Ducks Questions about "Back Doors" in Tech Products. Reuters, 28 October 2020.
Metze M (2014) Ingelijfd door de NSA. De Groene Amsterdammer. https://www.groene.nl/artikel/ingelijfd-door-de-nsa. Accessed 11 October 2020.
Miller G (2020) The CIA Secretly Bought a Company That Sold Encryption Devices across the World. Then Its Spies Sat Back and Listened. Washington Post, 11 February 2020.
Openbaar Ministerie (2019) Zelf fouten in ICT-systemen zoeken en melden.Openbaar Ministerie. https://www.om.nl/onderwerpen/cybercrime/fouten-ict-systemen/. Accessed 15 October 2019.
Modderkolk H (2020a) Nederland luisterde jarenlang landen af dankzij superchip. De Volkskrant, 20 February 2020.
Modderkolk H (2020b) Waarom criminelen geen WhatsApp gebruiken en meer over hoe de politie kon meelezen. De Volkskrant, 2 July 2020.
Modderkolk H (2020c) Plan Grapperhaus voor aftappen van Facebook en WhatsApp sneuvelt voortijdig. De Volkskrant, 7 December 2020.
Möller B, Duong T, Kotowicz K (2014) This POODLE Bites: Exploiting The SSL 3.0 Fallback. https://www.openssl.org/~bodo/ssl-poodle.pdf. Accessed 4 January 2024.
Monroy M (2022) "'Wicked Problem': Europol Considers Vulnerability Exploitation to Break Encryption", Security Architectures in the EU Blog 4 October 2022. https://digit.site36.net/2022/10/04/wicked-problem-europol-considers-vulnerability-exploitation-to-break-encryption. Accessed 4 January 2024.

Nakashima E (2020) NSA Found a Dangerous Microsoft Software Flaw and Alerted the Firm — Rather Than Weaponize It.Washington Post. https://www.washingtonpost.com/national-security/nsa-found-a-dangerous-microsoft-software-flaw-and-alerted-the-firm--rather-than-weaponize-it/2020/01/14/f024c926-3679-11ea-bb7b-265f4554af6d_story.html. Accessed 14 January 2020.

Neubert C (2015) "The Tail on the Hardware Dog". Historical Articulations of Computing Machinery, Software, and Services. In: Kaldrack I, Leeker M (eds) There Is No Software, There Are Just Services. Meson Press, Lüneburg.

NIST (2006) Recommendation for Random Number Generation Using Deterministic Random Bit Generators. https://www.nist.gov/publications/recommendation-random-number-generation-using-deterministic-random-bit-generators-2. Accessed 4 January 2024.

NIST (2013a) Cryptographic Standards Statement.https://www.nist.gov/news-events/news/2013/09/cryptographic-standards-statement. Accessed 12 June 2019.

NIST (2013b) Supplemental ITL Bulletin for September 2013. https://csrc.nist.gov/csrc/media/publications/shared/documents/itl-bulletin/itlbul2013-09-supplemental.pdf. 4 January 2024.

Norton-Taylor R (2010) Not So Secret: Deal at The heart of UK-US Intelligence.The Guardian. http://www.theguardian.com/world/2010/jun/25/intelligence-deal-uk-us-released. Accessed 6 October 2020.

NOS (2019) Politie keek live mee met geheime berichten criminelen. https://nos.nl/l/2258177. Accessed 3 July 2020.

NSA (2010a) Memo on Project Bullrun. https://archive.nytimes.com/www.nytimes.com/interactive/2013/09/05/us/documents-reveal-nsa-campaign-against-encryption.html. Accessed 4 January 2024.

NSA (2010b) Leaked NSA document: Stealthy Techniques Can Crack Some of SIGINT's Hardest Targets. https://www.eff.org/files/2015/01/27/20150117-spiegel-supply-chain_interdiction_-_stealthy_techniques_can_crack_some_of_sigints_hardest_targets.pdf. Accessed 4 January 2024.

OECD (1980) OECD Guidelines on the Protection of Privacy and Transborder Flows of Personal Data, 23 September 23, 1980.

OECD (1997) OECD Recommendation of the Council concerning Guidelines for Cryptography Policy, 27 March 27, 1997.

OECD (2008) OECD Recommendation of the Council on the Protection of Critical Information Infrastructures, C(2008)35, 17 June 17, 2008.

OECD (2021), Encouraging Vulnerability Treatment, 307, February 2021.

Olechowski A, Eppinger SD, Joglekar N (2015) Technology Readiness Levels at 40: A Study of State-of-the-Art Use, Challenges, and Opportunities. In: 2015 Proceedings of PICMET '15: Management of the Technology Age.

Openbaar Ministerie (2013) Beleidsbrief Responsible Disclosure (hoe te handelen bij "ethische" hackers?') (not accessible anymore online).

Openbaar Ministerie (2018) Zelf fouten in ICT-systemen zoeken en melden. In: Openbaar Ministerie. https://www.om.nl/onderwerpen/cybercrime/fouten-ict-systemen/. Accessed 13 December 2019.

Openbaar Ministerie (2020a) Beleidsbrief Coordinated Vulnerability Disclosure. https://www.om.nl/binaries/om/documenten/richtlijnen/2020/december/14/om-beleidsbrief-ethisch-hacken/OM+Beleidsbrief+Coordinated+Vulnerability+Disclosure+Dec+2020.pdf. Accessed 4 January 2024.

Openbaar Ministerie (2020b) Aardschok voor georganiseerde misdaad. https://www.om.nl/actueel/nieuws/2020/07/02/aardschok-voor-georganiseerde-misdaad. Accessed 3 July 2020.

Open Technology Institute (2019) Open Letter to GCHQ on the Threats Posed by the Ghost Proposal. Lawfare. https://www.lawfareblog.com/open-letter-gchq-threats-posed-ghost-proposal. Accessed 30 May 2019.

Opstelten IW (2012) Brief van de Minister van Veiligheid en Justitie: Naar een veiliger samenleving, 28 864/363.

Ozzie R (2017) Slides on CLEAR Proposal. https://github.com/rayozzie/clear. Accessed 4 January 2024.

Pannu M, Bird R, Gill B, Patel K (2015) Investigating Vulnerabilities in GSM Security. In: 2015 International Conference and Workshop on Computing and Communication (IEMCON). pp 1–7.

Park S, Albert K (2020) A Researcher's Guide to Some Legal Risks of Security Research. https://clinic.cyber.harvard.edu/wp-content/uploads/2020/10/Security_Researchers_Guide-2.pdf. Accessed 4 January 2024.

Perlroth N (2013a) Documents Reveal N.S.A. Campaign Against Encryption. New York Times, 5 September 2013.

Perlroth N (2013b) Government Announces Steps to Restore Confidence on Encryption Standards. Bits Blog. https://bits.blogs.nytimes.com/2013/09/10/government-announces-steps-to-restore-confidence-on-encryption-standards/. Accessed 12 June 2019.

Perlroth N, Larson J, Shane S (2013) N.S.A. Able to Foil Basic Safeguards of Privacy on Web. The New York Times, 5 September 2013.

Perrier E (2021) Ethical Quantum Computing: A Roadmap. arXiv:210200759 [quant-ph].

Peterson A (2015) Today's Internet Users Are Still Being Hurt by '90s-Era U.S. Encryption Policies.Washington Post. https://www.washingtonpost.com/news/the-switch/wp/2015/05/28/todays-internet-users-are-still-being-hurt-by-90s-era-u-s-encryption-policies/. Accessed 19 April 2019.

Peterson A, Nakashima E (2015) Obama Administration Explored Ways to Bypass Smartphone Encryption. Washington Post, 24 September 2015.

Pfefferkorn R (2020) The EARN IT Act Is a Disaster amid the COVID-19 Crisis. Brookings. https://www.brookings.edu/techstream/the-earn-it-act-is-a-disaster-amid-the-covid-19-crisis/. Accessed 25 September 2020.

Portnoy E (2019) Why Adding Client-Side Scanning Breaks End-to-End Encryption.Electronic Frontier Foundation. https://www.eff.org/de/deeplinks/2019/11/why-adding-client-side-scanning-breaks-end-end-encryption. Accessed 11 June 2020.

Poulsen K (2013) New Snowden Leak Reports "Groundbreaking" NSA Crypto-Cracking. Wired, 29 August 2013.

Presidency of the Council of Ministers (2020) Security through encryption and security despite encryption, 10728/20, 18 September 2020.

Presidency of the Council of the European Union (2021) Next steps on Encryption, 8519/21, 12 May 2021.

Reaves B, Vargas L, Scaife N et al. (2018) Characterizing the Security of the SMS Ecosystem with Public Gateways. ACM Transactions on Privacy and Security 22:2:1–2:31. https://doi.org/10.1145/3268932

Redactie (2011) Politie infiltreert Tor-netwerk Robert M. Security.nl. https://www.security.nl/posting/33368/Politie+infiltreert+Tor-netwerk+Robert+M_. Accessed 18 December 2019.

Reidenberg J (1997) Lex Informatica: The Formulation of Information Policy Rules through Technology. Texas Law Review 76:553.

Riley M (2014) NSA Said to Have Used Heartbleed Bug, Exposing Consumers. Bloomberg.com, 11 April 2014.

Rosenstein R (2017) Deputy Attorney General Rod J. Rosenstein Delivers Remarks on Encryption at the United States Naval Academy. https://www.justice.gov/opa/speech/deputy-attorney-general-rod-j-rosenstein-delivers-remarks-encryption-united-states-naval. Accessed 5 December 2018.

Rosenzweig P (2020) The Law and Policy of Client-Side Scanning.Lawfare. https://www.lawfareblog.com/law-and-policy-client-side-scanning. Accessed 15 October 2021.

Ruohonen J, Kimppa K (2019) Updating the Wassenaar Debate Once Again: Surveillance, Intrusion Software, and Ambiguity. Journal of Information Technology & Politics 16:169–186. https://doi.org/10.1080/19331681.2019.1616646

Saitta E (2014) Newly Controlled Items Under the Wassenaar Arrangement. In: Dymaxion. https://dymaxion.org/essays/wa-items.html. Accessed 23 September 2020.
Samuelson P (1999) Intellectual Property and the Digital Economy: Why the Anti-Circumvention Regulations Need to Be Revised. Berkeley Technology Law Journal 14:519–566.
Samuelson P (2003) DRM {and, or, vs.} the law. Communications of the ACM 46:41–45. https://doi.org/10.1145/641205.641229
Savage C (2018a) Justice Dept. Revives Push to Mandate a Way to Unlock Phones. The New York Times, 24 March 2018.
Savage S (2018b) Lawful Device Access without Mass Surveillance Risk: A Technical Design Discussion. In: Proceedings of the 2018 ACM SIGSAC Conference on Computer and Communications Security. ACM, Toronto Canada, pp 1761–1774.
Scahill J, Begley J (2015) How Spies Stole the Keys to the Encryption Castle.The Intercept. https://theintercept.com/2015/02/19/great-sim-heist/. Accessed 18 December 2019.
Schaake M (2013) First Steps towards Curbing Digital Arms Exports Welcome. https://www.marietjeschaake.eu/en/first-steps-towards-curbing-digital-arms-exports-welcome. Accessed 23 September 2020.
Schaake M, Pupillo L, Ferreira A, Varisco G (2018) Software Vulnerability Disclosure in Europe: Technology, Policies and Legal Challenges, CEPS 28 June 2018.
Schmid G (2001) Report on the existence of a global system for the interception of private and commercial communications (ECHELON interception system), 2001/2098 (INI), 11 July 2001.
Schneier B (2007) Did NSA Put a Secret Backdoor in New Encryption Standard? Wired.
Schneier B (2016) The NSA Is Hoarding Vulnerabilities. In: Schneier on Security. https://www.schneier.com/blog/archives/2016/08/the_nsa_is_hoar.html. Accessed 11 June 2021.
Schneier B (2019a) The Myth of Consumer-Grade Security. Schneier on Security. https://www.schneier.com/blog/archives/2019/08/the_myth_of_con.html. Accessed 23 October 2020.
Schneier B (2019b) Evaluating the GCHQ Exceptional Access Proposal. Lawfare. https://www.lawfareblog.com/evaluating-gchq-exceptional-access-proposal. Accessed 12 July 2019.
Schoenmakers B, Sidorenko A (2006) Cryptanalysis of the Dual Elliptic Curve Pseudorandom Generator, 29 May 2006. https://eprint.iacr.org/2006/190. Accessed 4 January 2024.
Schwartz A, Knake R (2016) Government's Role in Vulnerability Disclosure. https://www.belfercenter.org/sites/default/files/legacy/files/vulnerability-disclosure-web-final3.pdf. Accessed 4 January 2024.
Shetterly ML (2016) Hidden Figures: The Story of the African-American Women Who Helped Win the Space Race: The American Dream and the Untold Story of the Black Women Mathematicians Who Helped Win the Space Race. William Morrow Paperbacks, New York.
Shumow D, Ferguson N (2007) On the Possibility of a Back Door in the NIST SP800-90 Dual EC PRNG. https://rump2007.cr.yp.to/15-shumow.pdf. Accessed 4 January 2024.
Silfversten E, Jordan V, Martin K et al. (2020) Cybersecurity. A State-of-the-Art Review: Phase 2. https://repository.wodc.nl/bitstream/handle/20.500.12832/3016/3051-cybersecurity-a-state-of-the-art-review-full-text.pdf?sequence=13&isAllowed=y. Accessed 4 January 2024
Singh S (2000) The Code Book: The Science of Secrecy from Ancient Egypt to Quantum Cryptography. Anchor Books, New York.
SRF/jdp (2020) Second Swiss firm Allegedly Sold Encrypted Spying Devices. https://www.swissinfo.ch/eng/second-swiss-firm-allegedly-sold-encrypted-spying-devices/46186432. Accessed 8 January 2021.
Stolton S (2021) Commission Seeks to Calm Fears over Europol's Decryption Platform. Euractiv. https://www.euractiv.com/section/data-protection/news/commission-seeks-to-calm-fears-over-europols-decryption-platform/. Accessed 23 November 2021.
Stouffer K, Pillitteri V, Lightman S et al. (2015) Guide to Industrial Control Systems (ICS) Security, NIST SP 800-82r2.
Sullivan A, Satter R (2019) Dark Web Child Porn Bust Leads to 338 Arrests Worldwide. Reuters, 16 October 2019.

Terra F (2019) Responsible Disclosure voorbeeld tekst. Responsible Disclosure. https://responsibledisclosure.nl/. Accessed 18 October 2019.
Theis JM (1954) Practical Application of Electronic Equipment to Accounting. N.A.C.A. Bulletin, p 1739.
Timberg C, Soltani A (2013) By Cracking of A5/1 Cellphone Code, NSA Has Capability for Decoding Private Conversations. Washington Post, 13 December 2013.
Tromer E (2018) Eran Tromer's Attack on Ray Ozzie's CLEAR protocol. Steve Bellovin's blog. https://www.cs.columbia.edu/~smb/blog/2018-05/2018-05-02.html. Accessed 9 October 2020.
U.S. Copyright Office (2000) Joint Study of Section 1201(g) of The Digital Millennium Copyright Act. https://www.copyright.gov/reports/studies/dmca_report.html. Accessed 30 October 2019.
US Government (2017) Vulnerabilities Equities Policy and Process for the United States Government, 15 November 2017
van Alsenoy B (2016) Regulating Data Protection. The Allocation of Responsibility and Risk Among Actors Involved in Personal Data Processing. PhD thesis, KU Leuven, Leuven.
van Daalen O (2003) Technische voorzieningen en cryptografie-onderzoek (master thesis, unpublished, copy with author).
van Daalen O (2022), In Defense of Offense: Information Security Research under the Right to Science, Computer Law & Security Review 46: 105706.
van Daalen O (2023a) The Right to Encryption: Privacy as Preventing Unlawful Access, Computer Law & Security Review 49:105804.
van Daalen O (2023b) Fundamental Rights Assessment of the Framework for Detection Orders under the CSAM Proposal, April 2023. https://www.ivir.nl/publicaties/download/CSAMreport.pdf. Accessed 4 January 2024.
van Daalen O (2023c) The Right to Root: Constructing a Claim to Control Devices from the Right to Privacy. JIPITEC 14(2023:4): 580–593.
van Daalen O (2024) Developing a human-rights compatible governance framework for quantum computing, Research Directions: Quantum Technologies 2:2024.
van den Heuvel J, van Wely M (2019) Telefoons criminelen gekraakt dankzij IT'er. De Telegraaf, 26 April 2019.
van den Heuvel K (2018) Securing the Smart Home. A Study on Cybersecurity Problems in Smart Home Devices: Does European Product Liability Law Offer Meaningful Legal Solutions for Consumers? University of Amsterdam, Amsterdam.
Veen J, Boeke S (2020) No Backdoors: Investigating the Dutch Standpoint on Encryption. Policy & Internet. https://doi.org/10.1002/poi3.233
Verbruggen P, Wolters P, Sieburgh C, Jansen C (2016) Towards Harmonised Duties of Care and Diligence in Cybersecurity. SSRN Journal 78–107. https://doi.org/10.2139/ssrn.2814101
Waldfogel J (2017) How Digitization Has Created a Golden Age of Music, Movies, Books, and Television. Journal of Economic Perspectives 31:195–214. https://doi.org/10.1257/jep.31.3.195
Warner M (2015) Notes on the Evolution of Computer Security Policy in the US Government, 1965-2003. IEEE Annals of the History of Computing 37:8–18. https://doi.org/10.1109/MAHC.2015.25
WA Secretariat (2018) Wassenaar Arrangement on Export Controls for Conventional Arms and Dual-Use Goods and Technologies, see https://www.wassenaar.org/. Accessed 4 January 2024.
WA Secretariat (2020) Genesis of the Wassenaar Arrangement. The Wassenaar Arrangement. https://www.wassenaar.org/genesis-of-the-wassenaar-arrangement/. Accessed 23 September 2020.
Weinmann R-P (2015) Some Analysis of the Backdoored Backdoor. https://rpw.sh/blog/2015/12/21/the-backdoored-backdoor/. Accessed 12 July 2019.
White House (1999) Press Release on 1999 Crypto Export Policy (published on archived copy of EFF.org from 12 October 1999). https://web.archive.org/web/19991012125149/http://eff.org:80/pub/Privacy/ITAR_export/1999_export_policy/19990916_wh_cryptopolicy_pr.html. Accessed 30 November 2018.

Whittle M, Eager J, Lale-Demoz E et al. (2021) Impact Assessment on Increased Protection of Internet-Connected Radio Equipment and Wearable Radio Equipment. https://ec.europa.eu/docsroom/documents/40763. Accessed 4 January 2024.
Wilson Thompson A (2021) Assessing the Vulnerabilities Equities Process, Three Years After the VEP Charter. Lawfare. https://www.lawfareblog.com/assessing-vulnerabilities-equities-process-three-years-after-vep-charter. Accessed 11 June 2021.
Yost JR (2015) The Origin and Early History of the Computer Security Software Products Industry. IEEE Annals of the History of Computing 37:46–58. https://doi.org/10.1109/MAHC.2015.21
Zanero S (undated) Adverse Impacts of "Intrusion Software" Clause on Security Research
Zimmermann P (1991) Why I Wrote PGP. https://www.philzimmermann.com/EN/essays/WhyIWrotePGP.html. Accessed 18 October 2018.
Zimmermann P (1996) Phil Zimmermann's Senate Testimony, 26 June 1996. https://philzimmermann.com/EN/testimony/index.html. Accessed 4 January 2024.

Table of Cases: USA

6th Cir., Junger v Daley, Judgment of 4 April 2000, 209 F.3d 481.
9th Cir., Bernstein v U.S. Dept. of Justice, Judgment of 6 May 1999, 176 F.3d 1132.
D.D.C., Karn v U.S. Dept. of State, Judgment of 22 March 1996, 925 F.Supp. 1.

Table of Cases: National

Bundesverfassungsgericht (BVerfG), 2 BVR 2233/07, 2 BVR 1151/08 and 2 BVR 1524/08, F.W. and K. gegen §202c Abs. 1 Nr. 2 StGB, Judgment of 19 June 2009a.
Bundesverfassungsgericht (BVerfG), IT-Sicherheitslücken, Judgment of 8 June 2021, 1 BvR 2771/18.
District Court of Arnhem, ECLI:NL:RBARN:2008:BD7578, NXP / RUN (Mifare-chip), Judgment of 18 July 2008.
District Court of The Hague, ECLI:NL:RBDHA:2018:10451, Vriendendatabase, Judgment of 30 August 2018.
District Court of The Hague, ECLI:NL:RBSGR:2010:BN1963, Nintendo modchips, Judgment of 21 July 2010.
District Court Oost-Brabant, ECLI:NL:RBOBR:2013:BZ1157, Henk Krol, Judgment of 15 February 2013.
District Court the Hague, ECLI:NL:RBDHA:2014:15611, Groene Hart Ziekenhuis, Judgment of 17 December 2014.
District Court The Hague, ECLI:NL:RBDHA:2018:10451, Centraal Bureau voor Genealogie, Judgment of 30 August 2018.
District Court The Hague, ECLI:NL:RBDHA:2018:6310, Consumentenbond / Samsung, Judgment of 30 May 2018.
Landgericht München, 7 O 10502/12, TubeBox, Judgment of 26 July 2012.

Table of Cases: UK

Kabushiki Kaisha Sony Computer Entertainment Inc v Ball (Application for Summary Judgment), Judgment of 19 July 2004, [2004] EWHC 1738 (Ch).

Table of Cases: EU

CJEU, Case C-131/12, Google Spain, Judgment of 13 May 2014.
CJEU, Case C-210/16, Wirtschaftsakademie, Judgment of 5 June 2018.
CJEU, Case C-25/17, Jehova's witnesses, Judgment of 10 July 2018.
CJEU, Case C-355/12, Nintendo / PC Box, Judgment of 23 January 2014.
CJEU, Case C-40/17, Fashion-ID, Judgment of 29 July 2019.
CJEU, Case C-406/10, SAS / World Programming, Judgment of 2 May 2012.
High Court of Justice, HC09C00988, Nintendo Co Ltd v Playables Ltd, Judgment of 28 July 2010, [2010] EWHC 1932.

Part II
The Human Rights Framework

Chapter 4
Human Rights in Context

Contents

Abstract This chapter focuses on history and application of the European Convention of Human Rights and the Charter of Fundamental Rights of the European Union. It discusses the roots of these instruments, the interpretative methods which are generally applied, as well as the typologies of states duties. This serves as the backdrop for the other chapters which focus on the specific human rights to privacy, communications freedom and science.

Keywords History of human rights · Interpretative methods of human rights

4.1 Introduction

Human rights relate to information security, but this relation remains largely unexplored. In the coming chapters, I lay the foundation for an analysis of this relationship. I am particularly interested in those three human rights which have the strongest connection to the information security cycle: the right to privacy (and data protection), the right to communications freedom and the right to science.

Now to be clear, not all these rights are equally relevant to all parts of the information security cycle. At the first stage of the cycle, taking information security measures, the rights to privacy and data protection are most relevant since these

O. van Daalen, *From Encryption to Quantum Computing*, Information Technology and Law Series 38, https://doi.org/10.1007/978-94-6265-635-2_4

measures are at least partly applied to information in the private sphere. Historically, the right to communications freedom also covers the protection of *confidential* communications, and I will also touch on that. Then, at the next stages of the cycle, the research into information security measures and the publication of the research, the rights to communications freedom and the right to science are the most relevant. This is because these rights protect research activities and the sharing of information. And at the fourth stage of the cycle, taking mitigating measures, again the rights to data protection and privacy are the most important.

This means I also leave some rights out. Because of the widespread use of information security technologies, a number of other human rights are in theory also affected. Information security technologies are for instance strongly tied to the right to human dignity (Article 1 Charter), because they allow users to protect themselves against arbitrary interference. In a similar vein, these technologies are important for the right to respect for one's physical and mental integrity (Article 3 Charter), for instance allowing a person to protect medical data from unauthorised access. Information security technologies further support the right to freedom of thought, conscience and religion (Article 10 Charter, Article 9 Convention), because it allows people to develop and share their thoughts without outside interference. They also support freedom of assembly and association (Article 12 Charter, Article 11 Convention), because they enable people to meet in confidence, communicate and organise amongst themselves. These technologies are further important for the right to conduct a business (Article 16 Charter), because it enables businesses to store information and communicate with others while preventing unauthorised access (both internally and externally). Lastly, they are important for the right to a fair trial and the right of defence (Articles 47 and 48 Charter, Article 6 Convention), because they allow clients to communicate with their attorneys in confidence. For all these rights, however, the link with information security is more remote, while my analysis based on the rights to privacy, communications freedom and science will largely be relevant for an assessment under those other rights as well.

For my analysis, I focus on three human rights instruments. For the right to privacy and the right to communications freedom, the European Convention of Human Rights (the Convention) and the European Charter of Fundamental Rights (the Charter) will be discussed. For the right to science, I base my analysis mostly on the International Covenant on Economic, Social and Cultural Rights (the Covenant). In the following three chapters, these rights will be discussed separately. First, however, I discuss the origin and general principles of application of the Convention and the Charter.[1] I discuss the origin of the Convenant further in the chapter on the right to science.

---

[1] Parts of this chapter have already been published in Van Daalen 2022, 2023a, 2023b and 2024.

4.2 The Early Years of Human Rights

The Convention, Charter and Covenant do not stand in isolation, they are the result of a discourse on human rights which started during the Enlightenment and has not ended yet.[2] Although the roots of the concept of human rights might not necessarily lie in Europe, the origin of these particular human rights instruments can be traced back to the period from roughly the 15th to the 18th century in Western Europe. The revolutionary atmosphere of that era provided fertile soil for the nascence of an early codification of human rights.

This period firstly marked a shift from a feudal to a mercantile society—from a society where peasants depended on nobility for their livelihood, to the ascendance of merchants and rich farmers, the *bourgeoisie*, whose wealth depended on commerce, not royalty.[3] This increased importance of trading sparked a discourse on the existence of a right to private property, but more importantly, the shift in economic power also heralded a shift in political power; monarchies were under pressure and sometimes overthrown as something resembling parliamentary democracy gained in importance.

Human rights—or natural rights as they were called at that time—were intimately linked to this shift in power. Locke, Hobbes and Rousseau argued that citizens had natural rights, already present at birth, and the authority to govern was derived from a transfer of power from citizens to their government.[4] Simultaneously, the European continent was the theatre of multiple religious wars, as the power of the Catholic Church was under siege from the rise of Protestantism.[5] As a result, the concept of religious freedom and freedom of conscience gained prominence. And the rise of the printing press during that period not only allowed various forms of Protestantism to disperse widely, but also put censorship into stark focus, underlining the importance of freedom of expression (see further Chap. 6).

This revolutionary spirit eventually culminated in one of the most prominent early human rights instruments, the French *Déclaration des droits de l'homme et du citoyen* of 1789.[6] It can be read both as a formal indictment of the *ancien régime* and an ideal for a new society, with two main goals. It is firstly intended to *protect* against the arbitrary exercise of power—for example against arrests without a warrant, undue taxation, restrictions without legal basis and punishment without justification. And it supports a *restructuring* in power—considering that "men are born and remain free and equal in rights", and "social distinctions can be based on the common good", which was at odds with the idea of a ruling class of hereditary royalty. Other countries

---

[2] See Ishay 2009, Chap. 1 for earlier contributions to the human rights discourse and a much more comprehensive overview of the history of human rights.

[3] See ibid., Chap. 2; Greer 2006, pp. 2–5.

[4] Greer 2006, pp. 2–3.

[5] See Ishay 2009, Chap. 2.

[6] (1789) Déclaration des Droits de l'Homme et du Citoyen; see also Jefferson T (1776) Declaration of Independence; (1689) English Bill of Rights; (1215) Magna Carta.

followed the French example, as the idea of national constitutions encoding certain inalienable human rights gained traction.

Did these countries meanwhile live up to their lofty ideals? No. The application of many of the earlier instruments still reflected the political status quo.[7] Most importantly, the simple idea of *universality*—that all humans have the same rights—was only very partially embraced. The French *Déclaration* speaks of "*les droits naturels, inaliénables et sacrés de l'Homme*"—but French women could not vote.[8] The Dutch constitution of 1789 solemnly declared that each member of society has an equal claim to the advantages of society without distinction.[9] But Dutch traders were then still enslaving and selling thousands of people to work to their death on Dutch plantations—hanging them with hooks through their rib cages or burning them alive as punishment.[10]

4.3 The Universal Declaration of Human Rights

It was only after the Second World War that an attempt to formulate a global, coherent and truly universal human rights agenda was undertaken. Franklin Roosevelt in his 1941 "Four Freedoms"-speech outlined human rights as a post-war ideal, proclaiming that "freedom means the supremacy of human rights everywhere".[11] After the war, a global coalition of over 50 countries under the auspices of the newly founded United Nations set out to articulate this ideal in a human rights instrument. This work, chaired by Eleanor Roosevelt, wife of the by then deceased US president Franklin Roosevelt, resulted in 1948 in the adoption of the Universal Declaration of Human Rights (the Declaration).[12]

The Declaration differed from existing human rights instruments in three ways. It was driven by condemnation of the human rights abuses committed by Germany and others, and a shared conviction that human rights are instrumental to maintaining peace.[13] It was the outcome of international co-operation, bridging vast political and philosophical differences, from Communism to Capitalism, from Islam to Christianity.[14] And it was comprehensive, laying down a significant catalogue of human

---

[7] See for an overview of criticism on this view of human rights Orakhelashvili 2011, para 8.2.5.

[8] (1789) Déclaration des Droits de l'Homme et du Citoyen; Sémiramis 2014.

[9] (1789) Déclaration des Droits de l'Homme et du Citoyen.

[10] Kom and Esajas 2020.

[11] Roosevelt FD (1941) Four Freedoms speech.

[12] United Nations (1948) Universal Declaration of Human Rights; see Ishay 2009, p. 211 and further for a historical overview.

[13] Morsink 1999, Chap. 1; in United Nations (1948) Universal Declaration of Human Rights, recital 1 it is considered that "recognition of the inherent dignity and of the equal and inalienable rights of all members of the human family is the foundation of freedom, justice and peace in the world"; see further Mcguinness 2011.

[14] Glendon 2001, Chap. 6.

rights, grounded in analyses of different value systems.[15] But it was also a mere *declaration*—not binding on its signatories.

Fortunately, as the ink on the Declaration was still drying, an international human rights instrument with an obligatory character was also in the making. This movement originated, not surprisingly, on the European continent.[16] Just as Roosevelt during the war had envisaged cooperation between countries with a global scope, Churchill in 1943 had shared a post-war vision of a "Council of Europe, [...] a really effective league with all the strongest forces concerned woven into its texture with a high court to adjust disputes and with forces, armed forces, national or international or both, held ready to enforce these decisions and prevent renewed aggression and the preparation of future wars".[17] After the war, partly driven by the spectre of rising Soviet power, western European powers set out to co-operate in three different areas: economy, defence and human rights. This led to the creation of complicated patchwork of different institutions with overlapping competences, as we will see.

4.4 Human Rights Protection in Europe

As to the cooperation on *human rights*: this initially took shape through the founding of a "Council of Europe", echoing Churchill's wartime speech, in 1949. This organisation was founded by twelve western European countries: Belgium, Denmark, France, Ireland, Italy, Luxembourg, Netherlands, Norway, Sweden and the United Kingdom. At its core, the organisation was aimed at preventing war and protecting against the rise of the Eastern bloc, but what set it apart from the other newly founded European institutions, is that it considered human rights central to achieving these goals.

Thus, the first main project of the Council of Europe was developing a European human rights instrument. Within one year, this culminated in the European Convention on Human rights, adopted on 4 November 1950.[18] True to its roots, the Convention had three aims—to prevent future wars, as a bulwark against the spread of Communism, which by the drafters was considered less protective of human rights, and as an early detection mechanism of human rights violations.[19] It drew on the Declaration, transposing many of the rights, but where it diverged was in *enforcement*: the Convention also contained an adjudication mechanism through which member states can be held accountable before a special international court, the European Court of Human Rights.

---

[15] Ibid., Chap. 5; Greer 2006, p. 10.

[16] See Greer et al. 2018, pp. 8–17.

[17] (1943) National Address broadcast on radio. The International Churchill Society.

[18] Council of Europe, European Convention on Human Rights (as amended by Protocols Nos. 11 and 14 and supplemented by Protocols Nos. 1, 4, 6, 7, 12, 13 and 16), 1950.

[19] Greer 2006, p. 20.

The Convention has since become the most important human rights instrument across Europe, as the Council of Europe has grown to over 45 members. This includes all members of the other institutional framework of European cooperation, the European Union, which will be discussed below. It also includes non-EU members, such as Turkey. And the Convention has been ratified by all members of the Council of Europe—in fact, ratification is a condition of membership for the Council of Europe.[20] This means that these countries can also be brought before the European Court of Human Rights.

As mentioned, for those Council of Europe members who are also a member of the European Union, however, another European human rights instrument also applies. This instrument, the Charter of Fundamental Rights, has gained in importance since the beginning of this millennium and by now in some cases eclipses the Convention, as we will see in the coming chapters. As a result, the interplay between the Charter and the Convention has become an important factor in European human rights law. To understand this dynamic, it is necessary to also discuss the evolution of the other two domains of post-war cooperation in Western Europe: defence, and more importantly, economy.

Initially, collaboration in these two domains was intertwined: the Benelux-countries, France and the UK in March 1948 concluded the Brussels Treaty, which focused on economic as well as military cooperation,[21] But this rapidly changed. After one year, the military cooperation was subsumed under the mutual defence pact NATO, founded in 1949. The economic co-operation was partly implemented through the European Coal and Steel Community in 1951 (ECSC), founded by the Benelux-countries, France, West Germany and Italy.[22] The ECSC was essentially a peace project, as coal and steel were important elements for waging war, and the pact was intended to stave off conflict between France and Germany over these resources.[23]

In the following decade, however, this economic cooperation broadened, as the goal of maintaining peace in Europe shifted to the background. This led to two other treaties on economic cooperation, one regarding the European Atomic Energy Community (EURATOM) and one regarding the European Economic Community (EEC), both concluded in 1957.[24] Of these three treaties, the EEC was by far the most ambitious, aimed at establishing an internal market, free competition, a customs union, a common economic and social policy and coordinated international trade policy. It was also the treaty by which the European Court of Justice was instituted, which would come to adjudicate disputes over these treaties.

The EEC Treaty concerned itself with the European economy. But as the European Communities adopted policies to give effect to the EEC Treaty, it became clear

[20] Greer et al. 2018, p. 12.

[21] (1948) The Treaty of Economic, Social and Cultural Collaboration and Collective Self-Defence.

[22] (1951) Treaty establishing the European Coal and Steel Community.

[23] See on the role of coal during the war Levinsohn 1991.

[24] (1957) Treaty establishing the European Economic Community.

that even mere economic regulation also affects human rights.[25] For example, when European rules prescribed that butter be sold at a discount for persons receiving welfare, and the name of the recipient had to be mentioned on the coupon, it was argued before the European Court of Justice that this affected the privacy of the recipients.[26]

The problem was that at that time, human rights were only enshrined in national constitutions, not in the European Community treaties. The only concept approaching something like human rights in their effect were the "four fundamental freedoms" establishing the single European market: the free movement of goods, people (then still focused on workers), services and capital. These freedoms had a decidedly economic character, though, and the European Court of Justice thus was not well-equipped to address human rights complaints. At the same time, handing over constitutional review of European rules to the national courts would undermine the supremacy of the treaties.

The European Court of Justice attempted to resolve this dilemma by reading the protection of fundamental rights *into* the treaties.[27] It did so in an influential decision on the power of the German Constitutional Court to review the constutionality of European rules, *Internationale Handelsgesellschaft* (1970). In this case, the German Court had concluded that certain European export rules were contrary to the German constitution. The European Court of Justice considered that the validity of Community measures cannot be judged on the basis of national rules, because this would adversely affect the uniformity and efficacy of Community law. But it simultaneously concluded that "respect for fundamental rights forms an integral part of the general principles of law protected by the Court of Justice", and the "protection of such rights, whilst inspired by the constitutional traditions common to the member states, must be ensured within the framework of the structure and objectives of the community".[28] One obvious instrument setting out these fundamental rights was the Convention, even though the European Communities had not ratified

[25] See for a good overview of the early history Ferraro and Carmona 2015, Chap. 2; and Greer et al. 2018, Chap. 4. In the European Union context, the term "fundamental rights" is often used instead of "human rights". I will use both interchangeably. See for a discussion of the difference between "fundamental" and "human" rights; van der Sloot 2017; but also the answer of the FRA: "The term 'fundamental rights' is used in European Union (EU) to express the concept of 'human rights' within a specific EU internal context"; European Union Agency for Fundamental Rights (2012) Frequently asked questions. https://fra.europa.eu/en/about-fundamental-rights/frequently-asked-questions. Accessed 1 July 2020.

[26] CJEU, Case C-29/69, Erich Stauder v City of Ulm-Sozialamt, Judgment of 12 November 1969.

[27] See for a discussion of the case law Coppel and O'Neill 1992.

[28] CJEU, Case 11-70, Internationale Handelsgesellschaft (Solange I), Judgment of 17 December 1970, paras 3–4.

it.[29] This situation was not ideal, though, because the legal framework of the European Communities still lacked, in the words of the German Constitutional Court, a "catalogue of fundamental rights".[30]

As the European Communities developed, the need for such a catalogue was only becoming more urgent. Firstly, the *acquis communitaire*, the combined set of European rules grew. With this, the potential for human rights infringements also increased. Moreover, European cooperation was further intensified in pursuit of "an ever closer union", encompassing not only the internal market, but also justice and security, under the Treaty of Maastricht (1992) and the Treaty of Amsterdam (1997).[31] This meant that issues such as immigration, criminal justice and law enforcement all came within the purview of the EU, domains which obviously have a significant impact on human rights. Meanwhile, the legitimacy of the European project was increasingly contested.[32] Yet, while the treaties of Amsterdam and Maastricht required its members and potential members to respect human rights, they still did not introduce a catalogue of fundamental rights.[33]

This changed in 1999 when the European Council of Ministers under the German Presidency concluded that fundamental rights applicable at Union level should be consolidated in a Charter.[34] A wide group of representatives from national governments and parliaments and European Union institutions quickly began the drafting process.[35] After one year, on 7 December 2000, the Charter of Fundamental Rights of the European Union could be adopted.[36] The process did not end here, though, because the Charter was at that moment still only a "solemn proclamation" by the Council, the European Parliament and the Commission—it was decided that "the

[29] The Court in 1974 considered that international human rights treaties are "guidelines" which should be followed within the framework of community law when safeguarding these rights, thus opening the door for using the Convention as inspiration; CJEU, Case 4-73, J. Nold, Kohlen- und Baustoffgroßhandlung v Commission of the European Communities., Judgment of 14 May 1974, para 14. In 1975, the Court explicitly referred to the Convention in its reasoning; CJEU, Case 36/75, Roland Rutili v Ministre de l'intérieur, Judgment of 28 October 1975, para 32.

[30] Bundesverfassungsgericht (BverfG), BvL 52/71, Solange I-Beschluß, Judgment of 29 May 1974.

[31] (1992) Treaty on European Union; (1997) Treaty of Amsterdam Amending the Treaty on European Union, the Treaties Establishing the European Communities and Certain Related Acts.

[32] De Burca 2015; Alston et al. 1999, Chap. 1.

[33] The Maastricht Treaty only proclaimed that the EU shall respect as general principles of Community law, fundamental rights, as guaranteed by the Convention and the constitutional traditions common to the Member States; (1992) Treaty on European Union, Article F(2). The Amsterdam Treaty affirmed that the EU "is founded on the principles of liberty, democracy, respect for human rights and fundamental freedoms, and the rule of law, principles which are common to the Member States"; (1997) Treaty of Amsterdam Amending the Treaty on European Union, the Treaties Establishing the European Communities and Certain Related Acts, Article F(1) as amended. The European Union in 1992 furthermore declared respect for human rights and fundamental freedoms part of its external policy; (1992) Treaty on European Union, Article J.1(2).

[34] (1999) European Council. Conclusions of the Presidency, para 44.

[35] De Burca 2015.

[36] (2000) Charter of Fundamental Rights of the European Union.

question of the Charter's force" would be considered later.[37] *Much* later, as it turned out, because the Charter was to remain in this legal twilight zone until 2009, when the Charter was finally in the Lisbon Treaty elevated to "the same legal value as the Treaties".[38]

And with that proclamation, fundamental rights protection in the European Union came full circle, from something to be read into the treaties, to a full-blown human rights instrument binding all member states. Meanwhile, however, the earlier European human rights instrument, the Convention, is still in force, and all members of the EU are also a signatory to it. The Charter of Fundamental Rights incorporates the rights protected under the European Convention for Human Rights and extends it—for example including the right to data protection. This potentially leads to conflicts between the two instruments. The Charter partially resolves this by explicitly taking the Convention as the baseline protection.[39] But in order to further integrate the two human rights systems, it was also agreed in the Lisbon Treaty that the EU *itself* should accede to the Convention.[40] This accession to the Convention did not go as planned, however. When the European Court of Justice was asked to give its opinion on the draft accession agreement, it concluded in 2014 that the envisaged accession was bound to upset the legal framework of the EU and did not give it its seal of approval.[41] Whether the EU will eventually accede is still an open question.

Perhaps this question of accession will be rendered moot in the coming years, as the European Court of Justice has been gradually growing into its role as a human rights court in its own right, in particular when it comes to applying the rights to privacy, data protection and communications freedom. It has for example invalidated the European obligation to store communications data in bulk, leading to a string of constitutional cases in domestic courts.[42] And it has declared the European mechanism by which personal data could be transferred to the US invalid, not once but twice, deeply upsetting trans-Atlantic data flows.[43] These cases will be discussed in more detail in Chap. 5.

---

[37] European Council, Conclusions of the Presidency, 7 December 2000.

[38] (2007) Treaty of Lisbon amending the Treaty on European Union and the Treaty establishing the European Community, Article 6(1) as amended.

[39] European Union (2009) Charter of Fundamental Rights of the European Union, fifth paragraph of the preamble. The Charter in Article 52(3) makes it explicit that in so far as it "contains rights which correspond to rights guaranteed by the Convention for the Protection of Human Rights and Fundamental Freedoms, the meaning and scope of those rights shall be the same as those laid down by the said Convention".

[40] (2007) Treaty of Lisbon amending the Treaty on European Union and the Treaty establishing the European Community, Article 6(2) as amended.

[41] CJEU, Opinion 2/13 on accession to the Convention, Judgment of 18 December 2014a; see before CJEU, Opinion 2/94 on Accession by the Community to the European Convention for the Protection of Human Rights and Fundamental Freedoms, Judgment of 28 March 1996 where the Court still considered that the Community had no competence to accede to the Convention.

[42] CJEU, Cases C-293/12 and C-594/12, Digital Rights Ireland and others, Judgment of 8 April 2014.

[43] CJEU, Case C-311/18, Schrems II, Judgment of 16 July 2020; CJEU, Case C-362/14, Schrems I, Judgment of 6 October 2015.

Not only does the Court of Justice dare to take unpopular decisions, in the past few years it has also extended its competence with regard to the application of the Charter significantly. The Charter itself provides that it is only applicable to EU institutions and member states "when they are implementing Union law".[44] And the Court has inferred in *Åkerberg Fransson* (2013) that the Charter applies "where national legislation falls within the scope of European Union law", further noting in *Siragusa* (2014) that this "requires a certain degree of connection" between the measures in question and EU law.[45] It has also considered itself competent to apply the Charter to national laws which are not covered by European policy, where the national law affects one of the fundamental freedoms guaranteed by the Treaty.[46]

This new role as a human rights guardian is becoming more relevant by the day, as some EU member states such as Hungary and Poland are taking a totalitarian turn, flouting the rule of law, curtailing the independence of the judiciary and limiting civil society.[47] In the course of several infringement proceedings over the past years, the European Court of Justice has, in response, demonstrated it is not afraid to flex its constitutional muscle. In 2020, the Grand Chamber ruled that Hungary breached the Charter by adopting the Hungarian "Soros Law" which required NGOs to register, declare and publish the receipt of foreign funding, because this requirement was incompatible with the rights to association, to privacy and data protection.[48] In the same year, it ruled that Hungary's requirement that foreign universities can only offer their teaching in Hungary as long as they also offer it in the country where they have their seat (aimed at the Soros-funded Central European University), was incompatible with the right to academic freedom enshrined in the Charter.[49]

This history explains why we now in the European Union have two highest courts both dealing with human rights, one applying the Charter and the other applying the Convention. Their decisions often converge, and each Court increasingly refers to the case law of the other, as we will see in the coming chapters. It is useful to first discuss the interpretative principles applied by both Courts, where we can already see this cross-pollination in action.

---

[44] (2000) Charter of Fundamental Rights of the European Union, Article 51(1).

[45] CJEU, Case C-617/10, Åkerberg Fransson, Judgment of 26 February 2013, para 21; CJEU, Case C-206/13, Siragusa, Judgment of 6 March 2014, para 24.

[46] CJEU, Case C-66/18, European Commission v Hungary, Judgment of 6 October 2020; CJEU, Case C-78/18, European Commission v Hungary (Transparency of Associations), Judgment of 18 June 2020.

[47] See for example European Commission 2023.

[48] CJEU, Case C-78/18, European Commission v Hungary (Transparency of Associations), Judgment of 18 June 2020.

[49] CJEU, Case C-66/18, European Commission v Hungary, Judgment of 6 October 2020.

4.5 The Application of the Convention and the Charter

4.5.1 *Interpretative Principles Under the Convention and the Charter*

Broadly speaking, courts interpret the meaning of laws in four ways: by looking at the *text* of a provision (textual interpretation), by looking at its *context* within the legislative system (contextual interpretation), by *comparing* approaches in different countries (comparative interpretation) and by looking at the *goals* of a law (teleological interpretation, which may involve looking at the legislative history of a provision).[50] Of these four modes of interpretation, the *textual* and *contextual* approach have limited value for human rights decisions, because human rights norms are typically vague, not part of a highly structured system, more purpose-oriented and their meaning across languages may differ.[51]

The two other modes of interpretation are, however, applied frequently by the European Court of Human Rights and the European Court of Justice, and for this book, the *teleological* approach is especially relevant. This is because, firstly, the technologies discussed in this book are relatively new: quantum and encryption technologies have existed for only a few decades. Moreover, the rights discussed in this book conflict with each other: for example, a measure restricting the development of quantum technologies affects the right to *science*, but may be important to protect the right to *privacy*. In order to determine the scope of the human rights in in the context of these new technologies and to resolve conflicts between these human rights, the *goal* of the human rights is in many cases decisive. But how does this work in practice?

4.5.1.1 Interpretation by the European Court for Human Rights

The interpretative approach where the goal of a right takes centre stage is clearest in the case law of the European Court of Human Rights, which had already in its earlier years developed a clear set of principles for interpretation of the Convention.[52] In *Wemhoff* (1968), the Court underscored that it must not apply a restrictive interpretation of the Convention, but instead one which does justice to its purpose: it should "seek the interpretation that is most appropriate in order to realise the aim and achieve the object of the treaty, not that which would restrict to the greatest

---

[50] See Senden 2011, Chap. 4 for a discussion of these methods. Senden also mentions "autonomous" and "evolutive" interpretation as a particular approach, but for my purposes these categories do not stand on their own, because they say little about the way the substantive scope of a provision is determined; see also Article 31 of United Nations (1969) Vienna Convention on the Law of Treaties, which mentions the four modes also for the interpetation of international treaties.

[51] See Senden 2011, Chap. 4.3.1; Lenaerts and Gutiérrez-Fons 2013, Section 1.A.

[52] See ECHR 2011 for a useful overview; see also Senden 2011, Chap. 4.

possible degree the obligations undertaken by the Parties".[53] In 1975, the Court confirmed that the Convention should be interpreted in line with the Vienna Convention on the Law of Treaties, which means that it should be interpreted in good faith in accordance with the ordinary meaning to be given to the terms of the treaty in their context, and, in particular, in the light of its *object and purpose*.[54] In *Tyrer* (1978) the Court subsequently established the "living instrument"-doctrine, embracing the view that the Convention is a living instrument which must be interpreted in the light of present-day conditions.[55] The Court then supplemented this the following year with the effectiveness-doctrine in *Airey*, noting that the protection afforded by the Convention should not be illusory but "practical and effective".[56]

Among the counterweights balancing these expansive principles is the notion of the *margin of appreciation*, first developed by the Court in *Handyside* in 1976.[57] The Court in the context of freedom of expression under Article 10 of the Convention considered that "[b]y reason of their direct and continuous contact with the vital forces of their countries, State authorities are in principle in a better position than the international judge to give an opinion on the exact content of these requirements as well as on the "necessity" of a "restriction" or "penalty" intended to meet them. [...] Consequently, Article 10 para. 2 (Article 10-2) leaves to the Contracting States a margin of appreciation". But it also considers that this does not give the state an "unlimited power of appreciation"—the "domestic margin of appreciation thus goes hand in hand with a European supervision".

These considerations also apply to the other human rights protected under the Convention, describing one of the most prominent outer boundaries of review by the Court, outside of which the states are free to make their own policy affecting human rights. In the case-law developed since *Handyside*, this concept has been informed by the existence of European consensus on a particular social norm. Where this consensus exists, the margin of appreciation accorded to states is smaller, whereas in the absence of such a consensus, it is wider.[58] It is also informed by the importance of

[53] ECHR, Application no. 2122/64, Wemhoff v Germany, Judgment of 27 June 1968, para 8; see also (2011) What are the limits to the evolutive interpretation of the Convention? In: Dialogue Between Judges 2011. European Court of Human Rights, Strasbourg, p. 7.

[54] ECHR, Application no. 4451/70, Golder v United Kingdom, Judgment of 21 February 1975, para 34; and Article 31 of United Nations (1969) Vienna Convention on the Law of Treaties.

[55] See ECHR, Application no. 5856/72, Tyrer v UK, Judgment of 25 April 1978, para 31 and numerous subsequent decisions; see for an overview (2011) What are the limits to the evolutive interpretation of the Convention? In: Dialogue Between Judges 2011. European Court of Human Rights, Strasbourg, p. 7.

[56] See ECHR, Application no. 6289/73, Airey v Ireland, Judgment of 9 October 1979a, para 26 and numerous subsequent decisions. It built on *Golder* (1975), where the Court noted that "hindrance in fact can contravene the Convention just like a legal impediment"; ibid., para 25; see ECHR, Application no. 4451/70, Golder v United Kingdom, Judgment of 21 February 1975, para 26.

[57] ECHR, Application no. 5493/72, Handyside v the United Kingdom, Judgment of 7 December 1976, paras 48–49.

[58] See for an example of the first; ECHR, Marckx v Belgium, Judgment of 13 June 1979; and for an example of the latter ECHR, Application no. 5493/72, Handyside v the United Kingdom, Judgment of 7 December 1976.

the right: where a particularly significant aspect of a right comes into play, the margin of appreciation accorded to the state is diminished.[59] Where, on the other hand, the goal of the measures is significant, states are granted a greater margin of appreciation.[60] And where the national authorities have already performed a balancing exercise between different rights involved in line with the criteria set out by the Court, "the Court would require strong reasons to substitute its view for that of the domestic courts".[61]

4.5.1.2 Interpretation by the European Court of Justice

As discussed, the origin of the European Court of Justice can be traced back to the goal of economic cooperation, and the Court only recently took on its role as a human rights court. So while it has applied the teleological approach abundantly before the entry into force of the Charter, it has done so mostly in the context of applying the treaties.[62] By 1963 it considered that for the interpretation of the EEC Treaty, it was necessary to consider "the spirit, the general scheme and the wording" of the treaty, as well as the objective.[63] Similarly, where it concerns the interpretation of a provision of *EU law* (as opposed to the treaties itself), the Court considers it settled case law that "it is necessary not only to refer to its wording but also to consider its context and the objectives of the legislation of which it forms part, and in particular the origin of that legislation".[64] The Court has furthermore developed the *effet utile*-, or effectiveness-doctrine, where it not only looks at the *object and purpose* of a provision or particular legislative instrument, but also at implications of a certain interpretation for the system of EU law *as a whole*.[65] In the context of human rights, it has in the past repeatedly considered that the interpretation of such rights must be ensured "within the framework of the structure and objectives of the EU"—thus

---

[59] See for example ECHR, Application no. 7525/76, Dudgeon v United Kingdom, Judgment of 22 October 1981, para 52.

[60] See for example the case law on surveillance discussed in Chap. 5.

[61] ECHR, Applications nos. 40660/08 and 60641/08, Von Hannover v Germany (no. 2), Judgment of 7 February 2012, para 107.

[62] See for a discussion Senden 2011, Chap. 5.2.1 and Chap. 13. For completeness, the Court does not apply only the teleological method: positioned often as the arbiter between the national and European legislator, it is also familiar with the comparative analysis; see Lenaerts and Gutiérrez-Fons 2013 for a discussion, in particular pp. 35–36; and Lenaerts and Gutman 2016; and for an earlier analysis Lenaerts 2007.

[63] CJEU, Case C-26/62, Van Gend en Loos, Judgment of 5 February 1963, para 12.

[64] CJEU, Cases C-511/18, C-512/18 and C-520/18, La Quadrature du Net, Judgment of 6 October 2020, para 105; CJEU, C-414/16, Egenberger, Judgment of 17 April 2018, para 44.

[65] See for example CJEU, Case C-41/74, Van Duyn, Judgment of 4 December 1974, para 12, where the Court considered that the useful effect of a European Union act (e.g. a directive) would be weakened if it could not be invoked by individuals before national courts where the directive is not implemented; see Lasser 2009, Chap. 7; and Šadl 2015 for a discussion.

focusing not so much on the objectives of the human right, but of the legal framework of the EU.[66]

Since the Charter has come into effect, the teleological method is also becoming relevant for the interpretation of human rights under the Charter. Firstly, the Charter itself provides that its explanatory documents should be taken into account for the interpretation of its provisions.[67] And the Court in its decisions now occasionally refers to the objective of the Charter and the human rights it protects. In one case, it has attached weight to the preamble of the Charter, which states that it is necessary "to strengthen the protection of fundamental rights in the light of changes in society, social progress and scientific and technological developments".[68] In other cases, it has considered that rights under the Charter are not absolute, but must be considered in relation to their *function in society* or *social purpose*.[69]

Still, as we will see in the chapters that follow, the case law of the European Court of Justice is less useful when determining the scope of the rights under the Charter. Firstly, the Charter came into effect relatively recently, so the body of European Union case law focusing particularly on human rights is limited, having not yet crystallised into a coherent system. It also has not developed a generally applicable margin of appreciation-doctrine similar to that of the European Court of Human rights.[70] Moreover, the reasoning of the Court is more succinct, without the possibility for individual judges to publish dissenting and concurring opinions, which makes it more complex to understand the reasoning behind a certain decision.[71] Most decisions are difficult to read, with sentences easily spanning one paragraph, and it does not employ the colourful, rights-laden and sometimes sweeping language of its Strasbourg counterpart, making it more difficult to extrapolate case law to new contexts. Perhaps most importantly, in many of the cases where it applies the Charter, it has done so in response to a request for a preliminary ruling. This means that the scope of the questions put to it is determined by the referring domestic courts, and these questions often concern the *interpretation* of European rules, with the Charter only being one of the instruments to be applied. This is a crucial difference with the European Court for Human Rights, where cases can, and often are adjudicated

[66] CJEU, Opinion 2/13 on accession to the Convention, Judgment of 18 December 2014b, para 177; CJEU, Case 11-70, Internationale Handelsgesellschaft (Solange I), Judgment of 17 December 1970, para 4.

[67] European Union (2009) Charter of Fundamental Rights of the European Union, Article 52(7). The comparative method is also recognised explicitly in the Charter: in so far that the Charter recognises fundamental rights as they result from the constitutional traditions common to the member states, those rights shall be interpreted in harmony with those traditions; ibid., Article 52(4).

[68] CJEU, Opinion 1/15, Judgment of 26 July 2017, para 135.

[69] See for the first CJEU, Cases C-511/18, C-512/18 and C-520/18, La Quadrature du Net, Judgment of 6 October 2020, para 120; CJEU, Case C-311/18, Schrems II, Judgment of 16 July 2020, para 173; CJEU, Opinion 1/15, Judgment of 26 July 2017, para 136; CJEU, Case C-291/12, Schwarz v Bochum, Judgment of 17 October 2013, para 33; CJEU, Case C-92/09, Volker und Markus Schecke and Eifert, Judgment of 9 November 2010, para 48; and for the second CJEU, Case C-112/00, Schmidberger, Judgment of 12 June 2003, para 80.

[70] Greer et al. 2018, p. 319.

[71] See Senden 2011, p. 36.

on the basis of complaints by individuals, leaving much more room for the factual background of a case.

One could argue that in my analysis of the case law of the European Court of Justice in the chapters that follow, the decisions are read too specifically or that it is at any rate too early for such an exercise. I disagree: the European Court of Justice is quickly gaining importance in the application of human rights, and its decisions are already making themselves felt across the world. Close reading these decisions is instructive and will become more important in the coming years as the Court further establishes itself as a human rights court proper.

4.5.2 *Interference, Foreseeability and Legitimate Aims*

Not only do both Courts share a somewhat similar method of interpretation, they also partly apply the same tests when assessing the compatibility of a measure. This assessment consists of a more or less fixed set of steps.

Under the Convention, the European Court of Human Rights assesses first whether there is an "interference" with a right (unless it assesses the existence of a positive obligation, see below), and although the Charter speaks of "limitations" on a right, instead of "interferences", the European Court of Justice in its case law uses these terms interchangeably, thus suggesting that they have the same scope.[72]

If it has been established that there is an interference, both Courts will then usually proceed to investigate whether the interference is *prescribed by law* (under the Convention), or *provided for by law* (under the Charter). This requirement, also called the "foreseeability"-requirement, ensures that member states are bound by the rule of law. Countries may not interfere with a right without there being a law or similar instrument from which they derive the power to do so. This requirement was important in the first decades of the Convention, for example where the UK applied surveillance without a provision in the law. By now, this requirement is fading into the background, as member states do generally adopt certain laws to base these interferences on, as we will see in the discussion of the case law that follows. In particular, most of the measures discussed in Chap. 3 are based on a law, so this condition is fulfilled. But some of the examples in Chap. 3, such as of governments undermining encryption, are not necessarily based on a law, and where appropriate, I discuss this requirement as well.

This does not mean, of course, that states may interfere with a right as long as they do so on the basis of such a law. Both Courts apply two other conditions. First, the

[72] See for example the Court using the term "interference"; CJEU, Cases C-293/12 and C-594/12, Digital Rights Ireland and others, Judgment of 8 April 2014, para 32 and further; CJEU, Case C-362/14, Schrems I, Judgment of 6 October 2015, para 87 and further; CJEU, Opinion 1/15, Judgment of 26 July 2017, para 38 and further; CJEU, Case C-547/14, Philip Morris Brands SARL and Others v Secretary of State for Health, Judgment of 4 May 2016, para 150; CJEU, Cases C-203/15 and C-698/15, Tele2 Sverige and Watson and Others, Judgment of 21 December 2016, para 100 and further.

measure must also have one of the legitimate aims mentioned in the Convention and the Charter. Under the rights to privacy and communications freedom in the Convention, relevant legitimate aims are, among others, "national security", "public safety", the "prevention of disorder or crime" and the protection of "the rights of others". Under the Charter, measures must "genuinely meet objectives of general interest recognised by the Union or the need to protect the rights and freedoms of others".[73] These Union objectives include "maintaining law and order and safeguarding national security".[74] The main drivers behind measures in the domain of information security, encryption and quantum computing fall within one of these headers. In some cases, the margin of appreciation also differs, depending on the kind of aim that a state pursues. I discuss these differences in the chapters that follow.

4.5.3 *The Necessity Test*

More importantly, the interference also has to fulfil the so-called "necessity"-test, which is central to the application of human rights in both the Convention and the Charter. Under the Convention, any interference with the right to privacy and the right to communication freedom must be "necessary in a democratic society" for it to be compatible with the Convention. Under the Charter, limitations may be made only if they are "necessary" and subject to the principle of proportionality.[75] The question is what these requirements mean, and whether there is a difference between them.

For the Convention, the necessity-test is elaborated in the *Silver*-case (1983).[76] First, "the adjective 'necessary' is not synonymous with 'indispensable', neither has it the flexibility of such expressions as 'admissible', 'ordinary', 'useful', 'reasonable' or 'desirable'". Furthermore, "the phrase 'necessary in a democratic society' means that, to be compatible with the Convention, the interference must, inter alia, correspond to a 'pressing social need' and be 'proportionate to the legitimate aim pursued'". Both considerations clarify that the interest pursued by the restriction must be sufficiently important.[77] Embedded in this test, is also the requirement that states should use

[73] Praesidium of the European Convention (2007) Explanations Relating to the Charter of Fundamental Rights, explanation to Article 52.

[74] See Articles 3 and 4(1) of (1992) Treaty on European Union; see on "national security" CJEU, Cases C-511/18, C-512/18 and C-520/18, La Quadrature du Net, Judgment of 6 October 2020, para 134 and further and on law and order, or to be precise, "fight against serious crime and thus, ultimately, to public security"; CJEU, Cases C-293/12 and C-594/12, Digital Rights Ireland and others, Judgment of 8 April 2014, para 41.

[75] European Union (2009) Charter of Fundamental Rights of the European Union, Article 52(1).

[76] ECHR, Application nos. 5947/72; 6205/73; 7052/75; 7061/75; 7107/75; 7113/75; 7136/75, Silver and others v the United Kingdom, Judgment of 25 March 1983, para 97; with references to ECHR, Application no. 5493/72, Handyside v the United Kingdom, Judgment of 7 December 1976, paras 48–49; and ECHR, Klass and others v Germany, Judgment of 6 September 1978, para 42.

[77] See also Gerards 2013, p. 467.

the least restrictive or harmful measure.[78] The Court also underlines that exceptions to a right are to be narrowly interpreted. In *Z v. Finland* (1997), the Court further explains that in determining whether interferences are "necessary in a democratic society", it will consider whether, "in the light of the case as a whole, the reasons adduced to justify them were relevant and sufficient and whether the measures were proportionate to the legitimate aims pursued".[79] The respondent State will have to demonstrate the existence of the pressing social need behind the interference.[80]

The European Court of Justice has not elaborated on the concept of necessity as thoroughly, but it is reasonable to assume that in general the above interpretation applies.[81] In fact, this is one domain where the review applied by both Courts has explicitly converged in the past years. To be precise, the European Court of Justice in the context of privacy rights has consistently applied a particularly stringent necessity-test: in cases where the interference is especially serious, the Court requires that restrictions are "*strictly* necessary", not merely "necessary".[82] This principle can be found in a string of decisions from 2008 onwards, where the Court considers that "the protection of the fundamental right to respect for private life at EU level requires, in accordance with settled case-law of the Court, that *derogations from and limitations on* the protection of personal data should apply only in so far as is strictly necessary" (emphasis added), implying that restrictions should be subject to significant scrutiny.[83] In *Digital Rights Ireland* and *Schrems*, it also explains what this means: "in view of the important role played by the protection of personal data in the light of the fundamental right to respect for private life and the extent and

78 ECHR, Application no. 13590/88, Campbell v UK, Judgment of 25 March 1992, para 48.

79 ECHR, Application no. 22009/93, Z v Finland, Judgment of 25 February 1997, para 94.

80 ECHR, Application no. 20071/07, Piechowicz v Poland, Judgment of 17 April 2012, para 212; see also ECHR, Application no. 37444/97, Bagiński v Poland, Judgment of 11 October 2005, para 89.

81 If only because the Charter at least grants the same protection as the Convention does. See in the context of privacy and data protection also WP29 (2014) WP29 Opinion 01/2014 on the application of necessity and proportionality concepts and data protection within the law enforcement sector, para 4.2; and EDPS 2017, p. 6 for a similar interpretation.

82 See also CJEU, Case C-207/16, Ministerio Fiscal, Judgment of 2 October 2018, where the Court did not apply this standard to an interference it considered not "serious", para 56.

83 CJEU, Cases C-511/18, C-512/18 and C-520/18, La Quadrature du Net, Judgment of 6 October 2020, para 130; CJEU, Case C-623/17, Privacy International v United Kingdom, Judgment of 6 October 2020, para 67; CJEU, Case C-311/18, Schrems II, Judgment of 16 July 2020, para 176; CJEU, Opinion 1/15, Judgment of 26 July 2017, para 140; see before CJEU, Case C-73/07, Satamedia, Judgment of 16 December 2008, para 26; CJEU, Case C-92/09, Volker und Markus Schecke and Eifert, Judgment of 9 November 2010, para 77; CJEU, Case C-473/12, IPI, Judgment of 7 November 2013, para 39; CJEU, Cases C-293/12 and C-594/12, Digital Rights Ireland and others, Judgment of 8 April 2014, para 52; CJEU, Case C-362/14, Schrems I, Judgment of 6 October 2015, para 92; CJEU, Cases C-203/15 and C-698/15, Tele2 Sverige and Watson and Others, Judgment of 21 December 2016, para 96; see also CJEU, C-205/21, V.S. / Ministerstvo na vatreshnite raboti, Judgment of 26 January 2023.

seriousness of the interference with that right [...], the EU legislature's discretion is reduced, with the result that review of that discretion should be strict".[84]

This test has not remained confined to the European Court of Justice: in 2016 the European Court of Human Rights in *Szabó* explicitly endorsed this application of the "strict necessity"-requirement to privacy cases.[85] The Court in this case even developed the test further, requiring a double test: not only should the measure be strictly necessary for safeguarding of "democratic institutions", but it should also be strictly necessary for obtaining vital intelligence in an individual operation.[86] The European Court of Justice has not given a precise definition of what this strict scrutiny entails. It can at least be opposed to "marginal scrutiny", where the Court tests whether the measure in question is manifestly unreasonable or completely arbitrary.[87]

This development is not only an interesting example of each Court building on the case law of the other, it is also highly relevant for the substantive assessment of governance measures in this book. Given the convergence of the review standard of both Courts in privacy cases, I argue that this review requires a basic scepticism from the Court as to the necessity of a measure, as well as an in-depth examination of its necessity on the basis of empirical evidence. This is particularly relevant for this study, because claims of necessity of a certain measure, both under the Convention and the Charter, always need to be supported by a significant body of evidence. This is especially so where restrictions are particularly serious, for example in cases affecting the rights to privacy and data protection. As we will see in the chapters to come, some of the policies affecting information security and encryption in particular fall within that category.

4.5.4 *The Relevance of the Essence of a Right under the Charter*

While the Charter is quite similar to the Convention in its application, this does not mean that the *method of evaluating* the compatibility of measures is exactly the same. Under the Charter, one condition in addition to the steps discussed above must be satisfied. Not only must limitations on the exercise of a right or freedom be provided by law and be necessary, but they must also respect *the essence* of this right or freedom.[88]

---

[84] CJEU, Cases C-293/12 and C-594/12, Digital Rights Ireland and others, Judgment of 8 April 2014, para 48; see also CJEU, Case C-362/14, Schrems I, Judgment of 6 October 2015, para 78.

[85] In *Szabó*, the Court considered that, "given the particular character of the interference in question and the potential of cutting-edge surveillance technologies to invade citizens' privacy", the requirement "necessary in a democratic society" must be interpreted as requiring "strict necessity"; ECHR, Application no. 37138/14, Szabó and Vissy v Hungary, Judgment of 12 January 2016b, para 73.

[86] Ibid., para 73.

[87] Gerards 2004, p. 144; see Granger and Irion 2014, p. 846 on the strict scrutiny test in privacy cases.

[88] European Union (2009) Charter of Fundamental Rights of the European Union, Article 52(1).

The question is what the relevance of this notion of essence is, and how it relates to the notion of proportionality.[89] One could firstly argue that the proportionality test has to be applied to *all* limitations, but where the essence of the right or freedom is affected, the test itself will be more stringent (this is called the "relative" theory).[90] In contrast to this "relative" approach, one could argue that the requirement of respect for the essence means that this a step to be taken *before* the application of the proportionality test: only if a certain limitation respects the essence of a right or freedom, is it possible to apply the proportionality test (this is called the "absolute" theory).[91] The difference is significant, because under the absolute theory, if you can demonstrate that a measure does *not* respect the essence of a fundamental right, you do not need to demonstrate that the measure is disproportionate, something which is often difficult to do.

This latter interpretation is more convincing. Firstly, a literal interpretation of Article 52 of the Charter suggests that the absolute theory is correct.[92] The case law of the Court of Justice also appears to support this reading.[93] In this book, I will work therefore on the basis that the correct reading of the essence requirement under Article 52 of the Charter implies that it is a binary concept, to be applied separately from the application of the proportionality requirement.

4.6 Different Typologies of States' Duties

A last conceptual framework which cuts across the Convention and the Charter, is that of negative and positive obligations.[94] The term "negative obligation" refers to the duty of a state to *not do* something—for example, not to prohibit the circulation of a newspaper. A "positive obligation" refers to a state's duty to actually *do* something—for example, to protect protesters against counter-protestors in order to safeguard their freedom of expression. This is important for my assessment of the governance measures in this book, because I not only explore what governments cannot do, such as undermine encryption, but also whether they have an obligation to do things, such as investing in the development of encryption.

The text of many of the rights under the Convention appear to impose a solely negative obligation: everyone has a right to privacy, for example, and there "shall be no interference" with such right. But the European Court of Human Rights had already

---

[89] Brkan in a number of papers explores the origins and scope of the concept of the essence of a fundamental rights; Brkan 2017, 2018a, b.

[90] See Brkan 2018a, pp. 3–4. One can find support for this reasoning in the official explanations to the Charter; Praesidium of the European Convention (2007) Explanations Relating to the Charter of Fundamental Rights, explanation on Article 52 of the Charter.

[91] See Brkan 2018b.

[92] See Brkan 2018a, p. 4; see also the diagram on p. 73 of European Union Agency for Fundamental Rights 2020.

[93] See Brkan 2018a, pp. 5–6 for an in-depth discussion.

[94] See on positive and negative obligations under the Convention and the Charter Beijer 2017.

in its earlier case law contended that there may be positive obligations inherent in the effective respect of a right, regardless of whether there is an interference.[95] Since then, it has developed extensive case law on positive obligations. Now, the Court's case law is not always consistent, but I will attempt to derive some principles from the decisions in the chapters that follow.[96] Here, I only discuss the general structure of the Court's assessment of positive obligations.

The first question is what *kinds* of positive obligations the European Court of Human Rights recognises. The Court explained that "the notion of 'respect' is not clear-cut: having regard to the diversity of practices followed and the situations obtaining in the Contracting states, the notion's requirements will vary considerably from case to case".[97] Most importantly, the Court has considered that in "determining whether or not a positive obligation exists, regard must be had to the fair balance that has to be struck between the general interest of the community and the interests of the individual, the search for which balance is inherent in the whole of the Convention".[98] How this fair balance must be struck, depends on the right in question. In particular, the interests at stake must be weighed against the burden imposed on states: positive obligations may not impose an impossible or disproportionate burden on the authorities or the legislator.[99]

According to the Court, states in principle have a wide margin of appreciation in deciding on the *choice of means* by which they legislate.[100] States, as a result of "their direct and continuous contact with the vital forces of their countries" are, "in principle, in a better position than the international judge to give an opinion on how best to secure the right to respect for private life within the domestic legal order".[101] There are also considerations for widening the margin of appreciation even further. Firstly, this is so where there is no consensus between states, either with regard to the relative importance of the interest at stake, or—specifically relevant for positive

---

[95] See ECHR, Marckx v Belgium, Judgment of 13 June 1979, para 31; ECHR, Application no. 6289/73, Airey v Ireland, Judgment of 9 October 1979a, para 32; ECHR, Application no. 8978/80, X and Y v the Netherlands, Judgment of 26 March 1985, para 23.

[96] See for a critical discussion Beijer 2017, Chap. 4.7.

[97] ECHR, Application nos. 9214/80; 9473/81; 9474/81, Abdulaziz, Cabales and Balkandali v the United Kingdom, Judgment of 28 May 1985, para 67; ECHR, Application no. 28957/95, Christine Goodwin v the United Kingdom, Judgment of 11 July 2002, para 72; ECHR, Application no. 25579/05, A, B and C v Ireland, Judgment of 16 December 2010, para 248.

[98] ECHR, Application no. 9532/81, Rees v United Kingdom, Judgment of 17 October 1986, para 37.

[99] ECHR, Application no. 37359/09, Hämäläinen v Finland, Judgment of 16 July 2014, para 66; ECHR, Application no. 2872/02, K.U. v Finland, Judgment of 2 December 2008, para 48; ECHR, Application no. 28957/95, Christine Goodwin v the United Kingdom, Judgment of 11 July 2002, paras 86-88; ECHR, Application no. 9532/81, Rees v United Kingdom, Judgment of 17 October 1986, paras 43–44.

[100] ECHR, Application no. 5786/08, Söderman v Sweden, Judgment of 12 November 2013, paras 78–79.

[101] ECHR, Application no. 48009/08, Mosley v the United Kingdom, Judgment of 10 May 2011, para 108.

obligations—in relation to the best means of protecting it.[102] This is also the case where the interests at stake must be weighed against other, competing public or private interests or Convention rights and a "fair balance" must be struck.[103] In *Dickson*, the Court further specified that where a case raises complex issues and choices of social strategy, it would generally respect the policy choices of the legislator, unless it is "manifestly without reasonable foundation".[104]

The Court has also considered that the boundaries between positive and negative obligations do not lend themselves to "precise definition".[105] Given the difficulty of delineating the two, the question is whether this distinction matters at all. It does, because the Court does not usually assess positive obligations under the second paragraph of the provision setting out each right in the Convention (although the *aims* of the second paragraph are of "a certain relevance", according to the Court).[106] This is because this second paragraph explains under which circumstances an "interference" is allowed, whereas in the case of positive obligations there is no such interference. This means that the necessity and proportionality test is applied under the header of whether the obligation exists in the first place.[107] This explains the more open structure of the assessment of positive obligations in the case law of the Court.

The rich case law on positive obligations of the European Court of Human Rights can be contrasted with that of European Court of Justice, which until recently did

---

[102] ECHR, Application no. 37359/09, Hämäläinen v Finland, Judgment of 16 July 2014, para 67; referring to ECHR, Application no. 21830/93, X, Y and Z v the United Kingdom, Judgment of 22 April 1997, para 44; ECHR, Application no. 36515/97, Fretté v France, Judgment of 26 February 2002, para 41; ECHR, Application no. 28957/95, Christine Goodwin v the United Kingdom, Judgment of 11 July 2002, para 85.

[103] ECHR, Application no. 37359/09, Hämäläinen v Finland, Judgment of 16 July 2014, para 67; referring to *inter alia* ECHR, Application no. 36515/97, Fretté v France, Judgment of 26 February 2002, para 42; ECHR, Application no. 42326/98, Odièvre v France, Judgment of 13 February 2003, paras 44–39; ECHR, Application no. 6339/05, Evans v the United Kingdom, Judgment of 10 April 2007, para 77; ECHR, Application no. 44362/04), Dickson v the United Kingdom, Judgment of 4 December 2007, para 78; ECHR, Application no. 57813/00, S.H. and others v Austria, Judgment of 3 November 2011, para 94; see also ECHR, Application no. 48009/08, Mosley v the United Kingdom, Judgment of 10 May 2011, para 111; and ECHR, Applications nos. 40660/08 and 60641/08, Von Hannover v Germany (no. 2), Judgment of 7 February 2012, para 99.

[104] ECHR, Application no. 44362/04), Dickson v the United Kingdom, Judgment of 4 December 2007, para 78.

[105] ECHR, Application no. 42326/98, Odièvre v France, Judgment of 13 February 2003, para 40; ECHR, Application no. 6339/05, Evans v the United Kingdom, Judgment of 10 April 2007, paras 75 and 76.

[106] ECHR, Application no. 37359/09, Hämäläinen v Finland, Judgment of 16 July 2014, para 65; ECHR, Application no. 32555/96, Roche v the United Kingdom, Judgment of 19 October 2005, para 157; ECHR, Application no. 10454/83, Gaskin v the United Kingdom, Judgment of 7 July 1989, para 42.

[107] Because it is sometimes difficult to distinguish between positive and negative obligations, and since the framework for determining whether something is a positive obligation is not very consistent, Judge Wildhaber in a concurring opinion in *Stjerna* (1991) advocated for considering breaches of both positive and negative obligations under the heading of an "interference". See concurring opinion Judge Wildhaber in ECHR, Application no. 18131/91, Stjerna v Finland, Judgment of 25 November 1994. The Court, however, did not follow this suggestion since.

not mention the concept of positive obligations in the context of the Charter, perhaps partly because the Charter states that it "does not establish any new power or task for the Community or the Union, or modify powers and tasks defined by the Treaties".[108] But this, too, appears to be changing. In *La Quadrature du Net* (2020) it noted that positive obligations under Article 7 of the Charter may require public authorities to adopt legal measures to protect private life, family life, an individual's home and communications, considering that the Court must strike a fair balance between the positive obligations in question.[109]

For this book, what matters is not so much the distinction between positive and negative obligations, but that human rights in essence are aimed at providing effective protection, regardless of the header under which this protection falls. One framework of obligations which has proven useful in determining a broad catalogue of obligations is the widely accepted tripartite typology of duties to *respect*, *protect* and *fulfil* human rights.[110] To "respect" requires the state to not interfere with the freedoms of its citizens: the classic notion of negative obligations. To "protect" requires the state to take measures to prevent others from interfering with its citizens: a certain form of positive obligations, mostly focused on horizontal relationships. And to "fulfil" requires the state to take measures to ensure opportunities for its citizens to satisfy needs recognised in human rights instruments which they cannot secure by their own efforts: creating the opportunities for the enjoyment of human rights, in other words. This tripartite typology also plays a role in determining the substance of human rights obligations in the chapters below.

Having now set the stage by discussing the principles for application of the human rights in question, it is time to determine the relevant scope of these rights, starting with the right to privacy.

References

Articles, Books and Other Documents

Alston P, Bustelo MR, Heenan J (eds) (1999) The EU and Human Rights. Oxford University Press, Oxford, England; New York.

Beijer M (2017) The Limits of Fundamental Rights Protection by the EU: The Scope for the Development of Positive Obligations. Intersentia, Cambridge Antwerp Portland

Brkan M (2017) In Search of the Concept of Essence of EU Fundamental Rights through the Prism of Data Privacy. https://papers.ssrn.com/abstract=2900281. Accessed 4 January 2024

[108] (2000) Charter of Fundamental Rights of the European Union, Article 51(2); See for the assessment until 2018 Greer et al. 2018, p. 320; see also Beijer 2017, Chap. 10.

[109] CJEU, Cases C-511/18, C-512/18 and C-520/18, La Quadrature du Net, Judgment of 6 October 2020, paras 126–128; see before CJEU, Case C-78/18, European Commission v Hungary (Transparency of Associations), Judgment of 18 June 2020, para 123.

[110] Eide (1987), para 66 and further. This typology has subsequently been further refined; see for a discussion Koch 2009, Chap. 2.1.

Brkan M (2018a) The Essence of the Fundamental Rights to Privacy and Data Protection: Finding the Way through the Maze of the CJEU's Constitutional Reasoning. German Law Journal , 6: 864–883.

Brkan M (2018b) The Concept of Essence of Fundamental Rights in the EU Legal Order: Peeling the Onion to its Core. European Constitutional Law Review 14:332–368. https://doi.org/10.1017/S1574019618000159

Coppel J, O'Neill A (1992) The European Court of Justice: Taking Rights Seriously? Legal Studies 12:227–239. https://doi.org/10.1111/j.1748-121X.1992.tb00467.x

De Burca G (2015) The Drafting of the European Union Charter of Fundamental Rights. European Law Review 40:799–810.

ECHR (2011) What Are the Limits to the Evolutive Interpretation of the Convention? , Dialogue Between Judges 2011. https://www.echr.coe.int/documents/d/echr/Dialogue_between_judges_2011. Accessed 4 January 2024

EDPS (2017) Assessing the Necessity of Measures That Limit the Fundamental Right to the Protection of Personal Data: A Toolkit, 11 April 2017

Eide A (1987) Report on the Right to Adequate Food as a Human Right, E/CN.4/Sub.2/1987/23, 7 July 1987

European Commission (2023) 2023 Rule of Law Report. Country Chapter on the Rule of Law Situation in Poland' SWD(2023) 821 final, https://commission.europa.eu/system/files/2023-07/48_1_52627_coun_chap_poland_en.pdf. Accessed 6 July 2023

European Union Agency for Fundamental Rights (2020) Applying the Charter of Fundamental Rights of the European Union in law and policymaking at national level: guidance. Publications Office, LU.

Ferraro F, Carmona J (2015) Fundamental Rights in the European Union: The Role of the Charter after the Lisbon Treaty: In Depth Analysis. https://www.europarl.europa.eu/thinktank/en/document/EPRS_IDA(2015)554168. Accessed 4 January 2024

Gerards J (2013) How to Improve the Necessity Test of the European Court of Human Rights. International Journal of Constitutional Law 11:466–490. https://doi.org/10.1093/icon/mot004

Gerards JH (2004) Intensity of Judicial Review in Equal Treatment Cases. Netherlands International Law Review 51:135–183. https://doi.org/10.1017/S0165070X04001354

Glendon MA (2001) A World Made New: Eleanor Roosevelt and the Universal Declaration of Human Rights (1st edition, Random House 2001)

Granger M-P, Irion K (2014) The Court of Justice and the Data Retention Directive in Digital Rights Ireland: Telling Off the EU Legislator and Teaching a Lesson in Privacy and Data Protection. European Law Review 2014:835–850.

Greer SC (2006) The European Convention on Human Rights: Achievements, Problems and Prospects. Cambridge University Press, Cambridge, UK; New York.

Greer S, Gerards J, Slowe R (2018) Human Rights in the Council of Europe and the European Union: Achievements, Trends and Challenges. Cambridge University Press, Cambridge.

Ishay M (2009) The History of Human Rights: From Ancient Times to the Globalization Era, University of California Press, Berkeley.

Koch IE (2009) Human Rights as Indivisible Rights: The Protection of Socio-Economic Demands under the European Convention on Human Rights. Martinus Nijhoff Publishers

Kom A de, Esajas M (2020) Wij slaven van Suriname. Atlas Contact, Amsterdam.

Lasser M de S-O-l (2009) Judicial Deliberations: A Comparative Analysis of Transparency and Legitimacy. Oxford University Press

Lenaerts K (2007) Interpretation and the Court of Justice: A Basis for Comparative Reflection. The International Lawyer 41:1011.

Lenaerts K, Gutiérrez-Fons JA (2013) To Say What the Law of the EU is: Methods of Interpretation and the European Court of Justice. https://cadmus.eui.eu/handle/1814/28339. Accessed 4 January 2024

Lenaerts K, Gutman K (2016) The Comparative Law Method and the European Court of Justice: Echoes across the Atlantic. The American Journal of Comparative Law 64:841–864. https://doi.org/10.1093/ajcl/avw017
Levinsohn BL (1991) De kolencrisis van 1941. Een bestuurskundige case study over de beleidsopvattingen van ambtelijk middenkader. PhD thesis, University of Utrecht, Utrecht
Mcguinness ME (2011) Peace v. Justice: The Universal Declaration of Human Rights and the Modern Origins of the Debate. Diplomatic History 35:749–768. https://doi.org/10.1111/j.1467-7709.2011.00982.x
Morsink J (1999) The Universal Declaration of Human Rights: origins, drafting and intent. University of Pennsylvania Press, Philadelphia.
Orakhelashvili A (2011) Research Handbook on the Theory and History of International Law. Edward Elgar Publishing
Šadl U (2015) The Role of Effet Utile in Preserving the Continuity and Authority of European Union Law: Evidence from the Citation Web of the Pre-accession Case Law of the Court of Justice of the EU. European Journal of Legal Studies 8:18–45.
Sémiramis I (2014) 21 avril 1944: les Françaises ont (enfin) le droit de voter.TV5MONDE. https://information.tv5monde.com/terriennes/21-avril-1944-les-francaises-ont-enfin-le-droit-de-voter-3230. Accessed 12 June 2020
Senden H (2011) Interpretation of Fundamental Rights In A Multilevel Legal System: An Analysis of the European Court of Human Rights and the Court of Justice of the European Union. Intersentia, Cambridge.
van Daalen O (2022), In Defense of Offense: Information Security Research under the Right to Science, Computer Law & Security Review 46: 105706.
van Daalen O (2023a) The Right to Encryption: Privacy as Preventing Unlawful Access, Computer Law & Security Review 49:105804.
van Daalen O (2023b) The Right to Root: Constructing a Claim to Control Devices from the Right to Privacy. JIPITEC 14(2023:4): 580–593.
van Daalen O (2024) Developing a human-rights compatible governance framework for quantum computing. Research Directions: Quantum Technologies 2: 2024.
van der Sloot B (2017) Legal Fundamentalism: Is Data Protection Really a Fundamental Right? In: Leenes R, van Brakel R, Gutwirth S, De Hert P (eds) Data Protection and Privacy: (In)visibilities and Infrastructures. Springer International Publishing, Cham, pp 3–30.

Table of Cases: National

Bundesverfassungsgericht (BverfG), BvL 52/71, Solange I-Beschluß, Judgment of 29 May 1974.

Table of Cases: EU

CJEU, C-205/21, V.S. / Ministerstvo na vatreshnite raboti, Judgment of 26 January 2023.
CJEU, C-414/16, Egenberger, Judgment of 17 April 2018.
CJEU, Case 11-70, Internationale Handelsgesellschaft (Solange I), Judgment of 17 December 1970.
CJEU, Case 36/75, Roland Rutili v Ministre de l'intérieur, Judgment of 28 October 1975.
CJEU, Case 4-73, J. Nold, Kohlen- und Baustoffgroßhandlung v Commission of the European Communities., Judgment of 14 May 1974.
CJEU, Case C-112/00, Schmidberger, Judgment of 12 June 2003.
CJEU, Case C-206/13, Siragusa, Judgment of 6 March 2014.
CJEU, Case C-207/16, Ministerio Fiscal, Judgment of 2 October 2018.

CJEU, Case C-26/62, Van Gend en Loos, Judgment of 5 February 1963.
CJEU, Case C-29/69, Erich Stauder v City of Ulm-Sozialamt, Judgment of 12 November 1969.
CJEU, Case C-291/12, Schwarz v Bochum, Judgment of 17 October 2013.
CJEU, Case C-311/18, Schrems II, Judgment of 16 July 2020.
CJEU, Case C-362/14, Schrems I, Judgment of 6 October 2015.
CJEU, Case C-41/74, Van Duyn, Judgment of 4 December 1974.
CJEU, Case C-473/12, IPI, Judgment of 7 November 2013.
CJEU, Case C-547/14, Philip Morris Brands SARL and Others v Secretary of State for Health, Judgment of 4 May 2016.
CJEU, Case C-617/10, Åkerberg Fransson, Judgment of 26 February 2013.
CJEU, Case C-623/17, Privacy International v United Kingdom, Judgment of 6 October 2020.
CJEU, Case C-66/18, European Commission v Hungary, Judgment of 6 October 2020.
CJEU, Case C-73/07, Satamedia, Judgment of 16 December 2008.
CJEU, Case C-78/18, European Commission v Hungary (Transparency of Associations), Judgment of 18 June 2020.
CJEU, Case C-92/09, Volker und Markus Schecke and Eifert, Judgment of 9 November 2010.
CJEU, Cases C-203/15 and C-698/15, Tele2 Sverige and Watson and Others, Judgment of 21 December 2016.
CJEU, Cases C-293/12 and C-594/12, Digital Rights Ireland and others, Judgment of 8 April 2014.
CJEU, Cases C-511/18, C-512/18 and C-520/18, La Quadrature du Net, Judgment of 6 October 2020.
CJEU, Opinion 1/15, Judgment of 26 July 2017.
CJEU, Opinion 2/13 on accession to the Convention, Judgment of 18 December 2014a.
CJEU, Opinion 2/13 on accession to the Convention, Judgment of 18 December 2014b.
CJEU, Opinion 2/94 on Accession by the Community to the European Convention for the Protection of Human Rights and Fundamental Freedoms, Judgment of 28 March 1996.
ECHR, Application no. 10454/83, Gaskin v the United Kingdom, Judgment of 7 July 1989.
ECHR, Application no. 13590/88, Campbell v UK, Judgment of 25 March 1992.
ECHR, Application no. 18131/91, Stjerna v Finland, Judgment of 25 November 1994.
ECHR, Application no. 20071/07, Piechowicz v Poland, Judgment of 17 April 2012.
ECHR, Application no. 2122/64, Wemhoff v Germany, Judgment of 27 June 1968.
ECHR, Application no. 21830/93, X, Y and Z v the United Kingdom, Judgment of 22 April 1997.
ECHR, Application no. 22009/93, Z v Finland, Judgment of 25 February 1997.
ECHR, Application no. 25579/05, A, B and C v Ireland, Judgment of 16 December 2010.
ECHR, Application no. 2872/02, K.U. v Finland, Judgment of 2 December 2008.
ECHR, Application no. 28957/95, Christine Goodwin v the United Kingdom, Judgment of 11 July 2002.
ECHR, Application no. 32555/96, Roche v the United Kingdom, Judgment of 19 October 2005.
ECHR, Application no. 36515/97, Fretté v France, Judgment of 26 February 2002.
ECHR, Application no. 37138/14, Szabó and Vissy v Hungary, Judgment of 12 January 2016b.
ECHR, Application no. 37359/09, Hämäläinen v Finland, Judgment of 16 July 2014.
ECHR, Application no. 37444/97, Bagiński v Poland, Judgment of 11 October 2005.
ECHR, Application no. 42326/98, Odièvre v France, Judgment of 13 February 2003.
ECHR, Application no. 44362/04), Dickson v the United Kingdom, Judgment of 4 December 2007.
ECHR, Application no. 4451/70, Golder v United Kingdom, Judgment of 21 February 1975.
ECHR, Application no. 48009/08, Mosley v the United Kingdom, Judgment of 10 May 2011.
ECHR, Application no. 5493/72, Handyside v the United Kingdom, Judgment of 7 December 1976.
ECHR, Application no. 57813/00, S.H. and others v Austria, Judgment of 3 November 2011.
ECHR, Application no. 5786/08, Söderman v Sweden, Judgment of 12 November 2013.
ECHR, Application no. 5856/72, Tyrer v UK, Judgment of 25 April 1978.
ECHR, Application nos. 5947/72; 6205/73; 7052/75; 7061/75; 7107/75; 7113/75; 7136/75, Silver and others v the United Kingdom, Judgment of 25 March 1983.
ECHR, Application no. 6289/73, Airey v Ireland, Judgment of 9 October 1979a.

ECHR, Application no. 6339/05, Evans v the United Kingdom, Judgment of 10 April 2007.
ECHR, Application no. 7525/76, Dudgeon v United Kingdom, Judgment of 22 October 1981.
ECHR, Application no. 8978/80, X and Y v the Netherlands, Judgment of 26 March 1985.
ECHR, Application nos. 9214/80; 9473/81; 9474/81, Abdulaziz, Cabales and Balkandali v the United Kingdom, Judgment of 28 May 1985.
ECHR, Application no. 9532/81, Rees v United Kingdom, Judgment of 17 October 1986.
ECHR, Applications nos. 40660/08 and 60641/08, Von Hannover v Germany (no. 2), Judgment of 7 February 2012.
ECHR, Klass and others v Germany, Judgment of 6 September 1978.
ECHR, Marckx v Belgium, Judgment of 13 June 1979.

Chapter 5
The Right to Privacy and Data Protection

Contents

Abstract This chapter discusses the rights to privacy and data protection under the Convention and the Charter. It starts out with a discussion on the concept of privacy and describes the historical development of the idea. It then discusses how this concept has been embedded in human rights instruments, and how this has been applied over the decades. This analysis then leads to the conclusion that the rights to privacy and data protection protect against unlawful access to and control of information and systems, an insight which is highly relevant to information security measures which perform a similar function.

Keywords Privacy · Data protection · Unlawful access · Information security measures · Encryption

O. van Daalen, *From Encryption to Quantum Computing*, Information Technology and Law Series 38, https://doi.org/10.1007/978-94-6265-635-2_5

5.1 Introduction

In 2006, German authorities, obtained the power to hack computers.[1] The authorities had already accessed computers remotely in investigations before, but without an explicit legal basis. Now, the region of Nordrhein-Westfalen had adopted specific rules to this end. These became the subject of court proceedings, which ultimately reached the German Constitutional Court, the *Bundesverfassungsgericht*. There, renowned judges and a host of experts, including the leader of the German hacker association *Chaos Computer Club*, had to answer an important question: is this *Online Durchsuchung* allowed under the German Constitution?

This question touches on many aspects of the relationship between the information security cycle and privacy. The German authorities wanted to intercept messages on a device before they were encrypted. How does this relate to the confidentiality of communications? And after entering the device, the authorities could potentially access all stored information, even if they intended to monitor only specific communications. Is this intrusion in itself problematic from a privacy perspective, or should the focus be on the subsequent processing of the data? Moreover, the German authorities would exploit a vulnerability in a computer—thus keeping weaknesses secret and creating the risk that criminals could enter the unpatched computers of innocent people as well. How should the interests of these people—who are not a subject of an investigation—be weighed?

In Chap. 3, I discussed the governance of the information security cycle, encryption technologies and quantum computing. I concluded that there are important gaps. This affects information security research and impacts the level of information security in society. A central question of this book is, whether you can derive a set of obligations from the rights to privacy and data protection under the Convention and the Charter by which you can assess these shortcomings. In this chapter, I answer this question on the basis of case law of the European Court of Human Rights and the European Court of Justice.[2] As we will see, many of the considerations developed over the years come together in the decision of the *Bundesverfassungsgericht*, which I review at the end of this chapter.

The role of the rights to privacy and data protection can be split into two parts. First, as discussed, the Courts have to establish whether there is an interference. For most of the governance approaches discussed in Chap. 3, this is less obvious than it appears: regulations may create the possibility of future privacy interferences, but do they also constitute privacy interferences themselves? And even if it is established that some of these approaches should indeed be assessed under the rights to privacy and data protection, the second question is *how* these should be evaluated. This determination revolves around the necessity requirement and—for the Charter—around the "essence"-requirement. In this chapter, I develop the criteria by which

---

[1] Bundesverfassungsgericht, BVerfGE - 1 BvR 370/07 - 1 BvR 595/07-, Online-Durchsuchung, Judgment of 27 February 2008.

[2] Parts of this chapter have already been published in Van Daalen 2022, 2023a, 2023b and 2024.

these regulations can be assessed. In Chaps. 8–10, these criteria will be applied to different domains.

5.2 Concepts of Privacy

If you want to determine the scope of the human right to privacy (including the right to data protection), the Charter and Convention are an obvious place to start. I discuss these in the sections that follow. But first, I want to discuss the normative *concept* of privacy, not the *right* as laid down in the Convention and the Charter. Scholars have for decades valiantly attempted to make sense of the concept—outlining its dimensions, eliciting its values and categorising its functions.[3] Most start out simply enough—with a reference to an 1890-paper from two US lawyers.[4] But after that, many papers just add to the complexity. Fortunately, these theories of privacy are not developed in a vacuum. They are often drafted in response to societal and technological developments raising new privacy-related questions, and authors use these theories to argue for legislative protection of a not-yet-recognised privacy interest. Below, a selection of theories will be described which have a bearing on information security, concluding that all these privacy theories revolve around the concepts of *access* and *control*, which play an important role in my subsequent analysis.

5.2.1 *The Enlightenment*

This historical account starts somewhere between the 17th and 18th century. This was a time when the monarch was still powerful, but its power was under siege. Digital technologies were yet to be invented. In that era, privacy violations came primarily from the state: soldiers could enter your house, government officials could read your letters and spies could eavesdrop on your conversations.[5] The debate was mostly about whether citizens could claim protection against such unwarranted intrusion.

During this period, the contours of two important privacy interests, the home and of correspondence, were already taking shape. In 1763, when the British government wanted to tax not only the *commercial* production of cider, but also the *domestic* production, William Pitt made an impassioned plea for the sanctity of the home: "The poorest man may in his cottage bid defiance to all the force of the crown. It may be frail—its roof may shake—the wind may blow through it—the storm may enter, the rain may enter—but the King of England cannot enter—all his force

---

[3] See Sax 2018; Solove 2008; Holvast 2009; Blok 2002; Nissenbaum 2009; Koops et al. 2017.

[4] Warren and Brandeis 1890.

[5] Others could also intrude on your private affairs and use it for gain which in some situations resulted in a legal response, for example the criminalisation of blackmail; Solove 2008, pp. 95–96.

dares not cross the threshold of the ruined tenement".[6] And while many European states, such as England, France, Germany, the Italian states and the Dutch Republic, enlisted postal services to route, intercept and decrypt letters, this was not well-received either.[7] Many letters were exchanged in code, and a number of manuals on cryptography were printed during that time (see also the next chapter).[8] Martin Luther, who kindled the Protestant movement, is said to have been outraged at the interception of his correspondence by the Duke of Saxony: "a thief is a thief, whether he is a money thief or a letter thief".[9]

Infringements like these ultimately led to constitutional protection of the home and of correspondence across Europe and the United States, something which previously had only been recognised in specific legal doctrines.[10] In fact, these rights still figure prominently in the Convention and the Charter, as we will see. What sets the privacy violations of this age apart, is the limited role technology plays. Information *collection* methods were manual, information *storage* could not be done at scale, and information *distribution* was costly. You can describe the privacy of that era as *privacy as confidentiality*, or *privacy as secrecy*. The policy response was to constitutionally prohibit *access*, unless certain conditions were met—for example, you could not enter a home or open correspondence without a warrant.

5.2.2 The Era of Mass Communications

Then came the introduction of *mass communications*, from the 19th century onwards. As a host of new information distribution channels enveloped the world, from newspapers to radio, from cinema to television, it became clear that *access* to information, for example reading a letter, is not the only privacy problem. What set this era apart was that the broad reach of mass media meant that for the first time, *distribution*—including distribution of private information—could take place at scale.

Around this time, Warren and Brandeis published their oft-cited article arguing for a separate right to privacy, concerned about "instantaneous photographs and newspaper enterprises".[11] Their argument was largely intended to curtail the spread of private information via newspapers. This new thinking about privacy recognised not only the role of the state in privacy violations, but also the role of private parties, such as newspaper publishers. And the suggested policy response lay not so much in

---

[6] Cited in United States Supreme Court, Miller v v United States, Judgment of 23 June 1958, U.S. 357, p. 307; York 2005.

[7] De Leeuw 1999; Kahn 1996, Chap. 5; Iordanou 2018; see further Lang 2018, p. 126; Gürkan 2012.

[8] Lang 2018, Chaps. 4 and 6; Ellison 2011; Poole 2011.

[9] Quoted in Kahn 2006.

[10] See for the right to secrecy of correspondence; Steenbruggen 2009, Chap. 1.

[11] Warren and Brandeis 1890, p. 195.

restricting *access* to information but restricting *public distribution*. At the same time, it was realised that restrictions were not appropriate in all cases. Where information is in the public interest, Warren and Brandeis argued that distribution should not be limited, even where the information itself was confidential. Thus, privacy now also had to be explicitly balanced with freedom of expression. This new understanding of privacy could be framed as *privacy as reputation*, focusing on the Role of private information in public media.

5.2.3 The Introduction of Databases

A third way of thinking about privacy was triggered by the *introduction of electronic databases*, after the Second World War. This enabled storage of data at scale, heralding a boom in privacy scholarship, as it became clear that the understanding of *privacy as confidentiality* and *privacy as reputation* did not suffice anymore. People were providing *access* to their private information to have it stored in databases, for example to obtain government services, but on the condition that the *use* of that data would be restricted. The influential 1973 US-government report is illustrative: "Dictionary definitions of privacy uniformly speak in terms of seclusion, secrecy, and withdrawal from public view. They all denote a quality that is not inherent in most record-keeping systems".[12] A new concept was necessary.

The dominant policy response of that time was described by Westin, who in 1967 defined privacy as "the claim of individuals, groups, or institutions to determine for themselves when, how, and to what extent information about them is communicated to others".[13] This understanding shifted the concept from the *restriction* of access to information, to the *control* of its use. Under this thinking, the processing of private information is in principle allowed, but its use is subject to certain conditions. This means for example that personal data needs to be accurate and appropriately secured. This culminated in the data protection instruments discussed in Chap. 3. The concept has even been embraced by the German Constitutional court, which in 1983 recognised a right to "informational self-determination": the right of an individual to determine for themselves the disclosure and use of their personal data.[14] This era also planted the seeds for the right to data protection under the Charter, which I discuss further below. This understanding of privacy is commonly referred to as *privacy as informational self-determination*.

---

[12] Advisory Committee on Automated Personal Data Systems, *Records, Computers and the Rights of Citizens*, 1 July 1973, p. 38; also referred to in van der Sloot 2017a, b, p. 39.

[13] Westin 2015, p. 5; see also Fried 1968, p. 482.

[14] German Constitutional Court, German Census, Judgment of 15 December 1983, para 147.

5.2.4 *The Introduction of the Internet*

Then, as *networking technologies* started to spread, the connection of personal computers to the public internet raised two new privacy questions. First, the internet provides a channel through which users can interact *with* the outside world, reading websites, playing online games and publishing information. This allows the organisations providing those services to collect personal profiles, because if you use an online service, you necessarily give away information about yourself. Some of this you do voluntarily, for example through a carefully crafted social media-account. But much of it happens involuntarily: in the past decades a widespread data collection ecosystem has developed, through which companies monitor and then influence the behaviour of internet users on devices and websites.

One conceptual response to this development was to understand privacy as "the freedom from unreasonable constraints on the construction of one's own identity" as suggested by Agre and Rotenberg.[15] This concept is a variation on informational self-determination discussed above: it is still predicated on the idea that the individual is in charge, but they use and need this power to develop their personality. This understanding emphasises that privacy also has a role to play in the public sphere, not only as a shielding right (e.g. blocking a slanderous publication), but also by providing you with the possibilities to actively build your own identity. This means that, for example, algorithms which nudge your behaviour into a certain direction could under certain circumstances also be considered a violation of your privacy.[16]

The internet not only connected the computer *to* the outside world, however. It also provided a channel for outsiders *into* devices of internet users. Initially, when personal computers still were large aluminum things you put under your desk, this meant that outsiders could gain access to a domain people consider very private: the home. Later, as computers became mobile phones, this access broadened to include other domains as well, such as the office and the car. And many outsiders did, in fact, use this possibility to gain access. States, including the Dutch, have the power to intrude remotely on a device in the course of criminal investigations—similar to the power which was the subject of the case discussed in the introduction.[17] A more widespread practice of monitoring comes from the makers of devices and software. For example, the dominant smartphone platforms Android and iOS both provide fine-grained access to the sensors on a smartphone, enabling to read information such as the location, camera, files and battery level of the phone.[18]

The German Constitutional Court developed an important conceptual framework in response to this, in the *Online Durchsuchung* case discussed above. The Court in 2008 recognised a fundamental right to confidentiality and integrity of information

[15] Agre and Rotenberg 1997, p. 7; see for a discussion Zuiderveen Borgesius 2014, pp. 92 et seq.

[16] See for example Lanzing 2019; Yeung 2017.

[17] Gutheil et al. 2017.

[18] See Google 2021a, b, sections on Sensors, Location and Performance; Apple, SRSensor. The sensors an app can read. In: Apple Developer Documentation. https://developer.apple.com/documentation/sensorkit/srsensor#3681604. Accessed 22 June 2021.

technology systems.[19] In its decision, the Court observed that the currently recognised fundamental rights to confidential communication, inviolability of the home and informational self-determination do not provide sufficient protection against the state searching an IT-system remotely. This is because of the potentially wide-ranging nature of such a search. The Court in response recognised a fundamental right which protects against "access by the state in the area of information technology also insofar as the state has access to the information technology system as a *whole*, and not only to individual communication events or stored data" (emphasis mine).[20] I discuss this further at the end of this chapter.

But this was not only a constitutional development: you can also identify policy initiatives in response to these developments which were in the same vein: lawmakers started regulating the placing and reading of information on devices by third parties, and started regulating the sending of spam.[21] This understanding of privacy builds on the classical understanding of privacy in terms of access restrictions—in this case not to the home or to correspondence, but to computer systems.

5.2.5 The Connection of Everyday Objects with a Computer Chip

This understanding is also relevant for the last development we are currently in the midst of: the *connection of everyday objects with computer chips to the internet*. Objects we use in our everyday life, such as cars, bikes, thermostats and even fridges, increasingly contain a computer chip, and many of these chips are connected to the internet, often with cloud-based services. These chips will in the future undoubtedly even be installed in our bodies.[22] This development firstly makes it possible for companies to collect even more information about the private domain. Think, for example, about smart home devices with an always-on microphone which analyse everything being said in the living room.

What is new, is that the *functionality* of these objects is in many cases also controlled remotely by the manufacturer or the provider of online services, often in surprising ways. Lenders in the US have been known to remotely shut off the ignition of a car if the owner is late in payments.[23] Electronic car manufacturer Tesla not only collects detailed information on the car itself in real time—and has even used this to track the whereabouts of a critical journalist—but it also disables features of the car

[19] See Bundesverfassungsgericht, BVerfGE - 1 BvR 370/07 - 1 BvR 595/07-, Online-Durchsuchung, Judgment of 27 February 2008; Abel and Schafer 2009.

[20] Ibid., para 201.

[21] See for example González Fuster et al. 2010.

[22] See Yuste et al. 2017; see Strickland and Harris 2022 for a jarring example of bionic eyes functioning through a retinal implant which stopped working because the company behind them went bankrupt.

[23] Corkery and Silver-Greenberg 2019.

remotely, for example when a car changes hands.[24] Tesla even makes sure that when people try to upgrade their car themselves without paying for the functionality, this is logged centrally.[25] BMW and Audi similarly announced they can enable certain options, such as seat heating or parking assistance, remotely—thus also giving them power to *disable* functionality.[26] In 2009, Amazon removed copies of Orwell's *1984* (!) remotely from the e-readers of its customers over a copyright claim.[27] The list goes on. iOS updates from Apple have long been designed to block existing jailbreaking methods.[28] HP installed a "security update" which started rejecting all third-party ink cartridges five months after installation.[29] And Philips has released an update to its smart lamps which blocked lamps not approved by Philips from working.[30] All these examples are only possible because of measures which restrict the access to, and use of IT-systems: information security measures. If Tesla wants to ensure that only Tesla can grant certain car options, this means it needs to restrict access to the car software by others, including the car owner.

This development also has a relationship to privacy, but how exactly has not been explored: this development has received little to no attention from academic privacy scholars.[31] One community which has, however, seen this coming is the free software community.[32] The Free Software Foundation has for almost forty years explained why it is essential for freedom and privacy that people have control over their own devices—instead of yielding control to others such as the manufacturer. In their analysis, this problem of control takes many forms: users can be restricted via contracts, by not being able study and change the code, but also via technical means. The remote control enabled by information security technologies is a jarring example of the latter. And whereas the conceptual thinking on this is still mostly undeveloped, the policy response is completely absent. Conceptually, however, it is not hard to link this to privacy as a restriction of access to your device, in line with the German Constitutional Court decision.

Since this concept will come back in the subsequent analysis, it is helpful to introduce a term to describe the privacy, data protection and communications freedom interests affected by information security measures imposing control on systems. I group these interests under the header of *device self-determination*. I encountered the concept in the writings of Cory Doctorow, who explores this idea under the header

[24] Musk 2013; Gordon 2020a, b.

[25] Stumpf 2020.

[26] Stevens 2020; Audi 2020a, b.

[27] Johnson and Francisco 2009, Amazon in response said that it would change the systems so that this could not happen again.

[28] Gartenberg 2020a, b; Wortham 2009.

[29] Doctorow 2020a, b, c.

[30] Ward 2015.

[31] See Hoofnagle et al. 2019; and Graber 2015 for the only papers I am aware of, which discuss this issue somewhat.

[32] Stallman 2020.

of *technological self-determination* in relation to monopolies and interoperability.[33] For me, however, this concept is the information security corollary to the concept of informational self-determination discussed above. Whereas *informational* self-determination refers to the rights of individuals to determine for themselves how personal data is used and disclosed, *device self-determination* refers to the right to determine how you use your devices. It is related to another concept which is gaining traction in policy circles lately: the right to repair your own devices.[34] I explore policy responses to protect device self-determination in Chap. 8.

5.2.6 The Values of Privacy

I am leaving a lot out, such as the rise of dominant online platforms, the increase in disinformation, the growth in algorithmic nudging and the introduction of cloud computing. The discussion on new privacy concepts and new rules in response to these developments is still ongoing.[35] For now, this is sufficient. The only thing which is still helpful, is an answer to the question *why* privacy interests are worth protecting in the first place.[36]

One reason is that privacy serves to protect citizens against abuse of power by their governments, an argument which has become more important in the last decade, as totalitarianism is rising. Governments around the world have been deploying vast surveillance infrastructures to monitor and censor citizens and to repress dissent. China for example actively censors popular messaging app WeChat, blocking politically controversial messages, such as discussions on the detention (and in some cases vanishing) of over 300 human rights defenders in 2015—the so-called "709 crackdown".[37] The connection to democracy is obvious: the detained played an important role in safeguarding the rule of law and ensuring respect for human rights in China, and blocking public debate on their detention indirectly undermines these activities. Other examples of governments using spyware to hack dissidents have been discussed in Chap. 2. And as some states in Europe are also taking a totalitarian turn (see Chap. 3), privacy as a protection of democracy only gains in importance.

Of course, even in democratic states, privacy has important functions. Privacy is strongly connected to values such as individual liberty, dignity, autonomy, independence and self-development. A lack of privacy can have a chilling effect on the exercise of these values. When the Snowden-documents revealed the widespread

---

[33] See Doctorow 2020a, b, c; Doctorow 2021a, b, c. See for the development of a similar concept also Zittrain 2009, in particular Chap. 5.

[34] The European Commission announced a proposal to that effect for 2022; Von der Leyen U, Šefčovič M (2021) State of the Union.

[35] Hoepman and Koops 2020; Tene 2011; Barocas and Levy 2020; van der Sloot 2017a, b; Lanzing 2019.

[36] See Hughes 2015; Solove 2008, Chap. 4.

[37] Knockel et al. 2020; Ruan L et al. 2017; Ministry of Foreign Affairs of the Netherlands.

surveillance of internet communications, searches for sensitive terms in Google ("pipe bomb", "tax avoidance") and views of sensitive articles in Wikipedia ("Jihad", "Nationalism") dropped noticeably.[38] This points to another function of privacy: to provide a space where individuals can develop ideas and their personality without outside interference.[39]

Privacy is not only about the individual—it also has a public dimension. Privacy has value for society because it protects a space where ideas can be formed, for unorthodoxy.[40] The German Constitutional Court in the German census-case considered that if a person does not know whether information will be collected about them, they will try not to stand out.[41] Unorthodox ideas might in the end benefit society and may not have existed but for the seclusion in which they were developed.[42] Galilei encrypted some of his correspondence and hid manuscripts in a secretly built place under the stairs in his villa near Prato to escape the Inquisition's prying eyes.[43] And privacy creates spaces for social interaction on the terms of its participants.[44]

5.2.7 Summing Up

To sum up, throughout history, the different mechanisms through which (information-related) privacy is maintained in the information society can be roughly divided into two categories: the *restriction of access* and the *exercise of control*, over information and information systems.

Information security technologies play an important role in enabling both mechanisms. Restriction of access to information can for example be enforced via encryption technologies. Restriction of access to systems can for example be enforced by firewalls. Control over information can be exercised by segregating databases. Control over systems can be exercised by gaining full technological power over it—by gaining *root*.

Information security technologies can not only be used to protect *against* privacy violations: they also *enable* privacy violations. These technologies also enable

[38] Marthews and Tucker 2017; Penney 2016.

[39] See Richards 2015.

[40] Hughes 2015.

[41] German Constitutional Court, German Census, Judgment of 15 December 1983, para 146.

[42] Richards 2015.

[43] Marcus and Findlen 2019.

[44] As an example, extramarital dating site Ashley Madison was hacked in 2015; Zetter 2015. It's motto was "Life is short. Have an affair". Hackers posted details of over 30 million subscribers online, and others started browsing through the material, exposing its more high-profile customers. The private detective business reported an uptick in cases; O'Brien 2015. One can imagine this put marriages under strain, and one pastor in his suicide note even mentioned the hack as one of the reasons—the ultimate chilling effect; Segall 2015. This wouldn't have happened if the privacy of the subscribers was well protected.

control, over information and over systems. What matters is *who exercises* this control. The implications of this are worked out further in Chap. 8. First, however, I review to what extent the above conceptualisations of privacy are reflected in the Convention and the Charter.

5.3 The Right to Privacy Under the Convention

An analysis of the right to privacy under the Convention should start with the bad news: there *is* no right to privacy under the Convention. The Convention instead deals with four distinct concepts: private life, family life, home and correspondence.[45] The good news is that the Court has subsumed a lot of privacy-related concepts under these four headers, and it has even referred to a "right of privacy" under Article 8 of the Convention in some of its cases.[46] For this book, however, the case law on only two of these concepts is relevant: the right to "private life" and to "correspondence". The other two have too little bearing on information security to warrant separate discussion.[47]

5.3.1 The Scope of Private Life

As to the notion of "private life": the Court has repeatedly emphasised that it is a broad term not susceptible to exhaustive definition.[48] This is relevant, as it demonstrates that this concept lends itself well to the dynamic interpretation the Court has developed over the years. And as we will see, the Court has, through this dynamic interpretation,

---

[45] See ECHR 2022, Guide on Article 8 of the European Convention on Human Rights: Right to respect for privacy and family life, home and correspondence. Council of Europe for an overview of the case law of this provision.

[46] ECHR, Application no. 36919/02, Armonienė v v Lithuania, Judgment of 25 November 2008, para 42; ECHR, Application no. 931/13, Satakunnan Markkinapörssi Oy and Satamedia Oy v v Finland, Judgment of 27 June 2017, para 137.

[47] The concept of "family life" relates to issues such as marriages, relationships between children and other family members and family reunification; see ECHR 2022, Guide on Article 8 of the European Convention on Human Rights: Right to respect for privacy and family life, home and correspondence, Chap. III. The notion of the "home" revolves mostly around themes such as housing, the protection of homes of journalists and lawyers and the environment surrounding a home; see ibid., Chapter IV. There are instances where "home" or "family life" are discussed together with (one of) the other concepts (see for example; ECHR, Application no. 20511/03, I v v Finland, Judgment of 17 July 2008, para 38. Since then the more relevant concepts of "correspondence" and "private life" are also discussed, it is not useful to incorporate an in-depth discussion of the concepts of "home" and "family life" in isolation.

[48] ECHR, Application no. 13710/88, Niemietz v v Germany, Judgment of 16 December 1992, para 29; ECHR, Application no. 2346/02, Pretty v v the United Kingdom, Judgment of 29 April 2002, para 61.

applied many of the conceptual frameworks and values discussed in the previous section.

The Court, in its earlier cases on secret surveillance, described the strong relation between the right to privacy as protection against totalitarianism. In *Klass* (1978) it warned of the danger such measures pose of "undermining or even destroying democracy on the ground of defending it", considering that states may not, "in the name of the struggle against espionage and terrorism, adopt whatever measures they deem appropriate".[49] This is not surprising, as interferences with the right to privacy under the Convention must be necessary in a *democratic* society.

The Court has also recognised the individual aspect of privacy. It has repeatedly noted that the "very essence of the Convention is respect for human dignity and human freedom", also in the context of Article 8.[50] It has emphasised the importance of autonomy in cases focusing on the right to self-determination (euthanasia, discrimination of transgender people).[51] And the Court has considered that Article 8 includes "the right to live privately, away from unwanted attention".[52] As noted above, the role of information security in regulating *access*, both to information and to systems, is strongly related to this understanding of private life as a space of autonomy, self-development and seclusion.

The idea of private life does not *only* relate to such an "inner circle" in which "the individual may live his or her own personal life as he or she chooses, thus excluding entirely the outside world not encompassed within that circle".[53] In fact, the right to a private life is "primarily intended to ensure the development, without outside interference, of the personality of each individual in his relations with other

---

[49] ECHR, Klass and others v v Germany, Judgment of 6 September 1978, para 49; often repeated in later case law, for example ECHR, Application no. 47143/06, Roman Zakharov v v Russia, Judgment of 4 December 2015g, para 232.

[50] ECHR, Application no. 28957/95, Christine Goodwin v the United Kingdom, Judgment of 11 July 2002, para 90; ECHR, Application no. 2346/02, Pretty v the United Kingdom, Judgment of 29 April 2002, para 65. See later for similar wording; ECHR, Application no. 23380/09, Bouyid v Belgium, Judgment of 28 September 2015, para 89; ECHR, Application nos. 32541/08 and 43441/08, Svinarenko and Slyadnev c. Russia, Judgment of 17 July 2014, para 138; ECHR, Application no. 39630/09, El-Masri v the former Yugoslav Republic of Macedonia, Judgment of 13 December 2012, para 248. As follows from the wording of the Court, human dignity is a concept central to the entire Convention, but the above cases demonstrate that it is also central to informing the scope of the protection afforded under Article 8.

[51] ECHR, Application no. 2346/02, Pretty v the United Kingdom, Judgment of 29 April 2002, para 61; ECHR, Application no. 28957/95, Christine Goodwin v the United Kingdom, Judgment of 11 July 2002, para 90.

[52] Application nos. 46133/99 and 48183/99, Smirnova v Russia, Judgment of 24 July 2003, para 95; later reiterated in inter alia ECHR, Application no. 40454/07, Couderc and Hachette Filipacchi Associés v France, Judgment of 10 November 2015, para 83; ECHR, Application no. 931/13, Satakunnan Markkinapörssi Oy and Satamedia Oy v Finland, Judgment of 27 June 2017, para 130; ECHR, Application no. 35623/05, Bărbulescu v Romania, Judgment of 5 September 2017, para 70.

[53] ECHR, Application no. 35623/05, Bărbulescu v Romania, Judgment of 5 September 2017, para 70; referring to ECHR, Application no. 13710/88, Niemietz v Germany, Judgment of 16 December 1992, para 29.

human beings".[54] The Court has sometimes called this the right to lead a "private *social* life" (emphasis added), which comprises "the possibility for the individual to develop his or her social identity", and "the possibility of approaching others in order to establish and develop relationships with them".[55] Consequently, the private life may also be affected in a public context, and can include professional as well as commercial activities.[56] As discussed above, the role of information security in exercising *control* over information is strongly related to this notion of a private social life.

Lastly, the Court has more recently read into Article 8 "a form of informational self-determination, allowing individuals to rely on their right to privacy as regards data which, albeit neutral, are collected, processed and disseminated collectively and in such form or manner that their Article 8 rights may be engaged".[57] As explained above, this right to informational self-determination is predicated on the possibility of exercising control over private information after it has been collected by others.

5.3.2 The Scope of Correspondence

The related concept of "correspondence" under Article 8 does not rest on a similarly structured, systematic foundation: its content can only be divined through the varied case law.[58] It quickly becomes clear, though, that the Court has interpreted the concept broadly.

---

[54] ECHR, Application no. 2346/02, Pretty v the United Kingdom, Judgment of 29 April 2002, para 61; later confirmed in different wording in inter alia ECHR, Application no. 35623/05, Bărbulescu v Romania, Judgment of 5 September 2017, para 70; ECHR, Application nos. 40660/08 and 60641/08, Von Hannover v Germany (no. 2), Judgment of 7 February 2012, para 95; see before ECHR, Application no. 13710/88, Niemietz v Germany, Judgment of 16 December 1992, para 29.

[55] ECHR, Application no. 35623/05, Bărbulescu v Romania, Judgment of 5 September 2017, para 70; see in another context ECHR, Application no. 50001/12, Breyer v Germany, Judgment of 30 January 2020, para 73.

[56] ECHR, Application no. 35623/05, Bărbulescu v Romania, Judgment of 5 September 2017, paras 70–71; ECHR, Application no. 931/13, Satakunnan Markkinapörssi Oy and Satamedia Oy v Finland, Judgment of 27 June 2017, para 130; ECHR, Application no. 13710/88, Niemietz v Germany, Judgment of 16 December 1992, para 29.

[57] ECHR, Application no. 50001/12, Breyer v Germany, Judgment of 30 January 2020, para 75. This is salient, because the Convention does not have a right to data protection, whereas the Charter does. This new understanding allows the Court to take a more data protection-oriented approach under Article 8 of the Convention.

[58] See for an overview Schabas 2015, pp. 409–410; ECHR 2022, Guide on Article 8 of the European Convention on Human Rights: Right to respect for privacy and family life, home and correspondence, paras 392–395, on which the overview in this paragraph is based. In an attempt to synthesise this variety of cases, Arnbak considers the protection of "correspondence" a "first line of defense"—the protection applies, regardless of what the content or intent of the correspondence is; see for an analysis Arnbak 2016, pp. 134–135. The consequences of this analysis are not clear however: this does not mean, for example, that the courts can omit the proportionality assessment.

Firstly, the concept of "correspondence" covers a wide range of media: from physical letters, packages, telexes, telephone, pagers and private radio broadcasts, to email and internet use.[59] Furthermore, it covers real-time interception as well as searches of stored correspondence, and it covers storage on various types of media, including hard disks and floppy disks.[60] The Court has also found it important that in Article 8, the adjective "private" is mentioned in relation to "private life", but not in regard to "correspondence".[61] This led it to conclude that the *content* of correspondence is not relevant for the assessment of whether there is an interference.[62] The Court for example accords the same protection to professional and personal correspondence.[63] It also does not matter where the correspondence originated or was received—correspondence from the workplace, business premises or a lawyer's office is also protected.[64]

The thrust of this case law is, again, about the restricting of *access* (to correspondence). But inklings of the notion of privacy as the exercise of *control* can also be found in the case law, for example where the Court has considered that information *relating* to correspondence is also covered under Article 8.[65] This kind of

---

[59] Physical letters: see for example ECHR, Application no. 28825/02, Buglov v Ukraine, Judgment of 10 July 2014; packages; ECHR (Commission Decision), Application no. 7308/75, X. v the United Kingdom, Judgment of 12 October 1978, para 3; telexes; ECHR (Commission decision), Application no. 21482/93, Christie v the United Kingdom, Judgment of 27 June 1994; telephone; ECHR, Application no. 8691/79, Malone v the United Kingdom, Judgment of 2 August 1984, para 64; ECHR, Klass and others v Germany, Judgment of 6 September 1978, para 41; pagers; ECHR, Application no. 47114/99, Taylor-Sabori v the United Kingdom, Judgment of 22 October 2002, para 18; private communications by radio; ECHR (Commission decision), Application no. 8962/80, X. and Y. v Belgium, Judgment of 13 May 1982, para 4; email and internet usage; ECHR, Application no. 62617/00, Copland v the United Kingdom, Judgment of 3 April 2007, para 41; and ECHR, Application no. 35623/05, Bărbulescu v Romania, Judgment of 5 September 2017, para 72.

[60] See ECHR, Klass and others v Germany, Judgment of 6 September 1978 for an example of real-time interception; ECHR, Application no. 13710/88, Niemietz v Germany, Judgment of 16 December 1992, para 32, for an example of searches of physically stored correspondence; and ECHR, Application no. 74336/01, Wieser and Bicos Beteiligungen GmbH v Austria, Judgment of 16 October 2007, para 45; ECHR, Application no. 65755/01, Iliya Stefanov v Bulgaria, Judgment of 22 May 2008, para 34 for an example of searches of electronically stored correspondence.

[61] See recently ECHR, Application no. 35623/05, Bărbulescu v Romania, Judgment of 5 September 2017, para 72.

[62] ECHR, Application no. 70204/01, Frérot v France, Judgment of 12 June 2007, para 54; ECHR, Application nos. 15672/08, 24462/08, 27559/08, 28302/08, 28312/08, 34823/08, 40738/08, 41124/08, 43197/08, 51938/08 and 58170/08, Mehmet Nuri Özen and others v Turkey, Judgment of 11 January 2011, para 40.

[63] See as an example ECHR, Application no. 13710/88, Niemietz v Germany, Judgment of 16 December 1992, para 32.

[64] See for the workplace ECHR, Application no. 62617/00, Copland v the United Kingdom, Judgment of 3 April 2007, para 41; for business premises ECHR, Application no. 20605/92, Halford v the United Kingdom, Judgment of 25 June 1997, para 44 and further references therein; and for the lawyer's office ECHR, Application no. 13710/88, Niemietz v Germany, Judgment of 16 December 1992, para 32 and further references therein.

[65] See ECHR, Application no. 8691/79, Malone v the United Kingdom, Judgment of 2 August 1984, para 84; ECHR, Application no. 44787/98, P.G. and J.H. v the United Kingdom, Judgment

data, sometimes called metadata or behavioural data, may include the date, time, duration and parties to a communication. This metadata is unavoidably generated while communicating, and intermediaries will have to process it, even if minimally. As more communications have become digital, the amount of metadata generated has grown exponentially. Information security plays a role in exercising control over this data while it traverses across networks, similar to the conceptual framework applicable in the context of data protection discussed above.

Lastly, Article 8 not only relates to the *interception* of correspondence—it also extends to the *impeding* of correspondence (e.g. ensuring that someone is unable to correspond).[66] This has a strong link with the right to communications freedom discussed in Chap. 6: if you cannot send messages, your communications freedom is impeded. This is important, since surveillance often goes hand in hand with censorship, as in the example of WeChat above.

5.3.3 The Notion of Interference with the Right to Privacy Under the Convention

Thus the extensive interpretation of the right to private life and correspondence means that governmental approaches to information security could fall within their scope. But this is not sufficient for Article 8 to apply: the next question is whether there is an *interference* with the right to privacy. Answering that question is not as easy as it sounds.

Governmental approaches to information security can be categorised into three kinds of potential interferences, one by states and the other two also by non-state actors. Some governmental measures weaken the access or control function of information security to enable *lawful access* to information—that is, access by governments within the limits of their competence. A government may for example prohibit the use of strong encryption in smartphones: this makes it easier for law enforcement to collect data from a phone in a criminal investigation, in situations where they may legally exercise this power. But some of these measures also facilitate a second kind of potential interference: *unlawful* access to information. The prohibition of strong encryption may for instance make it easier for criminals to steal personal data when *they* find the phone. Or it could make it easier for governmental institutions to access information outside of the scope of their powers. Lastly, information security

of 25 September 2001, para 42; ECHR, Application no. 31446/12, Ben Faiza v France, Judgment of 8 February 2018, paras 66–68; and ECHR, Application nos. 58170/13, 62322/14 and 24960/15, Big Brother Watch and others v United Kingdom (Grand Chamber), Judgment of 25 May 2021h, para 342. It must be noted, however, that the Court in its earlier case law (Malone, P.G. and J.H.) distinguished contents and behavioural data, suggesting the latter was to be accorded less protection, but the Court later in Big Brother Watch (2021) suggested the interference with regard to both is the same; ibid., paras 342, 363.

[66] See ECHR, Application no. 4451/70, Golder v United Kingdom, Judgment of 21 February 1975, para 43.

technologies allow others to *control* the devices of citizens. This is a third kind of potential interference.

The laws and practices which lead to these interferences have, however, one thing in common: they merely create the *condition* for an interference. It is not self-evident that such a governmental measure also constitutes an interference *in itself* under Article 8. Legislation which restricts encryption technologies might create capabilities for actual surveillance, such as wiretapping. But it is uncertain whether such a measure also constitutes an interference. Similarly, the legal protection for copy protection not by itself restricts the freedom of its users: it merely creates the capability of restricting this freedom. In cases such as these, it is thus less clear *whether* someone will be harmed as a result of a measure, *who* will be harmed, and *what* the harm is. This makes it difficult to determine whether there is an interference under the Convention. Yet, these measures may impact the enjoyment of human rights of persons. The Court has, fortunately, also adjudicated cases in the face of this kind of uncertainty.[67]

Two types of cases under Article 8 are particularly relevant. The first batch relates to *secret surveillance*: governmental surveillance of persons who are kept in the dark that they are being surveilled. This case law is summarised in *Zakharov* (2015).[68] Here, the Court clarified under which circumstances an applicant can claim to be a victim of a violation of Article 8 in the context of secret surveillance.[69] This is a requirement under the Convention: only if you are a victim of a violation by one of the contracting parties, do you have standing before the Court (Article 34 of the Convention). And if you are a victim, this automatically means there was an interference. In these cases, the fear and chilling effect created by the possibility of secret surveillance in itself constitutes an interference. The Court considers that where it is not possible to challenge the application of secret surveillance at a domestic level, "widespread suspicion and concern among the general public that secret surveillance powers are being abused cannot be said to be unjustified", and there is a greater need for scrutiny by the Court.[70] It then continues that "the menace of surveillance can be claimed in itself to restrict free communication through the postal and telecommunication services, thereby constituting for all users or potential users a direct

[67] See for a discussion also van der Sloot 2018.

[68] *Zakharov* is the outcome of a line of cases starting with *Klass* (1978), through *Malone* (1984), to *Kennedy* (2010); see ECHR, Klass and others v Germany, Judgment of 6 September 1978, paras 36 and 41; ECHR, Application no. 8691/79, Malone v the United Kingdom, Judgment of 2 August 1984, para 48; ECHR, Application no. 26839/05, Kennedy v United Kingdom, Judgment of 18 May 2010, para 124 and further. In *Weber and Saravia*, the Court in 2006 repeated the formula of *Klass*, but it referred to the "threat of surveillance" instead of the "menace of surveillance"; ECHR, Application no. 54934/00, Weber and Saravia v Germany, Judgment of 29 June 2006, para 78; see later ECHR, Application no. 58243/00, Liberty and others v United Kingdom, Judgment of 1 July 2008, para 56; ECHR, Application no. 25198/02, Iordachi and others v Moldova, Judgment of 10 February 2009, para 34.

[69] ECHR, Application no. 47143/06, Roman Zakharov v Russia, Judgment of 4 December 2015.

[70] Ibid., para 169.

interference with the right guaranteed by Article 8".[71] This is important. While the Court does not mention the term "chilling effects", it alludes to the fact that people will act differently when they fear they are being spied upon.

The second set of case law relates to the *storage* of personal data.[72] In these cases, the Court considers that the storage of data in itself already is an interference, because of what might be done with the data in the future. The Court's decision in *S. and Marper* (2008) contains the most in-depth discussion.[73] Here, the Court had to determine whether the retention of DNA samples, DNA profiles (which contain information extracted from the DNA samples) and fingerprints for law enforcement purposes was compatible with Article 8. The question was whether the storage of this information was problematic in itself, or whether this depended on the subsequent use of the data. The Court concludes that the mere storage of information relating to the private life of an individual already constitutes an interference.[74] The

[71] The same approach can be found in the later cases *Szabó and Vissy* (2016), *Centrum för Rättvisa* (2021); ECHR, Application no. 37138/14, Szabó and Vissy v Hungary, Judgment of 12 January 2016; ECHR, Application no. 35252/08, Centrum för Rättvisa v Sweden (Grand Chamber), Judgment of 25 May 2021, para 167. In *Weber and Saravia*, the Court observed that not destroying gathered intelligence and refusing to notify the persons intercepted also amounted to an interference, because these may serve to *conceal* monitoring activities which interfere with the applicants' rights; see ECHR, Application no. 54934/00, Weber and Saravia v Germany, Judgment of 29 June 2006, para 79.

[72] In the first few judgments, the Court keeps it short. In the *Leander* judgment, the Court in 1987 simply concludes that the *mere storage* of personal data already amounts to an interference in the context of Article 8; ECHR, Application no. 9248/81, Leander v Sweden, Judgment of 26 March 1987, para 48; in the subsequent jurisprudence until 2008, it does not waste more words on this position. In *Kopp*, the Court considered that the subsequent use of interception data has no bearing on the finding that the interception itself is already an interference; ECHR, Application no. 13/1997/797/1000, Kopp v Switzerland, Judgment of 25 March 1998; see later ECHR, Application no. 16428/05, Gardel v France, Judgment of 17 December 2009, para 58. In both *Amann* and *Rotaru*, the Court in 2000 summarily confirms its view that the creating and storing by a public authority of a card containing data relating to the private life of an individual (in this case a record of a phone call) already amounts to an interference; ECHR, Application no. 27798/95, Amann v Switzerland, Judgment of 16 February 2000, para 70; ECHR, Application no. 28341/95, Rotaru v Romania, Judgment of 4 May 2000, paras 43 and 46. And in Segerstedt-Wiberg v Sweden, the Court again considers in a short sentence that it follows from its established case-law that the storage of the information relating to private life amounted to interference; ECHR, Application no. 62332/00, Segerstedt-Wiberg v Sweden, Judgment of 6 June 2006, para 76.

[73] ECHR, Application nos. 30562/04 and 30566/04, S and Marper v United Kingdom, Judgment of 4 December 2008i; see also ECHR, Application no. 29514/05, Van der Velden v the Netherlands, Judgment of 7 December 2006 for an earlier but less reasoned decision on the same topic; and ECHR, M.K. v France, Judgment of 18 April 2013, para 26 for a later confirmation of the reasoning; ECHR, Application no. 45245/15, Gaughran v the United Kingdom, Judgment of 13 February 2020j with regard to the indefinite retention of photographs of people taken in custody with the potential to apply facial mapping and facial recognition techniques; ibid., para 70; see further ECHR, Application no. 50001/12, Breyer v Germany, Judgment of 30 January 2020, para 81; ECHR, Application no. 35623/05, Uzun v Germany, Judgment of 2 September 2010; ECHR, Application no. 24029/07, M.M. v United Kingdom, Judgment of 30 November 2012, para 188.

[74] ECHR, Application nos. 30562/04 and 30566/04, S and Marper v United Kingdom, Judgment of 4 December 2008i, para 67. The Court also confirmed this reasoning later in *Big Brother Watch* (2021)

Court firstly attaches weight to the *perceptions* of the individual, noting that "an individual's concern about the possible future use of private information retained by the authorities [in this case DNA samples and profiles, OvD] is legitimate and relevant to a determination of the issue of whether there has been an interference".[75] This is reminiscent of the chilling effects-doctrine developed in the secret surveillance cases discussed above.

The Court also attaches weight to the *kinds of future use* which are made possible as a result of this storage. With regard to DNA profiles, the Court enumerates the things the state can already do with such stored information, such as searching for familial links in the database and assessing the likely ethnic origin of the donor.[76] This leads it to conclude that the *capacity* of DNA profiles to identify genetic relationships and ethnic origin is already sufficient to determine that their *retention* is an interference.[77] Similarly, with regard to fingerprints, it concludes that because fingerprints allow for identification of an individual with precision in a wide range of circumstances, they are *capable* of affecting her private life and their retention should also be considered an interference.[78]

This reasoning also applies to the three potential information security interferences described above—lawful access, unlawful access and device control. Restrictions on information security which facilitate lawful access, or increase the risk of unlawful access can have a chilling effect. You might not send a sensitive chat message, if you are uncertain whether it may be intercepted by a government. You might not store private information on your phone, if you fear that it may fall in the hands of criminals when you lose your phone. Similarly, governmental measures which enable others than the owner to control a device may in itself constitute an interference because, of the possibilities for future privacy violations through this control. You might not buy a car if at a future time some of its functionality may be disabled and you cannot do anything about it.

In the rest of this book, I contend that two types of measures constitute an interference. First, measures which facilitate lawful access and control, to information and systems protected by the right to privacy (and communications freedom, as we will see in the coming chapter), should be considered an interference. Second, measures which significantly increase the risk of unlawful access and control constitute an interference. Now, what are these information and systems? These primarily include information containing personal data or confidential communications, and systems

---

and *Centrum för Rättvisa* (2021); ECHR, Application nos. 58170/13, 62322/14 and 24960/15, Big Brother Watch and others v United Kingdom (Grand Chamber), Judgment of 25 May 2021h, para 330; ECHR, Application no. 35252/08, Centrum för Rättvisa v Sweden (Grand Chamber), Judgment of 25 May 2021, para 244. There, it considered all stages of communications surveillance, from interception, initial retention, selection, examination and subsequent retention to constitute forms of interference. It also did not matter that the data is initially in coded form.

[75] ECHR, Application nos. 30562/04 and 30566/04, S and Marper v United Kingdom, Judgment of 4 December 2008, para 71.

[76] Ibid., paras 75 and 76.

[77] Ibid., paras 75–77.

[78] Ibid., paras 84–86.

owned or used by individuals. As will be discussed further in Chap. 9, it is difficult to draw a clear line around these categories, primarily because governance measures in the information security cycle will apply to information and systems as deployed in a variety of contexts: some computers affected by governance measures may contain personal data, and others might not. What makes an increase in risk "significant"? This is the case where it leads to chilling effects on behaviour, which is for instance the case when it cannot be excluded that a well-resourced attacker will exploit a vulnerability. The intelligence agencies of other states are examples of such well-resourced attackers, and they, together with criminal organisations, play an important role in the analysis in the chapters that follow.

5.3.4 Negative Obligations Under Article 8 of the Convention

Still, establishing whether there is an interference is only the first step. The next step is to evaluate the *compatibility* of the measure. Here, the distinction between lawful and unlawful access (to information) is again relevant. The object of Article 8 is essentially to protect the individual against *arbitrary interference and abuse of power* by public authorities.[79] This means that the negative obligations under Article 8 are best suited for evaluating measures creating a risk of unlawful access by the *state*. Other forms of unlawful access and device control, by non-state actors, are best analysed under the positive obligations of Article 8, which I discuss in the next section.

The Court provides the most in-depth analysis of this risk of unlawful access in its case law on secret surveillance. It first delineates the conditions under which *lawful* access by the state may take place. It is essential to have clear, detailed rules on the application of surveillance powers, in view of the risks of arbitrariness as a result of secrecy.[80] This means that domestic law must give "an adequate indication as to the circumstances in which and the conditions on which public authorities are empowered to resort to" surveillance measures, and indicate the scope of the "discretion conferred on the competent authorities and the manner of its exercise with sufficient clarity".[81] The Court has provided detailed guidance on how lawful

---

[79] See ECHR, Application nos. 1474/62; 1677/62; 1691/62; 1769/63; 1994/63; 2126/64, Belgian Linguistic Case, Judgment of 23 July 1968, para 7; ECHR, Application no. 6289/73, Airey v Ireland, Judgment of 9 October 1979, para 32; ECHR, Marckx v Belgium, Judgment of 13 June 1979, para 31; ECHR, Application no. 18535/91, Kroon and Others v the Netherlands, Judgment of 27 October 1994, para 31; Schabas 2015, p. 366; and ECHR 2022, Guide on Article 8 of the European Convention on Human Rights: Right to respect for privacy and family life, home and correspondence, para 3.

[80] ECHR, Application no. 47143/06, Roman Zakharov v Russia, Judgment of 4 December 2015g, para 229. In earlier decisions, it assessed the quality of the law under the foreseeability requirement, but in most recent cases it combines the analysis of the quality of law- and the necessity-requirement; see ibid., para 236; see Eskens et al. 2015.

[81] ECHR, Application no. 47143/06, Roman Zakharov v Russia, Judgment of 4 December 2015g, paras 229–230; ECHR, Application no. 26839/05, Kennedy v United Kingdom, Judgment of 18

access must be circumscribed in legislation.[82] Even if a law is clear, this does not mean it is proportionate. Thus, the Court also performs a substantive review.

This involves a balancing exercise. On one side of the scale, the Court investigates the justification of the government for taking the measure. Where the aim is to protect national security, for example, member states enjoy a wide margin of appreciation in choosing how to do this, although this is sometimes preceded by the qualification that it is "fairly" wide, or it is a "certain" margin.[83] In the context of secret surveillance, the Court must be satisfied that there are adequate and effective guarantees against abuse.[84] This assessment "depends on all the circumstances of the case, such as the nature, scope and duration of the possible measures, the grounds required for ordering them, the authorities competent to authorise, carry out and supervise them, and the kind of remedy provided by the national law".[85]

May 2010, para 125; ECHR, Application no. 58243/00, Liberty and others v United Kingdom, Judgment of 1 July 2008, para 62; ECHR, Application no. 35623/05, Uzun v Germany, Judgment of 2 September 2010, para 61.

[82] ECHR, Application no. 47143/06, Roman Zakharov v Russia, Judgment of 4 December 2015g, para 231; ECHR, Application no. 35252/08, Centrum för Rättvisa v Sweden (Grand Chamber), Judgment of 25 May 2021, para 253; ECHR, Application no. 37138/14, Szabó and Vissy v Hungary, Judgment of 12 January 2016, para 56; ECHR, Application no. 54934/00, Weber and Saravia v Germany, Judgment of 29 June 2006, para 95; ECHR, Application no. 25198/02, Iordachi and others v Moldova, Judgment of 10 February 2009, para 39; ECHR, Application no. 62540/00, The Association for European Integration and Human Rights and Ekimdzhiev v Bulgaria, Judgment of 28 June 2007, para 76; ECHR, Application no. 11105/84, Huvig v France, Judgment of 24 April 1990, para 29 and further; see also ECHR, Application nos. 30562/04 and 30566/04, S and Marper v United Kingdom, Judgment of 4 December 2008i, para 99 where this case law is applied to the retention of data; ECHR, Application no. 35623/05, Uzun v Germany, Judgment of 2 September 2010, para 66; see ECHR, Application no. 9248/81, Leander v Sweden, Judgment of 26 March 1987, para 51 for the application of this principle in the context of secret controls of staff in the national security sector; see ECHR, Application no. 50001/12, Breyer v Germany, Judgment of 30 January 2020, para 83 for the application in the context of the obligatory storage of personal information (e.g. subscriber data); see for bulk surveillance ECHR, Application nos. 58170/13, 62322/14 and 24960/15, Big Brother Watch and others v United Kingdom (Grand Chamber), Judgment of 25 May 2021h, para 361; ECHR, Application no. 35252/08, Centrum för Rättvisa v Sweden (Grand Chamber), Judgment of 25 May 2021, para 275.

[83] ECHR, Application nos. 58170/13, 62322/14 and 24960/15, Big Brother Watch and others v United Kingdom (Grand Chamber), Judgment of 25 May 2021h, para 338; ECHR, Application no. 35252/08, Centrum för Rättvisa v Sweden (Grand Chamber), Judgment of 25 May 2021, para 252; ECHR, Application no. 54934/00, Weber and Saravia v Germany, Judgment of 29 June 2006, para 106.

[84] ECHR, Application no. 47143/06, Roman Zakharov v Russia, Judgment of 4 December 2015g, para 232.

[85] ECHR, Application no. 35252/08, Centrum för Rättvisa v Sweden (Grand Chamber), Judgment of 25 May 2021, para 253; ECHR, Application nos. 58170/13, 62322/14 and 24960/15, Big Brother Watch and others v United Kingdom (Grand Chamber), Judgment of 25 May 2021h, para 339; ECHR, Application no. 47143/06, Roman Zakharov v Russia, Judgment of 4 December 2015g, para 232; ECHR, Application no. 37138/14, Szabó and Vissy v Hungary, Judgment of 12 January 2016, para 57; ECHR, Application no. 54934/00, Weber and Saravia v Germany, Judgment of 29 June 2006, para 106; ECHR, Application no. 62540/00, The Association for European Integration

In doing this assessment, the Court generally investigates two factors: the potential privacy impact of *lawful* surveillance, and the risk of *unlawful* surveillance. The first factor, the potential privacy impact, depends on criteria such as the sensitivity and richness of the data, the number of people affected, the way the data is processed, the amount of data processed and the duration of the surveillance.[86] These considerations are also relevant for assessing measures aimed at information security. Where it can be expected that a measure affects many people or sensitive data, a stricter review of the measure is necessary.

The Court, however, also analyses the risks of abuse of surveillance powers—of *unlawful* access. Abuse can partly be prevented by supervision of the exercise of surveillance powers, for example by a court.[87] Technology also plays a role in the risk of unlawful access.

The Court has on the one hand shown it is willing to consider that *technologies in itself* already contribute to this risk. In *Szabó* (2016), the Court warned for example

---

and Human Rights and Ekimdzhiev v Bulgaria, Judgment of 28 June 2007, para 77; ECHR, Klass and others v Germany, Judgment of 6 September 1978, para 50.

[86] See for the nature of the data: ECHR, Application nos. 30562/04 and 30566/04, S and Marper v United Kingdom, Judgment of 4 December 2008i, para 104; ECHR, Application no. 50001/12, Breyer v Germany, Judgment of 30 January 2020, para 95; ECHR, Application no. 35623/05, Uzun v Germany, Judgment of 2 September 2010, para 72. See for the *number of people affected* ECHR, Application no. 37138/14, Szabó and Vissy v Hungary, Judgment of 12 January 2016, para 69; see also ECHR, Application nos. 30562/04 and 30566/04, S and Marper v United Kingdom, Judgment of 4 December 2008, paras 119, 245, 248. As to the amount of data being collected and retained; see ECHR, Application no. 47143/06, Roman Zakharov v Russia, Judgment of 4 December 2015g, para 255. And as to the duration of the surveillance; see for example ECHR, Application no. 35623/05, Uzun v Germany, Judgment of 2 September 2010, para 80. As to the way the data is processed; see ECHR, Application nos. 58170/13, 62322/14 and 24960/15, Big Brother Watch and others v United Kingdom (Grand Chamber), Judgment of 25 May 2021h, para 330.

[87] The Court, given that the review before and during the surveillance will take place in secret, considers it essential that the procedures "provide adequate and equivalent guarantees safeguarding his or her rights", adding that "the values of a democratic society must be followed as faithfully as possible in the supervisory procedures", and it is "in principle desirable to entrust supervisory control to a judge", which "offers the best guarantees of independence, impartiality and a proper procedure"; ECHR, Application no. 47143/06, Roman Zakharov v Russia, Judgment of 4 December 2015g, para 234; ECHR, Application no. 37138/14, Szabó and Vissy v Hungary, Judgment of 12 January 2016, para 77; ECHR, Application no. 26839/05, Kennedy v United Kingdom, Judgment of 18 May 2010, para 167; ECHR, Application no. 28341/95, Rotaru v Romania, Judgment of 4 May 2000, para 59; ECHR, Klass and others v Germany, Judgment of 6 September 1978, para 55. The review body must be "capable of verifying the existence of a reasonable suspicion against the person concerned"; ECHR, Application no. 47143/06, Roman Zakharov v Russia, Judgment of 4 December 2015g, para 260. The Court also attaches importance to obligations to individual notification of the surveillance measures and general transparency, since this allows for the existence of effective safeguards against abuse; ibid., para 234, para 283; ECHR, Application no. 54934/00, Weber and Saravia v Germany, Judgment of 29 June 2006, para 135. The more serious the interference, the stricter the supervision needs to be; in the case of bulk surveillance, the review needs to be subject to "end-to-end safeguards"; ECHR, Application nos. 58170/13, 62322/14 and 24960/15, Big Brother Watch and others v United Kingdom (Grand Chamber), Judgment of 25 May 2021, para 350; ECHR, Application no. 35252/08, Centrum för Rättvisa v Sweden (Grand Chamber), Judgment of 25 May 2021, para 264.

about the potential for abuse, given the "formidable technologies" at the disposal of governments and "the magnitude of the pool of information retrievable by the authorities applying highly efficient methods and processing masses of data, potentially about each person, should he be, one way or another, connected to suspected subjects or objects of planned terrorist attacks".[88] It has also repeatedly underlined that the continuously advancing sophistication of surveillance technologies increases the risk of arbitrariness.[89] In *Zakharov* (2015), it examined one particular aspect of this: where the security services and the police have direct technical access to communications and are thus in theory able to circumvent the judicial authorisation procedure, this makes the system particularly prone to abuse, especially since this access is not logged.[90]

Information security measures can also reduce the risk of abuse. In *Big Brother Watch* (2021), it examined the risk of abuse in the context of the transfer of intercepted communication to other intelligence services. Here, the Court noted that the transferring state must ensure that the receiving state, in handling the data, has "in place safeguards capable of preventing abuse and disproportionate interference", which means that it must guarantee the "secure storage" of the material and restrict onward disclosure.[91] Similarly, in *Centrum för Rättvisa* (2021), the Court considered that intelligence services should be obliged to retain logs and a detailed record of each step in bulk interception operations, to minimise the risk of unlawful access.[92]

In other words, the residual *risk* of unlawful access by states, even where there is clear legislation and (judicial) supervision, is an important part of the proportionality assessment under Article 8. This is relevant for the assessment of governmental measures aimed at information security, including encryption, because such measures may increase this risk. The risk of unlawful access depends on the chance of this happening and the impact when it happens. This impact arguably will depend partly

---

[88] ECHR, Application no. 37138/14, Szabó and Vissy v Hungary, Judgment of 12 January 2016, paras 73, 79.

[89] ECHR, Application no. 43514/15, Catt v the United Kingdom, Judgment of 24 January 2019, para 114; ECHR, Application nos. 58170/13, 62322/14 and 24960/15, Big Brother Watch and others v United Kingdom (Grand Chamber), Judgment of 25 May 2021h, para 322; ECHR, Application no. 35252/08, Centrum för Rättvisa v Sweden (Grand Chamber), Judgment of 25 May 2021, para 236; ECHR, Application no. 47143/06, Roman Zakharov v Russia, Judgment of 4 December 2015g, para 229; ECHR, Application no. 37138/14, Szabó and Vissy v Hungary, Judgment of 12 January 2016, para 62; see also the Court in ECHR, Application nos. 30562/04 and 30566/04, S and Marper v United Kingdom, Judgment of 4 December 2008, para 112.

[90] ECHR, Application no. 47143/06, Roman Zakharov v Russia, Judgment of 4 December 2015g, paras 270, 272. On the other hand, in Kennedy, the Court considered the fact that there was no evidence of abuse of the powers a reason for considering the measures compatible with Article 8; ECHR, Application no. 26839/05, Kennedy v United Kingdom, Judgment of 18 May 2010, para 168.

[91] ECHR, Application nos. 58170/13, 62322/14 and 24960/15, Big Brother Watch and others v United Kingdom (Grand Chamber), Judgment of 25 May 2021h, paras 362, 396–398.

[92] ECHR, Application no. 35252/08, Centrum för Rättvisa v Sweden (Grand Chamber), Judgment of 25 May 2021, paras 311–316. According to the Court, the already existent obligation under data protection rules to keep logs might be sufficient in this regard, though.

on the same criteria as those for lawful access discussed above: the sensitivity and richness of the data, the amount of data and the number of people affected. Arguably, it will also depend on the severity of the consequences *if* access takes place unlawfully: can it be used to blackmail people, to stalk them or in other ways make their life harder? The problem is that for many generic information security measures, it is impossible to determine the impact of unlawful access in advance, because these measures protects all kinds of information and systems. The consequences of this are further discussed in Chaps. 9 and 10.

5.3.5 Positive Obligations Under Article 8 of the Convention

As noted, the risk of unlawful access also plays an important role in the case law of the Court on *positive* obligations under Article 8—to the extent that this unlawful access is done by private parties. While, again, the object of Article 8 of the Convention is "essentially" to protect the individual against arbitrary interference, the Court has not shied away from reading into this provision a positive obligation to respect the rights therein.[93] The Court in the context of Article 8 has framed this question primarily in terms of whether member states are under circumstances obliged to take "measures designed to secure respect for private life even in the sphere of the relations of individuals between themselves".[94]

In general, the nature of the obligation (and the margin of appreciation) will depend on the particular aspect of private life which is at issue and the interests at stake.[95] Where "fundamental values" or "essential aspects" of private life are at stake (for instance the treatment of rape under the criminal justice system), states must ensure protection through effective criminal law provisions and effective investigation.[96] In the same vein, the margin of appreciation is also narrowed where "a particularly

---

[93] See ECHR, Marckx v Belgium, Judgment of 13 June 1979, para 31; see in the context of Article 6 ECHR, Application no. 6289/73, Airey v Ireland, Judgment of 9 October 1979, para 25; see further ECHR, Application no. 8978/80, X and Y v the Netherlands, Judgment of 26 March 1985, para 23.

[94] ECHR, Application no. 8978/80, X and Y v the Netherlands, Judgment of 26 March 1985, para 23; ECHR, Application no. 42326/98, Odièvre v France, Judgment of 13 February 2003, para 40; ECHR, Application no. 6339/05, Evans v the United Kingdom, Judgment of 10 April 2007, para 75.

[95] See ECHR, Application no. 37359/09, Hämäläinen v Finland, Judgment of 16 July 2014, paras 66–68 for a relatively recent overview of the case law; see ECHR, Application no. 8978/80, X and Y v the Netherlands, Judgment of 26 March 1985, para 24 for a first reference to the dependency on the particular aspect of private life which is at issue; see lastly ECHR, Application no. 25579/05, A, B and C v Ireland, Judgment of 16 December 2010, para 248 for a more concise and somewhat less recent enumeration.

[96] See ECHR, Application no. 8978/80, X and Y v the Netherlands, Judgment of 26 March 1985, para 27; ECHR, Application no. 39272/98, M.C. v Bulgaria, Judgment of 4 December 2003, paras 150 and 153; ECHR, Application no. 2872/02, K.U. v Finland, Judgment of 2 December 2008, paras 43 and 46; ECHR, Application no. 36934/08, I.C. v Romania, Judgment of 24 May 2016, paras 51 and 52.

important facet of an individual's existence or identity is at stake, or where the activities at stake involve a most intimate aspect of private life".[97] As to measures which are intended to protect children under Article 8, these should be "effective and include reasonable steps to prevent ill-treatment of which the authorities had, or ought to have had, knowledge and effective deterrence against such serious breaches of personal integrity".[98] States do not always have to take measures through criminal law, the Court has also recognised that for certain interests, civil law provisions can be sufficient to ensure respect for private life, for example in cases of unlawful publications.[99]

The Court has in two cases underlined that states have an obligation to protect private information against *unlawful access* by others, also in view of the public trust in security in the future. Both in *I v. Finland* (2008) and *Z v. Finland* (1997), the Court considered to what extent states have an obligation to take legislative measures to safeguard medical data.[100] The Court's considerations in *I v. Finland* are instructive, raising the bar for states when it comes to information security while underlining the role of information security when it comes to safeguarding trust:[101]

> The protection of personal data, in particular medical data, is of fundamental importance to a person's enjoyment of his or her right to respect for private and family life as guaranteed by Article 8 of the Convention. Respecting the confidentiality of health data is a vital principle in the legal systems of all the Contracting Parties to the Convention. It is crucial not only to respect the sense of privacy of a patient but also to preserve his or her confidence in the medical profession and in the health services in general. The above considerations are especially valid as regards protection of the confidentiality of information about a person's HIV infection, given the sensitive issues surrounding this disease. The domestic law must afford appropriate safeguards to prevent any such communication or disclosure of personal health data as may be inconsistent with the guarantees in Article 8 of the Convention [...].

The Court concluded that "the mere fact that the domestic legislation provided the applicant with an opportunity to claim compensation for damages caused by an

---

[97] ECHR, Application no. 5786/08, Söderman v Sweden, Judgment of 12 November 2013, para 79; see ECHR, Application no. 6339/05, Evans v the United Kingdom, Judgment of 10 April 2007, para 77 regarding "a particularly important facet of an individual's existence or identity"; later referred to in ECHR, Application no. 48009/08, Mosley v the United Kingdom, Judgment of 10 May 2011k, para 109; and see regarding "a most intimate aspect of private life"; ibid., para 109; referring to mutatis mutandis ECHR, Application no. 7525/76, Dudgeon v United Kingdom, Judgment of 22 October 1981, para 52.

[98] ECHR, Application no. 5786/08, Söderman v Sweden, Judgment of 12 November 2013, para 81; see also ECHR, Application no. 2872/02, K.U. v Finland, Judgment of 2 December 2008, para 46.

[99] See ECHR, Application no. 8978/80, X and Y v the Netherlands, Judgment of 26 March 1985, para 24: "Recourse to the criminal law is not necessarily the only answer"; later confirmed in inter alia ECHR, Application no. 42326/98, Odièvre v France, Judgment of 13 February 2003, para 46; ECHR, Application nos. 40660/08 and 60641/08, Von Hannover v Germany (no. 2), Judgment of 7 February 2012, para 104; and ECHR, Application no. 5786/08, Söderman v Sweden, Judgment of 12 November 2013, para 85.

[100] ECHR, Application no. 20511/03, I v Finland, Judgment of 17 July 2008; ECHR, Application no. 22009/93, Z v Finland, Judgment of 25 February 1997.

[101] ECHR, Application no. 20511/03, I v Finland, Judgment of 17 July 2008, para 38; see also Arnbak 2016, pp. 108–112.

alleged unlawful disclosure of personal data was not sufficient to protect her private life. What is required in this connection is practical and effective protection *to exclude any possibility of unauthorised access* occurring in the first place. Such protection was not given here" (emphasis added).[102]

This does not mean there is no room for balancing interests, for example between the right to confidential communications and the prevention of crime. The Court has in *K.U. v. Finland* (2008) considered that "[a]lthough freedom of expression and confidentiality of communications are primary considerations and users of telecommunications and Internet services must have a guarantee that their own privacy and freedom of expression will be respected, such guarantee cannot be absolute and must yield on occasion to other legitimate imperatives, such as the prevention of disorder or crime or the protection of the rights and freedoms of others".[103] It concluded that it is the task of the legislator to provide the framework for reconciling the various claims which compete for protection in this context.

Finally, there are no decisions directly applicable to the risk of *device control* discussed above, but the principles set out above map relatively well to this issue. Firstly, the *values* supported by the right to privacy align well—in particular autonomy and self-development—which imply having control over your own devices, deciding whether, when and how you use them. More importantly, this issue falls within the *scope* of the concept of private life. These devices are used in a private zone, often in or near one of the most private domains: the home and the body. Given the above case law, in which the Court presumably attached importance to the fact that this concerned access to medical data, one of the most sensitive categories of data, an argument can be made that states have a positive obligation to ensure that users retain control over their own devices. This argument in the context of information security is further discussed in Chap. 8.

5.4 The Rights to Privacy and Data Protection Under the Charter

As noted above, the Charter grants at least the same protection as the Convention. This means that the above case law under the Convention also applies for determining the scope of the right to privacy under the Charter. As explained in the prior chapter, the Charter can also provide protection which goes *beyond* the Convention. First, it contains a separate right to data protection, in addition to the right to privacy.[104] Second, interferences affecting the "essence" of a right are evaluated differently. As we will see, the European Court of Justice precisely with regard to these two topics has connected human rights to information security.

---

[102] ECHR, Application no. 20511/03, I v Finland, Judgment of 17 July 2008, para 38.

[103] ECHR, Application no. 2872/02, K.U. v Finland, Judgment of 2 December 2008, para 49.

[104] See Kokott and Sobotta 2013; Lynskey 2014; González Fuster 2014; van der Sloot 2017b, 2017b.

5.4.1 *The Scope of the Right to Privacy and Data Protection*

The right to *privacy* under Article 7 of the Charter refers to the same four concepts as its counterpart in the Convention: private life, family life, home and communications.[105] The European Court of Justice was able to build on decades of case law when it started to apply the right to privacy under Charter. The right to "the protection of personal data" has, on the other hand, only been enshrined in a human rights instrument since the adoption of the Charter in 2000. For this right, the Court had to develop its own case law.

Unfortunately, the confusing origin of the right to data protection has made this difficult. The right was recognised at a time when a significant body of data protection instruments was already in place.[106] And whereas existing fundamental rights had to be balanced against each other, these data protection instruments on which the new right to data protection is based, already reflected a balance between data protection and other rights.[107] This possibly explains why the Court of Justice barely distinguishes the right to privacy and data protection in its case law, making the scope

[105] "Communications" should be interpreted in the same manner as "correspondence"; see Praesidium of the European Convention 2007, Explanations Relating to the Charter of Fundamental Rights under Articles 7 and 8. For completeness: the Court has barely discussed the existence of positive obligations under the Charter, but this is changing. Twice, it has suggested that Article 7 may also impose on member states a positive obligation, in particular to adopt legislation to combat crimes against the person; CJEU, Cases C-511/18, C-512/18 and C-520/18, La Quadrature du Net, Judgment of 6 October 2020c, para 126; CJEU, Case C-78/18, European Commission v Hungary (Transparency of Associations), Judgment of 18 June 2020, para 123.

[106] The Court has also observed in some judgments that the legislative instruments, such as the Data Protection Directive, are in fact implementing the right to data protection (which is somewhat striking, since the Data Protection Directive was in place *before* the Charter). See to that effect CJEU, Case C-543/09, Deutsche Telekom, Judgment of 5 May 2011, para 50; and more clearly CJEU, Case C-131/12, Google Spain, Judgment of 13 May 2014, para 69; CJEU, Cases C-141/12 and C-372/12, YS v Minister voor Immigratie, Integratie en Asiel, and Minister voor Immigratie, Integratie en Asiel v M, S, Judgment of 17 July 2014, para 55; CJEU, Case C-398/15, Manni, Judgment of 9 March 2017, para 40.

[107] (1981) Convention for the Protection of Individuals with regard to Automatic Processing of Personal Data (Convention 108), last recital; (1995) Directive 95/46/EC of the European Parliament and of the Council of 24 October 1995 on the protection of individuals with regard to the processing of personal data and on the free movement of such data, recital 3; Regulation (EU) 2016/679 of the European Parliament and of the Council of 27 April 2016 on the protection of natural persons with regard to the processing of personal data and on the free movement of such data, and repealing Directive 95/46/EC (General Data Protection Regulation), recitals 10, 13; COE 2018, Convention for the protection of individuals with regard to the processing of personal data (Convention 108+), recitals 3 and 5; see Hijmans 2016, p. 62 for the same view and further literature.

of the right hard to grasp.[108] There are, however, two aspects where this right plays a distinct role in the case law of the Court.

5.4.1.1 The Concept of Interference

First, the right to data protection is relevant in the determination of an *interference*. The Court in many decisions applies a data protection-oriented approach, simply concluding that a measure which leads to the "processing" of personal data already in itself constitutes an interference. For example, the communication or retention of personal data to a third party is considered an interference, regardless of the subsequent use of the communicated information.[109] It also does not matter what the nature of the data is, and whether persons have been "inconvenienced" as a result of the interference.[110]

This approach is complemented by the decisions of the European Court of Justice where it, like the European Court of Human Rights, takes into account the *effect* of a measure in establishing an interference. The Court has for example considered the risk of abuse and unlawful access relevant to establish an interference.[111] And its case law contains traces of a chilling effect-doctrine, for example where the Court considers it relevant that a measure can generate a feeling of "constant surveillance".[112]

---

[108] CFI, T-194/04, Bavarian Lager, Judgment of 8 November 2007, para 118; CJEU, Case C-73/07, Satamedia, Judgment of 16 December 2008, para 52; CJEU, Case C-275/06, Promusicae, Judgment of 29 January 2008, para 63; CJEU, Case C-92/09, Volker und Markus Schecke and Eifert, Judgment of 9 November 2010, para 47; later repeated in CJEU, Cases C-468/10 and C-469/10, ASNEF, Judgment of 24 November 2011, para 41; CJEU, Case C-291/12, Schwarz v Bochum, Judgment of 17 October 2013, paras 25 and 26; CJEU, Case C-362/14, Schrems I, Judgment of 6 October 2015, para 91; CJEU, Cases C-203/15 and C-698/15, Tele2 Sverige and Watson and Others, Judgment of 21 December 2016, para 100. In later cases, it makes a somewhat clearer distinctoin; CJEU, Cases C-293/12 and C-594/12, Digital Rights Ireland and others, Judgment of 8 April 2014d, paras 34 and 35; ibid., para 36; CJEU, Opinion 1/15, Judgment of 26 July 2017, para 122; CJEU, Case C-207/16, Ministerio Fiscal, Judgment of 2 October 2018, para 51; CJEU, Cases C-203/15 and C-698/15, Tele2 Sverige and Watson and Others, Judgment of 21 December 2016, para 129; CJEU, Case C-78/18, European Commission v Hungary (Transparency of Associations), Judgment of 18 June 2020, paras 110–134.

[109] CJEU, Opinion 1/15, Judgment of 26 July 2017, para 124; similarly under Article 8 of the Charter CJEU, Case C-465/00, Rundfunk, Judgment of 20 May 2003, para 74; CJEU, Cases C-293/12 and C-594/12, Digital Rights Ireland and others, Judgment of 8 April 2014d, paras 34 and 35.

[110] CJEU, Case C-623/17, Privacy International v United Kingdom, Judgment of 6 October 2020, para 70; CJEU, Case C-207/16, Ministerio Fiscal, Judgment of 2 October 2018, para 51; CJEU, Opinion 1/15, Judgment of 26 July 2017, para 124; CJEU, Cases C-293/12 and C-594/12, Digital Rights Ireland and others, Judgment of 8 April 2014d, para 33; and under Article 8 of the Convention CJEU, Case C-465/00, Rundfunk, Judgment of 20 May 2003, para 75.

[111] CJEU, Case C-623/17, Privacy International v United Kingdom, Judgment of 6 October 2020, para 73; CJEU, Cases C-511/18, C-512/18 and C-520/18, La Quadrature du Net, Judgment of 6 October 2020c, para 119.

[112] CJEU, Cases C-293/12 and C-594/12, Digital Rights Ireland and others, Judgment of 8 April 2014, para 37; in CJEU, Cases C-511/18, C-512/18 and C-520/18, La Quadrature du Net, Judgment

5.4.1.2 The Essence of Articles 7 and 8 of the Charter

Second, the role of the *essence* of the right to data protection distinguishes the case law of the European Court of Justice from its counterpart. The essence of the right to *privacy* is as you would expect: if the privacy impact of a measure crosses a certain threshold, the essence is affected. The Court has touched on this a number of times. For example, in *Schrems I*, the Court had to review whether generalised access to the *content* of communication by the NSA affects the essence of the right to privacy. It did.[113] The Court in *Digital Rights Ireland* on the other hand had to review whether the indiscriminate obligatory retention of *behavioural data* affected the essence. It did not.[114] Similarly, it ruled that the transfer of *travel data* to Canada does not affect the essence of the right.[115]

The Court takes a different approach in determining the essence of the right to data protection under Article 8. The Court has, surprisingly connected the essence of the right to data protection to one particular aspect of the right: information security.[116] In *Digital Rights Ireland*, the Court reasons that the essence was not affected because in the challenged legislation "certain principles of data protection and data security must be respected", according to which member states "are to ensure that appropriate technical and organisational measures are adopted against accidental or unlawful destruction, accidental loss or alteration of the data".[117] The Court in

of 6 October 2020c, para 117 the Court also attached importance to the fact that a profile could be built in establishing an interference.

[113] CJEU, Case C-362/14, Schrems I, Judgment of 6 October 2015, para 94; See also European Court of Justice, Opinion of A-G Bot in Schrems, Judgment of 23 September 2015, para 177 who found it "extremely doubtful" whether the regulations at issue respected the essence of Articles 7 and 8 of the Charter. Surprisingly, as an illustration of this, the Court actually refers to Digital Rights Ireland in which it did not conclude that the essence was affected.

[114] CJEU, Cases C-293/12 and C-594/12, Digital Rights Ireland and others, Judgment of 8 April 2014d, para 39; A-G Cruz Villalón did not touch on this particular aspect, surprisingly; see CJEU, Cases C-293/12 and C-594/12, Opinion of A-G Cruz Villalón in Digital Rights Ireland, Judgment of 12 December 2013, para 107; CJEU, Cases C-203/15 and C-698/15, Tele2 Sverige and Watson and Others, Judgment of 21 December 2016, para 101; A-G Saugmandsgaard Øe also uncritically embraces the reasoning in Digital Rights Ireland; see CJEU, Cases C-203/15 and C-698/15, Opinion of A-G Saugmandsgaard Øe in Tele2 and Watson, Judgment of 19 July 2016, paras 155–160. It can be contested whether the retention of behavioural data has less privacy impact than the retention of communications data, but this not the place to discuss this.

[115] CJEU, Opinion 1/15, Judgment of 26 July 2017, para 151.

[116] For completeness, the Court possibly in 2011 already referred to the essence of Article 8 of the Charter in Deutsche Telekom: "Moreover, where a subscriber has consented to the passing of his personal data to a given undertaking with a view to their publication in a public directory of that undertaking, the passing of the same data to another undertaking intending to publish a public directory without renewed consent having been obtained from that subscriber is not capable of substantively impairing the right to protection of personal data, as recognised in Article 8 of the Charter".; CJEU, Case C-543/09, Deutsche Telekom, Judgment of 5 May 2011, para 66. The reference is so obscure and poorly reasoned, though, that it does not appear to merit the same level of scrutiny as the other cases.

[117] CJEU, Cases C-293/12 and C-594/12, Digital Rights Ireland and others, Judgment of 8 April 2014, para 40.

Opinion 1/15 considered that an envisaged agreement on the exchange of EU flight passenger data with Canada lays down "rules intended to ensure, inter alia, the security, confidentiality and integrity of that data, and to protect it against unlawful access and processing", implicitly concluding that the essence of Article 8 of the Charter is not affected because of this.[118] In *Ligue des Droits Humains*, it came to the same conclusion.[119]

It is unclear why the Court considers it a requirement to take information security measures in order to safeguard the essence of the right to data protection. It does not further explain itself. Perhaps the Court was inspired by the word "protection", reading it as protection against attacks against the confidentiality, integrity and availability of the data. Whatever the reason, it is safe to conclude that its decisions were not a coincidence. The Court had ample opportunity to elevate other principles to the essence of Article 8 of the Charter, but didn't. For example, a "particularly serious" interference "with the fundamental rights of practically the entire European population" in itself did not affect the essence.[120] Moreover, the absence of a requirement to retain personal data in Europe, as a result of which the control by an independent authority could not be fully ensured, also did not affect the essence, *even though* the Court explicitly mentions that this is required under Article 8(3) of the Charter.[121] Meanwhile, Article 8 says nothing about information security.

Three observations can be made. First, the Court in determining whether the essence is affected does not evaluate whether the processing *itself* is lawful (whether it is, for instance, proportionate), but it merely assesses whether the information security controls accurately reflect the choices made *with regard* to such processing. In other words, it focuses on the risk of unauthorised processing, primarily by the controller, but presumably also by others. Second, the Court does not raise the bar very high: the mere existence of provisions prescribing certain technical and organisational measures is already sufficient not to affect the essence of Article 8 of the Charter. At the same time, it also underlines that these measures need to be appropriate to the risk, which means that these considerations also play a role in the proportionality assessment, to be discussed below.

5.4.1.3 The Concept of Proportionality

Whereas the Court had to develop its own framework with regard to the *essence* of the rights to data protection and privacy, it applies a framework strongly inspired by the case law of the European Court of Human Rights with regard to *proportionality*. The review of proportionality firstly depends on the margin of appreciation afforded

[118] CJEU, Opinion 1/15, Judgment of 26 July 2017, para 150.

[119] CJEU (Grand Chamber), Case C-817/19, Ligue des Droits Humains v Conseil des Ministres (Belgian PNR Data), Judgment of 21 June 2022, para 120.

[120] CJEU, Cases C-293/12 and C-594/12, Digital Rights Ireland and others, Judgment of 8 April 2014d, para 56.

[121] Ibid., para 68.

to the legislature. As discussed, interferences with Articles 7 and 8 of the Charter must be "strictly necessary", which, I argue, requires an in-depth examination of the necessity of a measure, preferably on the basis of empirical evidence.

In practice, this assessment involves a balancing of the *objective* pursued by a measure against the nature and seriousness of the interference.[122] On one side of the scale, the Court assesses the importance of the objective. For example, if national security is at stake, the state has more leeway, and it is for instance allowed to retain the behavioural data of all users for a limited period.[123] By contrast, the protection against serious crime or the safeguarding of public security may only justify the *targeted* retention, of only a group of users, of behavioural data.[124]

On the other side of the scale, the Court assesses the *nature and the seriousness* of an interference. It firstly applies a quality of law-test similar to that developed by the European Court of Human Rights: privacy-restricting measures must be clearly circumscribed and provide safeguards against abuse and unlawful access, in particular where sensitive data is at stake and where data is subject to automated processing.[125]

It then assesses the seriousness of an interference. Similar to the case law of the European Court of Human Rights, the seriousness first depends on the impact of *lawful access*. This assessment involves aspects such as the number of people affected, the nature of the data, the duration of the measure and whether automated processing is applied.[126] Where the Court has added its own contribution to the

[122] Ibid., para 47.

[123] CJEU, Cases C-511/18, C-512/18 and C-520/18, La Quadrature du Net, Judgment of 6 October 2020c, paras 136–139, paras 177–179.

[124] Ibid., para 147; see further CJEU, Cases C-203/15 and C-698/15, Tele2 Sverige and Watson and Others, Judgment of 21 December 2016, para 102; CJEU, Case C-207/16, Ministerio Fiscal, Judgment of 2 October 2018, paras 56 and 62, where the interference was not serious, and thus it was not problematic "that the object was the preventing, investigating, detecting and prosecuting 'criminal offences' generally, without it being necessary that those offences be defined as 'serious'". See also the PNR-data opinion, where the Court considered that the "fight against terrorist offences and serious transnational crime" is capable of justifying even "serious interferences" with Articles 7 and 8 of the Charter; CJEU, Opinion 1/15, Judgment of 26 July 2017, para 149.

[125] See CJEU, Case C-623/17, Privacy International v United Kingdom, Judgment of 6 October 2020, para 68; CJEU, Cases C-511/18, C-512/18 and C-520/18, La Quadrature du Net, Judgment of 6 October 2020c, para 132; CJEU, Case C-311/18, Schrems II, Judgment of 16 July 2020, para 177; CJEU, Opinion 1/15, Judgment of 26 July 2017, para 141; see also CJEU, Case C-362/14, Schrems I, Judgment of 6 October 2015, para 91; CJEU, Cases C-293/12 and C-594/12, Digital Rights Ireland and others, Judgment of 8 April 2014d, paras 54–55; in the ibid., the Court considers that the rules should protect against both abuse and unlawful access, whereas in the other cases it considers that the rules should protect against abuse; see for an earlier decision CJEU, Case C-291/12, Schwarz v Bochum, Judgment of 17 October 2013, para 55.

[126] Regarding the number of people, see CJEU, Cases C-293/12 and C-594/12, Digital Rights Ireland and others, Judgment of 8 April 2014d, paras 58, 63; see similarly CJEU, Cases C-203/15 and C-698/15, Tele2 Sverige and Watson and Others, Judgment of 21 December 2016, paras 105, 107, 112; CJEU, Case C-362/14, Schrems I, Judgment of 6 October 2015, para 93; CJEU, Opinion 1/15, Judgment of 26 July 2017, para 187; CJEU, Case C-360/10, SABAM/Netlog, Judgment of 16 February 2012, paras 48–49; and see CJEU, Case C-70/10, Scarlet/SABAM, Judgment of 21

European Court of Human Rights case law, is in its considerations with regard to *unlawful access.*

Part of the risk of unlawful access can be mitigated by judicial review, which can ensure that, before or after access is granted, a court will check whether it does not go further than necessary—similar to the Convention-case law.[127] The Court has also considered other forms of unlawful access. First, it has assessed the risk of access to personal data by governments if the data were to be stored outside the EU—and the Court concluded that data should be stored in the EU, to enable the review of security compliance by an independent authority.[128] More importantly, the Court has investigated the security measures prescribed by the legislature. In *Digital Rights Ireland*, it considered the required security measures insufficient, in particular because they permit providers to take into account economic considerations when determining the level of security they apply.[129] In *Tele 2* it considered that, given "the quantity of retained data, the sensitivity of that data and the risk of unlawful access to it, the providers of electronic communications services must, in order to ensure the full integrity and confidentiality of that data, guarantee a particularly high level of protection and security by means of appropriate technical and organisational measures".[130] Thus, the Court in its proportionality assessment accords a central role to information security measures in preventing unlawful access, explicitly questioning whether costs may play a role when a particularly high level of protection is required. This strict test obviously has a bearing on the analysis of the governance of

November 2011, paras 50–51. Regarding the nature of the data: CJEU, Cases C-293/12 and C-594/12, Digital Rights Ireland and others, Judgment of 8 April 2014d, para 27; CJEU, Opinion 1/15, Judgment of 26 July 2017, para 165; CJEU, Case C-207/16, Ministerio Fiscal, Judgment of 2 October 2018, para 60; CJEU, Cases C-511/18, C-512/18 and C-520/18, La Quadrature du Net, Judgment of 6 October 2020c, para 175; regarding the duration of the measure, see ibid., para 137; CJEU, Opinion 1/15, Judgment of 26 July 2017, para 205; CJEU, Cases C-203/15 and C-698/15, Tele2 Sverige and Watson and Others, Judgment of 21 December 2016; CJEU, Cases C-293/12 and C-594/12, Digital Rights Ireland and others, Judgment of 8 April 2014d, para 64; and regarding automated processing; see CJEU, Cases C-511/18, C-512/18 and C-520/18, La Quadrature du Net, Judgment of 6 October 2020c, paras 181–182; CJEU, Opinion 1/15, Judgment of 26 July 2017, para 174.

127 Regarding judicial review, in *Digital Rights Ireland*, the Court considered it relevant that the Data Retention Directive did not provide that the conditions under which access may take place, or a prior review by a supervisory body before access; CJEU, Cases C-293/12 and C-594/12, Digital Rights Ireland and others, Judgment of 8 April 2014d, paras 61–62; see also CJEU, Cases C-203/15 and C-698/15, Tele2 Sverige and Watson and Others, Judgment of 21 December 2016, para 117; and CJEU, Opinion 1/15, Judgment of 26 July 2017, paras 201, 202 and 208; see further on judicial review CJEU, Case C-746/18, H.K. v Prokuratuur, Judgment of 2 March 2021.

128 CJEU, Cases C-203/15 and C-698/15, Tele2 Sverige and Watson and Others, Judgment of 21 December 2016, para 122; CJEU, Cases C-293/12 and C-594/12, Digital Rights Ireland and others, Judgment of 8 April 2014d, paras 67 and 68.

129 CJEU, Cases C-293/12 and C-594/12, Digital Rights Ireland and others, Judgment of 8 April 2014d, para 67.

130 See for similar consideration CJEU, Cases C-203/15 and C-698/15, Tele2 Sverige and Watson and Others, Judgment of 21 December 2016, para 122.

the information security cycle, encryption and quantum computing in the chapters that follow.

5.5 Conclusion

The above analysis resonates with the landmark decision of the Bundesverfassungsgericht of 2008 regarding online searches. As noted in the introduction, the German Constitutional Court in this decision recognized a new fundamental right to confidentiality and integrity of information technology systems.[131] This new right protects against "access by the state in the area of information technology also insofar as the state has access to the information technology system as a *whole*, and not only to individual communication events or stored data" (emphasis mine).[132] As explained in Chap. 2, these terms "confidentiality" and "integrity" are also central to information security.[133] According to the German Court, the application of existing fundamental rights do not provide sufficient protection against the state searching an IT-system remotely, because of the potentially wide-ranging nature of such a search. Even if the state sets out to only monitor *specific* communications after having gained access to a device, it potentially has access to *all* stored information. Such potential access, given the important role of information technology systems in our lives, has a far-ranging impact.[134] And these considerations underline the importance of taking into account the residual risk of unlawful access and control by the state described above.

However, the Constitutional Court in its reasoning also considers the implications for unlawful access by others. The Court considered that online searches are used to circumvent encryption, which undermines the measures people take to protect themselves against unauthorised access.[135] The fact that the measure prevents this "informational self-protection" increases the gravity of the interference. And online searches may also inflict other damage, in that governmental agencies might not share non-public security loopholes with software vendors (to retain access via vulnerabilities). This, according to the Court, might affect public trust in "state endeavours to ensure the greatest possible security of information technology".[136] It concludes

[131] See Bundesverfassungsgericht, BverfGE—1 BvR 370/07—1 BvR 595/07-, Online-Durchsuchung, Judgment of 27 February 2008; Abel and Schafer 2009.

[132] Bundesverfassungsgericht, BverfGE—1 BvR 370/07—1 BvR 595/07-, Online-Durchsuchung, Judgment of 27 February 2008, para 201.

[133] The aspect of "confidentiality", according to the Court, refers to the interest in ensuring that "data which are created, processed and stored by the information technology system that is covered by its scope of protection remain confidential". The "integrity" of an IT system is presumed to be affected where "its performance, functions and storage contents can be used by third parties"; ibid., para 204.

[134] See also to that effect EDPS 2022, p. 8.

[135] Bundesverfassungsgericht, BverfGE—1 BvR 370/07—1 BvR 595/07-, Online-Durchsuchung, Judgment of 27 February 2008, para 236.

[136] Ibid., para 241.

that such far-reaching powers may only be applied in the case of a concrete danger to "life, limb and freedom of the individual" and an "existential threat" to humanity or the state.[137]

Almost 15 years after the *Online Durchsuchung*-case discussed above, the German Constitutional Court issued a new decision. This time, it focused on the stockpiling of zero-days by the German government, developing its prior reasoning to also encompass positive obligations in the domain of information security.[138] In this decision, it underlined that the state bears a responsibility for the security of IT systems in the context of fundamental rights protection, and is obliged to help protect users of IT systems against attacks.[139] According to the Court, if a state is aware of an unknown vulnerability, the state is required to protect users from third-party infiltration via such unknown security vulnerabilities.[140] This is because vulnerabilities can cause major damage, to fundamental rights but also to things like critical infrastructure.[141] Meanwhile, normal users cannot protect themselves against this damage. In this particular case, the German Court determined that laws should prescribe how the authorities deal with security vulnerabilities of which the developers are not aware.[142]

In their decision, the German Courts point the way to further connecting the rights to privacy and data protection with information security. Even though the European Court of Human Rights and the European Court of Justice have not recognised the same right to confidentiality and integrity of IT-systems, such a right is also lying dormant in the Convention and the Charter. Both the European Court of Human Rights and the European Court of Justice have recognised the role of information security in safeguarding the privacy interests of individuals. In particular, the Courts have emphasised the risk of unlawful access in relation to the rights to privacy and data protection, translating it into negative and positive obligations under specific circumstances.

Information security measures provide ways to control information, determining who can do what with information and systems. They also enable people to determine who gains access to their private domain, in the form of private information, personal devices, etc. They enable others who gain *authorised* access to this private domain, to ensure respect for the privacy interests of these people, for example, by securing the personal data they collected. In an information society, information security can thus protect *individual interests*, such as the interest of autonomy and self-development, *social interests*, such as the development of oneself in relation to others, and *democracy*, as a bulwark against totalitarianism.

The risk of unlawful access has grown immensely as a result of bad information security practices. The implications of this for the information security cycle, and in

---

137 Ibid., paras 247–248.

138 Bundesverfassungsgericht, BVerfGE IT-Sicherheitslücken, Judgment of 8 June 2021, 1 BvR 2771/18.

139 Ibid., paras 25–26.

140 Ibid., para 34.

141 Ibid., paras 35–37.

142 Ibid., p. 41.

particular quantum computing and encryption, are discussed in Chaps. 8–10. First, however, I discuss the right to communications freedom.

References

Articles, Books and Other Documents

Abel W, Schafer B (2009) The German Constitutional Court on the Right in Confidentiality and Integrity of Information Technology Systems – A Case Report on BVerfG, NJW 2008, 822. SCRIPT-ed 6:106–123. https://doi.org/10.2966/scrip.060109.106

Advisory Committee on Automated Personal Data Systems (1973) Records, Computers and the Rights of Citizens, 1 July 1973. https://www.justice.gov/opcl/docs/rec-com-rights.pdf. Accessed 4 January 2024.

Agre P, Rotenberg M (eds) (1997) Technology and Privacy: The New Landscape. MIT Press, Cambridge, Mass.

Apple SRSensor (undated). The Sensors an App Can Read. Apple Developer Documentation. https://developer.apple.com/documentation/sensorkit/srsensor#3681604. Accessed 22 June 2021.

Arnbak AM (2016) Securing Private Communications: Protecting Private Communications Security in EU Law: Fundamental Rights, Functional Value Chains, and Market Incentives. Kluwer Law International, Alphen aan den Rijn, The Netherlands.

Audi (2020) Consistently Connected: Audi Introduces Functions on Demand. https://www.audi.com/en/company/investor-relations/talking-business/audi-functions-on-demand.html. Accessed 24 November 2020.

Audi (2020) Consistently connected: Audi introduces functions on demand. In: audi.com. https://www.audi.com/en/company/investor-relations/talking-business/audi-functions-on-demand.html. Accessed 24 November 2020.

Barocas S, Levy K (2020) Privacy Dependencies. Washington Law Review 95:63.

Blok PH (2002) Het recht op privacy: een onderzoek naar de betekenis van het begrip "privacy" in het Nederlandse en Amerikaanse recht. Boom Juridische uitgevers: Den Haag, 2002.

de Leeuw K (1999) The Black Chamber in the Dutch Republic during the War of the Spanish Succession and Its Aftermath, 1707-1715. The Historical Journal 42:133–156.

Doctorow (2021a) Technological self-determination. https://doctorow.medium.com/technological-self-determination-da7a04952fa. Accessed 9 September 2021.

Doctorow C (2020a) Ink-Stained Wretches: The Battle for the Soul of Digital Freedom Taking Place Inside Your Printer. In: Electronic Frontier Foundation. https://www.eff.org/deeplinks/2020/11/ink-stained-wretches-battle-soul-digital-freedom-taking-place-inside-your-printer. Accessed 18 November 2020.

Doctorow C (2020b) Ink-Stained Wretches: The Battle for the Soul of Digital Freedom Taking Place Inside Your Printer. Electronic Frontier Foundation. https://www.eff.org/deeplinks/2020/11/ink-stained-wretches-battle-soul-digital-freedom-taking-place-inside-your-printer. Accessed 18 November 2020.

Doctorow C (2020c) What Big Tech Does to Discourse, and the Forgotten Tech Tool That Can Make Tech Less Big. https://www.oii.ox.ac.uk/news-events/videos/what-big-tech-does-to-discourse-and-the-forgotten-tech-tool-that-can-make-tech-less-big-with-cory-doctorow/. Accessed 4 January 2024.

Doctorow C (2021b) Technological Self-Determination. https://doctorow.medium.com/technological-self-determination-da7a04952fa. Accessed 9 September 2021.

Doctorow C (2021c) Technology, Self-Determination, and the Future of the Future. https://scalar.usc.edu/works/refusal/technology-self-determination-and-the-future-of-the-future. Accessed 4 January 2024.

EDPS (2022) Preliminary Remarks on Modern Spyware, 15 February 2022. https://edps.europa.eu/data-protection/our-work/publications/papers/edps-preliminary-remarks-modern-spyware_en. Accessed 4 January 2024.
Ellison K (2011) Millions of Millions of Distinct Orders: Multimodality in Seventeenth-Century Cryptography Manuals. 14:1–24.
Eskens S, van Daalen O, van Eijk N (2015) Ten Standards for Oversight and Transparency of National Intelligence Services. https://www.ivir.nl/publicaties/download/1591.pdf. Accessed 4 January 2024.
Fried C (1968) Privacy. Yale Law Journal 1968:475.
Gartenberg C (2020) Apple Releases iOS 13.5.1, Patching out the UncOver Jailbreak. The Verge. https://www.theverge.com/2020/6/1/21277281/apple-ios-13-5-1-patch-unc0ver-jailbreak-update-software-install. Accessed 5 January 2021.
Gartenberg C (2020) Apple releases iOS 13.5.1, patching out the UncOver jailbreak. In: The Verge. https://www.theverge.com/2020/6/1/21277281/apple-ios-13-5-1-patch-unc0ver-jailbreak-update-software-install. Accessed 5 January 2021.
González Fuster G (2014) The Emergence of Personal Data Protection as a Fundamental Right of the EU. Springer International Publishing, Switzerland.
González Fuster G, Gutwirth S, Hert P de (2010) From Unsolicited Communications to Unsolicited Adjustments. In: Gutwirth S, Poullet Y, De Hert P (eds) Data Protection in a Profiled World. Springer Netherlands, Dordrecht, pp 105–117.
Google (2021a) Android Documentation. https://developer.android.com/guide/topics/sensors/sensors_overview. Accessed 5 January 2021.
Google (2021b) Android Documentation. In: Google. https://developer.android.com/guide/topics/sensors/sensors_overview. Accessed 5 January 2021, sections on Sensors, Location and Performance.
Gordon A (2020) People Are Jailbreaking Used Teslas to Get the Features They Expect. https://www.vice.com/en/article/y3mb3w/people-are-jailbreaking-used-teslas-to-get-the-features-they-expect. Accessed 18 November 2020.
Gordon A (2020) People Are Jailbreaking Used Teslas to Get the Features They Expect. In: Vice. https://www.vice.com/en/article/y3mb3w/people-are-jailbreaking-used-teslas-to-get-the-features-they-expect. Accessed 18 November 2020.
Graber CB (2015) Tethered Technologies, Cloud Strategies and the Future of the First Sale/Exhaustion Defence in Copyright Law. QMJIP 5:389–408. https://doi.org/10.4337/qmjip.2015.04.02
Gürkan E (2012) The Efficacy of Ottoman Counter-Intelligence in the 16th Century. Acta Orientalia Academiae Scientiarum Hungaricae 65:1–38. https://doi.org/10.1556/AOrient.65.2012.1.1
Gutheil M, Liger Q, Heetman A et al. (2017) Legal Frameworks for Hacking by Law Enforcement: Identification, Evaluation and Comparison of Practices. https://www.europarl.europa.eu/RegData/etudes/STUD/2017/583137/IPOL_STU(2017)583137_EN.pdf. Accessed 4 January 2024.
Hijmans H (2016) The European Union as a Constitutional Guardian of Internet Privacy and Data Protection: The Story of Article 16 TFEU. University of Amsterdam, Amsterdam.
Hoepman J-H, Koops B-J (2020) Offering "Home" Protection to Private Digital Storage Spaces. SCRIPTed 17:359–388. https://doi.org/10.2966/scrip.170220.359
Holvast J (2009) History of Privacy. In: Matyáš V, Fischer-Hübner S, Cvrček D, Švenda P (eds) The Future of Identity in the Information Society. Springer, Berlin, Heidelberg, pp 13–42.
Hoofnagle CJ, Kesari A, Perzanowski A (2019) The Tethered Economy. The George Washington Law Review 87:783
Hughes K (2015) The Social Value of Privacy, the Value of Privacy to Society and Human Rights Discourse. In: Roessler B, Mokrosinska D (eds) Social Dimensions of Privacy: Interdisciplinary Perspectives. Cambridge University Press, Cambridge, pp 225–243.
Iordanou I (2018) The Professionalization of Cryptology in Sixteenth-Century Venice. Enterprise & Society 19:979–1013. https://doi.org/10.1017/eso.2018.10

Johnson B, Francisco S (2009) Amazon Kindle Users Surprised by "Big Brother" Move. The Guardian, 17 July 2019
Kahn D (1996) The Codebreakers: The Story of Secret Writing, rev. edn. Scribner, New York.
Kahn D (2006) Back When Spies Played by the Rules. The New York Times, 13 January 2006
Knockel J, Parsons C, Ruan L et al. (2020) We Chat, They Watch. How International Users Unwittingly Build up WeChat's Chinese Censorship Apparatus, Citizen Lab, 7 May 2020.
Kokott J, Sobotta C (2013) The Distinction between Privacy and Data Protection in the Jurisprudence of the CJEU and the ECtHR. International Data Privacy Law 3:222–228. https://doi.org/10.1093/idpl/ipt017
Koops B-J, Newell B, Timan T et al. (2017) A Typology of Privacy. University of Pennsylvania Journal of International Law 38:483.
Lamont T (2016) Life after the Ashley Madison Affair. The Guardian. http://www.theguardian.com/technology/2016/feb/28/what-happened-after-ashley-madison-was-hacked. Accessed 25 November 2020.
Lang B (2018) Real Life Cryptology. Amsterdam University Press. http://www.jstor.org/stable/j.ctvfp6380
Lanzing M (2019) "Strongly Recommended" Revisiting Decisional Privacy to Judge Hypernudging in Self-Tracking Technologies. Philos Technol 32:549–568. https://doi.org/10.1007/s13347-018-0316-4
Lynskey O (2014) Deconstructing Data Protection: The "Added-Value" of a Right to Data Protection in the EU Legal Order. International and Comparative Law Quarterly 63:569–597. https://doi.org/10.1017/S0020589314000244
Marcus H, Findlen P (2019) Deciphering Galileo: Communication and Secrecy before and after the Trial. Renaissance Quarterly 72:953–995. https://doi.org/10.1017/rqx.2019.253
Marthews A, Tucker C (2017) Government Surveillance and Internet Search Behavior. Available at SSRN: https://ssrn.com/abstract=2412564 or https://doi.org/10.2139/ssrn.2412564
Ministry of Foreign Affairs of the Netherlands (2020) Statement on the 5th anniversary of the "709 crackdown" on human rights lawyers and defenders. https://www.netherlandsandyou.nl/latest-news/news/2020/07/10/statement-by-the-spokesperson-on-the-5th-anniversary-of-the-%E2%80%9C709-crackdown%E2%80%9D-on-human-rights-lawyers-and-defenders. Accessed 19 November 2020.
Musk E (2013) A Most Peculiar Test Drive. https://www.tesla.com/blog/most-peculiar-test-drive. Accessed 18 November 2020.
Nissenbaum H (2009) Privacy in Context: Technology, Policy, and the Integrity of Social Life. Stanford University Press, Stanford Law Books, Redwood City.
O'Brien SA (2015) Ashley Madison Hack Leads to Spike in Private Eye Requests. CNNMoney. https://money.cnn.com/2015/08/21/technology/trustify-private-investigator-ashley-madison/index.html. Accessed 25 November 2020.
Penney J (2016) Chilling Effects: Online Surveillance and Wikipedia Use. Berkeley Technology Law Journal 31:117.
Poole W (2011) A Late Sixteenth-Century Cryptographic Treatise: Jacobus Colius's "Tractatus De Fictis Characteribus" (1584–86). Journal of the Warburg and Courtauld Institutes 2011:213–239.
Richards N (2015) Intellectual Privacy: Rethinking Civil Liberties in the Digital Age. Oxford University Press, New York.
Ruan L, Knockel J, Crete-Nishihata M (2017) We (Can't) Chat, 91, Citizen Lab,13 April 2017.
Sax M (2018) Privacy from an Ethical Perspective. In: de Groot A, van der Sloot B (eds) The Handbook of Privacy Studies: An Interdisciplinary Introduction. Amsterdam University Press, Amsterdam.
Schabas W (2015) The European Convention on Human Rights: A Commentary, 1st edn. Oxford University Press, Oxford, United Kingdom.
Segall L (2015) Pastor Outed on Ashley Madison Commits Suicide. CNNMoney. https://money.cnn.com/2015/09/08/technology/ashley-madison-suicide/index.html. Accessed 25 November 2020.

Corkery M, Silver-Greenberg J (2019) Miss a Payment? Good Luck Moving That Car. In: DealBook. https://dealbook.nytimes.com/2014/09/24/miss-a-payment-good-luck-moving-that-car/. Accessed 18 November 2020.
Solove DJ (2008) Understanding Privacy. Harvard University Press, Cambridge, Mass.
Stallman R (2020) Free Software Is Even More Important Now. https://www.gnu.org/philosophy/free-software-even-more-important.html. Accessed 20 November 2020.
Steenbruggen W (2009) Publieke dimensies van privé-communicatie: een onderzoek naar de verantwoordelijkheid van de overheid bij de bescherming van vertrouwelijke communicatie in het digitale tijdperk. Cramwinckel, Amsterdam.
Stevens T (2020) Your Next BMW Might Only Have Heated Seats for 3 Months. Roadshow. https://www.cnet.com/roadshow/news/bmw-vehicle-as-a-platform/. Accessed 18 November 2020.
Strickland E, Harris M (2022) Their Bionic Eyes Are Now Obsolete and Unsupported. IEEE Spectrum. https://spectrum.ieee.org/bionic-eye-obsolete. Accessed 16 February 2022.
Stumpf R (2020) Tesla Can Detect Aftermarket Hacks Designed to Defeat EV Performance Paywalls. The Drive. https://www.thedrive.com/tech/35946/tesla-can-detect-aftermarket-hacks-designed-to-defeat-ev-performance-paywalls. Accessed 18 November 2020.
Tene O (2011) Privacy: The New Generations. International Data Privacy Law 1:15–27. https://doi.org/10.1093/idpl/ipq003
van Daalen O (2022), In Defense of Offense: Information Security Research under the Right to Science, Computer Law & Security Review 46: 105706.
van Daalen O (2023a) The Right to Encryption: Privacy as Preventing Unlawful Access, Computer Law & Security Review 49:105804.
van Daalen O (2023b) The Right to Root: Constructing a Claim to Control Devices from the Right to Privacy, JIPITEC 14(2023:4): 580–593.
van Daalen O (2024) Developing a human-rights compatible governance framework for quantum computing, Research Directions: Quantum Technologies 2: 2024.
van der Sloot B (2017a) Privacy as Virtue: Moving beyond the Individual in the Age of Big Data. PhD thesis, University of Amsterdam, Amsterdam.
van der Sloot B (2017b) Legal Fundamentalism: Is Data Protection Really a Fundamental Right? In: Leenes R, van Brakel R, Gutwirth S, De Hert P (eds) Data Protection and Privacy: (In)visibilities and Infrastructures. Springer International Publishing, Cham, pp 3–30.
van der Sloot B (2018) A New Approach to the Right to Privacy, or How the European Court of Human Rights Embraced the Non-Domination Principle. Computer Law & Security Review 34:539–549. https://doi.org/10.1016/j.clsr.2017.11.013
Ward J (2015) Philips Hue Excludes 3rd Party Bulbs With Firmware Update. Zatz Not Funny! https://zatznotfunny.com/2015-12/philips-hue-excludes-3rd-party-bulbs/. Accessed 18 November 2020.
Warren SD, Brandeis LD (1890) The Right to Privacy. Harvard Law Review 4:193–220.
Westin AF (2015) Privacy and Freedom. IG Publishing, New York.
Wortham J (2009) Unofficial Software Incurs Apple's Wrath. The New York Times, 12 May 2009.
Yeung K (2017) "Hypernudge": Big Data as a Mode of Regulation by Design. Information, Communication & Society 20:118–136. https://doi.org/10.1080/1369118X.2016.1186713
York N (2005) William Dowdeswell and the American Crisis, 1763–1775. History 90:507–531.
Yuste R, Goering S, Agüera y Arcas B et al. (2017) Four Ethical Priorities for Neurotechnologies and AI. Nature News 551:159. https://doi.org/10.1038/551159a
Zetter K (2015) Hackers Finally Post Stolen Ashley Madison Data. Wired, 18 August 2015.
Zittrain J (2009) The Future of the Internet - And How to Stop It. Online edition, New Haven, Conn. https://dash.harvard.edu/handle/1/4455262. Accessed 4 January 2024
Zuiderveen Borgesius FJ (2014) Improving Privacy Protection in the Area of Behavioural Targeting. PhD thesis, University of Amsterdam, Amsterdam.

Table of Cases: EU

ECHR, Application no. 36919/02, Armonienė v. Lithuania, Judgment of 25 November 2008.
ECHR, Application no. 931/13, Satakunnan Markkinapörssi Oy and Satamedia Oy v. Finland, Judgment of 27 June 2017.
ECHR, Application no. 20511/03, I v. Finland, Judgment of 17 July 2008.
ECHR, Application no. 13710/88, Niemietz v. Germany, Judgment of 16 December 1992.
ECHR, Application no. 2346/02, Pretty v. the United Kingdom, Judgment of 29 April 2002.
ECHR, Klass and others v. Germany, Judgment of 6 September 1978.
ECHR, Application no. 47143/06, Roman Zakharov v. Russia, Judgment of 4 December 2015.
ECHR, Application no. 28957/95, Christine Goodwin v. the United Kingdom, Judgment of 11 July 2002.
ECHR, Application no. 23380/09, Bouyid v. Belgium, Judgment of 28 September 2015.
ECHR, Applications nos. 32541/08 and 43441/08, Svinarenko and Slyadnev c. Russia, Judgment of 17 July 2014.
ECHR, Application no. 39630/09, El-Masri v. the former Yugoslav Republic of Macedonia, Judgment of 13 December 2012.
Applications nos. 46133/99 and 48183/99, Smirnova v. Russia, Judgment of 24 July 2003.
ECHR, Application no. 40454/07, Couderc and Hachette Filipacchi Associés v. France, Judgment of 10 November 2015.
ECHR, Application no. 35623/05, Bărbulescu v. Romania, Judgment of 5 September 2017.
ECHR, Applications nos. 40660/08 and 60641/08, Von Hannover v. Germany (no. 2), Judgment of 7 February 2012.
ECHR, Application no. 50001/12, Breyer v. Germany, Judgment of 30 January 2020.
ECHR, Application no. 28825/02, Buglov v. Ukraine, Judgment of 10 July 2014.
ECHR (Commission Decision), Application no. 7308/75, X. v. the United Kingdom, Judgment of 12 October 1978.
ECHR (Commission decision), Application No. 21482/93, Christie v. the United Kingdom, Judgment of 27 June 1994.
ECHR, Application no. 8691/79, Malone v. the United Kingdom, Judgment of 2 August 1984.
ECHR, Application no. 47114/99, Taylor-Sabori v. the United Kingdom, Judgment of 22 October 2002.
ECHR (Commission decision), Application no. 8962/80, X. and Y. v. Belgium, Judgment of 13 May 1982.
ECHR, Application no. 62617/00, Copland v. the United Kingdom, Judgment of 3 April 2007.
ECHR, Application no. 74336/01, Wieser and Bicos Beteiligungen GmbH v. Austria, Judgment of 16 October 2007.
ECHR, Application no. 65755/01, Iliya Stefanov v. Bulgaria, Judgment of 22 May 2008.
ECHR, Application no. 70204/01, Frérot v. France, Judgment of 12 June 2007.
ECHR, Applications nos. 15672/08, 24462/08, 27559/08, 28302/08, 28312/08, 34823/08, 40738/08, 41124/08, 43197/08, 51938/08 and 58170/08, Mehmet Nuri Özen and others v. Turkey, Judgment of 11 January 2011.
ECHR, Application no. 20605/92, Halford v. the United Kingdom, Judgment of 25 June 1997.
ECHR, Application no. 44787/98, P.G. and J.H. v. the United Kingdom, Judgment of 25 September 2001.
ECHR, Application no. 31446/12, Ben Faiza v. France, Judgment of 8 February 2018.
ECHR, Applications nos. 58170/13, 62322/14 and 24960/15, Big Brother Watch and others v. United Kingdom (Grand Chamber), Judgment of 25 May 2021.
ECHR, Application no. 4451/70, Golder v. United Kingdom, Judgment of 21 February 1975.
ECHR, Application no. 26839/05, Kennedy v. United Kingdom, Judgment of 18 May 2010.
ECHR, Application no. 54934/00, Weber and Saravia v. Germany, Judgment of 29 June 2006.
ECHR, Application no. 58243/00, Liberty and others v. United Kingdom, Judgment of 1 July 2008.
ECHR, Application no. 25198/02, Iordachi and others v. Moldova, Judgment of 10 February 2009.

ECHR, Application no. 37138/14, Szabó and Vissy v. Hungary, Judgment of 12 January 2016.
ECHR, Application no. 35252/08, Centrum för Rättvisa v. Sweden (Grand Chamber), Judgment of 25 May 2021.
ECHR, Application no. 9248/81, Leander v. Sweden, Judgment of 26 March 1987.
ECHR, Application no. 13/1997/797/1000, Kopp v. Switzerland, Judgment of 25 March 1998.
ECHR, Application no. 16428/05, Gardel v. France, Judgment of 17 December 2009.
ECHR, Application no. 27798/95, Amann v. Switzerland, Judgment of 16 February 2000.
ECHR, Application no. 28341/95, Rotaru v. Romania, Judgment of 4 May 2000.
ECHR, Application no. 62332/00, Segerstedt-Wiberg v. Sweden, Judgment of 6 June 2006.
ECHR, Applications nos. 30562/04 and 30566/04, S and Marper v. United Kingdom, Judgment of 4 December 2008h.
ECHR, Application no. 29514/05, Van der Velden v. the Netherlands, Judgment of 7 December 2006.
ECHR, M.K. v. France, Judgment of 18 April 2013.
ECHR, application no. 45245/15, Gaughran v. the United Kingdom, Judgment of 13 February 2020.
ECHR, Application no. 35623/05, Uzun v. Germany, Judgment of 2 September 2010.
ECHR, Application no. 24029/07, M.M. v. United Kingdom, Judgment of 30 November 2012.
ECHR, Application nos. 1474/62; 1677/62; 1691/62; 1769/63; 1994/63; 2126/64, Belgian Linguistic Case, Judgment of 23 July 1968.
ECHR, Application no. 6289/73, Airey v. Ireland, Judgment of 9 October 1979.
ECHR, Marckx v. Belgium, Judgment of 13 June 1979.
ECHR, Application no. 18535/91, Kroon and Others v. the Netherlands, Judgment of 27 October 1994.
ECHR, Application no. 62540/00, The Association for European Integration and Human Rights and Ekimdzhiev v. Bulgaria, Judgment of 28 June 2007.
ECHR, Application no. 11105/84, Huvig v. France, Judgment of 24 April 1990.
ECHR, Application no. 43514/15, Catt v. the United Kingdom, Judgment of 24 January 2019.
ECHR, Application no. 8978/80, X and Y v. the Netherlands, Judgment of 26 March 1985.
ECHR, Application no. 42326/98, Odièvre v. France, Judgment of 13 February 2003.
ECHR, Application no. 6339/05, Evans v. the United Kingdom, Judgment of 10 April 2007.
ECHR, Application no. 37359/09, Hämäläinen v. Finland, Judgment of 16 July 2014.
ECHR, Application no. 25579/05, A, B and C v. Ireland, Judgment of 16 December 2010.
ECHR, Application no. 39272/98, M.C. v. Bulgaria, Judgment of 4 December 2003.
ECHR, Application no. 2872/02, K.U. v. Finland, Judgment of 2 December 2008.
ECHR, Application no. 36934/08, I.C. v. Romania, Judgment of 24 May 2016.
ECHR, Application no. 5786/08, Söderman v. Sweden, Judgment of 12 November 2013.
ECHR, Application no. 48009/08, Mosley v. the United Kingdom, Judgment of 10 May 2011j.
ECHR, Application no. 7525/76, Dudgeon v. United Kingdom, Judgment of 22 October 1981.
ECHR, Application no. 22009/93, Z v. Finland, Judgment of 25 February 1997.
European Court of Justice, Opinion of A-G Bot in Schrems, Judgment of 23 September 2015.
BVerfG, - 1 BvR 370/07 - - 1 BvR 595/07 -, Online-Durchsuchung, Judgment of 27 February 2008a.
German Constitutional Court, German Census, Judgment of 15 December 1983.
BVerfG, IT-Sicherheitslücken, Judgment of 8 June 2021b, 1 BvR 2771/18.
CFI, T-194/04, Bavarian Lager, Judgment of 8 November 2007.
CJEU, Cases C-511/18, C-512/18 and C-520/18, La Quadrature du Net, Judgment of 6 October 2020c.
CJEU, Case C-78/18, European Commission v. Hungary (Transparency of Associations), Judgment of 18 June 2020.
CJEU, Case C-543/09, Deutsche Telekom, Judgment of 5 May 2011.
CJEU, Case C-131/12, Google Spain, Judgment of 13 May 2014.
CCJEU, Cases C-141/12 and C-372/12, YS v Minister voor Immigratie, Integratie en Asiel, and Minister voor Immigratie, Integratie en Asiel v M, S, Judgment of 17 July 2014.
CJEU, Case C-398/15, Manni, Judgment of 9 March 2017.

CJEU, Case C-73/07, Satamedia, Judgment of 16 December 2008.
CJEU, Case C-275/06, Promusicae, Judgment of 29 January 2008.
CJEU, Case C-92/09, Volker und Markus Schecke and Eifert, Judgment of 9 November 2010.
CJEU, Cases C-468/10 and C-469/10, ASNEF, Judgment of 24 November 2011.
CJEU, Case C-291/12, Schwarz v. Bochum, Judgment of 17 October 2013.
CJEU, Case C-362/14, Schrems I, Judgment of 6 October 2015.
CJEU, Cases C-203/15 and C-698/15, Tele2 Sverige and Watson and Others, Judgment of 21 December 2016.
CJEU, Cases C-293/12 and C-594/12, Digital Rights Ireland and others, Judgment of 8 April 2014d.
CJEU, Opinion 1/15, Judgment of 26 July 2017.
CJEU, Case C-207/16, Ministerio Fiscal, Judgment of 2 October 2018.
CJEU, Case C-465/00, Rundfunk, Judgment of 20 May 2003.
CJEU, Case C-623/17, Privacy International v. United Kingdom, Judgment of 6 October 2020.
CJEU (Grand Chamber), Case C-817/19, Ligue des Droits Humains v. Conseil des Ministres (Belgian PNR Data), Judgment of 21 June 2022.
CJEU, Case C-311/18, Schrems II, Judgment of 16 July 2020.
CJEU, Case C-360/10, SABAM / Netlog, Judgment of 16 February 2012.
CJEU, Case C-70/10, Scarlet / SABAM, Judgment of 21 November 2011.
CJEU, Case C-746/18, H.K. v. Prokuratuur, Judgment of 2 March 2021.

Table of Cases: Germany

BVerfG, 1 BvR 370/07, Online-Durchsuchung, Judgment of 27 February 2008.
BVerfG, 1 BvR 209, German Census, Judgment of 15 December 1983.
BVerfG, 1 BvR 1541/20, IT-Sicherheitslücken, Judgment of 8 June 2021.

Chapter 6
The Right to Communications Freedom

Contents

Abstract This chapter discusses the right to communications freedom under the Convention and the Charter. It starts with a historical analysis of the right, focusing on its relation to science and communications infrastructure. It then analyses how the right protects activities in the field of information security, while imposing a duty on researchers to mitigate the risks associated with those activities. It also discusses to what extent these rights can be invoked to restrict the application of information security measure or at least allow for their circumvention.

Keywords Communications freedom · Cryptography · Information security research · Duties and responsibilities · Access to information and information infrastructure

O. van Daalen, *From Encryption to Quantum Computing*, Information Technology and Law Series 38, https://doi.org/10.1007/978-94-6265-635-2_6

6.1 Introduction

At the beginning of the seventeenth century, censorship in England was rife.[1] Books had to be approved in advance, some were rewritten by the censors and others were never authorised for publication at all. Approved books could still be banned afterwards, sometimes publicly burned. Authors were beaten, mutilated and imprisoned, bookstores were closed, and even private houses raided. As the power of the English king waned and Parliament gained in importance in 1640, there was a temporary lull in censorship. Whereas around seven hundred books and pamphlets were printed annually in England in the 1630s, this grew to two thousand in 1641, and over four thousand in 1642.[2] Among the books printed that year was a manual on cryptography: *Mercury: or the Secret and Swift Messenger. Shewing, How a Man may with Privacy and Speed communicate his Thoughts to a Friend at Any Distance.*[3] It was written by John Wilkins, Bishop of Chester and one of the founders of the Royal Society.[4]

A number of books on cryptography had already been written at that time, but this was the first one in English. This is relevant—it was intended to be broadly read. In the introduction, Wilkins writes that knowledge on cryptography had traditionally been the domain of "Statesmen and Soldiers". He argued, however, that all "who profess the Knowledge of Nature or Reason" needed to understand this subject. Why? Because this knowledge formed part of the "Liberal Arts"—of established science, not of occult magic.[5] Simultaneously, however, Wilkins questioned the wisdom of making this kind of knowledge available to the general public, because it could be also be used for undesirable ends. Some decades earlier, Mary Queen of Scots' plot to assassinate and overthrow Queen Elisabeth I had been discovered by intercepting and deciphering her letters.[6] Wilkins published his book at a time when political tensions in the run-up to the English civil war were rapidly increasing. Wilkins was also undoubtedly thinking about people who would use this knowledge to discuss the regime in power, some perhaps even aiming to overthrow it.

Wilkins' deliberations echo one of the central questions of this book: what role does the right to communications freedom play with regard to information security? This relationship is a bit more complicated than the relationship between privacy and information security because the question can be answered on two levels. First, communications freedom has a relation to the *cycle* of information security, to the extent that it covers the research and disclosure of vulnerabilities. When you do research or you publish your findings, you can rely on the right to communications freedom.

---

[1] Cressy 2006, p. 290.

[2] Ibid., p. 292.

[3] Wilkins 1694; see on Wilkin's treatise Ellison 2011 and 2013.

[4] Bowen and Hartley 1960.

[5] Wilkins 1694, pp. 9, 11; Ellison 2016, p. 198; see on this further Ellison 2013.

[6] Singh 2000, Chap. 1.

Second, communications freedom also has a relation to the *application* of information security measures. In Chap. 5, I recognised two mechanisms through which privacy is maintained in the information society: through *restriction of access* and through *exercise of control*, both in regard to information and to systems, often enforced through information security measures. I also observed that these mechanisms can be used to *interfere* with privacy—for example if you are denied access to your data, or if others exercise control over your devices.

Now, just as the use of these mechanisms can affect privacy, their use can also affect communications freedom, often restricting it. For example, DRM-technologies which are applied to protect movies against unauthorised access through software and hardware limit the possibilities of users to share this information with others. And blocking websites negatively affects the possibilities of users to access information. But sometimes, these mechanisms support communications freedom—for example by ensuring you retain control over your own communication devices, or by shielding your chats from prying eyes. In this chapter, I explore this further.[7] I will first discuss the relationship between communications freedom and the information security *cycle*. Then the relationship with the application of information security will be discussed.

It should be noted that, just as there is no right to privacy under the Convention and the Charter, there is no right to communications freedom: under Article 10 of the Convention and Article 11 of the Charter everyone has the right to "freedom of expression". "Expressing" is something most people do in public, so the term "freedom of expression" on the surface might suggest that it only refers to the public dimension of communication. But people also communicate less freely in private if they are under surveillance.[8] Furthermore, the term "expression" refers to the sending phase of communications, whereas the right protected under the Convention and the Charter also includes the phase of receiving information. I therefore instead use the term "communications freedom", to emphasise not only the public dimension of communication, but also its private aspects, and to underline its importance throughout all phases of communication. At the same time, this chapter's main focus is the public aspects of communications freedom, because when the Court discusses the effects that privacy restrictions might have on confidential communications in

[7] Parts of this chapter have already been published in Van Daalen 2022, 2023a, 2023b and 2024.

[8] See Steenbruggen 2009, para 2.3; Zuiderveen Borgesius and Steenbruggen 2019, Sects. I and III for a discussion of this particular legal basis of communications secrecy; see Ruiz 1997, p. 147 who for reasons of internal coherence argued for the opposite position; see also Hofman 1995, pp. 90–91; and Asscher 2002, pp. 127–128; see also Arnbak 2016, p. 133; this is even more so, where communications are not only intercepted, but also tampered with. Ruiz further argues that since the right to freedom of expression also includes the right to be silent, communications freedom *a fortiori* also includes the right to speak in private; Ruiz 1997, p. 68; see also Asscher 2002, p. 18. Indeed, the right to confidentiality of communications at the time of framing the French *Declaration de Droits de l'Homme et du Citoyen de 1789* was regarded as part of the right to freedom of expression; Ruiz 1997, pp. 64–67.

the context of surveillance, it does so often under the header of Article 8 of the Convention, which has already been discussed in the previous chapter.[9]

6.2 Three Perspectives on Communications Freedom

Let me start with a short historical account of three perspectives on communications freedom, clarifying its relationship to information security. First, I will discuss print technology and censorship. Then, I will discuss communications networks and access to communications infrastructure. And I will conclude with the era of digitisation, and with it, the application of restrictive information security measures. This account is by no means complete but fulfils its role here. I wish to demonstrate how the concepts of access and control, over information and systems, play an important role in the enjoyment of communications freedom in the twenty-first century, just as they do when it comes to the right to privacy.

6.2.1 The Introduction of Print Technology

Communications freedom was initially about preventing censorship—censorship by public authorities, to be precise. In Western Europe, the idea that communication deserves protection from governmental interference is rooted in the Enlightenment, where a number of developments coalesced to bring this into focus.[10] First, the emancipation of a *bourgeois* class put existing power relations under strain, setting the scene for a clash between the monarchy, the Catholic church and the citizenry. An important factor in this clash was the advent of Protestantism and the widespread use of the new printing press. In 1517, Luther kindled the Protestant movement by nailing his *Ninety-Five Theses* to the church door at Wittenberg.[11] This new movement was facilitated by Gutenberg's invention of movable type in around 1440, which enabled information to be disseminated faster and more widely than ever before.[12] Luther turned out to be a master at this new medium—using it to strengthen his message, through his translation of the Bible and a continuous stream of religious pamphlets,

---

[9] See ECHR, Application no. 47143/06, Roman Zakharov v Russia, Judgment of 4 December 2015g, para 169; ECHR, Application no. 37138/14, Szabó and Vissy v Hungary, Judgment of 12 January 2016; ECHR, Application no. 35252/08, Centrum för Rättvisa v Sweden (Grand Chamber), Judgment of 25 May 2021, para 167; ECHR, Application nos. 58170/13, 62322/14 and 24960/15, Big Brother Watch and others v United Kingdom (Grand Chamber), Judgment of 25 May 2021h, para 450.

[10] Ishay 2009, Chap. 2; Dommering 2016, part 2; Starr 2004, Chap. 1.

[11] Leppin and Wengert 2015.

[12] His Chinese and Korean colleagues were earlier, but this knowledge had not dispersed to Europe yet; Daland 1931.

with one author calling these evangelisation efforts the "West's first large-scale media campaign".[13]

Book printing not only allowed Luther's proclamation to gain traction, it more generally heralded a new age of communication within Europe, enabling manuscripts to be printed at scale. Some of these manuscripts were political in nature, undermining the power of the ruling class. But book printing also facilitated the development of science—putting increasing strain on the Catholic church as experimental knowledge discovered by humanists was at odds with the worldview proclaimed by the Church. For example, the Church had always embraced the idea that the planets revolved around the Earth. Galileo's insight that the Earth revolved around the Sun, made possible by the invention of telescopes, was considered heresy.

In response, political and religious authorities throughout Europe applied a range of interventions to control the spread of printed information. As discussed in the introduction, reigning factions in England used censorship to protect their interests.[14] In Bourbon France, the monarchy "developed an elaborate system for channeling the power of the printed word" through royal privileges accorded to books, booksellers and guilds.[15] The Catholic Church also took action, first ordering Luther's books to be burned, later drawing up a more extensive list of prohibited books (only to be abandoned in 1966!).[16] A less spectacular but more influential practice of the Church was to correct books before publication, so-called "expurgation".[17] It was not only religious books that were the target of the censors—scientific works were also restricted. For example, the Catholic Church added all books espousing a heliocentric worldview—including Galileo's work—to the list of banned books on 5 May 1616.[18] And these measures also extended to other scientific areas, such as medicine.[19]

This was also the time when the seeds for modern copyright law were sown. The use of privileges for book printing was not merely a tool for censorship—it was also a way to protect the economic interests of the printers.[20] Initially, these two goals went hand in hand—authorities exerted strict control over books through these printing licenses, and privileged printers were able to recoup their investments

[13] Edwards 2004; Creasman 2018.

[14] See Clegg 2001, 2005, 2008; Cressy 2006, Chap. 12.

[15] See Darnton 2014, p. 29.

[16] The Catholic Church in 1521 convinced Emperor Charles V to ban all Luther's writings and ordered to have them burned; Creasman 2018; Charles V (1521) Edict of Worms on Condemning Heresy and Those Who Challenge Ecclesiastical and Secular Authority; later, under Pope Paul IV in 1559, the Catholic Church drew up a more general *List of Prohibited Books*, updated regularly since; see Marcus 2020, pp. 25, 35; Ottaviani 1966, *Notification regarding the abolition of the Index of books*, 14 June 1966. The *Index* also prescribed that books be burned, and the Roman Inquisition started incinerating entire personal libraries within two months after its first publication; Marcus 2020, p. 41.

[17] Marcus 2020, Chap. 2 and further.

[18] Heilbron 2010, p. 218. The Italian Inquisition in 1633 forced Galileo to condemn his findings and placed him under house arrest in his villa in the hills near Florence; Næss 2005, p. 175.

[19] See Marcus 2020, Chap. 1.

[20] See van Gompel 2011, Chap. 3 for a discussion.

through the exclusivity granted to them. In the centuries that followed, economic ordering and the protection of the rights of the author became the dominant goals of the privilege system. This evolved into the copyright laws we know today. The main way in which current copyright laws protect right holders is through restrictions on copying and accessing information (and less through remuneration). This betrays their censorial roots and is important for understanding how information security measures are now used to further these restrictions, something I will discuss in the section on digitisation.

Although the censorship measures discussed above came in various forms, they have one thing in common: authorities intervened because of the *content* of information, restricting access and exercising control over it. These kinds of restrictions are of course still with us today. They have gradually adapted to encompass new media, from cinema to the internet, and protect different interests, from public morals to privacy. These include the regulations limiting the sharing of results of information security research and information security tools, discussed in Chap. 3. It is not necessary to further discuss these restrictions here—all these limitations on the information security cycle are assessed under this classic understanding of communications freedom.

6.2.2 The Introduction of Communication Networks

At the end of the nineteenth century, however, a new dimension of communications freedom started to gain importance in response to the rise of electronic communications networks: communications freedom as *access to communications infrastructure*. This is because communications networks are expensive to build, and their value depends on how many people you can reach. Access to these networks was an important element in ensuring that the public could benefit fully from their value. At that time the debate was not yet framed in terms of fundamental rights. It revolved around economic ordering and regulation of market dominance. But it was already driven by the interest of the public in freedom of communication.

The development of the telegraph and telephone networks in the US was an important early example of this new thinking. In the US, the telegraph market was so fragmented in around 1850 that it was hard to make a profit, and communication between different networks was choppy at best.[21] This led to consolidation, and by 1866 one company, Western Union, had managed to acquire a network spanning the entire country.[22] Similarly, the first telephone networks in the US were fragmented across thousands of organisations, some of them grassroots initiatives of small groups of farmers using fence wire to transmit messages.[23] AT&T through a host of takeovers eventually came to own the entire US telephone network.

[21] Starr 2004, p. 172.

[22] Ibid., p. 175.

[23] Ibid., pp. 200–201.

This dominance prompted a debate on access: when should you be able to use the network, and under what conditions? A decision of the US Supreme Court of 1894 on the telegraph is illuminating: "Telegraph companies resemble railroad companies and other common carriers, in that they are instruments of commerce, and in that they exercise a public employment, and are therefore bound to serve all customers alike, without discrimination. They have, doubtless, a duty to the public to receive, to the extent of their capacity, all messages clearly and intelligibly written, and to transmit them upon reasonable terms."[24] This debate ultimately led US Congress to designate telegraph and telephone companies as so-called "common carriers" in 1910, as a result of which they were obliged to carry messages, as long as they were paid for carrying the message.[25] Meanwhile in Europe, telegraph and telephone networks were primarily in the hands of the governments (usually via the postal services). Mandatory access was presumably therefore less of a public concern. These separate networks across the continent did, however, have another problem: communication across borders was complex. This led to a different form of access regulation: interconnection agreements between the networks in different countries.[26]

The invention of wireless communications in the beginning of the twentieth century resulted in another example of access regulation: access to radio spectrum.[27] As the number of broadcasting stations multiplied, interference increased and governments around the world started granting radio licenses to prevent chaos, granting exclusive rights for the use of certain frequencies. This created artificial scarcity, which allowed governments to exercise significant control over communications, partly by denying licenses and partly by imposing conditions on licenses. But in contrast to the royal privileges accorded to printers during the Enlightenment, by this time, the right to communications freedom was enshrined in national constitutions, so broadcasting licenses had to be assessed against these constitutional principles.[28] One of the consequences of this, was the adoption of so-called must-carry rules, under which communication networks are obliged to grant access to a diverse range of broadcasters, usually public service broadcasters.

What all these examples have in common, is that they show that *access to systems*—in particular communications systems—can further communications freedom. And although initially the policy debate was framed mostly as matter of economic ordering—"maverick operators should gain access to incumbent networks"—it can also be a human rights issue. This has become more obvious as electronic communications networks have since come to play a central role in our society, which the discussion some years ago around net neutrality regulations demonstrate. In fact, the debate around net neutrality is not only an example of

---

24 Supreme Court, 59, Primrose v Western Union Telegraph Company, Judgment of 26 May 1894.

25 Starr 2004, p. 188; Wu 2013, Chap. 3.

26 See for example Standage 2014, Chap. 4 for examples in the telegraph market.

27 See Starr 2004, Chaps. 10 and 11; Lommers 2012; Wu 2013, Chaps. 2 and 9.

28 Starr 2004, pp. 365–366.

regulations aimed at ensuring access to infrastructure to safeguard communications freedom—it is arguably also an example of regulation of information security measures to achieve this goal. This movement was fueled by concerns that internet users and service providers would be excluded from this vital communications medium.[29] This would be done through contracts—for instance asking Netflix to pay extra if it wants preferential treatment in case of scarcity. It would also be done through technical measures—for instance by deliberately slowing down WhatsApp-traffic. These technical measures could be considered a form of information security measures. The resulting regulations were aimed partly at prohibiting internet service providers from blocking or throttling internet traffic—in other words, it prohibited them from applying certain security measures.

6.2.3 The Era of Digitisation

Not only have electronic communications *networks* become more important in our lives—increased digitisation has also made it easier to search, copy and share *information*. As discussed in Chap. 3, this affected the interests of the entertainment industry, who saw their control over content dissipate. It also increased the risks of other types of data leaking to the outside world, such as confidential data. To stem the tide, not only did organisations apply information security measures to restrict access and exercise control over information; policymakers also attempted to resolve these conflicts by granting legal protection to technical protection of copyrighted information.

As already alluded to in Chap. 3, the rules protecting technical measures sparked a serious debate on the implications for freedom of communications. These technical measures could restrict more access to information than was hitherto possible, also preventing information flows which were deemed to be in the public interest. In response, policymakers have introduced exemptions to the circumvention prohibitions to allow for "legitimate uses"—e.g. uses which were protected under the right to communications freedom—such as copying for personal use, jailbreaking and accessing personal data (see Chap. 3).

But even with these exemptions in place, the regulation of the tools used to perform this circumvention ignited a heated debate around access to information. For example, when US authorities arrested Russian cryptographer Dmitry Sklyarov after he gave a presentation on vulnerabilities in Adobe's eBook encryption scheme, there was

[29] See Sluijs 2011; van Eijk 2014; Nunziato 2009.

public outcry around the world.[30] Sklyarov became a political prisoner of sorts—activists started campaigning to "Free Sklyarov", making songs, stickers and banners, organising rallies from San Jose to Moscow, calling for a boycott of Adobe, all while internet luminaries such as Lessig weighed in.[31] Thus ultimately caused Adobe to withdraw its support of the criminal case.

A similar, though less heated, debate took place in the context of pay-TV, which is also based on restricting access to content. For example, in 2012, a Roman administrative court found that Italian public service broadcaster RAI acted in violation of must-carry (or rather "must-offer") rules by encrypting its free-to-air TV channels, necessitating customers of commercial satellite broadcaster Sky Italia to buy a separate dongle for the decryption of RAI channels.[32] The court noted that public service programming must be "universally accessible via all technology platforms", regardless of who owns them. Since then, these debates have become less contentious, as the range of legally available digital music, movies and books has grown. But the legal protection of technical measures is still in place, and the fundamental issues surrounding the restriction of information via these measures still has not been resolved. As a result, incidents such as the remote disabling of Orwell's 1984, mentioned in Chap. 3, still sometimes make the news.

These communications freedom interests can perhaps best be shared under the header of device self-determination, the concept introduced in Chap. 5. Device self-determination as I define it, has to do with the possibility of determining how you use digital technology. It not only protects the privacy of individuals; it also protects their communications freedom. It allows them to determine how they want to access, copy and share information, in particular using their own devices. I will discuss the consequences of this in the following sections.

One understanding of communications freedom, as *trust in communications*, is also worth mentioning in this context. The licensing systems described in the section above were not watertight: "piracy" was commonplace.[33] This not only undermined the businesses of licensed printers, but also called into question the authenticity of circulating copies. In response, printers developed printers' marks, which were supposed to attest to the authenticity of a text, but these were counterfeited too, even leading one printer to sign each book by hand.[34] This had a profound effect

---

[30] See Electronic Frontier Foundation 2002a; Lemos 2002; (2011) USA v Dmitry Sklyarov—Press Statement and Complaint. In: Cryptome. https://cryptome.org/usa-v-sklyarov.htm. Accessed 16 November 2019; Wilbur 2009. He was charged with violating the anti-circumvention provisions of the Digital Millennium Copyright Act, not for his research, but because he contributed to the "Advanced eBook Processor"—software sold by his employer Elcomsoft, which allowed people to read eBooks on any computer without paying; Electronic Frontier Foundation 2002a. The US Attorney subsequently agreed to drop the charges against Sklyarov, and in the trial against his employer, a federal jury in San Jose in 2002 eventually found Elcomsoft not guilty; Electronic Frontier Foundation 2002b, 2011.

[31] Free Dmitry Sklyarov! 2003; Smith 2001; Boycott Adobe 2001; Lessig (2001); see also Coleman 2013, Chap. 5.

[32] Moscon 2012.

[33] Johns 1998, Chap. 2.

[34] Ibid., pp. 173, 182.

on the trust in communications. Johns in his study on printing notes that in "an environment where unauthorized printing was seen as a real possibility, the identity of the author, the authenticity of the text, and the credibility of the knowledge contained in the text were all therefore destabilized".[35] Communications freedom, then, also is dependent on the ability to *trust* information. Trust in information has only become more relevant with the advent of the internet, as the ease with which information can be produced and distributed makes it increasingly difficult to distinguish between true and false, between authentic and forged. Yet, this relationship between trust and communications freedom is hardly studied. Trust has been merely recognised as one of the underlying rationales for the protection of private communications, and the role of trust at the intersection of information security and communications freedom has not been discussed at all.[36] I will not explore this further in this book, but this is a valuable topic for further research.

6.2.4 Three Justifications for Protection of Communications Freedom

Although the perspectives on communications freedom might have evolved in the past centuries, its justifications have remained by and large the same since the Enlightenment—its proponents have put forward three main considerations.[37] The first is the "argument from truth": freedom of communications supports the advancement of truth, because truth will replace falsehoods in an open debate.[38] The second argument centres around autonomy or self-development: communications freedom deserves special protection because it is necessary for an individual to develop themself, an idea strongly related to the argument from truth.[39] And the third justification—the "argument from democracy"—contends that communications freedom is necessary for a democracy to flourish, because it allows for deliberation on public affairs, such as laws and government policy.[40]

---

[35] Ibid., p. 620.

[36] Zuiderveen Borgesius and Steenbruggen 2019; Arnbak 2016, Chap. 9.

[37] See Barendt 2005, Chap. 1; Barendt mentions one additional argument—suspicion of government—but this arguably can also be subsumed under the other justifications; see also Alexander 2005, Chap. 7 for a broader set of arguments, including the fostering of tolerance and the promotion of virtue.

[38] See Milton 1644, Areopagitica; a Speech of Mr. John Milton for the Liberty of Unlicenc'd Printing, to the Parlament of England; Mill 1999, pp. 59–60. Supreme Court Justice Holmes in 1919 famously took the ball and ran with it, contending that "the ultimate good desired is better reached by free trade in ideas—the best test of truth is the power of the thought to get itself accepted in the competition of the market"; US Supreme Court, 250 U.S. 616 (1919), Dissenting opinion of Holmes in Abrams v United States, Judgment of 10 November 1919.

[39] See Brison 1998 for an overview of the different strands of this argument.

[40] See Schauer 1983, Sect. II. Already in 1689 the English Parliament claimed for itself the right to criticize the king, noting in the Bill of Rights that "the freedom of speech and debates or proceedings

While these considerations still ring true, there are also important limits to them. More communications do not always equal more truth—in fact, lies on social media spread "farther, faster, deeper, and more broadly than the truth".[41] The addictive properties of digital devices meanwhile have reduced our ability to think and act freely—more communications do not always equal more autonomy.[42] And disinformation has come to complement censorship as an important tool for the influencing of public opinion—more communications do not always equal more democracy. In fact, the Twitter and Facebook ban of former US president Trump in the aftermath of the election of his successor was done to *protect* democracy.[43] In other words: communications freedom is a necessary, but not a sufficient condition for achieving these three goals. In Chap. 8, I will also touch on enabling factors for communications freedom to thrive in the context of information security.

First, however, I will review the case law under the Charter and the Convention. As discussed in the introduction, this right to communications freedom has a relationship to both the *information security cycle* and the information security *application*. Both will be dealt separately, for each focusing on the question of interference and proportionality.

6.3 Communications Freedom and the Information Security Cycle

Recall that the information security cycle described in Chap. 2 consists of different phases: the taking of measures, the research into vulnerabilities, the publication of vulnerabilities and then taking new measures to address those vulnerabilities. Communications freedom is particularly relevant to two of these phases: the research and publication stage. As we will see, both activities fall squarely in the protection accorded under Article 10 of the Convention and Article 11 of the Charter.

6.3.1 The Qualification of Interferences with Regard to Information Security Research

The practice of publishing information security vulnerabilities is highly diverse. Some vulnerabilities are published in academic papers which have gone through

---

in parliament ought not to be impeached or questioned in any court or place out of parliament"; Bogen 1983, p. 433. This was also one of the main drivers behind the recognition in the French *Declaration* of the right to "*la libre communication des pensées et des opinions*"; (1789) Déclaration des Droits de l'Homme et du Citoyen, Article 11.

[41] Vosoughi et al. 2018

[42] See also Bastick 2021.

[43] Facebook Oversight Board, 2021-001-FB-FBR, Decision on Facebook's ban of president Trump, Judgment of 5 May 2021.

peer review. Other vulnerabilities have been published in online fora, or on mailing lists. Sometimes the authors merely state that there is a vulnerability, without alluding to the details. In other disclosures, the authors provide actual exploits to demonstrate their findings (which can of course be easily used for malicious purposes). This leads to the question to what extent these different kinds of publications are covered by Article 10.

Article 10 protects "information and ideas". In practice, a broad range of types of information is protected. This can vary from trivial information, to information which is only in the public interest, to information which is merely damaging.[44] One topic not yet handled by the Court, is whether information which is both functional and expressive, such as an executable exploit, is also protected. Given the sweeping considerations of the Court, however, the fact that information not only conveys knowledge, but also *does* something, should not exclude it from protection. This is also relevant for the assessment of export controls of encryption technology, which may focus on encryption *code*, not the mere encryption algorithms.

Furthermore, the form through which you express yourself also does not matter. The Court has considered that it follows from Article 10 that each person is free to choose the form for expressing information and ideas which they consider the most effective to reach the most persons.[45] This can range from text to pictures, from speech to symbols, from literary heritage to the right not to speak.[46] The Court even considers that protesting by physically impeding activities of which the applicants disapproved, constitutes expressions of opinion within the meaning of Article 10.[47]

This of course does not mean that all kinds of information are protected to the same degree. The degree of protection afforded to publications largely depends on the extent to which a publication contributes to the public interest. I discuss this further in the section below on proportionality.

The second question is to what extent restrictions on the information security cycle should be considered an interference. Under Article 10, "formalities, conditions, restrictions or penalties" are mentioned as examples of an interference. Thus, criminal convictions, orders to pay damage and publication prohibitions should, in principle, all be assessed under Article 10.[48] Furthermore, where there is a *potential* of a chilling effect on communications freedom, for example because an order is not yet enforced,

---

44 This includes information and ideas that offend, shock and disturb the state; ECHR, Application no. 5493/72, Handyside v the United Kingdom, Judgment of 7 December 1976l, para 49.

45 ECHR, Application no. 31276/05, Women on Waves and others v Portugal, Judgment of 3 February 2009, para 38.

46 See Bychawska-Siniarska 2017, pp. 17–18.

47 ECHR, 67/1997/851/1058, Steel and others v the United Kingdom, Judgment of 23 September 1998, para 92.

48 See ECHR 2020, para 50; for example ECHR, Application nos. 21279/02 and 36448/02, Lindon, Otchakovsky-Laurens and July v France, Judgment of 22 October 2007; ECHR, Application no. 18139/91, Tolstoy Miloslavsky v the United Kingdom, Judgment of 13 July 1995; ECHR, Application no. 28255/07, Cumhuriyet Vakfi and others v Turkey, Judgment of 8 October 2013.

this will often be considered an interference as well.[49] There are various kinds of restrictions on information security research, as outlined in Chap. 3. Only a few are outright prohibitions under criminal law—many are restrictions under civil law, such as copyright law, and some are imposed via contractual obligations (that is: service providers, or product manufacturers prohibit research in the contracts they conclude with their customers). Furthermore, many of these provisions have a chilling effect, as discussed in that chapter as well—it may lead to experts not doing the research at all, or not publishing parts of the research out of fear of repercussions. As a result, many of the research restrictions discussed in Chap. 3 should be considered an interference under Article 10.

For one type of interference, it is not so clear to what extent it falls under Article 10: the judicial enforcement of *contractual* restrictions. Under certain circumstances, these may also interfere with the right to communications freedom. The Court has in the past considered that states have a positive obligation to protect the right to freedom of expression even in the sphere of relations between individuals.[50] Similar to the right to privacy, the existence of this obligation depends on the fair balance between the general interest of the community and the interests of the individual, and should not impose an impossible or disproportionate burden on the authorities.[51] Whereas the Court has developed this doctrine in the context of public broadcasters—which have a certain relationship to the state—it has since considered that the right applies not only to employment relationships governed by public law, but also those governed by private law.[52] It has furthermore noted in the context of the protection of journalists that states should create "a favourable environment for participation in public debate

[49] In the *Financial Times* case, the Court found it immaterial for the establishment of an interference whether an order directed to a journalist to disclose its sources was actually enforced (it wasn't in this case), as there was still harm because the order was *capable* of being enforced; ECHR, Application no. 821/03, Financial Times Ltd. and others v the United Kingdom, Judgment of 15 December 2009, para 56; in Goodwin and subsequent cases, the Court accepted the argument that source disclosure orders on journalists can violate Article 10 of the Convention, see inter alia ECHR, Application no. 17488/90, Goodwin v the United Kingdom, Judgment of 27 March 1996, para 28; ECHR, Application no. 64752/01, Voskuil v the Netherlands, Judgment of 22 November 2007, para 49; ECHR, Application no. 39315/06, Telegraaf Media Nederland Landelijke Media B.V. and others v the Netherlands, Judgment of 22 November 2012, paras 84–88; ECHR, Application no. 21272/12, Becker v Norway, Judgment of 5 October 2017, para 59. Similarly, in Sanoma the Court analyses this further, noting that the Court in earlier case-law has considered "the extent to which the acts of compulsion resulted in the actual disclosure or prosecution of journalistic sources irrelevant for the purposes of determining whether there has been an interference with the right of journalists to protect them"; ECHR, Application no. 38224/03, Sanoma v The Netherlands, Judgment of 14 September 2010, para 67. In this case, the credible threat to issue an order to raid the offices of a newspaper is already sufficient to be considered an interference, because, the Court notes "a chilling effect will arise wherever journalists are seen to assist in the identification of anonymous sources"; ibid., para 71.

[50] ECHR, Application no. 39293/98, Fuentes Bobo v Spain, Judgment of 29 February 2000, para 38.

[51] ECHR, Application no. 23144/93, Özgür Gündem v Turkey, Judgment of 16 March 2000, para 43.

[52] The Court for instance assessed the dismissal of a journalist by a broadcaster for contract breach because of publication under Article 10; ECHR, Application no. 73571/10, Case of Matùz v

by all the persons concerned, enabling them to express their opinions and ideas without fear, even if they run counter to those defended by the official authorities or by a significant part of public opinion, or even irritating or shocking to the latter".[53] While the principle of contractual freedom will also have to be taken into account in this balancing act, it is likely that the judicial enforcement of contractual limitations on information security research should at least be considered an interference (or warrant discussion under the notion of positive obligations flowing from Article 10). This is especially so where publication is not only in the interest of the publisher, but also in the interest of the public, which will often be the case where the information security cycle is concerned.

Finally, not only is the act of publication covered by Article 10: the Court considers the research and disclosure stage to be highly intertwined. As discussed, Article 10 protects all phases of the communications cycle: "receiving" as well as "imparting" information. The Courts have interpreted this to mean that the preparatory stages of communication also fall within the scope of this provision. The Court has for example considered that in circumstances where access to government information is instrumental for the exercise of an applicant's right to receive and impart information, its denial may constitute an interference with that right.[54] This depends on factors such as the purpose and nature of an information request: access must be necessary and the information must be in the public interest.[55] Research activities in preparation of a publication, such as doing an investigation, are also covered by the right to communications freedom.[56] The Court has lastly repeatedly underscored

Hungary, Judgment of 21 October 2014, para 26; and it has considered the dismissal of an employee for publishing an offensive cartoon in a trade union magazine; ECHR, Application nos. 28955/06, 28957/06, 28959/06 and 28964/06, Palomo Sánchez and Others v Spain, Judgment of 12 September 2011; see on this topic further Mak 2007.

[53] ECHR, Application nos. 65286/13 and 57270/14, Khadija Ismayilova v Azerbaijan, Judgment of 10 January 2019, para 158.

[54] ECHR, Application no. 18030/11, Magyar Helsinki Bizottság v Hungary, Judgment of 8 November 2016n, para 155.

[55] Ibid., paras 159, 161.

[56] See e.g.; ECHR, Application no. 77551/01, Dammann v Switzerland, Judgment of 25 April 2006, para 52. The Court in *Leander* (1987) initially noted that this right basically prohibits a Government from restricting a person from receiving information that others wish or may be willing to impart to him; ECHR, Application no. 9248/81, Leander v Sweden, Judgment of 26 March 1987, para 74. It did not, according to the Court in earlier case-law, also impose a right to gain access to a register containing information on that person; see later ECHR, Application no. 10454/83, Gaskin v the United Kingdom, Judgment of 7 July 1989, para 51; ECHR, Roche v the United Kingdom, Judgment of 19 October 2005, para 72. In subsequent cases, it changed this position; ECHR, Application no. 37374/05, Társaság a Szabadságjogokért v Hungary, Judgment of 14 April 2009, para 35; ECHR, Application no. 39534/07, Österreichische Vereinigung zur Erhaltung, Stärkung und Schaffung Eines Wirtschaftlich Gesunden Land- Und Forst- Wirtschaftlichen Grundbesitzes/ Austria, Judgment of 28 November 2013, para 41; ECHR, Application no. 18030/11, Magyar Helsinki Bizottság v Hungary, Judgment of 8 November 2016n.

that academic freedom, both in the research and publication phase, is protected under Article 10 of the Convention.[57]

6.3.2 Proportionality of Restrictions on the Information Security Cycle

Having established that many information security research restrictions constitute an interference, the next question is whether these are proportionate, or, in the words of Article 10, whether an interference is "necessary in a democratic society".[58] This necessity must, according to the Court, be a "pressing social need" and, where the press is concerned, the most careful scrutiny is applied, which means that the margin of appreciation is restricted.[59] In its case law, the Court affirmed in strong language the central role of freedom of expression in the human rights framework: it constitutes one of the essential foundations of a democratic society and one of the basic conditions for its progress and for each individual's self-fulfillment.[60] The Court speaks of restrictions which could "only have been justified by imperative necessities since exceptions to the freedom of expression must be interpreted narrowly", and in another case notes that "supervision must be strict because of the importance—frequently stressed by the Court—of the rights in question", which means that the necessity for any restriction must be convincingly established.[61]

---

[57] See Laffranque 2017; ECHR, Application no. 2933/03, Cox v Turkey, Judgment of 20 May 2010; ECHR, Application nos. 346/04 39779/04, Mustafa Erdoğan and Others v Turkey, Judgment of 27 May 2014, para 40; ECHR, Application nos. 4149/04 41029/04, Aksu v Turkey, Judgment of 15 March 2012, para 71; ECHR, Application no. 40877/07, Hasan Yazici v Turkey, Judgment of 15 April 2014, para 55; ECHR, Application no. 17089/03, Sorguç v Turkey, Judgment of 23 June 2009; ECHR, Application no. 18030/11, Magyar Helsinki Bizottság v Hungary, Judgment of 8 November 2016n, para 168; ECHR, Application nos. 23536/94 and 24408/94, Başkaya and Okçuoğlu v Turkey, Judgment of 8 July 1999, para 65; ECHR, Application no. 31475/05, Kenedi v Hungary, Judgment of 26 May 2009, para 43; ECHR, Application no. 28396/95, Wille vs. Liechtenstein, Judgment of 28 October 1999; ECHR, Application no. 44102/04, Sapan v Turkey, Judgment of 8 June 2010, para 34; ECHR, Application no. 20233/06, Kula v Turkey, Judgment of 19 June 2018, para 38; ECHR, Application no. 39128/05, Lombardi Vallauri v Italy, Judgment of 20 October 2009, para 43; see for a discussion Groen 2015.

[58] ECHR, Application no. 5493/72, Handyside v the United Kingdom, Judgment of 7 December 1976l, para 49.

[59] Ibid., para 49; ECHR, Application no. 13585/88, Observer and Guardian v the United Kingdom, Judgment of 26 November 1991, para 60; ECHR, Application no. 13166/87, the Sunday Times v the United Kingdom, Judgment of 26 November 1991, para 51.

[60] ECHR, Application no. 5493/72, Handyside v the United Kingdom, Judgment of 7 December 1976, para 49.

[61] ECHR, Application no. 15153/89, Vereinigung Demokratischer Soldaten Österreichs and Gubi v Austria, Judgment of 19 December 1994, para 37; ECHR, Application no. 13914/88; 15041/89; 15717/89; 15779/89; 17207/90, Informationsverein Lentia and Others v Austria, Judgment of 24 November 1993, para 35.

While restrictions on communications freedom need to be subject to strict scrutiny, not all information is protected to the same degree. This involves a balancing exercise, weighing the interests in interference against the interests in communications freedom.[62] This also requires an analysis of the subsidiarity of the interference: there must be no other means of achieving the same end that would interfere less seriously with the fundamental right concerned.[63] Furthermore, as has also been discussed in Chap. 4, where Article 10 conflicts with another right under the Convention, such as the right to privacy, these rights deserve equal respect, and a wide margin of appreciation will usually be afforded by the Court in striking a balance between the two.[64]

At the heart of the proportionality analysis of the Court in the context of communications freedom lies the concept of the "*public interest*".[65] The more the dissemination of information is in the public interest, the more it can count on protection. According to the Court, the "public interest relates to matters which affect the public to such an extent that it may legitimately take an interest in them, which attract its attention or which concern it to a significant degree, especially in that they affect

[62] See for example ECHR, Application no. 69698/01, Stoll v Switzerland, Judgment of 10 December 2007o. The impact depends on various factors, including the nature and content of the speech, and the means of dissemination and the target audience. For example, in the context of reputation, the Court takes into account the extent to which attacks on someone's reputation seriously affect his or her life; ECHR, Application no. 26922/14, Toranzo Gomez v Spain, Judgment of 20 November 2018, para 51. In the context of protecting national security and preventing crime and disorder, the Court has investigated to what extent the texts taken as a whole can be considered as inciting to violence; ECHR, Application no. 23144/93, Özgür Gündem v Turkey, Judgment of 16 March 2000, para 63. As to the medium: publishing poetry has less impact than distributing leaflets; publishing a literary work less impact publishing on the internet; ECHR, Application no. 23168/94, Karataş v Turkey, Judgment of 8 July 1999, para 49; ECHR, Application no. 23500/94, Polat v Turkey, Judgment of 8 July 1999, para 47; ECHR, Application no. 64569/09, Case of Delfi AS v Estonia, Judgment of 16 June 2015, para 110.

[63] ECHR, Application no. 13444/04, Glor v Switzerland, Judgment of 30 April 2009, para 94.

[64] ECHR, Application nos. 40660/08 and 60641/08, Von Hannover v Germany (no. 2), Judgment of 7 February 2012, para 106; ECHR, Application no. 64569/09, Case of Delfi AS v Estonia, Judgment of 16 June 2015, para 139.

[65] For completeness: it need not only concern political issues or crimes but can concern things such as sporting issues or performing artists as well; ECHR, Application nos. 40660/08 and 60641/08, Von Hannover v Germany (no. 2), Judgment of 7 February 2012, para 109. Regarding art, the Court noted that "Article 10 includes freedom of artistic expression—notably within freedom to receive and impart information and ideas—which affords the opportunity to take part in the public exchange of cultural, political and social information and ideas of all kinds [...]. Those who create, perform, distribute or exhibit works of art contribute to the exchange of ideas and opinions which is essential for a democratic society. Hence there is an obligation on the State not to encroach unduly on the author's freedom of expression [...]"; ECHR, Application no. 40287/98, Alinak v Turkey, Judgment of 29 March 2005, para 42; see further the analysis in Council of Europe 2011, Chap. I. Where it concerns "commercial speech" (such as advertising), the Court applies a notably lower standard, affording a significant margin of appreciation to the member states and merely investigating for example whether "the measures taken at a national level are justifiable in principle and proportionate"; ECHR, Application no. 10572/83, Markt Intern Verlag Gmbh and Klaus Beermann v Germany, Judgment of 20 November 1989, para 33; ECHR, Application no. 15088/89, Jacubowski v Germany, Judgment of 23 June 1994, para 26.

the well-being of citizens or the life of the community".[66] This is also the case with regard to "matters which are capable of giving rise to considerable controversy, which concern an important social issue, or which involve a problem that the public would have an interest in being informed about."[67] Furthermore, the quest by the public to find *solutions* to problems through dialogue also thrives on freedom of expression.[68] All these considerations are relevant for the information security cycle: while vulnerabilities may appear to be highly technical issues only interesting to a limited group of experts, these can deeply affect individuals, organisations and governments alike. They have, in other words, a strong public interest dimension. Research and disclosure are an important way to address these vulnerabilities and the related public interest issues. This is particularly the case where information security measures support the enjoyment of fundamental rights, for example in the case of encryption technologies which protect the confidentiality of communications.

Another factor considered by the Court is the extent to which information contributes to the quest for truth: it has considered that "it is an integral part of freedom of expression to seek historical truth".[69] This emphasis on the discovery of truth can also be found in the case law on the evidence required to support public statements. The proportionality of prohibiting the publication of a "value judgment" (as opposed to a fact), depends on whether there is a sufficient "factual basis".[70] It follows that information that contributes to the quest for truth, or can be proven to be

---

[66] ECHR, Application no. 18030/11, Magyar Helsinki Bizottság v Hungary, Judgment of 8 November 2016n, para 162.

[67] Ibid., para 162 As an example, information meets a public-interest test where, inter alia, disclosure provides transparency on matters of interest for society as a whole and thereby allows participation in public governance by the public at large; ibid., para 161.

[68] ECHR, Application nos. 133/1996/752/951, United Communist Party of Turkey and Others v Turkey, Judgment of 30 January 1998, para 57: "The Court considers one of the principal characteristics of democracy to be the possibility it offers of resolving a country's problems through dialogue, without recourse to violence, even when they are irksome. Democracy thrives on freedom of expression. From that point of view, there can be no justification for hindering a political group solely because it seeks to debate in public the situation of part of the State's population and to take part in the nation's political life in order to find, according to democratic rules, solutions capable of satisfying everyone concerned."; See also ECHR, Application nos. 29221/95 and 29225/95, Stankov and the United Macedonian Organisation Ilinden v Bulgaria, Judgment of 2 October 2001, para 97: "The essence of democracy is its capacity to resolve problems through open debate.".

[69] ECHR, Application no. 64915/01, Chauvy and Others v France, Judgment of 29 June 2004, para 69. Conversely, "denying the reality of clearly established historical facts, such as the Holocaust [...] does not constitute historical research akin to a quest for the truth", and the Court considered such "attempts to deflect Article 10 of the Convention from its real purpose by using his right to freedom of expression for ends which are contrary to the text and spirit of the Convention"; ECHR, Application no. 65831/01, Garaudy v France, Judgment of 24 June 2003.

[70] ECHR, Application no. 29369/10, Morice v France, Judgment of 23 April 2015, para 126. In *Lingens* and *Oberschlick*, the Court for the first time made a distinction between factual statements on the one hand, and opinions or value judgments on the other hand—considering it disproportionate to ask for proof of value judgments; ECHR, Application no. 9815/82, Lingens v Austria, Judgment of 8 July 1986, para 46; and later ECHR, Application no. 11662/85, Oberschlick v Austria, Judgment of 23 May 1991, para 63. The Court in Salov considered that Article 10 Convention "does not prohibit discussion or dissemination of information received even if it is strongly suspected that this

true, should be accorded more protection. Lastly, the Court has considered that a criminal law system should allow for the *exceptio veritatis*—the defence of truth—with regard to provisions protecting the reputation of heads of state.[71] Research and publication of information security vulnerabilities contributes to a better understanding of the working of software and hardware, and thus of truth. This already is an important argument, but it becomes even more important because software and hardware play such a central role in our society, also for the enjoyment of other fundamental rights. Improving our understanding of the digital infrastructure we rely on every day also contributes to the enjoyment of these other fundamental rights.

Case law on the right to freedom of expression in relation to the publication of *confidential information* is also relevant. This is because some policy interventions in this cycle are predicated on the assumption that keeping information with regard to information security measures secret, is a good way to advance information security. The Court notes, however, that in the context of confidential information, there is "little scope" for restrictions on a debate of matters of public interest.[72] Furthermore, the Court is realistic when it comes to the question of whether information is still confidential—it looks to the actual dissemination and also takes into account the probability that information might not be confidential anymore.[73] This is relevant, because most vulnerabilities will eventually be published, sometimes anonymously, regardless of the existence of confidentiality obligations.

Lastly, the case law on who can profit from Article 10 is highly relevant. The Court initially accorded an important role to journalists working in the press media in spurring the debate on matters of public interest. According to the Court, the press played the vital role of "public watchdog".[74] As the internet became widely available, it gradually recognised that others could also perform this role. What matters is whether the activities of an organisation are an essential element of informed public

---

information might not be truthful"; ECHR, Application no. 65518/01, Salov v Ukraine, Judgment of 6 September 2005, para 113.

[71] ECHR, Application no. 51279/99, Colombani and others v France, Judgment of 25 June 2002, para 66.

[72] ECHR, Application no. 69698/01, Stoll v Switzerland, Judgment of 10 December 2007o, para 106. See also: "The conviction of a journalist for disclosing information considered to be confidential or secret may discourage those working in the media from informing the public on matters of public interest. As a result, the press may no longer be able to play its vital role as "public watchdog" and the ability of the press to provide accurate and reliable information may be adversely affected."; ibid., para 110.

[73] See ECHR, Application no. 13166/87, the Sunday Times v the United Kingdom, Judgment of 26 November 1991; ECHR, Application no. 13585/88, Observer and Guardian v the United Kingdom, Judgment of 26 November 1991; ECHR, Application no. 16616/90, Vereniging Weekblad Bluf! v the Netherlands, Judgment of 9 February 1995, para 45; ECHR, Application no. 39315/06, Telegraaf Media Nederland Landelijke Media B.V. and others v the Netherlands, Judgment of 22 November 2012, para 130.

[74] ECHR, Application no. 13585/88, Observer and Guardian v the United Kingdom, Judgment of 26 November 1991, para 59; ECHR, Application no. 13166/87, the Sunday Times v the United Kingdom, Judgment of 26 November 1991, para 50.

debate.[75] For example, NGOs can play such a role. As discussed in Chap. 2, in the context of information security, this "informed public debate" is fed by researchers from diverse backgrounds, some are self-taught independents, some are working in the commercial sector, some are from academia. All these researchers should be considered a "public watchdog" for the state of information security of our digital infrastructure, as long as they work towards strengthening this infrastructure, and as such are accorded the same protection under Article 10.

All in all, disclosure of vulnerabilities in digital infrastructure by researchers is a good example of an activity protected under Article 10.

6.3.3 Duties and Responsibilities and the Information Security Cycle

Now, the fact that communication may be protected under Article 10, does not mean that its beneficiaries can publish information at will. In fact, the limitation clause of Article 10 is more extensive than the limitation clause of the right to privacy under the Convention. It also emphasises the obligations of the person invoking the right: according to the Convention, the exercise of these freedoms carries with it "duties and responsibilities". The question is how these duties and responsibilities apply to information security research. In fact, since the information security cycle is predicated on improving information security in the long run, but publication may in the short term pose a risk, the brunt of the proportionality assessment in this context will in most cases be bourne by the scope of these duties and responsibilities.

Case law on the due diligence required by journalists when publishing information suggests that information security researchers have a duty of care when researching and disclosing vulnerabilities.[76] Journalists can profit from Article 10 when reporting on issues of general interest, but only as long as they are acting in good faith in order to provide accurate and reliable information in accordance with the ethics of journalism.[77] In the context of defamation by a newspaper, the due diligence required depends on different factors, such as the nature and degree of the defamation, the extent to which the newspaper could have reasonably regarded its sources as reliable, the authority of the source, the amount of research before publication, whether the

---

[75] ECHR, Application no. 18030/11, Magyar Helsinki Bizottság v Hungary, Judgment of 8 November 2016, para 167.

[76] The Court has also touched on the duties and responsibilities of others, such as employees towards their employers, see for example ECHR, Application no. 20436/02, Wojtas-Kaleta v Poland, Judgment of 16 July 2009.

[77] ECHR, Application no. 48723/07, Stankiewicz and others v Poland, Judgment of 14 October 2014, para 62; see before ECHR, Application no. 21980/93, Bladet Tromsø and Stensaas v Norway, Judgment of 20 May 1999, para 65; ECHR, Application no. 29183/95, Fressoz and Roire v France, Judgment of 21 January 1999, para 54.

story has been presented in a reasonably balanced manner and whether the newspaper gave the persons defamed the opportunity to defend themselves.[78] Where the allegations are particularly serious, for example allegations that a person supervised the deportation of Jews in the Second World War, "the utmost care and particular moderation" was required.[79] While most of the case law concerns journalists, the Court has determined that the same principles also apply to others, such as people distributing campaigning leaflets.[80]

This case law implies that information security researchers will in many cases have a duty to mitigate the risks associated with disclosure. The most important way to mitigate the risks, is by allowing a period of time to bring out a patch or fix a vulnerability before publishing it. But how much time should researchers grant the organisations to bring out a patch? The reference to the *ethics* in the case law above, could be read to imply that for journalists, this is partly a matter of what the profession itself considers to be acceptable. And the same would apply to information security researchers—commonly accepted standards should be considered relevant for this assessment. However, the Court's case law also provides some pointers. On the one hand, the *urgency* of publication is relevant—in other words, what would happen if publication were to be delayed? This question is mostly relevant in the context of so-called prior restraints: prohibiting a publication altogether, instead of interfering *after* a publication. Such prior restraints are not prohibited *per se*, but "the dangers inherent in prior restraints are such that they call for the most careful scrutiny on the part of the Court. This is especially true so as far as the press is concerned, for news is a perishable commodity and to delay its publication, even for a short period, may well deprive it of all its value and interest."[81] Where there is less urgency in publishing information, for example in the case of archives, the duty to "act in accordance with the principles of responsible journalism by ensuring the accuracy of historical, rather than perishable, information is likely to be more stringent".[82] One last aspect: in the preceding section, I argued that where information security measures protect fundamental rights, the research and disclosure of a vulnerability in order to patch a system will quickly be in the public interest. But is the converse also true? That is, where information security measures restrict fundamental rights, will research and disclosure *without* allowing for patching be considered a responsible approach? Not

---

[78] ECHR, Application no. 48723/07, Stankiewicz and others v Poland, Judgment of 14 October 2014, para 63 and cited case law.

[79] ECHR, Application no. 53984/00, Radio France and others v France, Judgment of 30 March 2004, para 39; See also ECHR, Application no. 25333/06, Europapress Holding D.O.O. v Croatia, Judgment of 22 October 2009, para 68.

[80] ECHR, Application no. 68416/01, Steel and Morris v United Kingdom, Judgment of 15 February 2005, para 90.

[81] ECHR, Application no. 3111/10, Ahmet Yildirim v Turkey, Judgment of 18 December 2012, para 47; see before ECHR, Application no. 13166/87, the Sunday Times v the United Kingdom, Judgment of 26 November 1991, para 51; and ECHR, Application no. 13585/88, Observer and Guardian v the United Kingdom, Judgment of 26 November 1991, para 60.

[82] ECHR, Application nos. 3002/03 and 23676/03, Times Newspapers Ltd. v the United Kingdom (Nos. 1 and 2), Judgment of 10 March 2009, para 45.

always, but the argument may be relevant in certain cases. I will discuss this further in Chap. 8.

Now, to be clear, there have also been cases where research and publication have gone too far. Sometimes, this is because of the damage resulting from a publication. For example, in *Hadjianastassiou* (1992), the Court considered that "the disclosure of the State's interest in a given weapon and that of the corresponding technical knowledge, which may give some indication of the state of progress in its manufacture, are capable of causing considerable damage to national security" and it found a five month-prison sentence for disclosing information justified.[83] This can also be the case where there are alternatives which achieve the same effect—something which is particularly relevant for performing research.[84] For example, the Court did not deem it necessary for journalists to actually buy a firearm (in violation of criminal law) in order to demonstrate that it was easy to purchase one, because this could have been illustrated in other ways.[85] The conviction of a journalist for carrying a weapon on an airplane (wanting to prove that airport security was bad) was also considered disproportionate, because the journalist could have revealed the security flaws at the airport without committing a criminal offence, for example by disposing of the knife after the security check-points.[86] Similarly, the conviction of journalists who owned and used scanners to intercept police traffic (to arrive at a crime scene in time) was also deemed proportionate, although the reasoning is succinct.[87] This means information security researchers must not go further than necessary, not with their methods, and not with their disclosure. So: no downloading a file if you just needed to show that the server was badly secured; no providing an exploit if you could prove your point with a description of what you found; and always documenting what you did, for later reference.

6.3.4 Positive Obligations Flowing from the Right to Communications Freedom

Lastly, case law on a so-called "right to reply" provides some inspiration for the question of whether states have an obligation to adopt coordinated vulnerability disclosure processes. The Court in one case notes that the state has a positive obligation to ensure that an author had a reasonable opportunity to exercise his right of reply in a newspaper, and to ensure that he had an opportunity before the domestic courts to contest

[83] ECHR, Application no. 12945/87, Hadjianastassiou v Greece, Judgment of 16 December 1992, para 45.

[84] See ECHR 2020, para 284 for an overview.

[85] ECHR, Application no. 33628/15, Salihu and others v Sweden, Judgment of 10 May 2016, para 57.

[86] ECHR, Application no. 56328/10, Erdtmann v Germany, Judgment of 5 January 2016, para 23.

[87] ECHR, Application no. 22567/09, Brambilla and others v Italy, Judgment of 23 June 2016.

the newspaper's refusal.[88] The Court considers that the right of reply, as an important element of freedom of expression, flows from the need not only to be able to contest untruthful information, but also to ensure a plurality of opinions, especially in matters of general interest such as literary and political debate.[89] In both cases, the national law provided for a right to reply, and the case centred around the question of whether its application was in line with Article 10, focusing on the role of the press. The cases arguably also underline that states have an obligation to structure other publication processes, not only of the press, in such a way that damage is minimised and the goals of this process—truth-seeking, plurality—are maximised. This broader understanding is also relevant for information security research—it is likely that states have a positive obligation to embed coordinated vulnerability disclosure procedures in their legal frameworks to ensure that information security research is channeled in the right direction. I will discuss how this can be done further in Chap. 8.

6.3.5 The Right to Communications Freedom Under the Charter

The case law on Article 10 of the Convention is as rich, as the case law on Article 11 of the Charter is limited (partly because these decisions stem from preliminary questions, see Chap. 4). As noted above, however, the meaning and scope of Article 11 of the Charter are the same as those guaranteed under the Convention.[90] And the Court of Justice also often refers to the European Court of Human Rights in its decisions.[91] In its case law to date, the European Court of Justice has furthermore not deviated from the line set out by the European Court of Human Rights. The European Court of Justice has called the principle of freedom of expression "one of the fundamental pillars of a democratic society", and has underlined the "essential role played by the press in a democratic society", communicating information and ideas and the public's right to receive them.[92] Restrictions on the press informing the public must

---

[88] ECHR, Application no. 28743/03, Melnychuk v Ukraine, Judgment of 5 July 2007p.

[89] Ibid., para 2; ECHR, Application no. 24016/05, Eker v Turkey, Judgment of 24 October 2017, para 43.

[90] Praesidium of the European Convention 2007, Explanations Relating to the Charter of Fundamental Rights, Explanations to Article 11. The European Court of Justice has also referred to case law on the Convention in its decisions; see for example CJEU, Case C-547/14, Philip Morris Brands SARL and Others v Secretary of State for Health, Judgment of 4 May 2016, para 147.

[91] For example, when balancing the right to privacy and the right to communications freedom in the context of publications, it refers to the criteria set out by the European Court of Human Rights; CJEU, Case C-345/17, Sergejs Buivids v Datu valsts inspekcija, Judgment of 14 February 2019, paras 65–66.

[92] CJEU, Case C-421/07, Damgaard, Judgment of 2 April 2009, para 26; CJEU, Case C-136/17, GC/CNIL, Judgment of 24 September 2019, para 76.

thus be "strictly necessary".[93] Similar to the case law on Article 10 of the Convention, whether a publication contributes to the public interest is an important factor.[94] Other factors include "the content, form and consequences of the publication, and the manner and circumstances in which the information was obtained and its veracity", as well as the possibility for an organisation "to adopt measures to mitigate the extent of the interference".[95] Conversely, when publication does not contribute to a discussion of public interest—as in the case of commercial information—member states have a broader discretion in determining which measures are appropriate, and review is limited to an examination of the reasonableness and proportionality of the interference.[96] In other words—it is not necessary to draw a clear line between the communications freedom case law under the Charter and under the Convention when it comes to assessing restrictions on the information security cycle. This is a bit different when it comes to communications freedom and the *application* of information security, as we will see.

6.4 Communications Freedom and the Application of Information Security

I discussed the relationship between the rights to communications freedom and information security research, but there is also another way in which information security is related to communications freedom: as a result of its *application*, namely to restrict access and exercise control in relation to information and systems. So, how does this application of information security relate to the right under the Convention and the Charter?

There are two variations to this question. First: is there an obligation on the part of organisations using information security measures to ensure that communications freedom is respected within their systems? You could call this a "communications

[93] CJEU, Case C-516/17, Spiegel Online GmbH v Volker Beck, Judgment of 29 July 2019, para 72; CJEU, Case C-145/10, Painer, Judgment of 1 December 2011, para 113; CJEU, Case C-73/07, Satamedia, Judgment of 16 December 2008, para 56; see similarly CJEU, Case C-283/11, Sky Österreich GmbH/Österreichischer Rundfunk, Judgment of 22 January 2013, para 52.

[94] CJEU, Case C-345/17, Sergejs Buivids v Datu valsts inspekcija, Judgment of 14 February 2019, para 66; see also CJEU, Case C-131/12, Google Spain, Judgment of 13 May 2014, para 81.

[95] CJEU, Case C-345/17, Sergejs Buivids v Datu valsts inspekcija, Judgment of 14 February 2019, para 66. In the context of the publication of information of criminal offences, the Court applies similar criteria; CJEU, Case C-136/17, GC/CNIL, Judgment of 24 September 2019, para 77. The nature of the speech or information is particularly important when striking a fair balance, for example "in political discourse and discourse concerning matters of the public interest"; CJEU, Case C-469/17, Funke Medien NRW GmbH v Bundesrepublik Deutschland, Judgment of 29 July 2019, para 74; CJEU, Case C-516/17, Spiegel Online GmbH v Volker Beck, Judgment of 29 July 2019, para 58.

[96] CJEU, Case C-421/07, Damgaard, Judgment of 2 April 2009, para 27; see also CJEU, Case C-157/14, Neptune Distribution SNC v Ministre de l'Économie et des Finances (Minister for Economic Affairs and Finance), Judgment of 17 December 2015, para 76.

freedom-by-design" obligation, similar to the way a privacy-by-design obligation can be constructed from the rights to privacy and data protection. Or, in the terms of the preceding chapter: whether the conditions of *access* of systems accurately reflect an appropriate balance between the interests of communications freedom and other interests (of rightsholders, for example, in the case of access to culture). A less far-reaching question is whether the circumvention of information security measures which do *not* strike this balance appropriately, may still be prohibited—and in the case of DRM even criminalised.

The answer to these questions has implications for the *measure taking*-phase, the *research*-phase and the *disclosure*-phase of the information security cycle. But whereas the activities described in the preceding section fall squarely within the protection accorded by both instruments, the Courts have barely discussed the application of information security under this provision, only touching on the understanding of communications freedom as *access*. Below, I make a first attempt to fill this gap.

6.4.1 The Case Law Under Article 10 of the Convention

One aspect of access to information under Article 10 has already been discussed in the preceding section: preventing access to information in the course of information security research. But what about access to other content, such as music, movies and books? Article 10 speaks of the right to "receive" information, after all. This does not prohibit organisations from—entirely on their own initiative—restricting the conditions under which they make information available through their platforms: *that* cannot be considered an interference.[97]

But what if circumvention of these information security measures is prohibited—could you then argue that this interferes with the right of people to circumvent information security measures to ensure they receive it? Generally speaking, no. For example, Helberger in her 2005 thesis concluded that a general "right of decryption" for access-controlled content cannot be derived from the right to communications freedom, primarily because it would be at odds with the balancing required under paragraph 2 of Article 10.[98] Subsequent case law does not lead to a wholly different conclusion. There might, however, be specific cases where circumvention is justified, as we will see.

This argument starts with a thirty-year-old case concerning licenses for the use of satellite dishes. Here, the Court determined that the scope of protection accorded under Article 10 of the Convention also extends to the *means* used to impart and

[97] The Court did rule, on the other hand, that a national court's decision to terminate a tenancy agreement because of the tenants' refusal to dismantle a satellite dish should be considered an interference; ECHR, Application no. 23883/06, Khurshid Mustafa and Tarzibachi v Sweden, Judgment of 16 December 2008, para 36.

[98] See Helberger N (2005) Controlling access to content: regulating conditional access in digital broadcasting. PhD thesis, University of Amsterdam, p. 76.

receive information, since any restriction imposed on the means necessarily interferes with the right to receive and impart information.[99] This at least suggests that information security *measures* which restrict access to information or infrastructure, or control information, may under some circumstances be considered an interference. Since then, the Court has on multiple occasions reviewed the blocking of websites and social media accounts, and these are even more relevant to this discussion.

In those decisions, the Court applies the framework it has developed in the context of prior restraints on print media. In particular, it investigates whether there are sufficient guarantees against of abuse of power by the government—reminiscent of the case law on privacy rights discussed in Chap. 5. In order to prevent such abuse, a legal framework is required which ensures first, tight control over the scope of bans and, second, effective judicial review. As to the scope of a ban, where the authorities have unfettered discretion to impose a ban, the Court is concerned that content will be blocked "arbitrarily and excessively".[100] When authorities do impose a ban, they are required to consider the fact that blocking may render large quantities of information inaccessible, thus substantially restricting the rights of internet users, with significant collateral effect on the material that has not been found to be illegal.[101] In one case where the legislation allowed for IP-based bans, which risked the blocking of legal websites because they would share a server with a website containing illegal information, the Court considered this to not fulfil the foreseeability requirement.[102] In the same vein, the Court has found it relevant whether a blocking order had been implemented without advance warning to those who would be affected.[103] With regard to the judicial review, the Court has considered that courts should strike a balance between competing interests on the basis of precise and specific rules.[104] In

---

[99] ECHR, Application no. 12726/87, Autronic v Switzerland, Judgment of 22 May 1990, para 47. The reasoning in Autronic is somewhat echoed by the ECHR in Groppera and the Court has reiterated it since then, recently in 2008; ECHR, Application no. 10890/84, Groppera v Switzerland, Judgment of 28 March 1990, paras 53–55; see later ECHR, Application no. 74243/01, Fevzi Saygili v Turkey, Judgment of 8 January 2008, para 29; ECHR, Application no. 22479/93, Öztürk v Turkey, Judgment of 28 September 1999, para 49. In Autronic, the Court also dismissed arguments from the Austrian government to the effect that the restriction was necessary to protect the confidentiality of encrypted broadcasts, because there was no risk that these could be decrypted by mere receipt; ECHR, Application no. 12726/87, Autronic v Switzerland, Judgment of 22 May 1990, para 63.

[100] ECHR, Application no. 10795/14, Vladimir Kharitonov v Russia, Judgment of 23 June 2020q, para 38.

[101] ECHR, Application nos. 48310/16 and 59663/17, Kablis v Russia, Judgment of 30 April 2019, para 94; ECHR, Application nos. 48226/10 and 14027/11, Case of Cengiz and Others v Turkey, Judgment of 1 December 2015, para 64; ECHR, Application no. 3111/10, Ahmet Yildirim v Turkey, Judgment of 18 December 2012, para 67.

[102] ECHR, Application no. 10795/14, Vladimir Kharitonov v Russia, Judgment of 23 June 2020q, para 42.

[103] Ibid., para 43.

[104] ECHR, Application nos. 48310/16 and 59663/17, Kablis v Russia, Judgment of 30 April 2019, para 92; ECHR, Application no. 3111/10, Ahmet Yildirim v Turkey, Judgment of 18 December 2012, para 64; ECHR, Application nos. 48226/10 and 14027/11, Case of Cengiz and Others v Turkey, Judgment of 1 December 2015, para 62; see in the context of print ECHR, Application no. 39288/98, Ekin v France, Judgment of 17 July 2001, para 58.

other words, the Court reviews to what extent *lawful* communication activities are prevented as a result of a measure, mirroring the review in the context of the right to privacy of the risk of *unlawful* access.

The central question for this book is *how much* lawful information may be blocked in order for a ban to still be considered proportionate. One factor the Court has considered in the past in the context of copyright infringement, is whether the lawful information remains available through other means. The Court has for example considered a request inadmissible where the complainant was blocked from accessing two music sites which contained copyright infringing material, because he could easily access music through other means without breaching copyright.[105] Similarly, The Court has considered the criminal conviction of *The Pirate Bay*'s founders for facilitation of copyright infringement an interference, but it at the same time considered the complaint manifestly unfounded because the measure was proportionate.[106] At the same time, the Court has in the past also taken into account the public's interest in accessing cultural works, for example where it reviewed whether a compulsory copyright licensing scheme struck a fair balance between the right to property and the public interest to have access to musical works.[107]

Where on the other hand a *lawful* website is blocked without being able to gain access through a different channel, the Court is less forgiving. The Court considers denying prisoners access to a specific website disproportionate, for example where they want to gain access to a website containing information on the rights of prisoners, or containing information necessary for their education.[108] In line with this, the Court more recently took a strict stance on blanket bans, noting that "*[a]ny* indiscriminate blocking measure which interferes with lawful content or websites as a collateral effect of a measure aimed at illegal content or websites amounts to arbitrary interference with the rights of owners of such websites" (emphasis added).[109] This wording echoes the language in *I v. Finland* in the context of Article 8, where the Court concluded that governments have an obligation to "exclude *any* possibility of unauthorised access" to medical data (emphasis added).[110]

[105] ECHR, Application no. 20877/1, Akdeniz v Turkey (dec.), Judgment of 11 March 2014.

[106] ECHR, Application no. 40397/12, Neij and Kolmissopi v Sweden, Judgment of 19 December 2013.

[107] See ECHR, Application no. 562/05, SIA AKKA/LAA v Latvia, Judgment of 12 July 2016.

[108] ECHR, Application no. 17429/10, Kalda v Estonia, Judgment of 19 January 2016; ECHR, Application no. 21575/08, Jankovskis v Lithuania, Judgment of 17 January 2017.

[109] ECHR, Application no. 10795/14, Vladimir Kharitonov v Russia, Judgment of 23 June 2020q, para 46.

[110] ECHR, Application no. 20511/03, I v Finland, Judgment of 17 July 2008, para 47.

6.4.2 The Case Law Under Article 11 of the Charter

The Court of Justice in its case law on Article 11 of the Charter applies similar principles in copyright enforcement cases. These cases are about the extent to which a court can impose security measures on parties which play a role in distribution chain. One thing which sets the case law of the Charter apart from the Convention in this context, is that the Court of Justice regularly elevates the right to intellectual property to the same level of importance as other fundamental rights protected under the Charter.[111] The Court in those cases thus reviews whether a fair balance is struck between the right to intellectual property, the freedom to conduct a business, the right to protection of personal data and the right to communications freedom.

In one case, the Court investigated whether a measure imposed on service providers is strictly targeted, "in the sense that it must serve to bring an end to a third party's infringement of copyright or of a related right but without thereby affecting the possibility of internet users lawfully accessing information using the provider's services".[112] In this regard, the Court also considers it relevant that statutory exceptions to copyright vary within member states, which means content in one country might be unlawful, but in another may be lawful.[113] The Court considered in another case that a requirement of password-protecting an internet connection (so that unauthorised users cannot go online) is capable of affecting the communications freedom of those users, but at the same time this requirement does not undermine the essence of this right and strikes a fair balance between copyright protection and communications freedom, particularly since users can also connect to the internet via other means.[114]

The Court of Justice has further recognised that restrictions on *confidential communications* can affect the right to communications freedom under the Charter. In *Digital Rights Ireland*, the Court, in reasoning reminiscent of *Autronic* (see above), considered that while the Data Retention Directive—mandating the retention of communications data on all telecommunication subscribers—"does not permit the retention of the content of the communication or of information consulted using an electronic communications network, it is not inconceivable that the retention of the data in question might have an effect on the use, by subscribers or registered users, of the means of communication covered by that directive and, consequently, on their exercise of the freedom of expression guaranteed by Article 11 of the Charter".[115]

---

[111] European Union (2009) Charter of Fundamental Rights of the European Union, Article 17(2).

[112] CJEU, Case C-484/14, Tobias Mc Fadden/Sony Music Entertainment Germany GmbH, Judgment of 15 September 2016, para 93; CJEU, Case C-314/12, UPC Telekabel Wien, Judgment of 27 March 2014, para 56.

[113] CJEU, Case C-70/10, Scarlet/SABAM, Judgment of 21 November 2011, para 52; CJEU, Case C-360/10, SABAM/Netlog, Judgment of 16 February 2012, para 50.

[114] CJEU, Case C-484/14, Tobias Mc Fadden/Sony Music Entertainment Germany GmbH, Judgment of 15 September 2016, para 92, para 94.

[115] CJEU, Cases C-293/12 and C-594/12, Digital Rights Ireland and others, Judgment of 8 April 2014, para 28. In *Tele2*, the Court repeats this reasoning; CJEU, Cases C-203/15 and C-698/15,

It is perhaps too early to draw conclusions on the basis of the limited case law. The Courts have not really faced the question of how the application of information security relates to communication freedom. What can be concluded, though, is that, firstly, communications freedom plays a certain role in ensuring that lawful information remains accessible; partly by ensuring that information security measures do not block too much, and partly by allowing for the circumvention of measures which *do* block too much. What this case law points to, is that where access to lawful information is prevented, for example by information security measures, it may be disproportionate to prohibit such access—especially if it is difficult to access the data via another way. This argument plays a role in the legal protection of copy protection discussed in Chap. 8. It can also be concluded that communications freedom is an argument for ensuring that private communications remain inaccessible. This argument plays a role in the regulation of encryption technologies. I will discuss the implications of this further in Chaps. 9 and 10.

6.5 Conclusion

In the introduction to this chapter, Wilkins asks himself whether knowledge on cryptography should be shared with the public, since it can also be used for malicious purposes. He concludes that the interests of truth and self-development must prevail[116]:

> If it be feared that this Discourse may unhappily advantage others, in such unlawful courses; 'tis considerable, that it does not only teach how to deceive, but consequently also how to discover Delusions. And then besides, the chief experiments are of such nature, that they cannot be frequently practiced, without just cause of suspicion, when as it is in the Magistrates power to prevent them. However, it will not follow, that everything must be supprest which may be abused. [...] If all those useful Inventions that are liable to abuse, should therefore be concealed, there is not any Art or Science which might be lawfully profest.

Wilkins' considerations still ring true today. The insight from the Enlightenment that truth is contestable—never absolute or finished, always open to new findings—has informed our modern understanding of science, including the science of information security. Security is never complete, always subject to the finding of new vulnerabilities or attacks, and it is precisely through the disclosure of such vulnerabilities that our knowledge can be refined. Many information security researchers will also consider their work as much a scientific endeavour as a form of personal development, and some might even call it Art—hacking for profit *and* fun.

Tele2 Sverige and Watson and Others, Judgment of 21 December 2016, para 101. While in *Digital Rights Ireland*, the Court did not examine the questions posed under Article 11 of the Charter since it already considered them under Articles 7 and 8 of the Charter, in *Tele2* it answered the questions in light of Articles 7, 8 *and* 11 of the Charter; CJEU, Cases C-293/12 and C-594/12, Digital Rights Ireland and others, Judgment of 8 April 2014d, para 70; and CJEU, Cases C-203/15 and C-698/15, Tele2 Sverige and Watson and Others, Judgment of 21 December 2016, dictum.

[116] Wilkins 1694, pp. 171–172.

This quest for truth, scientific progress and self-development is also embedded in the right to communications freedom. And another concept at the core of the right to communications freedom, the public interest, also resonates strongly with research into the information security cycle. Research aimed at making people aware of vulnerabilities will in many cases be considered to be in the public interest, since it can affect many people and it is very relevant for them to be informed about it. Conversely, this means that where research is *not* followed up with subsequent disclosure, or where no opportunity is given to mitigate the damage of disclosure, it is more questionable as to whether such research will be able to profit from the right to communications freedom.

There is also a second way in which communications freedom relates to the information security cycle—namely through the *application* of information security. Information security measures are a way to restrict the sharing of information. Some measures are at odds with this right—think of technological measures which prevent whistleblowers from leaking information in the public interest. Some measures may align with this right—think of encryption technologies which ensure the confidentiality of communications. The extent to which information security measures support communications freedom is relevant for governmental policy in relation to the first phase of the information security cycle, the taking of measures: which information security measures should get legal backing, which should be mandatory and which do not? I will discuss this further in Chap. 8.

This consideration is also relevant for governmental policy with regard to the other parts of the cycle: the research, disclosure and patching of vulnerabilities. When a researcher finds a vulnerability in an eBook-protection scheme which restricts lawful sharing, and it develops a tool to share books without authorisation, not only may publishing the *vulnerability* in itself be protected by communications freedom, because it furthers scientific development, but the protection of the *tool* will also have to be assessed under this right, because it creates new possibilities for legitimate sharing. The duty of the researcher to allow for the patching of these vulnerabilities may in such cases be informed by the fact that strengthening the effectiveness of the measure results in *restricting* communications freedom. On the other hand, where a researcher finds vulnerabilities in an encryption scheme used to ensure the confidentiality of messages, the publication of the vulnerabilities may be *protected* by the right to communications freedom, but the researchers' duty to mitigate the risk of disclosure will be greater due to the fundamental rights affected by the weakness. This required balancing will also be discussed further in Chap. 8.

In other words: the right to communications freedom plays a vital role in the information security cycle. This role can be easily applied to other scientific areas where research and disclosure are important. But the right also has its limits—it is about the way in which the *research and communication process* plays a role in the scientific endeavour. There is, of course, more to the relationship between science and human rights than this process. Science can contribute to human progress, but can also limit it, and even endanger the existence of humanity. The right to science provides pointers on how we should deal with this tension, giving a deeper understanding of states' obligations with regard to scientific endeavours. I discuss this in the next chapter.

References

Articles, Books and Other Documents

Adobe (2011) FAQ: ElcomSoft legal background (archived). https://web.archive.org/web/20111104031758/; http://www.adobe.com/aboutadobe/pressroom/pressreleases/200108/elcomsoftqa.html. Accessed 16 November 2019.
Alexander L (2005) Is There a Right of Freedom of Expression? Cambridge University Press, Cambridge.
Arnbak AM (2016) Securing Private Communications: Protecting Private Communications Security in EU Law: Fundamental Rights, Functional Value Chains, and Market Incentives. Kluwer Law International, Alphen aan den Rijn, The Netherlands.
Asscher LF (2002) Communicatiegrondrechten: een onderzoek naar de constitutionele bescherming van het recht op vrijheid van meningsuiting en het communicatiegeheim in de informatiesamenleving. Otto Cramwinckel, Amsterdam.
Barendt E (2005) Freedom of Speech, 2nd edn. Oxford University Press, Oxford; New York.
Bastick Z (2021) Would You Notice if Fake News Changed Your Behavior? An Experiment on the Unconscious Effects of Disinformation. Computers in Human Behavior 116:106633. https://doi.org/10.1016/j.chb.2020.106633
Bogen DS (1983) The Origins of Freedom of Speech and Press. Maryland Law Review 42:429–465.
Bowen EJ, Hartley H (1960) The Right Reverend John Wilkins, F.R.S. (1614-1672). Notes and Records of the Royal Society of London 15:47–56.
Boycott Adobe (2001) (archived). https://web.archive.org/web/20010925130705/; http://boycottadobe.com/. Accessed 16 November 2019.
Brison S (1998) The Autonomy Defense of Free Speech. Ethics 108:312–339. https://doi.org/10.1086/233807
Bychawska-Siniarska D (2017) Protecting the Right to Freedom of Expression under the European Convention on Human Rights: A Handbook for Legal Practitioners. Council of Europe, Strasbourg.
Clegg CS (2001) Press Censorship in Jacobean England. Cambridge University Press, Cambridge, UK.
Clegg CS (2005) Censorship and the Courts of Star Chamber and High Commission in England to 1640. Journal of Modern European History 3:50–80. https://doi.org/10.17104/1611-8944_2005_1_50
Clegg CS (2008) Press Censorship in Caroline England. Cambridge University Press, Cambridge.
Coleman EG (2013) Coding Freedom: The Ethics and Aesthetics of Hacking. Princeton University Press, Princeton.
Council of Europe (2011) Cultural rights in the case-law of the European Court of Human Rights. https://www.culturalpolicies.net/wp-content/uploads/2019/10/ECHR_Research_report_cultural_rights_ENG.pdf. Accessed 5 January 2024.
Creasman AF (2018) Martin Luther and the Printing Press. In: Whitford DM (ed) Martin Luther in Context, 1st edn. Cambridge University Press, pp 108–116.
Cressy D (2006) England on Edge: Crisis and Revolution; 1640–1642. Oxford University Press, Oxford.
Daland J (1931) The Evolution of Modern Printing and the Discovery of Movable Metal Type by the Chinese and Koreans in the Fourteenth Century. Journal of the Franklin Institute 209–234. https://doi.org/10.1016/S0016-0032(31)90851-X

Darnton R (2014) Censors at Work: How States Shaped Literature. The British Library, London.
Dommering EJ (2016) Het verschil van mening: geschiedenis van een verkeerd begrepen idee. Uitgeverij Bert Bakker, Amsterdam.
DTVE Reporter (2013) RAI Loses Appeal Against Encryption of Channels. https://www.digitaltveurope.com/2013/09/04/rai-loses-appeal-against-encryption-of-channels/. Accessed 30 April 2021.
Electronic Frontier Foundation (2002a) US v ElcomSoft & Sklyarov FAQ. https://www.eff.org/pages/us-v-elcomsoft-sklyarov-faq. Accessed 11 October 2019.
Edwards M (2004) Printing, Propaganda, and Martin Luther, Illustrated edn. Augsburg Fortress Publishers, Minneapolis.
Electronic Frontier Foundation (2002a) US v. ElcomSoft & Sklyarov FAQ. https://www.eff.org/pages/us-v-elcomsoft-sklyarov-faq. Accessed 11 October 2019.
Electronic Frontier Foundation (2002b) Jury Acquits Elcomsoft in eBook Copyright Case. https://www.eff.org/press/archives/2008/04/21. Accessed 16 November 2019.
Electronic Frontier Foundation (2011) US v. ElcomSoft Sklyarovhttps://www.eff.org/cases/us-v-elcomsoft-sklyarov. Accessed 16 November 2019.
Ellison K (2011) Millions of Millions of Distinct Orders: Multimodality in Seventeenth-Century Cryptography Manuals. 14:1–24.
Ellison K (2013) Digital Scholarship as Handwork and Brainwork: An Early Modern History of Cryptography. Journal for Early Modern Cultural Studies 13:29–46. https://doi.org/10.1353/jem.2013.0047
Ellison K (2016) A Cultural History of Early Modern English Cryptography Manuals. Routledge.
Free Dmitry Sklyarov! (2003) (archived). https://web.archive.org/web/20030201125121/; http://www.freesklyarov.org/. Accessed 16 November 2019.
Groen JR (2015) Academische vrijheid en wetenschappelijke integriteit: een onderzoek naar vrijheid en verantwoordelijkheid in wetenschappelijk onderwijs en onderzoek, Preadvies NVOR, September 2015.
Heilbron JL (2010) Galileo. Oxford University Press, Oxford [England]; New York.
Helberger N (2005) Controlling Access to Content: Regulating Conditional Access in Digital Broadcasting. PhD thesis, University of Amsterdam, Amsterdam.
Hofman JA (1995) Vertrouwelijke communicatie: een rechtsvergelijkende studie over de geheimhouding van communicatie in grondrechtelijk perspectief naar internationaal, Nederlands en Duits recht. W.E.J. Tjeenk Willink, Zwolle.
Ishay M (2009) The History of Human Rights: From Ancient Times to the Globalization Era, University of California Press, Berkeley.
Johns A (1998) The Nature of the Book: Print and Knowledge in the Making. University of Chicago Press, Chicago, Ill.
Laffranque J (2017) A Look at the European Court of Human Rights Case Law on Moral Issues and Academic Freedom. Juridica International 26:34–46. https://doi.org/10.12697/JI.2017.26.04
Lemos R (2002) Russian crypto expert arrested at Def Con. https://www.cnet.com/news/russian-crypto-expert-arrested-at-def-con/. Accessed 11 October 2019.
Leppin V, Wengert TJ (2015) Sources for and against the Posting of the Ninety-Five Theses. Lutheran Quarterly XXiX:26.
Lessig L (2001) Jail Time in the Digital Age. The New York Times, 30 July 2001.
Lommers S (2012) Europe–on Air: Interwar Projects for Radio Broadcasting. Amsterdam University Press, Amsterdam.
Mak C (2007) Fundamental Rights in European Contract Law. PhD thesis, University of Amsterdam, Amsterdam.
Marcus H (2020) Forbidden Knowledge: Medicine, Science, and Censorship in Early Modern Italy. University of Chicago Press, Chicago, Ill
Mill JS (1999) On Liberty. Broadview Press, Peterborough, Ont.
Moscon V (2012) Italian Broadcaster Rai Must Allow Sky Italia to Broadcast Its Channels Free-to-Air. IRIS 2012:21.

Næss A (2005) Galileo Galilei, When the World Stood Still. Springer, Berlin; New York.
Nunziato DC (2009) Virtual Freedom: Net Neutrality and Free Speech in the Internet Age. Stanford Law Books, Stanford, Calif.
Ottaviani A (1966) Notification Regarding the Abolition of the Index of Books, 14 June 1966. https://www.vatican.va/roman_curia/congregations/cfaith/documents/rc_con_cfaith_doc_19660614_de-indicis-libr-prohib_en.html. Accessed 5 January 2024.
Ruiz BR (1997) Privacy in Telecommunications: A European and an American Approach. Kluwer Law International, The Hague: Boston.
Schauer F (1983) Free Speech and the Argument from Democracy. Nomos 25:241–256.
Singh S (2000) The Code Book: The Science of Secrecy from Ancient Egypt to Quantum Cryptography. Anchor Books, New York.
Sluijs JP (2011) From Competition to Freedom of Expression: Introducing Art. 10 ECHR in the European Network Neutrality Debate, Human Rights Law Review 12:509–554.
Smith JT (2001) Free Dmitry Sklyarov Rally to Be Held Monday 23 July 2001 in New York City. https://www.linux.com/news/free-dmitry-sklyarov-rally-be-held-monday-23-july-2001-new-york-city/. Accessed 16 November 2019.
Standage T (2014) The Victorian Internet: The Remarkable Story of the Telegraph and the Nineteenth Century's Online Pioneers. Bloomsbury, New York, NY.
Starr P (2004) The Creation of the Media: Political Origins of Modern Communications. Basic Books, New York.
Steenbruggen W (2009) Publieke dimensies van privé-communicatie: een onderzoek naar de verantwoordelijkheid van de overheid bij de bescherming van vertrouwelijke communicatie in het digitale tijdperk. Otto Cramwinckel, Amsterdam.
van Daalen O (2022), In Defense of Offense: Information Security Research under the Right to Science, Computer Law & Security Review 46: 105706.
van Daalen O (2023a) The Right to Encryption: Privacy as Preventing Unlawful Access, Computer Law & Security Review 49:105804.
van Daalen O (2023b) The Right to Root: Constructing a Claim to Control Devices from the Right to Privacy, JIPITEC 14(2023:4): 580–593.
van Daalen O (2024) Developing a human-rights compatible governance framework for quantum computing, Research Directions: Quantum Technologies 2: 2024.
van Eijk N (2014) Net Neutrality in the Netherlands. Gyeongje Gyuje wa Beob = Journal of Law and Economic Regulation 7:146–162.
van Gompel S (2011) Formalities in Copyright Law: An Analysis of Their History, Rationales and Possible Future. PhD thesis, University of Amsterdam, Amsterdam.
Vosoughi S, Roy D, Aral S (2018) The Spread of True and False News Online. Science 359:1146–1151. https://doi.org/10.1126/science.aap9559
Wilbur M (2009) A Decade of the DMCA. Lulu.com, 2009.
Wilkins J (1694) Mercury: Or the Secret and Swift Messenger. Shewing, How a Man May with Privacy and Speed communicate His Thoughts to a Friend at Any Distance, 2nd edn. Richard Baldwin, London.
Wu T (2013) The Master Switch: The Rise and Fall of Information Empires. Vintage Books, New York.
Zuiderveen Borgesius FJ, Steenbruggen W (2019) The Right to Communications Confidentiality in Europe: Protecting Privacy, Freedom of Expression, and Trust. Theoretical Inquiries in Law 20:291–322. https://doi.org/10.1515/til-2019-0010

Table of Cases: EU

ECHR, Application no. 47143/06, Roman Zakharov v Russia, Judgment of 4 December 2015.
ECHR, Application no. 37138/14, Szabó and Vissy v Hungary, Judgment of 12 January 2016.

ECHR, Application no. 35252/08, Centrum för Rättvisa v Sweden (Grand Chamber), Judgment of 25 May 2021.
ECHR, Applications nos. 58170/13, 62322/14 and 24960/15, Big Brother Watch and others v United Kingdom (Grand Chamber), Judgment of 25 May 2021.
ECHR, Application no. 5493/72, Handyside v the United Kingdom, Judgment of 7 December 1976b.
ECHR, Application no. 31276/05, Women on Waves and others v Portugal, Judgment of 3 February 2009.
ECHR, 67/1997/851/1058, Steel and others v the United Kingdom, Judgment of 23 September 1998.
ECHR (2020) Guide on Article 10 of the European Convention on Human Rights. Council of Europe.
ECHR, Applications nos. 21279/02 and 36448/02, Lindon, Otchakovsky-Laurens and July v France, Judgment of 22 October 2007.
ECHR, Application no. 18139/91, Tolstoy Miloslavsky v the United Kingdom, Judgment of 13 July 1995.
ECHR, Application no. 28255/07, Cumhuriyet Vakfi and others v Turkey, Judgment of 8 October 2013.
ECHR, Application no. 821/03, Financial Times Ltd. and others v the United Kingdom, Judgment of 15 December 2009.
ECHR, Application no. 17488/90, Goodwin v the United Kingdom, Judgment of 27 March 1996.
ECHR, Application no. 64752/01, Voskuil v the Netherlands, Judgment of 22 November 2007.
ECHR, Application no. 39315/06, Telegraaf Media Nederland Landelijke Media B.V. and others v the Netherlands, Judgment of 22 November 2012.
ECHR, Application no. 21272/12, Becker v Norway, Judgment of 5 October 2017.
ECHR, Application no. 38224/03, Sanoma v The Netherlands, Judgment of 14 September 2010c.
ECHR, Application no. 39293/98, Fuentes Bobo v Spain, Judgment of 29 February 2000.
ECHR, Application no. 23144/93, Özgür Gündem v Turkey, Judgment of 16 March 2000.
ECHR, Application no. 73571/10, Case of Matùz v Hungary, Judgment of 21 October 2014.
ECHR, Applications nos. 28955/06, 28957/06, 28959/06 and 28964/06, Palomo Sánchez and Others v Spain, Judgment of 12 September 2011.
ECHR, Applications nos. 65286/13 and 57270/14, Khadija Ismayilova v Azerbaijan, Judgment of 10 January 2019.
ECHR, Application no. 18030/11, Magyar Helsinki Bizottság v Hungary, Judgment of 8 November 2016d.
ECHR, Application no. 77551/01, Dammann v Switzerland, Judgment of 25 April 2006.
ECHR, Application no. 9248/81, Leander v Sweden, Judgment of 26 March 1987.
ECHR, Application no. 10454/83, Gaskin v the United Kingdom, Judgment of 7 July 1989.
ECHR, Roche v the United Kingdom, Judgment of 19 October 2005.
ECHR, Application no. 37374/05, Társaság a Szabadságjogokért v Hungary, Judgment of 14 April 2009.
ECHR, Application no. 39534/07, Österreichische Vereinigung zur Erhaltung, Stärkung und Schaffung Eines Wirtschaftlich Gesunden Land- Und Forst- Wirtschaftlichen Grundbesitzes/Austria, Judgment of 28 November 2013.
ECHR, Application no. 2933/03, Cox v Turkey, Judgment of 20 May 2010.
ECHR, Application nos. 346/04 39779/04, Mustafa Erdoğan and Others v Turkey, Judgment of 27 May 2014.
ECHR, Application nos. 4149/04 41029/04, Aksu v Turkey, Judgment of 15 March 2012.
ECHR, Application no. 40877/07, Hasan Yazici v Turkey, Judgment of 15 April 2014.
ECHR, Application no. 17089/03, Sorguç v Turkey, Judgment of 23 June 2009.
ECHR, Applications nos. 23536/94 and 24408/94, Başkaya and Okçuoğlu v Turkey, Judgment of 8 July 1999.
ECHR, Application no. 31475/05, Kenedi v Hungary, Judgment of 26 May 2009.

ECHR, Application no. 28396/95, Wille vs. Liechtenstein, Judgment of 28 October 1999.
ECHR, Application no. 44102/04, Sapan vs. Turkey, Judgment of 8 June 2010.
ECHR, Application no. 20233/06, Kula v Turkey, Judgment of 19 June 2018.
ECHR, Application no. 39128/05, Lombardi Vallauri v Italy, Judgment of 20 October 2009.
ECHR, Application no. 13585/88, Observer and Guardian v the United Kingdom, Judgment of 26 November 1991.
ECHR, Application no. 13166/87, the Sunday Times v the United Kingdom, Judgment of 26 November 1991.
ECHR, Application no. 15153/89, Vereinigung Demokratischer Soldaten Österreichs and Gubi v Austria, Judgment of 19 December 1994.
ECHR, Application no. 13914/88; 15041/89; 15717/89; 15779/89; 17207/90, Informationsverein Lentia and Others v Austria, Judgment of 24 November 1993.
ECHR, Application no. 69698/01, Stoll v Switzerland, Judgment of 10 December 2007e.
ECHR, Application no. 26922/14, Toranzo Gomez v Spain, Judgment of 20 November 2018
ECHR, Application no. 23168/94, Karataş v Turkey, Judgment of 8 July 1999.
ECHR, Application no. 23500/94, Polat v Turkey, Judgment of 8 July 1999.
ECHR, Application no. 64569/09, Case of Delfi AS v Estonia, Judgment of 16 June 2015.
ECHR, Application no. 13444/04, Glor v Switzerland, Judgment of 30 April 2009.
ECHR, Applications nos. 40660/08 and 60641/08, Von Hannover v Germany (no. 2), Judgment of 7 February 2012.
ECHR, Application no. 40287/98, Alinak v Turkey, Judgment of 29 March 2005.
ECHR, Application no. 10572/83, Markt Intern Verlag Gmbh and Klaus Beermann v Germany, Judgment of 20 November 1989.
ECHR, Application no. 15088/89, Jacubowski v Germany, Judgment of 23 June 1994.
ECHR, Application nos. 133/1996/752/951, United Communist Party of Turkey and Others v Turkey, Judgment of 30 January 1998.
ECHR, Applications nos. 29221/95 and 29225/95, Stankov and the United Macedonian Organisation Ilinden v Bulgaria, Judgment of 2 October 2001.
ECHR, Application no. 64915/01, Chauvy and Others v France, Judgment of 29 June 2004.
ECHR, Application no. 65831/01, Garaudy v France, Judgment of 24 June 2003.
ECHR, Application no. 29369/10, Morice v France, Judgment of 23 April 2015.
ECHR, Application no. 9815/82, Lingens v Austria, Judgment of 8 July 1986.
ECHR, Application no. 11662/85, Oberschlick v Austria, Judgment of 23 May 1991.
ECHR, Application no. 65518/01, Salov v Ukraine, Judgment of 6 September 2005.
ECHR, Application no. 51279/99, Colombani and others v France, Judgment of 25 June 2002.
ECHR, Application no. 16616/90, Vereniging Weekblad Bluf! v the Netherlands, Judgment of 9 February 1995.
ECHR, Application no. 20436/02, Wojtas-Kaleta v Poland, Judgment of 16 July 2009.
ECHR, Application no. 48723/07, Stankiewicz and others v Poland, Judgment of 14 October 2014.
ECHR, Application no. 21980/93, Bladet Tromsø and Stensaas v Norway, Judgment of 20 May 1999.
ECHR, Application no. 29183/95, Fressoz and Roire v France, Judgment of 21 January 1999.
ECHR, Application no. 53984/00, Radio France and others v France, Judgment of 30 March 2004.
ECHR, Application no. 25333/06, Europapress Holding D.O.O. v Croatia, Judgment of 22 October 2009.
ECHR, Application no. 68416/01, Steel and Morris v United Kingdom, Judgment of 15 February 2005.
ECHR, Application no. 3111/10, Ahmet Yildirim v Turkey, Judgment of 18 December 2012.
ECHR, Applications nos. 3002/03 and 23676/03, Times Newspapers Ltd. v the United Kingdom (Nos. 1 and 2), Judgment of 10 March 2009.
ECHR, Application no. 12945/87, Hadjianastassiou v Greece, Judgment of 16 December 1992.
ECHR, Application no. 33628/15, Salihu and others v Sweden, Judgment of 10 May 2016
ECHR, Application no. 56328/10, Erdtmann v Germany, Judgment of 5 January 2016.

ECHR, Application no. 22567/09, Brambilla and others v Italy, Judgment of 23 June 2016.
ECHR, Application no. 28743/03, Melnychuk v Ukraine, Judgment of 5 July 2007f
ECHR, Application no. 24016/05, Eker v Turkey, Judgment of 24 October 2017.
ECHR, Application no. 23883/06, Khurshid Mustafa and Tarzibachi v Sweden, Judgment of 16 December 2008.
ECHR, Application no. 12726/87, Autronic v Switzerland, Judgment of 22 May 1990.
ECHR, Application no. 10890/84, Groppera v Switzerland, Judgment of 28 March 1990.
ECHR, Application no. 74243/01, Fevzi Saygili v Turkey, Judgment of 8 January 2008.
ECHR, Application no. 22479/93, Öztürk v Turkey, Judgment of 28 September 1999.
ECHR, Application no. 10795/14, Vladimir Kharitonov v Russia, Judgment of 23 June 2020g.
ECHR, Applications nos. 48310/16 and 59663/17, Kablis v Russia, Judgment of 30 April 2019.
ECHR, Applications nos. 48226/10 and 14027/11, Case of Cengiz and Others v Turkey, Judgment of 1 December 2015.
ECHR, Application no. 39288/98, Ekin v France, Judgment of 17 July 2001.
ECHR, Application no. 20877/1, Akdeniz v Turkey (Dec.), Judgment of 11 March 2014.
ECHR, Application no. 40397/12, Neij and Kolmissopi v Sweden, Judgment of 19 December 2013.
ECHR, Application no. 562/05, SIA AKKA/LAA v Latvia, Judgment of 12 July 2016.
ECHR, Application no. 17429/10, Kalda v Estonia, Judgment of 19 January 2016.
ECHR, Application no. 21575/08, Jankovskis v Lithuania, Judgment of 17 January 2017.
ECHR, Application no. 20511/03, I v Finland, Judgment of 17 July 2008.
CJEU, Case C-547/14, Philip Morris Brands SARL and Others v Secretary of State for Health, Judgment of 4 May 2016.
CJEU, Case C-345/17, Sergejs Buivids v Datu valsts inspekcija, Judgment of 14 February 2019.
CJEU, Case C-421/07, Damgaard, Judgment of 2 April 2009.
CJEU, Case C-136/17, GC / CNIL, Judgment of 24 September 2019.
CJEU, Case C-516/17, Spiegel Online GmbH v Volker Beck, Judgment of 29 July 2019.
CJEU, Case C-145/10, Painer, Judgment of 1 December 2011.
CJEU, Case C-73/07, Satamedia, Judgment of 16 December 2008.
CJEU, Case C-283/11, Sky Österreich GmbH / Österreichischer Rundfunk, Judgment of 22 January 2013.
CJEU, Case C-131/12, Google Spain, Judgment of 13 May 2014.
CJEU, Case C-469/17, Funke Medien NRW GmbH v Bundesrepublik Deutschland, Judgment of 29 July 2019.
CJEU, Case C-157/14, Neptune Distribution SNC v Ministre de l'Économie et des Finances (Minister for Economic Affairs and Finance), Judgment of 17 December 2015.
CJEU, Case C-484/14, Tobias Mc Fadden/Sony Music Entertainment Germany GmbH, Judgment of 15 September 2016.
CJEU, Case C-314/12, UPC Telekabel Wien, Judgment of 27 March 2014.
CJEU, Case C-70/10, Scarlet / SABAM, Judgment of 21 November 2011.
CJEU, Case C-360/10, SABAM/Netlog, Judgment of 16 February 2012.
CJEU, Cases C-293/12 and C-594/12, Digital Rights Ireland and others, Judgment of 8 April 2014.
CJEU, Cases C-203/15 and C-698/15, Tele2 Sverige and Watson and Others, Judgment of 21 December 2016.

Table of Cases: USA

Facebook Oversight Board, 2021-001-FB-FBR, Decision on Facebook's ban of president Trump, Judgment of 5 May 2021.
Supreme Court, 59, Primrose v Western Union Telegraph Company, Judgment of 26 May 1894.
US Supreme Court, 250 U.S. 616 (1919), Dissenting opinion of Holmes in Abrams v United States, Judgment of 10 November 1919.

Chapter 7
The Right to Science

Contents

Abstract This chapter discusses the right to science under the Convention for Economic, Social and Cultural Rights, as well as under the Charter. It discusses the origins of the right, the interpretative instruments relevant to the right and how this relates to the duty of researchers to perform scientific activities in the public interest. It concludes that under the right to science scientists should have the freedom to do scientific research, but that with this comes a responsibility to mitigate the risks associated with this research. This provides the normative framework for the subsequent analysis of the different governance options in relation to the information security cycle, encryption and quantum computing.

Keywords Right to science · Precautionary principle · Atomic bomb · Quantum computing · Encryption · Information security

7.1 Introduction

Not only did the Second World War kickstart modern computing, it also spurred the development of the atomic bomb.[1] On 2 August 1939, Albert Einstein (at the suggestion of a little-known scientist named Leo Szilard) warned the American

[1] Parts of this chapter have already been published in Van Daalen 2022, 2023a, 2023b and 2024.

O. van Daalen, *From Encryption to Quantum Computing*, Information Technology and Law Series 38, https://doi.org/10.1007/978-94-6265-635-2_7

government that "the element uranium may be turned into a new and important source of energy in the immediate future" and that "powerful bombs of a new type may thus be constructed", suggesting that Nazi Germany might already have started their research.[2] This set in motion the United States' effort to build the first nuclear bomb, the Manhattan Project.

The development of the atomic bomb was a quintessential product of science—from fundamental science, such as Einstein's famous theory of mass energy equivalence ($E = mc^2$), to experimental research on quantum physics. Whether the bombings of Hiroshima and Nagasaki, killing more than two hundred thousand people, hastened the end of the war was debated, but nobody disputed the destructive potential that was unleashed.[3] "*One is tempted to feel that Man is being punished, through the agency of his own evil passions, for impiety in inquiring too closely into the hidden secrets of nature*", wrote the English philosopher Bertrand Russell in 1945.[4] "*But such a feeling is unduly defeatist. Science is capable of conferring enormous boons: it can lighten labour, abolish poverty, and enormously diminish disease. But if science is to bring benefits instead of death, we must bring to bear upon social, and especially international, organization, intelligence of the same high order that has enabled us to discover the structure of the atom.*"

Thus, when in 1945 under the auspices of the United Nations a new organisation to promote peace was established, the United Nations Educational, Scientific and Cultural Organisation (UNESCO), the immoral application of science loomed large.[5] And when the United Nations discussed the incorporation of a "right to science" in the Universal Declaration of Human Rights (UDHR), the use of science for the public good took centre stage.[6]

7.2 Relevant Provisions

This was not the first time that a right to science gained legal recognition. The German concept of *Wissenschaftsfreiheit* as a constitutional right could already be found in the Frankfurt Imperial Constitution of 1849, and has been adopted in other national constitutions since.[7] It was the first time, however, that the right was recognised in a

---

[2] Lanouette et al. 2013, preface; Einstein 1939.

[3] See for a discussion on whether the bombings hastened the ending of the war; Wilson 2007.

[4] Russell 1945.

[5] See also Shaver 2010, pp. 13, 142. The founding Conference initially aimed at establishing UNECO—without the S. At the proposal of the British delegation, "science" was also included in the name, presumably because delegates still had the horrors of Hiroshima and Nagasaki fresh on their minds; UNESCO 2015, p. 20. UNESCO was founded to promote peace through "educational and scientific and cultural relations" among peoples of the world; UNESCO 1945, preamble.

[6] Morsink 1999, p. 219.

[7] Starck 2006, pp. 110–111.

truly international human rights instrument, in Article 27 of the Universal Declaration of Human Rights (the Declaration)[8]:

1. Everyone has the right freely to participate in the cultural life of the community, to enjoy the arts and to share in scientific advancement and its benefits.
2. Everyone has the right to the protection of the moral and material interests resulting from any scientific, literary or artistic production of which he is the author.

This was then later worked out in Article 15 of the International Covenant on Economic and Social Rights (the Covenant), signed in 1966, on which I will focus because it is more recent and more extensive, and because it has been ratified by all European Union member states. Article 15 reads[9]:

1. "The States Parties to the present Covenant recognize the right of everyone: [...]
   (b) To enjoy the benefits of scientific progress and its applications;
   (c) To benefit from the protection of the moral and material interests resulting from any scientific, literary or artistic production of which he is the author.
2. The steps to be taken by the States Parties to the present Covenant to achieve the full realization of this right shall include those necessary for the conservation, the development and the diffusion of science and culture.
3. The States Parties to the present Covenant undertake to respect the freedom indispensable for scientific research and creative activity.
4. The States Parties to the present Covenant recognize the benefits to be derived from the encouragement and development of international contacts and co-operation in the scientific and cultural fields."

Most recently, this right has been protected under the European Charter of Fundamental Rights in Article 13, which provides that the "arts and scientific research shall be free of constraint. Academic freedom shall be respected". The emphasis on academic freedom sets the Charter apart from the other instruments, and the significance of this is also discussed below.

---

[8] United Nations 1948. Before, it was already incorporated in Article 13 of the American Declaration of the Rights and Duties of Man: "every person has the right [...] to participate in the benefits that result from intellectual progress, especially scientific discoveries"; Ninth International Conference of American States (1948) American Declaration of the Rights and Duties of Man. See for literature on the right to science; Mann et al. 2020; Smith 2020a; Mann and Schmid 2018; Morgera 2015; Butenschon Skre and Eide 2013; Gran et al. 2013; Donders 2011; Müller 2010; Shaver 2010; Schabas 2007; see for an early analysis of scientific freedom Zoontjens 1993.

[9] United Nations 1976; see for a discussion of the *travaux préparatoires*; Shaver 2010; Smith 2020a, 2020b. I will not discuss the right to education as laid out in Article 13 Covenant because I consider the educational aspects of research and dissemination relating to information security research to be more properly discussed under the header of Article 15 Covenant; see on the ratification status; Egan et al. 2018.

7.3 Interpretation of the Right to Science

7.3.1 *Interpretation of the Right to Science Under the Covenant*

Legal scholars have imposed on the right to science a broad range of responsibilities in the recent years, claiming that it for example informs pandemic policy, extends clinical research, restricts scientific co-operation between governments and corporations, and that it promotes open access.[10] It was not always like this—not so long ago, the right to science was still called a "sleeping beauty", a right lying dormant, albeit with great potential.[11] During its slumber, the international human rights community built an edifice of legal scholarship around it, significantly developing the right along the way.

This goes in particular for one important theme throughout this chapter, the idea that science should have a *purpose*, namely to benefit humanity. The signatories at the time of drafting of the Declaration and the Covenant were not yet ready for that conclusion, as can be seen from the *travaux préparatoires*.[12] During both negotiations, the USSR pushed for a clarification that the purpose of science should be to benefit humanity, and that abuse of science should be prevented. Although the USSR had some allies, this proposal ultimately was not accepted by the signatories. The US' delegate response during the Covenant negotiations is telling: "The search for truth must remain unshackled."[13] However, in recent years, the thinking on this has progressed significantly.

Under the Covenant, the right to science is generally considered to have three components.[14] As we will see, these are all highly relevant to the topic of this book. The first is the *freedom of science*—this is about the activity of science, being able to choose your own lines of inquiry. This is relevant for information security researchers—allowing them to also do *offensive* security research and share the results. But it is also important because it supports the freedom to do research into quantum computers. The second is the right to enjoy the *benefits of science*—this is about the positive results of science, and it aligns well with the iterative nature of the information security cycle, and the third is the obligation to *protect against the risks of science*—this is about the negative effects of science. For the information security cycle, this implies that scientists must minimise the impact of disclosure of vulnerabilities and restrict the harm from tools. For quantum computing, this could imply that governments need to push for quantum-resistant encryption while developing the technology to break other kinds of encryption. I will work the application

---

[10] See for an overview Porsdam and Porsdam Mann 2021; see earlier Plozza 2021; Sianko et al. 2021; Almqvist 2020; Porsdam Mann et al. 2018, p. 10822; Eide and Skre 2013; and van Westendorp and Lierman 2020.

[11] Mann et al. 2020.

[12] See for an analysis; Smith 2020b.

[13] Ibid., p. 229.

[14] Beiter 2019, para 2.

of the right to science to these domains further out in part III. First, I will discuss the content of the right to science.

The first report in which the content of these themes is explored, is the Venice Statement, drawn up by human rights experts between June 2007 and July 2009.[15] According to the experts, the right to science compels states to create "an enabling and participatory environment" for science, ensure the enjoyment of the benefits of scientific progress, and to protect against its abuse and adverse effects.[16] Among the obligations which the experts derive from this, three stand out.

First, states have an obligation to respect scientific freedom: the obligation "to respect the freedoms indispensable for scientific research and creative activity, such as freedom of thought, to hold opinions without interference, and to seek, receive, and impart information and ideas of all kinds". Secondly, this freedom is not unfettered: states should at the same time take "appropriate measures to prevent the use of science and technology in a manner that could limit or interfere with the enjoyment of the human rights and fundamental freedoms".[17] Lastly, the experts emphasise the importance of knowledge sharing and diffusion, while respecting human rights: states have an obligation to "adopt a legal and policy framework and to establish institutions to promote the development and diffusion of science and technology in a manner consistent with fundamental human rights" and "to promote access to the benefits of science and its applications on a non-discriminatory basis".[18]

Special Rapporteur Farida Shaheed then developed this foundation further in her 2012-report on the right to science.[19] She embraced the findings of the Venice Commission, but also emphasised the right as a means for people to critically, and in an iterative manner reflect on the world and themselves.[20] She identified a strong connection between the right to science and the right to freedom of expression, self-determination and the right to participate in public affairs, noting that it imposes on states an obligation to allow people to reconsider, create, and contribute to "knowledge that is testable and refutable, including revisiting and refuting existing theorems and understandings",[21] She agreed with the Venice Commission that scientific freedom includes the right to freedom of inquiry, and underlines the importance of the freedom of sharing.[22] The rapporteur suggested where scientific progress should ultimately lead: the concept of "access to the benefits of science" points to "the idea of a positive impact on the well-being of people and the realization of their human

---

[15] UNESCO; see Müller 2010 for a discussion of the Venice Statement; see also for one of the reports leading up to the ultimate statement.

[16] UNESCO, para 13.

[17] Ibid., para 14(a) and (d).

[18] Ibid., para 16(a) and (b).

[19] Shaheed 2012; the appointment of the Special Rapporteur was a suggestion of the Venice Committee; see UNESCO 2009, Article 21.

[20] Shaheed 2012, para 18.

[21] Ibid., paras 18 and 21.

[22] See also Chapman 2009, p. 17; Shaheed 2012, para 41.

rights".[23] Conversely, states should protect from harm arising from the misuse of science.[24]

In 2017, UNESCO then adopted the Recommendation on Science and Scientific Researchers, setting out a detailed agenda for the right to science.[25] The themes of scientific freedom, access to science and science benefiting humanity are woven throughout the document. At the heart of the guidance lies the conceptualisation of science as a dynamic, iterative process—both the freedom of inquiry and the freedom to share results are a theme central to the report.[26] It is recommended that researchers "work in a spirit of intellectual freedom to pursue, expound and defend the scientific truth as they see it, an intellectual freedom which should include protection from undue influences on their independent judgement".[27] Member states should encourage and facilitate publication of results, data, methods and software, as well as access to knowledge.[28] Restrictions on publications must be strictly minimised and surrounded by appropriate safeguards.[29] Finally, the recommendations acknowledge the importance of scientific, social and ecological responsibility in science. This responsibility is informed by the promotion of themes such as peace, sustainable development, human welfare, dignity and human rights.[30]

Lastly, in 2020, the Committee on Economic, Social and Cultural Rights (CESCR) adopted a General Comment on Science and Economic, Social and Cultural rights.[31] The CESCR consists of 18 independent human rights experts, elected by the parties to the Covenant. The CESCR has the authority to interpret the Covenant, and its guidance thus carries significant weight. Unfortunately, the General Comment devotes significantly less attention to the scientific process than the preceding documents, focusing more on issues such as gender-based and disability-based discrimination in science, perhaps because the earlier documents already described this process in

[23] Shaheed 2012, para 24.

[24] Ibid., recommendation (m).

[25] UNESCO 2017.

[26] It is defined as "the enterprise whereby humankind, acting individually or in small or large groups, makes an organized attempt, by means of the objective study of observed phenomena and its validation through sharing of findings and data and through peer review, to discover and master the chain of causalities, relations or interactions; brings together in a coordinated form subsystems of knowledge by means of systematic reflection and conceptualization; and thereby furnishes itself with the opportunity of using, to its own advantage, understanding of the processes and phenomena occurring in nature and society"; ibid., para I(1)(a). The terms "research and development" are defined as "scientific research and experimental development for which "scientific research" signifies those processes of study, experiment, conceptualization, theory-testing and validation involved in the generation of scientific knowledge (…) and thus including both fundamental and applied research".

[27] Ibid., para 16.

[28] Ibid., paras 35 and 36.

[29] Ibid., para 38.

[30] Ibid., paras 18, 20.

[31] CESCR, General Comment No. 25 (2020) on Science and Economic, Social and Cultural Rights (Article 15(1)(b), (2), (3) and (4) of the International Covenant on Economic, Social and Cultural Rights), E/C.12/GC/25, 30 April 2020.

detail.[32] It does, however, emphasise the importance of freedom of research, noting that science is dependent on its "robust protection", and considering that this freedom includes the freedom to determine the direction and method of research and to share the results wherever possible.[33] Like the earlier documents, the CESCR considers that the development of science in the service of peace and human rights should be "prioritized" over other uses.[34] In particular, limitations on the applications of science "can be used to guarantee the safety and quality of products used by persons", for example through human rights impact assessments and limitations on the research process.[35] The report continues, "any limitation on the content of scientific research implies a strict burden of justification by States, in order to avoid infringing freedom of research".

The General Comment is perhaps most relevant for the attention devoted to the precautionary principle, which is described as the principle that "in the absence of full scientific certainty, when an action or policy may lead to unacceptable harm to the public or the environment, actions will be taken to avoid or diminish that harm".[36] The CESCR suggests that technological and human rights impact assessments can help to identify potential risks early in the process. It furthermore suggests the involvement of the public in balancing the interests of scientific freedom with potential risks, through "informed, transparent and participatory public deliberation".[37] I discuss the relevance of the precautionary principle further below.

Lastly, the CESCR mentions a couple of especially impactful scientific and technological advancements in particular, including quantum computers, noting that these might both enhance and restrict the enjoyment of economic, social and cultural rights.[38] It concludes that states have to adopt policies and measures that expand the benefits of these new technologies while reducing their risks.[39] It points to the importance of global cooperation to this end, noting that states should promote multilateral agreements to prevent these risks from materialising or to mitigate their effect.[40] And it emphasises the role that human rights play in these decisions, having attention for

---

32 The CESCR refers to the UNESCO Recommendation on Science and Scientific Researchers for its definition of science and notes that "knowledge should be considered as science only if it is based on critical inquiry and is open to falsifiability and testability", while simultaneously considering that not only scientific professionals can rely on the right, but also "citizen scientists" ibid., paras 5, 10.

33 Ibid., paras 13, 47, 50.

34 Ibid., para 6; see for a contrast with the *travaux préparatoires* Smith 2020b.

35 CESCR, General Comment No. 25 (2020) on Science and Economic, Social and Cultural Rights (Article 15(1)(b), (2), (3) and (4) of the International Covenant on Economic, Social and Cultural Rights), E/C.12/GC/25, 30 April 2020, para 22.

36 Ibid., para 56.

37 Ibid., para 57.

38 Ibid., para 73.

39 Ibid., para 74.

40 Ibid., paras 74, 81.

the unwarranted effects that some technologies might have on the enjoyment of those rights.[41]

7.3.2 *Interpretation of the Right to Science Under the Charter*

The guidance on Article 15 Covenant is in contrast to the cursory explanation given on its equivalent in the Charter, Article 13. It is merely noted in the explanatory memorandum that this right is deduced primarily from the right to freedom of thought and expression, to be exercised having regard to Article 1 (on human dignity) and subject to the limitations under Article 10 of the Convention.[42] Article 13 should of course be understood in light of the guidance on this right in the context of the Covenant.

There is, however, one difference between the two provisions: Article 13 not only protects "scientific research", but also explicitly protects "academic freedom". The relation between the right to science and academic freedom is unclear: both academic freedom and the right to science protect institutional and individual elements of the scientific endeavour.[43] The most relevant question for this book is whether research performed by academics is accorded *extra* protection, compared to research performed by others. According to Beiter, this is the case: academic freedom is a special, "enhanced" kind of scientific freedom, only applicable to academics.[44] The reasoning is that academics have the particular role of performing research in the public interest, but because of this role, they also require extra protection.[45] This is not convincing, if only because non-academic researchers *also* perform research bin the public interest. In fact, a significant amount of information security research takes place outside of academia, as has been discussed in Chap. 6. This is why I conclude that the concept of academic freedom merely *emphasises* the role of the right to science in the context of academia but does not accord it extra protection. Thus, the relevance for the information security cycle of this particular element of Article 13 is limited.

---

[41] Ibid., paras 74–76.

[42] Praesidium of the European Convention (2007) Explanations Relating to the Charter of Fundamental Rights.

[43] See on the difficulties of articulating the concept of academic freedom; Barendt 2010, Chap. 2; see further on this topic Beiter 2019; Beiter et al. 2016a, 2016b; Quinn and Levine 2014; Groen 2015, pp. 9–10. The Court on Article 13 has underlined that academic freedom also incorporates an "institutional and organisational dimension"; CJEU, Case C-66/18, European Commission v Hungary, Judgment of 6 October 2020, para 227.

[44] Beiter 2019, p. 237.

[45] See also Beiter et al. 2018, p. 173.

7.4 Relation Between the Right to Science and Communications Freedom

As noted above, an important part of the right to science is scientific freedom: the right to determine your own lines of inquiry and share the results of this inquiry with others. This obviously is strongly related to the right to communications freedom under the Convention and the Charter, as is also clear from the Court of Justice's considerations on Article 13 in *European Commission v Hungary* (2020)[46]:

> [A]cademic freedom in research and in teaching should guarantee freedom of expression and of action, freedom to disseminate information and freedom to conduct research and to distribute knowledge and truth without restriction, although it should be made clear that that freedom is not restricted to academic or scientific research, but that it also extends to academics' freedom to express freely their views and opinions.

Although this quote focuses on academic freedom due to the particulars of the case, one could easily replace *academic* with *scientific* and it would still work. So what does the right to science add to the right to communications freedom?[47]

First, the right to science protects all phases of scientific inquiry equally. The research stage is explicitly mentioned in the Covenant: it includes an undertaking on member states to "respect the freedom indispensable for scientific research and creative activity".[48] By contrast, the activities traditionally protected under the right to communications freedom are mostly related to the disclosure phase, and the protection of the preparatory stages can be derived from protection of the disclosure phase (see Chap. 6). This further extends protection to research activities in the information security context and the domain of quantum computing, especially where this research may never lead to a publication at all.

Second, not only do scientists have a right to perform research, but everyone has a right to enjoy the benefits of that research, of "scientific progress". You can enjoy the benefits through products and services which are based on the insights of that research. And you can also enjoy scientific progress by learning about the state of science, and, where necessary, improve on it. This iterative nature of the scientific process is at the heart of the right to science.

But the state of science can of course only improve, if researchers indeed *contribute* their findings to what is already known. Thus, I argue that the right to science under most circumstances imposes an obligation on researchers to disclose

---

[46] CJEU, Case C-66/18, European Commission v Hungary, Judgment of 6 October 2020, para 225.

[47] I do not discuss here the way in which the right to science prescribes how governments must organise their educational institutions; see Beiter 2019 for an analysis. In this article, Beiter also claims that scientific and academic freedom entail more robust speech rights than are afforded under the right to communications freedom. Based on the case law discussed in Chap. 6, I do no think that this conclusion is warranted.

[48] United Nations 1976, Article 19(3); see for a similar argument Groen 2015, pp. 10–11; Similar reasoning is applied by Barendt in regard to the relation between "academic freedom" and freedom of expression, who notes that many forms of academic activity involve conduct rather than speech; Barendt 2010, p. 21; See also Beiter et al., Chap. IV.B.

their results (and an obligation on states to adopt a framework which promotes the diffusion of knowledge). This understanding is not yet recognised in the literature, but it squares with the fundamental values underlying the right to science: the pursuit of truth in service of humanity. Now, under what circumstances is there such an obligation?

To start with the most obvious scenario: if someone claims immunity from liability under the right to science, such immunity can only be granted under the condition that the public enjoys the benefits of their scientific work, for example through a publication. This principle can be extended to dual use research more generally—research which has outcomes that can be used for both malicious and beneficial purposes. In that case, the right to science requires that the findings are disclosed to ensure that the public can benefit from them in three ways: science can further build on these insights, useful technologies can be developed from these insights, and measures can be taken to mitigate the risks from them. Thus, I argue that the right to science implies that information security researchers have an obligation to disclose their findings. This argument becomes even stronger when read in conjunction with the "duties and responsibilities"-clause under the right to communications freedom, which also imposes on researchers a general duty of care when invoking their rights to communications freedom. I will work out the implications of this for information security in Chap. 8.

At the same time, governments must not grant scientists a blank cheque. The right to science also *shapes* research—through a version of the precautionary principle. This is something different from the "duties and responsibilities" which come with the right to communications freedom discussed in Chap. 6 (and can also be read into the right to science). The duty of care in the context of communications freedom is directed towards those who claim protection, such as researchers. In the context of information security, it mostly affects the *research methods*—which may not go further than necessary—and the *disclosure*—which must be done in such a way as to mitigate the risks related to publication. The precautionary principle, in contrast, has its origins in public policy, providing a framework for how states should deal with risks, such as environmental risks.[49] Although the principle is about risk mitigation, similar to the duty of care, it is about a more cautious version of risk mitigation. It is about mitigating risks, even if it is uncertain that something is a risk, or even when it is uncertain that a mitigating measure works—because if the risk were to materialise, it would be disastrous.[50] This means that, where science poses significant risks, states must mitigate those risks, which can be through regulation of the research, but can

[49] For example, environmental policy of the EU should be based on the "precautionary principle", see Article 191 EU Treaty on the Functioning of the European Union, 2009.

[50] There are numerous definitions of the precautionary principle, mostly differing in terms of the uncertainty one is willing to accept, but this is a rough description which aligns with policy guidance from the European Commission, UNESCO and the CESCR; European Commission 2000, p. 7; Fenstad and Matsuura; CESCR, General Comment No. 25 (2020) on Science and Economic, Social and Cultural Rights (Article 15(1)(b), (2), (3) and (4) of the International Covenant on Economic, Social and Cultural Rights), E/C.12/GC/25, 30 April 2020, para 56; see before UNESCO 2009, Section 12(g); see on other definitions Clarke 2013; Persson 2016; and Hartzell-Nichols 2013.

also be done by making mitigating technology available. And where mitigation is impossible, prohibiting the research must be considered.

This is relevant to vulnerability disclosure in the information security cycle—where the way you disclose vulnerabilities can limit the risk of unlawful access. It is also relevant to the tools being used in information security—which can be used to attack and defend. And it is relevant for research into quantum computing—which can break conventional encryption, and thus may imply an obligation for governments to simultaneously push for post-quantum encryption.

The right to science also shapes the direction of research in another way. Although states must on the one hand apply the precautionary principle to risky science, they are at the same time required to—in the words of the CESCR—"prioritise" science for peace and human rights. The main way in which they can do this, is through funding, giving grants to research which is likely to contribute to those goals. This also means that states should be even more cautious than normal in curtailing the disclosure of research in this area. This is similar to the argument in Chap. 6 that researchers' duty of care is less stringent when publishing vulnerabilities which create space for the exercise of human rights.

7.5 Limitations on the Right to Science

It is acknowledged in the guiding documents that there is a tension between scientific freedom and the principle of mitigating the risks of scientific research. This tension is particularly clear in the case of scientific results with a dual use. Research regarding information security measures is an example of this: its results can be used to strengthen the effectiveness of security measures but can also be used to exploit those measures. Research into quantum computing is another example: this can be used to develop new medicines or break encryption. The limitations system under the Declaration, the Charter and the Covenant in theory provides a framework for assessing under which circumstances the benefits outweigh the risks. In practice, however, only the Charter has a sufficiently mature framework for evaluating limitations.

In the Declaration, Article 29 states in paragraph 2 that "everyone shall be subject only to such limitations as are determined by law solely for the purpose of securing due recognition and respect for the rights and freedoms of others and of meeting the just requirements of morality, public order and the general welfare in a democratic society". The list of legitimate aims is quite limited. The proportionality requirement must be read into the provision, since it does not refer to limitations which must be 'necessary'.

In the Covenant, Article 4 sets out that the "States Parties to the present Covenant recognize that, in the enjoyment of those rights provided by the State in conformity with the present Covenant, the State may subject such rights only to such limitations as are determined by law only in so far as this may be compatible with the nature of these rights and solely for the purpose of promoting the general welfare in a democratic society." Here, the legitimate aim, "general welfare", is even more limited, and does not include, for example, national security.[51] This appears to be a deliberate choice by the drafters, who were convinced that economic and social rights could not be restricted by such aims.[52] This interpretation in retrospect seems unwise, as there can be other legitimate aims for restrictions on the right to science, which cannot easily be grouped under the header of 'general welfare.'[53] And here as well, the provision does not refer to limitations "necessary" in a democratic society, but one can read a proportionality test into the wording of Article 4 of the Covenant.[54]

One important principle which informs the proportionality test under the right to science is, again, the precautionary principle. This principle plays a role in setting the science agenda—see above—but also can help in determining how states may limit the right to science.[55] The CESCR for example suggested that when the precautionary principle is at odds with scientific freedom, "participation and transparency become crucial because the risks and potential of some technical advances or some scientific research should be made public in order to enable society, through informed, transparent and participatory public deliberation, to decide whether or not the risks are acceptable".[56] There is, unfortunately, very little other guidance on how to balance scientific freedom with the precautionary principle under the right to science.[57]

One peculiarity under Article 4 of the Covenant is worth mentioning: it is required that limitations should be "compatible with the nature of these [...] rights". This can be compared to the "essence"-requirement of the Charter (see above)—it is intended to ensure that minimum core obligations, for example the obligation to ensure a minimum essential level of water, cannot be limited, regardless of the circumstances.[58] The CESCR has in its General Comment identified a number of core obligations under the right to science. The one most relevant for this book, on doing research, is unfortunately self-referential: states should remove limitations to the freedom of scientific research "that are incompatible with article 4 of the Covenant" (which contains the reference to core obligations).[59]

---

[51] Müller 2009, p. 573.

[52] Ibid., p. 571; Donders 2015, p. 497.

[53] See also Donders 2015, p. 498.

[54] Müller 2009, pp. 577, 583.

[55] Some have argued that the precautionary principle also implies that states must be precautious when restricting science; see Baldoli and Radaelli 2019; and Sunstein 2002, but this complicates the analysis quite a bit and is not necessary for our purposes.

[56] CECR, General Comment No. 25 (2020) on Science and Economic, Social and Cultural Rights (Article 15(1)(b), (2), (3) and (4) of the International Covenant on Economic, Social and Cultural Rights), E/C.12/GC/25, 30 April 2020, para 57.

[57] In two of the preceding reports, it was merely mentioned; Shaheed 2012, para 50; UNESCO 2009, Section 12(g).

[58] Müller 2009, pp. 579–580.

[59] CESCR, General Comment No. 25 (2020) on Science and Economic, Social and Cultural Rights (Article 15(1)(b), (2), (3) and (4) of the International Covenant on Economic, Social and Cultural

Lastly, under the Charter, the right to science is limited by the framework of Article 52, discussed in Chap. 4. Given the strong connections between the right to science and the right to communications freedom, one could for the Charter fall back on the considerations developed in the case law on communications freedom discussed in Chap. 6. This means that the principles of necessity, proportionality and subsidiarity apply to all limitations on the right. I discuss what this means for governance in the fields of information security, encryption technologies and quantum computing in the concluding chapters.

7.6 Conclusion: A Marriage of Science and Conscience

Immediately after the Second World War, science was in crisis. On 2 November 1945, Oppenheimer, the physicist leading the Manhattan Project, gave a speech to the Association of Los Alamos Scientists, acknowledging that what was created had profoundly changed the world for the worse.[60] Yet, he called for us not to yield our belief in the value of science, instead arguing that this value must be derived from its significance to humanity. Alas, it was to no avail—scientists in the years that followed continued developing a far more potent bomb, the hydrogen bomb.

Thus, Einstein, fifteen years after his warning letter to the US government, again issued an urgent plea, this time in the form of a manifesto, written together with Bertrand Russell and addressed to the whole world.[61] While the ultimate aim was similar to the letter of 1939, its message was starkly different. The effects of the atomic bomb at Hiroshima were devastating, but Einstein and Russell argued that the potential future use of the hydrogen bomb, thousands of times more explosive, threatened the existence of humankind. Pandora's box was opened and could not be closed. Fearing that a new world war would ultimately escalate into a nuclear one, the authors did not call for nuclear disarmament—instead they called for world peace.

The right to science should be seen in that light. It stands on its own as a human right, since it protects the scientific process, the continuous cycle of falsification in the quest for truth. This means the right must protect this process in all its stages—from research to publication, from development to testing. Yet at the same time, it does not protect all *types* of scientific endeavours equally—prioritising the protection of those scientific activities whose aim is to benefit humanity, and only if performed in a responsible manner, protecting human rights and other values.

This distinction imposes a burden on government—to direct research towards societal progress. And it imposes a responsibility on scientists themselves—it is not possible to absolve responsibility for the potential uses of future technologies,

Rights), E/C.12/GC/25, 30 April 2020, para 52. Shaver has earlier on attempted to construe the minimum core content of the right to science; Shaver 2015.

[60] Oppenheimer JR (1945) Speech to the Association of Los Alamos Scientists.

[61] Russell and Einstein 1955.

similar to journalists who have a duty of care as a public watchdog. One important way of respecting scientific freedom while safeguarding the public interest, is by the recognition of a duty to disclose: this enables the progress of science. This has consequences for research into information security. But this duty to disclose is accompanied by an obligation to mitigate the risks—disclosing your findings may lead to new risks, and researchers should minimise those risks. This, as discussed, is relevant to information security and quantum computing. The right, in short, calls for the marriage of *science* with *conscience*. How this can be operationalised in the context of information security, encryption and quantum computing, will be discussed in the concluding three chapters.

References

Articles, Books and Other Documents

Almqvist J (2020) COVID-19 and Human Rights: Conjuring up a Defence of the Right to Science. Expert Comments of the Elcano Royal Institute 38/2020.

Baldoli R, Radaelli CM (2019) Evidence-Based Policy and the Precautionary Principle: Friends or Foes. In: Giordano S, Harris J, Piccirillo L (eds) The Freedom of Scientific Research: Bridging the Gap between Science and Society. Manchester University Press, Manchester.

Barendt EM (2010) Academic Freedom and the Law: A Comparative Study. Hart Pub, Oxford; Portland, Or.

Beiter KD, Karran T, Appiagyei-Atua K (2016a) "Measuring" the Erosion of Academic Freedom as an International Human Right: A Report on the Legal Protection of Academic Freedom in Europe. Vanderbilt Journal of Transnational Law 49:597–691.

Beiter KD, Karran T, Appiagyei-Atua K (2016b) Academic Freedom and Its Protection in the Law of European States. European Journal of Comparative Law and Governance 3:254–345. https://doi.org/10.1163/22134514-00303001

Beiter KD, Karran T, Appiagyei-Atua K (2018) Yearning to Belong: Finding a "Home" for the Right to Academic Freedom in the U.N. Human Rights Covenants. Intercultural Human Rights Law Review 11:107–188.

Beiter KD (2019) Where Have All the Scientific and Academic Freedoms Gone? And What Is "Adequate for Science"? The Right to Enjoy the Benefits of Scientific Progress and Its Applications. Israel Law Review 52:233–291. https://doi.org/10.1017/S0021223719000062

Butenschon Skre A, Eide A (2013) The Human Right to Benefit from Advances in Science and Promotion of Openly Accessible Publications. Nordic Journal of Human Rights 31: 427–453.

Chapman AR (2009) Towards an Understanding of the Right to Enjoy the Benefits of Scientific Progress and Its Applications. Journal of Human Rights 8:1–36. https://doi.org/10.1080/14754830802701200

Clarke S (2013) The Precautionary Principle and the Dual-Use Dilemma. In: Rappert B, Selgelid MJ (eds) On the Dual Uses of Science and Ethics: Principles, Practices, and Prospects. ANU Press.

Donders Y (2011) The Right to Enjoy the Benefits of Scientific Progress: In Search of State Obligations in Relation to Health. Medicine, Health Care and Philosophy. 14:371. https://doi.org/10.1007/s11019-011-9327-y

Donders Y (2015) Balancing Interests: Limitations to the Right to Enjoy the Benefits of Scientific Progress and Its Applications/Une balance des intérêts - Les restrictions au droit de bénéficier du progrès scientifique et de ses applications. Journal Européen des Droits de l'Homme 2015:486–503.

Egan A, Pech L, O'Cinneide C (2018) Enhancing EU Actions on Economic, Social and Cultural Rights within Its Human Rights Policy, February 2018. https://www.europarl.europa.eu/RegData/etudes/STUD/2018/603838/EXPO_STU(2018)603838_EN.pdf. Accessed 5 January 2024.

Eide A, Skre AB (2013) The Human Right to Benefit from Advances in Science and Promotion of Openly Accessible Publications. Nordic Journal of Human Rights 31:427–454.

Einstein A (1939) Letter to President Roosevelt.

European Commission (2000) Communication from the Commission on the Precautionary Principle. https://eur-lex.europa.eu/LexUriServ/LexUriServ.do?uri=COM:2000:0001:FIN:en:PDF. Accessed 5 January 2024.

Fenstad JE, Matsuura K (2005) The Precautionary Principle, World Commission on the Ethics of Scientific Knowledge and Technology, March 2005. https://unesdoc.unesco.org/ark:/48223/pf0000139578. Accessed 5 January 2024.

Gran B, Waltz M, Renzhofer H (2013) A Child's Right to Enjoy Benefits of Scientific Progress and Its Applications. The International Journal of Children's Rights 21:323–344. https://doi.org/10.1163/15718182-02102002

Groen JR (2015) Academische vrijheid en wetenschappelijke integriteit: een onderzoek naar vrijheid en verantwoordelijkheid in wetenschappelijk onderwijs en onderzoek, Preadvies NVOR, September 2015.

Hartzell-Nichols L (2013) From "the" Precautionary Principle to Precautionary Principles. Ethics, Policy & Environment 16:308–320. https://doi.org/10.1080/21550085.2013.844569

Lanouette W, Szilard BA, Salk J, Szilard L (2013) Genius in the Shadows: A Biography of Leo Szilard, the Man behind the Bomb, Revised and updated edition. Skyhorse Publishing, New York, NY.

Mann SP, Schmid MM (2018) Health Research Priority Setting: State Obligations and the Human Right to Science. The American Journal of Bioethics 18:33–35. https://doi.org/10.1080/15265161.2018.1523492

Mann SP, Porsdam H, Donders Y (2020) "Sleeping Beauty": The Right to Science as a Global Ethical Discourse. Human Rights Quarterly 42:332–356. https://doi.org/10.1353/hrq.2020.0020

Morgera E (2015) Fair and Equitable Benefit-Sharing at the Cross-Roads of the Human Right to Science and International Biodiversity Law. Laws 4:803–831. https://doi.org/10.3390/laws4040803

Morsink J (1999) The Universal Declaration of Human Rights: Origins, Drafting and Intent. University of Pennsylvania Press, Philadelphia.

Müller A (2009) Limitations to and Derogations from Economic, Social and Cultural Rights. Human Rights Law Review 9:557–601. https://doi.org/10.1093/hrlr/ngp027

Müller A (2010) Remarks on the Venice Statement on the Right to Enjoy the Benefits of Scientific Progress and Its Applications (Article 15(1)(b) ICESCR). Human Rights Law Review 10:765–784. https://doi.org/10.1093/hrlr/ngq033

Persson E (2016) What Are the Core Ideas behind the Precautionary Principle? Science of The Total Environment 557-558:134–141. https://doi.org/10.1016/j.scitotenv.2016.03.034

Plozza M (2021) Awakening from "Sleeping Beauty's" Slumber: Curtain ip for the Human Right to Science. Völkerrechtsblog. https://doi.org/10.5281/zenodo.4692465

Porsdam H, Porsdam Mann S (eds) (2021) The Right to Science: Then and Now, 1st edn. Cambridge University Press.

Porsdam Mann S, Donders Y, Mitchell C et al. (2018) Opinion: Advocating for Science Progress as a Human Right. Proceedings of the National Academy of Sciences 115:10820–10823. https://doi.org/10.1073/pnas.1816320115
Quinn R, Levine J (2014) Intellectual-HRDs and Claims for Academic Freedom under Human Rights Law. The International Journal of Human Rights 18:898–920. https://doi.org/10.1080/13642987.2014.976203
Russell B (1945) The Bomb and Civilization. http://www.personal.kent.edu/~rmuhamma/Philosophy/RBwritings/bombCivilization.htm. Accessed 7 November 2019.
Russell B, Einstein A (1955) Russell-Einstein Manifesto. http://www.spokesmanbooks.com/Spokesman/PDF/85russein.pdf. Accessed 5 January 2024.
Schabas W (2007) Study of the Right to Enjoy the Benefits of Scientific and Technological Progress and its Applications. In: Donders Y, Volodin V (eds) Human Rights in Education, Science, and Culture: Legal Developments and Challenges. Ashgate Publishing, pp 273–308.
Shaheed F (2012) The Right to Enjoy the Benefits of Scientific Progress and Its Applications, https://doi.org/10.1163/2210-7975_HRD-9970-2016149
Shaver L (2010) The Right to Science and Culture. Wisconsin Law Review 2010:121–184.
Shaver L (2015) The Right to Science : Ensuring that Everyone Benefits from Scientific and Technological Progress. European Journal of Human Rights 2015:411–430.
Sianko N, Balidemaj Basha A, Small M (2021) The Importance of the Right to Science During Pandemics. Kontakt 23:59–61. https://doi.org/10.32725/kont.2021.012
Smith T (2020a) Understanding the Nature and Scope of the Right to Science through the Travaux Préparatoires of the Universal Declaration of Human Rights and the International Covenant on Economic, Social and Cultural Rights. The International Journal of Human Rights 24:1156–1179. https://doi.org/10.1080/13642987.2020.1715947
Smith T (2020b) Scientific Purpose and Human Rights: Evaluating General Comment No 25 in Light of Major Discussions in the Travaux Préparatoires of the Universal Declaration of Human Rights and International Covenant on Economic, Social, and Cultural Rights. Nordic Journal of Human Rights 38:221–236. https://doi.org/10.1080/18918131.2021.1882757
Starck C (2006) Freedom of Scientific Research and Its Restrictions in German Constitutional Law Special Issue: In Honor of Professor Claude Klein. Israel Law Review 39:110–126.
Sunstein CR (2002) The Paralyzing Principle. Does the Precautionary Principle Point Us in Any Helpful Direction? Regulation Winter 2002-2003: 32–38.
UNESCO (1945) Constitution of the United Nations Educational, Scientific and Cultural Organization.
United Nations (1948) Universal Declaration of Human Rights.
United Nations (1976) International Covenant on Economic, Social and Cultural Rights.
UNESCO 2007, Report of the Experts' Meeting on The Right to Enjoy the Benefits of Scientific Progress and its Applications, June 7, 2007. https://unesdoc.unesco.org/ark:/48223/pf0000154583. Accessed 5 January 2024.
UNESCO 2009, The Right to enjoy the benefits of scientific progress and its applications, 16 July 2009. https://unesdoc.unesco.org/ark:/48223/pf0000185558 Accessed 5 January 2024.
UNESCO (ed) (2015) From ideas to actions: 70 years of UNESCO = Des idées aux actes: 70 années d'UNESCO = De ideias a ações: 70 anos da UNESCO. UNESCO Publishing ; Editora Brasileira, Paris: São Paulo.
UNESCO 2017, Recommendation on Science and Scientific Researchers, 13 November 2017. https://unesdoc.unesco.org/ark:/48223/pf0000263618. Accessed 5 January 2024.
van Daalen O (2022), In Defense of Offense: Information Security Research under the Right to Science, Computer Law & Security Review 46: 105706.
van Daalen O (2023a) The Right to Encryption: Privacy as Preventing Unlawful Access, Computer Law & Security Review 49:105804.
van Daalen O (2023b) The Right to Root: Constructing a Claim to Control Devices from the Right to Privacy, JIPITEC 14(2023:4): 580–593.
van Daalen O (2024) Developing a human-rights compatible governance framework for quantum computing, Research Directions: Quantum Technologies 2: 2024.

van Westendorp M, Lierman S (2020) Walking the Line: Balancing Access to Research and Protecting Prisoners. Medical Law Review 28:65–92. https://doi.org/10.1093/medlaw/fwy041
Wilson W (2007) The Winning Weapon? Rethinking Nuclear Weapons in Light of Hiroshima. International Security 31:162–179. https://doi.org/10.1162/isec.2007.31.4.162
Zoontjens PJJ (1993) Vrijheid van wetenschap: juridische beschouwingen over wetenschapsbeleid en hoger onderwijs. W.E.J. Tjeenk Willink.

Table of Cases: EU

CJEU, Case C-66/18, European Commission v Hungary, Judgment of 6 October 2020

Part III
Synthesis

Chapter 8
Human Rights-Compatible Information Security Cycle Governance

Contents

Abstract This chapter takes the normative framework under the rights to privacy, data protection, communications freedom and the right to science. It then applies this framework to the governance measures with regard to the information security cycle. It discusses the taking of measures, where it concludes that current governance measures focus too much on a sectoral approach, whereas it also follows from the rights to privacy and communications freedom that a more horizontal approach is warranted, For the offensive side of information security, it concludes that researchers under this normative framework are protected in doing research into information security and publishing the findings, but that governments and researchers have a duty to mitigate the risks following from this research.

Keywords Information security · Coordinated vulnerability disclosure · Vulnerability equities process · Communications freedom · Privacy · Right to science

O. van Daalen, *From Encryption to Quantum Computing*, Information Technology and Law Series 38, https://doi.org/10.1007/978-94-6265-635-2_8

8.1 Introduction

In the following chapters, I will develop a synthesis of the findings of the earlier chapters. Each chapter is dedicated to one domain: the information security cycle, encryption technologies and quantum computing. To make sure that the reasoning can be followed, I reiterate some of these earlier findings.

For each chapter, I will follow the structure employed throughout this book—first I discuss the characteristics of the landscape, both the technologies and the governance. Then, I review the human rights standards by which the governance measures have to be assessed, and in the concluding section, policy recommendations which follow from these requirements will be provided. In this first chapter, I discuss governmental obligations in the realm of the information security cycle.[1]

8.2 The Information Security Cycle Landscape

8.2.1 *The Technological Landscape*

A central starting point of this book is that information security should be approached as a continuous process. I described this process, which I call the information security cycle, in Chap. 2. This process can be roughly divided into two phases: a phase where security measures are taken, and a phase where vulnerabilities are discovered. I call it a *cycle*, because findings in the second phase may—and often will—be fed back into the first phase. Security professionals have for decades organised their processes around this cycle, assuming that vulnerabilities will inevitably be found, and planning how their organisations should deal with them.

The reason why vulnerabilities will inevitably be found, is that it is much more difficult to defend against attacks, than it is to perform attacks. An attacker only needs one weakness to enter a system—those parts of the system which are exposed to attacks are together called the *attack surface*. A defender will need to plug all potential holes in the attack surface to prevent someone from coming in. In other words: the security of a system is as strong as its weakest link. As systems have grown in complexity, often consisting of components from hundreds of vendors, it has become increasingly difficult for organisations to manage the exposure of a system to attacks. It has also become quite challenging to allocate responsibilities among different suppliers. This means there are a lot of vulnerabilities lying around in our digital infrastructure. Meanwhile, as discussed in, many people are looking for these vulnerabilities.

---

[1] Parts of this chapter have already been published in Van Daalen 2022, 2023a, 2023b and 2024.

As set out in Chap. 2, when a researcher finds a bug, they often disclose it in a way which allows others to fix it before the vulnerability becomes public knowledge. This prevents exploitation by others and is called coordinated vulnerability disclosure (CVD)—*coordinated*, because researchers have to coordinate the timing of disclosure with vendors who want to bring out a fix. Although many experts agree in principle on the utility of processes, there is no consensus on two key elements. First, it is not always clear how long a vendor may take to fix a vulnerability before a researcher is allowed to disclose their findings to the world. This means vendors can in theory drag this process out, while systems remain at risk. Second, it is not always clear which vendor is responsible for fixing a weakness in a system, a problem which has become more acute as the number of vendors supplying components to any system has grown.

Sometimes, bugs are instead exploited, for example, by intelligence agencies targeting dissidents, or by criminals holding companies to ransom. Information about vulnerabilities can spread rapidly, sometimes across domains—malware originally developed by intelligence agencies can for instance be repurposed as ransomware. Because almost everything has a computer or is a computer—even cars and buildings—, the impact of a breach is becoming increasingly severe. As a result, not a week goes by without a major security breach in the news.

8.2.2 The Governance Landscape

The EU governance of the information security cycle has not kept up with these developments, as discussed in Chap. 3. Three aspects of the current EU governance of the information security cycle stand out.

First, historically there was no horizontal governance of information security—meaning the rules on information security do not apply to all sectors equally, although this is changing. There are mostly specific rules for specific domains, such as rules for systems processing personal data and rules for online consumer products. The requirements with regard to taking security measures, fixing vulnerabilities and notifying vulnerabilities differ across these domains. The rules often do not clearly require the impact of poor security on society at large to be taken into account. They do not provide clear guidelines on how to deal with obligations to take measures which conflict with each other. Because of the emphasis on this domain-specific regulation, it is uncertain whether all potentially vulnerable systems are regulated by these frameworks.

Second, the current governance framework does not extend to all components of the attack surface. The organisation *using* digital infrastructure is generally responsible for the security of a system. Although the vendors of generic components of digital infrastructure, such as SSDs, memory chips and CPUs, may in the future be required to take security measures, fix holes or notify vulnerabilities to interested parties.

And while the governance of the first phase of the cycle might have its flaws, for the second phase, the discovery of vulnerabilities, the situation is worse: research and disclosure into information security measures can currently lead to criminal and civil liability in the EU, without an exception for research =in the public interest. There is also no obligation to disclose vulnerabilities when they are found. There have been proposals to facilitate processes at an EU level, for example by setting up a central point for disclosure of vulnerabilities, but these have not been adopted yet at the time of writing. Similarly, rules on how *governments* (in particular law enforcement and intelligence agencies) should deal with the knowledge of vulnerabilities have only in recent years become a topic of debate, and then primarily at the national level.

This means the information security cycle is not functioning as well as it could be. I argue that it is time to change this. This is not only because the implicit goal of EU policymaking is generally to increase the information security of digital infrastructure—and improving the information security cycle contributes to that goal. As it is demonstrated in this book, a badly functioning information security cycle also negatively affects the human rights to privacy (and data protection), communications freedom and science. If obligations in the measure taking-phase only extend to sections of our digital infrastructure, this will increase the risk of vulnerabilities being exploited, which has an impact on the rights to privacy and communications freedom. If governance measures prevent research into vulnerabilities, or disclosure of the results of this research, this impacts the rights to communications freedom and science.

Currently, however, there are only some initiatives at the EU level to fundamentally address the issues identified above. The European Commission in its 2020 Cybersecurity strategy still focuses on strengthening specific sectors, such as critical infrastructure and consumer electronics.[2] It does not consider information security as a cyclical process, does not protect research into information security and does not explicitly consider frameworks for feeding back vulnerabilities into the cycle (although coordinated vulnerability disclosure does play a role in the future Cyber Resilience Act and the NIS2 Directive. Even this legislation has given little attention to the research stage of the cycle.

There are some proposals from experts on improving information security rules, but they address only parts of the problem. A proposal by the European consumer organisation for a new, "horizontal" cybersecurity law provides a useful starting point, but it would only apply to consumer devices, and does not explicitly protect the research side of the information security cycle.[3] Similarly, the authors of a policy paper in 2016 focus on duties of care and diligence in cybersecurity with regard to consumer products and services.[4] Although in 2020, the Dutch Cybersecurity

[2] High Representative of the Union for Foreign Affairs and Security Policy, The EU's Cybersecurity Strategy for the Digital Decade, JOIN(2020) 18 final, December 16, 2020; see for an analysis of the development of this policy Fuster and Jasmontaite 2020; see for an early analysis of the European Parliament Meulen et al. 2015.

[3] Oliveira da Silva 2019.

[4] Verbruggen et al. 2016.

Council advocated an integral, wide-ranging approach to improve cybersecurity in the Netherlands, its advice is high level, and as a result does not address the gaps identified above.[5] A broad analysis of the European Court of Auditors in 2019 also touches on some of the issues identified in this book, but does not take the cyclical nature of information security as its starting point.[6] A Dutch policy proposal of 2018 is also limited to a specific area, emphasising standardisation, the monitoring and testing of products, and liability for insecure products.[7] Lastly, the thorough 2018 study on vulnerability disclosure in the EU shares some of the recommendations of this book, but does not focus on the measure taking-phase.[8] What is needed is a more broadly applicable framework for information security—so how can this be fixed?

8.2.3 The Role of the State and of the EU in the Information Security Cycle

This is where human rights obligations come in. Human rights play a role in the political arena in several ways. Some laws are incompatible with human rights. But human rights may also provide support for particular legislation, in some cases even requiring that this legislation is adopted. Where politicians do not live up to these standards, courts can in some cases enforce human rights. Below, I develop the contours of a policy framework for states, building from these human rights. Let me acknowledge at the outset, however, that the development of this framework is just the start, and that implementation is fraught with a number of societal and legal challenges. I discuss three of these challenges.

First, states are obviously not the only stakeholder influencing how the information security cycle works. As discussed in Chaps. 2 and 3, the functioning of the information security cycle is the outcome of interventions by a variety of stakeholders. These include standard-setting bodies, which develop security standards and specifications for certain technologies, such as and post-quantum cryptography; large global corporations, such as Google and Apple, who decide which security technology to apply; small national initiatives, such as telecom providers exchanging IP-addresses of infected computers; the global community of security researchers, who collectively push the direction of research; and bodies active in coordinating responses to vulnerabilities (s), which in most countries are governmental organisations, but in some cases are s. This book is not about the dynamics and roles of these different institutions. Suffice it to say that they all have different interests, partially at odds with the suggestions proposed below, and many of these stakeholders are active globally.

---

5 Cyber Security Raad 2021.

6 European Court of Auditors 2019.

7 Ministry of Economic Affairs and Climate and the Ministry of Justice and Security of the Netherlands 2018.

8 Schaake et al. 2018.

As a result, there is currently a limit to what states can do in this domain—they may appear to be but one player in this complex ecosystem. The global standards referred to above are often set in international fora, largely outside public view. The technology companies may appear to set the pace, with the legislature merely following in their wake: when Google and Apple decide to apply encryption by default in their devices, users just have to accept that. Furthermore, some of the institutions in this landscape, such as, have a history of favouring self-regulation over governmental intervention.

At the same time, if my analysis below holds, some significant changes in the governance of the information security cycle are necessary. If that means that the current ecosystem needs to be radically readjusted, the state is the only institution theoretically capable of doing so. States have the authority to steer standard-setting processes, to shape private initiatives, and direct research. Just as the European Court of Human Rights has considered that states are the *ultimate guarantor* of pluralism under the right to communications freedom, so does the state have an essential role to play in ensuring an appropriate level of information security for the persons and organisations falling within its jurisdiction.[9]

At the same time, states cannot do this alone—one isolated country does not wield sufficient power to steer the field of information security. Information security is dominated by global interests, from intelligence agencies to multinationals, from Russian malware criminals to Israeli spyware vendors. A response needs to cross borders, if it is to have a chance of success. This is an important reason why measures in these domains are preferably to be taken at the EU level, if they cannot be taken at a global level. Harmonising at the EU level crosses some of these borders, provides the negotiation clout to influence policy on a global level, and serves as an important focal point for regulation outside of the EU—similar to the way the set a global standard for data protection rules. There are also two other reasons why intervention at the EU level is preferable. Most of the regulations in this area already come from the EU (see Chap. 3). More fundamentally, since information security deeply affects cross-border products and services within the EU, a well-functioning internal market also calls for intervention at the EU level.

Even if we accept, in theory, that governance should come from the EU, there is one other obstacle, though—doubts about whether the competence to regulate in this domain lies exclusively with member states. The Treaty of the European Union asserts that the Union shall respect the states' function of maintaining "law and order and safeguarding national security", noting that national security remains the sole responsibility of each member state.[10] A high level of information security might, on the surface, seem to be contrary to the goal of maintaining national security—if you make it difficult for organised crime to access information and systems, you also make it more difficult for states to do so. Thus, because national security falls

---

[9] See ECHR, Application nos. 13914/88; 15041/89; 15717/89; 15779/89; 17207/90, Informationsverein Lentia and Others v Austria, Judgment of 24 November 1993, para 38; ECHR, Application no. 13936/02, Manole and Others v. Moldova, Judgment of 17 September 2009, para 99.

[10] Consolidated version of the Treaty on the European Union, Article 4.

within the sole competence of the member states, the EU cannot intervene, or so it goes.

A reluctance to intervene on an EU level for this reason is misplaced.[11] A high level of information security is not at odds with law and order and national security. On the contrary: a digital infrastructure which is secured against attacks, is also in the interest of law and order (because it obstructs criminals) and national security (because it obstructs attacks from nation states and attacks with a nation-wide impact). There is only one instance where this may be different: where a state wants to retain a vulnerability for itself instead of disclosing it. Although there are good reasons for claiming that keeping vulnerabilities secret is bad for national security, it is a valid question whether the EU does have competence in this area—at first glance it does not. For that situation, member states will have to develop their own legislation.

In this respect, it is also important that the EU apparently considers itself to be competent to regulate the protection of critical infrastructure, which is connected to national security, via its internal market powers—as this is the basis of the current directive.[12] The Court of Justice has clarified that just because a national measure is intended to safeguard national security, this cannot render EU law inapplicable and exempt a member state from its obligation to comply with that law.[13] Similarly, the European Parliament and the Council may adopt rules on criminal offences and sanctions in the area of computer crime—in fact, this was the basis for the Cybercrime Directive.[14] If you have the legislative competence to impose liability for committing computer crimes, you also have the power to introduce an exemption to that liability.

Even if you conclude that the EU in theory has the *competence* to follow up on the suggestions below, it is also relevant to know whether it has a legal basis and an obligation to intervene, and whether this can be enforced in court. The problem here is that the Convention and the Covenant do not bind the EU; only the Charter does. An argument can be made, however, that the Charter provides a legal basis for the implementation of positive obligations in the field of information security, although I should note that this is not well-established yet. The EU Treaty states that fundamental rights, as guaranteed by the Convention and as they result from the constitutional traditions common to the member states, shall constitute general principles of the Union's law.[15] The Charter must furthermore be interpreted in line

---

[11] See on the competence of the EU in the area of "cyberspace" Bendiek and Maat 2019.

[12] EU (2009) Treaty on the Functioning of the European Union, Articles 114 jo. 26; (2016) Directive (EU) 2016/1148 of the European Parliament and of the Council of 6 July 2016 Concerning Measures for a High Common Level of Security of Network and Information Systems Across the Union; see Fuster and Jasmontaite 2020, para 5.4 on this.

[13] CJEU, Case C-623/17, Privacy International v United Kingdom, Judgment of 6 October 2020, para 44; CJEU, Cases C-511/18, C-512/18 and C-520/18, La Quadrature du Net, Judgment of 6 October 2020, para 99; see Zalnieriute 2022 for an analysis of this aspect.

[14] EU (2009) Treaty on the Functioning of the European Union, Article 83(1).

[15] Consolidated version of the Treaty on the European Union, Article 7(3).

with the Convention as discussed in Chap. 4.[16] As discussed in the same chapter, the European Court of Human Rights has developed a mature doctrine of positive obligations. It is not surprising then, that the European Court of Justice recently, in *La Quadrature du Net*, can be seen to apply the concept of positive obligations under the Charter, from which it could be concluded that the Charter also forms a legal basis for such interventions, in addition to the TFEU.[17]

Through similar reasoning, one could also conclude that the Covenant supports enforceable positive obligations under the Charter. States under the Covenant have a duty to respect, protect and fulfil the right to science.[18] And the Charter may not restrict or adversely affect human rights recognised by international agreements to which all member states are party.[19] The Court has already considered that it takes into account the Covenant when applying the general principles to which the EU Treaty refers (because these bind all member states).[20] It could on the basis of this reasoning also rely on the Covenant (which has also been ratified by all EU member states), when applying the Charter, particularly for the right to science, which is also recognised under the Charter.[21]

Based on all these considerations, one could argue that the Charter provides a legal basis for the implementation of positive obligations in the realm of information security. Even if this conclusion is not warranted and not all of my suggestions below can be considered judiciable positive obligations at the EU level, it is certain that the absence of these measures cannot be considered to be compatible with the human rights instruments discussed in this book. This means that the EU should be the primary legislator—to the extent that it is competent to do so—and in those cases where the EU does not provide protection, this means that member states need to step in. So the question is then: to what extent are the EU and member states under the Charter, the Convention and the Covenant required to fix the gaps in the information cycle? This is discussed further below.

[16] (2000) Charter of Fundamental Rights of the European Union, Article 52(3).

[17] CJEU, Cases C-511/18, C-512/18 and C-520/18, La Quadrature du Net, Judgment of 6 October 2020, para 126–127.

[18] CESCR, General Comment No. 25 (2020) on Science and Economic, Social and Cultural Rights (Article 15 (1) (b), (2), (3) and (4) of the International Covenant on Economic, Social and Cultural Rights), E /C.12/GC/25, April 30, 2020, para 41 and further.

[19] (2000) Charter of Fundamental Rights of the European Union, Article 53.

[20] CJEU, Case C-540/03, European Parliament v Council of the European Union, Judgment of 27 June 2006, para 37.

[21] See also European Union Agency for Fundamental Rights. (2020) Applying the Charter of Fundamental Rights of the European Union in law and policymaking at national level: guidance. Publications Office, LU, p. 23.

8.3 Human Rights Requirements for Information Security Cycle Governance

One key to answering this question lies in the observation that not all information security measures have the same impact on human rights (in particular the rights to privacy, data protection and communications freedom). For example, where a bank applies measures to defend against unauthorised transactions by criminals, this *protects* the privacy and data protection interests of individuals. There are also examples of information security measures where ordinary individuals, not criminals, are considered to be—in information security lingo—*adversaries*. In those cases, these security measures are designed to restrict the possible uses of digital infrastructure by these individuals. These kinds of measures can *negatively* impact human rights. For instance, where software restricts the possibility of sharing information with friends and family, or where security measures restrict the possibility of whistleblowers leaking data to the press, this affects the right to communications freedom (see Chap. 6).

Furthermore, determining states' obligation in regard to the information security cycle also requires an analysis of the extent to which the cycle *itself*—not the measures which are subject to the cycle—serves human rights. Generally speaking, this cycle does indeed serve human rights, as explained in Chap. 6. Firstly, where information security measures protect human rights, strengthening these measures through the information security cycle means further protecting those interests. Fixing a hole in the security measures of a bank to protect against unauthorised transactions by criminals, strengthens the protection of the rights of individuals whose transactions are at risk. Secondly, research into information security measures and subsequent disclosure is protected by the rights to communications freedom and science, because it contributes to scientific development.

As described above, disclosing a vulnerability and strengthening a security measure can in some cases be at odds with other interests. These can be human rights interests, for example, when you patch a hole to make it more difficult for whistleblowers to leak data to the press, or you disclose a vulnerability for which there is no fix yet. These can be public interests, such as national security or the prevention of crime, for example when closing a vulnerability affects the ability of the police to investigate a case.

So in short, protecting human rights in this context means the information security cycle should be shaped towards *strengthening security measures* which protect human rights, and under certain circumstances *weakening the impact of security measures* which negatively affect human rights. Meanwhile, these goals should be further balanced against other interests. For this book, three interests are particularly relevant: the rights of researchers to investigate and disclose vulnerabilities, the aim of states to protect national security and to prevent crime, and the rights of others. One group of "rights of others" which merits particular attention in this context are intellectual property rights. Under the Charter, intellectual property rights have gained specific recognition, arguably placing them on par with other fundamental rights in the Charter.[22] The explicit recognition of intellectual property rights in the Charter leads to the question of how balancing these interests should be done. In this book, I will not go into the particulars of this specific balancing, but instead consider it merely one example of the balancing required when devising policy for the information security cycle. The general outlines of this balancing exercise are described below, starting with the obligation to strengthen measures, then discussing the obligation to weaken the negative impact of security measures, and then analysing the relationship to the information security cycle.

8.3.1 Strengthening Security Measures Protecting Human Rights

The first step in this balancing exercise requires an understanding of the obligations of states to *strengthen* security measures which protect human rights. In Chaps. 5 and 6, I described what a human rights assessment under the rights to privacy and communications freedom in the context of information security looks like. This requires an analysis of the potential for *access* to, and *control* of information and systems protected by privacy and communications freedom interests (by both governments and others, which I will discuss further below). This is firstly because governmental measures which facilitate lawful access or control, or significantly increase the risk of unlawful access or control should be considered an interference. Secondly, this is because the proportionality analysis of governance measures in this context also depends on these considerations. Below, I will refer to both access and control as *access*.

As discussed in Chap. 5, the proportionality analysis revolves around the residual risk of unlawful access. With *residual*, I mean that there remains a risk, even in the face of governance measures which decrease the risk, such as clear legislation and judicial supervision. *Unlawful* can mean two different things. For governmental institutions, it means that access takes place beyond the powers granted to the governmental institutions doing surveillance. But the rights to privacy, data protection and communications freedom also impose obligations on states to exclude unlawful access by others—such as criminals and other states. This obviously includes access which is prohibited by law, such as intercepting phone conversations. But for many types of access, whether it is prohibited by law depends on the internal information security policy—the policy which determines that, for example, doctors may be allowed to gain access to a medical file, whereas the receptionist may not. So this also includes many forms of *unauthorised* access, access in contravention of a security policy, to the extent that this is prohibited by law. I will group both forms of unlawful access to information and systems protected by the rights to privacy, data protection and communications freedom under the header of *unlawful access*.

Now, although governments have an obligation to minimise the risk of unlawful access, this obligation has its limits. Determining these limits involves a balancing

[22] (2000) Charter of Fundamental Rights of the European Union, Article 17(2).

exercise—of striking a "fair balance" between the interest of the public and the interest of the individual. The interest of the public can be in reducing the burden on the state. On this side of the equation, several factors play a role. A measure may cost the state more money: it perhaps needs to build new institutions which enforce the new rules. Or a measure can cost others more—organisations may have to attract new people to comply with the new rules. Or a measure imposes other kinds of burdens—stringent security rules may hinder innovation or affect freedom of expression. What matters is that where the burden imposed on the public is very high and the measures only achieve a limited effect in preventing unlawful access, there is less of an obligation to intervene. Similarly, where the impact of unlawful access is limited, the obligation is also less present.

The determination of the impact poses a problem in this context. As discussed in Chap. 5, this impact depends on criteria such as the sensitivity and amount of data, the number of people affected and the severity of the consequences of a breach. Where unlawful access only affects a few people and the consequences of a breach for those people remains limited, more risk can be accepted than if a vulnerability concerns, for example, all Android-smartphone users in the world. In another example, the impact of remotely halting a car in the middle of a highway would be far greater than decrypting an invoice for groceries without authorisation.

The problem when determining the risk, is that most governance measures in the information security cycle affect technologies *as deployed in numerous instances.* If you leave vulnerabilities in software which is broadly used, you cannot really assess what information and devices you put at risk. This is firstly because you do not know in advance what information is protected by the software—for some, the vulnerability might expose family pictures, whereas for others it might expose their medical data. In addition, the security of a *system* is as strong as its weakest link, so you cannot really know in which way a vulnerability in one particular software package will affect security of the overall system. It is thus largely impossible to differentiate beforehand between the risks of unlawful access for different kinds of data and devices.

This has two implications. First, as discussed in Chap. 5, governance measures in the information security cycle which increase the risk of unlawful access should be considered an *interference* with the rights to privacy, data protection and communications freedom (with regard to confidential communications). This is different where this unlawful access remains restricted to information or devices with no underlying privacy or communications freedom interest whatsoever. It is difficult to think about a plausible scenario where this is the case—even malware developed by the leaked and used by criminals (see Chap. 2). Arguably, even the deployment of highly targeted malware, constitutes an interference with the rights to privacy, data protection and human rights, because it *increases* the risk of vulnerabilities leaking towards the civilian domain. A more important implication is that the proportionality assessment of the risk of unlawful access will in many cases have to take as a starting point that the security of very sensitive data is at stake.

Now, there are different ways of dealing with this uncertainty from a policy perspective, if you have to decide what level of risk of unlawful access is acceptable.

You could take a chance, assuming that in most cases only not-so sensitive data or devices will be affected—but at the same time increasing the risk that sensitive data or devices would in some cases be unlawfully accessed. It is doubtful whether such an approach is compatible with human rights requirements, looking at the cases discussed in Chap. 3. A more defensible approach is that where sensitive data is *potentially* at stake, you will have to assume that there is a risk that this kind of data may be accessed. In other words—as a lawmaker, from an information security perspective you have to protect your most vulnerable individuals and organisations, and a high level of protection is warranted.

Still, a policymaker will also have other aims, and these sometimes clash with this goal of protecting individuals and organisations. When a state undermines an information security measure, or keeps a vulnerability to itself in order to exploit it, it will often do so in the name of national security or the prevention of crime. Doing so may also increase the risk of unlawful access as described above. As discussed in Chap. 3, the importance of such objectives is not sufficient to justify deliberately weakening information security measures (or deliberately keeping them weak), because this increases the risk of unlawful access significantly (including by not disclosing knowledge of a vulnerability which puts people at risk). The Courts have in the past considered policies which increased this risk of unlawful access to be disproportionate, even for important goals such as national security, where the sensitive data of a large part of the population was at stake. This means that governments who knowingly retain vulnerabilities in digital infrastructure or even insert them act at odds with this case law.

8.3.2 Weakening the Negative Impact on Human Rights of Security Measures

As discussed above, there are also examples where information security measures negatively impact human rights. Some of these affect communications freedom—for example measures which prevent people from sharing information with friends and family (such as home movies). Others restrict privacy—think for example of organisations having the ability to remotely turn off a device (such as a thermostat or a car). Both examples roughly fall under the header of device self-determination as discussed in Chap. 5. Furthermore, as discussed in Chap. 3, many of these measures are fortified by legal protection against circumvention.

This is a serious problem. Many of the devices we use, we do not control. Our cars, our refrigerators, our pacemakers; we are considered the adversary, dependent on the goodwill of the manufacturer for updates and functionality. How to deal with this under the Convention and the Charter has barely come up before the courts. There have been some cases relating to the rights to communications freedom where the outlines of the concept of device self-determination could be discerned (see Chap. 5). Courts have, for example, considered under which circumstances the governmental blocking of a website would violate the right to communications freedom. The way in which the courts evaluate these measures, somewhat mirrors the way in which the courts review state restrictions on the right to privacy. Under the right to privacy, the risk of unlawful access is central to the Courts' analysis. However, under the right to communications freedom, the risk of preventing lawful access by users is the central topic. And just as states must take measures to exclude the risk of unlawful access to private information, measures which prevent lawful access may under certain circumstances considered to be disproportionate.

The question of course is, under which circumstances? The starting point for this analysis is that, in an ideal world, all activities which are lawful would not be restricted by security measures: let us call this the *communication freedom by design* approach. Just as the principle of *privacy by design* requires that technological measures mirror the privacy protection afforded by rules, *communication freedom by design* would require organisations to ensure that users are afforded the rights to communications freedom they have under applicable legal frameworks. In an ideal world, this would for example mean that all applicable copyright exceptions should in theory be respected in technological frameworks, and that systems should always provide a way for legitimate whistleblowers to siphon off information in the public interest without detection.

That principle, however, is difficult, if not impossible, to implement in practice. It is challenging to determine in advance under which circumstances you can rely on a copyright exception via technological means. It is impossible to distinguish between legitimate whistleblowing and illegitimate hacking in advance. Furthermore, it is questionable whether such an approach strikes the right balance with the rights of others (such as the right to conduct a business, the right to intellectual property and the right to property).

Because of the difficulties in striking the right balance between these interests, I suggest three more proportionate policy interventions when it comes to restrictive information security measures in devices. First, organisations will have to at least provide a manual override of certain security measures, in line with Doctorow's analysis.[23] Related to this, where circumvention of certain measures affects the privacy and communications freedom rights of individuals, there is a stronger reason for researchers to ensure that a patch has been made available before disclosure. But where circumvention as a result of disclosure is in the public interest, for example to allow the exercise of lawful uses of information or a device, there is less of a duty of care for researchers to wait until a patch has been published. The contours of these proposals will be discussed below.

---

[23] See Doctorow 2021.

8.3.3 Promoting the Rights of Researchers in the Research and Disclosure Phase

The final way in which human rights play a role in the information security cycle is by creating space for the research and disclosure phase. As discussed in Chaps. 6 and 7, limitations on information security research and disclosure—through criminal and civil liability—are an interference with the right to communications freedom and the right to science.[24] This also applies to restrictions on the creation of new information security technologies, and the development, possession and use of tools for this research.

In this analysis, it is useful to make a distinction between the right to communications freedom and the right to science, because they do not overlap completely. First, the right to communications freedom will be discussed and then the right to science. At the heart of the proportionality analysis of restrictions on research and disclosure under the right to communications freedom lies the concept of "public interest". Knowledge of vulnerabilities should be considered to be in the public interest for two reasons. First, information which leads to a better understanding of reality should in general be considered to be in the public interest. Second, knowledge about risks to individuals or organisations should be considered to be in the public interest, because of the potential damage from exploitation and because this knowledge allows things to be fixed. Where research and disclosure is in the public interest, limits on these activities will often be considered disproportionate.

Then again, doing research in the public interest also comes with certain duties, comparable to the duty of care of journalists when relying on the right to communications freedom. First, researchers have a duty to *mitigate the risks* of research and disclosure. This is because those who claim protection under the right to communications freedom have a duty to protect the interests of others. It also follows from the fact that the research and disclosure of vulnerabilities could increase the risk of unlawful access and thus affect privacy and data protection. It follows from the idea that the right to science, comes with a duty to ensure that the results benefit humanity. Second, researchers have a *duty to disclose* vulnerabilities. This primarily comes from the right to science, which supports the dynamic and iterative nature of the scientific process—you may do research, as long as you perform this research to benefit humanity. Benefiting humanity in this case means sharing your findings with the world. This is further underscored by the importance of the human rights affected by bad security, combined with the difficulty of determining whether a vulnerability affects these interests (see above).

In practice, this means a number of things. Firstly, researchers have to minimise the damage when doing their *research*. For example, if a researcher wants to demonstrate a vulnerability in the server, they may not download sensitive data from the server if this is not necessary to demonstrate the vulnerability. It also means that researchers have to minimise the damage when *disclosing* their findings. This requires

---

[24] See for an earlier analysis with a US-focus; Granick 2005; and Preston and Lofton 2002.

balancing the risk of disclosure against the risk of non-disclosure. As discussed, delaying publication until a patch has been published is usually the best way to mitigate the damage, but this depends on the facts of a case. If there are indications that a certain vulnerability is already being exploited in the wild, this means the vulnerability should be disclosed quickly, because it allows vulnerable organisations to mitigate the risk themselves. Also where there are less infringing ways to demonstrate the existence of a vulnerability, research and disclosure will generally not be considered proportionate.

The duty to disclose implies that governance measures should be aimed at rapid disclosure and patching of vulnerabilities to strengthen security measures. It also means that states may not keep vulnerabilities found through research under wraps for offensive purposes (and holds even more for *inserting* vulnerabilities, something which will be discussed further in the next chapter on encryption and human rights). This does not mean, by the way, that *all* information needs to be disclosed: perhaps it is sufficient to publicly disclose just the information needed to allow organisations to determine whether they are affected, whereas vendors also need to obtain a working exploit. If on the other hand, disclosing would merely increase the risk of unauthorised access, but not allow people to mitigate this risk, this would argue against publication.

Now, researchers are not expected to determine entirely on their own how they should give effect to these duties. Given the interests at stake, and the complex balancing required when devising -processes, the human rights discussed in this book also imply a governmental obligation to devise -policies and embed them in a legal framework. By doing so, states can further ensure that research towards vulnerabilities is used to strengthen security measures, especially those which protect human rights.

To be clear: this framework for research activities does not distinguish between protected and unprotected research activities, or between protected and unprotected researchers. It is not based on formal criteria, such as whether a researcher is affiliated with a university. Instead, what matters for this framework is whether a vulnerability has been discovered, and how the person handles that discovery.

Now, a large part of information security research is not aimed at discovering vulnerabilities or mitigating them. Sometimes it is aimed at developing the tools used to find vulnerabilities. Although this activity does not fall squarely under the right to communications freedom, it is protected under the right to science. And while many tools can only be used in the public interest, some may also be used for undesirable activities, such as attacking networks or exploiting software. In that case, the right to science also imposes a duty of care—a duty to minimise harmful use of the tool while maximising the benefits of the tool. The damage can be minimised by tweaking the tool, but can in some cases also be addressed by simultaneously creating alternative technologies which protect against harmful use.

Finally, the three human rights discussed in this book also steer funding policy in this domain. Governments' obligation to strengthen security measures which protect the human rights discussed above not only requires them to minimise the risk of unlawful access—to develop new security technologies and *patch* holes in existing technologies. It also requires governments to promote *research and disclosure* into unlawful access—to *find* holes and *disclose* them, so they can be patched. States obviously have quite some leeway in shaping science policy, even if it affects human rights. But if a state simply does *not* invest in research into information security technologies which protect privacy, data protection and communications freedom, it undoubtedly does not fulfill its obligations under these rights.

The above analysis calls for closing the gaps in the governance of the information security cycle identified in this book, especially when the current gaps expose human rights interests. I explore the translation of these state duties further in the following sections.

8.4 Recommendations for Human Rights-Compatible Governance

Now, translating state duties means devising governance measures, and devising governance measures is complicated. You have to take into account a broad range of interests and embed your measures in a framework of previously existing regulations. This book is not the place to provide a fully worked out legislative proposal; instead, the suggestions should be understood as guiding principles for shaping policy across domains, in the hope that the legislator will use these as inspiration. Where the legislator does not take this role, these principles can also serve as reference points in court cases over the obligations of states in this domain. Of course, the details are important, but perhaps more important is the shift they represent: a shift towards viewing security as a dynamic process which affects systems across sectors. For instance, although I propose the development of an omnibus regulation of the information security cycle, if this turns out to be politically unfeasible, then at least you can apply this perspective of information security as a cycle to each sectoral regulation which affects information security.

Some of these proposals may appear quite radical, but that is simply because the stakes are so high and the gaps are so big. As I have previously explained in this book, vulnerabilities in digital infrastructure negatively impact human rights, in particular the rights to privacy, data protection and communications freedom. I have also identified a number of significant gaps in the current governance approach to information security, as a result of which there are currently many of these vulnerabilities to be found in digital infrastructure. In view of states' obligations to minimise the risk of unlawful access, as described above, a number of significant changes are required.

8.4.1 Introduce Horizontal Governance of the Information Security Cycle

As discussed, one of the main problems with the current governance of the information security cycle is that regulation is restricted to certain segments. There are good explanations for this—importantly, the competence for regulating the internal market is different from those regulating criminal matters. This piecemeal approach does not work when domains are so difficult to keep apart. One obvious way to address this, is by adopting EU legislation which encompasses all domains where information security plays a role. From the perspective of the effectiveness of information security, there is no good reason to approach security differently across sectors—as long as, that is, the rules themselves are sufficiently flexible to account for the differences within those sectors.

The scope of the rules should be focused on the risk of unlawful access as defined above: it should thus cover all systems where there is a risk of access or control of systems or information in violation of laws or internal policies. This can range from computers to cars, from nuclear plants to -cameras. For these new rules, the function of a system does not matter: it applies to systems which process personal data, to systems which support critical infrastructure and to systems which protect ordinary websites.

The required security standard—focusing on taking measures—should remain risk-based, building on the current security standards for personal data processing and critical infrastructure. This means, in short, that the organisations which fall within the new scope of these rules must still take "appropriate technical and organisational measures" to secure the systems they operate, sell or supply. Such a risk-based approach to the required security standard provides flexibility and has already been in use for many years.

There are, however, three elements in this risk-based security standard which require reconsideration in the context of human rights: the role of *costs*, the impact of bad security on *others* and the *balancing* of different goals when devising a policy. First, offsetting the risks of unlawful access against the costs of a security measure has traditionally been an important aspect for determining what is an appropriate level of security. But taking the human rights of individuals as the starting point for protection means that a high level of protection is required when it comes to vulnerabilities in digital infrastructure. Given the considerations of the Court in *Digital Rights Ireland* (see Chap. 5), it is questionable as to whether costs can still be a decisive factor in this context. Wholly excluding the factor of costs would not do justice to the fact that one can never ensure 100% security. It would also not do justice to other fundamental rights, such as the right to property and the right to conduct a business.[25] Instead, I contend that for measures which are directed at preventing and fixing vulnerabilities in digital infrastructure that potentially affect human rights, the factor of costs must not be eliminated entirely, but must be relegated

[25] See Articles 17 resp. 16 (2000) Charter of Fundamental Rights of the European Union.

to the background. Furthermore, it should be clarified that the risk of unlawful access should also take into account the risks to *other* persons or organisations, not only the risk to the organisation doing the assessment. Where security requirements conflict—the budget for improving resilience against attacks may for instance be competing with the budget for preventing attacks in the first place –, it should be clarified that the requirement which offers the most human rights protection takes precedence. This means that the requirement of resilience will often lose out. The legislator will have to further work out these three points in guidance.

When it comes to *fixing of vulnerabilities*, I propose a more radical overhaul. I argue, firstly, that new rules with regard to this part of the information security cycle take as the atomic unit of regulation the *attack surface* of a system—that part of a system which is exposed to attacks. This is, after all, where the problems of unlawful access and control arise in the first place. This immediately leads to the question of what is still considered a *system* when determining how big the attack surface is. An isolated app on a smartphone which does not rely on online services has relatively well-defined boundaries—the attack surface would probably include all input and output elements of the app on the phone. But which app nowadays is not in one way or another connected to the internet? And what is the attack surface of a financial transaction system of a bank? Does this include the call centre providing customer support? Does it include the physical retail banking offices? This would need to be explored in further research.

It is important to define the attack surface well, though, because I argue that these rules relating to fixing vulnerabilities should apply to all organisations that play a role in this attack surface. This includes at least three significant stakeholders. First, the organisations which operate a system—the hospital which runs a database with health files, the online shop offering a website. Second, the organisations which sell a system—the vendor of a -camera system or the provider of an operating system. Third, in order to address the problem that the attack surface of a system depends on the security of its components, the rules should also apply to organisations which supply the components which are incorporated in these systems—these include for example and chip manufacturers. In what follows, I call these *operators*, *vendors* and *suppliers*.

To be clear: I am not arguing that all these parties are responsible for taking *initial* measures to secure the attack surface of a system, if only because suppliers and vendors cannot know in advance how their products or services will be incorporated into specific systems. But, as I explained in Chap. 3, *fixing* a vulnerability after discovery requires coordination. Sometimes it is easier to patch the hardware; sometimes it is quicker to patch the software; and sometimes you might want to have the users of the system take organisational measures. This is why I propose as a guiding principle, that the responsibility of these organisations for fixing vulnerabilities in the attack surface should be *joint*. All parties responsible for the attack surface would have a joint obligation to secure it when vulnerabilities are found, and each organisation who plays a role in the attack surface can be considered jointly and severally liable when the attack surface remains insecure. This would mean that it would not work for one organisation to blame the other for poor security—if things go wrong, both are responsible.

This joint responsibility for fixing vulnerabilities in the attack surface could solve current allocation issues between different organisations who play a role in the attack surface. It would mean, for example, that an supplier is responsible for bad encryption in s, but so is the operating system vendor who offers this encryption as a functionality in its software. And it should address the oft-recurring issue of who has to provide security updates for devices, such as phones. Under this approach, the device vendor *and* the operating system supplier both have a responsibility to close holes which are discovered in the system—the phone—through updates.

Of course, this obligation to secure the attack surface need not mean that operators, vendors and suppliers are *internally* responsible, in the same way, for fixing the holes in someone else's system. The requirement that security measures are "appropriate" means that the *internal* allocation of responsibility can differ according to the context. This would be similar to joint controllership under the: the data subject can hold both controllers liable, but—in the words of the Court—"the existence of joint liability does not necessarily imply equal responsibility of the various operators engaged in the processing of personal data", and the level of liability of each of them must be assessed with regard to the circumstances of the case.[26] The general civil law doctrine of joint liability and internal allocation of damages is also relevant and needs to be further explored.[27] As an example, factors which at first sight could play a role in the internal allocation of responsibility are:

- The *proximity* of the organisation to the potential vulnerability: where a certain vendor was the original developer of code, which was later found to contain a flaw, it makes sense that this vendor is primarily responsible for this part of the attack surface;
- The *costs* of maintaining the attack surface: where for example organisation A would be overburdened by mitigating a vulnerability and organisation B can easily bring out a patch, this speaks for allocating the responsibility for fixing it to organisation B;
- The *benefits* of a measure: the organisation which stands to benefit the most from the intervention arguably should bear the brunt of the costs;
- The *scale* of a measure: if organisation A can only maintain the attack surface of its own system, whereas organisation B can maintain *all* affected systems, this favours allocating the responsibility to organisation B; and
- The *speed* of maintenance: where organisation A can bring out a fix in one day, and organisation B takes a week, this favours allocating responsibility to organisation A.

The particulars of this internal allocation of responsibility is a topic for further study, also in light of the Cyber Resilience Act which is being negotiated at the time

[26] CJEU, Case C-40/17, Fashion-ID, Judgment of 29 July 2019, para 70.

[27] See for instance van Alsenoy 2016 for the conclusion that liability under data protection law is compatible with the non-binding Principles of European Tort Law.

of writing and should adress some of the issues relating to the protection of the attack surface.

Furthermore, I propose that this responsibility for the attack surface must not diminish over time. A CCTV camera remains a threat to information security, even—or particularly when—it is not being supported anymore. Sustainable information security governance means that the security of a product needs to be maintained as long as it still contains an attack surface. A possible solution for connected devices to prevent organisations having to support products indefinitely is to remotely disable the internet connection after a certain period, thus removing a significant part of the attack surface. Another option could be to hand over the maintenance of the security of a product to the user by providing access to the source code and giving the user the power to install their own software. This obviously requires further study as well.

8.4.2 Promote Research and Disclosure of Vulnerabilities

Governments can not only strengthen information security by taking measures—they can also promote research which uncovers vulnerabilities. In other words, they can put offensive information security research on equal footing with defensive information security research.[28]

One way of doing this, would be to simply make circumvention of security measures lawful, under both criminal and civil law, regardless of intent and regardless of what you do with your knowledge of the vulnerability. This would not be in line with the human rights obligations discussed in Chaps. 5 and 6: states are required to provide practical and effective protection to if not exclude, then at least minimise the risk of unlawful access.[29] Now, technical and organisational measures are one way to provide such protection; prohibiting circumvention of these measures is another way. There is, of course, an interaction between both levers: if you have strong security measures, you need less law enforcement, and if you have strong law enforcement this may decrease the need for good security. You will always need some legal rules aimed at prohibition: what is important for the information security cycle, is that knowledge of vulnerabilities are fed back into the system again.

A more proportionate approach is therefore to introduce an exception to liability for information security research in the public interest, as worked out below.[30] Such an exception should extend to both criminal and civil liability—which means that researchers cannot be prosecuted or held liable in any other way for doing their research. This also means that contractual restrictions on research and disclosure

---

[28] Bratus et al. 2014.

[29] The Court speaks of "unauthorised" access, but for clarity I use the same terminology as in the sections above; ECHR, Application no. 20511/03, I v Finland, Judgment of 17 July 2008, para 47; ECHR, Application no. 2872/02, K.U. v Finland, Judgment of 2 December 2008, para 49.

[30] See also ENISA 2018; ENISA 2013, para 2.4.3; Schaake et al. 2018, para 6.2.2; and OECD 2021, para 3.3; see also Zhao et al. 2017 which suggests the same because it would support the effectiveness of bug-bounty programs.

in line with the exception should be considered void, and, in their contracts with suppliers, states should not restrict research which falls within this exception.

The exception can be modelled along the lines of the guidelines for the non-prosecution of information security research by the Dutch public prosecutor. This means that information security research and disclosure is in the public interest if three conditions are met. Firstly, the activities may not go further than necessary for the goal of demonstrating the existence of vulnerabilities (proportionality). If research causes damage to a system, this should be considered disproportionate. Secondly, there is no other way to demonstrate the existence of vulnerabilities with less impact (subsidiarity). Lastly, the findings of the research must be disclosed in line with applicable coordinated vulnerability disclosure policies (more on this below). For evidence purposes, this also means that researchers will have to structure their research in such a way that they will subsequently be able to demonstrate that they acted in line with these principles. Putting the public interest at the core of this exception also implies that there is room to take into account the positive human rights impacts of disclosing a vulnerability in some cases.

Making the exception dependent on the disclosure of vulnerabilities is important: this is a translation of the idea under the right to science that research is dependent on an iterative process of sharing information and falsification. Merely doing information security research without disclosing your findings would not do justice to this principle. But I contend that this obligation to disclose on the basis of the right to communications freedom and the right to science goes further: it should apply, regardless of how you obtained knowledge of vulnerabilities, not only when you claim protection under these rights.

This means the rule should also apply to states: states should—*in principle, see below*—no longer be able to hoard vulnerabilities, and should instead disclose those vulnerabilities they are aware of. This policy follows as much from the right to science as it follows from the rights to privacy and communications freedom (because hoarding vulnerabilities increases the risk of unlawful access too much). One important question is what would the impact be on the work of national intelligence agencies when accessing adversaries' systems: to what extent do they rely on non-disclosed vulnerabilities, or can they simply rely on disclosed vulnerabilities which have not yet been patched and badly configured infrastructure? In 2021, the German Constitutional Court concluded that the fundamental right to confidentiality and integrity of systems does not require authorities to notify "any security vulnerabilities immediately and in all circumstances".[31] The Court continues that delaying notification must, however, be based on a legal framework that resolves the conflict between the different interests involved:

> It must be ensured that every time the authority decides whether to keep an unknown security vulnerability open, it assesses the risk of the vulnerability's existence becoming more widely known and it determines, in qualitative and quantitative terms, the benefit of potential state infiltration measures exploiting the vulnerability. Following a weighing of the risks and

[31] Bundesverfassungsgericht (BVerfG), IT-Sicherheitslücken, Judgment of 8 June 2021, 1 BvR 2771/18, paras 43–44.

benefits, the authority must report the security vulnerability to the developer unless the interest in keeping it open outweighs the risks.

Whether this conclusion is correct requires further research. My initial assessment is that the German Court gives too much leeway to states in this regard: on balance, the public interest favours immediate disclosure, and the burden rests on governments to demonstrate otherwise. This, given the poor state of information security, will be difficult to accomplish.

There is one important exception to the duty to disclose: if this is a vulnerability in a configuration of a single system of one organisation, disclosing would not necessarily help others with improving their own systems (unless this is a common mistake). In that case, it is questionable whether this can be derived from human rights obligations, because it does not affect the right to science, and the right to privacy and communications freedom do not call for such transparency. Thus, private organisations would not have to disclose the results of their pentesting (unless they uncover an actual, notifiable security breach, not a mere vulnerability). But if this is a vulnerability which is present across many organisations—a form of *class break* I discussed in Chap. 3–, then disclosing enables others to patch their systems.

I recognise that such a duty to disclose may have side effects. First, it may lead to less research on vulnerabilities. If you need to disclose a vulnerability, you might not want to be aware of its existence it in the first place—so you'd rather not investigate it.[32] It would also be likely to lower the price for bug bounties significantly—you have to disclose vulnerabilities anyway, so there is no point in asking for remuneration.[33] This measure will lastly limit the market for zero day exploits.[34] It also means that it is not useful for governments to insert vulnerabilities in systems on purpose. But what if some states are obliged to do this, but others are not, for example? A cynic might conclude that in that case, EU citizens would be less secure than the citizens of their adversaries, because EU intelligence agencies could not use knowledge of vulnerabilities as leverage against their counterparts. These effects need to be investigated further.

Another way in which governments can support the research and disclosure of vulnerabilities is by funding it. The European Union and member states need to dedicate a significant amount of money to prevent the introduction of weaknesses and have researchers investigate weaknesses in digital infrastructure.[35] Preventing weaknesses could be improved by emphasising training in formal methods and investing in a more secure architecture. In order to maximise the impact of this, the focus

[32] See for an older economics analysis of mandatory disclosure Choi et al. 2010.

[33] See on the economics of the market for bug bounties; Zhao et al. 2017; Zhou and Hui 2019.

[34] See Fidler 2015 for another approach to the market for zero days, advocating more enforcement for possession and use of exploits, as well as export control. See further Herr and Rosenzweig 2014, also advocating export control of exploits.

[35] It has also been suggested that states buy up zero days—this would not only lead to undesirable incentives (leaving bad code in software on purpose) but also strengthens the market for zero days, whereas I think the market should rather be weakened; Geer 2014; see Denning 2015 for a different perspective.

should initially be on systems which are integral to a large part of the infrastructure—for example encryption and authentication libraries, firewall code and access management systems. The findings of the research should of course be fed back into the system in order to fix any holes which are found.

Furthermore, it should be clarified that researchers—in the broad sense, meaning from an academic, professional or amateur background—should be free to develop, share and use tools for information security research, even if these tools could also be used for malicious purposes. In fact, governments could also consider funding some of the research tools to accelerate the cycle and close gaps more quickly. At the same time, the duty of care of researchers also requires them to mitigate the risk that tools will be used for this purpose, either by simultaneously offering a defence against abuse or by restricting the possibilities of the tool.

Lastly, in order to ensure that research interests are sufficiently reflected in policy making and that governance measures do not inadvertently affect legitimate activities, information security researchers should also be involved in this policymaking.

8.4.3 Fix Vulnerabilities When They Are Found

The framework for the research of vulnerabilities should be complemented with a framework for disclosing and acting on knowledge of vulnerabilities. At the core of this framework lies the idea that -policies (which are currently voluntary principles), should be embedded in a legal framework. This framework should apply to all organisations which play a role in the attack surface—the operator, vendor and supplier—and contain at least three main elements.[36]

First, it is important that each organisation should create a publicly available contact point for disclosing vulnerabilities and that reporting of vulnerabilities is standardised—this could, for instance, be done through an online form on the website of the organisation, through which everyone could submit vulnerabilities.[37] This would allow researchers to easily submit vulnerability reports and allow organisations to ensure they receive the right information. Researchers would at the same time, be required to submit vulnerability reports through these reporting mechanisms, to ensure that the knowledge of a vulnerability would reach the right person quickly.

A second element of this framework would be an obligation on the part of these organisations to act on the knowledge of a vulnerability.[38] This could be partly construed via a clarification of the obligation to take security measures—when you

[36] This paragraph sets out the major elements of such a framework—useful standards for details, such as how to secure the submission of vulnerabilities, are for example worked out in ISO. See also for similar suggestions ENISA 2018; Schaake et al. 2018; Herpig 2018; OECD 2021 (although the authors argue for voluntary, not mandatory notification of vulnerabilities).

[37] See also Oliveira da Silva 2019 for a similar recommendation.

[38] This has already been proposed as early as 2008; Anderson et al. 2008, para 6.5.1.

learn something has a weakness, and you do not act on it, this may imply that your level of security is no longer appropriate. But since the system also extends to other parties who play a role in the attack surface, this means that these parties would now have a joint responsibility to act on this knowledge—coordinating and sharing information among themselves where necessary. This also requires that these organisations should not be held liable for sharing information on vulnerabilities for coordination purposes. Some have suggested that s should play this role.[39] Whether this is a good idea would depend on the institutional governance structure—something which is beyond the scope of this book but is a worthy topic for further research.

The speed with which organisations have to handle a vulnerability report would depend on a number of factors, with the potential risk of exploitation being the primary factor. This risk depends partly on the severity of the impact: where for example this affects many devices, or many people, or important infrastructure, or human rights, this calls for a swift response. It depends in part on the likelihood of exploitation: where a vulnerability has already been exploited in the wild, this implies that a quick response is necessary, although one generally should assume that vulnerabilities are already being exploited.[40] Another factor is the costs of implementing a fix, and—related to this—the complexity of the coordination between different organisations in the attack surface. In order to ensure that organisations cannot drag this process out, the burden of proof to demonstrate that a response was appropriate would rest with the organisation which has learned of the vulnerability.

A third element of a legal framework would consist of measures to increase transparency about vulnerabilities. This could be done by officially recognising a central repository of vulnerabilities, to which operators, vendors and suppliers must report vulnerabilities they have learned of, including when they have been fixed. There are already central registers, such as the register, but these are privately run and not recognised in legislation. And the NIS2 Directive also accords ENISA a role in registering vulnerabilities, but only in the context of NIS2. This can be extended: this officially recognised repository would not only keep track of all vulnerabilities but would also disclose them for easy reference and provide aggregate reports on the time it takes to fix a vulnerability. This would improve the possibilities for enforcement and allow for further tweaking of the framework in the future.

8.4.4 Mandate a Manual Override

The last policy proposal which follows from the analysis above, is the introduction of a manual override for security measures, something which has been proposed by Cory Doctorow and the Electronic Frontier Foundation.[41] A manual override should

[39] See for example ENISA 2015, para 6.4.

[40] See also ISO, ISO/IEC 29147:2014—Information technology—Security techniques—Vulnerability disclosure, 15 February 2014, para 5.9.

[41] See Doctorow 2012; Portnoy and Eckersley 2017.

under certain circumstances allow users to *gain root*, to take control of a system and override restrictions on its use.

Under certain circumstances, because this obviously does not work for everything. In multi-user systems, there are good reasons for security restrictions—to prevent people from snooping in files without authorisation, for example, or to prevent them from spending money of others. Here, a manual override of security measures would only create a huge security hole, without much gain in individual freedom. These are not the places to impose a manual override obligation.

This is different where only one person uses a system. Here, security measures are not intended to protect the privacy of others; they are intended to protect the system against the user. This can be done for example to restrict the functionality of the device, usually for economic reasons—and these restrictions are usually imposed by a vendor or supplier of a device. For instance, the driving range of Tesla's cars partly depends on their software settings.[42] Another reason can be to protect people against themselves. For example, Apple currently only allows you to install apps from their app store on your iPhone, supposedly because these have been scanned for security threats.[43]

Whatever the reason, the interests of autonomy and self-determination in principle favour gaining control of a device and providing a manual override in single user systems would be the most proportionate way of doing so. Conversely, security measures which restrict human rights but do *not* provide this override would be allowed to be circumvented, and tools to circumvent measures which do not have an override should be allowed to be distributed and used.

Still, there are tricky implementation questions, and the economic consequences need to be thought through. May the manual override be subject to conditions? For example, can use of the override void the warranty or terminate the services being supplied? Similarly, if gaining root makes it impossible for organisations to protect the content being streamed to a device, may a content provider suspend the streaming? Another issue is related to the scope of this manual override: should a user be able to gain root of their electronic bike for example, overriding public safety measures such as a digitally enforced speed limit? A bike is a single user system, but overriding the speed limit can affect the safety of others. And what if your business model relies on locking down your device—will such a mandatory override then have the effect of people not being able to buy the device at all because it is too expensive? These are all valuable topics for further study.

42 See for example Moon 2020.

43 Apple 2021.

8.5 Topics for Further Research

This analysis only touches on some of the gaps in EU governance of the information security cycle. A lot of potential topics in this domain still remain to be explored. First, in this book I have barely discussed the relationship between trust, information security and human rights (in particular the rights to communications freedom). Information security can play an important role in ensuring trust in information and communications—for example, by ensuring that information has not been tampered with, or that it comes from a certain person. This also has an impact on communications freedom: generally speaking, measures which increase trust in communications are also supportive of communications freedom. On the other hand, the same security measures can also be used to disable or discourage anonymous or pseudonymous communications, something which affects communications freedom negatively. This is a topic worth further exploration.

Another topic which has not been touched on, is digital sovereignty—a term referring to regions and countries running their "own" digital infrastructure. Many countries in the EU are currently using technology provided by suppliers based outside the EU, including suppliers from countries who are not considered political allies. For example, some European states are using (or considering using) equipment from Huawei for their networks. There have been persistent rumours that Huawei's products contain backdoors that can be exploited by the Chinese government. In a worst case scenario, this would allow China to monitor and turn off a country's communications. One response would be switching to EU-made technology, although even this would not provide guarantees against hacking because, of course, states within the EU often have conflicting interests as well.

When states meddle with the digital infrastructure of other states, this can also have grave implications for human rights. If China switches off the mobile networks of the Netherlands, this obviously affects the right to communications freedom of all Dutch citizens (and others using those networks). I have not touched on what this means for EU governance of the information security cycle, but some observations can be made. First, if digital sovereignty in the EU is the aim, one should be hesitant to cooperate with countries such as the US and the UK, who have proven to be untrustworthy in this regard (see Chap. 3 for NSA's and GCHQ's attempts to undermine key information security technologies). The same is even more true for countries that are not considered political allies of the EU, such as China. Thus, it is doubtful that the EU's currently ongoing "sovereign cloud" project, which welcomes China and the US as technological partners, will deliver the digital sovereignty that the EU is aiming for.[44] Second, this sovereignty should extend to all parts of the attack surface, and thus calls for complete vertical integration of "digitally sovereign" products. This means that countries or at least regions will have to have their own manufacturing capabilities for a broad range of building blocks for digital infrastructure.

This also points to another aspect which I barely touch on in this book, namely the relationship between other aspects of information security, such as availability, and

---

[44] Grüll and Stolton 2020; see for a more limited and earlier analysis Maurer et al. 2015.

human rights. As illustrated by the above example, these aspects also have strong relationship to human rights, primarily to the right to communications freedom. It can be explored further how issues like the switching off of communications services remotely, or the disabling of online services through denial-of-services-attacks, relate to the human rights obligations of states, and in particular whether states have a responsibility to prevent this from happening.

The last point, which is worth exploring further, is the international aspect of the governance of the EU information security cycle. Vulnerabilities do not stay within country borders and the market for zero days is global. Updating governance in the EU would only address part of the problem—another part would have to be the international co-ordination of governance frameworks. One key issue is the non-proliferation of exploits via export-control: this is currently done through the Wassenaar Arrangement, but countries with large purveyors of malware, such as Israel, are not a party to this arrangement. Another key issue is the divergence in required security measures across regions. It is therefore worthwhile to explore the creation of an international treaty on the governance of the information security cycle.

References

Articles, Books and Other Documents

Anderson R, Böhme R, Clayton R, Moore T (2008) Security Economics and the Internal Market, 31 January 2008. https://www.enisa.europa.eu/publications/archive/economics-sec. Accessed 5 January 2024.

Apple (2021) Building a Trusted Ecosystem for Millions of Apps: A Threat Analysis of Side-loading, October 2021. https://www.apple.com/privacy/docs/Building_a_Trusted_Ecosystem_for_Millions_of_Apps_A_Threat_Analysis_of_Sideloading.pdf. Accessed 5 January 2024.

Bendiek A, Maat EP (2019) The EU's Regulatory Approach to Cyber-Security, SWP Working Paper, October 2019.

Bratus S, Arce I, Locasto ME, Zanero S (2014) Why Offensive Security Needs Engineering Textbooks. Or, How to Avoid a Replay of "Crypto Wars" in Security Research.;login: 39:6–11.

Choi JP, Fershtman C, Gandal N (2010) Network Security: Vulnerabilities and Disclosure Policy. The Journal of Industrial Economics 58:868–894. https://doi.org/10.1111/j.1467-6451.2010.00435.x

Cyber Security Raad (2021) Adviesrapport Integrale Aanpak Cyberweerbaarheid. https://www.rijksoverheid.nl/documenten/rapporten/2021/04/06/tk-bijlage-csr-adviesrapport-integrale-aanpak-cyberweerbaarheid. Accessed 5 January 2024.

Denning DE (2015) Toward More Secure Software. Communications ACM 58:24–26. https://doi.org/10.1145/2736281

Doctorow C (2012) The Coming Civil War over General Purpose Computing. https://memex.craphound.com/2012/08/23/the-coming-civil-war-over-general-purpose-computing/. Accessed 28 May 2021.

Doctorow C (2021) Neofeudalism and the Digital Manor. https://locusmag.com/2021/01/cory-doctorow-neofeudalism-and-the-digital-manor/. Accessed 2 July 2021.

ENISA (2013) The Directive on attacks against information systems: a good practice collection for CERTs on the Directive on attacks against information systems.

ENISA (2015) Good practice guide on vulnerability disclosure: from challenges to recommendations.

ENISA (2018) Economics of Vulnerability Disclosure, 14 December 2018. https://www.enisa.europa.eu/publications/economics-of-vulnerability-disclosure. Accessed 5 January 2024.

Fidler M (2015) Regulating the Zero-Day Vulnerability Trade: A Preliminary Analysis. Journal of Law and Policy for the Information Society (ISJLP) 11:405–484.

Fuster GG, Jasmontaite L (2020) Cybersecurity Regulation in the European Union: The Digital, the Critical and Fundamental Rights. In: Christen M, Gordijn B, Loi M (eds) The Ethics of Cybersecurity. Springer International Publishing, Cham, pp 97–115.

Geer D (2014) Cybersecurity as Realpolitik. https://media.kasperskycontenthub.com/wp-content/uploads/sites/63/2014/08/21032558/geer.blackhat.6viii14.txt. Accessed 5 January 2024.

Granick JS (2005) The Price of Restricting Vulnerability Publications. International Journal of Communications Law & Policy. 9:1–35.

Grüll P, Stolton S (2020) US and Chinese Tech Giants Welcomed into "EU Sovereign" Cloud Project. https://www.euractiv.com/section/digital/news/us-and-chinese-tech-giants-welcomed-into-eu-sovereign-cloud-project/. Accessed 23 October 2020.

Herpig S (2018) Governmental Vulnerability Assessment and Management, August 2018. https://www.stiftung-nv.de/sites/default/files/vulnerability_management.pdf. Accessed 5 January 2024.

Herr T, Rosenzweig P (2014) Cyber Weapons and Export Control: Incorporating Dual Use with the PrEP Model. SSRN Journal 8:301. https://doi.org/10.2139/ssrn.2501789

Maurer T, Skierka I, Morgus R, Hohmann M (2015) Technological Sovereignty: Missing the Point? In: 2015 7th International Conference on Cyber Conflict: Architectures in Cyberspace. IEEE, Tallinn, Estonia, pp 53–68.

Meulen N van der, A Jo E, Soesanto S (2015) Cybersecurity in the European Union and Beyond: Exploring the Threats and Policy Responses. https://www.europarl.europa.eu/RegData/etudes/STUD/2015/536470/IPOL_STU(2015)536470_EN.pdf. Accessed 5 January 2024.

Moon M (2020) Tesla Software Update Will Show Range Increase for the 2021 Model 3. https://www.engadget.com/tesla-software-update-range-increase-2021-model-3-094041207.html. Accessed 19 January 2022.

OECD (2021) Encouraging Vulnerability Treatment, 307, February 2021. https://www.oecd-ilibrary.org/science-and-technology/encouraging-vulnerability-treatment_0e2615ba-en. Accessed 5 January 2024.

Oliveira da Silva F (2019) Keeping Consumers Secure. How to Tackle Cybersecurity Threats through EU Law, BEUC-X-2019-066, 5 November 2019.

Portnoy E, Eckersley P (2017) Intel's Management Engine Is a Security Hazard, and Users Need a Way to Disable It. Electronic Frontier Foundation. https://www.eff.org/deeplinks/2017/05/intels-management-engine-security-hazard-and-users-need-way-disable-it. Accessed 28 December 2021.

Preston E, Lofton J (2002) Computer Security Publications: Information Economics, Shifting Liability and the First Amendment. Whittier Law Review 24:72.

Schaake M, Pupillo L, Ferreira A, Varisco G (2018) Software Vulnerability Disclosure in Europe: Technology, Policies and Legal Challenges, CEPS June 2018.

van Alsenoy B (2016) Liability under EU Data Protection Law. Jipitec 7:18.

van Daalen O (2022), In Defense of Offense: Information Security Research under the Right to Science, Computer Law & Security Review 46: 105706.

van Daalen O (2023a) The Right to Encryption: Privacy as Preventing Unlawful Access, Computer Law & Security Review 49:105804.

van Daalen O (2023b) The Right to Root: Constructing a Claim to Control Devices from the Right to Privacy, JIPITEC 14(2023:4): 580–593.

van Daalen O (2024) Developing a human-rights compatible governance framework for quantum computing, Research Directions: Quantum Technologies 2: 2024.

Verbruggen P, Wolters P, Sieburgh C, Jansen C (2016) Towards Harmonised Duties of Care and Diligence in Cybersecurity. SSRN Journal 78–107. https://doi.org/10.2139/ssrn.2814101
Zalnieriute M (2022) A Struggle for Competence: National Security, Surveillance and the Scope of EU Law at the Court of Justice of European Union. The Modern Law Review 85:1. https://doi.org/10.1111/1468-2230.12652
Zhao M, Laszka A, Grossklags J (2017) Devising Effective Policies for Bug-Bounty Platforms and Security Vulnerability Discovery. Journal of Information Policy 7:372–418. https://doi.org/10.5325/jinfopoli.7.2017.0372
Zhou J, Hui K-L (2019) Bug Bounty Programs, Security Investment and Law Enforcement: A Security Game Perspective. WEIS 2016. https://weis2016.econinfosec.org/wp-content/uploads/sites/6/2019/05/WEIS_2019_paper_36.pdf. Accessed 5 January 2024.
European Court of Auditors 2019, *Challenges to effective EU cybersecurity policy*, March 2019.
Ministry of Economic Affairs and Climate and the Ministry of Justice and Security of the Netherlands 2018, *Roadmap Digitaal Veilige Hard- en Software*, April 2018.

Table of Cases: National

Bundesverfassungsgericht (BVerfG), IT-Sicherheitslücken, Judgment of 8 June 2021, 1 BvR 2771/18.

Table of Cases: EU

CJEU, Case C-40/17, Fashion-ID, Judgment of 29 July 2019.
CJEU, Case C-540/03, European Parliament v Council of the European Union, Judgment of 27 June 2006.
CJEU, Case C-623/17, Privacy International v United Kingdom, Judgment of 6 October 2020.
CJEU, Cases C-511/18, C-512/18 and C-520/18, La Quadrature du Net, Judgment of 6 October 2020.
ECHR, Application nos. 13914/88; 15041/89; 15717/89; 15779/89; 17207/90, Informationsverein Lentia and Others v Austria, Judgment of 24 November 1993.
ECHR, Application no. 13936/02, Manole and Others v Moldova, Judgment of 17 September 2009.
ECHR, Application no. 20511/03, I v Finland, Judgment of 17 July 2008.
ECHR, Application no. 2872/02, K.U. v Finland, Judgment of 2 December 2008.

Chapter 9
Human Rights-Compatible Encryption Governance

Contents

Abstract This chapter takes the rights to privacy, data protection, communications freedom and science as a normative framework. It then applies this to the governance landscape with regard to encryption. It concludes that governance measures should be aimed at minimising the risks of unlawful access. This in practice means, given the pivotal role of encryption in information security, that governments cannot take measures which restrict the application of encryption technologies. Instead, governments should invest in the development and adoption of encryption technologies to minimise the risk of unlawful access.

Keywords Encryption · Unlawful access · Right to privacy and data protection · Confidentiality · Governance

O. van Daalen, *From Encryption to Quantum Computing*, Information Technology and Law Series 38, https://doi.org/10.1007/978-94-6265-635-2_9

9.1 Introduction

By a truly unbelievable coincidence, security researcher Moxie Marlinspike writes, he saw a small package fall of a truck in front him.[1] The package bore a name familiar to the surveillance cognoscenti: Cellebrite. It contained something unique: the tools used by police around the world to hack phones. Marlinspike was the boss of Signal, one of the worlds most popular encrypted communication apps, and there was evidence that Cellebrite could also extract Signal's encrypted messages from phones.[2] So he analysed the tool and this resulted in something surprising—the software was full of holes, which could be exploited by feeding the extraction machine with innocuous-looking files from a connected phone. Needless to say, this fundamentally affected the reliability of the evidence the police collected via Cellebrite's machines. At the end of his blog, Marlinspike announced something "completely unrelated":

> upcoming versions of Signal will be periodically fetching files to place in app storage. These files are never used for anything inside Signal and never interact with Signal software or data, but they look nice, and aesthetics are important in software. [...] There is no other significance to these files.

Of course this was in jest—there *was* significance to these files. If the police were to connect a Cellebrite machine to a phone which contained such a file, there now was a chance that the evidence collected via the machine would be destroyed, damaged or changed. The mere possibility of this happening was already sufficient to cast the evidence gathered via Cellebrite's machines in doubt.

Casting doubt on the validity of obtained data in such a way, in response to attempts to break your security, is not just an artful hack. It also illustrates that, just as the information security cycle is a continuous cycle of making and breaking, so encryption technologies are the subject of an ongoing arms race which has been going on for three decades. This arms race is fought both in the policy domain—by governments pushing for regulation, and civil society organisations and technology companies pushing back—and it is fought on the ground—by intelligence agencies secretly undermining these technologies, followed by technology companies developing defences. Meanwhile, the importance of encryption technologies to protect human rights has only grown. The question is what this means for the human rights-compatibility of governance in this domain? That is the topic of this chapter.

As noted previously, this chapter builds on the work of the earlier chapters.[3] In particular, because the interplay between encryption technologies and quantum computing is an example of the information security cycle in action, I will draw on the analysis of human rights-compatible governance of the information security cycle from the previous chapter. Mirroring the structure of the earlier chapter, I will first discuss the technological and regulatory landscape of encryption, then focus on

---

[1] Marlinspike 2021.

[2] Brewster 2021.

[3] Parts of this chapter have already been published in Van Daalen 2022, 2023a, 2023b and 2024.

the human rights requirements for encryption and then conclude with an analysis of human rights-compatible governance in this field (including suggestions for further research).

9.2 The Encryption Landscape

9.2.1 Positioning this Book in the Broader Literature

In the encryption governance debate, you essentially find two strands of argument. One is fundamental and non-negotiable. The other is about finding balance. The fundamental strand can be traced back to the 1990s. Here, on one side you have self-proclaimed libertarians and "cypherpunks" fantasising about "Crypto Anarchy"—a world in which the spread of cryptography would herald a new age of anonymity and confidentiality, severely undermining the power of governments and corporations. The Crypto Anarchist Manifesto, written in 1992 by an active contributor to the Cypherpunks mailing list, sums it up[4]:

> A specter is haunting the modern world, the specter of crypto anarchy. Computer technology is on the verge of providing the ability for individuals and groups to communicate and interact with each other in a totally anonymous manner. Two persons may exchange messages, conduct business, and negotiate electronic contracts without ever knowing the True Name, or legal identity, of the other. Interactions over networks will be untraceable, via extensive re-routing of encrypted packets and tamper-proof boxes which implement cryptographic protocols with nearly perfect assurance against any tampering. Reputations will be of central importance, far more important in dealings than even the credit ratings of today. These developments will alter completely the nature of government regulation, the ability to tax and control economic interactions, the ability to keep information secret, and will even alter the nature of trust and reputation.

These ideals have not lost traction since. Wikileaks' Julian Assange, in his introduction to a collection of conversations on internet freedom, wrote in 2012[5]:

> But we discovered something. Our one hope against total domination. A hope that with courage, insight and solidarity we could use to resist. A strange property of the physical universe that we live in. The universe believes in encryption. It is easier to encrypt information than it is to decrypt it. We saw we could use this strange property to create the laws of a new world. To abstract away our new platonic realm from its base underpinnings of satellites, undersea cables and their controllers. To fortify our space behind a cryptographic veil. To create new lands barred to those who control physical reality, because to follow us into them would require infinite resources. And in this manner to declare independence.

These are not mere observations or wishes about the power of cryptography—the authors have a vision on the role of government in an information society. *Lawful* access to encrypted information is not acceptable, because government meddling

[4] May 1992.

[5] Assange et al. 2012, p. 4.

should be kept to a minimum, period. Ideals on the role of state, however, also lead to an equally fundamental, opposite argument, one embraced by governments pushing for encryption restrictions: there can be—in the words of ex-FBI director Comey—no "law-free zones", no places which a government cannot reach.[6] This sentiment was echoed by Dutch minister Grapperhaus, when he said there can be "no excuse" for the communications of people sharing child sexual abuse material being inaccessible.[7] Let us call these positions *fundamental*—they take a principled position as the starting point and argue from there. And these fundamental positions have played an important role in the public debate on encryption governance since the nineties (see Chap. 3).

These fundamental approaches can be contrasted with a line of reasoning based on *balancing* costs and benefits. Here, the idea of lawful access to encrypted information is not dismissed out of principle. Instead, devising encryption policy is a matter of weighing the costs and benefits of enabling access to information. These balancing arguments also have a rich history, mostly in favour of strong encryption, which I discussed in Chap. 3. You can distinguish authors according to two things: the *factors* they emphasise when doing the balancing, and the *outcome* of the balancing. Let us provide a short recap here.

Some authors emphasise the *risks* of unlawful access—the *costs*. From a technical perspective, the papers by Abelson et al. deserve particular mention.[8] Other authors have extended this argument, for example arguing that information security will only become more important, and thus the impact of unlawful access will grow.[9] Hoepman on the other hand suggests that many of the risks of unlawful access can be overcome through smart engineering.[10] Lastly, there are authors who connect the risks to lawful access solutions with human rights, something I will discuss further in the coming sections.[11]

There are also authors who downplay the problem of going dark—the *benefits*. Some for example emphasise the value of non-encrypted information—we already live in a "golden age of surveillance".[12] Others emphasise alternative ways to gain access to encrypted information, which do not affect encryption technologies—"encryption workarounds"—such as guessing the key, compelling the key and exploiting a flaw in encryption software.[13] Some also expect that access will remain

[6] Comey 2014.

[7] Bouma 2019.

[8] Abelson et al. 1997, 2015, 2021.

[9] Landau 2017.

[10] Hoepman 2015.

[11] Andersen and Alisson-Hope 2022; Schulz and van Hoboken 2016; Kaye D, Report on encryption, anonymity, and the human rights framework, A/HRC/29/32, 22 May 2015; Elsayed-Ali 2016; Arnbak 2016, Chap. 4.1.

[12] Swire 2011.

[13] Kerr and Schneier 2018.

possible in the future, if only because service providers are economically dependent on retaining access themselves.[14]

As mentioned, not only do different authors emphasise different factors when doing the balancing: the *outcome* of this balancing exercise also differs. Most of those in favour of balancing argue for a hands-off approach: because the costs outweigh the benefits, governments must not interfere with encryption technologies. This starts with Koops, who concluded in 1999 that, given the circumstances at the time, such as the threats which would be addressed with regulation, the investigative powers available to authorities and the level of security of the digital infrastructure, the equities appear to favour not regulating encryption technologies.[15] It continues with digital rights organisations, such as the Electronic Frontier Foundation, Bits of Freedom, European Digital Rights initiative (EDRi) and Amnesty.[16] Arnbak argues, building on the work of De Hert and Hildebrandt, that states have a "system responsibility" when it comes to communications security—meaning that they not only must refrain from interfering with communications, but must also ensure that private parties protect communications security.[17] They can do so through a range of measures, and Arnbak considers that encryption by default "should count as a constitutional first line of defense".[18] Even Hoepman, who is critical of the technical objections raised against encryption proposals, concludes that the societal and ethical costs offset the gains of lawful access.[19]

Only a few groups come to a different conclusion. A US-based group of experts calling itself the Encryption Working Group is making an earnest attempt to see whether something other than a hands-off approach is viable. They conclude that the problem of granting access to data at rest on mobile devices via key escrow appears to be the most tractable, suggesting that further research in this area needs to be done.[20] Another position which you often hear in policy circles, is that governments should have the powers to hack computers and devices, instead of restricting encryption, which also means not sharing vulnerabilities with organisations.[21]

My analysis finds itself in Team Balance. Legislators who argue that as a matter of principle there cannot be "law-free zones" do not deserve to be taken seriously. Similarly, those who present the rights to privacy and communications freedom as absolute, have a political vision of government to which I do not subscribe. The goals of national security and law enforcement are a good reason to at least consider

---

[14] Gasser et al. 2016; Encryption Working Group 2019a, 2019b.

[15] Koops 1999, Chap. 11.

[16] Mckinney and Falcon 2021; Bits of Freedom Bits of Freedom's Encryption Archive. In: Bits of Freedom. https://www.bitsoffreedom.nl/tag/encryptie/. Accessed 19 January 2022; Elsayed-Ali 2016; European Digital Rights (EDRi) Encryption Archives. https://edri.org/tag/encryption/. Accessed 19 January 2022.

[17] Arnbak 2016, Sect. 4.6.

[18] Ibid., p. 212.

[19] Hoepman 2015.

[20] Encryption Working Group 2019a, 2019b.

[21] See for example Bellovin et al. 2014; see also Kerr and Schneier 2018 for a number of other approaches as an alternative to encryption.

granting lawful access to information and systems. But these need to be weighed against other risks, however, and I come to the conclusion that—given the human rights at stake—we need *more*, not less encryption. This is also where my analysis can be distinguished from previous literature on this topic. First, I develop the connection between human rights and encryption, building on the distinction between lawful and unlawful access developed in Chaps. 5 and 6. Second, I go further than a mere hands-off approach, developing the positive obligations of states with regard to encryption. This will be explained further below.

9.2.2 Even with Good Governance, Security Breaches Remain

In Chap. 2, it was concluded that information security is in a poor state—vulnerabilities are everywhere and policymakers are not doing enough about it. But even if they were, and the governance proposals of Chap. 3 provide an outline for this, security breaches will remain. Sometimes, it is just bad luck or stupidity. You lose your phone, or someone writes their password on a note and sticks it to their screen.

There are also more fundamental reasons. First, supply chains in digital infrastructure are complex. One device may contain thousands of components of hundreds of suppliers. Many of these suppliers provide drivers which use publicly available libraries from other developers, and the services running on top of this hardware use a stack of software components, developed and maintained by many more organisations, possibly hundreds more. It is already difficult to ensure that no vulnerabilities exist in one element of a system. It is even more difficult to verify that there are no vulnerabilities in a system *as a whole*, due to the complex interaction between different elements. This is why I proposed in the previous chapter that policymakers should approach information security governance as a cycle of making and breaking, because there will inevitably be a lot of breaking.

Second, information sent from system to system over the internet traverses many nodes spanning the globe. These nodes are operated by all kinds of organisations, many of which cannot be trusted, and each of which can be subverted.[22] Even if the EU took all the measures proposed in the previous chapter, it would not affect a significant chunk of the digital infrastructure which European citizens and organisations depend on. All this means that the current IT-landscape creates a serious risk of unlawful access, and things will stay that way in the future.

---

[22] See for a historical analysis of the design choice to place security at the edge of the network DuPont and Fidler 2016.

9.2.3 Encryption Technologies Restrict Unlawful Access

This is why encryption technologies are important: encryption technologies provide a modicum of security in an insecure world. Information security architects have long advocated the use of *defense-in-depth strategies* for protecting systems.[23] This means that you create a range of obstacles for attackers, so that if one protection measure fails, it does not take down the entire system. Encryption technologies can play a significant role there: even if an attacker is able to enter, say, an online system, if the data on the system is well encrypted, and the key is stored somewhere else, the attacker still can not access it.

This is also why encryption technologies are adopted in a variety of domains. First, encryption technologies are recognised as an important security measure in data protection regulation (see Chap. 3). For instance, the European Data Protection Board (EDPB) recognises it as defence against communication over insecure lines and storage in jurisdictions where governments may access the data contrary to European human rights laws. Recall that the European Court of Justice concluded that the transfer of personal data to the US was problematic under the GDPR in *Schrems I* and *Schrems II* due to US surveillance laws.[24] The EDPB in response to these decisions considered what safeguards were necessary to protect against such surveillance. It noted that well-implemented encryption can enable the transfer of personal data to the US, at least for backup purposes (because the NSA cannot access it).[25] But encryption technologies do not only protect against unlawful access by governments. They also protect against surveillance by others, such as cloud providers automatically analysing your data when you back it up, or network providers spying on your communications. Lastly, encryption technologies play a significant role in securing devices against loss. If you lose your phone or laptop, and it is not encrypted, it is relatively simple to extract all their data. Because our mobile devices contain a lot of sensitive data and information—family pictures, messages, passwords and even access to your bank account—if others are extracting this data, it can be disastrous. With encryption, you can make sure that even if you lose your device, you do not lose your data. That is why the dominant operating systems for laptops and phones (Apple, Google, Microsoft and Linux), all apply device encryption, in some cases by default (see Chap. 2).

9.2.4 And Encryption Technologies Restrict Lawful Access

The thing is, encryption technologies protect not only against *unlawful* access—they also protect against *lawful* access. They are a dual use-technology *par excellence.*

---

[23] See Schneier 2003, Chap. 8.

[24] CJEU, Case C-362/14, Schrems I, Judgment of 6 October 2015; CJEU, Case C-311/18, Schrems II, Judgment of 16 July 2020.

[25] EDPB 2020, para 79.

They restrict a whistleblower from sharing information with the press, even if it concerns information which everyone should know (see prior chapter). They restrict users who want to legally share culture with family and friends. And what about the organisations who are the victim of a ransomware attack? They are a victim of encryption technologies used to shut *them* out.

Now, this could provide a lot of issues for policymakers to be concerned about. But that is not what is driving the public debate. What concerns policymakers, and has kept them concerned for some decades, is how encryption technologies limit one particular form of lawful access: access by law enforcement and intelligence agencies. This is especially the case for the *user-controlled encryption technologies* discussed in Chap. 2 —technologies where only the users of the encryption have the decryption key. These user-controlled encryption technologies simply do not allow the possibility of accessing information lawfully, at least not without the cooperation of the user. As discussed, these kinds of technologies are increasingly applied by default, both in devices and messaging apps. This is why governments have been signaling that they are encountering more encryption in their investigations, which is making their lives more difficult (see Chap. 3).

9.2.5 *Encryption Makes Investigations More Difficult, Not Impossible*

To be sure, encryption undoubtedly affects the ability of law enforcement and intelligence agencies to do their work. It is not clear, though, to what extent these technologies merely make an investigation more *difficult*, or *impossible*. We depend on governments to provide the evidence; they are the ones who encounter encryption in their work, after all. The problem is that governments pushing for encryption regulation have made only a small amount of empirical data available, and what little data there is, does not support the conclusion that ubiquitous encryption prevents the solving of investigations—instead, it suggests that encryption technologies merely make investigations more challenging (see Chap. 3).

This makes sense. First, investigations are generally not dependent *only* on information which is encrypted. By investigating other sources—tracking phones, checking accounts, measuring internet traffic, accessing camera recordings, interviewing witnesses—you may still see what your suspects are *doing*, even if you do not know what they are *saying*. Encrypted data is just a piece of a large store of information, a store which arguably has grown in the past decades as digitisation has ushered in the "golden age of surveillance" I referred to earlier.[26]

Second, as discussed in Chap. 3, data may be encrypted, yet still be accessible. This is partly because encryption technologies do not work in isolation; there are various points of interaction in a broader system where the technologies can fail. A user may

[26] Swire and Ahmad 2011, in particular pp. 466–470; Swire 2011.

have chosen a weak password; the encryption algorithm was not implemented properly; or the key was not stored securely, etc. We also know that some of the encryption technologies which were presented as secure, were in fact undermined by intelligence agencies, or their keys were stolen. And law enforcement agencies in the EU have been running fake encrypted messaging services to snare criminals. Furthermore, some governmental agencies have the legal competence to exploit weaknesses in information security, to gain access and read information *before* it is encrypted—by hacking a device.

Lastly, governments invest a lot of money into computing power to attack encrypted data with brute force (see also Chap. 3). They might already be cracking some of the encryption measures in criminal investigations, for all we know. One of these brute force attacks may come from quantum computers, something which I discuss further in the next chapter.

9.2.5.1 Nevertheless, Governments Still Call for Curbing Encryption Technologies

The question as to whether encryption technologies merely make investigations challenging, or prevents them from doing their work is important, because not only are governments claiming that encryption prevents them from solving cases it is also the reason behind a concerted global effort to curb the use of encryption technologies. This started in the nineties, during the first "Crypto Wars". Governments around the world then attempted to mandate the use of weakened algorithms, to limit key length and to oblige the storage of keys with a third party.

Many opposed this. They did so primarily because it would increase the risk of unlawful access. Because if you make *lawful* access easier, you also increase the risk of *unlawful* access. If encryption can be broken by US intelligence agencies, why should it withstand attacks from Chinese intelligence agencies, now and in the future? And if you store keys with a third party provider, how can you make sure that the keys remain secure? But another concern was that it was ineffective: why would criminals start using these weakened encryption technologies if they can easily find stronger technologies online? Ultimately, the EU and US backed down in the face of broad resistance from commercial and human rights interests. There still are laws in some countries which limit the export, distribution and even *use* of certain encryption technologies, but in the US and the EU, at least, encryption technologies are at the time of writing still largely unregulated (see Chap. 3).

Recently, however, there has been a renewed push to ensure lawful access to encrypted information by law enforcement and intelligence agencies, a push which this time originates from policymakers in the EU and the US. In this new round, a number of approaches have been proposed which, its proponents hope, will prevent a rerun of the previous Crypto Wars. In particular, legislators are anxious to clarify that they do not propose weakening algorithms or mandating key lengths, presumably because it would increase the risk of unlawful access too much. Instead, one approach which has been the subject of public debate recently is scanning the information on a device before it is encrypted—client-side-scanning. Another is to amend the software so that you can covertly add others to a conversation, secretly generating keys for the silent participants. Finally, for device encryption, storing the keys with the technology provider is suggested.

What all these approaches have in common, though, is that they still increase the risk of *unlawful* access. To be clear, these approaches do not affect the encryption technologies themselves—and thus limit the risk of unlawful access by organised crime through brute force attacks. These approaches still introduce central points of attack that were not there before—an intelligence agency can try to gain access to the key provisioning service (for silently adding participants to chats and decrypting devices), to the monitoring lists (for client-side scanning) and to the keys stored with the provider (for device encryption).

In fact, some of the arguments which carried the day in the nineties, when the first proposals to curb encryption technologies were debated, have only become more convincing. If you store keys with a provider, these keys might be stolen (as has happened at times already, see Chap. 3). Similarly, if you create avenues for accessing communications, these may be exploited. Traditional wiretapping methods of course also create a risk, but this is particularly so for introducing new digital methods which enable *class breaks*, bulk access to data. Meanwhile, encryption technologies have now come to play a significant role in information security governance, and thus the stakes have only become higher. At the same time, the digital infrastructure has become even more difficult to secure. Connected to this is also another consideration, one which has not gotten much attention in this debate. Silently adding functionality to apps also affects the trust of the public in digital infrastructure, and in updating mechanisms in particular, while these mechanisms are essential to keep digital infrastructure secure.

The issues around *lawful* access have become more complicated as well. Encryption technologies are now deployed globally. Ensuring access to encrypted information requires a global effort. But this also means that you need to think about the circumstances under which governments may access this data. Can Saudi-Arabia gain access to monitor persons it considers a threat to the security of the state? Can China monitor the communications of Uyghurs? And who decides what should be on a client side scanning list? These questions obviously have a human-rights dimension.

Lastly, the saying from the nineties, that *if you outlaw strong crypto, only outlaws will still have strong crypto*, still rings true. If you force dominant communication providers to downgrade their encryption, ordinary people have little choice but to stay—because all their friends are on the same network. Criminals, on the other hand, can easily switch to a new network, one with strong encryption in place, because all their criminal friends have also switched. Thus, the effectiveness of these measures is still uncertain. The question is, what these considerations imply for a legal analysis under the Convention and the Charter. This will be explored further below.

9.3 Human Rights Requirements for Encryption Governance

Understanding the human rights implications of the governance of encryption technologies, requires an understanding of the function of encryption. Schulz and Van Hoboken in their study on encryption and human rights, make the connection between encryption and human rights by focusing on "human-facing communications (and information) properties, like confidentiality, privacy, authenticity, availability, integrity, anonymity" which these technologies protect.[27] They call this *human-facing*, to distinguish it from cases where humans do not benefit from its application (think of ransomware). They argue that these properties deserve protection against state interference, because they "effectuate" the protection of human rights.[28] In this book, I focus on one way in which encryption technologies effectuate this protection: by restricting access to information—in other words, I focus on the *confidentiality* of information. For other information properties that encryption technologies may provide, such as authenticity and integrity, this analysis may also be useful, but this requires further study.

Now, encryption technologies may restrict access, but the human rights impact depends on who is doing the restricting. If only spies are using encryption, there are not many human rights involved. But if ordinary people are using it, then indeed there are. One author who put these considerations squarely on the map is Rogaway. In *The Moral Character of Cryptographic Work*, he sounded the alarm—underscoring that cryptography research, which may appear to be neutrally solving mathematical puzzles, always benefits one side more than the other.[29] In the words of Rogaway: "Cryptography rearranges power: it configures who can do what, from what." As we will see, this notion plays a central role in the human rights assessment of the governance of encryption technologies.

The assessment I will set out below, follows the same approach as the assessment of information security cycle governance, building on the work by Schulz and Van Hoboken.[30] For the evaluation of restrictive measures under states' negative obligations, the first question is whether these measures should be considered an interference? Second, you need to determine whether the interference is necessary in a democratic society. For encryption technologies, this question of necessity is a serious hurdle to clear: policymakers must demonstrate that they cannot achieve their goals—solving cases, gathering intelligence—without such restrictions (see Chap. 3). And third, you need to determine whether a measure is proportionate. In

[27] Schulz and van Hoboken 2016, p. 13.

[28] Ibid., p. 53.

[29] Rogaway 2015; see Narayanan 2013a and 2013b for a somewhat related set of articles on the societal function of cryptography.

[30] Schulz and van Hoboken 2016; see for an earlier analysis Kaye D, Report on encryption, anonymity, and the human rights framework, A/HRC/29/32, 22 May 2015; and for a somewhat similar, though US-focused approach Landau 2017.

all cases, the risk of unlawful access plays a central role in this analysis, as we will see below.

This risk of unlawful access also plays a central role in the assessment of *positive obligations*. The question there is: to what extent do states have an obligation to minimise this risk, through measures strengthening encryption technologies? As set out in the previous chapter, this requires a balancing of, on the one hand, the current risks of unlawful access, and on the other hand, the interests of the public in not strengthening these measures. The considerations in *I. v. Finland* and *K.U. v. Finland* are an important yardstick: what is required is "practical and effective protection to exclude any possibility of unauthorised access occurring in the first place", but the right to privacy and communications freedom "must yield on occasion to other legitimate imperatives, such as the prevention of disorder or crime or the protection of the rights and freedoms of others".[31]

These elements will be discussed below. Before we begin, let me acknowledge that the assessment of states' obligations under human rights law of course ultimately depends on the specifics of particular governance measures and the factual circumstances. But I believe that the role of encryption technologies is so important, that it is possible to provide more general guidance to policymakers.

9.3.1 The Assessment of an Interference

First, the question of interference. As discussed in Chap. 3, there is a problem there, because restrictive governance measures aimed at encryption technologies merely create the *possibility* of surveillance, they do not constitute surveillance themselves. In my analysis of case law under the Convention and the Charter, however, I conclude that the mere existence of this possibility should be considered an interference. As discussed in the previous chapter, courts have reviewed surveillance powers in abstract as an interference in itself, and they have considered the mere storage of personal data to be an interference, because of what might be done with it in the future. The reason for this, is that it may lead to *chilling effects*, to a general fear in the population that their data may be accessed—and as a result people will not store certain information or communicate certain things.

Consequently, as set out in Chap. 5, the central question here is whether a measure significantly increases the risk of unlawful access to privacy and communications freedom interests, even in the face of governmental measures to prevent this? To be clear: the risk of *lawful* access need not be taken into account for this analysis—the risk of *unlawful* access is already sufficient to constitute an interference. If, however, such a measure increases the chance of lawful access as well, this may also constitute an interference under the analysis in Chaps. 5 and 6. This is because these measures also have chilling effects—for instance, if you know that your communication *may* be

[31] ECHR, Application no. 20511/03, I v Finland, Judgment of 17 July 2008, para 47; ECHR, Application no. 2872/02, K.U. v Finland, Judgment of 2 December 2008, para 49.

increasingly surveilled because your encryption is weakened, even if this surveillance is lawful, you might think twice before saying something controversial. This is similar to the argument put forward by Schulz and Van Hoboken: measures which restrict the use and deployment of encryption, restrict "uninhibited communications", and therefore constitute an interference with the right to privacy and communications freedom.[32] Just to be clear, if there is an interference, this does not necessarily mean that this interference is disproportionate—this requires a separate assessment.

Based on the reasoning above, I conclude that governance measures that negatively impact the availability, application or effectiveness of encryption technologies are an interference with the rights to privacy and communications freedom.[33] I mention the *availability* because, first, you need to have access to these technologies. But then the *application* becomes important, because even if you have access, you must be able to use these technologies. Even if you are allowed to use them, they must work well—this is why I also mention the *effectiveness*. And the reason why these are considered an interference is because, as discussed above, such measures significantly increase the risk of unlawful access to information protected by privacy and communications freedom.

Similarly, where measures are aimed at obliging software companies to introduce new functionality for monitoring information on user devices, this should also be considered an interference with the rights to privacy and communications freedom. This is relevant, for example, where states oblige client-side scanning on a device: pushing this functionality and monitoring lists on a phone is already an interference. The same goes for measures that oblige providers to update their chat software, so that participants can be silently added. The reason why this is an interference has nothing to do with an increase in unlawful or lawful access—it is an interference because it affects the right to device self-determination discussed in Chap. 5, as it restricts your control over your own device. I will touch on this in the section below, but this is a topic worthy of further research.

9.3.1.1 Domestic Restrictions

Under the analysis above, many regulatory measures proposed by governments in relation to encryption technologies should be considered an interference (see Chap. 5). All these measures significantly increase the risk of unlawful access, as explained in Chaps. 5 and 6. This firstly goes for historically proposed measures, such as mandating weakened algorithms and imposing maximum key lengths for domestic use or distribution. Here, it is to be expected that foreign adversaries and

32 See Schulz and van Hoboken 2016, p. 55.

33 You might ask whether it is possible to direct measures to only certain *classes* of encryption technologies, namely those which do not protect human rights interests. This is not what policymakers want, though. The types of encryption technologies governments are focusing on, are encryption technologies used by ordinary individuals, precisely because they can also be used by criminals. It is much less interesting for law enforcement and intelligence agencies to gain access to encryption technologies which are only used in, say, an industrial context.

criminals will exploit the imposed weaknesses. This also goes for measures to store keys with a third party—we know that foreign adversaries have no qualms breaking into these repositories either.

This also applies to the newly proposed measures discussed in this book: client-side scanning, covertly adding governmental agencies to a conversation and storing the keys with a provider. As discussed, from a human rights perspective these measures have one advantage over previously proposed approaches—they leave the encryption unaffected. Still, just as in the previous chapter I proposed that the *attack surface* should be the atomic unit for assessing measures in the information security cycle, so must the attack surface be the unit by which measures with regard to encryption must be evaluated. From this perspective, these newly proposed measures primarily *shift* the point of attack, but do not reduce the attack surface. For client-side scanning and covertly adding new participants, attackers will focus on surreptitiously changing client software and exploiting the mechanisms for monitoring communications at the endpoint. This not only increases the risk of unlawful access of information—it also increases the risk of unlawful control of a device. And when storing the key with providers, attackers will focus on the key repositories—as the exploits of the NSA and GCHQ in Chap. 3 demonstrate. This is exactly why user-controlled encryption is so important, because for those technologies there is no central key repository.

Now, it is not only *regulation* aimed at encryption technologies that can be an interference—the same goes for covert actions to undermine the availability or effectiveness of these technologies, as documented in Chap. 3. Secretly weakening encryption standards by bribing companies or by subverting the standard-setting process fall under this header. Similarly, acquiring a communications company to install backdoored crypto, or purchasing the entire stock of communication technology with strong encryption technologies, thus forcing people to use weaker encryption, can be considered an interference. The reason, again, is that these measures significantly increase the risk of unlawful access. As a sidenote, it is uncertain whether all state interventions in the encryption landscape that we know of (for instance where the Dutch police have been secretly running encrypted messaging services), comply with the foreseeability requirement under the Convention and the Charter; this is something worth investigating in specific cases. This will not be discussed further in this book.

One governance measure which does *not* necessarily constitute an interference, is the research and development of computing power to attack encrypted information with brute force. Developing these machines *in itself* does not increase the risk of unlawful access. The opportunity for criminals or intelligence agencies—other than the one operating these computers—to covertly use these computers to decrypt information, is small. This may be different where this power is used to create large collections of keys to later decrypt information, because those keys can be easily stolen, creating an attractive target for adversaries (see above).

Where the *application* of this computing power is used to decrypt particular information protected by human rights, however, such as private communication, this *should* be considered an interference, because you gain access to something which was not previously accessible. Given that I concluded above that a significant increase in *lawful access* may also constitute an interference, there could be situations where the development of this computing power in itself should already be considered an interference. I discuss the conditions for the application of this power below.

9.3.1.2 Export Restrictions

The assessment of the control of exports outside the EU warrants separate analysis, if only because export control measures of civilian encryption technologies still exist in some parts of the world, and the EU might consider reintroducing this as well (see Chap. 3).[34] The issue here is that at first sight the control of exports outside of the EU also has an impact outside of the EU, and it is uncertain to what extent European human rights instruments apply there. The protection under the Convention focuses—roughly speaking—on people in Europe.[35] For the Charter, this is more complex. There are good arguments why the Charter's applicability extends beyond the border of the EU.[36] For one, the Charter does not explicitly restrict its territorial scope. The European Commission has also indicated that respect for the Charter is a "binding legal requirement in relation to both internal and external policies".[37] The Treaty on the European Union also requires that EU external action must be "guided" by human rights and fundamental freedoms, and that the EU shall contribute to the protection of human rights in its relations with the wider world.[38] This is also why the EU has curbed the export of cyber-surveillance technologies in its Dual-Use Regulation.[39]

However, even if the EU has *no* responsibility whatsoever to protect the human rights of people outside of the EU, a case can still be made that export control on encryption technologies constitutes an interference. Generally speaking, it makes no sense to interpret territorial restrictions strictly where technologies are globally available and communications span the globe. To put it bluntly: if the EU has its privacy and security protections in order, but these are undermined as soon as people, products or data leave the EU, then the protections within the EU do not amount to much. This is clearly the case for encryption technologies which are used in communications between people inside and outside of the EU. Here, export measures affect the privacy and communications freedom interests of people in the EU, because these people in the EU are not able to communicate securely with their counterparts

[34] See for a partly similar analysis Budish et al. 2018.

[35] Article 1 of the Convention obliges parties to secure the rights of the Convention to "everyone within their jurisdiction".

[36] See further the analysis in van Daalen et al. 2021, para 2.4; Kassoti 2020.

[37] See DG Trade 2015, p. 5.

[38] Consolidated version of the Treaty of the European Union, Article 3(5) and Article 20.

[39] (2021) Regulation of the European Parliament and of the Council Setting up a Union Regime for the Control of Exports, Brokering, Technical Assistance, Transit and Transfer of Dual-Use Items (Recast); see on this van Daalen et al. 2021.

outside of the EU. An example of this are the downgrade attacks discussed in Chap. 3, where an attacker could force the browser to use a communications protocol which was weakened in order to comply with export control regulations. You could also argue that export control constitutes an interference, where the EU prohibits the export of certain strong encryption technologies and as a result only weak encryption technologies will be incorporated by default in products, which are then imported in the EU again. One could also argue that when people from the EU visit a country with weaker encryption technology due to EU export restrictions, their human rights under the Convention and the Charter are also affected. Lastly, you could argue that strong encryption technologies are important for securing the data of EU citizens transferred outside of the EU—the GDPR requires that the transfer of data outside of the EU remains sufficiently protected after all.

It is not necessary to pursue this argument further, because limiting the export of these kinds of technologies outside of the EU should also be considered an interference with the right to communications freedom and the right to science of people in the EU. This was also the reasoning on which a US court struck down export control regulations on the basis of the First Amendment of the US constitution in *Bernstein* in 1999.[40] The assessment under the First Amendment of course differs from that under the Convention, the Charter and the Covenant. It is clear that encryption technologies embody the results of scientific findings, and these are also protected by the right to communications freedom and science under European human rights instruments. The fact that these findings not only constitute knowledge, but also *do* something does not matter for this assessment. Sure, you might say, but quantum computers also "embody" knowledge—are then export controls of quantum computers also an interference with the right to communications freedom? No—there is an important difference between quantum computers and encryption software: the latter is information, and the first is not. This means that here, export controls on elements of quantum computers are primarily governed by the right to science, something I will discuss in the following chapter.

9.3.2 The Assessment of Necessity

After having established that there is an interference, you will then have to first assess whether these measures are "necessary" under the Convention, Charter and Covenant. This means that there must be "a pressing social need", that restrictions on the right to privacy must be "strictly necessary" and that the reasons justifying a measure must be relevant and sufficient (see Chaps. 4 and 5). Whether something is "necessary", is difficult to determine, however, at least in the abstract. For this, we are heavily dependent on information from governments, requiring a case-by-case analysis of proposed measures in a specific context.

[40] 9th Cir., Bernstein v U.S. Dept. of Justice, Judgment of 6 May 1999, 176 F.3d 1132.

What can be said, is that the already presented body of evidence in support of new measures by policymakers falls short of the mark (discussed in Chap. 3). The evidence presented does not answer the question of whether restrictions on encryption technologies are *necessary*. Instead, these documents in the most favourable reading merely makes the case for them being *useful*. Encryption may result in an investigation requiring more time, or more manpower, but solving a case is almost never a binary question of having access to encrypted information. This in itself would already be sufficient for any interference to be incompatible with the discussed human rights under the Convention and the Charter: the *need* to impose these restrictive measures has simply not been demonstrated.

So, what do governments actually need to demonstrate to live up to this high standard? In *Szabó*, the Court clarified that in privacy cases, a measure should not only be necessary for safeguarding democratic institutions, but also be strictly necessary for obtaining vital intelligence *in an individual operation*.[41] This consideration is also relevant for the governance of encryption technologies. This doesn't mean that you need to review the compatibility of a governmental measure on the basis of individual operations, but it does mean that a review cannot be abstract and has to take account of how a competence is applied in individual cases. This means, firstly, that a government must show that the investigative powers it already has, do not suffice. This is not only a matter of showing in the abstract that they are missing an important piece of the puzzle from the available data. They also need to account for the powers already granted to them as a government. Here, the adoption of new powers to hack computers, as discussed in Chap. 3, merits special attention. These laws provide a specific method to gain access to information *before* it is encrypted. Where a government, such as the Netherlands, has adopted such laws, any proposal to curb encryption technologies must also contain an analysis that these laws *have been used* where this was warranted, and still it is necessary to obtain the power to decrypt information.

In addition to an analysis of the *powers* a government has, it is also necessary to review the *capabilities* of a government—that is, the people and tools available to a government to prevent crime and protect national security. Of course, this largely falls within the margin of appreciation accorded to each state: every state may decide for itself how it allocates its budget between different departments. To the extent that a government has made a specific choice with regard to certain capabilities, it needs to at least demonstrate that these currently available capabilities do not suffice. For example, if a government has already invested in brute force capability to decrypt information, then this is an important consideration when determining whether a measure weakening encryption is necessary.

[41] ECHR, Application no. 37138/14, Szabó and Vissy v Hungary, Judgment of 12 January 2016, para 85.

9.3.3 *The Assessment of Proportionality*

But even if a measure is necessary, it must also be proportionate. This question is the most difficult to assess in the abstract: it depends on the specifics of a technology and what a government is trying to achieve. In general, though, the risk of residual unlawful access and control created by the measure, must be balanced against the aim of the measure, such as law enforcement or national security. I discuss this balance in the sections below. First the focus will be on the practical issue of enabling lawful access and control in a global world. I then discuss the role of encryption technologies in empowering individuals against unlawful access. Then different governance approaches—such as export control or undermining encryption technologies—will be assessed against the human rights framework set out above.

9.3.3.1 The Global Governance of Encryption Technologies

First, a difficult practical problem: how to shape the framework for lawful access and control in a world where encryption technologies are used globally? There are basically two options here. One option is to impose a single framework for lawful access which is based on the requirements for lawful access in one particular country or region, such as the EU. This would mean the Chinese could only gain access to encrypted data where the required safeguards for lawful access under the Convention and the Charter are in place. This would be problematic from a political perspective. Say, for instance, that the US and the EU would be driving this effort. Their respective surveillance frameworks are already sufficiently different so as to be incompatible (see *Schrems I* and *II*).[42]

The alternative approach—granting access and control pursuant to different frameworks per region—would be even worse from a human rights perspective. Then the Chinese state could under their own surveillance laws gain access to the communications of Uyghur persons, and the Saudi government could gain access to the communications of political dissidents under *their* laws. Of course, these countries could already attempt to force service providers to provide access to information and communication under their own laws, but at least there is the possibility for people to, perhaps in secret, apply user-controlled encryption technologies.

The question thus becomes, under which circumstances may the EU or its member states agree to a surveillance framework for lawful access and control incorporated into globally adopted encryption technologies? Must such a framework comply with the safeguards required in the Convention and the Charter, even if this surveillance regime is only applied to persons or situations which are not protected under the Convention and the Charter? As noted, there will be little political appetite at the EU level for this. The European Union sees itself as a defender of human rights outside of

[42] CJEU, Case C-362/14, Schrems I, Judgment of 6 October 2015; CJEU, Case C-311/18, Schrems II, Judgment of 16 July 2020.

the region, as the adoption of export control of cyber-surveillance items in the Dual-Use Regulation demonstrates. But as set out above, good arguments can also be made that the Convention and the Charter would stand in the way. First, these instruments apply to the external policies of the EU and its member states. This means that the EU—which would be driving the effort for such a lawful access framework—has a responsibility under the Charter to prevent human rights infringements of people outside of the EU. What's more: in a globalised world, it is likely that people in the EU would also be subject to the surveillance framework of countries outside of the EU—for instance when communicating with people outside of the EU, when using services outside of the EU or when their data travels outside of the EU.

9.3.3.2 Encryption as Empowering Technology in a World of Insecurity

Even if you were to succeed in solving this conundrum, there is also a more fundamental argument to reckon with. Encryption technologies are not merely *a* technology protecting against unlawful access: they are *the core technology*. Encryption technologies are the technological embodiment of the principle of informational self-determination as well as protection against arbitrary interference and against abuse of surveillance powers. This is also echoed in the judgment of the German Constitutional Court on the right to confidentiality and integrity of IT-systems, discussed in Chap. 5.[43] This is what Rogaway speaks of, when he says encryption is about power. By enabling persons to determine with whom they want to share information, encryption technologies empower individuals, against governments and organisations.

Empowering individuals has never been more important. As discussed above, our digital infrastructure is already now notoriously insecure; encryption is one of the few technologies which can provide a measure of protection against unlawful access. This will become even more important in the future. The private and public surveillance, both lawful and unlawful, of our digital infrastructure is on the rise. There is no reason to think that the upward trajectory of collecting and analysing ever more data will be reversed in the future. Data on citizens may be collected lawfully now but could be used against them if a more totalitarian regime takes power, in violation of the Convention and the Charter. What is more, we do not even need a future government to make the argument—there are already governments which have no qualms about killing their political opponents on the basis of covertly collected data, even outside of their own border: think of Saudi Arabia killing Khashoggi in Turkey (see Chap. 3). Encryption can provide some protection, against some of these practices (but probably would not have saved Khashoggi).

This brings me to the most fundamental argument, an argument which does not really depend on the specifics of governance measures of encryption technologies.

[43] See also Schulz and van Hoboken 2016, p. 38: "In summary, it can be said that in the digital environment, the right to informational self-determination in Germany implies the right to use encryption with regard to its IT system."

Given the above considerations, the importance of empowering ordinary individuals and organisations through encryption technologies simply outweighs the other interests at stake. This means that governance measures that negatively and significantly impact the availability, application or effectiveness of encryption technologies are disproportionate. We simply cannot afford to expand the attack surface or increase the risk of unlawful access or control of information and systems protected by the rights to privacy and communications freedom. This argument holds, even if the risks of unlawful surveillance by *governments* is minimised, because it still increases the risk of unlawful access by other parties, in particular by state actors. Simply put—we need more encryption, not less, and any governance measures which lead to less encryption go too far. So what are these measures?

9.3.3.3 An Analysis of Different Government Measures

Measures affecting encryption technologies. Most importantly, this includes regulatory measures which prohibit or make it more difficult to distribute or apply user-controlled encryption technologies. As discussed, user-controlled encryption technologies are particularly important in empowering the user, because only the user gets to decide who can gain access. If you *directly* prohibit distribution or use of these technologies, this should be considered disproportionate.

Similar measures which do not focus on encryption technologies as such, but still negatively impact the security of the system as a whole, are less problematic but not compatible with human rights requirements either. These include measures such as mandatory client-side scanning, changing software to enable covertly joining a call and obliging key storage with a provider. These measures are less problematic because they still allow the application of user-controlled encryption technologies in communications and in device storage, thus still protecting against private surveillance and device loss. In that sense, these measures maintain some of the protection provided by user-controlled encryption technologies. But as discussed above, they simultaneously undermine the effect of these technologies by enabling access through other means; they increase the attack surface elsewhere. As a result, they still significantly increase the risk of unlawful access, in particular by powerful attackers, such as intelligence agencies and well-resourced criminals—it's just that the attack has shifted to a different part of the infrastructure. In fact, because this measure not only affects *access* to encrypted information, but also *control* of the devices used to encrypt the information, the impact may be even worse from a human rights perspective.

The same goes for measures which *in practice* affect the application of these technologies. This includes measures mandating that certain technologies should not be turned on by default. It also includes measures in which governments treat encrypted data with fewer safeguards than non-encrypted data, for example where the use of encryption is considered suspicious, or where it justifies storing the data indefinitely.[44] This also makes it more difficult to apply user-controlled encryption technologies.

Non-regulatory measures that negatively impact the effectiveness of encryption technologies in a significant way should also be considered disproportionate. These include covertly subverting encryption technologies, rigging standard setting processes and the hoarding of weaknesses of encryption technologies.

And what about pre-existing rules which weaken encryption technologies, such as those which currently oblige telecommunications providers to use encryption which can be broken at the request of law enforcement or intelligence agencies—are these also disproportionate? Not necessarily. The thing is that telecommunication providers transporting traffic as intermediaries simply cannot apply user-controlled encryption technologies—their reach currently does not extend to the devices of people. Conversely, users have nothing to say about what happens on a network. Nodes of telecommunications networks, including those operated by telecommunications providers, should therefore be considered untrusted anyway. This why it is much more important to facilitate the application of user-controlled encryption to communications traversing over these networks, in particular by applying encryption by default. This also explains why it is important that user-controlled encryption technologies remain available, effective and can be easily applied.

Advanced decryption capabilities. The application of advanced decryption capabilities, such as through brute force attacks, requires a different analysis. As discussed above, the development of these capabilities may be an interference where they significantly increase the risk of *lawful access*. But then, the proportionality of that interference revolves around the application of surveillance frameworks for such lawful access (if it concerns encrypted information which is protected by the right to communications freedom and privacy). Here, the requirements under the Convention and the Charter with regard to lawful access in the context of secret surveillance apply (see Chap. 5, in particular *Zakharov*).

First, brute force attacks are inherently limited because it costs money and effort to use them, which already ensures a modicum of proportionality. This does not mean, however, that there can be no abuse of this power in individual circumstances. Therefore, persons should be given adequate protection against arbitrary interference. This can be done by clearly circumscribing the conditions under which this power may be applied; setting out the nature of the offence; the scope of people who may be subject to an order; limiting the duration; defining a procedure for storing, examining and using decrypted data; determining how the data must be communicated; and the circumstances in which data may or must be deleted. Second, there need to be adequate and effective measures against the abuse of surveillance powers. This assessment is dependant on all the circumstances of the case, such as the nature,

[44] The ECHR addressed this question once, but in a different case, namely where an encryption service had been specially designed for and exclusively used by a criminal organisation, and with regard to a different right (Article 5 Convention). It, however, also concluded that the mere fact that someone had used an encrypted service, without additional evidence, cannot lead to a "reasonable suspicion"; ECHR, Application no. 19699/18, Akgün v Turkey, Judgment of 20 July 2021, paras 178–181.

scope and duration of the possible measures, the grounds required for ordering them, the authorities competent to authorise, carry out and supervise them, and the kind of remedy provided by the national law. The exercise of these powers needs to be supervised before, during and after decryption, by an independent and impartial body, preferably a judge. When it is possible, subjects need to be notified after decryption has taken place.

There is a problem with this supervision. Because information is encrypted, you cannot know in advance what data you are decrypting, how many people it concerns and how sensitive it is. You might be able to guess, in certain cases, but you cannot know for sure. As a result, you might inadvertently be decrypting information which is protected by legal privilege, such as attorney-client communications, or that otherwise requires special treatment, such as communication between a journalist and a whistleblower. This means that for the decryption of this data, the most stringent regime must apply. Decryption must firstly be restricted to specific files. As noted above, it is also important that the decryption be supervised by a judge or other independent and impartial body before, during and after the process. Where there is a risk that the decryption might unlock information which is covered by special duties of confidentiality, such as information revealing journalistic sources and attorney-client communication, this court or other independent and impartial body must also *preview* the decrypted information beforehand.[45] Furthermore, the subject must be notified as soon as this can be done without jeopardising the investigation.

Research of encryption technologies. Finally, measures which negatively impact the *research* into encryption technologies are in most cases incompatible with the Convention and the Charter. These include measures limiting research into cryptography and sharing the findings thereof, and also through export control of encryption technologies. This is not—or not primarily—because these measures interfere with the rights to privacy, but because the research activity is protected by the right to science and the right to communications freedom. Cryptography research is a prime example of the cyclical nature of information security. To the extent that this research is focused on encryption technologies which protect the rights to privacy and communications freedom, this argument becomes even stronger. In the words of Rogaway, looking for ways to break encryption—cryptanalysis—*supports* encryption[46]:

> One might misinterpret the academic cryptanalytic undertaking as an attack on the privacy of legitimate users—an attack on the inoffensive Alice and Bob—which would thus seem to favor power. But this is the opposite of the right view. The reason that academic cryptographers do cryptanalysis is to better inform the designers and users of cryptosystems about what is and what is not safe to do. The activity is not done to surveil people, but to help ensure that people are not surveilled—at least by cryptanalytic means. And the work routinely has exactly that effect.

[45] See ECHR, Applications nos. 58170/13, 62322/14 and 24960/15, Big Brother Watch and others v United Kingdom (Grand Chamber), Judgment of 25 May 2021, para 445.

[46] Rogaway 2015, p. 23.

Restricting the right of researchers to choose their own lines of enquiry, and communicate the results interferes with this cycle and need to be assessed against the framework described in the previous chapter. This means, in short, that doing cryptographic research and sharing the results must be permitted, as long as researchers minimise damage while doing the research, and while disclosing their findings.

9.4 Recommendations for Human-Rights Compatible Governance

What must governments do in view of these human rights requirements? I argue that governments have positive obligations to safeguard a vibrant encryption landscape, to minimise the risk of unlawful access as explained in Chaps. 5 and 6. As noted in Chap. 4, the doctrine of positive obligations has been developed in the context of the Convention. It is only recently that the European Court of Justice has considered that the Charter also imposes positive obligations. This means that in practice, the analysis below will currently be more relevant to states' obligation under the Convention, and less so under the Charter, although this may change in the future. So what is a *vibrant encryption landscape*?

This is a landscape where there is a virtuous cycle of continuously strengthening encryption technologies, giving users and organisations a variety of cryptographical technologies at their disposal and where governments actively promote the use of these technologies. To be clear, not all of these encryption technologies need to be *user-controlled*—this depends on the risk of unlawful access of the information and the particular context in which the encryption is applied. But there needs to be a wide range of encryption technologies available, so that for each situation, the appropriate technology can be applied. And by *wide*, I mean that these options must always include user-controlled encryption—this, I argue, is a requirement which proceeds from the human rights framework I have analysed above.

This implies that governments are required, firstly, to strengthen and where possible increase the range of encryption technologies available to organisations. Part of this involves recognising in law that the application of all kinds of encryption technologies, including user-controlled encryption, is legal. This also implies prohibiting technical and contractual measures which hinder or prevent the application of these technologies. Perhaps more importantly, states have a role to play in strengthening the encryption landscape itself, through research funding. The Dutch government and the European Commission are already doing that to a certain extent, as discussed in Chap. 3, but this should be extended. In those funding programmes, particular attention should be paid to those encryption technologies which are widely adopted, yet maintained by individuals, often volunteers: after a vulnerability in the widely used OpenSSL encryption library was discovered, one journalist quipped that the internet is protected by two guys called Steve (who maintain the library).[47] Of

[47] Stokel-Walker 2014.

course, states have considerable freedom in determining which projects to fund, and how to organise this funding, but at the very least they should have a well-considered policy in place.

Another way is to ensure that encryption technologies are not encumbered by intellectual property rights. Publicly funded research on encryption technologies may be structured in such a way that the results can be applied without restrictions, financial or otherwise. The same goes for encryption technologies that are developed by the private sector, but are then elevated to a technological standard, for example in standard-setting fora or through the dominance of specific companies. In particular, there should be no patent covering the application of any post-quantum cryptography that is adopted as a standard by NIST—this would hinder its adoption, and go against the requirement to prevent unlawful access.

Thirdly, governments must promote the use of strong encryption technologies. Part of this can be done by mandating the application of encryption technologies by organisations providing products and services to users. This is important when embracing the horizontal governance approach to the information security cycle described in the previous chapter, and when the government maintains a patchwork of legislative measures governing the information security cycle. Furthermore, part of this can be done through education and media campaigns, while noting that it is not the responsibility of users to apply encryption technologies—these should be applied by default. Lastly, part of it can be done by having governments adopt it themselves and by promoting the use of encryption technologies internationally. Again, states can decide for themselves *how* to give effect to this requirement, but they need to at least be able to explain their decisions.

9.5 Topics for Further Research

The above analysis centres around *encryption* technologies, but encryption technologies are a mere subset of cryptographic technologies. For example, it is interesting to understand how lawful access proposals affect authentication mechanisms. I expect that the regulation of other cryptographic technologies, such as technologies for authentication and verification, can be assessed under a framework which builds on the one developed in this chapter. In particular, the distinction between *lawful* and *unlawful* activities—introduced in—for determining compatibility with human rights instruments may serve as a useful analytical tool. This can be further investigated.

Another point which is not explored in this analysis, is the role of trust in relation to these measures. As mentioned above, some of the envisaged governance measures, such as covertly adding new functionality with a new update, not only affect the security of a system—they also affect the trust in digital infrastructure. It is interesting to explore how this factors in the human rights assessment.

Lastly, I have touched on the issue of unlawful *control* of devices, but I have not thoroughly examined this aspect of the relationship between encryption governance measures and human rights—I have reviewed the confidentiality function of encryption in relation to human rights. It is worth researching how the right to device self-determination limits what governments may do in this domain. This is particularly interesting because governments are increasingly focusing on regulating the "end points"—the devices of users—instead of intermediary nodes (such as telecommunications providers). This development goes hand in hand with a shift by industry towards locking down devices, something which has significant implications for communications freedom and privacy.

References

Articles, Books and Other Documents

Abelson H, Anderson R, Bellovin SM et al. (1997) *The Risks of Key Recovery, Key Escrow, and Trusted Third-Party Encryption*, 27 May 1997.

Abelson H, Anderson R, Bellovin SM et al. (2015) Keys under Doormats: Mandating Insecurity by Requiring Government Access to All Data and Communications, MIT-CSAIL-TR-2015-026, 6 July 2015.

Abelson H, Anderson R, Bellovin SM et al. (2021) Bugs in our Pockets: The Risks of Client-Side Scanning. arXiv:211007450 [cs] 2021.

Andersen L, Alisson-Hope D (2022) Human Rights Impact Assessment: Meta's Expansion of End-to-End Encryption, 4 April 2022.

Arnbak AM (2016) Securing Private Communications: Protecting Private Communications Security in EU Law: Fundamental Rights, Functional Value Chains, and Market Incentives. Kluwer Law International, Alphen aan den Rijn, The Netherlands.

Assange J, Appelbaum J, Muller-Maguhn A, Zimmermann J (2012) Cypherpunks: Freedom and the Future of the Internet. OR Books, New York, NY.

Bellovin SM, Blaze M, Clark S, Landau S (2014) Lawful Hacking: Using Existing Vulnerabilities for Wiretapping on the Internet. Northwestern Journal of Technology and Intellectual Property 12:1. https://doi.org/10.2139/ssrn.2312107

Bouma R (2019) Minister Grapperhaus wil toegang tot chat- en berichtendiensten. https://nos.nl/l/2308847. Accessed 25 November 2021.

Brewster T (2021) Can The FBI Hack Into Private Signal Messages on a Locked iPhone? Evidence Indicates Yes. https://www.forbes.com/sites/thomasbrewster/2021/02/08/can-the-fbi-can-hack-into-private-signal-messages-on-a-locked-iphone-evidence-indicates-yes/. Accessed 2 July 2021.

Budish R, Burkert H, Gasser U (2018) Encryption Policy and Its International Impacts: A Framework for Understanding Extraterritorial Ripple Effects, 1804. https://s3.documentcloud.org/documents/4450501/Budish-Aegis-Paper-May-2018.pdf. Accessed 5 January 2024.

Comey J (2014) Going Dark: Are Technology, Privacy, and Public Safety on a Collision Course?. https://www.fbi.gov/news/speeches/going-dark-are-technology-privacy-and-public-safety-on-a-collision-course/. Accessed 5 January 2024.

DG Trade (2015) Guidelines on the Analysis of Human Rights Impacts in Impact Assessments for Trade-Related Policy Initiatives. https://circabc.europa.eu/ui/group/7fc51410-46a1-4871-8979-20cce8df0896/library/991d8e1d-dbaa-49d6-8582-bb3aab2cab48/details. Accessed 5 January 2024.

DuPont Q, Fidler B (2016) Edge Cryptography and the Codevelopment of Computer Networks and Cybersecurity. IEEE Annals of the History of Computing 38:55–73. https://doi.org/10.1109/MAHC.2016.49

EDPB (2020) Recommendations 01/2020 on measures that supplement transfer tools to ensure compliance with the EU level of protection of personal data.

Elsayed-Ali S (2016) Encryption: A Matter of Human Rights. https://www.amnesty.nl/content/uploads/2016/03/160322_encryption_-_a_matter_of_human_rights_-_def.pdf. Accessed 5 January 2024.

Encryption Working Group (2019a) Likely Future Adoption of User-Controlled Encryption April.

Encryption Working Group (2019b) Moving the Encryption Policy Conversation Forward. https://carnegieendowment.org/2019/04/25/likely-future-adoption-of-user-controlled-encryption-pub-78986. Accessed 5 January 2024.

Gasser U, Gertner N, Goldsmith JL et al. (2016) Don't Panic: Making Progress on the "Going Dark" Debate. Berkman Center Research Publication. https://dash.harvard.edu/handle/1/28552576. Accessed 5 January 2024.

Hoepman J-H (2015) The Second Crypto War Is Not about Crypto. On Privacy, Security & .... https://blog.xot.nl/2015/12/08/the-second-crypto-war-is-not-about-crypto/index.html. Accessed 23 November 2021.

Kassoti E (2020) The Extraterritorial Applicability of the EU Charter of Fundamental Rights: Some Reflections in the Aftermath of the Front Polisario Saga. European Journal of Legal Studies 12:117–141. https://doi.org/10.2924/EJLS.2019.022

Kerr OS, Schneier B (2018) Encryption Workarounds. The Georgetown Law Journal 106:989.

Koops B-J (1999) The Crypto Controversy: A Key Conflict in the Information Society. Kluwer Law International, The Hague, London, Boston.

Landau S (2017) Listening in: Cybersecurity in an Insecure Age. Yale University Press, New Haven.

Marlinspike M (2021) Exploiting vulnerabilities in Cellebrite UFED and Physical Analyzer from an App's Perspective. Signal Messenger Blog. https://signal.org/blog/cellebrite-vulnerabilities/. Accessed 2 July 2021.

May TC (1992) The Crypto Anarchist Manifesto. https://groups.csail.mit.edu/mac/classes/6.805/articles/crypto/cypherpunks/may-crypto-manifesto.html. Accessed 5 January 2024.

Mckinney I, Falcon E (2021) EFF Transition Memo to Incoming Biden Administration. Electronic Frontier Foundation. https://www.eff.org/wp/eff-transition-memo-incoming-biden-administration. Accessed 19 January 2022.

Narayanan A (2013a) What Happened to the Crypto Dream? Part 1. On the Horizon 2. https://www.cs.princeton.edu/~arvindn/publications/crypto-dream-part1.pdf. Accessed 5 January 2024.

Narayanan A (2013b) What Happened to the Crypto Dream? Part 2. On the Horizon 4. https://www.cs.princeton.edu/~arvindn/publications/crypto-dream-part2.pdf. Accessed 5 January 2024.

Rogaway P (2015) The Moral Character of Cryptographic Work. https://eprint.iacr.org/2015/1162. Accessed 5 January 2024.

Schneier B (2003) Beyond Fear: Thinking Sensibly about Security in an Uncertain World. Copernicus Books, New York.

Schulz W, van Hoboken J (2016) Human Rights and Encryption. https://unesdoc.unesco.org/ark:/48223/pf0000246527. Accessed 5 January 2024.

Stokel-Walker C (2014) The Internet Is Being Protected by Two Guys Named Steve. https://www.buzzfeed.com/chrisstokelwalker/the-internet-is-being-protected-by-two-guys-named-st. Accessed 2 November 2021.

Swire P (2011) "Going Dark" versus a "Golden Age for Surveillance".Center for Democracy & Technology. https://cdt.org/blog/%e2%80%98going-dark%e2%80%99-versus-a-%e2%80%98golden-age-for-surveillance%e2%80%99/. Accessed 6 December 2018.

Swire P, Ahmad K (2011) Encryption and Globalization. The Columbia Science & Technology Law Review XIII:2. https://doi.org/10.7916/stlr.v13i2.3964

van Daalen OL, van Hoboken JVJ, Koot M, Rucz M (2021) The New Rules for Export Control Cyber-Surveillance Items in the EU, June 2021. https://open.overheid.nl/documenten/ronl-f616bafb-c268-436c-b926-3bacd98da61b/pdf. Accessed 5 January 2024.
van Daalen O (2022), In Defense of Offense: Information Security Research under the Right to Science, Computer Law & Security Review 46: 105706.
van Daalen O (2023a) The Right to Encryption: Privacy as Preventing Unlawful Access, Computer Law & Security Review 49:105804.
van Daalen O (2023b) The Right to Root: Constructing a Claim to Control Devices from the Right to Privacy, JIPITEC 14(2023:4): 580–593.
van Daalen O (2024) Developing a human-rights compatible governance framework for quantum computing, Research Directions: Quantum Technologies 2: 2024.

Table of Cases: USA

9th Cir., Bernstein v. U.S. Dept. of Justice, Judgment of 6 May 1999, 176 F.3d 1132.

Table of Cases: EU

CJEU, Case C-311/18, Schrems II, Judgment of 16 July 2020.
CJEU, Case C-362/14, Schrems I, Judgment of 6 October 2015.
ECHR, Application no. 19699/18, Akgün v Turkey, Judgment of 20 July 2021.
ECHR, Application no. 20511/03, I v Finland, Judgment of 17 July 2008.
ECHR, Application no. 2872/02, K.U. v Finland, Judgment of 2 December 2008.
ECHR, Application no. 37138/14, Szabó and Vissy v Hungary, Judgment of 12 January 2016.
ECHR, Applications nos. 58170/13, 62322/14 and 24960/15, Big Brother Watch and others v United Kingdom (Grand Chamber), Judgment of 25 May 2021.

Chapter 10
Human Rights-Compatible Quantum Computing Governance

Contents

Abstract This chapter takes the normative framework of the rights to privacy, data protection, communications freedom and science, and applies it to quantum computing governance. It concludes that there is very little governance currently on this topic. It also concludes that the obligation of governments to minimise the risk of unlawful access to private information in this case means that governments must invest in the development and deployment of cryptography which is resistant to attacks by quantum computers (in particular post-quantum cryptography). At the same time, governments under these rights may under certain strict circumstances deploy quantum computers for decryption purposes in specific cases.

Keywords Quantum computing · Privacy · Decryption · Post-quantum cryptography · Governance

10.1 Introduction

Quantum-level research during the Second World War yielded access to immense kinetic power; similar research might now unlock significant computing power. This power will not be as deadly as the nuclear bomb, but it promises to be seriously disruptive. It could result in breakthrough technological innovations in fields from medicine to fertilisers, but it could also break a foundational technology of information security: public key encryption. So, considering these impacts, what do the human rights to privacy, communications freedom and science require from governments when it comes to the development and application of quantum computing?

O. van Daalen, *From Encryption to Quantum Computing*, Information Technology and Law Series 38, https://doi.org/10.1007/978-94-6265-635-2_10

This is the topic of this chapter. Because this chapter builds on the legal analysis of the preceding chapters on the information security cycle and on encryption, this chapter will be shorter, and should be read together with Chaps. 8 and 9.[1]

10.2 The Quantum Computing Landscape

As discussed in Chap. 2, quantum computers work differently from the computers we use every day—*classical computers*. Classical computers derive their power from the properties of nature above atomic scale; quantum computers are based on the behaviour of the world on a sub-atomic, or quantum level. With quantum computers, you can use the peculiar properties of particles at the quantum level to—in theory—rapidly solve problems which take a lot of time with classical computers.

Not all problems are suitable for quantum computers. So far, it is expected that they will excel in two kinds of things (see Chap. 2). The first is simulating other quantum systems, such as the interaction of molecules. This could lead to breakthroughs in fields as diverse as health (developing better drugs), agriculture (developing cheaper ways to create fertiliser) and materials (developing cheaper solar panels). These computers are also expected to be significantly faster in solving certain optimisation and search problems. This is useful for problems in fields such as logistics (planning fastest distribution routes) and finance (valuing derivatives).

One of the applications in the field of optimisation and search, the application which is relevant to this book, is the breaking of particular forms of encryption. In particular, *public key encryption* is at risk from quantum computers. Currently, public key encryption technologies are based on the assumption that factoring primes and finding discrete logarithms takes so much time with classical computers that these algorithms can in practice not be broken. As discussed in Chap. 2, Shor in 1994 developed an algorithm to quickly factor primes and find discrete logarithms with a quantum computer. While breaking one public key would take years with a classical computer, it would take hours or seconds with a quantum computer. And this attack cannot be mitigated by lengthening the key size. As a sidenote, quantum computers also have an impact on *symmetric encryption*—Grover in 1996 developed an algorithm which accelerates the breaking of this as well—, but this can be mitigated by making the key size longer.

As it has been explained in the previous chapters, quantum computers are currently still deep in the proof-of-concept stage. This is because the potential power of these computers largely depends on the number of *qubits* used to perform calculations. And at the time of writing, qubits are not stable enough to perform calculations without errors: many of them fall apart before the calculation is finished. To address this, researchers are combining many physical qubits into one logical qubit via error-correction codes: they use around thousand *physical* qubits to make one *logical* qubit.

[1] Parts of this chapter have already been published in Van Daalen 2022, 2023a, 2023b and 2024.

But quantum computers would need thousands of *logical* qubits to perform useful calculations. For example, you would need over 8000 logical qubits to crack a 4096-bit RSA key. This means a quantum computer would need *millions* of physical qubits to do this; currently, quantum computers have hundreds at most. And the problem is: scientists do not yet know how to make bigger computers.

So, are we ever going to have a quantum computer this large, and if so—when? That's difficult to say. We do know that billions of Euros are being invested in the development of these new technologies—by states (notably the US, China, the EU and its member states), companies (such as Google, IBM and Rigetti) and universities. What makes it difficult to make predictions, is that these technologies are so new that you cannot extrapolate their development trajectory on the basis of the past. Moreover, the technologies on which quantum computers are based differ fundamentally from each other; some may use the polarisation states of a photon for doing calculations, whereas others may use something completely different, such as the spin direction of an electron. As a result, the technological trajectory for each approach also differs. Still, while experts do not agree on a specific timeline for a quantum computer which can attack the commonly used 2048-bit RSA key, the majority agree that at some point in the coming decades, such a computer will eventually be built (see Chap. 2). That is sufficient for this book, because it leads to the next question: what are the consequences when quantum computers become powerful enough to break commonly used public key encryption?

This partly depends on who gets to develop it and who gets to use it. In Chap. 2, I described four possible scenarios. In the *state takes all* scenario, one powerful country will be the first to develop a quantum computer and use this advantage to consolidate its technological and geopolitical power. By contrast, in the *corporation takes all* scenario, a single company will be the first to develop it, using it to further its commercial power. In the *public-private development* scenario, both states and corporations will simultaneously develop these computers, possibly in partnership. Lastly, in *quantum winter*, these computers will simply not be built.

In all scenarios except *quantum winter*, there is the possibility that governments will use these computers to crack encryption. This is particularly so in the *state takes all* scenario, with its military overtones. But it is also a realistic possibility in the *public-private development* scenario, in which states could, for example, develop these computers themselves (and keep them secret), or enlist the computers developed by the private sector for this purpose. Even in the *corporation takes all* scenario, if the company that developed a quantum computer makes it available through the cloud to others, this could in theory also allow others to use it for decryption purposes.

Regardless of which scenario plays out, you have to contend with the possibility that one or more governments will use these quantum computers for cracking codes, and that they will do so in a targeted way. This is because there will be only a few large quantum computers, and cracking one key will initially take hours. As they grow stronger, cracking codes will take a matter of seconds. So while attacks will initially be targeted, they will later become indiscriminate. Moreover, if the *public-private development* scenario plays out, these computers will grow more ubiquitous, and will then become cheaper. You will eventually have to contend with the possibility that criminal organisations may also gain access to this power.

Still, that does not mean that *all* information which was previously encrypted will then become transparent. Decrypting information requires collecting the information in the first place, and this is quite difficult. At least, it is something that governments can more easily do than criminal organisations; criminal organisations are not necessarily in the business of intercepting communications. But we suspect governments are already storing encrypted data for decryption later, so this is something to be contended with. There is also a more fundamental consequence of the development of these computers: because you cannot *know* whether you are being targeted, the threat of decryption will undermine trust in currently available public key encryption technologies.

This is why experts recommend switching as quickly as possible to encryption technologies which are *quantum-resistant*—meaning that they cannot be broken by quantum computers. One of these approaches is based on software: *post quantum cryptography*, or PQC. This refers to a group of algorithms incorporating mathematical problems that cannot be easily solved with quantum computers. The other is based on hardware: quantum key distribution, or QKD. These technologies use quantum level effects to enable the secure exchange of cryptographical keys, which can then be used for symmetrical encryption (which as discussed above is more resistant to quantum attacks).

These technologies are, however, not yet ready to fully replace the public key encryption technologies now in use. PQC algorithms are currently still being vetted by cryptography experts before they can be designated as standards. Even when they are in theory ready for mass adoption, this will require a formidable effort: previous transitions to new cryptographic algorithms took decades, not years. Furthermore, QKD technologies currently require dedicated infrastructure and can still only span a limited range, which limits their application.

The fact that we are still at an early stage of quantum computing also explains why there is so little governance in this field as yet (see Chap. 3). Currently, there are essentially two governance approaches in the EU: research funding (which also include use restrictions) and export control. The European Union is financing the development of powerful computers, including quantum computers, under the EuroHPC project. This funding already restricts their use to "primarily" civilian applications, which still allows their use for decryption by the state. Some of the building blocks of quantum computers are subject to export control under the Wassenaar Arrangement and the Dual-Use Regulation.

The question is whether we will see more governance measures on quantum computing in the coming decade? Highly probable. As quantum computers grow more powerful, a wide range of governance questions will come to the fore.[2] It is to be expected that governments will want to retain tight control over the proliferation of these computers—just as the machines used to make semiconductors for classical

[2] See for an overview World Economic Forum 2022; Hoofnagle and Garfinkel 2021, Chap. 9; Perrier 2021; van Apeldoorn and van Daalen 2020; Johnson 2019; de Wolf 2017.

computers are the subject of a heated export control debate.[3] Also, governments will want to ensure that computers within their jurisdiction are not used against the public interest—a nuclear scientist from Iran will probably not be allowed to perform nuclear simulations on Google's machines.[4] If these machines allow for the rapid development of new chemical and biological materials, it is likely that some of these inventions will be protected by intellectual property rights. Who should have these rights—the owner of the computer, or the person using the computer to create these inventions? Furthermore, a public debate on the accessibility of these computers can also be expected—if for instance only Microsoft has such a computer, and can decide the terms of its use, there is ample room for their abuse, for example making it very expensive to use the computer, or imposing anti-competitive restrictions on what you can do with the computer. Perhaps it could even be argued that governments must ensure access on reasonable and non-discriminatory terms for the use of their quantum computing resources. Lastly, there are questions around verification—how can you be sure that a quantum computer works as it is supposed to do? These are all fruitful topics for further research.

One thing governments are *not* likely to do, at least not on their own initiative, is to restrict their powers to decrypt information with these computers. In fact, funding rules for the EuroHPC project do not preclude its use for non-civilian applications—which may include decryption for surveillance purposes. Thus, the question is what the contours of human rights-compatible governance of quantum computing in the context of encryption technologies looks like? That is the topic of the next section.

10.3 Human Rights Requirements for Quantum Computing Governance

Any human rights evaluation of quantum computing governance must first address the elephant in the room—is it a good idea to develop quantum computers in the first place? The large sums of money currently being invested could be used for all kinds of things which clearly further human rights—providing food, housing and education to those who need it *right now*. Is it then useful to spend all this on a project which is partly driven by military goals, and may not yield any results whatsoever?[5]

It remains important to carefully review the societal merits of these kinds of moonshot projects. But human rights are not the most appropriate framework for

---

3 See for instance Cerulus 2021; Alper et al. 2020.

4 See van Apeldoorn and van Daalen 2020 for this example.

5 This question is not new. As an example, the 1969 lunar landing was hailed by Armstrong as a "giant leap for mankind", but many of the Black community did not judge it as favourably; see for example Jackson, 1969; the interviews in (2021) Summer of Soul (...Or, When the Revolution Could Not Be Televised). Mass Distraction Media, Concordia Studio, RadicalMedia; and Black artist Gil Scott-Heron's *Whitey on the Moon*, which goes in part: *The man jus' upped my rent las' night. // 'cause Whitey's on the moon // No hot water, no toilets, no lights. // but Whitey's on the moon*; Scott-Heron G (1970) Whitey on the Moon. BMG Music.

evaluating such high-level policy decisions, because states under this framework have a large margin of appreciation when it comes to deciding how to allocate funding for scientific research.

On the other hand, the human rights discussed above do impose requirements relating to the *results* of this research, via the right to science. Because just as the development of the atomic bomb was a product of years of scientific research, the development of quantum computers is a deeply scientific undertaking. In order for these computers to work, we need to understand at a subatomic level how nature works and can be manipulated. This requires fundamental scientific research. For a human rights assessment of governance in this domain, this means that the right to science is an important yardstick, and—related to this—so is the right to communications freedom.

As explained above, the right to science is firstly about using science for the benefit of humanity—this means *all* of humanity. In addition, the freedom to practice science comes with a responsibility to mitigate the risks of exercising this freedom. And lastly, as discussed in the previous chapters, where technologies have a dual use, the development of their beneficial use must also be accompanied by measures taken to mitigate the risks posed by their harmful use.

Of these three aspects of the right to science, the obligation to benefit humanity is the most flexible. As set out in Chap. 7, it has been argued that this right requires states to promote access to the benefits of science on a non-discriminatory basis.[6] And the CESCR in its General Comment, has underlined that states must adopt policies and measures that expand the benefits of quantum computers, also noting the importance of non-discrimination.[7] But these formulations leave much leeway to governments—which is understandable, because measures which ensure that people benefit from the results of science, can be at odds with other interests, such as the right to intellectual property, the right to property and the right to conduct a business. This will often require finding a fair balance between the different interests involved, especially when it comes to governing the private sector. There is, however, one scenario where the government has more room to govern: when it itself is funding research into quantum computers. This topic will be touched upon in the next section.

As to the obligations relating to the risk of quantum computers: these computers have various potentially harmful uses—think of the development of biochemical weapons or more powerful explosives—but the one I am concerned about, is the breaking of public key encryption. This could not only upset economic and political stability, it could also be a threat to the right to privacy and the right to communications freedom. This is why you also have to determine how the development of quantum computing relates to states' obligations under the right to privacy and the right to communications freedom. These obligations firstly set the conditions for decrypting information *lawfully*, meaning decryption within the powers granted by law to a

[6] See Shaheed 2012.

[7] CESCR, General Comment No. 25 (2020) on Science and Economic, Social and Cultural Rights (Article 15(1)(b), (2), (3) and (4) of the International Covenant on Economic, Social and Cultural Rights), E/C.12/GC/25, 30 April 2020, para 73.

government—this analysis is similar to the use of classical computing power to crack encryption with brute force, discussed in the previous chapter. I provide policy recommendations for this in the next sections.

More complex is what the obligation to minimise the risk of *unlawful* access implies for states with regard to quantum computing. Here the central question is: how do quantum computers increase the risk of unlawful access exactly? I can think of three ways. Firstly, governments will probably want to store the information they have decrypted lawfully, and this information may, as a result be, stolen more easily. The chances of this happening on a large scale are not too high, if only because the exfiltration of large amounts of data is difficult to do without detection. Nevertheless, decrypted information should be well secured, as also follows from the considerations in *Digital Rights Ireland*.[8]

Secondly, when quantum computers become more broadly accessible, organised crime may also use these computers to decrypt information that they have collected. The chances of this happening are slim, if only because the expertise needed to operate a quantum computer for this purpose will be relatively scarce, but also because it is difficult to collect encrypted data. However, the possibility that well-organised criminals could intercept communications (for instance, over the air) for later decryption, cannot be discounted.

My main concern, however, is *other* governments, governments not bound by European human rights instruments, decrypting the information of people in the EU (for example, because they intercepted the information in transit). This is bound to happen—if it is not happening already. And it is likely that some of these activities would be considered a form of unlawful access under European human rights instruments: as discussed in Chap. 5, the Court of Justice already considers some of the surveillance powers of the US government to be contrary to the Charter.

So, knowing the potential risks of breaking encryption, is it perhaps prudent to immediately cease all research on quantum computers altogether? Here, the precautionary principle under the right to science is relevant. As discussed in Chap. 7, this principle dictates that where science poses significant risks, state must mitigate those risks. This can be done through regulating the research, or by making mitigating technology available.

Regulating the research and development of quantum computers would of course be difficult and require legislative intervention and enforcement on an international scale, given the global scope of these activities. This would be very difficult. More importantly, as discussed in Chap. 2, it is expected that quantum computers will have many potential uses which are in the public interest. Moreover, the insights gained in researching these technologies may lead to new applications in other fields as well. And the need for technological breakthroughs will become more urgent as the climate crisis unfolds in the coming decades. Not so much as to invent our way out of it, but at least to mitigate it, creating more efficient technologies, so we can better use our dwindling resources, such as arable land and clean water. The dual use—or

[8] CJEU, Cases C-293/12 and C-594/12, Digital Rights Ireland and others, Judgment of 8 April 2014, paras 66–69.

multi use—nature of quantum computers stands in the way of an outright prohibition on their development. So what must states do instead?

10.4 Recommendations for Human Rights-Compatible Governance

The most effective way to minimise the risk of unlawful access as a result of the use of quantum computers, is to accelerate the development and adoption of PQC and QKD technologies. If these work as expected, they would provide at least the same level of protection as public key encryption currently does. An important way to accelerate the *development* of these technologies, is through funding. The European Commission is already doing this, to a certain extent.[9] And to ensure that people can build on the findings of others, the results of publicly-funded research in this domain should be made freely available. Furthermore, to spur on scientific development in this field, governments should make it easy for researchers from other countries to work in this domain. Still another way of minimising th risks of unlawful access, is not to restrict the sharing of the scientific findings of this research.

Most of the gains, however, can be achieved by spurring on the *adoption* of quantum-resistant technologies. As discussed in Chap. 2, switching to new encryption algorithms in the past took decades. We need to switch to new algorithms as quickly as possible, because data which is now being encrypted with a classical encryption algorithm can be stored and later decrypted.[10] Here, a fully-fledged push from governments is necessary.[11] This can be firstly done through regulation (broadly mandating the use of post-quantum cryptography), requiring its use in public procurement and through standardisation (ensuring that widely adopted information and communications technologies use PQC). Funding the development of tools to make the switch and educating people who can help to make the switch is also important. In addition, governments must explore the possibility of declaring any intellectual property rights which hinder the adoption of these technologies void. Lastly, governments should organise campaigns to underscore the urgency of making these changes, and keep track of the roll out of PQC through annual reports.

As a sidenote: whether this obligation to develop and adopt quantum-resistant encryption technologies can be enforced in court is another matter. This is because, as noted above, governments have a large margin of appreciation in deciding how they distribute their monies in this domain. Doing nothing to develop and adopt quantum resistant encryption technologies would be quite likely to be a violation of Convention and the Charter, but that is not the problem here—the problem is

[9] See European Commission 2022.

[10] See also Vermeer and Peet 2020, p. 2, where the authors conclude that "we judge the threat to be urgent. There is little to no margin of safety for beginning the migration to PQC".

[11] See World Economic Forum 2022, pp. 24–26 for similar recommendations.

that progress is not being made fast enough. This is a question which courts are ill-equipped to judge, meaning they will probably often defer to the legislature.

Hoofnagle and Garfinkel also suggest that getting rid of data is a way to protect against attacks by quantum computers.[12] This appears to be a solution to a problem which exists less in the EU than it does in the US—in the EU organisations under the GDPR are already obliged to delete data as soon as it is not necessary to retain it for the purposes for which it was collected. Nevertheless, the advent of quantum computing is another good reason to enforce these rules.

Another way to minimise the risk of other governments decrypting information in violation of European human rights instruments, is via export control. As discussed above, currently only some elements of quantum computers are subject to export control. But there is a clear momentum in favour of curbing the export of more technologies which are important for these computers. This is primarily driven by national security interests—because quantum computers may upset the geopolitical balance of power, countries will think twice before giving this power to others. This is also driven by human rights considerations—the export control of cybersurveillance items in the new Dual Use Regulation is a testament to that.[13] Because one of the most important applications of quantum computers currently is breaking encryption, systems and elements which constitute chokepoint technologies for quantum computers should be subject to export control.[14]

Of course, these controls would also have an impact on the right to science. In this early phase of fundamental research, talent is scarce and breakthroughs can come from anywhere in the world. Co-operating and procuring elements for your research across borders is an important way to accelerate discovery. Hoofnagle and Garfinkel quote the Chinese father of "quantum", Jian-Wei Pan, noting "As a physicist who has been devoted to quantum information research for 20 years, I would like to emphasize that quantum information technology has a long way to go before it can be widely used. Active international cooperation and open exchanges are imperative."[15] When these technologies have developed further, export control could make it impossible to enjoy the beneficial uses of this technology.

To be clear, making these technologies subject to export control means that an authorisation is required for the export, it does not mean that export is prohibited. In assessing whether a license should be granted, governments will have to review both the end-use and end-user of technologies being exported, also taking into account the human rights record of the importing country. Where the possibility that the items will be used to decrypt information in violation of European human rights interests cannot be excluded, an export license should be denied. Where, on the other hand, it can be demonstrated that these will be used for scientific purposes in the public interest—not to develop better nuclear bombs, for instance –, a license should be granted. And

[12] Hoofnagle and Garfinkel 2021, para 9.5.2.

[13] See van Daalen et al. 2021.

[14] It is not likely that these technologies can be considered "cybersurveillance-items" under the Dual Use-Regulation, because they are not "specially designed" for surveillance, see ibid., para 2.3.

[15] Hoofnagle and Garfinkel 2021, p. 408.

where a risk remains that the relevant components could be used for purposes which would undermine the public interest (including national security), one could consider asking for legal commitments from the importing country that restrict the ways in which the computer may be used. Whether this is an effective deterrent, though, requires further investigation—when governments have such potentially powerful technology at their disposal, they may not be so keen on honouring agreements.

Furthermore, governments will also have an obligation to limit the use of quantum computers for decryption purposes by non-governmental parties, because this increases the risk of unlawful access. It is difficult to think of a good reason for giving private parties these powerful decryption tools—perhaps if you have lost certain very important passwords? Governments must restrict the use of quantum computers operated by private parties to decrypt information, not only through contractual terms, but if possible also through technical recognition of the application of problematic algorithms. These restrictions should ensure that only governments use quantum computers to decrypt information without authorisation, and that others may only use this decryption power with authorisation of the persons whose device is being decrypted. The exact conditions for ensuring this, and the technical limitations in preventing certain algorithms from being run, is a topic for further research.

This leads us to the next question: under which conditions may governments themselves use this power to decrypt information? This question remains relevant, even after people have switched to PQC encryption, because governments are likely to have intercepted and retained classically encrypted messages, which they could then try to decrypt. From the perspective of privacy and communications freedom, quantum computing is just another form of brute force decryption technology. The conditions for the use of this power have already been discussed in the previous chapter. In short, it depends on whether this happens within the boundaries set for lawful access under the right to privacy and communications freedom. It is important to provide adequate protection against arbitrary interference, by clearly circumscribing the conditions under which this decryption power may be applied. Second, there need to be adequate and effective measures against the abuse of this decryption power. I have discussed this extensively in Chap. 5, and this analysis applies here as well.

There are, however, three issues in relation to lawful access which are particular to quantum computing.[16] The first is how to deal with the byproduct of the decryption: the public-private keypairs which are generated to decrypt the information. In order to ensure that these cannot be stolen, they should be deleted after they have been used to decrypt information.

The second issue has to do with the collection of the data. Was it only collected *because* it was encrypted, not for any other reason, for example because it came from a suspect? That in itself would be problematic. Because people will want to avoid their data being collected, it would hinder the application of encryption, and this would—given the analysis in the prior chapter—be a violation of the rights to privacy and communications freedom. A related question is: how long may encrypted data

[16] See also Hoofnagle and Garfinkel 2021, para 9.5.2.

be retained? States might want retain the data for years in anticipation of the development of large enough quantum computers—much longer than they would store any unencrypted data they intercepted. This, too, would be problematic, because it would deter people from applying encryption in the first place. This is therefore not permitted under the human rights framework discussed above. So, in short: states may not under this human rights framework distinguish between encrypted and unencrypted information in their collection and retention practices.

The most difficult question is which countries may use a quantum computer in a certain jurisdiction? If, for example, the Netherlands developed a quantum computer with which it could decrypt information—could the NSA then request that the Netherlands perform cryptanalysis for the US? I would argue that this requires the same approach as other foreign requests for evidence, for which two distinct frameworks apply, one for law enforcement and one for intelligence agencies. For decryption by law enforcement agencies, this can only be based on a mutual legal assistance treaty (MLAT), specifically providing the power to do this. For intelligence agencies, this needs to be based on specific arrangements with partner agencies. As sidenote: I do not make a distinction in this analysis with regard to quantum computers developed in the private realm (e.g. Google, Microsoft) or in the public realm (e.g. at universities, or built with public funding). The reason is that in both cases I expect governments to enlist their potential for decryption purposes, and as demonstrated above, if done with sufficient safeguards, this decryption should be considered lawful (enlisting private property might not).

Finally, states must give effect to the requirement that science benefits humanity in the context of quantum computing. As noted above, when it comes to regulating research by the private sector, this will be very much a matter of balancing different interests in specific cases, partly depending on which quantum scenario unfolds. One measure, however, which governments can—and arguably must—take, is ensuring that the results of *government*-funded research are shared freely and without discrimination, through conditions imposed on funding. The case for such an obligation is most clear for theoretical research, such as new quantum algorithms, because such sharing enables further development of science. The case could perhaps also be made for an obligation to ensure access to applied research, such as actual quantum computers, given the potential impact of these computers and the risk of market concentration. But this would also require a balancing with other fundamental rights, such as the right to property and the right to conduct a business. The necessity and specifics of policy measures in this context warrant further research.

10.5 Topics for Further Research

First, as mentioned above, the development of quantum computers is driven not only by the prospect that they can be used to break encryption: it is also driven by other interests, such as commercial interests, and the potential to benefit the public interest through breakthroughs in a range of scientific fields. These could have far-reaching impacts. Further research is necessary to understand what the implications of these impacts could be from a human rights perspective, and what the required governance response must be. Hoofnagle and Garfinkel provide an outline of policy questions in the quantum age, also focusing on other quantum technologies such as quantum sensing.[17] This is a fruitful area of further research.

Second, it is clear that the development of quantum computing is global in nature, and effective regulation would require a global response. But quantum computing has an effect on domains which are typically considered to form part of the realm of sovereign states, such as national security. And these technologies may have far-reaching impacts on geopolitical relations. Research on the international and geopolitical aspects of quantum computing governance is necessary, in particular focusing on the possibility of developing an international treaty on the governance of quantum computing, taking inspiration from similar domains such as nuclear anti-proliferation treaties—while being aware of the difficulties inherent in such an exercise.

Lastly, the issue of trust is important for the assessment of quantum computing in relation to human rights. As in the prior chapter, this is not a topic that has been explored in existing literature. You can easily poison the well of trust in security by sowing doubt about the efficacy of a security measure; quantum computing does exactly that. Further research is necessary to understand how the *potential* of quantum computers to break public key encryption also has an impact on trust in digital infrastructure, and what the implications of this are from a human rights perspective.

References

Articles, Books and Other Documents

Alper A, Sterling T, Nellis S (2020) Trump Administration Pressed Dutch Hard to Cancel China Chip-Equipment Sale: Sources. Reuters, 5 January 2020.

Cerulus L (2021) Chipmaker CEO Says Washington's Anti-China Tech Blockade Is a Bad Idea. https://www.politico.eu/article/europe-tech-sovereignty-china-peter-wennink-asml/. Accessed 5 November 2021.

de Wolf R (2017) The Potential Impact of Quantum Computers on Society. arXiv:171205380 [quant-ph].

European Commission (2022) Funding & Tenders Page on Transition towards Quantum-Resistant Cryptography. https://ec.europa.eu/info/funding-tenders/opportunities/portal/screen/opportunities/topic-details/horizon-cl3-2022-cs-01-03. Accessed 19 January 2022

Hoofnagle CJ, Garfinkel S (2021) Law and Policy for the Quantum Age, 1st edn. Cambridge University Press, New York.

Jackson J (1969) Comment on Moon Landing. The New York Times, 21 July 1969. http://timesmachine.nytimes.com/timesmachine/1969/07/21/90114418.pdf?pdf_redirect=true&ip=0. Accessed 31 March 2022.

Johnson WG (2019) Governance Tools for the Second Quantum Revolution. Jurimetrics 59:4.

Perrier E (2021) Ethical Quantum Computing: A Roadmap. arXiv:210200759 [quant-ph].

---

[17] Ibid., Chap. 9.

Shaheed F (2012) The Right to Enjoy the Benefits of Scientific Progress and Its Applications. https://doi.org/10.1163/2210-7975_HRD-9970-2016149
van Apeldoorn J, van Daalen O (2020) Kwantumcomputing heeft juridisch kader nodig. AG Connect 2020:73–74.
van Daalen OL, van Hoboken JVJ, Koot M, Rucz M (2021) The New Rules for Export Control Cyber-Surveillance Items in the EU. https://open.overheid.nl/documenten/ronl-f616bafb-c268-436c-b926-3bacd98da61b/pdf. Accessed 5 January 2024
van Daalen O (2022), In Defense of Offense: Information Security Research under the Right to Science, Computer Law & Security Review 46: 105706.
van Daalen O (2023a) The Right to Encryption: Privacy as Preventing Unlawful Access, Computer Law & Security Review 49:105804.
van Daalen O (2023b) The Right to Root: Constructing a Claim to Control Devices from the Right to Privacy, JIPITEC 14(2023:4): 580–593.
van Daalen O (2024) Developing a human-rights compatible governance framework for quantum computing, Research Directions: Quantum Technologies 2: 2024.
Vermeer M, Peet E (2020) Securing Communications in the Quantum Computing Age: Managing the Risks to Encryption. https://www.rand.org/pubs/research_reports/RR3102.html. Accessed 5 January 2024.
World Economic Forum (2022) Quantum Computing Governance Principles. https://www3.weforum.org/docs/WEF_Quantum_Computing_2022.pdf. Accessed 5 January 2024.

Table of Cases: EU

CJEU, Cases C-293/12 and C-594/12, Digital Rights Ireland and others, Judgment of 8 April 2014.

Chapter 11
Summary and Conclusion

Contents

Abstract This chapter provides a summary and conclusion of the analysis in the preceding chapters relating to the dynamic and complex relationship between information security, human rights, and the continuous cycle of making and breaking security measures. It outlines the landscape of information security, including encryption technologies and quantum computing, alongside governmental rules and practices. It introduces the human rights framework, delving into the rights of privacy, communication freedom, and science. The final part synthesizes these elements, applying the human rights framework to governance measures in the fields of information security, encryption technologies, and quantum computing. In an ideal world, the process of making and breaking should form a virtuous cycle, enhancing rather than inhibiting human rights. Policymakers play a crucial role in facilitating this cycle, sometimes by intervening, sometimes by refraining from doing so.

Keywords Encryption · Quantum computing · Information security · Human rights · Governance · Privacy · Communications freedom · Right to science · Data protection · Virology

O. van Daalen, *From Encryption to Quantum Computing*, Information Technology and Law Series 38, https://doi.org/10.1007/978-94-6265-635-2_11

11.1 Introduction

This book might appear to lie at the heart of a highly improbable Venn diagram—one about information security *and* encryption technologies *and* quantum computing *and* privacy *and* data protection *and* communications freedom *and* science. But in essence, it is a book about the cycle of making and breaking, about taking security measures, which are then circumvented, leading to new security measures, *et cetera*—a process I call the information security cycle. Although governments have adopted various laws and practices relating to isolated parts of this cycle, they rarely take a step back and consider how their policies fit into this cycle as a whole. What's more, the relationship between this cycle and human rights have remained largely unexplored. This book is intended to fill both gaps.[1]

The central question of this book is what constitutes human-rights compatible governance of the information security cycle. In developing the human rights framework, I take an information-centric approach, focusing on three human rights which have a particular relationship to the creation, distribution and use of information: the rights to privacy (and data protection), the right to communications freedom and the right to science. I then apply these to the governance of the information security cycle itself, as well as to two specific examples of this cycle: encryption technologies and quantum computing.

The book consists of three parts. In the first part, I describe the *landscape*: what the information security cycle is, what encryption technologies do and what quantum computing is about. In this first part, I also discuss the governmental rules and practices relating to these topics, i.e. the governance. Then, in the second part, I describe the *human rights framework*: in this case the rights to privacy and data protection, communication freedom and science. In the final part, the *synthesis*, I apply this framework to governance measures in these domains.

My main conclusion is that in an ideal world, making and breaking complement each other in a virtuous cycle, one which works for, not against humans, and supports their enjoyment of human rights. I conclude that policymakers can facilitate this cycle, sometimes by intervening, sometimes by refraining from intervening. Below, these findings will be summarised, first describing the information security cycle, then discussing the human rights framework and then developing human-rights compatible governance measures with regard to the information security cycle, encryption technologies and quantum computing.

[1] Parts of this chapter have already been published in Van Daalen 2022, 2023a, 2023b and 2024.

11.2 The Information Security Cycle

As mentioned in the introduction, an important part of this book is centered around the idea that information security should be considered a continuous process, which I develop in Chap. 2. This idea of a cycle is deeply ingrained in the practice of information security and is also reflected in the *plan-do-check-act* approach applied by security experts. You first *plan*, meaning you determine what measures you want to take in view of the risks. Then you *do*, meaning that you take these measures to defend against attacks. But there is always a risk that your measures are attacked. This means you will also have to periodically review whether your measures still suffice in view of the developing risks, and if necessary, take new measures—you also have to *check* and *act*.

The reason why you need to review these measures periodically is that there is a serious risk that your systems will be attacked. There are many people looking for vulnerabilities in systems, especially because most of these systems are connected to the internet nowadays. Intelligence agencies are looking for bugs to gain access to their adversaries' systems; academics are looking for weaknesses in order to gain academic acclaim; organised crime does so to exploit their victims; and security consultants may do so to bolster their reputation or for other commercial reasons.

Whatever the reason, weaknesses will invariably be exploited, sometimes to devastating effects. An attack can disrupt infrastructure, result in data breaches, and it can even lead to death, as the targeting of political dissidents by Saudi Arabia demonstrates. However, not all exploits are bad. They can also be used in the public interest—for instance, when a phone owner takes full control over their device, something called *jailbreaking*, or when a whistleblower removes tracking measures from documents they want to leak.

This continuous cat-and-mouse game between offence and defence is a large part of what information security is about. This was the case when computers were still the size of a large room in the 1970s, and now that computers fit in your pocket and have become ubiquitous, the stakes have only increased. As a result, we read almost weekly about significant vulnerabilities in digital infrastructure.

All these exploits are possible because the security of digital infrastructure is in poor shape, and there are a number of reasons for this. As computers and software have become more complex, the likelihood of a system containing bugs has grown. In the early computing days, all parts of a system used to be made by one company, and they consisted of few elements and minimal code. This is no longer the case: hundreds of suppliers are involved now, some developing part of the hardware, some developing libraries, and some just integrating all these parts together. As a result, keeping systems secure has become very challenging. At the same time, the security of a system is as strong as its weakest link. You need only one vulnerability to enter a system—but you need to fix all holes to defend it. This means that it is much more difficult to defend against an attack than it is to perform an attack.

It is not only difficult to secure things in the first place; it is also difficult to deal with vulnerabilities when they arise. Some vulnerabilities cannot be fixed, some are hard to fix, and some fixes affect system performance negatively. Furthermore, the increased complexity of the supply chain also means that it has become difficult to decide who should provide the fix. Even when a patch has been developed, you also have to *apply* the patch, which is not always done. All the while, users of a system remain exposed.

Whether this exposure is a risk depends on whether the vulnerability is known to others (who can then exploit it). Sometimes, the vulnerability has been publicly disclosed—then you must assume that it is being exploited. In other cases, the weakness is not yet publicly known, and then the question becomes whether someone else will discover the bug independently. Since there are always those looking for weaknesses to exploit, there is a good chance that this will happen. This is relevant because researchers who want to publicly disclose a vulnerability will sometimes give the responsible organisation time to bring out a fix. The longer you wait to publish information on the vulnerability, however, the bigger the chance is that others will discover the bug on their own as well. Often, researchers will then find themselves negotiating with the organisation to whom they disclosed the vulnerability—coordinating things like the most appropriate way to fix it, when it should be fixed and who should fix it. This process is called coordinated vulnerability disclosure (CVD).

If you look at this cycle from a distance, you will notice that this constant arms race is omnipresent in digital infrastructure. A central example explored in this book is how encryption technologies can restrict access to information and how quantum computing can break these restrictions. Below, I analyse these processes further and develop human-rights compatible governance for these domains. Let me first, however, summarise my findings with regard to the human rights framework.

11.3 The Human Rights Framework

As noted above, the human rights framework for this book consists of three partly overlapping rights. It consists, firstly, of the right to privacy, which also includes the right to data protection, both discussed in Chap. 5. It also consists of the right to communications freedom—a term not used in human rights instruments but which I employ to emphasise that this right protects both public and private communication throughout all phases of the communication process (Chap. 6). And it finally consists of the right to science (Chap. 7).

My analysis is focused on human rights-compatible governance of European Union member states. This is why the focus is on three human rights instruments: the European Convention on Human Rights (the Convention), the Charter of Fundamental Rights of the European Union (the Charter) and the International Covenant on Economic, Social and Cultural Rights (the Covenant). The protection afforded under these instruments overlaps to a certain extent. The Convention protects the right to privacy and the right to communications freedom. The Covenant is relevant because it protects the right to science. And the Charter protects all: the right to privacy, the right to data protection, the rights to communications freedom and the right to science. Now, there is a difference between the right to privacy and the right to data protection: under the Charter, limitations may not affect the "essence" of a right, and it is notable that the European Court of Justice considered that information security has something to do with the essence of the right to data protection. For this book, however, the distinction is not really relevant, because according to the European Court of Justice, the mere existence of provisions prescribing certain security measures already suffices to ensure that the essence is not affected. That is why, in this conclusion, I will just refer to the right to privacy, not the right to data protection.

11.3.1 The Right to Privacy

I develop the relationship between information security and the right to privacy by first highlighting a number of ways in which people understand the *concept* of privacy in relation to information. These understandings vary widely, ranging from *privacy as confidentiality*, to *privacy as reputation*, to *privacy as informational self-determination*. These also include *privacy as device control*, a new concept I employ to refer to the privacy interests in controlling your own devices, such as your phone.

For this book, however, all these understandings of privacy can be brought back to two concepts—they are about restricting *access to*, and *control of* information and systems. This is relevant because this is also, to a large extent, what information security is about. These concepts of access and control play an important role in my subsequent analysis and they can also be found in the case law under the Convention and the Charter on the rights to privacy and data protection. To make this chapter more readable, I will subsequently refer to both access and control, to both information and systems, as *access*.

This concept of access is firstly relevant for the determination of the existence of an *interference* (as it is called under the Convention). It is not immediately obvious that governance measures with regard to the information security cycle, encryption technologies and quantum computing constitute such an interference. For instance, if a governance measure weakens the effectiveness of encryption technologies, new possibilities for an interference might be created, but is this also an interference itself? From the case law on surveillance under the Convention and the Charter, however, I conclude that this is the case (see primarily Chap. 5). Not only is surveillance itself an interference, but creating the *risk* of surveillance can also be an interference. Similarly, the storage of personal data is considered an interference under this case law, primarily because of what might be done with the data in the future. In both cases, the courts have applied the doctrine of chilling effects to come to this conclusion—the mere existence of surveillance *powers* or technical *capabilities* has already created a concern in the population that these may be abused.

Based on this analysis, I conclude that information security governance measures which *facilitate lawful access* to information and systems protected under the right to privacy constitute an interference. A simple example of this is legislation mandating the use of an algorithm with a backdoor, something I explore further in my analysis on encryption governance measures. I also conclude that measures which significantly increase the *risk of unlawful access* constitute an interference—for example when this backdoor increases the risk of access by organised crime. I consider this risk to be "significant" if it leads to chilling effects.

This analysis about the possibility of access is, however, not only relevant for the determination of interference: it is also relevant when it comes to proportionality. When reviewing surveillance powers, which are generally about *access* to private information, the courts under the Convention and the Charter are concerned with two things. First, the conditions for lawful access must be clearly circumscribed, to protect against arbitrary interference. What is more interesting for our purposes, though, is that the law must also provide safeguards against the *abuse* of power—it must prevent against *unlawful access*. In my analysis, I conclude that the residual risk of unlawful access—the risk that remains after you have taken measures to prevent arbitrary and abusive interference—is an important part of the proportionality assessment under the right to privacy. This, to a large extent, is what information security is about—preventing the residual risk of unlawful access.

This is firstly about unlawful access by the state itself—state officials nosing through citizens' files without proper authorisation. But the right to privacy does not only entail negative obligations incumbent on the state. It also entails positive obligations, meaning that states under this right may have to *do* things to prevent interferences with this right. In particular, in the context of information security, the courts have assumed a responsibility of states to minimise the risk of unlawful access to information by others than the state. In one case, the European Court of Human Rights even required states to "exclude any possibility of unauthorised access occurring", although in later decisions it has clarified that this goal must be balanced against other interests. Both these negative and positive aspects of the right to privacy play an important role in my subsequent analysis of human-rights compatible governance of the information security cycle.

There are a number of other interests against which such balancing must occur, such as the protection of national security, the prevention of crime and the protection of the rights of others. Depending on the interest at stake, there may be limited instances where these interests outweigh the residual risk of unlawful access. But the test to be applied leaves little leeway to the state—these measures must be "strictly necessary" in a democratic society. This imposes a heavy burden on the state to demonstrate that interferences are necessary, something I assess in the context of the information security cycle and encryption technologies in the next sections.

My analysis on the right to privacy as providing protection against unlawful access is an important contribution to the thinking on the relationship between privacy and information security. It provides a useful framework for policymakers when devising governance measures in the realm of information security, and for courts when assessing states' obligations in this domain. It also raises new questions with regard to the role of the state in ordering information society, something I analyse further at the end of this conclusion.

11.3.2 The Right to Communications Freedom

Building on the analytical framework developed under the right to privacy, I then develop the relationship between information security and communications freedom (Chap. 8). The right to communications freedom is relevant to information security in two ways. First, it is relevant to *doing research* on information security and sharing the results thereof. It is also relevant to the *application* of information security measures. As I set out above, these measures can restrict access and control to information and systems and this can negatively impact communications freedom.

I start my analysis with three understandings of the concept of communications freedom (in Chap. 6). For restrictions on doing research, the classic understanding of communications freedom as prevention of censorship is relevant. For restrictions on application of information security measures, two other perspectives are relevant: how communications freedom under certain circumstances entails a right of access to communications infrastructure, and how it arguably encompasses a right to device self-determination, determining how you use digital technology.

I conclude that the research and disclosure of vulnerabilities in digital infrastructure is an eminent example of an activity protected under the right to communications freedom under the Convention and the Charter (Chap. 6). This is because it can improve our understanding of reality, and it can reduce the risks of poor information security, thus benefiting the public interest. As a result, different kinds of restrictions on research, ranging from outright prohibitions to contractual restrictions, should be considered an interference. And I conclude on the basis of the case law that these interferences must be "strictly necessary"—there is very little room for member states to limit this research.

This freedom, however, also comes with a duty of care. In order to claim protection under this right, researchers must mitigate the risks associated with disclosure, ensuring their activities do not go further than necessary. What is more, the case law also suggests that states have an obligation to adopt a CVD framework to ensure that security researchers can take these measures to mitigate the risks of disclosure. I develop the implications of this for governance in the realm of information security later in the book, and provide a summary in the next sections.

With regard to the *application* of information security, my analysis is that information security measures which restrict communications freedom are not necessarily an interference, let alone disproportionate (Chap. 6). This is particularly so where communications freedom and privacy overlap, in the case of confidential communications, the application of information security measures to protect the confidentiality of this communication supports both rights. There are, however, some limited cases where prohibiting the circumvention of information security measures can be considered an interference, in particular where lawful communication activities are impeded significantly. I conclude that the case law on this is still developing, but that in those situations where access to lawful information is completely prevented, or where it is very difficult to access the data through other means, it would be disproportionate to restrict such access through information security measures.

Both conclusions are highly relevant to the analysis of governance measures in the realm of information security. First, as we will see, a lot of governance measures currently result in curtailing information research and disclosure. Many of these should be considered disproportionate. Second, the idea that the constraints in software and hardware can function as regulatory mechanisms—*code as law*—is generally accepted, but its relationship to European human rights is less explored. Information security measures, however, are an important example of such code. The evaluation framework for these measures where they restrict freedom of communication, provides a useful analytical tool to think about some of these constraints.

11.3.3 The Right to Science

The last right I discuss is the right to science, as laid down in the Covenant and the Charter (Chap. 7). This right is about three things: it protects the freedom of practicing science, it ensures that people can profit from the benefits of science, and it protects against the risks of science. Thus, it is broader than the right to communications freedom: the core of the right to science is about scientific *progress* to benefit humanity in an iterative process which leads to an improved understanding of reality. In short, the author argues that the right to science calls for the marriage of science with conscience—and provides an important perspective for the development of governance measures in these domains.

This firstly means that the right to science shapes the direction of research through funding, focusing funds on science which supports peace and human rights, and requiring that the results of this funding are made broadly accessible. Secondly, I argue that the right to science under certain circumstances also involves a duty to disclose the findings of your research—this follows from the way that the right protects this iterative process of developing knowledge. This duty to disclose is an important element of the right to science which until now has not gained much attention. I analyse the governance implications of this duty to disclose further in this book and summarise the findings below. The last aspect of the right to science that is relevant for this book, is the precautionary principle, which reflects the idea that people should be protected from the risks of science. This principle implies that not all science activities are protected equally: scientific research that carries a lot of risk should be critically assessed, for example when governments are considering funding it. Often, however, the question is not so much whether the risk of scientific research is acceptable as such, the question instead is whether there is an obligation on the part of states to take measures which mitigate this risk. I argue that this obligation is inherent in the right to science.

11.4 Human Rights-Compatible Governance of the Information Security Cycle

So, what does all this mean for governance with regard to the information security cycle, encryption technologies and quantum computing? With regard to the information security cycle, I conclude that currently existing governance measures do not approach information security as a continuous process. There are only some rules on *taking* security measures, and when it comes to *breaking* them, well, that is mostly forbidden.

I analyse obligations to take information security measures in the context of the processing of personal data, critical infrastructure and consumer devices (Chap. 3). I conclude that even in those domains, where it is commonly accepted that information security plays an important role, the obligation to take information security measures does not cover all relevant organisations. Moreover, it does not cover all the ways in which a system can be attacked. An example I use throughout this book is the case of encryption applied in SSDs manufactured by Samsung. When it turned out that this encryption contained a flaw, it was uncertain who should be responsible for fixing it. Ultimately, Microsoft changed its settings to address the vulnerability. I also note that the standards for taking security measures differ per domain, and for no good reason. Although for the processing of personal data and critical infrastructures, the standard is risk-based, for consumer devices, the expectation of the consumer with regard to the level of security is leading. The problem is: everything is connected, and flaws in consumer devices can be used to attack critical infrastructure, so there's a need for a broadly applicable standard.

While the obligation to take security measures might be incomplete and inconsistent, the governance framework for *dealing* with vulnerabilities is even less developed. To start with, the obligation to fix vulnerabilities could be clearer (see Chap. 8). More importantly, researchers currently have no obligation to notify people if they become aware of a vulnerability. What is more, the processes for coordinating vulnerability disclosure are only beginning to be embedded in a legal framework. Finally, information security research may lead to civil and criminal liability, even when it furthers human rights.

I argue in Chap. 8 that it proceeds from the rights to privacy, communications freedom and science that this needs to be fixed. Because the information security cycle does not work well, our digital infrastructure is badly secured. This has a significantly negative impact on the rights to privacy and communications freedom, because it increases the risk of unlawful access to, and control of information and systems protected by these rights. What is important for our purposes, however, is that the rights to privacy and communications freedom not only entail negative obligations for states; it follows from these rights that states have positive obligations to minimise this risk of unlawful access and control. Conversely, these rights also imply that people, under certain circumstances, have a right to gain access to lawful information and take lawful control over their own devices—something which information security measures sometimes prevent.

To address this, I conclude that the EU must first ensure that information security measures are taken across all domains where information security plays a role. The historical emphasis on a sector-based approaches does not fit well with this, because all digital infrastructure can be exploited, and sometimes gaps in one part of the infrastructure can also be used to attack other parts. Fortunately, the EU appears to be addressing this, for example in the Cyber Resilience Act which is being negotiated at the time of writing.

I also conclude that the substance of the rules should be changed. I propose that these rules should be centered around the atomic unit of the "attack surface", which is basically all the ways in which a system may be compromised. Currently, not all organisations which contribute elements to the attack surface are considered responsible for its security. To fix this, governments must ensure that the entire attack surface of a system is covered by these security obligations. Fixing only part of the attack surface is not sufficient because this would still leave a system open for attack.

This has one important consequence, though: if you broaden the security obligations to encompass the entire attack surface, the rules also affect more organisations. The question is how you should deal with this. I propose making all organisations that contribute elements to the attack surface, *jointly* responsible for fixing vulnerabilities in this attack surface. I also offer in this book suggestions on how to allocate this responsibility internally—this could for example depend on who can fix the vulnerability the quickest, and who can do it the cheapest. I also suggest that the responsibility for the attack surface does not diminish over time—it remains important to secure the surface throughout the entire lifecycle of a system. I acknowledge that this is a radical overhaul of current information security governance (part of it may be implemented in the CRA which is currently being negotiated). I am convinced, however, that this approach does justice to the requirement that governments must minimise the risk of unlawful access and control.

I also provide some suggestions for changing the standard by which security measures are assessed to better protect human rights. I contend that the risk-based approach which can be found in various regulatory instruments works well: it is sufficiently flexible and has already been used for years. It is important to reconsider the role of costs in this approach—given the interests of human rights at play in badly secured systems, I contend that this cannot be a decisive factor in determining appropriate measures. A factor which should also be taken into account is the risk of badly secured infrastructure to other people, not only the risk of the organisation doing the assessment. And it should be clarified that where requirements conflict, the requirement which offers the most human rights protection takes precedence.

I further conclude that governments must promote *research* which uncovers vulnerabilities. This conclusion is based on the right to science, in combination with the right to communications freedom. As mentioned above, the scope of the right to communications freedom covers doing research and sharing findings in this domain. But the right to science provides further depth to this analysis. Under the right to science, governments firstly have an obligation to fund research and provide protection for research tools. This is also relevant for the field of information security and suggests that governments should increase funding of the development of high-impact information security technologies.

Where the right to science shines in providing guidance, however, is in fields which work as a cycle; where new scientific insight builds on or replaces existing insights. Of course, the information security cycle is a prime example of that. Here, knowledge of vulnerabilities serves as the input for hardening security measures, which then leads to the discovery of new vulnerabilities. The problem is that, currently, as discussed above, researchers can be held liable for doing such research. This means that governments should change the rules to make researchers not liable—not via criminal law, not through tort and not through contracts.

Simultaneously, the application of the right to science in this field also emphasises another aspect—the duty of care which comes with practicing science. The development of the atomic bomb put the spotlight on the ways in which the results of science can be used for the benefit or detriment of humankind. The duty of care inherent in the right to science, especially if read in combination with the right to communications freedom, can be read to imply that the benefits of science should be maximised and the negative effects should be minimised.

When you apply this duty of care to the information security cycle, this means that information security researchers have a number of obligations when doing research. Firstly—they have an obligation to ensure that their research does not go further than necessary and that there are no other ways of proving their point with less impact. Secondly, they have to disclose their findings, in order to ensure that any weaknesses they have discovered can be fixed. I acknowledge that this is a far-reaching conclusion, and there will be exceptions to this rule. For example, privately-funded research into private systems should probably not fall under this rule. In addition, such a duty to disclose would also affect the current practice of governments hoarding vulnerabilities for offensive purposes. The question is, under which circumstances governments can justify retaining vulnerabilities for a limited time, if strictly necessary? This is a topic for further study, probably distinguishing between a vulnerability leading to a *class break*—a weakness in many systems at once—and a vulnerability in one particular server, for example as a result of a wrong configuration. The starting point in all cases should be, however, that if one finds a weakness, it must be disclosed, and exceptions to this rule—if any—should be narrowly circumscribed.

Another part of the obligation to minimise the risk of unlawful access and control, is that governments must ensure that vulnerabilities are fixed when found. This is currently not working well—there are only limited frameworks for vulnerability disclosure. I propose that governments do three things. First, states must oblige all organisations to create a publicly available contact point for notifying of vulnerabilities. Second, it must be clarified that organisations are required to act on the knowledge of a vulnerability: if they are aware of a vulnerability, they should take measures to address it, possibly coordinating among all those responsible for the attack surface. And third, states must increase transparency on vulnerability disclosures through a central registration point. Fortunately, the NIS2 Directive addresses this partly, but it emphasises particular sectors, and leaves much leeway to member states to implement these mechanisms.

Lastly, the author proposes mitigating some of the negative impacts which information security measures may have on people, in particular where it concerns measures which lock down their devices. Currently, it is often difficult for users to take full control of their devices, because information security measures prevent them from doing so. You might own a phone, but in many cases, you do not fully control it. I conclude that the rights to privacy and communications freedom imply that governments must mandate a manual override of security measures which restrict the use of single-user systems (such as a phone, laptop or e-reader). This also requires a radically different approach to securing such systems, and drawing the boundaries of this right requires further research. Should you be allowed, for example, to change the maximum speed of an electric bike? But as more security shifts to the endpoints of the network, and more devices come online, the possibility of gaining full control over devices will become an increasingly important condition for the enjoyment of human rights and governments must devise policies in this regard.

11.5 Human Rights-Compatible Governance of Encryption

As discussed above, the interaction between encryption technologies and quantum computing is an example of the information security cycle at work. In fact, encryption technologies play an important role in information security. These technologies can for instance ensure that information has not been tampered with, or that a message comes from a specific sender. The function I am focusing on in this book, however, is *confidentiality*: they can restrict access to information. Now, encryption technologies can restrict two kinds of access. They can restrict *unlawful* access—by organised crime, for example. This serves to ensure that, when you lose your phone, you do not lose your pictures. But they can also restrict *lawful* access—by governments, for example, in the course of an investigation. And when it comes to preventing this lawful access, one particular form of encryption technologies, where only the users have the key—user-controlled encryption—is the most challenging for governments.

Because encryption technologies can prevent both unlawful and lawful access, governments' approach with regard to these technologies is complicated. On the one hand, states want to retain access to information where necessary. This favours *limiting* the availability, effectiveness and application of encryption technologies. On the other hand, states want to prevent others from gaining unauthorised access to information. This favours *supporting* these technologies.

Policies on encryption technologies have always reflected this tension. Before the 1970s, encryption policy was mostly about spies listening to their adversaries. States developed strong encryption technologies for themselves, while secretly backdooring encryption for others and subjecting the export of these technologies to a licensing regime. But things became more complex when cryptographers outside the intelligence agencies invented new, unbreakable encryption technologies, and it later became possible to share these widely through the internet.

In response, policymakers across the world in the nineties attempted to curtail not only the export, but also the use of these newly developed technologies. States imposed maximum key lengths, mandated weakened algorithms and obliged the storage of keys with a third party (key escrow). These attempts faced strong push-back, though, from civil society and commercial interests. One important objection was that these approaches would not only allow governments to *lawfully* access information; they also increased the risks that others—for example, intelligence services and organised crime—could access encrypted data *unlawfully*. Ultimately, at the beginning of this century, these regulatory efforts to restrict encryption technologies were mostly suspended in the US and the EU.

In fact, as our society became increasingly digital, EU policymakers started to embrace encryption as an important instrument to protect information and systems. For instance, encryption now plays a role in EU data protection rules, the GDPR, and the protection of critical infrastructure, the NIS directive. In addition, governments in the EU invest in the development of encryption technologies.

At the same time, however, governments secretly invested in breaking encryption technologies. From the Snowden leaks, we have learned that GCHQ and the NSA spent a lot of money undermining encryption technologies, for example by covertly introducing backdoors through standardisation. They are now also investing in attacking encryption with brute force: we know the EU is developing a computer platform for this purpose, and the NSA is also probably doing this. Furthermore, law enforcement agencies in the EU have been known to run fake encrypted communications services marketed to criminals.

And not only that: governments have also started pushing again for regulatory measures aimed at encryption. As encryption is now increasingly applied by default in communications and on devices, US and EU lawmakers are calling for policy interventions which would make it possible to gain access. Technological experts have also proposed a number of technological approaches to retaining access. These are, firstly, monitoring communications on the device itself—and although this is called *client-side* scanning, it usually involves some form of reporting back to a *server*, for instance to the police, when forbidden material is detected. The second option which has been proposed, is to covertly add participants to a chat—this would require amending chat software so that user does not see that the secret participant, for instance the police, has been added. Lastly, storing keys with a provider has been proposed (for device encryption). This would mean that when the authorities require access to an encrypted device in the course of an investigation, they would need to contact the manufacturer of the device (for instance, Apple) to assist in decryption by providing the required key.

It turns out that the Crypto Wars were never won at all, and they might even be back. This leads to the next question: what does human-rights compatible governance of encryption technologies entail? Some proponents of encryption restrictions argue that as a matter of principle, there should be no place which governments cannot reach. Others argue the opposite, that encryption finally provides an impenetrable shield to keep governments out. Building on the framework developed in the context of the information security cycle, I contend that devising human rights-compatible governance for encryption technologies requires an analysis of the *risks* of unlawful access and the *need* for lawful access.

Because encryption technology is a core information security component in our information society, I conclude that governance measures which negatively impact the availability, application or effectiveness of encryption technologies should be considered contrary to the rights to privacy and communications freedom. Not out of principle, but because this proceeds from the obligation to reduce the risk of *unlawful* access to information, as discussed above, combined with the poor state of information security of our digital infrastructure.

The main argument for this conclusion has little to do with the particular technological solutions proposed. I argue that the security of our digital infrastructure is in such bad shape, that we simply need more encryption, not less—and the available encryption technologies should always include user-controlled encryption technologies. To be fair, the three newly proposed technological solutions for lawful access fare better than previous approaches when it comes to preventing *unlawful* access: these new proposals do not weaken the encryption itself. But even these new proposals have one fundamental weakness: the existence of lawful access avenues that also increase the risk that powerful adversaries, in particular foreign intelligence services, will exploit them. The same goes for other measures aimed at weakening encryption technologies, such as covertly inserting a backdoor into encryption standards or into encryption software. And this applies to measures aimed at the application of these technologies, for example prohibiting application by default, storing encrypted information longer or subjecting it to more scrutiny than non-encrypted information. Because it is so difficult to secure information systems well, I argue that all these kinds of measures pose a serious risk to the security of our digital infrastructure, and thus to the enjoyment of human rights which is reliant on the security of that infrastructure.

There are also other reasons why the current push by governments to curb encryption technologies is at odds with the human rights to privacy and communications freedom. Firstly, governments have not yet demonstrated that restrictions on encryption technologies are necessary in a democratic society. Gaining access to encrypted information is only part of the toolbox available to law enforcement and intelligence agencies, a toolbox which has been gradually expanding, as more data on people becomes available because of increased digitisation. The burden of proof to show that access to encrypted data is "strictly necessary" rests with those proposing limitations on encryption technologies, and so far, governments have not succeeded. I also argue that, given the strict test applied by the courts, it is important to consider the legal powers (including the power to hack computers) and capabilities (including the capability to perform brute force attacks on encryption) which a government already has, when considering new measures in this domain. There are also questions around the effectiveness of these regulations, because strong encryption technologies will be likely to remain available online. Even if all these hurdles can be taken, the global nature of encryption technologies poses a difficult political problem. The EU can arguably only agree to a global *lawful* access regime which is compatible with the Convention and the Charter, but other countries will want to impose their own regime, and some of these may be at odds with these instruments. This challenge will be difficult to overcome.

Instead, it follows from the rights to privacy and communications freedom that governments have an obligation to safeguard a vibrant encryption landscape, where there is a virtuous cycle of strengthening encryption technologies, making them available and promoting their use. Governments should ensure that a wide range of encryption technologies is available, some of them user-controlled. They can do so, by clarifying that it is legal to apply all forms of encryption. They can also do this through funding research in this field and investigating limiting intellectual property rights on the technologies incorporated in encryption standards. This can, moreover, be done by further mandating the use of these technologies, investing in education, and having governments adopt these technologies themselves. Lastly, this can be done by promoting these technologies internationally.

This does not mean that governments are totally powerless when it comes to accessing encrypted information. States may still develop and use advanced decryption capabilities based on brute force attacks, as long as their use is subject to the required safeguards for secret surveillance developed in the case law under the Convention and the Charter. This means clearly limiting the cases in which this power may be applied and adopting safeguards against abuse. Because you cannot know in advance which data you are decrypting, these safeguards need to be tailored around the possibility that the most sensitive information will be decrypted—for example, communications between journalists and sources, or between lawyers and clients. This is why oversight by an independent and impartial body, preferably a judge, plays an important role here, especially by having this body *preview* decrypted information beforehand.

11.6 Human Rights-Compatible Governance of Quantum Computers

The above analysis is also relevant to another kind of technology: quantum computing. As explained in Chap. 2, quantum computers are not like regular computers: they can only be used for a limited number of applications. They can firstly be used to simulate other quantum systems—which could lead to inventions in molecular chemistry, such as better fertilisers, or more efficient solar cells. Secondly, they can be used for certain mathematical problems, such as solving logistical challenges. This also includes the reason why I am discussing them in this book: quantum computers could, in theory, break a broadly used kind of encryption technology: public key encryption.

In theory, because these computers are not yet able to do much at all, quantum computers currently barely exist. This is because quantum computers work differently from the classical computers we are used to: these new kinds of computers are based on the behaviour of particles on a quantum level. Doing calculations with these new computers is difficult. This is because the elements with which calculations are made, called *quantum bits*, or *qubits*, break down very quickly, which leads to calculation errors. In order to address this, scientists are applying error correction techniques, combining multiple *physical* qubits into one *logical* qubit. Currently, however, you would need around 1000 physical qubits to make one logical qubit, and you would need thousands of logical qubits to break regularly used public key encryption (with a strength of 2048 or 4096 bits). This means that you would need a quantum computer of millions of physical qubits. The computers that currently exist have hundreds. So, we are still far from a world where these computers pose a threat to public key encryption technologies.

Still, governments around the world, including the US, EU and China, are investing billions of euros in the development of these machines. They do so not only because of the key-cracking potential—they also expect these computers to lead to breakthrough innovations in other fields. As a result of these investments, many experts estimate that in the coming decades, quantum computers with thousands of stable qubits will be built. When they are developed, this would be a problem for information security. It would allow for the decryption of encrypted communications, and it would undermine the trust in a core information security technology—public key cryptography. It would allow for the calculation of private keys on the basis of public keys, something which is not currently possible, and this impossibility is exactly why public key encryption currently works as a security technology.

What does this mean for human rights-compatible governance of quantum computing? This has been answered in Chap. 10. An initial observation is that there is currently almost no governance in this field at all. Most of it is through governmental funding, and the conditions attached to this funding. One notable example is that the European Commission in its funding of supercomputers under the EuroHPC project, leaves open the possibility that quantum computers could be used for military purposes—which of course would include decryption activities. In addition, there is some export control of some of the elements of quantum computers. Generally, it is an unregulated space.

This needs to change—states must start developing governance measures around quantum computing to shape its development and use, informed by the impact that quantum computers may have on human rights. Generally speaking, this requires balancing the *risks* of quantum computing—in particular the breaking of public key encryption—with the *potential* of these technologies. As noted above, although fully developed quantum computers will not be able to perform every kind of computation quickly, their application could lead to important breakthroughs in a variety of fields, from medicine to agriculture, from finance to logistics. In other words, quantum computing provides a significant opportunity for societal progress. But, as set out above, one of the applications is breaking public key encryption, a fundamental technology in our information society. This has serious implications. The question is how governments should deal with this, given the rights to privacy, communications freedom and science?

I conclude that the right to science stands in the way of curbing the currently ongoing kind of fundamental research into quantum computers. The broad promise of these new technologies offsets the potential risks which will be introduced as a result of the development of quantum computers. At the same time, because those technologies may eventually impact the security of encryption technologies, investments into the development of quantum computing must be paired with strong investments by states in alternative encryption technologies which are not breakable by quantum computers. This not only follows from the duty of care under the right to science, to mitigate the negative impact of scientific development, but also from the obligation of states under the Convention and the Charter to minimise the risk of unlawful access, as discussed above.

This implies that governments should invest in the development of quantum-resistant technologies and encourage their adoption. Most of the energy should be directed towards *post quantum cryptography*, as these kinds of technologies are the most versatile and most widely applicable. For some applications, *quantum key distribution* may also be a way to mitigate the risk posed by quantum computers. Development can be facilitated by funding research, by allowing researchers from other countries to work, by not restricting scientific research, and by sharing results in this domain.

I am particularly concerned, about the adoption—it has previously taken decades to switch to different encryption algorithms. Adversaries are currently storing encrypted information that they have already intercepted, to be decrypted later. If we want to prevent valuable information from falling into the hands of powerful adversaries in the future, we should switch as quickly as possible to quantum-resistant encryption technologies. This means that governments will have to use all the tools available to them to accelerate this switch, including through regulation, standardisation, funding, training and campaigning.

Export control offers another way to limit the risk of unlawful access, subjecting the export of elements of these technologies to authorisation. There is a tension here with the right to science because these items might also be used for other purposes. Requiring an export licence does not mean that these exports will always have to be limited—this will depend on the risk that the goods will be used for unlawful decryption. Governments can decide on this on a case-by-case basis, looking at the end-user and the end-use of the good, and then taking into account the human rights impact of a certain export.

When these computers are eventually built, their application to decrypt information may only take place under limited circumstances. Governments should in principle prevent the use of quantum computers by *private parties* for decryption purposes without governmental authorisation. As for decryption by *governments*, I discussed the conditions for this in the section above. Something that merits attention in the context of quantum computing is how to deal with the storage of decrypted keys. Because these pose an attractive target for adversaries, I conclude that a decrypted keypair should be deleted immediately after it has been used for decryption purposes.

I further conclude that encrypted information may not be collected only because it is encrypted. Lastly, where governments will want to use each other's quantum computers to decrypt information, I contend that they may only do so on the basis of a mutual legal assistance treaty.

Finally, I contend that the obligation of governments to ensure that science benefits humanity, translates into one particular requirement when it comes to the domain of quantum computing: when funding research and development in this domain, states must impose conditions to ensure that the results are made accessible to all. This is particularly so for the results of theoretical research, such as research on algorithms. Whether such an obligation may also exist for the results of applied research, such as the building of actual quantum computers, warrants further investigation.

11.7 Peering into the Future

I started this book with the observation that everything consists of information and computers. This will only become more so in the coming years—more things will be digitised; more things will contain a CPU. As a result, information security will become even more important—as a force which protects human rights, and as one which restricts the enjoyment of human rights. Finding the right balance between the two will be a challenging but crucial task for everyone involved in governance of information security—states, NGOs and companies alike. This will also involve implementing human rights into information security measures, into code.

We have one prominent example of an attempt to embed fundamental rights into code—*privacy-by-design*. Here, the idea is to implement privacy-respecting principles, such as data minimisation, into a system in the design phase. If, for instance, you do not collect personal data in the first place, there is no risk that this data will be abused later on. As information security measures become even more ubiquitous, it is important to extend this idea of privacy-by-design to other realms—to have human-rights-by-design as a guiding principle for the development of digital infrastructure.

The experience of the past thirty years does not bode well, though. Even now that privacy-by-design has been elevated from a principle to an obligation under the GDPR, there are remarkably few organisations that take pains to ensure their systems are designed in a privacy-respecting way. Privacy-by-design still mostly remains an ideal, not a hard requirement.

Going forward, however, we will not have the luxury of depending on the goodwill of the organisations designing digital infrastructure to enjoy human rights—if we are to enjoy human rights in the coming centuries, the implications for human rights of information security need to be thoroughly scrutinised and steered in the right direction. Hopefully, this book provides a first analytical framework for this task.

This also means having a fruitful *debate* about the role of human rights in our digital infrastructure. This is often lacking. The history of encryption governance is emblematic of the shortcomings in much of the debate on digital rights. The principled positions of some of the proponents and opponents of encryption restrictions stand in the way of a human rights assessment balancing a broad range of interests. If we are to prevent a rerun from the first iterations of the Crypto Wars, it is imperative that states depart from these principled positions, instead weighing the risks of encryption restrictions against the benefits. The history of export control of hacking software provides another example. Here, the information security research community was involved only at a later stage of policymaking, which resulted in export controls potentially affecting legitimate information security research. This also needs to change—information security experts need to be more actively involved in the development of governance measures in these domains.

Fortunately, quantum computing provides a relatively clean slate for governance measures—governments can still develop rules which respect human rights, because there are currently so few rules. But states should step in quickly. The money being poured into quantum computers by private companies is so enormous, that there is a serious risk that they will shape the field of quantum computing in ways which are hard to reverse. Now is the time to start developing governance in this domain, governance which respects human rights and ensures fair and equitable access to quantum computing infrastructure. Policymakers should seize this opportunity.

11.8 Making and Breaking with Science and Conscience

Let me conclude with a case study from an entirely different field—the field of biological viruses. In 2011, virology researcher Robert Fouchier and his colleagues from the Erasmus Medical Centre in Rotterdam tested whether the H5N1 avian flu-virus could become airborne. Some of Fouchier's colleagues had thought that the virus could not become transmissible over the air. Fouchier proved them wrong.[2] He did so by passing the virus from ferret to ferret, and after a number of generations, it spread via the air.[3] Another researcher, Yoshihiro Kawaoka, together with his team from the University of Wisconsin, achieved the same feat, also in 2011. This sparked a debate on *gain-of-function* research, research to add new characteristics to viruses—a debate which has become newly relevant since the start of the covid-pandemic.

The considerations in that debate are remarkably similar to those in the information security debate—I am not the first to notice the similarities.[4] Research into gain-of-function is in the public interest, virologists argue. It can show the effectiveness of current vaccines and medicines, enable the creation of new ones, and allow for early detection of new strains.[5] But things can also go horribly wrong. An influenza pandemic in 1977–78, killing an estimated 700,000 people, is suspected to have come

[2] Grady and McNeil Jr. 2011.

[3] Enserink 2011a.

[4] See Schneier 2019; and for an older comparison Granick 2005.

[5] See for example Selgelid 2016; Davis et al. 2014.

from a virus strain from the 1950s that was stored in a lab, and was used, unwisely, in vaccine trials.[6] There have also been numerous close calls, where a deadly virus coming from a lab was nearly unleashed on the world.[7] It makes you wonder. Can virologists learn anything from how this works in information security?

Probably they can. But first, how did the avian flu controversy of a decade ago pan out? Fouchier wanted to publish his findings in *Science* in 2011; Kawaoka wanted to publish his in *Nature*.[8] But others considered the research too dangerous. An advisory body to the US government on biosecurity had the authors revise their manuscript before publication.[9] In addition, the Dutch government contended that Fouchier needed an export licence for sending the article to *Science* (the licence was granted).[10] The controversy also led the researchers to announce a self-imposed 60-day moratorium on avian flu transmission studies—a moratorium which ended lasting a year.[11]

Looking back, the debate seemed oddly abstract. When I started writing this book, everyone could still gather in close spaces. When this book was finished, we were in the middle of a pandemic which to date has claimed the lives of millions of people (over 15 million in one estimate), made many more ill and uprooted society in ways previously unimaginable.[12] All this probably started at the end of 2019 in Wuhan, China, spreading around the globe since. It is possible, and can at the very least not be excluded, that the virus has escaped from a lab in Wuhan.[13] We will probably never know for sure. What we *do* understand better by now, more than we would have liked to, are the extreme risks of this kind of research.

---

[6] Rozo and Gronvall 2015.

[7] See the examples in Tufekci 2021.

[8] See for an overview Ehrlich 2014; Sleator 2012; see for the article on Fouchiers research Herfst et al. 2012; and an accompanying article on whether the virus could transmit from human to human; Russell et al. 2012; see for a history of the tension between academic freedom and export control in the US Evans and Valdivia 2012.

[9] The National Science Advisory Board for Biosecurity (NSABB) reviewed the manuscripts, to see whether they contained information too dangerous to publish. At the end of 2011, the NSABB recommended that the manuscripts "not include the methodological and other details that could enable replication of the experiments by those who would seek to do harm". Enserink 2011b. The authors and publishers then agreed to redact their articles, on the condition that a process would be created for ensuring access to the redacted information where necessary. The authors submitted revised manuscripts to the NSABB, and the NSABB three months later recommended publication; Malakoff 2012.

[10] Enserink 2012. Although the licence was granted and the article published, Fouchier appealed, arguing that this publication should rely on the exemption for "fundamental scientific research" under the export rules. The court disagreed: this exemption only applies where the research is so abstractly worded, that there is no danger for proliferation or terrorism; District Court Noord-Holland, ECLI:NL:RBNHO:2013:8527, Fouchier v Dutch Ministry of Foreign Affairs, Judgment of 20 September 2013.

[11] Fouchier et al. 2012; Grady 2012.

[12] The Economist 2021.

[13] See for an overview Tufekci 2021.

This is where insights from the information security cycle have something to offer. The policy response on gain-of-function-research has been mostly focused on mitigating the risks of a leak.[14] By contrast, using the findings to improve societal resilience against new viruses have gotten less attention. Procedures for coordinated vulnerability disclosure in the virology domain are far less developed than those in information security. In the US, funding is for example currently granted on the condition that results should be "responsibly communicated, in compliance with applicable laws, regulations, and policies, and any terms and conditions of funding, in order to realize their potential benefit"—a weak requirement at best.[15]

Viruses will continue to spring up, just like software vulnerabilities will continue to be exploited. You could argue that there is a good reason to do gain-of-function-research—the viruses will be there anyway, and it's better to be prepared. But there is also another argument, one that is worthy of attention. The merits of creating viruses which are likely to not have occurred naturally is less obvious, similar to the merits of deliberately introducing weaknesses into computer systems. At the very least, this would require very strict risk mitigation measures.

This also has something to do with the question as to whether new diseases can be prevented with a vaccine. The speed with which vaccines can now be developed and tested appears to have dropped—it dropped from 8 years to 1.5 years, and the development of initial covid vaccines took a couple of weeks.[16] This, of course, was partly because research on earlier coronavirus vaccines started more than a decade earlier. An important question is whether a virus researcher can wait for a vaccine to be developed.

Feeding back scientific findings in the virology security cycle is arguably as important as mitigating the risks that gain-of-function research goes wrong. This will only become more relevant as this whole cycle digitises further—viruses can already be easily sequenced digitally (increasing the risks of a leak), and *making* viruses and vaccines will in the future probably be a matter of printing the right sequence.[17] In fact, virology research in the future may shift from the big labs to amateurs, as the required technology becomes cheaper, which will also lead to more gain-of-function-research, this time taking place in basements instead of labs.

At the height of the bird flu-controversy, scientific institutions organised many public debates on the issue. During one such debate at the Dutch Royal Academy of Sciences, the KNAW, a proponent for doing the research, claimed that "you cannot stop science and scientific curiosity".[18] But can you not, really? One of the main

---

[14] For example, in the letter where the avian-flu researchers announced the lifting of their moratorium, they emphasised lab safety measures, Fouchier et al. 2013; the European Academies' Science Advisory Council (EASAC) in October 2015 issued a number of recommendations, emphasising self-regulation and risk mitigation, EASAC 2015; see also Chap. 2 of Harris 2016 for an overview of primarily US-focused governance in 2016—Table 6 on pp. 164–167 *only* lists control measures, no mitigation measures.

[15] U.S. Department of Health and Human Services 2017, p. 6.

[16] Kis et al. 2020.

[17] Bert Hubert is for instance writing about the "source code" of mRNA vaccines; Hubert 2020.

[18] Van der Bruggen 2014, p. 6.

points of this book is that science for the sake of curiosity is not sufficient to justify high-risk research—the right to science comes with a duty of care. Breaking *is* an integral part of making, but the process only benefits society, if science is done with conscience.

References

Articles, Books and Other Documents

Davis CT, Chen L-M, Pappas C et al. (2014) Use of Highly Pathogenic Avian Influenza A(H5N1) Gain-Of-Function Studies for Molecular-Based Surveillance and Pandemic Preparedness. mBio 5:e02431–14. https://doi.org/10.1128/mBio.02431-14

EASAC 2015, *Gain of Function: Experimental Applications Relating to Potentially Pandemic Pathogens*, 27, October 2015. https://microbiologysociety.org/asset/FE35D386-C3EE-4018-A19D8C167D939B81/. Accessed 5 January 2024.

Ehrlich SA (2014) H5N1: A Cautionary Tale. Front Public Health 2:117. https://doi.org/10.3389/fpubh.2014.00117

Enserink M (2011a) Scientists Brace for Media Storm around Controversial Flu Studies. https://www.sciencemag.org/news/2011/11/scientists-brace-media-storm-around-controversial-flu-studies. Accessed 25 June 2021.

Enserink M (2011b) Grudgingly, Virologists Agree to Redact Details in Sensitive Flu Papers. https://www.sciencemag.org/news/2011/12/grudgingly-virologists-agree-redact-details-sensitive-flu-papers. Accessed 27 June 2021.

Enserink M (2012) Dutch Government OK's Publication of H5N1 Study. https://www.sciencemag.org/news/2012/04/dutch-government-oks-publication-h5n1-study. Accessed 26 June 2021.

Evans SAW, Valdivia WD (2012) Export Controls and the Tensions between Academic Freedom and National Security. Minerva 50:169–190. https://doi.org/10.1007/s11024-012-9196-4

Fouchier RAM, Garcia-Sastre A, Kawaoka Y et al. (2012) Pause on Avian Flu Transmission Research. Science 335:400–401. https://doi.org/10.1126/science.1219412

Fouchier RAM, García-Sastre A, Kawaoka Y et al. (2013) Transmission Studies Resume for Avian Flu. Science 339:520–521. https://doi.org/10.1126/science.1235140

Grady D (2012) Scientists to Pause Research on Deadly Strain of Bird Flu. The New York Times, 20 January 2011.

Grady D, McNeil Jr DG (2011) Debate Persists on Deadly Flu Made Airborne. The New York Times, 26 December 2011.

Granick JS (2005) The Price of Restricting Vulnerability Publications. International Journal of Communications Law & Policy, 9:1.

Harris ED (ed) (2016) Governance of Dual-Use Technologies: Theory and Practice. American Academy of Arts & Sciences. https://www.amacad.org/publication/governance-dual-use-technologies-theory-and-practice. Accessed 5 January 2024.

Herfst S, Schrauwen EJA, Linster M et al. (2012) Airborne Transmission of Influenza A/H5N1 Virus between Ferrets. Science 336:1534–1541. https://doi.org/10.1126/science.1213362

Hubert B (2020) Reverse Engineering the Source Code of the BioNTech/Pfizer SARS-CoV-2 Vaccine. Bert Hubert's writings. https://berthub.eu/articles/posts/reverse-engineering-source-code-of-the-biontech-pfizer-vaccine/. Accessed 30 June 2021.

Kis Z, Kontoravdi C, Dey AK et al. (2020) Rapid Development and Deployment of High-Volume Vaccines for Pandemic Response. Journal of Advanced Manufacturing and Processing 2:3 https://doi.org/10.1002/amp2.10060

Malakoff D (2012) Breaking News: NSABB Reverses Position on Flu Papers. https://www.sciencemag.org/news/2012/03/breaking-news-nsabb-reverses-position-flu-papers. Accessed 26 June 2021.

Rozo M, Gronvall GK (2015) The Reemergent 1977 H1N1 Strain and the Gain-of-Function Debate. mBio 6:e01013–15. https://doi.org/10.1128/mBio.01013-15

Russell CA, Fonville JM, Brown AEX et al. (2012) The Potential for Respiratory Droplet–Transmissible A/H5N1 Influenza Virus to Evolve in a Mammalian Host. Science 336:1541–1547. https://doi.org/10.1126/science.1222526

Schneier B (2019) What Digital Nerds and Bio Geeks Have to Worry About. Schneier on Security. https://www.schneier.com/essays/archives/2019/09/what_digital_nerds_a.html. Accessed 14 November 2021.

Selgelid MJ (2016) Gain-of-Function Research: Ethical Analysis. Science and Engineering Ethics 22:923–964. https://doi.org/10.1007/s11948-016-9810-1

Sleator RD (2012) Ferretting Out the Facts behind the H5N1 Controversy. Bioengineered Bugs 3:139–143. https://doi.org/10.4161/bbug.19943

Tufekci Z (2021) Where Did the Coronavirus Come From? What We Already Know Is Troubling. The New York Times, 25 January 2021.

The Economist (2021) The pandemic's true death toll. The Economist.

van Daalen O (2022), In Defense of Offense: Information Security Research under the Right to Science, Computer Law & Security Review 46: 105706.

van Daalen O (2023a) The Right to Encryption: Privacy as Preventing Unlawful Access, Computer Law & Security Review 49:105804.

van Daalen O (2023b) The Right to Root: Constructing a Claim to Control Devices from the Right to Privacy, JIPITEC 14(2023:4): 580–593.

van Daalen O (2024) Developing a human-rights compatible governance framework for quantum computing, Research Directions: Quantum Technologies 2: 2024.

van der Bruggen K (2014) Gain-of-Function Research. Report of a Debate between Prof. Giorgio Palù and Prof Simon Wain-Hobson, 25 June 2014. https://www.knaw.nl/shared/resources/actueel/bestanden/Reportdebategainoffunctionresearch25June2014.pdf. Accessed 27 June 2021.

U.S. Department of Health and Human Services 2017, *Framework for Guiding Funding Decisions about Proposed Research Involving Enhanced Potential Pandemic Pathogens*, 2017. https://www.phe.gov/s3/dualuse/Documents/P3CO.pdf. Accessed 5 January 2024.

Table of Cases: National

District Court Noord-Holland, ECLI:NL:RBNHO:2013:8527, Fouchier v Dutch Ministry of Foreign Affairs, Judgment of 20 September 2013.

MIX
Papier aus verantwortungsvollen Quellen
Paper from responsible sources
FSC® C105338

If you have any concerns about our products,
you can contact us on
ProductSafety@springernature.com

In case Publisher is established outside the EU,
the EU authorized representative is:
Springer Nature Customer Service Center GmbH
Europaplatz 3, 69115 Heidelberg, Germany

Printed by Libri Plureos GmbH
in Hamburg, Germany